Grammar *in use* Intermediate

Self-study reference and practice for students of North American English

THIRD
EDITION

with answers

Raymond Murphy
with William R. Smalzer

CAMBRIDGE
UNIVERSITY PRESS

CAMBRIDGE
UNIVERSITY PRESS

79 Anson Road, #06-04/06, Singapore 079906

Cambridge University Press is part of the University of Cambridge.

It furthers the University's mission by disseminating knowledge in the pursuit of education, learning and research at the highest international levels of excellence.

www.cambridge.org
Information on this title: www.cambridge.org/9780521734769

First published 1989
Second edition 2000
Third edition 2009
13th printing 2014

Printed in Singapore by Markono Print Media Pte Ltd

A catalog record for this publication is available from the British Library

ISBN 978-0-521-73476-9 Student's Book with answers
ISBN 978-0-521-73477-6 Student's Book with answers and CD-ROM
ISBN 978-0-521-75936-6 Student's Book with CD-ROM
ISBN 978-0-521-73478-3 Workbook with answers
ISBN 978-0-521-73479-0 Workbook

Cambridge University Press has no responsibility for the persistence or accuracy of URLs for external or third-party internet websites referred to in this publication, and does not guarantee that any content on such websites is, or will remain, accurate or appropriate.

Book design and layout: Adventure House, NYC
Audio production: Richard LePage & Associates

Illustration credits: Carlos Castellanos, Tim Foley, Marty Harris, Randy Jones, Kamae Designs, Roger Penwill, Lisa Smith, and Simon Williams

Contents

If you are not sure which units you need to study, use the **STUDY GUIDE** on page 319.

Prepositions

Phrasal Verbs

To the Student

This book is for students who want help with English grammar. It is written for you to use without a teacher.

The book will be useful for you if you are not sure of the answers to questions like these:

- What is the difference between *I did* and *I have done*?
- When do we use *will* for the future?
- What is the structure after *I wish*?
- When do we say *used to do* and when do we say *used to doing*?
- When do we use *the*?
- What is the difference between *like* and *as*?

These and many other points of English grammar are explained in the book, and there are exercises on each point.

Level

The book is intended mainly for *intermediate* students (students who have already studied the basic grammar of English). It concentrates on those structures that intermediate students want to use, but that often cause difficulty. Some advanced students who have problems with grammar will also find the book useful.

The book is *not* suitable for beginning learners.

How the Book Is Organized

There are 142 units in the book. Each unit concentrates on a particular point of grammar. Some problems (for example, the present perfect or the use of *the*) are covered in more than one unit. For a list of units, see the *Contents* at the beginning of the book.

Each unit consists of two facing pages. On the left there are explanations and examples; on the right there are exercises. At the back of the book there is an *Answer Key* for you to check your answers to the exercises (page 328).

There are also seven *Appendices* at the back of the book (pages 286–295). These include irregular verbs, summaries of verb forms, spelling, and British English.

Finally, there is a detailed *Index* at the back of the book (pages 363–369).

How to Use the Book

The units are *not* in order of difficulty, so it is *not* intended that you work through the book from beginning to end. Every learner has different problems, and you should use this book to help you with the grammar that *you* find difficult.

It is suggested that you work in this way:

- Use the *Contents* and/or *Index* to find which unit deals with the point you are interested in.
- If you are not sure which units you need to study, use the *Study Guide* on page 319.
- Study the explanations and examples on the left-hand page of the unit you have chosen.
- Do the exercises on the right-hand page.
- Check your answers with the *Answer Key*.
- If your answers are not correct, study the left-hand page again to see what went wrong.

You can, of course, use the book simply as a reference book without doing the exercises.

Additional Exercises ————————————————————

At the back of the book there are *Additional Exercises* (pages 296–318). These exercises bring together some of the grammar points from a number of different units. For example, Exercise 16 brings together grammar points from Units 25–34. You can use these exercises for extra practice after you have studied and practiced the grammar in the units concerned.

CD-ROM ————————————————————

The book is sold with or without a CD-ROM. On the CD-ROM, you will find more exercises on all the units. There are also more than 500 test questions that you can use to make your own tests, as well as three interactive games.

To the Teacher

Grammar in Use Intermediate was written as a self-study grammar book, but teachers may also find it useful as additional course material in cases where further work on grammar is necessary.

The book will probably be most useful at middle- and upper-intermediate levels (where all or nearly all of the material will be relevant), and can serve both as a basis for revision and as a means for practicing new structures. It will also be useful for some more advanced students who have problems with grammar and need a book for reference and practice. The book is not intended to be used by beginning learners.

The units are organized in grammatical categories (*Present and Past, Articles and Nouns, Prepositions*, etc.). They are not ordered according to level of difficulty, so the book should not be worked through from beginning to end. It should be used selectively and flexibly in accordance with the grammar syllabus being used and the difficulties students are having.

The book can be used for immediate consolidation or for later revision or remedial work. It might be used by the whole class or by individual students needing extra help. The left-hand pages (explanations and examples) are written for the student to use individually, but they may of course be used by the teacher as a source of ideas and information on which to base a lesson. The student then has the left-hand page as a record of what has been taught and can refer to it in the future. The exercises can be done individually, in class or as homework. Alternatively (and additionally), individual students can be directed to study certain units of the book by themselves if they have particular difficulties not shared by other students in their class. Don't forget the *Additional Exercises* at the back of the book (see **To the Student**).

The forms presented in *Grammar in Use* are those that are most used and generally accepted in standard spoken North American English. Some native speakers may regard some of the usages as "incorrect," for example, the use of *who* as an object pronoun, or the use of *they* to mean "he or she." In this book, such usages are treated as standard.

The book is sold with or without a CD-ROM. The CD-ROM contains further exercises on all the units in the book, a bank of more than 500 test questions from which users can select to compile their own tests, and three interactive games.

An edition of *Grammar in Use Intermediate* without the *Answer Key* is also available. Some teachers may prefer this for use with their students.

Grammar in Use Intermediate Third Edition

This is a new edition of *Grammar in Use Intermediate*. The differences between this edition and the second edition are:

- There are eight new units on phrasal verbs (Units 134–142). There is also a new unit on *Wish* (Unit 39). Units 40–79 and 81–134 all have different numbers from the second edition.

- Some of the material has been revised or reorganized, and in most units there are minor changes in the examples, explanations, and exercises.

- The *Additional Exercises* have been extended. The new exercises are 14–16, 25, 30–31, and 37–41.

- The book has been redesigned with new color illustrations.

- There is a new CD-ROM with further exercises to accompany the book.

Grammar *in use* Intermediate

Present Continuous (I am doing)

A Study this example situation:

Sarah is in her car. She is on her way to work.
She **is driving** to work.

This means: she is driving *now*, at the time of speaking.
The action is not finished.

Am/is/are + **-ing** is the *present continuous*:

I	**am**	(= I**'m**)	driv**ing**
he/she/it	**is**	(= he**'s**, etc.)	work**ing**
we/you/they	**are**	(= we**'re**, etc.)	do**ing**, etc.

B **I am doing** something = I'm in the middle of doing it; I've started doing it and I haven't finished yet:

- Please don't make so much noise. I**'m trying** to work. (*not* I try)
- "Where's Mark?" "He**'s taking** a shower." (*not* He takes a shower)
- Let's go out now. It **isn't raining** anymore. (*not* It doesn't rain)
- *(at a party)* Hello, Jane. **Are** you **enjoying** the party? (*not* Do you enjoy)
- What's all that noise? What**'s going** on? (= What's happening?)

The action is not necessarily happening at the time of speaking. For example:

Steve is talking to a friend on the phone. He says:

> I**'m reading** a really good book at the moment. It's about a man who . . . .

Steve is not reading the book at the time of speaking.
He means that he has started it but has not finished it yet.
He is in the middle of reading it.

Some more examples:

- Kate wants to work in Italy, so she**'s studying** Italian. (but perhaps she isn't studying Italian at the time of speaking)
- Some friends of mine **are building** their own house. They hope to finish it next summer.

C You can use the present continuous with **today** / **this week** / **this year**, etc. (periods around now):

- *A:* You**'re working** hard **today**. (*not* You work hard today)
  B: Yes, I have a lot to do.
- The company I work for **isn't doing** so well **this year**.

D We use the present continuous when we talk about changes happening around now, especially with these verbs:

get	change	become	increase	rise
fall	grow	improve	begin	start

- **Is** your English **getting** better? (*not* Does your English get better)
- The population of the world **is increasing** very fast. (*not* increases)
- At first I didn't like my job, but I**'m beginning** to enjoy it now. (*not* I begin)

Exercises

1.1 Complete the sentences with the following verbs in the correct form:

> get   happen   look   lose   make   start   stay   try   ~~work~~

1. "You _'re working_____ hard today." "Yes, I have a lot to do."
2. I _____ for Christine. Do you know where she is?
3. It _____ dark. Should I turn on the light?
4. They don't have anywhere to live at the moment. They _____ with friends until they find a place.
5. Things are not so good at work. The company _____ money.
6. Do you have an umbrella? It _____ to rain.
7. You _____ a lot of noise. Can you be quieter? I _____ to concentrate.
8. Why are all these people here? What _____ ?

1.2 Put the verb into the correct form. Sometimes you need the negative (*I'm not doing*, etc.).

1. Please don't make so much noise. I _'m trying_____ (try) to work.
2. Let's go out now. It _isn't raining___ (rain) anymore.
3. You can turn off the radio. I _____ (listen) to it.
4. Kate called me last night. She's on vacation in Quebec. She _____ (have) a great time and doesn't want to come home.
5. I want to lose weight, so this week I _____ (eat) lunch.
6. Andrew has just started evening classes. He _____ (study) German.
7. Paul and Sally had an argument. They _____ (speak) to each other.
8. I _____ (get) tired. I need a break.
9. Tim _____ (work) this week. He has a week off.

1.3 Complete the conversations.

1. *A:* I saw Brian a few days ago.
   B: Oh, did you? _What's he doing_____ these days? (what / he / do)
   A: He's in college now.
   B: _____ ? (what / he / study)
   A: Psychology.
   B: _____ it? (he / enjoy)
   A: Yes, he says _____ a lot. (he / learn)

2. *A:* Hi, Liz. How _____ ? (your new job / go)
   B: Not bad. It wasn't so good at first, but _____ better now. (it / get)
   A: What about Jonathan? Is he OK?
   B: Yes, but _____ his work at the moment. (he / not / enjoy) He's been in the same job for a long time, and _____ to get bored with it. (he / begin)

1.4 Complete the sentences using the following verbs:

> begin   change   get   ~~increase~~   rise

1. The population of the world _is increasing_____ very fast.
2. The world _____ . Things never stay the same.
3. The situation is already bad and it _____ worse.
4. The cost of living _____ . Every year things are more expensive.
5. The weather _____ to improve. The rain has stopped, and the wind isn't as strong.

Simple Present (I do)

A Study this example situation:

Alex is a bus driver, but now he is in bed asleep.

He is not driving a bus. (He is asleep.)

but He **drives** a bus. (He is a bus driver.)

Drive(s)/work(s)/do(es), etc., is the *simple present*:

I/we/you/they	**drive/work/do**, etc.
he/she/it	**drives/works/does**, etc.

B We use the simple present to talk about things in general. We use it to say that something happens all the time or repeatedly, or that something is true in general:

- ■ Nurses **take** care of patients in hospitals.
- ■ I usually **leave** for work at 8 a.m.
- ■ The earth **goes** around the sun.
- ■ The coffee shop **opens** at 7:30 in the morning.

Remember:

 I **work** . . . *but* He **works** . . .   They **teach** . . . *but* My sister **teaches** . . .

For spelling (**-s** or **-es**), see Appendix 6.

C We use **do** / **does** to make questions and negative sentences:

do	I/we/you/they	**work?**
does	he/she/it	**drive?**
		do?

	I/we/you/they	**don't**	**work**
	he/she/it	**doesn't**	**drive**
			do

- ■ I come from Japan. Where **do** you **come** from?
- ■ I **don't go** to church very often.
- ■ What **does** this word **mean**? (*not* What means this word?)
- ■ Rice **doesn't grow** in cold climates.

In the following examples, **do** is also the main verb (do you **do** / doesn't **do**, etc.):

- ■ "What **do** you **do**?" "I work in a department store."
- ■ He's always so lazy. He **doesn't do** anything to help.

D We use the simple present to say how often we do things:

- ■ I **get** up at 8:00 **every morning**.
- ■ **How often do** you **go** to the dentist?
- ■ Julie **doesn't drink** tea **very often**.
- ■ Robert usually **plays** tennis **two or three times a week** in the summer.

E **I promise / I apologize**, etc.

Sometimes we do things by saying them. For example, when you promise to do something, you can say "I promise . . . "; when you suggest something, you can say, "I suggest . . .":

- ■ **I promise** I won't be late. (*not* I'm promising)
- ■ "What do you **suggest** I do?" "**I suggest** that you spend less money."

In the same way, we say: **I advise** . . . / **I insist** . . . / **I refuse** . . . / **I suppose** . . . , etc.

Exercises

2.1 Complete the sentences using the following verbs:

cause(s)   connect(s)   drink(s)   live(s)   open(s)   ~~speak(s)~~   take(s)

1. Tanya __*speaks*__ German very well.
2. I don't _____ much coffee.
3. The swimming pool _____ at 7:30 every morning.
4. Bad driving _____ many accidents.
5. My parents _____ in a very small apartment.
6. The Olympic Games _____ place every four years.
7. The Panama Canal _____ the Atlantic and Pacific Oceans.

2.2 Put the verb into the correct form.

1. Julie __*doesn't drink*__ (not / drink) tea very often.
2. What time _____ (the banks / close) here?
3. I have a TV, but I _____ (not / watch) it much.
4. "Where _____ (Ricardo / come) from?" "He's Cuban."
5. "What _____ (you / do)?" "I'm an electrician."
6. It _____ (take) me an hour to get to work. How long _____ (it / take) you?
7. Look at this sentence. What _____ (this word / mean)?
8. David isn't in very good shape. He _____ (not / exercise).

2.3 Use the following verbs to complete the sentences. Sometimes you need the negative:

believe   eat   flow   ~~go~~   ~~grow~~   make   rise   tell   translate

1. The earth __*goes*__ around the sun.
2. Rice __*doesn't grow*__ in Canada.
3. The sun _____ in the east.
4. Bees _____ honey.
5. Vegetarians _____ meat.
6. An atheist _____ in God.
7. An interpreter _____ from one language into another.
8. Liars are people who _____ the truth.
9. The Amazon River _____ into the Atlantic Ocean.

2.4 You ask Liz questions about herself and her family. Write the questions.

1. You know that Liz plays tennis. You want to know how often. Ask her.
   How often __*do you play tennis*__ ?
2. Perhaps Liz's sister plays tennis, too. You want to know. Ask Liz.
   _____ your sister _____ ?
3. You know that Liz reads a newspaper every day. You want to know which one. Ask her.
   _____ ?
4. You know that Liz's brother works. You want to know what he does. Ask Liz.
   _____ ?
5. You know that Liz goes to the movies a lot. You want to know how often. Ask her.
   _____ ?
6. You don't know where Liz's grandparents live. You want to know. Ask Liz.
   _____ ?

2.5 Complete using the following:

I apologize   I insist   I promise   I recommend   ~~I suggest~~

1. It's a nice day. __*I suggest*__ we go for a walk.
2. I won't tell anybody what you said. _____ .
3. I won't let you pay for the meal. _____ that you let me pay.
4. _____ for what I did. It won't happen again.
5. The new restaurant downtown is very good. _____ it highly.

Present Continuous and Simple Present 1 (**I am doing** and **I do**)

Compare:

Present continuous (**I am doing**)

We use the continuous for things happening at or around the time of speaking. The action is not complete.

I am doing

past	now	future

- The water **is boiling**. Can you turn it off?
- Listen to those people. What language **are** they **speaking**?
- Let's go out. It **isn't raining** now.
- "I'm busy." "What **are you doing**?"
- **I'm getting** hungry. Let's eat.
- Kate wants to work in Italy, so she**'s learning** Italian.
- The population of the world **is increasing** very fast.

We use the present continuous for *temporary* situations:

- **I'm living** with some friends until I find a place of my own.
- *A:* You**'re working** hard today.
  B: Yes, I have a lot to do.

See Unit 1 for more information.

Simple present (**I do**)

We use the simple for things in general or things that happen repeatedly.

I do

past	now	future

- Water **boils** at 100 degrees Celsius.
- Excuse me, **do** you **speak** English?
- It **doesn't rain** very much in summer.
- What **do** you usually **do** after work?
- I always **get** hungry in the afternoon.
- Most people **learn** to swim when they are children.
- Every day the population of the world **increases** by about 200,000 people.

We use the simple present for *permanent* situations:

- My parents **live** in Vancouver. They have lived there all their lives.
- John isn't lazy. He **works** hard most of the time.

See Unit 2 for more information.

I always do and **I'm always doing**

I always do (something) = I do it every time:

- **I always drive** to work. (*not* I'm always driving)

"**I'm always doing** something" has a different meaning. For example:

I've lost my key again. **I'm always losing** things.

I'm always losing things = I lose things very often, perhaps too often, or more often than normal.

Two more examples:

- You**'re always watching** television. You should do something more active.
  (= You watch too much television)
- Tim is never satisfied. He**'s always complaining**. (= He complains too much)

Present Continuous and Simple Present 2 Unit 4   Present Tenses with a Future Meaning Unit 18

Exercises

3.1 Are the <u>underlined</u> verbs right or wrong? Correct them where necessary.

1. Water <u>boils</u> at 212 degrees Fahrenheit. _____*OK*_____
2. The water <u>boils</u>. Can you turn it off? _____*is boiling*_____
3. Look! That man <u>tries</u> to open the door of your car. _____
4. Can you hear those people? What <u>do</u> they <u>talk</u> about? _____
5. The moon <u>goes</u> around the earth in about 27 days. _____
6. I have to go now. It <u>gets</u> late. _____
7. I usually <u>drive</u> to work. _____
8. "Hurry up! It's time to leave." "OK, I <u>come</u>." _____
9. I hear you've got a new job. How <u>does</u> it <u>go</u>? _____
10. Paul is never late. He<u>'s</u> always <u>getting</u> to work on time. _____
11. They don't get along well. They<u>'re</u> always <u>arguing</u>. _____

3.2 Put the verb into the correct form, present continuous or simple present.

1. Let's go out. It __*isn't raining*__ (not / rain) now.
2. Julia is very good at languages. She __*speaks*__ (speak) four languages very well.
3. Hurry up! Everybody _____ (wait) for you.
4. "_____ (you / listen) to the radio?" "No, you can turn it off."
5. "_____ (you / listen) to the radio every day?" "No, just occasionally."
6. The River Nile _____ (flow) into the Mediterranean.
7. The river _____ (flow) very fast today – much faster than usual.
8. We usually _____ (grow) vegetables in our garden, but this year we _____ (not / grow) any.
9. A: How's your English?
   B: Not bad. I think it _____ (improve) slowly.
10. Rachel is in New York right now. She _____ (stay) at the Park Hotel. She always _____ (stay) there when she's in New York.
11. Can we stop walking soon? I _____ (start) to feel tired.
12. A: Can you drive?
    B: I _____ (learn). My father _____ (teach) me.
13. Normally I _____ (finish) work at five, but this week I _____ (work) until six to earn a little more money.
14. My parents _____ (live) in Taipei. They were born there and have never lived anywhere else. Where _____ (your parents / live)?
15. Sonia _____ (look) for a place to live. She _____ (stay) with her sister until she finds a place.
16. A: What _____ (your brother / do)?
    B: He's an architect, but he _____ (not / work) right now.
17. *(at a party)* I usually _____ (enjoy) parties, but I _____ (not / enjoy) this one very much.

3.3 Finish B's sentences. Use *always -ing*.

1. A: I've lost my keys again.
   B: Not again! __*You're always losing your keys*__ .
2. A: The car has broken down again.
   B: That car is useless. It _____ .
3. A: Look! You made the same mistake again.
   B: Oh no, not again! I _____ .
4. A: Oh, I forgot my glasses again.
   B: That's typical! _____ .

Present Continuous and Simple Present 2 (I am doing and I do)

A

We use continuous forms for actions and happenings that have started but not finished (they **are eating** / it **is raining**, etc.). Some verbs (for example, **know** and **like**) are not normally used in this way. We do not say "I am knowing" or "they are liking"; we say I **know**, they **like**.

The following verbs are not normally used in the present continuous:

like	love	hate	want	need	prefer	
know	realize	suppose	mean	understand	believe	remember
belong	fit	contain	consist	seem		

- I'm hungry. I **want** something to eat. (*not* I'm wanting)
- **Do** you **understand** what I **mean**?
- Ann **doesn't seem** very happy.

B

Think

When **think** means "believe" or "have an opinion," we do not use the continuous:
- I **think** Mary is Canadian, but I'm not sure. (*not* I'm thinking)
- What **do** you **think** about my plan? (= What is your opinion?)

When **think** means "consider," the continuous is possible:
- **I'm thinking** about what happened. I often **think** about it.
- Nicky **is thinking** of quitting her job. (= she is considering it)

C

He is selfish and He is being selfish

He**'s being** = He's behaving / He's acting. Compare:
- I can't understand why he**'s being** so selfish. He isn't usually like that.
  (**being** selfish = behaving selfishly at the moment)
- He never thinks about other people. He **is** very selfish. (*not* He is being)
  (= He is selfish generally, not only at the moment)

We use **am** / **is** / **are being** to say how somebody is *behaving*. It is not usually possible in other sentences:
- It**'s** hot today. (*not* It's being hot)
- Sarah **is** very tired. (*not* is being tired)

D

See   hear   smell   taste

We normally use the simple present (not continuous) with these verbs:
- **Do** you **see** that man over there? (*not* Are you seeing)
- This room **smells**. Let's open a window.

We often use **can** + **see** / **hear** / **smell** / **taste**:
- I **can hear** a strange noise. **Can** you **hear** it?

E

Look   feel

You can use the simple present or continuous to say how somebody looks or feels now:
- You **look** good today.   *or*   You**'re looking** good today.
- How **do** you **feel** now?   *or*   How **are** you **feeling** now?

but
- I usually **feel** tired in the morning. (*not* I'm usually feeling)

Exercises

4.1 Are the <u>underlined</u> verbs right or wrong? Correct them where necessary.

1. Nicky <u>is thinking</u> of giving up her job.   _____OK_____
2. <u>Are</u> you <u>believing</u> in God? _____
3. <u>I'm feeling</u> hungry. Is there anything to eat? _____
4. This sauce is great. It<u>'s tasting</u> really good. _____
5. <u>I'm thinking</u> this is your key. Is it? _____

4.2 Use the words in parentheses to make sentences. (You should also study Unit 3 before you do this exercise.)

1. (you / not / seem / very happy today)
   You don't seem very happy today.

2. (what / you / do?)
   _____
   _____
   Be quiet! (I / think)
   _____

3. (who / this umbrella / belong to?)
   _____
   _____
   I have no idea.

4. (dinner / smell / good)
   _____
   _____

5. Excuse me. (anybody / sit / there?)
   _____
   _____
   No, go ahead.

6. Ladies Gloves
   (these gloves / not / fit / me)
   _____
   _____
   They're too small.

4.3 Put the verb into the correct form, present continuous or simple present.

1. Are you hungry? _Do you want_ (you / want) something to eat?
2. Don't put the dictionary away. I _____ (use) it.
3. Don't put the dictionary away. I _____ (need) it.
4. Who is that man? What _____ (he / want)?
5. Who is that man? Why _____ (he / look) at us?
6. Alan says he's 80 years old, but nobody _____ (believe) him.
7. She told me her name, but I _____ (not / remember) it now.
8. I _____ (think) of selling my car. Are you interested in buying it?
9. I _____ (think) you should sell your car. You _____ (not / use) it very often.
10. Air _____ (consist) mainly of nitrogen and oxygen.

4.4 Complete the sentences using the most appropriate form of *be*, simple present *(am/is/are)* or present continuous *(am/is/are being)*.

1. I can't understand why _he's being_ so selfish. He isn't usually like that.
2. Sarah _____ very nice to me these days. I wonder why.
3. You'll like Debbie when you meet her. She _____ very nice.
4. You're usually very patient, so why _____ unreasonable about waiting 10 more minutes?
5. Why isn't Steve at work today? _____ sick?

Simple Past (**I did**)

Study this example:

> Wolfgang Amadeus Mozart was an Austrian musician and composer. He **lived** from 1756 to 1791. He **started** composing at the age of five and **wrote** more than 600 pieces of music. He **was** only 35 years old when he **died**.
>
> **Lived/started/wrote/was/died** are all *simple past*.

Wolfgang A. Mozart
1756-1791

Very often the simple past ends in **–ed** (*regular* verbs):

- ■ I work in a travel agency now. I **worked** in a department store before.
- ■ We **invited** them to our party, but they **decided** not to come.
- ■ The police **stopped** me on my way home last night.
- ■ Laura **passed** her exam because she **studied** very hard.

For spelling (sto**pp**ed, stud**ied**, etc.), see Appendix 6.

But many verbs are *irregular*. This means the simple past does *not* end in **–ed**. For example:

write	→ **wrote**	■	Mozart **wrote** more than 600 pieces of music.
see	→ **saw**	■	We **saw** Rose at the mall a few days ago.
go	→ **went**	■	I **went** to the movies three times last week.
shut	→ **shut**	■	It **was** cold, so I **shut** the window.

For a list of irregular verbs, see Appendix 1.

In questions and negatives we use **did** / **didn't** + *base form* (**enjoy** / **see** / **go**, etc.):

I	enjoy**ed**
she	**saw**
they	**went**

	you	**enjoy**?
did	she	**see**?
	they	**go**?

I		**enjoy**
she	**didn't**	**see**
they		**go**

- ■ *A:* **Did** you **go** out last night?
  B: Yes, I **went** to the movies, but I **didn't enjoy** the film much.
- ■ "When **did** Mr. Thomas **die**?" "About 10 years ago."
- ■ They **didn't invite** her to the party, so she **didn't go**.
- ■ "**Did** you **have** time to write the letter?" "No, I **didn't**."

In the following examples, **do** is the main verb in the sentence (**did** . . . **do** / **didn't do**):

- ■ What **did** you **do** on the weekend? (*not* What did you on the weekend?)
- ■ I **didn't do** anything. (*not* I didn't anything)

The past of **be** (**am** / **is** / **are**) is **was** / **were**:

I/he/she/it	**was**/**wasn't**
we/you/they	**were**/**weren't**

was	I/he/she/it?
were	we/you/they?

Note that we do not use **did** in negatives and questions with **was** / **were**:

- ■ I **was** angry because they **were** late.
- ■ **Was** the weather good when you **were** on vacation?
- ■ They **weren't** able to come because they **were** so busy.
- ■ Did you go out last night, or **were** you too tired?

Exercises

5.1 Read what Debbie says about a typical working day:

I usually get up at 7:00 and have a big breakfast. I walk to work, which takes me about half an hour. I start work at 8:45. I never have lunch. I finish work at 5:00. I'm always tired when I get home. I usually cook dinner a little later. I don't usually go out. I go to bed around 11:00, and I always sleep well.

Debbie

Yesterday was a typical working day for Debbie. Write what she did or didn't do yesterday.

1. ___*She got up at 7:00.*___
2. She _____ a big breakfast.
3. She _____ .
4. It _____ to get to work.
5. _____ at 8:45.
6. _____ lunch.
7. _____ at 5:00.
8. _____ tired when _____ home.
9. _____ dinner a little later.
10. _____ out last night.
11. _____ at 11:00.
12. _____ well last night.

5.2 Complete the sentences using the following verbs in the correct form:

buy   catch   cost   fall   hurt   sell   spend   teach   throw   ~~write~~

1. Mozart __*wrote*__ more than 600 pieces of music.
2. "How did you learn to drive?" "My father _____ me."
3. We couldn't afford to keep our car, so we _____ it.
4. Dave _____ down the stairs this morning and _____ his leg.
5. Jim _____ the ball to Sue, who _____ it.
6. Ann _____ a lot of money yesterday. She _____ a dress that _____ $200.

5.3 You ask James about his vacation. Write your questions.

Hi. How are things?
    Fine, thanks. I've just had a great vacation.
1. Where __*did you go*__ ?
    We went on a trip from San Francisco to Denver.
2. How _____ ? By car?
    Yes, we rented a car in San Francisco.
3. It's a long way to drive. How long _____ ?
    Two weeks.
4. Where _____ ? In hotels?
    Yes, small hotels or motels.
5. _____ ?
    It was very hot – sometimes too hot.
6. _____ the Grand Canyon?
    Of course. It was wonderful.

5.4 Complete the sentences. Put the verb into the correct form, positive or negative.

1. It was warm, so I __*took*__ off my coat. (take)
2. The movie wasn't very good. I __*didn't enjoy*__ it very much. (enjoy)
3. I knew Sarah was very busy, so I _____ her. (disturb)
4. I was very tired, so I _____ the party early. (leave)
5. The bed was very uncomfortable. I _____ very well. (sleep)
6. The window was open and a bird _____ into the room. (fly)
7. The hotel wasn't very expensive. It _____ very much. (cost)
8. I was in a hurry, so I _____ time to call you. (have)
9. It was hard carrying the bags. They _____ very heavy. (be)

11

Past Continuous (**I was doing**)

A Study this example situation:

Yesterday Karen and Jim played tennis. They began at 10:00 and finished at 11:30. So, at 10:30 they **were playing** tennis.

They **were playing** = they were in the middle of playing. They had not finished playing.

Was / were –ing is the *past continuous*:

I/he/she/it	**was**	play**ing**
we/you/they	**were**	do**ing**
		work**ing**, etc.

B I **was doing** something = I was in the middle of doing something at a certain time. The action or situation had already started before this time, but had not finished:

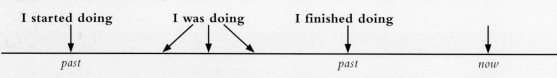

I started doing	**I was doing**	**I finished doing**	
past		*past*	*now*

- This time last year I **was living** in Brazil.
- What **were** you **doing** at 10:00 last night?
- I waved to Helen, but she **wasn't looking**.

C Compare the *past continuous* (**I was doing**) and *simple past* (**I did**):

Past continuous (in the middle of an action)	*Simple past* (complete action)
■ I **was walking** home when I met Dave.	■ I **walked** home after the party last night.
■ Kate **was watching** television when we arrived.	■ Kate **watched** television a lot when she was sick last year.

D We often use the simple past and the past continuous together to say that something happened in the middle of something else:

- Matt **burned** his hand while he **was cooking** dinner.
- It **was raining** when I **got** up.
- I **saw** you in the park yesterday. You **were sitting** on the grass and **reading** a book.
- I **hurt** my back while I **was working** in the garden.

But we use the simple past to say that one thing happened after another:

- I **was walking** downtown when I **saw** Dave. So I **stopped**, and we **talked** for a while.

Compare:

■ When Karen arrived, we **were having** dinner. (= we had already started before she arrived)	■ When Karen arrived, we **had** dinner. (= Karen arrived, and then we had dinner together.)

E Some verbs (for example, **know** and **want**) are not normally used in the continuous (see Unit 4A):

- We were good friends. We **knew** each other well. (*not* We were knowing)
- I was having a good time at the party, but Chris **wanted** to go home. (*not* was wanting)

Exercises

6.1 What were you doing at these times? Write sentences as in the examples. The past continuous is not always necessary (see the second example).

1. (at 8:00 last night) _I was having dinner._
2. (at 5:00 last Monday) _I was on a bus on my way home._
3. (at 10:15 yesterday morning) _____
4. (at 4:30 this morning) _____
5. (at 7:45 last night) _____
6. (half an hour ago) _____

6.2 Use your own ideas to complete the sentences. Use the past continuous.

1. Matt burned his hand while he _was cooking dinner_____ .
2. The doorbell rang while I _____ .
3. We saw an accident while we _____ .
4. Lauren fell asleep while she _____ .
5. The television was on, but nobody _____ .

6.3 Put the verb into the correct form, past continuous or simple past.

1.

I _saw_ (see) Sue in town yesterday, but she _____ (not / see) me. She _____ (look) the other way.

2.

I _____ (meet) Tom and Jane at the airport a few weeks ago. They _____ (go) to Boston and I _____ (go) to Montreal. We _____ (talk) while we _____ (wait) for our flights.

3.

I _____ (ride) my bicycle yesterday when a man _____ (step) out into the street in front of me. I _____ (go) pretty fast, but luckily I _____ (manage) to stop in time and _____ (not / hit) him.

6.4 Put the verb into the correct form, past continuous or simple past.

1. Jane _was waiting_ (wait) for me when I _arrived_ (arrive).
2. "What _____ (you / do) at this time yesterday?" "I was asleep."
3. "_____ (you / go) out last night?" "No, I was too tired."
4. How fast _____ (you / drive) when the accident _____ (happen)?
5. Sam _____ (take) a picture of me while I _____ (not / look).
6. We were in a very difficult position. We _____ (not / know) what to do.
7. I haven't seen David for ages. The last time I _____ (see) him, he _____ (try) to find a job in Miami.
8. I _____ (walk) along the street when suddenly I _____ (hear) footsteps behind me. Somebody _____ (follow) me. I was scared and I _____ (start) to run.
9. When I was young, I _____ (want) to be a pilot.
10. Last night I _____ (drop) a plate while I _____ (do) the dishes. Fortunately it _____ (not / break).

Present Perfect (I have done)

A

Study this example conversation:

Dave: **Have** you **traveled** a lot, Jane?
Jane: Yes, I**'ve been** to lots of places.
Dave: Really? **Have** you ever **been** to China?
Jane: Yes, I**'ve been** to China twice.
Dave: What about India?
Jane: No, I **haven't been** to India.

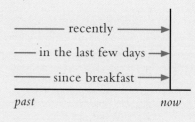

Jane's life
(a period until now)

past   now

Have/has + **traveled/been/done**, etc., *(past participle)* is the present perfect:

I/we/they/you **have** (= I**'ve**, etc.)	**traveled**
he/she/it **has** (= he**'s**, etc.)	**been**
	done, etc.

The past participle often ends in **-ed** (travel**ed**/decid**ed**, etc.), but many important verbs are *irregular* (**been/done/written**, etc.). For a list of irregular verbs, see Appendix 1.

B

We use the *present perfect* when we talk about a period of time that continues from the past until now. In the conversation in **A**, Dave and Jane are talking about the places Jane has visited in her life – which is a period that continues until now. Some more examples:

- **Have** you ever **eaten** caviar? (in your life)
- We**'ve** never **had** a car.
- "**Have** you **read** *Hamlet*?" "No, I **haven't read** any of Shakespeare's plays."
- Susan really loves that movie. She**'s seen** it eight times!
- What a boring movie! It's the most boring movie I**'ve** ever **seen**.

C

In the following examples, too, the speakers are talking about a period that continues until now (**recently** / **in the last few days** / **so far** / **since breakfast**, etc.).

- **Have** you **heard** from Brian **recently**?
- I**'ve met** a lot of people **in the last few days**.
- Everything is going well. We **haven't had** any problems **so far**.
- I'm hungry. I **haven't eaten** anything **since breakfast**.
- It's nice to see you again. We **haven't seen** each other **for a long time**.

——— recently ———

— in the last few days —

——— since breakfast ———

past   now

D

We use the present perfect with **today** / **this morning** / **this year**, etc., when these periods are not finished at the time of speaking (see also Unit 9B):

- I**'ve drunk** four cups of coffee **today**.
- **Have** you **had** a vacation **this year** (yet)?
- I **haven't seen** Tom **this morning**. **Have** you?
- Rob **hasn't studied** very hard **this semester**.

——— today ———

past   now

E

We say: It's the (first) time something **has happened**. For example:

- Don is taking a driving lesson. It's his first one.
  It's the first time he **has driven** a car. (*not* drives)
- *or* He **has never driven** a car **before**.

- Sarah has lost her passport again. This is the second time this **has happened**. (*not* happens)
- Bill is calling his girlfriend again. That's the third time he**'s called** her **tonight**.

This is the first time
I**'ve driven** a car.

STUDENT DRIVER

Present Perfect and Past Units 8–9   **Present Perfect Continuous** Units 10–11

Exercises

7.1 You are asking people questions about things they have done. Make questions with *ever* using the words in parentheses.

1. (ride / horse?) _Have you ever ridden a horse?_
2. (be / Mexico?) Have _____
3. (run / marathon?) _____
4. (speak / famous person?) _____
5. (most beautiful place / visit?) What's _____

7.2 Complete B's answers. Some sentences are positive and some negative. Use the following verbs:

| be | be | eat | happen | have | ~~meet~~ | play | read | see | see | try |

A   B

1. What's Mark's sister like?   I have no idea. _I've never met_ her.
2. How is Diane these days?   I don't know. I _____ her recently.
3. Are you hungry?   Yes. I _____ much today.
4. Can you play chess?   Yes, but _____ in ages.
5. Are you enjoying your vacation?   Yes, it's the best vacation _____ for a long time.
6. What's that book like?   I don't know. _____ it.
7. Is Sydney an interesting place?   I have no idea. _____ there.
8. Mike was late for work again today.   Again? He _____ late every day this week.
9. Do you like caviar?   I don't know. _____ it.
10. I hear your car broke down again yesterday.   Yes, it's the second time _____ this week.
11. Who's that woman by the door?   I don't know. _____ her before.

7.3 Complete the sentences using *today* / *this year* / *this semester*, etc.

1. I saw Tom yesterday, but _I haven't seen him today_ .
2. I read a newspaper yesterday, but I _____ today.
3. Last year the company made a profit, but this year _____ .
4. Tracy worked hard at school last semester, but _____ .
5. It snowed a lot last winter, but _____ .
6. Our football team won a lot of games last season, but we _____ .

7.4 Read the situations and write sentences as shown in the example.

1. Jack is driving a car, but he's very nervous and not sure what to do.
   You ask: _Have you driven a car before?_
   He says: _No, this is the first time I've driven a car._
2. Ben is playing tennis. He's not good at it, and he doesn't know the rules.
   You ask: Have _____
   He says: No, this is the first _____
3. Sue is riding a horse. She doesn't look very confident or comfortable.
   You ask: _____
   She says: _____
4. Maria is in Los Angeles. She has just arrived, and it's very new for her.
   You ask: _____
   She says: _____

Present Perfect and Past 1
(I have done and I did)

You can use the present perfect (**I have done**) for new or recent happenings:

- **I've lost** my keys. **Have** you **seen** them?
- "Is Sally here?"   "No, she**'s gone** out."
- The police **have arrested** two people in connection with the robbery.

You can also use the simple past (**I lost**, **she went**, etc.):

- I **lost** my keys. **Did** you **see** them?
- "Is Sally here?"   "No, she **went** out."
- The police **arrested** two people in connection with the robbery.

When we say that "something has happened," this is new information:

- Have you heard? Bill and Sarah **have won** the lottery!
  (*or* Bill and Sarah **won** . . .)
- The road is closed. There**'s been** (there **has been**) an accident.
  (*or* There **was** an accident)

Use the simple past only (*not* the present perfect) for things that are not recent or new:

- Mozart **was** a composer. He **wrote** more than 600 pieces of music.
  (*not* has been . . . has written)
- My mother **grew** up in Chile. (*not* has grown)

Compare:

- Shakespeare **wrote** many plays.
- My brother is a writer. He **has written** many books. (he still writes books)

The present perfect always tells us something about now:

- I'm sorry, but I**'ve forgotten** your name. (= I can't remember it *now*)
- Sally isn't here. She**'s gone** out. (= she is out *now*)
- I can't find my bag. **Have** you **seen** it? (= do you know where it is *now*?)

You can also use the simple past in all these examples ("I **forgot** your name," etc.).

Use the simple past only (*not* the present perfect) if the situation now is different.
Compare:

- It **has stopped** raining, so you don't need the umbrella.

  It **stopped** raining for a while, but now it's raining again.

You can use the simple past or present perfect with **just**, **already**, and **yet**.

Just = a short time ago:

- *A:* Are you hungry?
  B: No, I **just had** lunch.   *or*   I**'ve just had** lunch.
- *A:* Why are you so happy?
  B: I **just heard** some good news.   *or*   I**'ve just heard** some good news.

We use **already** to say that something happened sooner than expected:

- *A:* Don't forget to mail the letter.
  B: I **already mailed** it.   *or*   I**'ve already mailed** it.
- *A:* What time is Mark leaving?
  B: He **already left**.   *or*   He**'s already left**.

Yet = until now. **Yet** shows that the speaker is expecting something to happen. Use **yet** only in questions and negative sentences:

- **Did** it **stop** raining **yet**?   *or*   **Has** it **stopped** raining **yet**?
- I wrote the letter, but I **didn't mail** it **yet**.   *or*   . . . I **haven't mailed** it **yet**.

Simple Past Unit 5   **Present Perfect** Unit 7   **Present Perfect and Past 2** Unit 9   **British English** Appendix 7

Exercises

8.1 Complete the sentences using the verbs in parentheses. Use the present perfect where possible. Otherwise, use the simple past.

1. It ___has stopped___ (stop) raining, so you don't need your umbrella.

2. *before* / *now*
   The town is very different now. It _____ (change) a lot.

3. I meant to call you last night, but I _____ . (forget)

4. Mary
   Mary _____ (go) to Peru for a vacation, but she's back home in Austin now.

5. Are you OK?
   Yes. I _____ (have) a headache, but I feel fine now.

6. You look great! You _____ (lost) weight.

8.2 Which sentence is correct: (a), (b), or both of them?

1. a) My mother has grown up in Chile.   b) My mother grew up in Chile.   ___b___
2. a) Did you see my purse?   b) Have you seen my purse?   ___both___
3. a) I already paid the gas bill.   b) I've already paid the gas bill.   _____
4. a) The Chinese invented paper.   b) The Chinese have invented paper.   _____
5. a) Where have you been born?   b) Where were you born?   _____
6. a) Ow! I cut my finger.   b) Ow! I've cut my finger.   _____
7. a) I forgot Jerry's address.   b) I've forgotten Jerry's address.   _____
8. a) Did you go to the store yet?   b) Have you gone to the store yet?   _____
9. a) Albert Einstein has been the scientist who has developed the theory of relativity.   b) Albert Einstein was the scientist who developed the theory of relativity.   _____
10. a) My father was raised by his aunt.   b) My father has been raised by his aunt.   _____

8.3 Read the situations and write sentences with *just*, *already*, or *yet*. You can use the present perfect or simple past.

1. After lunch you go to see a friend at her house. She says, "Would you like something to eat?"
   You say: No, thank you. __I've just had lunch OR I just had lunch__ . (have lunch)
2. Joe goes out. Five minutes later, the phone rings and the caller says, "Can I speak to Joe?"
   You say: I'm sorry, _____ . (go out)
3. You are eating in a restaurant. The waiter thinks you have finished and starts to clear the table.
   You say: Wait a minute! _____ . (not / finish)
4. You are going to a restaurant tonight. You call to reserve a table. Later your friend says,
   "Should I call to reserve a table?" You say: No, _____ . (do it)
5. You know that a friend of yours is looking for a place to live. Perhaps she has been successful.
   Ask her. You say: _____ ? (find)
6. You are still thinking about where to go on vacation. A friend asks, "Where are you going
   on vacation?" You say: _____ . (not / decide)
7. Linda went to the bank, but a few minutes ago she returned. Somebody asks, "Is Linda still
   at the bank?" You say: No, _____ . (come back)
8. Yesterday Carol invited you to a party on Saturday. Now another friend is inviting you to the
   same party. You say: Thanks, but Carol _____ . (invite)

Present Perfect and Past 2
(I have done and I did)

Do not use the present perfect (**I have done**) when you talk about a *finished* time (for example, **yesterday / 10 minutes ago / in 1999 / when I was a child**). Use a past tense:

- It **was** very cold **yesterday**. (*not* has been)
- Paul and Lucy **went** out **10 minutes ago**. (*not* have gone)
- **Did** you **eat** a lot of candy **when you were a child**? (*not* have you eaten)
- I **got** home late **last night**. I **was** very tired and **went** straight to bed.

Use the simple past to ask **When . . . ?** *or* **What time . . . ?**:

- **When did** your friends **get** here? (*not* have . . . gotten)
- **What time did** you **finish** work?

Compare:

Present Perfect or Simple Past	Simple Past only
■ Tom **has lost** his key. He can't get into the house. (*or* Tom **lost** . . .)	■ Tom **lost** his key **yesterday**. He couldn't get into the house.
■ Is Carla here or **has** she **left**? (*or* **Did** she **leave**?)	■ **When did** Carla **leave**?

Compare:

Present Perfect (have done)

- **I've done** a lot of work **today**.

We use the present perfect for a period of time that continues *until now*. For example: **today / this week / since 1999**.

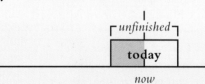

past   *now*

- It **hasn't rained this week**.
- **Have** you **seen** Lisa **this morning**? (It is still morning)
- **Have** you **seen** Tim **recently**?
- I don't know where Lisa is. I **haven't seen** her. (= I haven't seen her recently)
- We've **been waiting for an hour**. (We are still waiting now)
- John lives in Los Angeles. He **has lived** there **for seven years**.
- I **have never played golf**. (in my life)
- *It's the last day of your vacation. You say:* It**'s been** a really good vacation. I**'ve** really **enjoyed** it.

Simple Past (did)

- I **did** a lot of work **yesterday**.

We use the simple past for a *finished* time in the past. For example: **yesterday / last week / from 1999 to 2005**.

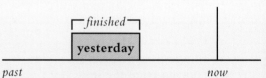

past   *now*

- It **didn't rain last week**.
- **Did** you **see** Lisa **this morning**? (It is now afternoon or evening)
- **Did** you **see** Tim **on Sunday**?
- *A:* **Was** Lisa at the party **on Sunday**? *B:* I don't think so. I **didn't see** her.
- We **waited** (*or* **were waiting**) **for an hour**. (We are no longer waiting)
- John **lived** in New York **for 10 years**. Now he lives in Los Angeles.
- I **didn't play** golf **last summer**.
- *After you come back from vacation, you say:* It **was** a really good vacation. I really **enjoyed** it.

Simple Past Unit 5   **Present Perfect** Unit 7   **Present Perfect and Past 1** Unit 8   **Present Perfect Continuous** Units 10–11

Exercises

9.1 Are the <u>underlined</u> parts of these sentences right or wrong? Correct them where necessary.

1. <u>I've lost</u> my key. I can't find it anywhere.   *OK*
2. <u>Have you eaten</u> a lot of candy when you were a child?   *Did you eat*
3. <u>I've bought</u> a new car. You have to come and see it.   _____
4. <u>I've bought</u> a new car last week.   _____
5. Where <u>have you been</u> last night?   _____
6. Maria <u>has graduated</u> from high school in 2004.   _____
7. I'm looking for Mike. <u>Have you seen</u> him?   _____
8. "<u>Have you been</u> to Paris?" "Yes, many times."   _____
9. I'm very hungry. <u>I haven't eaten</u> much today.   _____
10. When <u>has this book been</u> published?   _____

9.2 Make sentences from the words in parentheses. Use the present perfect or simple past.

1. (it / not / rain / this week) ___*It hasn't rained this week.*_____
2. (the weather / be / cold / recently) The weather _____
3. (it / cold / last week) It _____
4. (I / not / read / a newspaper yesterday) I _____
5. (I / not / read / a newspaper today) _____
6. (Kate / make / a lot of money / this year) _____
7. (she / not / make / so much / last year) _____
8. (you / take / a vacation recently?) _____

9.3 Put the verb into the correct form, present perfect or simple past.

1. I don't know where Lisa is. ___*Have you seen*___ (you / see) her?
2. When I _____ (get) home last night, I _____ (be) very tired, so I _____ (go) straight to bed.
3. *A:* _____ (you / eat) at the new sushi place on Joe's birthday?
   B: No, but _____ (we / be) there twice this month.
4. There was a bus drivers' strike last week. There _____ (not / be) any buses.
5. Mr. Lee _____ (work) in a bank for 15 years. Then he quit.
6. Kelly lives in Toronto. She _____ (live) there all her life.
7. *A:* _____ (you / go) to the movies last night?
   B: Yes, but it _____ (be) a mistake. The movie _____ (be) awful.
8. My grandfather _____ (die) before I was born. I _____ _____ (never / meet) him.
9. I don't know Karen's husband. I _____ (never / meet) him.
10. It's nearly lunchtime, and I _____ (not / see) Martin all morning. I wonder where he is.
11. *A:* Where do you live?
    B: In Rio de Janeiro.
    A: How long _____ (you / live) there?
    B: Five years.
    A: Where _____ (you / live) before that?
    B: In Buenos Aires.
    A: And how long _____ (you / live) there?
    B: Two years.

9.4 Write sentences about yourself using the ideas in parentheses.

1. (something you haven't done today) ___*I haven't eaten any fruit today.*_____
2. (something you haven't done today) _____
3. (something you didn't do yesterday) _____
4. (something you did last night) _____
5. (something you haven't done recently) _____
6. (something you've done a lot recently) _____

Present Perfect Continuous (I have been doing)

A

It has been raining.

Study this example situation:

Is it raining?
No, but the ground is wet.

It **has been raining**.

Have/has been –ing is the *present perfect continuous*:

I/we/they/you	**have**	(= I've, etc.)	**been**	do**ing**
he/she/it	**has**	(= he's, etc.)		wait**ing**
				play**ing**, etc.

We use the present perfect continuous for an activity that has recently stopped or just stopped. There is a connection with *now*:

- You're out of breath. **Have** you **been running**? (= you're out of breath *now*)
- Jason is very tired. He**'s been working** very hard. (= he's tired *now*)
- Why are your clothes so dirty? What **have** you **been doing**?
- *(on the phone)* I'm glad you called. **I've been thinking** about calling you . . .
- Where have you been? **I've been looking** everywhere for you.

B

It has been raining for two hours.

Study this example situation:

It began raining two hours ago, and it is still raining.

How long **has** it **been raining**?
It **has been raining** for two hours.

We use the present perfect continuous in this way with **how long**, **for**, and **since**. The activity is still happening (as in this example) or has just stopped.

- **How long have** you **been studying** English? (= you're still studying English)
- Tim is still watching television. He**'s been watching** television **all day**.
- Where have you been? **I've been looking** for you **for the last half hour**.
- Christopher **hasn't been feeling** well **recently**.

You can use the present prefect continuous for actions repeated over a period of time:

- Debbie is a very good tennis player. She**'s been playing since she was eight**.
- Every morning they meet in the same café. They**'ve been going** there **for years**.

C

Compare **I am doing** (see Unit 1) and **I have been doing**:

I am doing	**I have been doing**
present continuous	*present perfect continuous*
↓	→
now	*now*

- Don't bother me now. **I'm working**.

- We need an umbrella. It**'s raining**.
- Hurry up! We**'re waiting**.

- **I've been working** hard. Now I'm going to take a break.
- The ground is wet. It**'s been raining**.
- We**'ve been waiting** for an hour.

Present Perfect Simple and Continuous Units 11–12 Present Perfect with *for* / *since* Units 12–13

Exercises

10.1 What have these people been doing or what has been happening?

1. *earlier* / *now*

They *'ve been shopping.*

2. *earlier* / *now*

She _____

3. *earlier* / *now*

They _____

4. *earlier* / *now*

He _____

10.2 Write a question for each situation.

1. You meet Paul as he is leaving the swimming pool.
   You ask: (you / swim?) _Have you been swimming?_
2. You have just arrived to meet a friend who is waiting for you.
   You ask: (you / wait / long?) _____
3. You meet a friend at the store. His face and hands are very dirty.
   You ask: (what / you / do?) _____
4. A friend of yours is now working at a gym. You want to know how long.
   You ask: (how long / you / work / there?) _____
5. A friend tells you about his job – he sells computers. You want to know how long.
   You ask: (how long / you / sell / computers?) _____

10.3 Read the situations and complete the sentences.

1. It's raining. The rain started two hours ago.
   It _'s been raining_ for two hours.
2. We are waiting for the bus. We got to the bus stop 20 minutes ago.
   We _____ for 20 minutes.
3. I'm studying Spanish. I started classes in December.
   I _____ since December.
4. Jessica is working in Tokyo. She started working there on January 18.
   _____ since January 18.
5. Our friends always spend their summers in the mountains. They started going there
   years ago. _____ for years.

10.4 Put the verb into the present continuous (*I am -ing*) or present perfect continuous
(*I have been -ing*).

1. _Maria has been studying_ (Maria / study) English for two years.
2. Hello, Tom. _____ (I / look) for you all morning. Where have
   you been?
3. Why _____ (you / look) at me like that? Stop it!
4. Linda is a teacher. _____ (she / teach) for 10 years.
5. _____ (I / think) about what you said, and I've decided to take
   your advice.
6. "Is Kim on vacation this week?" "No, _____ (she / work)."
7. Sarah is very tired. _____ (she / work) very hard recently.

Present Perfect Continuous and Simple (**I have been doing** and **I have done**)

A Study this example situation:

Ling's clothes are covered with paint. She **has been painting** the ceiling.	The ceiling was white. Now it is red. She **has painted** the ceiling.
Has been painting is the *present perfect continuous*.	**Has painted** is the *present perfect simple*.
We are interested in the activity. It does not matter whether something has been finished or not. In this example, the activity (painting the ceiling) has not been finished.	Here, the important thing is that something has been finished. **Has painted** is a completed action. We are interested in the result of the activity (the painted ceiling), not the activity itself.

Compare these examples:

■ My hands are very dirty. **I've been fixing** the car.	■ The car is OK again now. **I've fixed** it.
■ Joe **has been eating** too much recently. He should eat less.	■ Somebody **has eaten** all my candy. The box is empty.
■ It's nice to see you again. What **have** you **been doing** since the last time we saw you?	■ Where's the book I gave you? What **have** you **done** with it?
■ Where have you been? **Have** you **been playing** tennis?	■ **Have** you ever **played** tennis?

B

We use the continuous to say or ask *how long* (for an activity that is still happening):	We use the simple to say or ask *how much, how many,* or *how many times* (for completed actions):
■ How long **have** you **been reading** that book?	■ How much of that book **have** you **read**?
■ Lisa is still writing her report. She**'s been writing** it **all day**.	■ Lisa **has written** 10 pages today.
■ They**'ve been playing** tennis **since 2:00**.	■ They**'ve played** tennis three times this week.
■ I'm studying Spanish, but I **haven't been studying** it very long.	■ I'm studying Spanish, but I **haven't learned** very much yet.

C Some verbs (for example, **know/like/believe**) are not normally used in the continuous:

■ **I've known** about it for a long time. (*not* I've been knowing)

For a list of these verbs, see Unit 4A. But note that you *can* use **want** and **mean** in the present perfect continuous:

■ **I've been meaning** to phone Pat, but I keep forgetting.

Simple Present Perfect Units 7–8   **Present Perfect Continuous** Unit 10   **Present Perfect with** *for / since* Units 12–13

Exercises

11.1 For each situation, write two sentences using the words in parentheses.

1. Luis started reading a book two hours ago. He is still reading it, and now he is on page 53.
   (read / for two hours) *He has been reading for two hours.*
   (read / 53 pages so far) *He has read 53 pages so far.*

2. Min is from Korea. She is traveling around Asia right now. She began her trip three months ago.
   (travel / for three months) She _____
   (visit / six countries so far) _____

3. Jimmy is a tennis player. He began playing tennis when he was 10 years old. This year he is national champion again – for the fourth time.
   (win / the national championships / four times) _____
   (play / tennis since he was 10) _____

4. When they graduated from college, Lisa and Amy started making movies together. They still make movies.
   (make / five movies since they finished college) They _____
   _____
   (make / movies since they finished college) _____
   _____

11.2 For each situation, ask a question using the words in parentheses.

1. You have a friend who is studying Arabic. You ask:
   (how long / study / Arabic?) *How long have you been studying Arabic?*

2. You have just arrived to meet a friend. She is waiting for you. You ask:
   (wait / long?) Have _____

3. You see somebody fishing by the river. You ask:
   (catch / any fish?) _____

4. Some friends of yours are having a party next week. You ask:
   (how many people / invite?) _____

5. A friend of yours is a teacher. You ask:
   (how long / teach?) _____

6. You meet somebody who is a writer. You ask:
   (how many books / write?) _____
   (how long / write / books?) _____

7. A friend of yours is saving money to take a trip. You ask:
   (how long / save?) _____
   (how much money / save?) _____

11.3 Put the verb into the more appropriate form, present perfect simple (*I have done*) or continuous (*I have been doing*).

1. Where have you been? *Have you been playing* (you / play) tennis?
2. Look! _____ (somebody / break) that window.
3. You look tired. _____ (you / work) hard?
4. "_____ (you / ever / work) in a factory?" "No, never."
5. "Hi, is Sam there?" "No, he _____ (go) for a run."
6. My brother is an actor. _____ (he / appear) in several films.
7. "Sorry I'm late." "That's all right. _____ (I / not / wait) long."
8. "Is it still raining?" "No, _____ (it / stop)."
9. _____ (I / lose) my cell phone. _____ (you / see) it anywhere?
10. _____ (I / read) the book you lent me, but _____ (I / not / finish) it yet. It's very interesting.
11. _____ (I / read) the book you lent me, so you can have it back now.

How long have you (been) . . . ?

A

Study this example situation:

Bob and Alice are married. They got married exactly 20 years ago, so today is their 20th wedding anniversary. They **have been** married for **20 years**.

We say: They are married. *(present)*

but **How long have** they **been** married? *(present perfect)*
(*not* How long are they married?)

They **have been** married for **20 years**.
(*not* They are married for 20 years)

We use the present perfect (especially with **how long**, **for**, and **since**) to talk about something that began in the past and continues to the present time. Compare the *present* and the *present perfect*:

■ Bill is in the hospital.
but He **has been** in the hospital **since Monday**.
(*not* Bill is in the hospital since Monday)

■ **Do** you **know** each other well?
but **Have** you **known** each other **for a long time**?
(*not* Do you know)

■ She's **waiting** for somebody.
but She's **been waiting all morning**.

■ **Do** they **have** a car?
but **How long have** they **had** their car?

past ——————— *present*

present perfect ➡

now

B

I have known/had/lived, etc., is the *present perfect simple*.

I have been learning / been waiting / been doing, etc., is the *present perfect continuous*.

When we ask or say "how long," the continuous is more common (see Unit 10):
■ **I've been studying** English **for six months**.
■ It's **been raining since lunchtime**.
■ Richard **has been doing** the same job **for 20 years**.
■ "**How long have** you **been driving**?" "**Since I was 17**."

Some verbs (for example, **know/like/believe**) are not normally used in the continuous:
■ How long **have** you **known** Emily? (*not* have you been knowing)
■ **I've had** a stomachache all day. (*not* I've been having)

See also Units 4A and 10C. For **have**, see Unit 16A.

C

You can use either the present perfect continuous or simple with **live** and **work**:
■ John **has been living / has lived** in Montreal for a long time.
■ How long **have** you **been working / have** you **worked** here?

But we use the simple (**I've lived / I've done**, etc.) with **always**:
■ **Have** you **always lived** in the country? (*not* always been living)

D

We say "I **haven't done** something **since/for** . . . " *(present perfect simple)*:
■ I **haven't seen** Tom **since** Monday. (= Monday was the last time I saw him)
■ Sue **hasn't called for** ages. (= the last time she called was ages ago)

Exercises

12.1 Are the <u>underlined</u> verbs right or wrong? Correct them where necessary.

1. Bob is a friend of mine. <u>I know him</u> very well.   *OK*
2. Bob is a friend of mine. <u>I know him</u> for a long time.   *I've known him*
3. Sue and Scott <u>are married</u> since July.   _____
4. The weather is awful. <u>It's raining</u> again.   _____
5. The weather is awful. <u>It's raining</u> all day.   _____
6. I like your house. How long <u>are you living</u> there?   _____
7. Gary <u>is working</u> in a store for the last few months.   _____
8. <u>I don't know</u> Tim well. We've only met a few times.   _____
9. I quit drinking coffee. <u>I don't drink</u> it for a year.   _____
10. That's a very old bike. How long <u>do you have</u> it?   _____

12.2 Read the situations and write questions from the words in parentheses.

1. John tells you that his mother is in the hospital. You ask him:
    (how long / be / in the hospital?)   *How long has your mother been in the hospital?*
2. You meet a woman who tells you that she teaches English. You ask her:
    (how long / teach / English?) _____
3. You know that Erica is a good friend of Carol's. You ask Erica:
    (how long / know / Carol?) _____
4. Your friend's brother moved to Costa Rica a while ago. You ask your friend:
    (how long / be / in Costa Rica?) _____
5. Chris drives a very old car. You ask him:
    (how long / have / that car?) _____
6. You are talking to a friend about Scott. Scott now works at the airport. You ask your friend:
    (how long / work / at the airport?) _____
7. A friend of yours is taking guitar lessons. You ask him:
    (how long / take / guitar lessons?) _____
8. You meet somebody on a plane. She says that she lives in Chicago. You ask her:
    (always / live / in Chicago?) _____

12.3 Complete B's answers to A's questions.

	A	B
1.	Amy is in the hospital, isn't she?	Yes, she *has been* in the hospital since Monday.
2.	Do you see Ann very often?	No, I *haven't seen* her for three months.
3.	Is Margaret married?	Yes, she _____ married for 10 years.
4.	Are you waiting for me?	Yes, I _____ for the last half hour.
5.	You know Linda, don't you?	Yes, we _____ each other a long time.
6.	Do you still play tennis?	No, I _____ tennis for years.
7.	Is Jim watching TV?	Yes, he _____ TV all night.
8.	Do you watch TV a lot?	No, I _____ TV for ages.
9.	Do you have a headache?	Yes, I _____ a headache all morning.
10.	George is never sick, is he?	No, he _____ sick since I met him.
11.	Are you feeling sick?	Yes, I _____ sick all day.
12.	Sue lives in Miami, doesn't she?	Yes, she _____ in Miami for the last few years.
13.	Do you go to the movies a lot?	No, I _____ to the movies for ages.
14.	Would you like to go to Taiwan one day?	Yes, I _____ to go to Taiwan. (*use* **always / want**)

For and since
When . . . ? and How long . . . ?

A

We use **for** and **since** to say how long something has been happening.

We use **for** + a period of time (**two hours**, **six weeks**, etc.): ■ I've been waiting **for two hours**.	We use **since** + the start of a period (**8:00**, **Monday**, **1999**, etc.): ■ I've been waiting **since 8:00**.

for two hours		since 8:00	
two hours ago ──────► *now*		*8:00* ──────► *now*	

for			**since**		
two hours	a long time	a week	8:00	April	lunchtime
20 minutes	six months	ages	Monday	1985	we arrived
five days	50 years	years	May 12	Christmas	yesterday

■ Kelly has been working here **for six months**. (*not* since six months)
■ I haven't seen Tom **for three days**.

■ Kelly has been working here **since April**. (= from April until now)
■ I haven't seen Tom **since Monday**.

It is possible to leave out **for** (but not in negative sentences):
■ They've been married (for) **10 years**. (with or without **for**)
■ They **haven't had** a vacation **for** 10 years. (you must use **for**)

We do *not* use **for** + all . . . (**all day** / **all my life**, etc.):
■ I've lived here **all my life**. (*not* for all my life)

You can use **in** instead of **for** in negative sentences:
■ They **haven't had** a vacation **in 10 years**.

B

Compare **When . . . ?** (+ *simple past*) and **How long . . . ?** (+ *present perfect*):

A: **When** did it start raining?
B: It started raining **an hour ago** / **at 1:00**.

A: **How long** has it been raining?
B: It's been raining **for an hour** / **since 1:00**.

A: **When** did Joe and Carol first meet?
B: They first met { a long time **ago**. / **when** they were in high school.

A: **How long** have they **known** each other?
B: They**'ve known** each other { **for** a long time. / **since** they were in high school.

C

We say "**It's** (= It has) **been a long time** / **two years**, etc., **since** something happened":
■ **It's been two years since** I saw Joe. (= I **haven't seen** Joe for two years)
■ **It's been ages since** we went to the movies. (= We **haven't gone** to the movies for ages)

You can ask "**How long has it been since . . . ?**":
■ **How long has it been since** you saw Joe? (= When did you last see Joe?)
■ **How long has it been since** Mrs. Hill died? (= When did Mrs. Hill die?)

Exercises

13.1 Write *for* or *since*.

1. It's been raining __*since*__ lunchtime.
2. Sarah has lived in Chicago _____ 1995.
3. Joe has lived in Dallas _____ 10 years.
4. I'm tired of waiting. We've been sitting here _____ an hour.
5. Kevin has been looking for a job _____ he graduated.
6. I haven't been to a party _____ ages.
7. I wonder how Joe is. I haven't seen him _____ last week.
8. Jane is away at college. She's been away _____ last August.
9. The weather is dry. It hasn't rained _____ a few weeks.

13.2 Write questions with *how long* and *when*.

1. It's raining.
   (how long?) __*How long has it been raining?*_____
   (when?) __*When did it start raining?*_____
2. Kate is studying Japanese.
   (how long / study?) _____
   (when / start?) _____
3. I know Jeff.
   (how long / you / know?) _____
   (when / you / meet?) _____
4. Rebecca and David are married.
   (how long?) _____
   (when / get?) _____

13.3 Read the situations and complete the sentences.

1. It's raining. It's been raining since lunchtime. It __*started raining*_____ at lunchtime.
2. Ann and Sue are friends. They met years ago. __*They've been friends for*_____ years.
3. Mark is sick. He got sick on Sunday. He has _____ Sunday.
4. Mark is sick. He got sick a few days ago. He has _____ a few days.
5. Sarah is married. She's been married for a year. She got _____ .
6. You have a headache. It started when you woke up.
   I've _____ I woke up.
7. Megan has been in France for the last three weeks.
   She went _____ .
8. You're working in a hotel. You started six months ago.
   I've _____ .

13.4 Write B's sentences using the words in parentheses.

1. *A:* Do you take vacations often?
   B: (no / five years) __*No, I haven't taken a vacation for five years.*_____
2. *A:* Do you see Laura often?
   B: (no / about a month) _____
3. *A:* Do you go to the movies often?
   B: (no / a long time) _____
4. *A:* Do you eat out often?
   B: (no / ages) _____

Now write B's answers again. This time use *It's been . . . since . . . .*

5. (1) __*No, it's been five years since I took a vacation.*_____
6. (2) No, it's _____
7. (3) No, _____
8. (4) _____

Past Perfect (I had done)

A

Study this example situation:

At 10:30
Bye!
Eric

At 11:00
Hi!
Sarah

Sarah went to a party last week. Eric went to the party, too, but they didn't see each other. Eric left the party at 10:30 and Sarah got there at 11:00. So: When Sarah got to the party, Eric wasn't there.

He **had gone** home.

Had gone is the *past perfect (simple):*

I/we/they/you he/she/it	**had**	(= I'**d**, etc.) (= he'**d**, etc.)	**gone seen finished**, etc.

The past perfect is **had** + *past participle* (**gone** / **seen** / **finished**, etc).

Sometimes we talk about something that happened in the past:

- Sarah **got** to the party.

This is the starting point of the story. Then, if we want to talk about things that happened *before* this time, we use the past perfect (**had** . . .):

- When Sarah arrived at the party, Eric **had** already **gone** home.

Some more examples:

- When we got home last night, we found that somebody **had broken** into our house.
- Karen didn't want to go to the movies with us because she'**d** already **seen** the film.
- At first I thought I'**d done** the right thing, but I soon realized that I'**d made** a big mistake.
- The man sitting next to me on the plane was very nervous. He **hadn't flown** before.
  or . . . He **had** never **flown** before.

B

Compare the *present perfect* (**have seen**, etc.) and the *past perfect* (**had seen**, etc.):

Present Perfect

have seen →

past   *now*

- Who is that woman? I'**ve** never **seen** her before.
- We aren't hungry. We'**ve** just **had** lunch.
- The house is dirty. They **haven't cleaned** it for weeks.

Past Perfect

had seen →

past   *now*

- I didn't know who she was. I'**d** never **seen** her before. (= before that time)
- We weren't hungry. We'**d** just **had** lunch.
- The house was dirty. They **hadn't cleaned** it for weeks.

C

Compare the *simple past* (**left**, **was**, etc.) and the *past perfect* (**had left**, **had been**, etc.):

- *A:* Was Tom there when you arrived?
  B: Yes, but he **left** a little later.

- Amy **wasn't** at home when I called. She **was** at her mother's house.

- *A:* Was Tom there when you arrived?
  B: No, he **had** already **left**.

- Amy **had** just **gotten** home when I called. She **had been** at her mother's house.

Past Perfect Continuous Unit 15   **Irregular Verbs** (*had gone, had seen*, etc.) Appendix 1

Exercises

14.1 Read the situations and write sentences using the words in parentheses.

1. You went to Jill's house, but she wasn't there.
   (she / go / out) _She had gone out._
2. You went back to your hometown after many years. It wasn't the same as before.
   (it / change / a lot) _____
3. I invited Rachel to the party, but she couldn't come.
   (she / make / plans to do something else) _____
4. You went to the movies last night. You got there late.
   (the movie / already / begin) _____
5. It was nice to see Daniel again after such a long time.
   (I / not / see / him in five years) _____
6. I offered Sue something to eat, but she wasn't hungry.
   (she / just / have / breakfast) _____

14.2 For each situation, write a sentence ending with **never . . . before**. Use the verb in parentheses.

1. The man sitting next to you on the plane was very nervous. It was his first flight.
   (fly) _He had never flown before._
2. A woman walked into the room. She was a complete stranger to me.
   (see) I _____ before.
3. Sam played tennis yesterday. He wasn't very good at it because it was his first game.
   (play) He _____
4. Last year we went to Mexico. It was our first time there.
   (be there) We _____

14.3 Use the sentences on the left to complete the paragraphs on the right. These sentences are in the order in which they happened – so (1) happened before (2), (2) before (3), etc. But your paragraph begins with the underlined sentence, so sometimes you need the past perfect.

1. (1) Somebody broke into the office during the night.
   (2) <u>We arrived at work in the morning</u>.
   (3) We called the police.

   We arrived at work in the morning and found that somebody _had broken_ into the office during the night. So we _____ .

2. (1) Laura went out this morning.
   (2) <u>I tried to call her</u>.
   (3) There was no answer.

   I tried to call Laura this morning, but _____ no answer. She _____ out.

3. (1) Jim came back from vacation a few days ago.
   (2) <u>I met him the same day</u>.
   (3) He looked relaxed.

   I met Jim a few days ago. _____ just _____ vacation. _____ relaxed.

4. (1) Kevin sent Sally lots of e-mails.
   (2) She never answered them.
   (3) <u>Yesterday he got a phone call from her</u>.
   (4) He was very surprised.

   Yesterday Kevin _____ from Sally. He _____ very surprised. He _____ lots of e-mails, but she _____ .

14.4 Put the verb into the correct form, past perfect (**I had done**) or simple past (**I did**).

1. "Was Ben at the party when you got there?" "No, he _had gone_ (go) home."
2. I felt very tired when I got home, so I _____ (go) straight to bed.
3. The house was very quiet when I got home. Everybody _____ (go) to bed.
4. Sorry I'm late. My car _____ (break) down on the way here.
5. We were driving on the highway when we _____ (see) a car that _____ (break) down, so we _____ (stop) to help.

UNIT 15

Past Perfect Continuous (I had been doing)

A

Study this example situation:

Yesterday morning

Yesterday morning I got up and looked out of the window. The sun was shining, but the ground was very wet.

It **had been raining**.

It was *not* raining when I looked out of the window; the sun was shining. But it **had been raining** before.

Had been –ing is the *past perfect continuous:*

I/we/you/they he/she/it	**had**	(= I**'d**, etc.) (= he**'d**, etc.)	**been**	do**ing** work**ing** play**ing**, etc.

Some more examples:
- When the boys came into the house, their clothes were dirty, their hair was messy, and one of them had a black eye. They**'d been fighting**.
- I was very tired when I got home. I**'d been working** hard all day.
- When I went to Tokyo a few years ago, I stayed with a friend of mine. She**'d been living** there only a short time but knew the city very well.

B

You can say that something **had been happening** for a period of time before something else happened:
- We**'d been playing** tennis for about half an hour when it started to rain hard.
- Jim went to the doctor last Friday. He **hadn't been feeling** well for some time.

C

Compare **have been –ing** (*present perfect continuous*) and **had been –ing** (*past perfect continuous*):

Present Perfect Continuous

I have been -ing →

past ——————————— *now*

- I hope the bus comes soon. I**'ve been waiting** for 20 minutes. *(before now)*
- James is out of breath. He **has been running**.

Past Perfect Continuous

I had been –ing →

past ———————— *now*

- The bus finally came. I**'d been waiting** for 20 minutes. *(before the bus came)*
- James was out of breath. He **had been running**.

D

Compare **was –ing** (*past continuous*) and **had been –ing**:
- It **wasn't raining** when we went out. The sun **was shining**. But it **had been raining**, so the ground was wet.
- Stephanie **was sitting** in an armchair resting. She was tired because she**'d been working** very hard.

E

Some verbs (for example, **know** and **like**) are not normally used in the continuous:
- We were good friends. We **had known** each other for years. (*not* had been knowing)

For a list of these verbs, see Unit 4A.

Exercises

15.1 Read the situations and make sentences from the words in parentheses.

1. I was very tired when I got home.
   (I / work / hard all day) _I'd been working hard all day._
2. The two boys came into the house. They had a soccer ball, and they were both very tired.
   (they / play / soccer) _____
3. I was disappointed when I had to cancel my vacation.
   (I / look / forward to it) _____
4. Ann woke up in the middle of the night. She was scared and didn't know where she was.
   (she / dream) _____
5. When I got home, Mike was sitting in front of the TV. He had just turned it off.
   (he / watch / a DVD) _____

15.2 Read the situations and complete the sentences.

1. We played tennis yesterday. Half an hour after we began playing, it started to rain.
   We _had been playing for half an hour_ when _it started to rain_ .
2. I had arranged to meet Robert in a restaurant. I arrived and waited for him. After 20
   minutes I suddenly realized that I was in the wrong restaurant.
   I _____ for 20 minutes when I _____
   _____ the wrong restaurant.
3. Sarah got a job in a factory. Five years later the factory closed down.
   When the factory _____ , Sarah _____
   _____ there for five years.
4. I went to a concert last week. The orchestra began playing. After about 10 minutes a man in
   the audience suddenly started shouting.
   The orchestra _____
   when _____

This time make your own sentence:

5. I began driving home from work. I _____
   when _____

15.3 Put the verb into the most appropriate form, past continuous (*I was doing*), past perfect
(*I had done*), or past perfect continuous (*I had been doing*).

1. It was very noisy next door. Our neighbors _were having_ (have) a party.
2. We were good friends. We _had known_ (know) each other for years.
3. John and I went for a walk. I had trouble keeping up with him because he
   _____ (walk) so fast.
4. Sue was sitting on the ground. She was out of breath. She _____ (run).
5. When I arrived, everybody was sitting around the table with their mouths full. They
   _____ (eat).
6. When I arrived, everybody was sitting around the table and talking. Their mouths were
   empty, but their stomachs were full. They _____ (eat).
7. Jim was on his hands and knees on the floor. He _____ (look)
   for his contact lens.
8. When I arrived, Kate _____ (wait) for me. She was upset with
   me because I was late and she _____ (wait) for a long time.
9. I was sad when I sold my car. I _____ (have) it for a long time.
10. We were exhausted at the end of our trip. We _____ (travel) for
    more than 24 hours.

Have and have got

Have and **have got** (for possession, relationships, illnesses, etc.)

You can use **have got** or **have** (without **got**). There is no difference in meaning:

> *I **have** a new cell phone.*
>
> *I**'ve got** a new cell phone, too.*

- They **have** a new car.   *or*   They**'ve got** a new car.
- Nancy **has** two sisters.   *or*   Nancy **has got** two sisters.
- I **have** a headache.   *or*   I**'ve got** a headache.
- He **has** a few problems.   *or*   He**'s got** a few problems.
- Our house **has** a big yard.   *or*   Our house **has got** a big yard.

When **have** means "possess," etc., you cannot use continuous forms (**is having** / **are having**, etc.):

- We're enjoying our vacation. We **have** / **have got** a nice room in the hotel. (*not* We're having)

In questions and negative sentences there are two possible forms:

Do you **have** any questions?	**Have** you **got** any questions?
I **don't have** any questions.	I **haven't got** any questions.
Does she **have** a car?	**Has** she **got** a car?
She **doesn't have** a car.	She **hasn't got** a car.

For the past we use **had** (without **got**):
- Ann **had** long hair when she was a child.

In past questions and negative sentences, we use **did/didn't**:
- **Did** they **have** a car when they were living in Miami?
- I **didn't have** a watch, so I didn't know what time it was.
- Ann **had** long hair, **didn't** she?

Have breakfast / **have trouble** / **have a good time**, etc.

We also use **have** (*but not* **have got**) for many actions and experiences. For example:

have	**breakfast** / **dinner** / **a cup of coffee** / **something to eat** **a party** / **a safe trip** / **a good flight** **an accident** / **an experience** / **a dream** **a look** (at something) **a conversation** / **a discussion** / **a talk** (with somebody) **trouble** / **difficulty** / **fun** / **a good time**, etc. **a baby** (= give birth to a baby) / **an operation**

Have got is *not* possible in the expressions in the box. Compare:
- Sometimes I **have** (= eat) a sandwich for lunch. (*not* I've got)

but   I**'ve got** / I **have** some sandwiches. Would you like one?

You can use continuous forms (**am having**, etc.) with the expressions in the box:
- We're enjoying our vacation. We**'re having** a great time. (*not* We have)
- Mike **is having** trouble with his car. He often has trouble with his car.

In questions and negative sentences, we use **do/does/did**:
- I **don't** usually **have** a big breakfast. (*not* I usually haven't)
- What time **does** Ann **have** lunch? (*not* has Ann lunch)
- **Did** you **have** any trouble finding a place to live?

Have to . . . Unit 30

Exercises

16.1 Write negative sentences with *have*. Some are present (*can't*) and some are past (*couldn't*).

1. I can't get into the house. (a key) _I don't have a key._
2. I couldn't read the letter. (my glasses) _I didn't have my glasses._
3. I can't climb up on the roof. (a ladder) _____
4. We couldn't visit the museum. (enough time) We _____
5. He couldn't find our house. (a map) _____
6. She can't pay her bills. (any money) _____
7. I can't fix the car tonight. (enough energy) _____
8. They couldn't take any pictures. (a camera) _____

16.2 Complete the questions with *have*. Some are present and some are past.

1. Excuse me, _do you have_ a pen I could borrow?
2. Why are you holding your face like that? _____ a toothache?
3. _____ a lot of toys when you were a child?
4. *A:* _____ the time, please?
   B: Yes, it's ten after seven.
5. I need a stamp for this letter. _____ one?
6. When you took the test, _____ time to answer all the questions?
7. *A:* It started to rain very hard while I was taking a walk.
   B: Did it? _____ an umbrella?

16.3 Write sentences about yourself. Do you have these things now? Did you have them 10 years ago? Write two sentences each time using *I have* / *I don't have* and *I had* / *I didn't have*.

Now	*10 years ago (or 5 if you're young)*
1. (a car) _I have a car. OR I've got a car._	_I didn't have a car._
2. (a bike) I _____	I _____
3. (a cell phone) _____	_____
4. (a dog) _____	_____
5. (a guitar) _____	_____
6. (long hair) _____	_____
7. (a driver's license) _____	_____

16.4 Complete the sentences. Use an expression from the list and put the verb into the correct form where necessary.

have a baby	**have a dream**	**have a talk**	**have trouble**	**have a good flight**
have a look	~~have lunch~~	**have a party**	**have a nice time**	**have dinner**

1. I don't eat much during the day. I never _have lunch_ .
2. If you're angry with your friend, it might be a good idea to sit down and _____ with her.
3. We _____ last week. It was great – we invited lots of people.
4. Excuse me, can I _____ at your newspaper, please?
5. Jim is on vacation in Hawaii. I hope he _____ .
6. I didn't sleep well last night. I _____ about my exam.
7. *A:* _____ finding the book you wanted?
   B: No, I found it OK.
8. Crystal _____ a few weeks ago. It's her second child.
9. *A:* Why didn't you answer the phone?
   B: We _____ with friends.
10. *You meet your friend Sally at the airport. She has just arrived. You say:*
    Hi, Sally. How are you? _____ ?

Used to (do)

A

Study this example situation:

A few years ago

these days

David quit jogging two years ago. He doesn't jog anymore.
But he **used to jog**.
He **used to jog** three miles a day.
He **used to jog** = he jogged regularly in the past, but he doesn't jog now.

he used to jog

he doesn't jog now

| past | 2 years ago | now |

B

Something **used** to happen = it happened regularly in the past but no longer happens:

- I **used to play** tennis a lot, but I don't play very often now.
- David **used to spend** a lot of money on clothes. These days he can't afford it.
- "Do you go to the movies much?"   "Not anymore, but I **used to**." (= I used to go)

We also use **used to . . .** for something that was true but is not true anymore:

- This building is now a furniture store. It **used to be** a movie theater.
- I **used to think** Mark was unfriendly, but now I realize he's a very nice person.
- I've started drinking coffee recently. I never **used to like** it before.
- Nicole **used to have** very long hair when she was a child.

C

"**I used to do something**" is past. There is no present form. You cannot say "I use to do."
To talk about the present, use the simple present (**I do**). Compare:

Past	he **used to play**	we **used to live**	there **used to be**
Present	he **plays**	we **live**	there **is**

- We **used to live** in a small town, but now we **live** in Chicago.
- There **used to be** four movie theaters in town. Now there is only one.

D

The normal question form is **did** (you) **use to . . . ?**:

- **Did** you **use to eat** a lot of candy when you were a child?

The negative form is **didn't use to . . .** :

- I **didn't use to like** him.

E

Compare **I used to do** and **I was doing**:

- I **used to watch** TV a lot when I was little. (= I watched TV regularly in the past, but I no longer do this)
- I **was watching** TV when Mike called. (= I was in the middle of watching a program)

F

Do not confuse **I used to do** and **I am used to doing** (see Unit 59). The structures and meanings are different:

- I **used to live** alone. (= I lived alone in the past, but I no longer live alone.)
- I **am used to living** alone. (= I live alone, and I don't find it strange or difficult because I've been living alone for some time.)

Past Continuous (*I was doing*) Unit 6   *Would* (= *used to*) Unit 34C   *Be / get used to (doing) something* Unit 59

Exercises

17.1 Complete the sentences with **use(d) to** + an appropriate verb.

1. David quit jogging two years ago. He ___used to jog___ three miles a day.
2. Liz _____ a motorcycle, but last year she sold it and bought a car.
3. We moved to Spain a few years ago. We _____ in Paris.
4. I seldom eat ice cream now, but I _____ it when I was a child.
5. Tracy _____ my best friend, but we aren't friends anymore.
6. It only takes me about 40 minutes to get to work now that the new highway is open. It _____ more than an hour.
7. There _____ a hotel near the airport, but it closed a long time ago.
8. When you lived in New York, _____ to the theater very often?

17.2 Matt changed his lifestyle. He stopped doing some things and started doing other things:

He stopped ⎰ ~~studying hard~~   He started ⎰ ~~sleeping late~~
            going to bed early   going out every night
            running three miles every morning   spending a lot of money

Write sentences about Matt with **used to** and **didn't use to**.

1. ___He used to study hard.___
2. ___He didn't use to sleep late.___
3. _____
4. _____
5. _____
6. _____

17.3 Compare what Karen said five years ago and what she says today:

Now write sentences about how Karen has changed. Use **used to / didn't use to / never used to** in the first part of your sentence.

1. ___She used to travel a lot___ , but ___she doesn't take many trips these days.___
2. She _____ , but _____
3. She _____ , but _____
4. She _____ , but _____
5. She _____ , but _____
6. She _____ , but _____
7. She _____ , but _____
8. She _____ , but _____
9. She _____ , but _____
10. She _____ , but _____

Present Tenses (I am doing / I do) with a Future Meaning

A

Present continuous (**I am doing**) with a future meaning

This is Ben's calendar for next week.

He **is playing** tennis on Monday afternoon.
He **is going** to the dentist on Tuesday morning.
He **is having** dinner with Ann on Friday.

In all these examples, Ben has already decided and arranged to do these things.

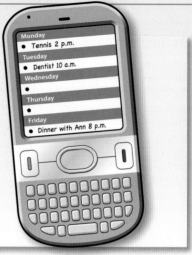

Monday
● Tennis 2 p.m.
Tuesday
● Dentist 10 a.m.
Wednesday
●
Thursday
●
Friday
● Dinner with Ann 8 p.m.

I'm doing something (tomorrow) = I have already decided and arranged to do it:
- *A:* What **are** you **doing** Saturday night? (*not* What do you do)
  B: **I'm going** to the theater. (*not* I go)
- *A:* What time **is** Cathy **arriving** tomorrow?
  B: At 10:30. **I'm meeting** her at the airport.
- **I'm not working** tomorrow, so we can go out somewhere.
- Sam **isn't playing** football next Saturday. He hurt his leg.

"**I'm going to** (do)" is also possible in these sentences:
- What **are** you **going to do** Saturday night?

But the present continuous is more natural for arrangements. See also Unit 19B.

Do not use **will** to talk about what you have arranged to do:
- What **are** you **doing** tonight? (*not* What will you do)
- Eric **is getting** married next month. (*not* will get)

You can also use the present continuous for an action *just before you begin to do it*. This happens especially with verbs of movement (**go/come/leave**, etc.):
- I'm tired. **I'm going** to bed now. Goodnight. (*not* I go to bed now)
- "Tina, are you ready yet?" "Yes, **I'm coming**." (*not* I come)

B

Simple present (**I do**) with a future meaning

You can use the simple present when you talk about schedules, programs, etc. (for public transportation, movies, etc.):
- My flight **leaves** at 11:30, so I need to get to the airport by 10:00.
- What time **does** the movie **begin**?
- It's Wednesday tomorrow. / Tomorrow **is** Wednesday.

You can use the simple present to talk about people if their plans are fixed like a schedule:
- I **start** my new job on Monday.
- What time **do** you **finish** work tomorrow?

But the continuous is more commonly used for personal arrangements:
- What time **are** you **meeting** Ann tomorrow? (*not* do you meet)

Compare:

Present Continuous	Simple Present
■ What time **are** you arriving?	■ What time **does** the plane **arrive**?
■ **I'm going** to the movies tonight.	■ The movie **starts** at 8:15 (tonight).

I'm going to Units 19, 22 *Will* Units 20–22 **Simple Present after *when* / *if*, etc.** Unit 24

Exercises

18.1 A friend of yours is planning to go on vacation soon. Ask her about her plans. Use the words in parentheses to make your questions.

1. (where / go?) _Where are you going?_____ Quebec.
2. (how long / stay?) _____ Ten days.
3. (when / leave?) _____ Next Friday.
4. (go / alone?) _____ No, with a friend.
5. (travel / by car?) _____ No, by plane.
6. (where / stay?) _____ In a hotel.

18.2 Ben wants you to visit him, but you are very busy. Look at your calendar for the next few days and explain to him why you can't come.

Monday
● Volleyball 7:30 p.m.
Tuesday
● Work late until 9 p.m.
Wednesday
● Theater
Thursday
● Meet Julia 8 p.m.
Friday
●

Ben: Can you come over on Monday night?
You: Sorry, but _I'm playing volleyball_____ . (1)
Ben: What about Tuesday night then?
You: No, not Tuesday. I _____ . (2)
Ben: And Wednesday night?
You: _____ . (3)
Ben: Well, are you free on Thursday?
You: I'm afraid not. _____ . (4)

18.3 Have you arranged to do anything at these times? Write true sentences about yourself.

1. (tonight) _I'm going out tonight._ OR _I'm not doing anything tonight._____
2. (tomorrow morning) I _____
3. (tomorrow night) _____
4. (next Sunday) _____
5. (*choose another day or time*) _____

18.4 Put the verb into the more appropriate form, present continuous or simple present.

1. I _'m going_____ (go) to the movies tonight.
2. _Does the movie begin_____ (the movie / begin) at 3:30 or 4:30?
3. We _____ (have) a party next Saturday. Would you like to come?
4. The art exhibit _____ (open) on May 3.
5. I _____ (not / go) out tonight. I _____ (stay) at home.
6. "_____ (you / do) anything tomorrow morning?" "No, I'm free. Why?"
7. We _____ (go) to a concert tonight. It _____ (start) at 7:30.
8. I _____ (leave) now. I came to say goodbye.
9. *A:* Have you seen Liz recently?
   B: No, but we _____ (meet) for lunch next week.
10. *You are on the train to Boston and you ask another passenger:*
    Excuse me. What time _____ (this train / get) to Boston?
11. *You are talking to Julie:*
    Julie, I _____ (go) to the store now. _____ (you / come) with me?
12. *You and a friend are watching television. You say:*
    I'm bored with this show. What time _____ (it / end)?
13. I _____ (not / use) the car tonight, so you can have it.
14. Sue _____ (come) to see us tomorrow. She _____ (fly) from Seattle, and her plane _____ (arrive) at 10:15 a.m.

(I'm) going to (do)

A

I am going to do something = I have already decided to do it, I intend to do it:

- ■ *A:* **Are** you **going to watch** the football game on TV tonight?
  B: No, I**'m going to go** to bed early. I'm tired from my trip.
- ■ *A:* I heard Lisa won some money. What **is** she **going to do** with it?
  B: She**'s going to buy** a new car.
- ■ I**'m going to make** a quick phone call. Can you wait for me?
- ■ This cheese smells awful. I**'m not going to eat** it.

B

I am doing and **I am going to do**

We use **I am doing** *(present continuous)* when we say what we have *arranged* to do – for example, arranged to meet somebody, arranged to go somewhere:

- ■ What time **are** you **meeting** Amanda tonight?
- ■ I**'m leaving** tomorrow. I already have my plane ticket.

I am going to do something = I've decided to do it (but perhaps not *arranged* to do it):

- ■ "The windows are dirty." "Yes, I know. I**'m going to wash** them later."
  (= I've decided to wash them, but I haven't *arranged* to wash them)
- ■ I've decided not to stay here any longer. Tomorrow I**'m going to look** for another place to live.

Often the difference is very small and either form is possible.

C

You can also say that "something **is going to happen**" in the future. For example:

The man can't see the wall in front of him.

He **is going to walk** into the wall.

When we say that "something **is going to happen**," the situation *now* makes us believe this. The man is walking toward the wall now, so we can see that he **is going to walk** into it.

situation now　　　　*future happening*

Some more examples:

- ■ Look at those dark clouds! It**'s going to rain**. (the clouds are there now)
- ■ I feel awful. I think I**'m going to be sick**. (I feel awful now)
- ■ The economic situation is bad now, and things **are going to get** worse.

D

I was going to (do something) = I intended to do it, but didn't do it:

- ■ We **were going to fly** to New York, but then we decided to drive instead.
- ■ Peter **was going to take** the exam, but he changed his mind.
- ■ I **was** just **going to cross** the street when somebody shouted, "Stop!"

You can say that "something **was going to happen**" (but didn't happen):

- ■ I thought it **was going to rain**, but it didn't.

I am doing* with a Future Meaning** Unit 18A　***I will* and *I'm going to Unit 22

Exercises

19.1 Write a question with *going to* for each situation.

1. Your friend has won some money. You ask:
    (what / do with it?) __*What are you going to do with it?*__
2. Your friend is going to a party tonight.
    You ask: (what / wear?) _____
3. Your friend has just bought a new table.
    You ask: (where / put it?) _____
4. Your friend has decided to have a party.
    You ask: (who / invite?) _____

19.2 Read the situations and complete the dialogs. Use *going to*.

1. You have decided to clean your room this morning.
    Friend: Are you going out this morning?
    You: No, __*I'm going to clean my room.*_____
2. You bought a sweater, but it doesn't fit you very well. You have decided to return it.
    Friend: That sweater is too big for you.
    You: I know. _____
3. You have been offered a job, but you have decided not to take it.
    Friend: I hear you've been offered a job.
    You: That's right, but _____
4. You have to call Sarah. It's morning now, and you intend to call her tonight.
    Friend: Have you called Sarah yet?
    You: No, _____
5. You are in a restaurant. The food is awful and you've decided to complain.
    Friend: This food is awful, isn't it?
    You: Yes, it's disgusting. _____

19.3 What is going to happen in these situations? Use the words in parentheses.

1. There are a lot of dark clouds in the sky.
    (rain) __*It's going to rain.*_____
2. It is 8:30. Tom is leaving his house. He should be at work at 8:45, but it takes him
    30 minutes to get there. (late) He _____
3. There is a hole in the bottom of the boat. A lot of water is coming in through the hole.
    (sink) The boat _____
4. Erica and Chris are driving in the country. There is very little gas left in the tank. The nearest
    gas station is miles away.
    (run out) They _____

19.4 Complete the sentences with *was / were going to* + the following verbs:

    buy   **call**   ~~**fly**~~   **have**   **play**   **quit**

1. We __*were going to fly*___ to New York, but then we decided to drive instead.
2. I _____ some new clothes yesterday, but I was very busy and
    didn't have time to go shopping.
3. Joshua and I _____ tennis last week, but he hurt his ankle.
4. I _____ Jane, but I decided to e-mail her instead.
5. *A:* The last time I saw Bob, he _____ his job.
    B: That's right, but in the end he decided not to.
6. We _____ a party last week, but some of our friends couldn't
    come, so we changed our minds.

Will 1

A

We use **I'll** (= **I will**) when we decide to do something at the time of speaking:

- Oh, I left the door open. **I'll go** and shut it.
- "What would you like to drink?" "**I'll have** some orange juice, please."
- "Did you call Julie?" "Oh no, I forgot. **I'll call** her now."

You cannot use the *simple present* (**I do** / **I go**, etc.) in these sentences:

- **I'll go** and shut the door. (*not* I go and shut)

We often use **I think I'll . . .** and **I don't think I'll . . .** :

- I am a little hungry. **I think I'll have** something to eat.
- **I don't think I'll go** out tonight. I'm too tired. (*not* I think I won't go out . . .)

In spoken English, the negative of **will** is usually **won't** (= **will not**):

- I can see you're busy, so **I won't stay** long.

B

Do *not* use **will** to talk about what you have already decided or arranged to do
(see Units 18–19):

- **I'm going** on vacation next Saturday. (*not* I'll go)
- **Are** you **working** tomorrow? (*not* Will you work)

C

We often use **will** in these situations:

Offering to do something
- That bag looks heavy. **I'll help** you with it. (*not* I help)

Agreeing to do something
- *A:* Can you give Tim this book?
- *B:* Sure, **I'll give** it to him when I see him this afternoon.

Promising to do something
- Thanks for lending me the money. **I'll pay** you back on Friday.
- I **won't tell** anyone what happened. I promise.

Asking somebody to do something (**Will you . . . ?**)
- **Will you** please **be** quiet? I'm trying to concentrate.
- **Will you shut** the door, please?

You can use **won't** to say that somebody refuses to do something:

- I've tried to give her advice, but she **won't listen**.
- The car **won't start**. (= the car "refuses" to start)

D

Shall I . . . ?   Shall we . . . ?

Shall is used in the questions **Shall I . . . ?** / **Shall we . . . ?** to ask somebody's opinion
(especially in offers or suggestions):

- **Shall I open** the window? (= Do you want me to open the window?)
- "Where **shall we have** lunch?" "Let's go to Marino's."

We use **should** more often in the same situations:

- **Should I open** the window? (= Do you want me to open it?)
- Where **should we have** lunch?

Exercises

20.1 Complete the sentences with *I'll* + an appropriate verb.

1. I'm too tired to walk home. I think ___I'll take___ a taxi.
2. "It's a little cold in this room." "You're right. _____ on the heat."
3. "We don't have any milk." "We don't? _____ and get some now."
4. "Can I wash the dishes for you?" "No, that's all right. _____ it later."
5. "I don't know how to use this computer." "Don't worry, _____ you."
6. "Would you like tea or coffee?" "_____ coffee, please."
7. "Goodbye! Have a nice trip." "Thanks. _____ you a postcard."
8. Thanks for letting me borrow your camera. _____ it back to you on Monday, OK?
9. "Are you coming with us?" "No, I think _____ here."

20.2 Read the situations and write sentences with *I think I'll . . .* or *I don't think I'll . . . .*

1. It's a little cold. The window is open, and you decide to close it. You say:
   ___I think I'll close the window.___
2. You're tired, and it's getting late. You decide to go to bed. You say:
   I think _____
3. A friend of yours offers you a ride in his car, but you decide to walk. You say:
   Thank you, but I think _____
4. You arranged to play tennis today. Now you decide that you don't want to play. You say:
   I don't think _____
5. You were going to go swimming. Now you decide that you don't want to go. You say:
   _____

20.3 Which is correct? (If necessary, study Units 18–19 first.)

1. "Did you call Julie?" "Oh no, I forgot. ~~I call~~ / I'll call her now." (*I'll call* is correct)
2. I can't meet you tomorrow. I'm playing / ~~I'll play~~ tennis. (*I'm playing* is correct)
3. "I meet / I'll meet you outside the hotel in half an hour, OK?" "Yes, that's fine."
4. "I need some money." "OK, I'm lending / I'll lend you some. How much do you need?"
5. I'm having / I'll have a party next Saturday. I hope you can come.
6. "Remember to get a newspaper when you go out." "OK. I don't forget / I won't forget."
7. What time does your plane leave / will your plane leave tomorrow?
8. I asked Sue what happened, but she doesn't tell / won't tell me.
9. "Are you doing / Will you do anything tomorrow night?" "No, I'm free. Why?"
10. I don't want to go out alone. Do you come / Will you come with me?

20.4 Complete the sentences with *I'll* / *I won't* / *shall I* / *shall we* + an appropriate verb.

1. *A:* Where ___shall we have___ lunch?
   B: Let's go to that new restaurant on North Street.
2. *A:* It's Mark's birthday soon, and I want to get him a present.
   What _____ him?
   B: I don't know. I never know what to give people.
3. *A:* Do you want me to put these groceries away?
   B: No that's OK. _____ it later.
4. *A:* Let's go out tonight.
   B: OK, where _____ ?
5. *A:* What I've told you is a secret. I don't want anybody else to know.
   B: Don't worry. _____ anybody.
6. *A:* I know you're busy, but can you finish this report this afternoon?
   B: Well, _____ , but I can't promise.

Will 2

A

We do not use **will** to say what somebody has already arranged or decided to do in the future:

■ Ann **is working** next week. (*not* Ann will work)
■ **Are** you **going to watch** television tonight? (*not* Will you watch)

For **"is working"** and **"Are** you **going to . . . ?"**, see Units 18–19.

But often, when we talk about the future, we are *not* talking about what somebody has decided to do. For example:

Joe and a friend are waiting in line at a movie theater.

This is a very long line!

Don't worry. We**'ll get in**.

Joe

We'll get in does *not* mean "we have decided to get in." Joe is saying what he knows or thinks will happen. He is predicting the future.

When we predict a future happening or situation, we use **will/won't**.

Some more examples:

■ Jill has lived abroad for a long time. When she comes back, she**'ll find** a lot of changes here.
■ "Where **will** you **be** this time next year?" "I**'ll be** in Japan."
■ That plate is hot. If you touch it, you**'ll burn** yourself.
■ Tom **won't pass** the exam. He hasn't studied hard enough.
■ When **will** you **find out** how you did on the exam?

B

We often use **will** (**'ll**) with:

probably	■ I**'ll probably** be home late tonight.
I expect	■ **I expect** the test **will** take two hours.
I'm sure	■ Don't worry about the exam. **I'm sure** you**'ll** pass.
I think	■ **Do you think** Sarah **will** like the present we bought her?
I don't think	■ **I don't think** the exam **will** be very difficult.
I guess	■ **I guess** your parents **will** be tired after their trip.
I suppose	■ When **do you suppose** Jan and Mark **will** get married?
I doubt	■ **I doubt** you**'ll** need a heavy coat in Las Vegas. It's usually warm there.
I wonder	■ I worry about those people who lost their jobs. **I wonder** what **will** happen to them.

After **I hope**, we generally use the present:

■ **I hope** Kate **passes** the exam.
■ **I hope** it **doesn't rain** tomorrow.

Will 1 Unit 20   *I will* and *I'm going to* Unit 22   *Will be doing* and *will have done* Unit 23
The Future Appendix 3   **British English** Appendix 7

Exercises

21.1 Which form of the verb is correct (or more natural) in these sentences?

1. Diane isn't free on Saturday. ~~She'll work~~ / She's working. (*She's working* is correct)
2. I'll go / I'm going to a party tomorrow night. Would you like to come, too?
3. I think Amy will get / is getting the job. She has a lot of experience.
4. I can't meet you tonight. A friend of mine will come / is coming over.
5. *A:* Have you decided where to go on vacation?
   B: Yes, we'll go / we are going to Italy.
6. Don't be afraid of the dog. It won't hurt / It isn't hurting you.

21.2 Complete the sentences with *will ('ll)* + the following verbs:

come   get   like   live   look   ~~pass~~   see   take

1. Don't worry about the exam. I'm sure you *'ll pass* .
2. Why don't you try on this jacket? It _____ nice on you.
3. I want you to meet Brandon sometime. I think you _____ him.
4. It's raining. Don't go out. You _____ wet.
5. Do you think people _____ longer in the future?
6. Goodbye. I'm sure we _____ each other again soon.
7. I invited Sue to the party, but I don't think she _____ .
8. When the new road is finished, I expect that my trip to work _____ less time.

21.3 Write *will ('ll)* or *won't*.

1. Can you wait for me? I ___won't___ be very long.
2. You don't need to take an umbrella along. It _____ rain.
3. If you don't eat anything now, you _____ be hungry later.
4. I'm sorry about what happened yesterday. It _____ happen again.
5. I've got some incredible news! You _____ never believe what happened.
6. There's no more bread. I guess we _____ have to go shopping before we eat.
7. Don't ask Amanda for advice. She _____ know what to do.
8. Jack doesn't like crowds. I don't think he _____ come with us to the party.

21.4 Where do you think you will be at these times? Write true sentences about yourself. Use:

I'll be . . .   I'll probably be . . .   I don't know where I'll be . . .   I guess I'll be . . .

1. (next Monday night at 7:45)
   I'll be at home. OR I guess I'll be at home. OR I don't know where I'll be.
2. (at 5:00 tomorrow morning)
   _____
3. (at 10:30 tomorrow morning)
   _____
4. (next Saturday afternoon at 4:15)
   _____
5. (this time next year)
   _____

21.5 Write questions using *do you think . . . will . . . ?* + the following verbs:

be back   cost   end   get married   happen   ~~like~~   rain

1. I bought Rosa a present. *Do you think she'll like it* ?
2. The sky is dark and cloudy. Do you _____ ?
3. The meeting is still going on. When do you _____ ?
4. My car needs to be fixed. How much _____ ?
5. Sally and David are in love. Do _____ ?
6. "I'm going out now." "OK. What time _____ ?"
7. The future is uncertain. What _____ ?

I will and I'm going to

Future actions

Study the difference between **will** and **(be) going to**:

Sue is talking to Erica:

Let's have a party.

That's a great idea. We**'ll invite** lots of people.

Sue   Erica

will ('ll): We use **will** when we decide to do something at the time of speaking. The speaker has not decided before. The party is a new idea.

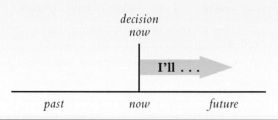

decision now

I'll . . .

past   now   future

Later that day, Erica meets Dave:

Sue and I have decided to have a party. We**'re going to invite** lots of people.

Erica   Dave

(be) going to: We use **(be) going to** when we have *already* decided to do something. Erica had already decided to invite lots of people *before* she spoke to Dave.

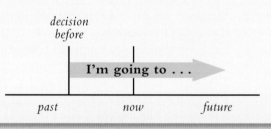

decision before

I'm going to . . .

past   now   future

Compare:
- "Daniel called while you were out."   "OK. I**'ll call** him back."
  "Daniel called while you were out."   "Yes, I know. I**'m going to call** him back."
- "Anna is in the hospital."   "Oh really? I didn't know. I**'ll go** and visit her."
  "Anna is in the hospital."   "Yes, I know. I**'m going to visit** her tonight."

Future happenings and situations (predicting the future)

Sometimes there is not much difference between **will** and **going to**. For example, you can say:
- I think the weather **will** be nice later.
- I think the weather **is going to** be nice later.

When we say something **is going to** happen, we think this because of the situation now (see Unit 19C):
- Look at those black clouds. It**'s going to rain**. (*not* It will rain)
  (We can see that it **is going to** rain from the clouds that are in the sky *now*.)
- I feel terrible. I think I**'m going to be** sick. (*not* I think I'll be sick)
  (I think I**'m going to be** sick because I feel terrible *now*.)

Do not use **will** in this type of situation.

In other situations, use **will**:
- Tom **will** probably **get** here at about 8:00.
- I think Jessica **will like** the present we bought for her.
- These shoes are very well made. They**'ll last** a long time.

Exercises

22.1 Complete the sentences using *will ('ll)* or *going to.*

1. *A:* Why are you turning on the television?
   B: ___I'm going to watch___ the news. (I / watch)
2. *A:* Oh, I just realized. I don't have any money.
   B: You don't? Well, don't worry. _____ you some. (I / lend)
3. *A:* I have a headache.
   B: You do? Wait a second and _____ an aspirin for you. (I / get)
4. *A:* Why are you filling that bucket with water?
   B: _____ the car. (I / wash)
5. *A:* I've decided to paint this room.
   B: Oh, really? What color _____ it? (you / paint)
6. *A:* Where are you going? Are you going shopping?
   B: Yes, _____ some things for dinner. (I / buy)
7. *A:* I don't know how to use this camera.
   B: It's easy. _____ you. (I / show)
8. *A:* Did you mail that letter for me?
   B: Oh, I'm sorry. I completely forgot. _____ it now. (I / do)
9. *A:* The ceiling in this room doesn't look very safe, does it?
   B: No, it looks as if _____ down. (it / fall)
10. *A:* Has Dan decided what to do when he finishes high school?
    B: Yes. Everything is planned. _____ a few months
        off. (he / take) Then _____ classes at the community
        college. (he / start)

22.2 Read the situations and complete the sentences using *will ('ll)* or *going to.*

1. The phone rings and you answer. Somebody wants to speak to Jim.
   Caller: Hello. Can I speak to Jim, please?
   You: Just a minute. ___I'll get___ him. (I / get)
2. It's a nice day, so you have decided to take a walk. Just before you go, you tell your friend.
   You: The weather's too nice to stay indoors. _____ a
          walk. (I / take)
   Friend: Good idea. I think _____ you. (I / join)
3. Your friend is worried because she has lost an important letter.
   You: Don't worry about the letter. I'm sure _____ it.
          (you / find)
4. There was a job advertised in the newspaper recently. At first you were interested, but then
   you decided not to apply.
   Friend: Have you decided what to do about that job you were interested in?
   You: Yes, _____ for it. (I / not / apply)
5. You and a friend come home very late. Other people in the house are asleep. Your friend
   is noisy.
   You: Shh! Don't make so much noise. _____ everybody up.
          (you / wake)
6. John has to go to the airport to catch a plane tomorrow morning.
   John: Ann, I need a ride to the airport tomorrow morning.
   Ann: That's no problem. _____ you. (I / take)
          What time is your flight?
   John: 10:50.
   Ann: OK, _____ at about 8:00. (we / leave)
   Later that day, Joe offers John a ride to the airport.
   Joe: John, do you want me to take you to the airport?
   John: No thanks, Joe. _____ me. (Ann / take)

Will be doing and will have done

A

Study this example situation:

These people are standing in line to get into the stadium.

now

An hour from now, the stadium will be full.
Everyone **will be watching** the game.

an hour from now

Three hours from now, the stadium will be empty.
The game **will have ended**.
Everyone **will have gone** home.

three hours from now

B

I will be doing something *(future continuous)* = I will be in the middle of doing it:
- I'm leaving on vacation this Saturday. This time next week, **I'll be lying** on the beach or **swimming** in the ocean.
- You have no chance of getting the job. You**'ll be wasting** your time if you apply for it.

Compare **will be doing** and **will do**:
- Don't call me between 7 and 8. We**'ll be having** dinner.
- Let's wait for Maria to arrive, and then we**'ll have** dinner.

Compare **will be doing** with other continuous forms:
- At 10:00 yesterday, Kelly **was** at the office. She **was working**. *(past)*
  It's 10:00 now. She **is** at the office. She **is working**. *(present)*
  At 10:00 tomorrow, she **will be** at the office. She **will be working**. *(future)*

C

We also use **will be -ing** to talk about complete actions in the future.
For example:
- The government **will be making** a statement about the crisis later today.
- **Will** you **be going** away this summer?
- Later in the program, **I'll be talking** to the Minister of Education . . .
- Our best player is injured and **won't be playing** in the game on Saturday.

In these examples, **will be -ing** is similar to **(be) going to . . .**

Later in the program, I'll be talking to . . .

D

We use **will have done** *(future perfect)* to say that something will already be complete before a time in the future. For example:
- Sally always leaves for work at 8:30 in the morning. She won't be at home at 9:00 – she**'ll have gone** to work.
- We're late. The movie **will** already **have started** by the time we get to the theater.

Compare **will have done** with other perfect forms:
- Ted and Amy **have been** married for 24 years. *(present perfect)*
  Next year they **will have been** married for 25 years. *(future perfect)*
  When their first child was born, they **had been** married for three years. *(past perfect)*

Exercises

23.1 Read about Josh. Then put a check (✓) by the sentences that are true. In each group of sentences, at least one is true.

Josh goes to work every day. After breakfast, he leaves home at 8:00 and arrives at work at about 8:45. He starts work immediately and continues until 12:30, when he has lunch (which takes about half an hour). He starts work again at 1:15 and goes home at exactly 4:30. Every day he follows the same routine, and tomorrow will be no exception.

1.  **At 7:45**
   a) he'll be leaving the house
   b) he'll have left the house
   c) he'll be at home ✓
   d) he'll be having breakfast ✓

4. **At 12:45**
   a) he'll have lunch
   b) he'll be having lunch
   c) he'll have finished his lunch
   d) he'll have started his lunch

2.  **At 8:15**
   a) he'll be leaving the house
   b) he'll have left the house
   c) he'll have arrived at work
   d) he'll be arriving at work

5.  **At 4:00**
   a) he'll have finished work
   b) he'll finish work
   c) he'll be working
   d) he won't have finished work

3. **At 9:15**
   a) he'll be working
   b) he'll start work
   c) he'll have started work
   d) he'll be arriving at work

6. **At 4:45**
   a) he'll leave work
   b) he'll be leaving work
   c) he'll have left work
   d) he'll have arrived home

23.2 Put the verb into the correct form, *will be (do)ing* or *will have (done)*.

1. Don't call me between 7 and 8. __*We'll be having*__ (we / have) dinner then.
2. Call me after 8:00. _____ (we / finish) dinner by then.
3. Tomorrow afternoon we're going to play tennis from 3:00 until 4:30. So at 4:00, _____ (we / play) tennis.
4. *A:* Can we meet tomorrow afternoon?
   B: I'm sorry I can't. _____ (I / work).
5. *B has to go to a meeting that begins at 10:00. It will last about an hour.*
   A: Will you be free at 11:30?
   B: Yes, _____ (the meeting / end) by then.
6. Ben is on vacation, and he is spending his money very quickly. If he continues like this, _____ (he / spend) all his money before the end of his vacation.
7. Do you think _____ (you / still / do) the same job 10 years from now?
8. Lisa is from New Zealand. She is traveling around South America right now. So far she has traveled about 1,000 miles. By the end of the trip, _____ (she / travel) more than 3,000 miles.
9. If you need to contact me, _____ (I / stay) at the Bellmore Hotel until Friday.
10. *A:* _____ (you / see) Laura tomorrow?
    B: Yes, probably. Why?
    A: I borrowed this CD from her. Can you give it back to her?

When I do / When I've done
When and if

Study this example:

Will you call me tomorrow?

Yes, I'll call you **when I get** home from work.

"I'll call you when I get home from work" is a sentence with two parts:

the main part: I'll call you

and the **when** part: **when I get** home from work

The time in the sentence is future (tomorrow), but we use a *present* tense (**I get**) in the **when** part of the sentence.

We do *not* use **will** in the **when** part of the sentence.

Some more examples:

- We'll go out **when** it **stops** raining. (*not* when it will stop)
- **When** you **are** in Los Angeles again, give us a call. (*not* When you will be)
- (*said to a child*) What do you want to be **when** you **grow** up? (*not* will grow)

The same thing happens after **while / before / after / as soon as / until** or **till**:

- I'm going to read a lot of books **while I'm** on vacation. (*not* while I will be)
- I'll probably go back home on Sunday. **Before** I **go**, I'd like to visit a museum.
- Wait here **until** (*or* **till**) I **come** back.

You can also use the present perfect (**have done**) after **when / after / until / as soon as**:

- Can I borrow that book **when** you**'ve finished** it?
- Don't say anything while Ben is here. Wait **until** he **has gone**.

If you use the present perfect, one thing must be complete *before* the other (so the two things do not happen together):

- **When I've called** Kate, we can have dinner.
  (= First I'll call Kate, and *after that* we can have dinner.)

Do not use the present perfect if the two things happen together:

- **When I call** Kate, I'll ask her about the party. (*not* When I've called)

It is often possible to use either the simple present or the present perfect:

- I'll come **as soon as** I **finish**. *or* I'll come **as soon as** I**'ve finished**.
- You'll feel better **after** you *or* You'll feel better **after** you**'ve**
  have something to eat. **had** something to eat.

After **if**, we normally use the simple present (**if I do / if I see**, etc.) for the future:

- It's raining hard. We'll get wet **if** we **go** out. (*not* if we will go)
- I'll be angry **if** it **happens** again. (*not* if it will happen)
- Hurry up! **If** we **don't hurry**, we'll be late.

Compare **when** and **if**:

We use **when** for things that are *sure* to happen:

- I'm going shopping later. (for sure) **When** I go shopping, I'll get some cheese.

We use **if** (*not* when) for things that will *possibly* happen:

- I might go shopping later. (it's possible) **If** I go shopping, I'll get some cheese.
- **If** it is raining tonight, I won't go out. (*not* When it is raining)
- Don't worry **if** I'm late tonight. (*not* when I'm late)
- **If** they don't come soon, I'm not going to wait. (*not* When they don't come)

Exercises

24.1 Complete the sentences using the verbs in parentheses. All the sentences are about the future. Use **will / won't** or the simple present (**I see / he plays / it is**, etc.).

1. I _'ll call_ (call) you when I __get__ (get) home from work.
2. I want to see Jennifer before she _____ (go) out.
3. We're going on a trip tomorrow. I _____ (tell) you all about it when we _____ (come) back.
4. Brian looks very different now. When you _____ (see) him again, you _____ (not / recognize) him.
5. _____ (you / miss) me while I _____ (be) away?
6. We should do something soon before it _____ (be) too late.
7. I don't want to go without you. I _____ (wait) until you _____ (be) ready.
8. Sue has applied for the job, but she isn't very well qualified for it. I _____ (be) surprised if she _____ (get) it.
9. I'd like to play tennis tomorrow if the weather _____ (be) nice.
10. I'm going out now. If anybody _____ (call) while I _____ (be) out, can you take a message?

24.2 Make one sentence from two.

1. You'll be in Los Angeles again. Give us a call.
   Give us a call when _you are in Los Angeles again_ .
2. I'll find a place to live. Then I'll give you my address.
   I _____ when _____ .
3. I'll go shopping. Then I'll come straight home.
   _____ after _____ .
4. It's going to get dark. Let's go home before that.
   _____ before _____ .
5. She must apologize to me first. I won't speak to her until then.
   _____ until _____ .

24.3 Read the situations and complete the sentences.

1. A friend of yours is going on vacation. You want to know what she is going to do. You ask:
   What are you going to do when _you go on vacation_ ?
2. A friend of yours is visiting you. She has to go soon, but you'd like to show her some pictures. You ask:
   Do you have time to look at some pictures before _____ ?
3. You want to sell your car. Jim is interested in buying it, but he hasn't decided yet. You ask:
   Can you let me know as soon as _____ ?
4. A friend of yours is going to visit Hong Kong. You want to know where she is going to stay. You ask:
   Where are you going to stay when _____ ?
5. The traffic is very bad in your town, but they are going to build a new road. You say:
   I think things will be better when they _____ .

24.4 Put in **when** or **if**.

1. Don't worry __if__ I'm late tonight.
2. Chris might call while I'm out tonight. _____ he does, can you take a message?
3. I'm going to Tokyo next week. _____ I'm there, I hope to visit a friend of mine.
4. I think Beth will get the job. I'll be very surprised _____ she doesn't get it.
5. I'm going shopping. _____ you want anything, I can get it for you.
6. I'm going away for a few days. I'll call you _____ I get back.
7. I want you to come to the party, but _____ you don't want to come, that's all right.
8. We can eat at home or, _____ you prefer, we can go to a restaurant.

Can, could, and (be) able to

A

We use **can** to say that something is possible or allowed, or that somebody has the ability to do something. We use **can** + *base form* (**can do** / **can see**, etc.):

- We **can see** the ocean from our hotel window.
- "I don't have a pen." "You **can use** mine."
- **Can** you **speak** any foreign languages?
- I **can come** and help you tomorrow if you want.
- The word "dream" **can be** a noun or a verb.

The negative is **can't** (= cannot):

- I'm afraid I **can't come** to your party on Friday.

B

You can say that somebody **is able to** do something, but **can** is more common:

- We **are able to see** the ocean from our hotel window.

But **can** has only two forms: **can** *(present)* and **could** *(past)*. So sometimes it is necessary to use **(be) able to**. Compare:

■ I **can't** sleep.	■ I **haven't been able to** sleep recently.
■ Tom **can** come tomorrow.	■ Tom **might be able to** come tomorrow.
■ Maria **can** speak French, Spanish, and English.	■ Applicants for the job **must be able to** speak two foreign languages.

C

Could

Sometimes **could** is the past of **can**. We use **could** especially with:

see   hear   smell   taste   feel   remember   understand

- We had a nice room in the hotel. We **could see** the ocean.
- As soon as I walked into the room, I **could smell** gas.
- She spoke in a very soft voice, so I **couldn't understand** what she said.

We also use **could** to say that somebody had the general ability or permission to do something:

- My grandfather **could speak** five languages.
- We were totally free. We **could do** what we wanted. (= we were allowed to do)

D

Could and **was able to**

We use **could** for general ability. But if you want to say that somebody did something in a specific situation, use **was/were able to** or **managed to** (*not* could):

- The fire spread through the building very quickly, but fortunately everybody **was able to escape** / **managed to escape**. (*not* could escape)
- We didn't know where David was, but we **managed to find** / **were able to find** him in the end. (*not* could find)

Compare:

- Jack was an excellent tennis player when he was younger. He **could beat** anybody. (= he had the general ability to beat anybody)
- *but* Jack and Ted played tennis yesterday. Ted played very well, but Jack **managed to** / **was able to beat** him. (= he managed to beat him this time)

The negative **couldn't** (**could not**) is possible in all situations:

- My grandfather **couldn't swim**.
- We looked for David everywhere, but we **couldn't find** him.
- Ted played well, but he **couldn't beat** Jack.

Exercises

25.1 Complete the sentences using *can* or *(be) able to*. Use *can* if possible; otherwise use *(be) able to*.

1. Eric has traveled a lot. He __*can*__ speak four languages.
2. I haven't __*been able to*__ sleep very well recently.
3. Nicole _____ drive, but she doesn't have a car.
4. I used to _____ stand on my head, but I can't do it anymore.
5. I can't understand Michael. I've never _____ understand him.
6. I can't see you on Friday, but I _____ meet you on Saturday morning.
7. Ask Catherine about your problem. She might _____ help you.

25.2 Write sentences about yourself using the ideas in parentheses.

1. (something you used to be able to do)
   __*I used to be able to sing well.*_____
2. (something you used to be able to do)
   I used _____
3. (something you would like to be able to do)
   I'd _____
4. (something you have never been able to do)
   I've _____

25.3 Complete the sentences with *can/can't/could/couldn't* + the following verbs:

~~come~~   eat   hear   run   sleep   wait

1. I'm sorry I __*can't come*__ to your party next week.
2. When Bob was 16, he _____ 100 meters in 11 seconds.
3. "Are you in a hurry?" "No, I've got plenty of time. I _____."
4. I felt sick yesterday. I _____ anything.
5. Can you speak a little louder? I _____ you very well.
6. "You look tired." "Yes, I _____ last night."

25.4 Complete the answers to the questions with *was/were able to*.

1. *A:* Did everybody escape from the fire?
   B: Yes. Although the fire spread quickly, everybody __*was able to escape*__ .
2. *A:* Did you finish your homework this afternoon?
   B: Yes, nobody was around to disturb me, so I _____ .
3. *A:* Did you have any trouble finding Amy's house?
   B: Not really. She'd given us good directions, so we _____ .
4. *A:* Did the thief get away?
   B: Yes. No one realized what was happening, and the thief _____ .

25.5 Complete the sentences using *could*, *couldn't*, or *managed to*.

1. My grandfather traveled a lot. He __*could*__ speak five languages.
2. I looked everywhere for the book, but I __*couldn't*__ find it.
3. They didn't want to come with us at first, but we __*managed to*__ persuade them.
4. Laura had hurt her leg and _____ walk very well.
5. Sue wasn't at home when I called, but I _____ contact her at her office.
6. I looked very carefully, and I _____ see someone in the distance.
7. I wanted to buy some tomatoes. The first store I went to didn't have any good ones, but I _____ get some at the next place.
8. My grandmother loved music. She _____ play the piano very well.
9. A girl fell into the river, but fortunately we _____ rescue her.
10. I had forgotten to bring my camera, so I _____ take any photos.

Could (do) and could have (done)

A

We use **could** in a number of ways. Sometimes **could** is the past of **can** (see Unit 25C):

- Listen. I **can hear** something. *(now)*
- I listened. I **could hear** something. *(past)*

But **could** is not only used in this way. We also use **could** to talk about possible actions now or in the future (especially to make suggestions). For example:

- *A:* What would you like to do tonight?
  B: We **could go** to the movies.
- *A:* When you go to New York next month, you **could stay** with Candice.
  B: Yes, I guess I **could.**

Can is also possible in these sentences (We **can go** to the movies, etc.). **Could** is less sure than **can.**

What would you like to do tonight?

We **could go** to the movies.

B

We also use **could** (*not* can) for actions which are not realistic. For example:

- I'm so tired, I **could sleep** for a week. (*not* I can sleep for a week)

Compare **can** and **could**:

- I **can stay** with Candice when I go to New York. (realistic)
- Maybe I **could stay** with Candice when I go to New York. (possible, but less sure)
- This is a wonderful place. I **could stay** here forever. (unrealistic)

C

We also use **could** (*not* can) to say that something is possible now or in the future. The meaning is similar to **might** or **may** (see Units 28–29):

- The story **could be** true, but I don't think it is. (*not* can be true)
- I don't know what time Liz is coming. She **could get** here at any time.

D

We use **could have** (done) to talk about the past. Compare:

- I'm so tired, I **could sleep** for a week. *(now)*
  I was so tired, I **could have slept** for a week. *(past)*
- The situation is bad, but it **could be** worse. *(now)*
  The situation was bad, but it **could have been** worse. *(past)*

Something **could have** happened = it was possible but did not happen:

- Why did you stay at a hotel when you were in New York? You **could have stayed** with Candice. (you didn't stay with her)
- I didn't know that you wanted to go to the concert. I **could have gotten** you a free ticket. (I didn't get you a ticket)
- Dave was lucky. He **could have hurt** himself when he fell, but he's OK.

E

We use **couldn't** to say that something would not be possible now:

- I **couldn't live** in a big city. I'd hate it. (= it wouldn't be possible for me)
- Everything is fine right now. Things **couldn't be** better.

For the past, we use **couldn't have** (done):

- We had a really good vacation. It **couldn't have been** better.
- The trip was canceled last week. Paul **couldn't have gone** anyway because he was sick. (= it would not have been possible for him to go)

Exercises

26.1 Answer the questions with a suggestion. Use *could* and the words in parentheses.

1.	Where would you like to go on vacation?	(to San Diego) *We could go to San Diego.*
2.	What should we have for dinner tonight?	(fish) We _____
3.	When should I call Angela?	(now) You _____
4.	What should I give Ana for her birthday?	(a book) _____
5.	When should we go and see Tom?	(on Friday) _____

26.2 In some of these sentences, you need *could* (not *can*). Change the sentences where necessary.

1. The story can be true but I don't think it is.   *could be true*
2. It's a nice day. We can go for a walk.   *OK* (could go *is also possible*)
3. I'm so angry I can scream.   _____
4. If you're hungry, we can have dinner now.   _____
5. It's so nice here. I can stay here all day,
   but unfortunately I have to go.   _____
6. *A:* Where's my bag. Have you seen it?
   B: No, but it can be in the car.   _____
7. Peter is a good musician. He plays the flute,
   and he can also play the piano.   _____
8. *A:* I need to borrow a camera.
   B: You can borrow mine.   _____
9. The weather is nice now, but it can change later.   _____

26.3 Complete the sentences. Use *could* or *could have* + appropriate verbs.

1. *A:* What should we do tonight?
   B: We _could go_ to the movies.
2. *A:* I spent a very boring evening at home yesterday.
   B: Why did you stay at home? You _____ out with us.
3. *A:* There's a job advertised in the paper that I think you are really qualified for.
   B: I guess I _____ for it, but I like my present job.
4. *A:* How was your test? Was it hard?
   B: It wasn't so bad. It _____ worse.
5. *A:* I got very wet walking home in the rain last night.
   B: Why did you walk? You _____ a taxi.
6. *A:* Where should we meet tomorrow?
   B: Well, I _____ to your house if you want.

26.4 Complete the sentences. Use *couldn't* or *couldn't have* + these verbs in the correct form:

~~be~~   be   come   find   get   ~~live~~   wear

1. I _couldn't live_ in a big city. I'd hate it.
2. We had a really good vacation. It _couldn't have been_ better.
3. I _____ that hat. I'd look silly, and people would laugh at me.
4. We managed to find the restaurant you recommended, but we _____ it without the map that you drew for us.
5. Paul has to get up at 4:00 every morning. I don't know how he does it. I _____ up at that time every day.
6. The staff at the hotel was really nice when we stayed there last summer. They _____ more helpful.
7. *A:* I tried to call you last week. We had a party, and I wanted to invite you.
   B: That's nice of you, but I _____ anyway. I was away all last week.

Must (You must be tired, etc.)

A

Must (not)

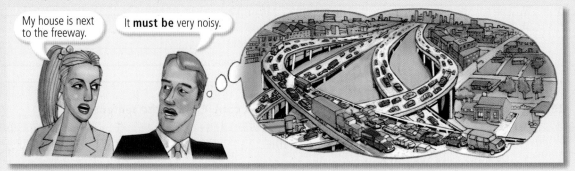

My house is next to the freeway.

It **must be** very noisy.

We use **must** to say that we feel sure something is true:

- You've been traveling all day. You **must be** tired.
  (Traveling is tiring and you've been traveling all day, so you **must be** tired.)
- "Jim is a hard worker." "Jim? You **must be** joking. He's very lazy."
- I'm sure Sally gave me her phone number. I **must have** it somewhere.

We use **must not** to say that we feel sure something is not true:

- Their car isn't outside their house. They **must not be** home. (= They **must be** out)
- Brian said he would be here by 9:30. It's 10:00 now, and he's never late. He **must not be coming**.
- They haven't lived here very long. They **must not know** many people.

Study the structure:

I/you/he (etc.)	must (not)	**be** (tired / hungry / home, etc.) **be** (**doing** / **coming** / **joking**, etc.) **do** / **get** / **know** / **have**, etc.

B

Must (not) have done

For the past, we use **must (not) have done**:

- "We used to live close to the freeway." "Did you? It **must have been** noisy."
- There's nobody at home. They **must have gone** out.
- I've lost one of my gloves. I **must have dropped** it somewhere.
- She walked past me without speaking. She **must not have seen** me.
- Tom walked into a wall. He **must not have been looking** where he was going.

Study the structure:

I/you/he (etc.)	must (not)	have	**been** (tired / hungry / noisy, etc.) **been** (**doing** / **coming** / **looking**, etc.) **gone** / **dropped** / **seen**, etc.

C

Can't and must not

It **can't be** true = I believe it is impossible:

- How can you say such a thing? You **can't be** serious!

Compare **can't** and **must not**:

- A: Joe wants something to eat.
- B: But he just had lunch. He **can't be** hungry already. (= it's impossible that he is hungry because he just had lunch)
- A: I offered Bill something to eat, but he didn't want anything.
- B: He **must not be** hungry. (= I'm sure he is not hungry – otherwise he would eat something)

Can't (I can't swim, etc.) Unit 25A, B   *Must (I must go, etc.)* Unit 30B, C   **British English** Appendix 7

Exercises

27.1 Put in *must* or *must not*.

1. You've been traveling all day. You ___*must*___ be tired.
2. That restaurant _____ be very good. It's always full of people.
3. That restaurant _____ be very good. It's always empty.
4. You _____ be looking forward to going on vacation next week.
5. It rained every day during their vacation, so they _____ have had a very nice time.
6. You got here very quickly. You _____ have walked very fast.

27.2 Complete each sentence with a verb (one or two words) in the correct form.

1. I've lost one of my gloves. I must __*have dropped*___ it somewhere.
2. They haven't lived here very long. They must not __*know*___ many people.
3. Ted isn't at work today. He must _____ sick.
4. Ted wasn't at work last week. He must _____ sick.
5. Sarah knows a lot about movies. She must _____ to the movies a lot.
6. Look. James is putting on his hat and coat. He must _____ out.
7. I left my bike outside last night and now it is gone. Somebody must _____ it.
8. Sue was in a difficult situation when she lost her job. It must not _____ easy for her.
9. There is a man walking behind us. He has been walking behind us for the last 20 minutes. He must _____ us.

27.3 Read the situations and use the words in parentheses to write sentences with *must have* and *must not have*.

1. The phone rang, but I didn't hear it. (I / asleep) __*I must have been asleep.*___
2. Julie walked past me without speaking. (she / see / me) __*She must not have seen me.*___
3. The jacket you bought is very good quality. (it / very expensive)
   _____
4. I can't find my umbrella. (I / leave / it in the restaurant last night)
   _____
5. Dave passed the exam without studying for it. (the exam / very difficult)
   _____
6. She knew everything about our plans. (she / listen / to our conversation)
   _____
7. Rachel did the opposite of what I asked her to do. (she / understand / what I said)
   _____
8. When I woke up this morning, the light was on. (I / forget / to turn it off)
   _____
9. I was awakened in the night by loud music next door. (the neighbors / have / a party)
   _____

27.4 Complete the sentences with *must not* or *can't*.

1. How can you say such a thing? You __*can't*___ be serious!
2. Their car isn't outside their house. They __*must not*___ be home.
3. I just bought a box of cereal yesterday. It _____ be empty already.
4. The Smiths always go on vacation this time of year, but they are still home.
   They _____ be taking a vacation this year.
5. You just started filling out your tax forms 10 minutes ago.
   You _____ be finished with them already!
6. Eric is a good friend of Ann's, but he hasn't visited her in the hospital.
   He _____ know she's in the hospital.

May and might 1

Study this example situation:

> You are looking for Bob. Nobody is sure where he is, but you get some suggestions.
>
> Where's Bob?
>
> He **may be** in his office.   (= perhaps he is in his office)
>
> He **might be having** lunch.   (= perhaps he is having lunch)
>
> Ask Ann. She **might know**.   (= perhaps she knows)

We use **may** or **might** to say that something is a possibility. Usually, you can use **may** or **might**, so you can say:

- It **may** be true. *or* It **might** be true. (= perhaps it is true)
- She **might** know. *or* She **may** know.

The negative forms are **may not** and **might not**:

- It **may not** be true. (= perhaps it isn't true)
- She **might not** work here anymore. (= perhaps she doesn't work here)

Study the structure:

I/you/he (etc.)	**may** **might**	(**not**)	**be** (true / in his office, etc.) **be** (**doing** / **working** / **having**, etc.) **do** / **know** / **work** / **want**, etc.

For the past we use **may have done** or **might have done**:

- *A:* I wonder why Kate didn't answer the phone.
  B: She **may have been** asleep. (= perhaps she was asleep)
- *A:* I can't find my bag anywhere.
  B: You **might have left** it in the store. (= perhaps you left it in the store)
- *A:* I was surprised that Sarah wasn't at the meeting yesterday.
  B: She **might not have known** about it. (= perhaps she didn't know)
- *A:* I wonder why David was in such a bad mood yesterday.
  B: He **may not have been feeling** well. (= perhaps he wasn't feeling well)

Study the structure:

I/you/he (etc.)	**may** **might**	(**not**) **have**	**been** (asleep / at home, etc.) **been** (**doing** / **working** / **feeling**, etc.) **known** / **had** / **wanted** / **left**, etc.

Could is similar to **may** and **might**:

- It's a strange story, but it **could be** true. (= it may/might be true)
- You **could have left** your bag in the store. (= you may/might have left it there)

But **couldn't** *(negative)* is different from **may not** and **might not**. Compare:

- Sarah **couldn't have gotten** my message. Otherwise she would have called me.
  (= it is not possible that she got my message)
- I wonder why Sarah hasn't called me. I suppose she **might not have gotten** my message. (= perhaps she didn't get it, and perhaps she did)

Could Unit 26   *May / might 2* Unit 29   *May I . . . ?* Unit 35   *Might* with *if* Units 29B, 36C, 38D
Modal Verbs (*can/could/will/would*, etc.) Appendix 4

Exercises

28.1 Write these sentences in a different way using **may** or **might**.

1. Perhaps Elizabeth is in her office. _She might be in her office._ OR _She may be . . ._
2. Perhaps Elizabeth is busy. _____
3. Perhaps she is working. _____
4. Perhaps she wants to be alone. _____
5. Perhaps she was sick yesterday. _____
6. Perhaps she went home early. _____
7. Perhaps she had to go home early. _____
8. Perhaps she was working yesterday. _____

In sentences 9–11, use **may not** or **might not**.

9. Perhaps she doesn't want to see me. _____
10. Perhaps she isn't working today. _____
11. Perhaps she wasn't feeling well yesterday. _____

28.2 Complete each sentence with a verb in the correct form.

1. "Where's Sam?" "I'm not sure. He might _be having_ lunch."
2. "Who is that man with Anna?" "I'm not sure. It might _____ her brother."
3. "Who was the man we saw with Anna yesterday?" "I'm not sure. It may _____ her brother."
4. "What are those people doing by the side of the road?" "I don't know. They might _____ for a bus."
5. "Do you have a stamp?" "No, but ask Sam. He may _____ one."

28.3 Read the situations and make sentences from the words in parentheses. Use **may** or **might**.

1. I can't find Jeff anywhere. I wonder where he is.
   a) (he / go / shopping) _He may have gone shopping._
   b) (he / play / tennis) _He might be playing tennis._
2. I'm looking for Tiffany. Do you know where she is?
   a) (she / watch / TV / in her room) _____
   b) (she / go / out) _____
3. I can't find my umbrella. Have you seen it?
   a) (it / be / in the car) _____
   b) (you / leave / in the restaurant last night) _____
4. Why didn't Dave answer the doorbell? I'm sure he was at home at the time.
   a) (he / not / hear / the doorbell) _____
   b) (he / be / in the shower) _____

28.4 Complete the sentences using **might not have** . . . or **couldn't have** . . . .

1. A: Do you think Sarah got the message we left her?
   B: No, she would have contacted us. _She couldn't have gotten it._
2. A: I was surprised Kate wasn't at the meeting. Perhaps she didn't know about it.
   B: That's possible. _She might not have known about it._
3. A: I wonder why they never replied to our letter. Do you think they received it?
   B: Maybe not. They _____ .
4. A: I wonder how the fire started. Was it an accident?
   B: No, the police say it _____ .
5. A: Mike says he needs to see you. He tried to find you yesterday.
   B: Well, he _____ very hard. I was in my office all day.
6. A: The man you spoke to – are you sure he was Chinese?
   B: No, I'm not sure. He _____ .

May and might 2

A

We use **may** and **might** to talk about possible actions or happenings in the future:

- I haven't decided yet where to go on vacation. I **may go** to Hawaii.
  (= perhaps I will go there)
- Take an umbrella with you. It **might rain** later. (= perhaps it will rain)
- The bus isn't always on time. We **might have** to wait a few minutes.
  (= perhaps we will have to wait)

The negative forms are **may not** and **might not**:

- Ann **may not go** out tonight. She isn't feeling well. (= perhaps she will not go out)
- There **might not be** enough time to discuss everything at the meeting.

Compare **will** and **may/might**:

- I'**ll be** late this evening. (for sure)
- I **may/might** be late this evening. (possible)

B

Usually you can use **may** or **might**. So you can say:

- I **may go** to Hawaii.   *or*   I **might go** to Hawaii.
- Lisa **might be** able to help you.   *or*   Lisa **may be** able to help you.

But we use only **might** (*not* **may**) when the situation is *not real*:

- If I were in Tom's position, I think I **might** look for another job.

The situation here is not real because I am *not* in Tom's position (so I'm not going to look for another job). **May** is not possible in this example.

C

There is also a continuous form: **may/might be –ing**. Compare this with **will be –ing**:

- Don't call me at 8:30. I'**ll be watching** the baseball game on TV.
- Don't call me at 8:30. I **might be watching** (*or* I **may be watching**) the baseball game on TV. (= perhaps I'll be watching it)

We also use **may/might be –ing** for possible plans. Compare:

- I'**m going** to Hawaii in July. (for sure)
- I **may be going** (*or* I **might be going**) to Hawaii in July. (possible)

But you can also say "I **may go** (*or* I **might go**) to Hawaii" with little difference in meaning.

D

Might as well / may as well

Rosa and Maria have just missed the bus.
The buses run every hour.

What should we do? Should we walk?

We **might as well**. It's a nice day, and I don't want to wait here for an hour.

We **might as well** do something = We should do it because there is no better alternative. There is no reason not to do it. **May as well** is also possible.

- *A:* You'll have to wait two hours to see the doctor.
  B: I **might as well go** home and come back.
- Rents are so high these days, you **may as well buy** a house.
  (= buying a house is as good, no more expensive)

Exercises

29.1 Write sentences with *may* or *might*.

1. Where are you going on vacation? (to Hawaii??)
   I haven't decided yet. *I might go to Hawaii.*
2. What kind of car are you going to buy? (a Toyota??)
   I'm not sure yet. I _____
3. What are you doing this weekend? (go to the movies??)
   I haven't made up my mind yet. _____
4. When is Jim coming to see us? (on Saturday??)
   I don't know for sure. _____
5. Where are you going to hang that picture? (in the dining room??)
   I haven't made up my mind yet. _____
6. What is Julia going to do when she graduates from high school? (go to college??)
   She's still thinking about it. _____

29.2 Complete the sentences using *might* + the following:

   bite   break   need   ~~rain~~   slip   wake up

1. Take an umbrella with you when you go out. It *might rain* later.
2. Don't make too much noise. You _____ the baby.
3. Watch out for that dog. It _____ you.
4. I don't think we should throw that letter away. We _____ it later.
5. Be careful. The sidewalk is very icy. You _____ .
6. I don't want the children to play in this room. They _____ something.

29.3 Complete the sentences using *might be able to* or *might have to* + appropriate verbs.

1. I can't help you, but why don't you ask Jane? She *might be able to help* you.
2. I can't meet you tonight, but I _____ you tomorrow.
3. I'm not working on Saturday, but I _____ on Sunday.
4. I can come to the meeting, but I _____ before the end.

29.4 Write sentences with *might not*.

1. I'm not sure that Ann will come to the party.
   Ann might not come to the party.
2. I'm not sure that I'll go out tonight.
   I _____
3. You don't know if Sam will like the present you bought for him.
   Sam _____
4. We don't know if Sue will be able to get together with us tonight.
   _____

29.5 Read the situations and make sentences with *might as well*.

1. You and a friend have just missed the bus. The buses run every hour.
   You say: We'll have to wait an hour for the next bus. *We might as well walk.*
2. You have a free ticket for a concert. You're not very excited about the concert, but you decide to go.
   You say: I _____ . It's a shame to waste a free ticket.
3. You've just painted your kitchen. You still have a lot of paint, so why not paint the bathroom, too?
   You say: We _____ . There's plenty of paint left.
4. You and a friend are at home. You're bored. There's a movie on TV starting in a few minutes.
   You say: _____ . There's nothing else to do.

Have to and **must**

A

I **have to do** something = it is necessary to do it, I am obliged to do it:

- You can't turn right here. You **have to turn** left.
- I **have to get up** early tomorrow. My flight leaves at 7:30.
- Jason can't meet us tonight. He **has to work** late.
- Last week Nicole broke her arm and **had to go** to the hospital.
- Have you ever **had to go** to the hospital?

We use **do/does/did** in questions (for the present and past simple):

- What **do I have to do** to get a driver's license?
  (*not* What have I to do?)
- **Does** Kimberly **have to work** tomorrow?
- Why **did** you **have to leave** early?

In negative sentences, we use **don't/doesn't/didn't**:

- I **don't have to get up** early tomorrow.
  (*not* I haven't to)
- Kimberly **doesn't have to work** on Saturdays.
- We **didn't have to pay** to park the car.

You can say:
I'll have to / I won't have to . . .
I'm going to have to . . .
I **might/may have to** . . . (= perhaps I'll have to)

- They can't fix my computer, so **I'll have to buy** a new one. *or*
  . . . so **I'm going to have to buy** a new one.
- I **might have to leave** the meeting early. *or* I **may have to leave** . . .

You **have to turn** left here.

B

Must is similar to **have to**:

- The economic situation is bad. The government **must do** something about it. *or*
  The government **has to do** . . .
- If you go to New York, you really **must visit** the Empire State Building.
  (*or* . . . you really **have to** visit . . .)

But **have to** is more common than **must**.

We use **must** especially in written rules and instructions:

- Answer all the questions. You **must write** your answers in ink.
- Applications for the job **must be received** by May 18.

C

You **must not** do something = it is necessary that you *not* do it (so don't do it):

- Students **must not use** cell phones in class. (= it is not allowed)

Compare **must not** and **don't have to**:

- You **must keep** this a secret. You **must not tell** anybody.
  (= don't tell anybody)
- You **don't have to tell** Tim about what happened. I can tell him myself.
  (= you don't need to tell him, but it's OK if you do)

D

You can use **have got to** instead of **have to**. So you can say:

- I**'ve got to work** tomorrow. *or* I **have to work** tomorrow.
- He**'s got to visit** his aunt tonight. *or* He **has to visit** his aunt tonight.

Must (You must be tired) Unit 27

Exercises

UNIT **30**

30.1 Complete the sentences with *have to* / *has to* / *had to*.

1. Jason can't join us tonight. He __has to__ work late.
2. Beth left before the end of the meeting. She _____ go home early.
3. I don't have much time. I _____ go soon.
4. Kathy may _____ go out of town on business next week.
5. Eric is usually free on weekends, but sometimes he _____ work.
6. There was nobody to help me. I _____ do everything by myself.
7. Julie has _____ wear glasses since she was a small child.
8. Jeff can't pay his bills. He's going to _____ sell his car.

30.2 Complete the questions with a form of *have to* + the words in parentheses.

1. "I broke my arm last week." "__Did you have to go__ (you / go) to the hospital?"
2. "I'm sorry I can't stay very long." "What time _____ (you / go)?"
3. _____ (you / wait) long for the bus last night?
4. How old _____ (you / be) to drive in your country?
5. How does Chris like his new job? _____ (he / travel) a lot?

30.3 Complete the sentences using *have to* + the verbs in the list. Some sentences are positive
(I *have to* . . . etc.) and some are negative (I *don't have to* . . . etc.).

   ask   do   ~~get up~~   go   make   make   shave   ~~show~~

1. I'm not working tomorrow, so I __don't have to get up__ early.
2. Steve didn't know how to use the computer, so I __had to show__ him.
3. Excuse me for a minute – I _____ a phone call.
4. I couldn't find the street I wanted. I _____ somebody for directions.
5. Jack has a beard, so he _____ .
6. A man was injured in the accident, but he _____ to the hospital
   because it wasn't serious.
7. Sue is the vice president of the company. She _____ important decisions.
8. I'm not so busy. I have a few things to do, but I _____ them now.

30.4 Complete the sentences with *might have to*, *will have to*, or *won't have to*.

1. They can't fix my computer, so I __'ll have to__ buy a new one.
2. I __might have to__ leave the party early. My son is going to call me if he needs a
   ride home.
3. We _____ take the train downtown instead of driving. It depends on
   the traffic.
4. Sam _____ go to jail if he doesn't pay all his old parking tickets.
5. Unfortunately, my father _____ stay in the hospital another week. The
   doctor is going to decide tomorrow.
6. If it snows all night, we _____ go to class tomorrow. It will be
   canceled.

30.5 Complete the sentences with *must not* or *don't* / *doesn't have to*.

1. I don't want anyone to know about this. You __must not__ tell anyone.
2. He __doesn't have to__ wear a suit to work, but he usually does.
3. I can sleep late tomorrow morning because I _____ go to work.
4. Whatever you do, you _____ touch that switch. It's very dangerous.
5. There's an elevator in the building, so we _____ climb the stairs.
6. You _____ forget what I told you. It's very important.
7. Lauren _____ get up early, but she usually does.
8. You _____ eat or drink on buses. It's not allowed.
9. You _____ be a good player to enjoy a game of tennis.

Additional Exercise 16 **(pages 305-306)**

61

Should

A You **should do** something = it is a good thing to do or the right thing to do.

You can use **should** to give advice or to give an opinion:
- You look tired. You **should go** to bed.
- The government **should do** more to reduce crime.
- "**Should** we **invite** Susan to the party?" "Yes, I think we **should**."

We often use **should** with **I think / I don't think / Do you think . . . ?**:
- **I think** the government **should do** more to reduce crime.
- **I don't think** you **should work** so hard.
- "**Do you think** I **should apply** for this job?" "Yes, **I think** you **should**."

You **shouldn't do** something = it isn't a good thing to do:
- You **shouldn't believe** everything you read in the newspapers.

Should is not as strong as **must** or **have to**:
- You **should** apologize. (= it would be a good thing to do)
- You **must** apologize. / You **have to** apologize. (= you have no alternative)

B We also use **should** when something is not right or not what we expect:
- I wonder where Liz is. She **should be** here by now.
  (= she isn't here yet, and this is not normal)
- The price on this package is wrong. It **should be** $1.29, not $1.59.
- That man on the motorcycle **should be wearing** a helmet.

We also use **should** to say that we expect something to happen:
- She's been studying hard for the exam, so she **should pass**.
  (= I expect her to pass)
- There are plenty of hotels in this city. It **shouldn't be** hard to find a place to stay. (= I don't expect it to be hard)

C You **should have done** something = you didn't do it, but it would have been the right thing to do:
- You missed a great party last night. You **should have come**. Why didn't you?
  (= you didn't come, but it would have been good to come)
- I wonder why they're so late. They **should have been** here an hour ago.

You **shouldn't have done** something = you did it, but it was the wrong thing to do:
- I feel sick. I **shouldn't have eaten** so much. (= I ate too much)
- She **shouldn't have been listening** to our conversation. It was private.

Compare **should** (do) and **should have** (done):
- You look tired. You **should go** to bed now.
- You went to bed very late last night. You **should have gone** to bed earlier.

D **Ought to . . .**

You can use **ought to** instead of **should**. We say "ought **to** do" (with **to**):
- Do you think I **ought to apply** for this job?
  (= Do you think I **should apply**?)
- That's a terrible thing to say. You **ought to be** ashamed of yourself!
- She's been studying hard for the exam, so she **ought to pass**.

Exercises

31.1 For each situation, write a sentence with **should** or **shouldn't** + one of the following:

~~go away for a few days~~   go to bed so late   look for another job
put some pictures on the walls   take a photo   use her car so much

1. Liz needs a change. _She should go away for a few days._
2. Your salary is too low. You _____
3. Eric always has trouble getting up. He _____
4. What a beautiful view! You _____
5. Sue drives everywhere. She never walks. She _____
6. Bill's room isn't very interesting. He _____

31.2 Read the situations and write sentences with **I think / I don't think . . . should . . . .**

1. Chris and Amy are planning to get married. You think it's a bad idea.
   I don't think they should get married.
2. I have a bad cold but plan to go out tonight. You don't think this is a good idea.
   You say to me: _____
3. Peter needs a job. He's just seen an ad for a job which you think would be
   ideal for him, but he's not sure whether to apply or not. You say to him: I think
   _____
4. The government wants to raise taxes, but you don't think this is a good idea.
   _____

31.3 Complete each sentence with **should (have)** + the verb in parentheses.

1. Tracy _should pass_ the exam. She's been studying very hard. (pass)
2. You missed a great party last night. _You should have come._ (come)
3. We don't see you enough. You _____ and see us more often. (come)
4. I'm in a difficult position. What do you think I _____ ? (do)
5. I'm sorry that I didn't follow your advice. I _____ what you
   said. (do)
6. We lost the game, but we _____ . Our team is better than theirs. (win)
7. "Is John here yet?" "Not yet, but he _____ here soon." (be)
8. I mailed the letter three days ago, so it _____ by now. (arrive)

31.4 Read the situations and write sentences with **should / shouldn't**. Some of the sentences
are past and some are present.

1. I'm feeling sick. I ate too much. _I shouldn't have eaten so much._
2. That man on the motorcycle isn't wearing a helmet. That's dangerous.
   He _should be wearing a helmet._
3. When we got to the restaurant, there were no free tables. We hadn't reserved one.
   We _____
4. The sign says that the store opens every day at 8:30. It is 9:00 now, but the store isn't
   open yet.
   _____
5. The speed limit is 30 miles an hour, but Kate is driving 50.
   She _____
6. Mai gave me her e-mail address, but I didn't write it down. Now I can't remember it.
   I _____
7. I was driving right behind another car. Suddenly, the driver in front of me stopped,
   and I drove into the back of his car. It was my fault.
   _____
8. I walked into a wall. I wasn't looking where I was going.
   _____

Subjunctive (I suggest you do)

A

Study this example:

Why don't you buy some nice clothes?

Lisa said to Mary, "Why don't you buy some nice clothes?"

Lisa suggested that Mary **buy** some nice clothes.

In this example, **buy** is the *subjunctive*. The *subjunctive* is always the same as the *base form* (I **buy**, he **buy**, she **buy**, etc.):

I/he/she/it we/you/they	**do/buy/be**, etc.

B

We use the subjunctive after these verbs:

demand	**insist**	**propose**	**recommend**	**suggest**

- I **insisted** he **have** dinner with us.
- The doctor **recommended** that I **rest** for a few days.
- John **demanded** that Lisa **apologize** to him.
- What do you **suggest** I **do**?

We also say **It's essential/imperative/important/necessary/vital** (that) something **happen**:

- **It's essential** that everyone **be** at work by 9:00 tomorrow morning. No exceptions.
- **It's imperative** that the government **do** something about health care.

You can also say:

- **It's essential for** everyone **to** be at work by 9:00 tomorrow morning.
- **It's imperative for** the government **to** do something about health care.

C

The negative is **not** + *base form* (I **not be**, you **not leave**, she **not go**, etc.):

- The doctor strongly **recommended** that I **not go** to work for two days.
- **It's** very **important** that you **not miss** this appointment with your eye doctor.

You can use the subjunctive for the present, past, or future:

- I **insist** you **come** with us.
- They **insisted** I **go** with them.

Note the subjunctive **be** (often passive):

- I **insisted** that something **be done** about the problem.
- **It's essential** that this medicine not **be taken** on an empty stomach.
- The airline **recommended** we **be** at the airport two hours before our flight.

D

Other structures are possible after **insist** and **suggest**:

- They **insisted on paying** for dinner. (see Unit 60A)
- It is a beautiful evening, so I **suggest going** for a walk. (see Unit 51)

You cannot use the *infinitive* (**to . . .**) after **suggest** or **insist**:

- She **suggested that he buy** some new clothes. (*not* suggested him to buy)
- He **insists on going** with us. (*not* he insists to go)

Exercises

32.1 Write a sentence that means the same as the first sentence. Begin in the way shown.

1. "Why don't you buy some new clothes?" said Lisa to Mary.
   Lisa suggested that ___*Mary buy some new clothes.*___

2. "I don't think you should go to work for two days," the doctor said to me.
   The doctor recommended that ___*I not go to work for two days.*___

3. "You really must stay a little longer," she said to me.
   She insisted that _____

4. "Why don't you visit the museum after lunch?" I said to her.
   I suggested that _____

5. "I think it would be a good idea to see a specialist," the doctor said to me.
   The doctor recommended that _____

6. "I think it would be a good idea for you not to lift anything heavy," the specialist said to me.
   The specialist recommended that _____

7. "You have to pay the rent by Friday at the latest," the landlord said to us.
   The landlord demanded that _____

8. "Why don't you go away for a few days?" Josh said to me.
   Josh suggested that _____

9. "I don't think you should give your children snacks right before mealtime," the doctor told me.
   The doctor suggested that _____

10. "Let's have dinner early," Sarah said to us.
    Sarah proposed that _____

32.2 Complete these sentences with appropriate verbs:

1. It's imperative that the government ___*do*___ something about health care.
2. I insisted that something ___*be*___ done about the problem.
3. Our friends recommended that we _____ our vacation in the mountains.
4. Since Dave hurt Tracy's feelings, I stongly recommended that he _____ to her.
5. The workers at the factory are demanding that their wages _____ raised.
6. Lisa wanted to walk home alone, but we insisted that she _____ for us.
7. The city council has proposed that a new convention center _____ built.
8. What do you suggest I _____ to the party? Something casual?
9. It is essential that every child _____ the opportunity to get a good education.
10. Brad forgot his wife's birthday last year, so it's really important he _____ it this year.
11. It is vital that every runner _____ water during the marathon.

32.3 Tom wants to get healthy. His friends have made some suggestions:

Why don't you try jogging? — Linda

How about walking to work in the morning? — Sandra

Eat more fruit and vegetables. — Bill

Why don't you take vitamins? — Anna

Write sentences telling what Tom's friends suggested.

1. Linda suggested that he ___*try jogging.*___
2. Sandra suggested that he _____
3. Bill suggested _____
4. Anna _____

Had better   It's time . . .

A

Had better (I'**d better** / you'**d better**, etc.)

I'**d better do** something = it is advisable to do it. If I don't, there will be a problem or a danger:

- I have to meet Amy in 10 minutes. I'**d better go** now or I'll be late.
- "Do you think I should take an umbrella?"   "Yes, you'**d better**. It might rain."
- We'**d better stop** for gas soon. The tank is almost empty.

The negative is I'**d better not** (= I had better not):

- "Are you going out tonight?"   "I'**d better not**. I've got a lot of work to do."
- You don't look very well. You'**d better not go** to work today.

Remember that:

> The form is "**had** better" (usually I'**d** better / you'**d** better, etc., in spoken English):
> - I'**d better** go now = I **had** better go now.
>
> **Had** is normally past, but the meaning of **had better** is present or future, not past:
> - I'**d better go** to the bank now / tomorrow.
>
> We say I'**d better do** (*not* to do):
> - It might rain. We'**d better take** an umbrella. (*not* We'd better to take)

B

Had better and **should**

Had better is similar to **should** but not exactly the same. We use **had better** only for a specific situation (not for things in general). You can use **should** in all types of situations to give an opinion or give advice:

- It's cold. You'**d better wear** a coat when you go out. (a specific situation)
- You're always at home. You **should go** out more often. (in general – *not* "had better go")

Also, with **had better**, there is always a danger or a problem if you don't follow the advice. **Should** only means "it is a good thing to do." Compare:

- It's a great movie. You **should** go and see it. (but no problem if you don't)
- The movie starts at 8:30. You'**d better** go now, or you'll be late.

C

It's time . . .

You can say **It's time** (for somebody) **to do** something:

- It's time **to go** home. / It's time for us **to go** home.

You can also say:

- It's late. It's time we **went** home.

Here we use the past (**went**), but the meaning is present, not past:

- It's 10:00 and he's still in bed. **It's time** he **got** up. (*not* It's time he gets up)

It's time you did something = you should have already done it or started it. We often use this structure to criticize or to complain:

- **It's time** you **changed** the oil in the car. It hasn't been changed in a long time.
- The windows are very dirty. I think **it's time** they **were washed**.

You can also say **It's about time** . . . . This makes the criticism stronger:

- Jack is a great talker. But **it's about time** he **did** something instead of just talking.

Should Unit 31

Exercises

33.1 Read the situations and write sentences with *had better (not)*. Use the words in parentheses.

1. You're going out for a walk with Tom. It looks as if it might rain. You say to Tom:
   (an umbrella) *We'd better take an umbrella.*
2. Alex has just cut himself. It's a bad cut. You say to him:
   (a bandage) _____
3. You and Kate plan to go to a restaurant tonight. It's a popular restaurant. You say to Kate:
   (make a reservation) We _____
4. Jill doesn't look very well – not well enough to go to work. You say to her:
   (work) _____
5. You received your phone bill four weeks ago, but you haven't paid it yet. If you don't pay soon, you could be in trouble. You say to yourself:
   (pay) _____
6. You want to go out, but you're expecting an important phone call. You say to your friend:
   (go out) I _____
7. You and Jeff are going to the theater. You've missed the bus, and you don't want to be late. You say to Jeff: (a taxi) _____

33.2 Put in *had better* where appropriate. If *had better* is not appropriate, use *should*.

1. I have an appointment in 10 minutes. I *'d better* go now or I'll be late.
2. It's a great movie. You *should* go and see it. You'll really like it.
3. You _____ set your alarm. You'll never wake up on time if you don't.
4. When people are driving, they _____ keep their eyes on the road.
5. I'm glad you came to see us. You _____ come more often.
6. She'll be hurt if we don't invite her to the wedding, so we _____ invite her.
7. These cookies are delicious. You _____ try one.
8. I think everybody _____ learn a foreign language.

33.3 Complete the sentences. Sometimes you need only one word, sometimes two.

1. a) I need some money. I'd better *go* to the bank.
   b) John is expecting you to call him. You _____ better call him now.
   c) "Should I leave the window open?" "No, you'd better _____ it."
2. a) It's time the government _____ something about the problem.
   b) It's time something _____ about the problem.
   c) I think it's about time you _____ about other people instead of only thinking about yourself.

33.4 Read the situations and write sentences with *It's time . . . .*

1. You think the children should be in bed. It's already 11 o'clock.
   It's time the children were in bed.
2. You haven't taken a vacation in ages. You need one now.
   It's time I _____
3. You're sitting on a train waiting for it to leave. It should have left five minutes ago.
   _____
4. You enjoy having parties. You haven't had one for a long time.
   _____
5. The company you work for is badly managed. You think some changes should be made.
   _____
6. Andrew has been doing the same job for the last 10 years. He should try something else.
   _____

Would

A

We use **would ('d) / wouldn't** when we imagine a situation or action
(= we think of something that is not real):

- It **would be** nice to buy a new car, but we can't afford it.
- I**'d love** to live by the ocean.
- *A:* Should I tell Chris what happened?
  B: No, I **wouldn't say** anything.
  (= I wouldn't say anything in your situation)

We use **would have (done)** when we imagine situations or
actions in the past (= things that didn't happen):

- They helped us a lot. I don't know what we **would have
  done** without their help.
- I didn't tell Sam what happened. He **wouldn't have
  been** pleased.

Compare **would (do)** and **would have (done)**:

- I **would call** Sue, but I don't have her number. *(now)*
  I **would have called** Sue, but I didn't have her number. *(past)*
- I'm not going to invite them to the party. They **wouldn't come** anyway.
  I didn't invite them to the party. They **wouldn't have come** anyway.

We often use **would** in sentences with **if** (see Units 36–38):

- I **would call** Sue **if** I had her number.
- I **would have called** Sue **if** I'd had her number.

B

Compare **will ('ll)** and **would ('d)**:

- I**'ll stay** a little longer. I've got plenty of time.
  I**'d stay** a little longer, but I really have to go now. (so I can't stay longer)
- I**'ll call** Sue. I've got her number.
  I**'d call** Sue, but I don't have her number. (so I can't call her)

Sometimes **would / wouldn't** is the past of **will / won't**.
Compare:

Present	Past
■ *Tom:* I**'ll call** you on Sunday. →	Tom said he**'d call** me on Sunday.
■ *Ann:* I promise I **won't be** late. →	Ann promised that she **wouldn't be** late.
■ *Liz:* Darn! The car **won't start**. →	Liz was annoyed because her car **wouldn't start**.

C

Somebody **wouldn't do** something = he/she refused to do it:

- I tried to warn him, but he **wouldn't listen** to me. (= he refused to listen)
- The car **wouldn't start**. (= it "refused" to start)

You can also use **would** when you talk about things that happened regularly in the past:

- When we were children, we lived by the ocean. In summer, if the weather was nice,
  we **would** all get up early and go for a swim. (= we did this regularly)
- Whenever Richard was angry, he **would** walk out of the room.

With this meaning, **would** is similar to **used to** (see Unit 17):

- Whenever Richard was angry, he **used to walk** out of the room.

Will Units 20–21   *Would you . . . ?* Unit 35A   *Would . . . if* Units 36–38   *Wish . . . would* Unit 39
Would like Units 35E, 56   *Would prefer / would rather* Unit 57

Exercises

34.1 Write sentences about yourself. Imagine things you would like or wouldn't like.

1. (a place you'd love to live) _I'd love to live by the ocean._
2. (a job you wouldn't like to do) _____
3. (something you would love to do) _____
4. (something that would be nice to have) _____
5. (a place you'd like to go to) _____

34.2 Complete the sentences using *would* + the following verbs (in the correct form):

   be   be   ~~do~~   do   enjoy   enjoy   have   pass   stop

1. They helped us a lot. I don't know what we _would have done_ without their help.
2. You should go and see the movie. You _____ it.
3. It's too bad you couldn't come to the concert yesterday. You _____ it.
4. Do you think I should apply for the job? What _____ you _____ in my position?
5. I was in a hurry when I saw you. Otherwise, I _____ to talk.
6. We took a taxi home last night but got stuck in the traffic. It _____ quicker to walk.
7. Why don't you go and see Claire? She _____ very pleased to see you.
8. Why didn't you take the exam? I'm sure you _____ it.
9. In an ideal world, everybody _____ enough to eat.

34.3 Each sentence on the right follows a sentence on the left. Which follows which?

1. ~~I'd like to go to Australia one day.~~	a) It wouldn't have been very pleasant. ___
2. I wouldn't like to live on a busy street.	b) It would have been fun. ___
3. I'm sorry the trip was canceled.	c) ~~It would be nice.~~ _c_
4. I'm looking forward to going out tonight.	d) It won't be much fun. ___
5. I'm glad we didn't go out in the rain.	e) It wouldn't be very pleasant. ___
6. I'm not looking forward to the trip.	f) It will be fun. ___

34.4 Write sentences using *promised* + *would / wouldn't*.

1. I wonder why Laura is late. _She promised she wouldn't be late._
2. I wonder why Steve hasn't called. He promised _____
3. Why did you tell Jane what I said? You _____
4. I'm surprised they didn't wait for us. They _____

34.5 Complete the sentences. Use *wouldn't* + a suitable verb.

1. I tried to warn him, but he _wouldn't listen_ to me.
2. I asked Amanda what had happened, but she _____ me.
3. Paul was very angry about what I'd said and _____ to me for two weeks.
4. Martina insisted on carrying all her luggage. She _____ me help her.

34.6 These sentences are about things that happened many times in the past. Complete the sentences using *would* + the following:

   forget   help   shake   share   ~~walk~~

1. Whenever Richard was angry, he _would walk_ out of the room.
2. We used to live next to railroad tracks. Every time a train went by, the house _____ .
3. George was a very kind man. He _____ always _____ you if you had a problem.
4. Brenda was always very generous. She didn't have much, but she _____ what she had with everyone else.
5. You could never rely on Joe. It didn't matter how many times you reminded him to do something, he _____ always _____ .

Can/Could/Would you . . . ?, etc.
(Requests, Offers, Permission, and Invitations)

A Asking people to do things (requests)

We use **can** or **could** to ask people to do things:
- **Can you** wait a minute, please?
or - **Could you** wait a minute, please?
- Liz, **can you** do me a favor?
- Excuse me, **could you** tell me how to get to the airport?
- I wonder if **you could** help me.

Could you open the door, please?

Note that we say **Do you think you could . . . ?**
(*not usually* can):
- **Do you think you could** lend me some money until next week?

We also use **will** and **would** to ask people to do things
(but **can/could** are more common):
- Liz, **will you** do me a favor?
- **Would you** please be quiet? I'm trying to concentrate.

B Asking for things

To ask for something, we use **Can I have . . . ?** / **Could I have . . . ?** or **Can I get . . . ?**:
- (*in a gift shop*) **Can I have** these postcards, please? (*or* **Can I get . . . ?**)
- (*during a meal*) **Could I have** the salt, please?

May I have . . . ? is also possible:
- **May I have** these postcards, please?

C Asking to do things

To ask to do something, we use **can**, **could**, or **may**:
- (*on the phone*) Hello, **can I** speak to Tom, please?
- "**Could I** use your phone?" "Yes, of course."
- **Do you think I could** borrow your bike?
- "**May I** come in?" "Yes, please do."

May is formal and less common than **can** or **could**.

To ask to do something, you can also say **Do you mind if I . . . ?** *or*
Is it all right / Is it OK if I . . . ?:
- "**Do you mind if I** use your phone?" "No. Not at all."
- "**Is it all right if I** come in?" "Yes, of course."

D Offering to do things

We use **Can I . . . ?** *or* **May I . . . ?** when we offer to do things:
- "**Can I** get you a cup of coffee?" "Yes, that would be very nice."
- (*in a store*) "**May I** help you?" "No, thanks. I'm being helped."

May is more formal than **can**.

E Offering and inviting

To offer or to invite, we use **Would you like . . . ?** (*not* Do you like):
- "**Would you like** a cup of coffee?" "Yes, please."
- "**Would you like** to go to the movies with us tonight?" "Yes, I'd love to."

I'd like . . . is a polite way of saying what you want:
- (*at a tourist information center*) **I'd like** some information about hotels, please.
- (*in a store*) **I'd like** to try on this jacket, please.

Exercises

35.1 Read the situations and write questions beginning with *Can . . .* or *Could . . . .*

1. You're carrying a lot of things. You can't open the door yourself. There's a man standing near the door. You say to him:
   Can you open the door, please? OR Could you open the door, please?

2. You phone Ann, but somebody else answers. Ann isn't there. You want to leave a message for her. You say: _____

3. You're a tourist. You want to go to the post office, but you don't know how to get there. You ask at your hotel: _____

4. You are in a department store. You see some pants you like, and you want to try them on. You say to the salesperson: _____

5. You need a ride home from a party. John drove to the party and lives near you. You say to him: _____

35.2 Read the situation and write a question using the word in parentheses.

1. You want to borrow your friend's camera. What do you say to him?
   (think) _Do you think I could borrow your camera?_

2. You are at a friend's house and you want to use her phone. What do you say?
   (all right) _Is it all right if I use your phone?_

3. You've written a letter in English. Before you send it, you want a friend to check it for you. What do you ask?
   (think) _____

4. You want to leave work early. What do you ask your boss?
   (mind) _____

5. The woman in the next room is playing music. It's very loud. You want her to turn it down. What do you say to her?
   (think) _____

6. You are calling the owner of an apartment that was advertised in the newspaper. You are interested in the apartment and want to see it today. What do you say to the owner?
   (OK) _____

7. You're on a train. The woman next to you has finished reading her newspaper, and you'd like to have a look at it. You ask her.
   (think) _____

35.3 What would you say in these situations?

1. Paul has come to see you. You offer him something to eat.
   You: _Would you like something to eat_ ?
   Paul: No, thank you. I've just eaten.

2. You need help replacing the memory card in your camera. You ask Kate.
   You: I don't know how to replace the memory card. _____ ?
   Kate: Sure. It's easy. All you have to do is this.

3. You're on a bus. You have a seat, but an elderly man is standing. You offer him your seat.
   You: _____ ?
   Man: Oh, that's very nice of you. Thank you very much.

4. You're the passenger in a car. Your friend is driving very fast. You ask her to slow down.
   You: You're making me very nervous. _____ ?
   Driver: Oh, I'm sorry. I didn't realize I was going so fast.

5. You've finished your meal in a restaurant and now you want the check. You ask the waiter:
   You: _____ ?
   Waiter: Sure. I'll get it for you now.

6. A friend of yours is interested in one of your books. You invite him to borrow it.
   Friend: This book looks very interesting.
   You: Yes, it's very good. _____ ?

If I do . . . and If I did . . .

A

Compare these examples:

1) Sue has lost her watch. She tells Ann:

   Sue: I think I left my watch at your house. Have you seen it?
   Ann: No, but I'll look when I get home. **If I find** it, I'll tell you.

   In this example, Ann feels there is a real possibility that she will find the watch. So she says:
   If I find . . . , I'll . . . .

2) Carol says:

   If I found a wallet in the street, I'd take it to the police station.

   This is a different type of situation. Here, Carol doesn't expect to find a wallet in the street.
   She is imagining a situation that will probably not happen. So she says:
   If I found . . . , I'd (= I would) **. . . .** (*not* if I find . . . , I'll . . .)

When you imagine something like this, you use **if** + *past*
(**if** I **found** / **if** there **was** / **if** we **didn't**, etc.).

But the meaning is *not* past:
- What would you do **if** you **won** a million dollars?
  (we don't really expect this to happen)
- I don't really want to go to their party, but I
  probably will go. They'd be hurt **if** I **didn't go**.
- **If** there **was** (*or* **were**) an election tomorrow,
  who would you vote for?

For **if . . . was/were**, see Unit 37C.

If I **won** a million dollars . . . .

B

We do not normally use **would** in the **if** part of the sentence:
- I'd be very frightened **if** somebody **pointed** a gun at me. (*not* if somebody would point)
- **If** I **didn't go** to their party, they'd be hurt. (*not* If I wouldn't go)

C

In the other part of the sentence (not the **if** part) we use **would ('d)** / **wouldn't**:
- If you got more exercise, you'**d feel** better.
- I'm not tired. If I went to bed now, I **wouldn't sleep**.
- **Would** you **mind** if I used your phone?

Could and **might** are also possible:
- If you got more exercise, you **might feel** better. (= it is possible that you would feel better)
- If it stopped raining, we **could go** out. (= we would be able to go out)

D

Do not use **when** in sentences like the ones on this page:
- They'd be hurt **if** I didn't go to their party. (*not* when I didn't go)
- What would you do **if** you were bitten by a snake? (*not* when you were bitten)

Would Units 34, 39   ***If I knew*** Unit 37   ***If I had known*** Unit 38

Exercises

36.1 Put the verb into the correct form.

1. They would be hurt if _I didn't go_ to their party. (not / go)
2. If you got more exercise, you _would feel_ better. (feel)
3. If they offered me the job, I think I _____ it. (take)
4. A lot of people would be out of work if the car factory _____ . (close down)
5. If I sold my car, I _____ much money for it. (not / get)
6. *(in an elevator)* What would happen if somebody _____ that red button? (press)
7. I'm sure Amy will lend you the money. I'd be very surprised if she _____ . (refuse)
8. Liz gave me this ring. She _____ very upset if I lost it. (be)
9. Dave and Kate are expecting us. They would be very disappointed if we _____ . (not / come)
10. Would Bob mind if I _____ his bike without asking him? (borrow)
11. What would you do if somebody _____ in here with a gun? (walk)
12. I'm sure Sue _____ if you explained the situation to her. (understand)

36.2 You ask a friend to imagine these situations. You ask *What would you do if . . . ?*

1. (imagine – you win a lot of money)
    What would you do if you won a lot of money?
2. (imagine – you lose your passport)
    What _____
3. (imagine – there's a fire in the building)
    _____
4. (imagine – you're in an elevator and it stops between floors)
    _____

36.3 Answer the questions in the way shown.

1. *A:* Should we catch the 10:30 train?
    B: No. (arrive too early) _If we caught the 10:30 train, we'd arrive too early._
2. *A:* Is Ken going to take the driver's test?
    B: No. (fail) If he _____
3. *A:* Why don't we stay at a hotel?
    B: No. (cost too much) If _____
4. *A:* Is Sally going to apply for the job?
    B: No. (not / get it) If _____
5. *A:* Let's tell them the truth.
    B: No. (not / believe us) If _____
6. *A:* Why don't we invite Bill to the party?
    B: No. (have to invite his friends, too) _____

36.4 Use your own ideas to complete these sentences.

1. If you got more exercise, _you'd feel better._
2. I'd feel very angry if _____
3. If I didn't go to work tomorrow, _____
4. Would you go to the party if _____
5. If you bought a car, _____
6. Would you mind if _____

If I knew . . .   I wish I knew . . .

A

Study this example situation:

Sue wants to call Paul, but she can't do this because she doesn't know his phone number. She says:

If I knew his number, I **would call** him.

Sue says: **If I knew** his number . . . . This tells us that she doesn't know his number. She is imagining the situation.

If I **knew** his number . . . .

When you imagine a situation like this, you use **if** + *past* (**if I knew** / **if** you **were** / **if** we **didn't**, etc.). But the meaning is present, not past:

- Tom would read more **if** he **had** more time. (but he doesn't have much time)
- **If** I **didn't** want to go to the party, I wouldn't go. (but I want to go)
- We wouldn't have any money **if** we **didn't** work. (but we work)
- **If** you **were** in my position, what would you do?
- It's a shame you can't drive. It would be helpful **if** you **could**.

B

We use the past in the same way after **wish** (**I wish** I **knew** / **I wish** you **were**, etc.). We use **wish** to say that we regret something, that something is not as we would like it to be:

- **I wish** I **knew** Paul's phone number.
  (= I don't know it and I regret this)
- Do you ever **wish** you **could** fly? (you can't fly)
- It rains a lot here. I **wish** it **didn't** rain so often.
- It's very crowded here. I **wish** there **weren't** so many people.
- **I wish** I **didn't** have to work tomorrow, but unfortunately, I do.

I **wish** I **had** an umbrella.

C

If I **was** / If I **were**

After **if** and **wish**, we use **was** or **were** with **I/he/she/it**. **Was** is more informal. So you can say:

- **If I was** you, I wouldn't buy that coat.   *or*   **If I were** you, . . .
- I'd go out **if it wasn't** so cold.   *or*   . . . **if it weren't** so cold.
- **I wish Carol was** here.   *or*   **I wish Carol were** here.

D

We do not normally use **would** in the **if** part of the sentence or after **wish**:

- **If I were** rich, I **would** have a yacht. (*not* If I would be rich)
- **I wish I had** something to read. (*not* I wish I would have)

Sometimes **wish . . . would** is possible: **I wish you would listen**. See Unit 39D.

E

Could sometimes means "would be able to" and sometimes "was / were able to":

- You **could** get a better job   (you **could** get = you would be able to get)
  if you **could** use a computer.   (you **could** use = you were able to use)

Exercises

37.1 Put the verb into the correct form.

1. If I __*knew*__ (know) his phone number, I would call him.
2. I __*wouldn't buy*__ (not / buy) that coat if I were you.
3. I _____ (help) you if I could, but I'm afraid I can't.
4. We would need a car if we _____ (live) in the country.
5. If we had the choice, we _____ (live) in the country.
6. This soup isn't very good. It _____ (taste) better if it weren't so salty.
7. I wouldn't mind living in Maine if the weather _____ (be) better.
8. If I were you, I _____ (not / wait). I _____ (go) now.
9. You're always tired. If you _____ (not / go) to bed so late every night, you wouldn't be tired all the time.
10. I think there are too many cars. If there _____ (not / be) so many cars, there _____ (not / be) so much pollution.

37.2 Write a sentence with *if* . . . for each situation.

1. We don't see you very often because you live so far away.
   __*If you didn't live so far away, we'd see you more often.*__
2. This book is expensive, so I'm not going to buy it.
   I'd _____ if _____
3. We don't go out to eat because we can't afford it.
   We _____
4. I can't meet you tomorrow. I have to work late.
   If _____
5. It's raining, so we can't have lunch on the patio.
   We _____
6. I don't want his advice, and that's why I'm not going to ask for it.
   If _____

37.3 Write sentences beginning with *I wish* . . . .

1. I don't know many people (and I'm lonely). __*I wish I knew more people.*__
2. I don't have a cell phone (and I need one). I wish _____
3. Amanda isn't here (and I need to see her). _____
4. It's cold (and I hate cold weather). _____
5. I live in a big city (and I don't like it). _____
6. I can't go to the party (and I'd like to). _____
7. I have to work tomorrow (but I'd like to stay in bed).
   _____
8. I don't know anything about cars (and my car has just broken down).
   _____
9. I'm not feeling well (and that's not pleasant).
   _____

37.4 Write your own sentences beginning with *I wish* . . . .

1. (somewhere you'd like to be now – on the beach, in Vietnam, in bed, etc.)
   I wish I __*were at home in bed now.*__
2. (something you'd like to have – a computer, a good job, more friends, etc.)
   _____
3. (something you'd like to be able to do – sing, speak a language, fly, etc.)
   _____
4. (something you'd like to be – beautiful, strong, rich, etc.)
   _____

If I had known . . .   I wish I had known . . .

A

Study this example situation:

> Last month Brian was in the hospital for a few days. Liz didn't know this, so she didn't go to see him. They met a few days ago. Liz said:
>
> **If I had known** you were in the hospital, **I would have gone** to see you.
>
> Liz said, "**If I had known** you were in the hospital . . ." So she *didn't* know he was in the hospital.

We use **if** + **had ('d)** . . . to talk about the past (**if I had known/been/done**, etc.):
- I didn't see you when you passed me in the street. **If I'd seen you**, of course I would have said hello. (but I didn't see you)
- I didn't go out last night. I would have gone out **if** I **hadn't been** so tired. (but I was tired)
- **If he had been looking** where he was going, he wouldn't have walked into the wall. (but he wasn't looking)
- The view was wonderful. **If I'd had** a camera, I would have taken some pictures. (but I didn't have a camera)

Compare:
- I'm not hungry. **If** I **was** hungry, I would eat something. *(now)*
- I wasn't hungry. **If** I **had been** hungry, I would have eaten something. *(past)*

B

Do not use **would** in the **if**-part of the sentence. We use **would** in the other part of the sentence:
- **If** I **had seen** you, I **would have said** hello. (*not* If I would have seen you)

Note that **'d** can be **would** or **had**:
- **If I'd seen** you,   (I'd seen = I **had** seen)
  I'd **have said** hello. (I'd have said = I **would** have said)

C

We use **had** (**done**) in the same way after **wish**. I **wish** something **had happened** = I am sorry that it didn't happen:
- I **wish I'd known** that Brian was sick. I would have gone to see him. (but I didn't know)
- I feel sick. I **wish** I **hadn't eaten** so much cake. (I ate too much cake)
- Do you **wish** you **had studied** science instead of languages? (you didn't study science)

Do not use **would have** . . . after **wish**:
- The weather was cold on our vacation. I wish it **had been** warmer. (*not* I wish it would have been)

D

Compare **would** (**do**) and **would have** (**done**):
- If I had gone to the party last night, I **would be** tired now. (I am not tired now – *present*)
- If I had gone to the party last night, I **would have met** lots of people. (I didn't meet lots of people – *past*)

Compare **would have**, **could have**, and **might have**:

- If the weather hadn't been so bad,
  - we **would have gone** out.
  - we **could have gone** out.
    (= we would have been able to go out)
  - we **might have gone** out.
    (= maybe we would have gone out)

Had done Unit 14   *If I do* and *if I did* Unit 36   *If I knew / I wish I knew* Unit 37   *Wish* Unit 39

Exercises

38.1 Put the verb into the correct form.

1. I didn't know you were in the hospital. If ___I'd known___ (I / know), ___I would have gone___ (I / go) to see you.
2. John got to the station in time to catch the train. If _____ (he / miss) the train, _____ (he / be) late for his interview.
3. I'm glad that you reminded me about Rachel's birthday. _____ (I / forget) if _____ (you / not / remind) me.
4. Unfortunately, I didn't have my address book with me when I was on vacation. If _____ (I / have) your address, _____ (I / send) you a postcard.
5. *A:* How was your trip? Did you have a nice time?
   B: It was OK, but _____ (we / enjoy) it more if _____ (the weather / be) nicer.
6. I took a taxi to the hotel, but the traffic was bad. _____ (it / be) quicker if _____ (I / walk).
7. I'm not tired. If _____ (I / be) tired, I'd go home now.
8. I wasn't tired last night. If _____ (I / be) tired, I would have gone home earlier.

38.2 Write a sentence starting with *If* for each situation.

1. I wasn't hungry, so I didn't eat anything.
   ___If I'd been hungry, I would have eaten something.___
2. The accident happened because the road was icy.
   If the road _____
3. I didn't know that Matt had to get up early, so I didn't wake him up.
   If I _____
4. I was able to buy the car only because Jim lent me the money.
   _____
5. Michelle wasn't injured in the crash because she was wearing a seat belt.
   _____
6. You didn't have any breakfast – that's why you're hungry now.
   _____
7. I didn't take a taxi because I didn't have any money.
   _____

38.3 Imagine that you are in these situations. For each situation, write a sentence with *I wish*.

1. You've eaten too much and now you feel sick. You say:
   ___I wish I hadn't eaten so much.___
2. There was a job advertised in the newspaper. You decided not to apply for it. Now you think that your decision was wrong. You say:
   I wish I _____
3. When you were younger, you didn't learn to play a musical instrument. Now you regret this. You say:
   _____
4. You've painted the door red. Now you think that red was the wrong color. You say:
   _____
5. You are walking in the country. You'd like to take some pictures, but you didn't bring your camera. You say:
   _____
6. You have some unexpected guests. They didn't call to say they were coming. You are very busy and you are not prepared for them. You say (to yourself):
   _____

Wish

A

You can say "**I wish you luck / all the best / success / a happy birthday**," etc.:

- ■ **I wish you all the best** in the future.
- ■ I saw Tim before the exam, and **he wished me luck**.

We say "wish somebody *something*" (**luck / a happy birthday**, etc.). But you cannot "wish that something *happens*." We use **hope** in this situation. For example:

- ■ I **hope** you **get** this letter before you leave town. (*not* I wish you get)

Compare **I wish** and **I hope**:

- ■ **I wish** you **a pleasant stay** here.
- ■ **I hope** you **have** a pleasant stay here. (*not* I wish you have)

B

We also use **wish** to say that we regret something, that something is not the way we would like it. When we use **wish** in this way, we use the *past* (**knew/lived**, etc.), but the meaning is *present*:

- ■ **I wish** I **knew** what to do about the problem. (I don't know and I regret this)
- ■ **I wish** you **didn't** have to go so soon. (you have to go)
- ■ Do you **wish** you **lived** near the ocean? (you don't live near the ocean)
- ■ Jack's going on a trip to Mexico soon. I **wish** I **was** going too. (I'm not going)

To say that we regret something in the past, we use **wish** + **had . . .** (**had known / had said**), etc.:

- ■ **I wish** I**'d known** about the party. I would have gone if I'd known. (I didn't know)
- ■ It was a stupid thing to say. I **wish** I **hadn't said** it. (I said it)

For more examples, see Units 37 and 38.

C

I wish I could (**do** something) = I regret that I cannot do it:

- ■ I'm sorry I have to go. I **wish** I **could stay** longer. (but I can't)
- ■ I've met that man before. I **wish** I **could remember** his name. (but I can't)

I wish I could have (**done** something) = I regret that I could not do it:

- ■ I hear the party was great. I **wish** I **could have gone**. (but I couldn't go)

D

You can say "**I wish** (somebody) **would** (do something)." For example:

I wish it **would stop** raining.

It's been raining all day. Jill doesn't like it. She says:

I wish it **would stop** raining.

Jill would like the rain to stop, but this will probably not happen.

We use **I wish . . . would** when we would like something to happen or change. Usually, the speaker doesn't expect this to happen.

We often use **I wish . . . would** to complain about a situation:

- ■ The phone has been ringing for five minutes. **I wish** somebody **would answer** it.
- ■ **I wish** you **would do** something instead of just sitting and doing nothing.

You can use **I wish . . . wouldn't . . .** to complain about things that people do repeatedly:

- ■ **I wish** you **wouldn't keep interrupting** me.

We use **I wish . . . would . . .** for actions and changes, not situations. Compare:

- ■ **I wish** Sarah **would** come. (= I want her to come)
- *but* ■ **I wish** Sarah **was** (*or* **were**) here now. (*not* I wish Sarah would be)
- ■ **I wish** somebody **would buy** me a car.
- *but* ■ **I wish** I **had** a car. (*not* I wish I would have)

Exercises

39.1 Put in *wish(ed)* or *hope(d)*.

1. I <u>*wish*</u> you a pleasant stay here.
2. Enjoy your vacation. I _____ you have a great time.
3. Goodbye. I _____ you all the best.
4. We said goodbye to each other and _____ each other luck.
5. We're going on a picnic tomorrow, so I _____ the weather is nice.
6. I _____ you luck in your new job. I _____ it works out well for you.

39.2 What do you say in these situations? Write sentences with *I wish . . . would . . . .*

1. It's raining. You want to go out, but not in the rain.
   You say: <u>*I wish it would stop raining.*</u>
2. You're waiting for Jane. She's late and you're getting impatient.
   You say to yourself: I wish _____
3. You're looking for a job – so far without success. Nobody will give you a job.
   You say: I wish somebody _____
4. You can hear a baby crying. It's been crying for a long time and you're trying to study.
   You say: _____

For the following situations, write sentences with *I wish . . . wouldn't . . . .*

5. Your friend drives very fast. You don't like this.
   You say to your friend: I wish you _____
6. Joe leaves the door open all the time. This annoys you.
   You say to Joe: _____
7. A lot of people drop litter in the street. You don't like this.
   You say: I wish people _____

39.3 Are these sentences right or wrong? Correct them where necessary.

1. I wish Sarah would be here now.   <u>*I wish Sarah were here now.*</u>
2. I wish you would listen to me.   _____
3. I wish I would have more free time.   _____
4. I wish our house would be a little bigger. _____
5. I wish the weather would change.   _____
6. I wish you wouldn't complain all the time. _____
7. I wish everything wouldn't be so expensive. _____

39.4 Put the verb into the correct form.

1. It was a stupid thing to say. I wish <u>*I hadn't said*</u> it. (I / not / say)
2. I'm fed up with this rain. I wish <u>*it would stop*</u> . (it / stop)
3. It's a difficult question. I wish _____ the answer. (I / know)
4. I should have listened to you. I wish _____ your advice. (I / take)
5. You're lucky to be going to Peru. I wish _____ with you.
   (I / can / come)
6. I have absolutely no energy. I wish _____ so tired. (I / not / be)
7. Aren't they ready yet? I wish _____ up. (they / hurry)
8. It would be nice to stay here longer. I wish _____ to go now.
   (we / not / have)
9. When we were in Cairo last year, we didn't have time to see all the things we wanted to see.
   I wish _____ longer. (we / can / stay)
10. It's freezing today. I wish _____ so cold. I hate cold weather.
    (it / not / be)
11. Joe still doesn't know what he wants to do. I wish _____ .
    (he / decide)
12. I really didn't enjoy the party. I wish _____ . (we / not / go)

Passive 1 (is done / was done)

A Study this example:

This house **was built** in 1935.

Was built is *passive*.

Compare *active* and *passive*:

Somebody **built** this house in 1935. *(active)*
subject *object*

This house **was built** in 1935. *(passive)*
subject

When we use an active verb, we say what the subject does:
- ◼ My grandfather was a builder. **He built** this house in 1935.
- ◼ It's a big company. **It employs** two hundred people.

When we use a passive verb, we say *what happens to the subject*:
- ◼ This house is pretty old. **It was built** in 1935.
- ◼ Two hundred people **are employed** by the company.

B When we use the passive, who or what causes the action is often unknown or unimportant:
- ◼ A lot of money **was stolen** in the robbery.
  (somebody stole it, but we don't know who)
- ◼ **Is** this room **cleaned** every day? (does somebody clean it? – it's not important who)

If we want to say who does or what causes the action, we use **by**:
- ◼ This house was built **by my grandfather**.
- ◼ Two hundred people are employed **by the company**.

C The passive is **be** (**is/was**, etc.) + *past participle* (**done/cleaned/seen**, etc.):

(be) done   **(be) cleaned**   **(be) damaged**   **(be) built**   **(be) seen**, etc.

For irregular past participles (**done/seen/known**, etc.), see Appendix 1.

Study the active and passive forms of the *simple present* and *simple past*:

Simple Present

  active: **clean(s)** / **see(s)**, etc.   Somebody **cleans** this room every day.

  passive: **am/is/are** + **cleaned/seen**, etc.   This room **is cleaned** every day.

- ◼ Many accidents **are caused** by careless driving.
- ◼ **I'm not** often **invited** to parties.
- ◼ How **is** this word **pronounced**?

Simple Past

  active: **cleaned/saw**, etc.   Somebody **cleaned** this room yesterday.

  passive: **was/were** + **cleaned/seen**, etc.   This room **was cleaned** yesterday.

- ◼ We **were woken** up by a loud noise during the night.
- ◼ "Did you go to the party?" "No, I **wasn't invited**."
- ◼ How much money **was stolen** in the robbery?

Passive 2–3 Units 41–42 **By** Unit 125

Exercises

40.1 Complete the sentences using these verbs in the correct form, present or past:

cause	damage	hold	invite	make
pass	show	surround	translate	write

1. Many accidents _are caused_ by dangerous driving.
2. Cheese _____ from milk.
3. The roof of the building _____ in a storm a few days ago.
4. You _____ to the wedding. Why didn't you go?
5. A movie theater is a place where films _____ .
6. In the United States, elections for president _____ every four years.
7. Originally the book _____ in Spanish, and a few years ago it _____ into English.
8. Although we were driving pretty fast, we _____ by a lot of other cars.
9. You can't see the house from the road. It _____ by trees.

40.2 Write questions using the passive. Some are present and some are past.

1. Ask about glass. (how / make?) _How is glass made?_
2. Ask about television. (when / invent?) _____
3. Ask about mountains. (how / form?) _____
4. Ask about the planet Neptune. (when / discover?) _____
5. Ask about silver. (what / use for?) _____

40.3 Put the verb into the correct form, simple present or simple past, active or passive.

1. It's a big factory. Five hundred people _are employed_ (employ) there.
2. _Did somebody clean_ (somebody / clean) this room yesterday?
3. Water _____ (cover) most of the Earth's surface.
4. How much of the Earth's surface _____ (cover) by water?
5. The park gates _____ (lock) at 6:30 p.m. every evening.
6. The letter _____ (mail) a week ago, and it _____ (arrive) yesterday.
7. The boat hit a rock and _____ (sink) quickly. Fortunately everybody _____ (rescue).
8. Ron's parents _____ (die) when he was very young. He and his sister _____ (bring up) by their grandparents.
9. I was born in Chicago, but I _____ (grow up) in Houston.
10. While I was on vacation, my camera _____ (steal) from my hotel room.
11. While I was on vacation, my camera _____ (disappear) from my hotel room.
12. Why _____ (Sue / quit) her job? Didn't she like it?
13. Why _____ (Bill / fire) from his job? What did he do wrong?
14. The company is not independent. It _____ (own) by a much larger company.
15. I saw an accident last night. Somebody _____ (call) an ambulance, but nobody _____ (injure), so the ambulance _____ (not / need).
16. Where _____ (these pictures / take)? In Hong Kong? _____ (you / take) them?

40.4 Rewrite these sentences. Instead of using *somebody/they/people*, etc., write a passive sentence.

1. Somebody cleans the room every day. _The room is cleaned every day._
2. They canceled all flights because of fog. All _____
3. People don't use this road much. _____
4. Somebody accused me of stealing money. I _____
5. How do people learn languages? How _____
6. People warned us not to go out alone. _____

81

Passive 2 (be done / been done / being done)

Study the following active and passive forms:

After **will / can / must / going to / want to**, etc.

active: **do/clean/see**, etc.	Somebody **will clean** this room later.
passive: **be + done/cleaned/seen**, etc.	This room **will be cleaned** later.

- The situation is serious. Something must **be done** before it's too late.
- A mystery is something that can't **be explained**.
- The music was very loud and could **be heard** from far away.
- A new supermarket is going to **be built** next year.
- Please go away. I want to **be left** alone.

After **should have / might have / would have / seem to have**, etc.

active: **done/cleaned/seen**, etc.	Somebody **should have cleaned** this room.
passive: **been + done/cleaned/seen**, etc.	This room **should have been cleaned**.

- I haven't received the letter yet. It might **have been sent** to the wrong address.
- If you had locked the car, it wouldn't **have been stolen**.
- There were some problems at first, but they seem to **have been solved**.

Present Perfect

active: **have/has + (done)**, etc.	The room looks nice. Somebody **has cleaned** it.
passive: **have/has been + (done)**, etc.	The room looks nice. It **has been cleaned**.

- Have you heard? The concert **has been canceled**.
- **Have** you ever **been bitten** by a dog?
- "Are you going to the party?" "No, I **haven't been invited**."

Past Perfect

active: **had + (done)**, etc.	The room looked nice. Somebody **had cleaned** it.
passive: **had been + (done)**, etc.	The room looks nice. It **had been cleaned**.

- The vegetables didn't taste very good. They **had been cooked** too long.
- The car was three years old but **hadn't been used** very much.

Present Continuous

active: **am/is/are + (do)ing**	Somebody **is cleaning** this room right now.
passive: **am/is/are + being (done)**	This room **is being cleaned** right now.

- There's somebody walking behind us. I think we **are being followed**.
- *(in a shop)* "Can I help you?" "No, thank you. I'**m being helped**."

Past Continuous

active: **was/were + (do)ing**	Somebody **was cleaning** this room when I arrived.
passive: **was/were + being (done)**	This room **was being cleaned** when I arrived.

- There was somebody walking behind us. We **were being followed**.

Passive 1, 3 Units 40, 42

Exercises

41.1 What do these words mean? Use *it can . . .* or *it can't . . . .* Use a dictionary if necessary.

If something is

1. washable, *it can be washed.* .
2. unbreakable, it _____ .
3. edible, _____ .
4. unusable, _____ .
5. invisible, _____ .
6. portable, _____ .

41.2 Complete these sentences with the following verbs (in the correct form):

arrest   carry   cause   ~~do~~   make   repair   ~~send~~   spend   wake up

Sometimes you need *have* (*might have*, *should have*, etc.).

1. The situation is serious. Something must _be done_ before it's too late.
2. I haven't received the letter. It might _have been sent_ to the wrong address.
3. A decision will not _____ until the next meeting.
4. Do you think that more money should _____ on education?
5. This road is in very bad condition. It should _____ a long time ago.
6. The injured man couldn't walk and had to _____ .
7. I told the hotel desk clerk I wanted to _____ at 6:30 the next morning.
8. If you hadn't pushed the policeman, you wouldn't _____ .
9. It's not certain how the fire started, but it might _____ by an electrical short circuit.

41.3 Rewrite these sentences. Instead of using *somebody* or *they*, write a passive sentence.

1. Somebody has cleaned the room. _The room has been cleaned._
2. Somebody is using the computer right now.
   The computer _____
3. I didn't realize that somebody was recording our conversation.
   I didn't realize that _____
4. When we got to the stadium, we found that they had canceled the game.
   When we got to the stadium, we found that _____
5. They are building a new highway around the city.
   _____
6. They have built a new hospital near the airport.
   _____

41.4 Make sentences from the words in parentheses. Sometimes the verb is active, sometimes passive.

1. There's somebody behind us. (I think / we / follow) _I think we're being followed._
2. This room looks different. (you / paint / the walls?) _Have you painted the walls?_
3. My car has disappeared. (it / steal!)
   It _____
4. My umbrella has disappeared. (somebody / take)
   Somebody _____
5. When I went into the room, I saw that the table and chairs were not in the same place.
   (the furniture / move) The _____
6. The man next door disappeared six months ago. (he / not / see / since then)
   He _____
7. I wonder how Jane is these days. (I / not / see / for ages)
   I _____
8. I wanted to use a computer at the library last night, but I wasn't able to.
   (the computers / use) All _____
9. Ann can't use her office this week. (it / redecorate)
   It _____
10. The photocopier broke down yesterday, but now it's OK. (it / work / again; it / repair)
    It _____ . It _____
11. A friend of mine was mugged on his way home a few nights ago. (you / ever / mug?)
    _____

Passive 3

A

I was offered . . . / we were given . . . , etc.

Some verbs can have two objects. For example, **give**:

- Someone gave **the police** **the information**. (= Someone gave the information to the police)

  object 1   *object 2*

So it is possible to make two passive sentences:

- **The police** were given the information.   *or*
  The information was given to the police.

Other verbs that can have two objects are:

ask   offer   pay   show   teach   tell

When we use these verbs in the passive, most often we begin with the *person*:

- **I was offered** the job, but I refused it. (= they offered me the job)
- **You will be given** plenty of time to decide. (= we will give you plenty of time)
- **Have you been shown** the new machine? (= has anybody shown you?)
- **The men were paid** $200 to do the work. (= somebody paid the men $200)

B

I don't like being . . .

The passive of **doing/seeing**, etc., is **being done / being seen**, etc. Compare:

active: I don't like **people telling me** what to do.

passive: I don't like **being told** what to do.

- I remember **being taken** to the zoo when I was a child.
  (= I remember somebody taking me to the zoo)
- Steve hates **being kept** waiting. (= he hates people keeping him waiting)
- We managed to climb over the wall without **being seen**. (= without anybody seeing us)

C

I was born . . .

We say I **was born** . . . (*not* I am born):

- I **was born** in Chicago.
- Where **were** you **born**? (*not* Where are you born?) } *past*

but

- How many babies **are born** every day?   *present*

D

Get

You can use **get** instead of **be** in the passive:

- There was a fight at the game, but nobody **got hurt**. (= nobody **was hurt**)
- I don't often **get invited** to parties. (= I'm not often invited)
- I'm surprised Ann **didn't get offered** the job. (= Ann **wasn't offered** the job)

You can use **get** only when things happen or change. For example, you cannot use **get** in the following sentences:

- Jill **is liked** by everybody. (*not* gets liked – this is not a "happening")
- He was a mystery man. Very little **was known** about him. (*not* got known)

We use **get** mainly in informal spoken English. You can use **be** in all situations.

We also use **get** in the following expressions (which are not passive in meaning):

get married, **get divorced**   **get lost** (= not know where you are)
get dressed (= put on your clothes)   **get changed** (= change your clothes)

Passive 1, 2 Units 40, 41

Exercises

42.1 Write these sentences using the passive, beginning in the way shown.

1. They didn't give me the information I needed.
   I *wasn't given the information I needed.*
2. They asked me some difficult questions at the interview.
   I _____
3. Jessica's colleagues gave her a present when she retired.
   Jessica _____
4. Nobody told me about the meeting.
   I wasn't _____
5. How much will they pay you for your work?
   How much will you _____
6. I think they should have offered John the job.
   I think John _____
7. Has anybody shown you what to do?
   Have you _____

42.2 Complete the sentences using *being* + the following (in the correct form):

   give   hit   invite   ~~keep~~   pay   treat

1. Steve hates *being kept* waiting.
2. We went to the party without _____ .
3. I like giving presents, and I also like _____ them.
4. It's a busy road and I don't like crossing it. I'm afraid of _____ .
5. I'm an adult. I don't like _____ like a child.
6. Few people are prepared to work without _____ .

42.3 When were they born? Choose five of these people and write a sentence for each.
(Two of them were born in the same year.)

Beethoven	Galileo	Elvis Presley	1452	1869
John Lennon	Mahatma Gandhi	Leonardo da Vinci	1564	~~1901~~
~~Walt Disney~~	Martin Luther King Jr.	William Shakespeare	1770	1940
			1929	1935

1. *Walt Disney was born in 1901.* _____
2. _____
3. _____
4. _____
5. _____
6. _____
7. And you? I _____

42.4 Complete the sentences using *get/got* + the following verbs (in the correct form):

   ask   damage   ~~hurt~~   pay   steal   sting   stop   use

1. There was a fight at the game, but nobody *got hurt* .
2. Ted _____ by a bee while he was sitting in the yard.
3. These tennis courts don't _____ very often. Not many people want to play.
4. I used to have a bicycle, but it _____ a few months ago.
5. Rachel works hard but doesn't _____ very much.
6. Last night I _____ by the police as I was driving home. One of the lights on my car wasn't working.
7. Please pack these things very carefully. I don't want them to _____ .
8. People often want to know what my job is. I often _____ that question.

It is said that . . .   He is said to . . .
He is supposed to . . .

Study this example situation:

Henry is very old. Nobody knows exactly how old he is, but:

It is said that he is 108 years old.

or   He **is said to be** 108 years old.

Both these sentences mean: People say that he is 108 years old.

You can use these structures with a number of other verbs, especially:

alleged   believed   considered   expected   known   reported   thought   understood

Compare the two structures:

- Cathy works very hard.
  It is said that she works 16 hours a day.   *or*   She **is said to work** 16 hours a day.
- The police are looking for a missing boy.
  It is believed that the boy is wearing a   *or*   The boy **is believed to be wearing** white sweater and blue jeans.   a white sweater and blue jeans.
- The strike started three weeks ago.
  It is expected that it will end soon.   *or*   The strike **is expected to end** soon.
- A friend of mine has been arrested.
  It is alleged that he hit a police officer.   *or*   He **is alleged to have hit** a police officer.
- The two houses belong to the same family.
  It is said that there is a secret tunnel   *or*   There **is said to be** a secret tunnel between them.   between them.

These structures are often used in news reports. For example, in a report about an accident:

- **It is reported that** two people were   *or*   Two people **are reported to have** injured in the explosion.   **been injured** in the explosion.

(Be) supposed to

Sometimes **(it is) supposed to . . .** = (it is) said to . . . :

- Let's go and see that movie. It**'s supposed to be** good.   (= it is said to be good)
- Mark **is supposed to have hit** a police officer, but I don't believe it.

But sometimes **supposed to** has a different meaning. We use **supposed to** to say what is intended, arranged, or expected. Often this is different from the real situation:

- The plan **is supposed to be** a secret, but everybody seems to know about it.
  (= the plan is intended to be a secret)
- What are you doing at work? You**'re supposed to be** on vacation.
  (= you arranged to be on vacation)
- Jane **was supposed to call** me last night, but she didn't.
- Our guests **were supposed to come** at 7:30, but they were late.
- I'd better hurry. I**'m supposed to meet** Chris in 10 minutes.

You**'re not supposed to** do something = it is not allowed or advisable:

- You**'re not supposed to park** your car here. It's private parking only.
- Mr. Bruno is much better after his operation, but he**'s still not supposed to do** any heavy work.

Exercises

43.1 Write these sentences in another way, beginning as shown. Use the <u>underlined</u> words.

1. It is <u>expected</u> that the strike will end soon. The strike _is expected to end soon._

2. It is <u>thought</u> that the prisoner escaped by climbing over a wall.
   The prisoner _is thought to have escaped by climbing over a wall._

3. It is <u>reported</u> that many people are homeless after the floods.
   Many people _____

4. It is <u>alleged</u> that the man robbed the store of $3,000.
   The man _____

5. It is <u>reported</u> that the building was badly damaged by the fire.
   The building _____

6. a) It is <u>said</u> that the company is losing a lot of money.
      The company _____
   b) It is <u>believed</u> that the company lost a lot of money last year.
      The company _____
   c) It is <u>expected</u> that the company will lose money this year.
      The company _____

43.2 There are a lot of rumors about Stan. Here are some of the things people say about him:

1. Stan speaks 10 languages.
2. He knows a lot of famous people.
3. He is very rich.
4. He has 12 children.
5. He was an actor when he was younger.

Stan

Nobody is sure whether these things are true. Write sentences about Stan using **supposed to**.

1. _Stan is supposed to speak 10 languages._
2. He _____
3. _____
4. _____
5. _____

43.3 Complete the sentences using **supposed to be** + the following:

on a diet   a flower   my friend   a joke   ~~on vacation~~   working

1. What are you doing at work? You _are supposed to be on vacation._
2. You shouldn't criticize me all the time. You _____
3. I really shouldn't be eating this cake. I _____
4. I'm sorry about what I said. I was trying to be funny. It _____
5. What's this drawing? Is it a tree? Or maybe it _____
6. You shouldn't be reading the paper now. You _____

43.4 Write sentences with **supposed to** + the following verbs:

arrive   block   call   ~~park~~   start

Use the negative (**not supposed to**) where necessary.

1. You _'re not supposed to park_____ here. It's private parking only.
2. We _____ work at 8:15, but we rarely do anything before 8:30.
3. Oh, I _____ Helen, but I completely forgot.
4. This door is a fire exit. You _____ it.
5. My train _____ at 11:30, but it was an hour late.

Have/get something done

Study this example situation:

Lisa

The roof of Lisa's house was damaged in a storm. Yesterday a worker came and repaired it.

Lisa **had** the roof **repaired** yesterday.

This means: Lisa arranged for somebody else to repair the roof. She didn't repair it herself.

We use **have something done** to say that we arrange for somebody else to do something for us. Compare:

- Lisa **repaired** the roof. (= she repaired it herself)
  Lisa **had** the roof **repaired**. (= she arranged for somebody else to repair it)
- "Did you **paint** your apartment yourself?" "Yes, I like doing things like that."
  "Did you **have** your apartment **painted**?" "No, I painted it myself."

B

Be careful with word order. The *past participle* (**repaired/cut**, etc.) is after the *object*:

have	Object	Past Participle
Lisa **had**	the roof	**repaired** yesterday.
Where did you **have**	your hair	**cut**?
Our neighbor has just **had**	air conditioning	**installed** in her house.
We are **having**	the house	**painted** this week.
How often do you **have**	your car	**serviced**?
Why don't you **have**	that coat	**cleaned**?
I don't like **having**	my picture	**taken**.

C

Get something done

You can also say "**get** something done" instead of "**have** something done" (mainly in informal spoken English):

- When are you going to **get the roof repaired**? (= have the roof repaired)
- I think you should **get your hair cut** really short.

D

Sometimes **have** (*or* **get**) **something done** has a different meaning. For example:

- Eric **had his license taken away** for driving too fast again and again.
- *or* Eric **got his license taken away** for driving . . .

This does not mean that he arranged for somebody to take his license away. It means that his license was taken away by the police.

With this meaning, we use **have** (*or* **get**) **something done** to say that something happens to somebody or their belongings. Usually what happens is not nice:

- James **got** his passport **stolen**. (= his passport was stolen)
- Have you ever **had** your flight **canceled**? (= has your flight ever been canceled?)

Exercises

44.1 Check (✓) the correct sentence, (a) or (b), for each picture.

1.
   Sarah

   a) Sarah is cutting her hair.
   b) Sarah is having her hair cut.

2.
   Bill

   a) Bill is cutting his hair.
   b) Bill is having his hair cut.

3.
   John

   a) John is shining his shoes.
   b) John is having his shoes shined.

4.
   Sue

   a) Sue is taking a picture.
   b) Sue is having her picture taken.

44.2 Answer the questions using *To have something done*. Choose from the boxes:

~~my car~~	my eyes	my jacket	my watch		clean	repair	~~service~~	test

1. Why did you go to the garage? _To have my car serviced._
2. Why did you go to the cleaner's? To _____
3. Why did you go to the jeweler's? _____
4. Why did you go to the optician's? _____

44.3 Write sentences in the way shown.

1. Lisa didn't repair the roof herself. _She had it repaired._
2. I didn't cut my hair myself. I _____
3. They didn't paint the house themselves. They _____
4. John didn't build that wall himself. _____
5. I didn't deliver the flowers myself. _____

44.4 Use the words in parentheses to complete the sentences. Use the structure *have something done*.

1. We _are having the house painted_ (the house / paint) this week.
2. I lost my key. I'll have to _____ (another key / make).
3. When was the last time you _____ (your hair / cut)?
4. _____ (you / a newspaper / deliver) to your house every day, or do you go out and buy one?
5. *A:* What are those workers doing at your house?
   B: Oh, we _____ (garage / build).
6. You can't see that sign from here? You should _____ (your eyes / check).

In the following sentences use *get something done*.

7. How often _do you get your car serviced_ (your car / service)?
8. This coat is dirty. I should _____ (it / clean).
9. If you want to wear earrings, why don't you _____ (your ears / pierce)?
10. *A:* I heard your computer wasn't working.
    B: That's right, but it's OK now. I _____ (it / repair).

In these items, use *have something done* with its second meaning (see Section D).

11. Did you hear about Pete? _He had his license taken away_ (license / take away).
12. Did I tell you about Jane? She _____ (her purse / steal) last week.
13. Gary was in a fight last night. _____ (his nose / break).

Reported Speech 1 (He said that . . .)

A

Study this example situation:

I'm feeling sick.

Tom

You want to tell somebody what Tom said. There are two ways of doing this:

You can repeat Tom's words (*direct* speech): Tom said, **"I'm feeling sick."**

Or you can use *reported* speech: Tom said **that he was feeling sick.**

Compare

direct: Tom said, " I am feeling sick."

reported: Tom said that he was feeling sick.

In writing we use these quotation marks to show direct speech.

B

When we use reported speech, the main verb of the sentence is usually past (Tom **said** that . . . / I **told** her that . . . , etc.). The rest of the sentence is usually past, too:

■ Tom **said** that he **was feeling** sick.
■ I **told** her that I **didn't have** any money.

You can leave out **that**. So you can say:

■ Tom **said that** he was feeling sick. *or* Tom **said** he was feeling sick.

In general, the *present* form in direct speech changes to the *past* form in reported speech:

am/is → **was**   do/does → **did**   will → **would**
are → **were**   have/has → **had**   can → **could**
want/know/go, etc. → **wanted/knew/went**, etc.

Compare direct speech and reported speech:

You met Jenny. Here are some of the things she said to you in *direct* speech:

"My parents **are** fine."

"I**'m** going to learn to drive."

"I **want** to buy a car."

"John **has** quit his job."

"I **can't** come to the party on Friday."

"I **don't** have much free time."

"I**'m** going away for a few days. I**'ll** call you when I **get** back."

Jenny

Later you tell somebody what Jenny said. You use *reported* speech:

■ Jenny said that her parents **were** fine.
■ She said that she **was** going to learn to drive.
■ She said that she **wanted** to buy a car.
■ She said that John **had** quit his job.
■ She said that she **couldn't** come to the party on Friday.
■ She said she **didn't** have much free time.
■ She said that she **was** going away for a few days and **would** call me when she **got** back.

C

The *simple past* (**did/saw/knew**, etc.) can usually stay the same in reported speech, or you can change it to the *past perfect* (**had done / had seen / had known**, etc.):

■ *direct:*   Tom said, "I **woke** up feeling sick, so I **didn't go** to work."
   reported: Tom said (that) he **woke** up feeling sick, so he **didn't go** to work. *or*
              Tom said (that) he **had woken** up feeling sick, so he **hadn't gone** to work.

Exercises

45.1 Yesterday you met a friend of yours, Rob. You hadn't seen him for a long time. Here are some of the things Rob said to you:

1. I'm living in my own apartment now.
6. I saw Nicole at a party in June, and she seemed fine.
8. I'm not enjoying my job very much.
2. My father isn't very well.
9. You can come and stay at my place if you're ever in Chicago.
3. Amanda and Paul are getting married next month.
4. My sister has had a baby.
10. My car was stolen a few days ago.
5. I don't know what Eric is doing.
7. I haven't seen Diane recently.
11. I want to take a trip, but I can't afford it.
12. I'll tell Amy I saw you.

Rob

Later that day you tell another friend what Rob said. Use reported speech.

1. _Rob said that he was living in his own apartment now._
2. He said that _____
3. He _____
4. _____
5. _____
6. _____
7. _____
8. _____
9. _____
10. _____
11. _____
12. _____

45.2 Somebody says something to you that is the opposite of what they said before. Complete the answers.

1. *A:* That restaurant is expensive.
   B: It is? _I thought you said it was cheap_ .
2. *A:* Sue is coming to the party tonight.
   B: She is? I thought you said she _____ .
3. *A:* Ann likes Paul.
   B: She does? Last week you said _____ .
4. *A:* I know lots of people.
   B: You do? I thought you said _____ .
5. *A:* Pat will be here next week.
   B: She will? But didn't you say _____ ?
6. *A:* I'm going out tonight.
   B: You are? But you said _____ .
7. *A:* I can speak a little French.
   B: You can? But earlier you said _____ .
8. *A:* I haven't been to the movies in ages.
   B: You haven't? I thought you said _____ .

Reported Speech 2

UNIT 46

A

It is not always necessary to change the verb in reported speech. If you report something and the situation *hasn't changed*, you do not need to change the verb to the past:

- *direct:*   Tom said, "My new job **is** very interesting."
  reported: Tom said that his new job **is** very interesting.
  (The situation hasn't changed. His job **is** still interesting.)

- *direct:*   Ann said, "**I want** to go to South America next year."
  reported: Ann told me that **she wants** to go to South America next year.
  (Ann still wants to go to South America next year.)

You can also change the verb to the past:

- Tom said that his new job **was** very interesting.
- Ann told me that she **wanted** to go to South America next year.

But if you are reporting a finished situation, you *must* use a past verb:

- Paul left the room suddenly. He said **he had** to go. (*not* has to go)

B

You need to use a past form when there is a difference between what was said and what is really true. For example:

You met Sonia a few days ago.
She said: "**Joe is in the hospital**." *(direct speech)*

Later that day you meet Joe in the street. You say: "I didn't expect to see you, Joe. Sonia said you **were** in the hospital." (*not* "Sonia said you are in the hospital," because he clearly is not)

 Joe is in the hospital.

 Sonia said you **were** in the hospital.

Sonia   Joe

C

Say and **tell**

If you say *who* somebody is talking to, use **tell**:

- Sonia **told me** that you were in the hospital. (*not* Sonia said me)
- What did you **tell the police**? (*not* say the police)

TELL <u>SOMEBODY</u>

Otherwise use **say**:

- Sonia **said** that you were in the hospital. (*not* Sonia told that . . .)
- What did you **say**?

SAY ~~SOMEBODY~~

But you can **say** something **to** somebody:

- Ann **said** goodbye **to** me and left. (*not* Ann said me goodbye)
- What did you **say to** the police?

D

Tell/ask somebody **to** do something

We also use the infinitive (**to do** / **to stay**, etc.) in reported speech, especially with **tell** and **ask** (for orders and requests):

- *direct:*   "**Stay** in bed for a few days," the doctor said to me.
  reported: The doctor **told me to** stay in bed for a few days.
- *direct:*   "**Don't shout**," I said to Jim.
  reported: I **told** Jim **not to** shout.
- *direct:*   "Please **don't tell** anybody what happened," Jackie said to me.
  reported: Jackie **asked me not to** tell anybody what (had) happened.

You can also say "Somebody **said** (not) **to** do something":

- Jackie **said** not **to tell anyone**. (*but not* Jackie said me)

92   **Reported Speech 1** Unit 45   **Reported Questions** Unit 48B

Exercises

46.1 Here are some things that Ann said to you:

I've never been to South America.   I don't have any brothers or sisters.

I can't drive.   I don't like fish.   Rosa has a very well-paid job.

I'm working tomorrow night.   Rosa is a friend of mine.   ~~Dave is lazy.~~

Ann

But later Ann says something different. What do you say?

Ann	You
1. Dave works very hard.	*But you said he was lazy.*
2. Let's have fish for dinner.	But _____
3. I'm going to buy a car.	_____
4. Rosa is always short of money.	_____
5. My sister lives in Tokyo.	_____
6. I think Peru is a great place.	_____
7. Let's go out tomorrow night.	_____
8. I've never spoken to Rosa.	_____

46.2 Complete the sentences with *say* or *tell* (in the correct form). Use only one word each time.

1. Ann ___*said*___ goodbye to me and left.
2. _____ us about your vacation. Did you have a good time?
3. Don't just stand there! _____ something!
4. I wonder where Sue is. She _____ she would be here at 8:00.
5. Jack _____ me that he was fed up with his job.
6. The doctor _____ that I should rest for at least a week.
7. Don't _____ anybody what I _____ . It's a secret just between us.
8. "Did she _____ you what happened?" "No, she didn't _____ anything to me."
9. Jason couldn't help me. He _____ me to ask Kate.
10. Gary couldn't help me. He _____ to ask Caroline.

46.3 The following sentences are direct speech:

Don't wait for me if I'm late.   Mind your own business.   Don't worry, Sue.

Can you open your bag, please?   ~~Hurry up!~~

Please slow down!   Will you marry me?   Do you think you could give me a hand, Tom?

Choose one of these to complete each sentence below. Use reported speech.

1. Bill was taking a long time to get ready, so I told ___*him to hurry up*_____ .
2. Sarah was driving too fast, so I asked _____ .
3. Sue was nervous about the situation. I told _____ .
4. I couldn't move the piano alone, so I _____ .
5. The customs officer looked at me suspiciously and _____ .
6. The man started asking me personal questions, so I _____ .
7. John was in love with Maria, so he _____ .
8. I didn't want to delay Helen, so I _____ .

Questions 1

A In questions we usually put the subject after the first verb:

Subject + Verb			Verb + Subject	
Tom	will	→	will	Tom?
you	have	→	have	you?
the house	was	→	was	the house?

- **Will Tom** be here tomorrow?
- **Have you** been working hard?
- When **was the house** built?

Remember that the subject comes after the *first* verb:
- **Is Catherine** working today? (*not* Is working Catherine)

B In *simple present* questions, we use **do/does**:

you	live	→	**do**	you live?
the film	begins	→	**does**	the film begin?

- **Do** you **live** near here?
- What time **does** the film **begin**?

In *simple past* questions, we use **did**:

you	sold	→	**did**	you sell?
the train	stopped	→	**did**	the train stop?

- **Did** you **sell** your car?
- Why **did** the train **stop**?

But do not use **do/does/did** if **who/what**, etc., is the subject of the sentence. Compare:

who *object*
Sarah called somebody .
— *object* —
Who **did** Sarah **call**?

who *subject*
Somebody called Sarah.
subject
Who **called** Sarah?

In these examples, **who/what**, etc., is the *subject*:
- **Who wants** something to eat? (*not* Who does want)
- **What happened** to you last night? (*not* What did happen)
- **How many people came** to the meeting? (*not* did come)
- **Which bus goes** downtown? (*not* does go)

C Note the position of prepositions in questions beginning **Who/What/Which/Where . . . ?**:
- **Who** do you want to speak **to**?
- **Which** job has Ann applied **for**?
- **What** was the weather **like** yesterday?
- **Where** are you **from**?

You can use *preposition* + **whom** in formal style:
- **To whom** do you wish to speak?

D **Isn't it . . . ?** / **Didn't you . . . ?**, etc. (negative questions)

We use negative questions especially to show surprise:
- **Didn't you** hear the doorbell? I rang it three times.

or when we expect the listener to agree with us:
- "**Haven't we** met somewhere before?" "Yes, I think we have."

Note the meaning of **yes** and **no** in answers to negative questions:
- **Don't you** want to go to the party? { **Yes.** (= Yes, I want to go) / **No.** (= No, I don't want to go) }

Note the word order in negative questions beginning **Why . . . ?**:
- **Why don't we** go out for a meal tonight? (*not* Why we don't go)
- **Why wasn't Mary** at work yesterday? (*not* Why Mary wasn't)

Exercises

47.1 Ask Joe questions. (Look at his answers before you write the questions.)

1. (where / live?) _Where do you live?_   In Vancouver.
2. (born there?) _____ No, I was born in Toronto.
3. (married?) _____ Yes.
4. (how long / married?) _____ 17 years.
   _____
5. (children?) _____ Yes, two boys.
   _____
6. (how old / they?) _____ 12 and 15.
7. (what / do?) _____ I'm a journalist.
8. (what / wife / do?)_____ She's a doctor.
   _____

Joe

47.2 Make questions with *who* or *what*.

1.   Somebody hit me.   _Who hit you?_
2.   I hit somebody.   _Who did you hit?_
3.   Somebody paid the bill.   Who _____
4.   Something happened.   What _____
5.   Diane said something.   _____
6. This book belongs to somebody.   _____
7. Somebody lives in that house.   _____
8.   I fell over something.   _____
9.   Something fell on the floor.   _____
10.   This word means something.   _____
11. I borrowed the money from somebody.   _____
12.   I'm worried about something.   _____

47.3 Put the words in parentheses in the correct order. All the sentences are questions.

1. (when / was / built / this house) _When was this house built?_
2. (how / cheese / is / made) _____
3. (when / invented / the computer / was) _____
4. (why / Sue / working / isn't / today) _____
5. (what time / coming / your friends / are) _____
6. (why / was / canceled / the concert) _____
7. (where / your mother / was / born) _____
8. (why / you / to the party / didn't / come) _____
9. (how / the accident / did / happen) _____
10. (why / this machine / doesn't / work) _____

47.4 Write negative questions from the words in parentheses. In each situation you
are surprised.

1. *A:* We won't see Ann tonight.
   B: Why not?   (she / not / come / to the party?) _Isn't she coming to the party?_
2. *A:* I hope we don't see Brian tonight.
   B: Why?   (you / not / like / him?) _____
3. *A:* Don't go and see that movie.
   B: Why not?   (it / not / good?) _____
4. *A:* I'll have to borrow some money.
   B: Why?   (you / not / have / any?) _____

Questions 2 (Do you know where . . . ? / He asked me where . . .)

A

Do you know where . . . ? / I don't know why . . . / Could you tell me what . . . ?, etc.

We say: Where **has Tom** gone?

but **Do you know** where **Tom has** gone? (*not* Do you know where has Tom gone?)

When the question (**Where has Tom gone?**) is part of a longer sentence (**Do you know . . . ? / I don't know . . . / Can you tell me . . . ?**, etc.), the word order changes. Compare:

■ What time **is it**?	*but* **Do you know** what time **it is**?
■ Who **are those people**?	**I don't know** who **those people are**.
■ Where **can I** find Linda?	**Can you tell me** where **I can** find Linda?
■ How much **will it** cost?	**Do you have any idea** how much **it will** cost?

Be careful with **do/does/did** questions. We say:

■ What **time does the movie begin**?	*but* **Do you know** what time **the movie begins**? (*not* does the movie begin)
■ What **do you mean**?	**Please explain** what **you mean**.
■ Why **did she leave** early?	**I wonder** why **she left** early.

Use **if** or **whether** where there is no other question word (**what**, **why**, etc.):

■ Did anybody see you?	*but* **Do you know if** anybody saw you?
	or . . . **whether** anybody saw you?

B

He asked me where . . . (reported questions)

The same changes in word order happen in *reported* questions. Compare:

■ *direct:* The police officer said to us, "Where **are you going** ?"

reported: The police officer asked us where **we were going** .

■ *direct:* Claire asked, "What time **do the banks close** ?"

reported: Claire wanted to know what time **the banks closed** .

In reported questions, the verb usually changes to the past (**were**, **closed**, etc.). See Unit 45.

Study these examples. You had an interview for a job, and these were some of the questions the interviewer asked you:

What **do you** do in your spare time?

Can you speak another language?

Are you willing to travel?

Why **did you** apply for the job?

How long **have you** been working at your present job?

Do you have a driver's license?

Later you tell a friend what the interviewer asked you. You use *reported* speech:

- She asked if (*or* whether) **I was** willing to travel.
- She wanted to know what **I did** in my spare time.
- She asked how long **I had** been working at my present job.
- She asked why **I had** applied for the job. (*or* . . . why **I applied**)
- She wanted to know if (*or* whether) **I could** speak another language.
- She asked if (*or* whether) **I had** a driver's license.

Reported Speech Units 45–46

Exercises

48.1 Make a new sentence from the question in brackets.

1. (Where has Tom gone?) Do you know _where Tom has gone?_____
2. (Where is the post office?) Could you tell me _____
3. (What time is it?) I wonder _____
4. (What does this word mean?) I want to know _____
5. (Has the plane left yet?) Do you know _____
6. (Is Sue going out tonight?) I don't know _____
7. (Where does Carol live?) Do you have any idea _____
8. (Where did I park the car?) I can't remember _____
9. (Is there a bank near here?) Can you tell me _____
10. (What do you want?) Tell me _____
11. (Why didn't Kelly come to the party?) I don't know _____
12. (How much does it cost to park here?) Do you know _____
13. (Who is that woman?) I have no idea _____
14. (Did Ann get my letter?) Do you know _____
15. (How far is it to the airport?) Can you tell me _____

48.2 You are making a phone call. You want to speak to Amy, but she isn't there. Somebody else answers the phone. You want to know three things:

(1) Where is Amy? (2) When will she be back? and **(3) Did she go out alone?**

Complete the conversation:

A: Do you know where _____ ? (1)
B: Sorry, I have no idea.
A: That's all right. I don't suppose you know _____ . (2)
B: No, I'm afraid I don't.
A: One more thing. Do you happen to know _____ ? (3)
B: I'm sorry. I didn't see her go out. But I'll tell her you called.

48.3 You have been away for a while and have just come back to your hometown. You meet Tony, a friend of yours. He asks you a lot of questions:

1. How are you?
5. Why did you come back?
6. Where are you living?
2. Where have you been?
7. Are you glad to be back?
3. How long have you been back?
8. Do you plan to stay for a while?
4. What are you doing now?
9. Can you lend me some money?

Tony

Now tell another friend what Tony asked you. Use reported speech.

1. _He asked me how I was._____
2. He asked me _____
3. He _____
4. _____
5. _____
6. _____
7. _____
8. _____
9. _____

Auxiliary Verbs (**have/do/can**, etc.)
I think so / I hope so, etc.

A

In each of these sentences there is an auxiliary verb and a main verb:

I	**have**	**lost**	my keys.
She	**can't**	**come**	to the party.
The hotel	**was**	**built**	ten years ago.
Where	**do** you	**live**?	

In these examples **have/can't/was/do** are auxiliary (= helping) verbs.

You can use an auxiliary verb when you do not want to repeat something:

- "Have you locked the door?" "Yes, I **have**." (=I have *locked the door*)
- George wasn't working, but Janet **was**. (=Janet was *working*)
- She could lend me the money, but she **won't**. (= she won't *lend me the money*)

Use **do/does/did** for the simple present and past:

- "Do you like onions?" "Yes, I **do**." (= I *like onions*)
- "Does Mark play soccer?" "He **did**, but he **doesn't** anymore."

You can use auxiliary verbs to deny what somebody says (= say it is not true):

- "You're sitting in my place." "No, I**'m not**." (= I'm not *sitting in your place*)
- "You didn't lock the door before you left." "Yes, I **did**." (= I *locked the door*)

B

We use **You have? / She isn't? / They do?**, etc., to show interest in what somebody has said:

- "I've just seen David." "**You have**? How is he?"
- "Liz isn't feeling very well today." "**She isn't**? What's wrong with her?"
- "It rained every day during our vacation." "**It did**? What a shame!"
- "Jim and Karen are getting married." "**They are**? Really?"

C

We use auxiliary verbs with **so** and **neither**:

- "I'm tired." "**So am I**." (= I'm tired, too)
- "I never read newspapers." "**Neither do I**." (= I never read newspapers either)
- Sue doesn't have a car, and **neither does Mark**.

Note the word order after **so** and **neither** (verb before subject):

- I passed the exam, and **so did Paul**. (*not* so Paul did)

You can also use **not . . . either** instead of **neither**:

- "I don't have any money." "**Neither do I**." *or* "I do**n't either**."

D

I think so / I hope so, etc.

After some verbs you can use **so** when you do not want to repeat something:

- "Are those people Australian?" "**I think so**." (= I think they are Australian)
- "Will you be home tomorrow morning?" "**I guess so**." (= I guess I'll be home . . .)
- "Do you think Kate has been invited to the party?" "**I suppose so**."

You can also say: **I hope so** and **I'm afraid so**.

The usual negative forms are:

I think so	→	**I don't think so**
I hope so / I'm afraid so / I guess so	→	**I hope not / I'm afraid not / I guess not**
I suppose so	→	**I suppose not**

- "Is that woman French?" "**I think so. / I don't think so**."
- "Do you think it will rain?" "**I hope so. / I hope not**." (*not* I don't hope so)

Exercises

49.1 Complete each sentence with an auxiliary verb (**do/was/could/should**, etc.).
Sometimes the verb must be negative (**don't/wasn't**, etc.).

1. I wasn't tired, but my friends __were__ .
2. I like hot weather, but Ann _____ .
3. "Is Eric here?" "He _____ five minutes ago, but I think he's gone."
4. Liz said she might call later on tonight, but I don't think she _____ .
5. "Are you and Chris coming to the party?" "I _____ , but Chris _____ ."
6. I don't know whether to apply for the job or not. Do you think I _____ ?
7. "Please don't tell anybody what I said." "Don't worry. I _____ ."
8. "You never listen to me." "Yes, I _____ !"
9. "Can you play a musical instrument?" "No, but I wish I _____ ."
10. "Please help me." "I'm sorry. I _____ if I _____ , but I _____ ."

49.2 You never agree with Alex. Answer in the way shown.

1. I'm hungry.   _You are? I'm not._
2. I'm not tired.   _You aren't? I am._
3. I like baseball.   _____
4. I didn't like the movie. _____   You
5. Alex I've never been to South America. _____
6. I thought the exam was easy. _____

49.3 You are talking to Lisa. If you're in the same position as Lisa, reply with **So . . .** or
Neither . . . as in the first example. Otherwise, ask questions as in the second example.

1. I feel really tired.   _So do I._
2. I'm working hard.   _You are? What are you doing?_
3. I watched TV last night.   _____
4. I won't be at home tomorrow. _____
5. Lisa I like to read. I read a lot. _____   You
6. I'd like to live somewhere else. _____
7. I can't go out tonight.   _____

49.4 In these conversations, you are B. Read the information in parentheses and then answer
with **I think so**, **I hope not**, etc.

1. (You don't like rain.)
   A: Is it going to rain? B: (hope) __I hope not.__
2. (You're not sure Sarah will get the job she applied for, but her chances look pretty good.)
   A: Do you think Sarah will get the job? B: (guess) _____
3. (You're not sure whether Amy is married – probably not.)
   A: Is Amy married? B: (think) _____
4. (You need more money quickly.)
   A: Do you think you'll get a raise soon? B: (hope) _____
5. (You're a hotel desk clerk. The hotel is full.)
   A: Do you have a room for tonight? B: (afraid) _____
6. (You're at a party. You have to leave early.)
   A: Do you have to leave already? B: (afraid) _____
7. (You are going to a party. You can't stand John.)
   A: Do you think John will be at the party? B: (hope) _____
8. (You're not sure what time the concert is – probably 7:30.)
   A: Is the concert at 7:30? B: (think) _____
9. (Ann normally works every day, Monday to Friday. Tomorrow is Wednesday.)
   A: Is Ann working tomorrow? B: (suppose) _____

Tag Questions (**do you?** / **isn't it?**, etc.)

A

Study these examples:

You haven't seen Maria today, **have you**?

No, I haven't.

It was a good movie, **wasn't it**?

Yes, I loved it.

Have you? and **wasn't it?** are *tags* (= mini-questions that we often put on the end of a sentence in spoken English). In these tags, we use an auxiliary verb (**have/was/will**, etc.).

We use **do/does/did** for the present and simple past (see Unit 49):

■ "Lauren plays the piano, **does**n't she?" "Well, yes, but not very well."
■ "You didn't lock the door, **did** you?" "No, I forgot."

B

Normally we use a *negative* question tag after a *positive* sentence:

Positive Sentence + Negative Tag	
Maria **will** be here soon,	**won't she?**
There **was** a lot of traffic,	**wasn't there?**
Jim **should** take his medicine,	**shouldn't he?**

. . . and a *positive* question tag after a *negative* sentence:

Negative Sentence + Positive Tag	
Kate **won't** be late,	**will she?**
They **don't** like us,	**do they?**
You **haven't** paid the gas bill,	**have you?**

Notice the meaning of **yes** and **no** in answer to a negative sentence:

■ You're **not** going out today, **are you?**   **Yes.** (= Yes, I am going out)
  No. (= No, I am not going out)

C

The meaning of a tag depends on how you say it. If your voice goes *down*, you are not really asking a question; you are inviting the listener to agree with you:

■ "It's a nice day, **isn't it**?" "Yes, beautiful."
■ "Eric doesn't look too good today, **does he**?" "No, he looks very tired."
■ She's very funny. She has a wonderful sense of humor, **doesn't she**?

But if the voice goes *up*, it is a real question:

■ "You haven't seen Lisa today, **have you**?" "No, I haven't."
(= Have you seen Lisa today by any chance?)

You can use a *negative sentence + positive tag* to ask for things or information or to ask somebody to do something. The voice goes *up* at the end of the tag in sentences like these:

■ "You wouldn't have a pen, **would you**?" "Yes, here you are."
■ "You couldn't lend me some money, **could you**?" "It depends how much."
■ "You don't know where Lauren is, **do you**?" "Sorry, I have no idea."

D

After **Let's . . .** the tag is **shall we**:

■ **Let's** go for a walk, **shall we**? (the voice goes *up*)

After **Do/Listen/Give . . .** , etc. (imperative), the tag is usually **will you**:

■ **Listen** to me, **will you**? (the voice goes *up*)

After **I'm . . .** , the negative tag is **aren't I**? (= am I not?):

■ "**I'm** right, **aren't I**?" "Yes, you are."

Exercises

50.1 Put a tag question at the end of each sentence.

1.	Tom won't be late,	_will he_ ?	No, he's never late.
2.	You're tired,	_aren't you_ ?	Yes, a little.
3.	You've lived here a long time,	?	Yes, 20 years.
4.	You weren't listening,	?	Yes, I was!
5.	Sue doesn't know Ann,	?	No, they've never met.
6.	Jack's on vacation,	?	Yes, he's in Peru.
7.	Mike hasn't called today,	?	No, I don't think so.
8.	You can speak Spanish,	?	Yes, but not fluently.
9.	He won't mind if I use his phone,	?	No, of course he won't.
10.	There are a lot of people here,	?	Yes, more than I expected.
11.	Let's go out tonight,	?	Yes, that would be great.
12.	This isn't very interesting,	?	No, not at all.
13.	I'm too impatient,	?	Yes, you are sometimes.
14.	You wouldn't tell anyone,	?	No, of course not.
15.	Listen to me,	?	OK, I'm listening.
16.	I shouldn't have lost my temper,	?	No, but that's all right.
17.	He'd never met her before,	?	No, that was the first time.

50.2 Read the situation and write a sentence with a tag question. In each situation you are asking your friend to agree with you.

1. You look out of the window. The sky is blue and the sun is shining. What do you say to your friend? (beautiful day) _It's a beautiful day, isn't it?_

2. You're with a friend outside a restaurant. You're looking at the prices, which are very high. What do you say? (expensive) It _____

3. You and a colleague have just finished a training course. You really enjoyed it. What do you say to your colleague? (great) The course _____

4. Your friend's hair is much shorter than when you last met. What do you say to her/him? (have / your hair / cut) You _____

5. You and a friend are listening to a woman singing. You like her voice very much. What do you say to your friend? (a good voice) She _____

6. You are trying on a jacket in a store. You look in the mirror, and you don't like what you see. What do you say to your friend? (not / look / very good) It _____

7. You and a friend are walking over a small wooden bridge. The bridge is very old and some parts are broken. What do you say? (not / very safe) This bridge _____

50.3 In these situations you are asking for information and asking people to do things.

1. You need a pen. Maybe Kelly has one. Ask her.
   Kelly, you don't have a pen, do you?

2. The cashier is putting your groceries in a plastic bag, but maybe he could give you a paper bag. Ask him.
   Excuse me, you _____

3. You're looking for Ann. Maybe Kate knows where she is. Ask her.
   Kate, you _____

4. You need a bicycle pump. Maybe Nicole has one. Ask her.
   Nicole, _____

5. You're looking for your keys. Maybe Robert has seen them. Ask him.
   Robert, _____

6. Ann has a car and you need a ride to the station. Maybe she'll take you. Ask her.
   Ann, _____

Verb + -ing (enjoy doing / stop doing, etc.)

A

Look at these examples:

- I **enjoy** read**ing**. (*not* I enjoy to read)
- Would you **mind** clos**ing** the door?
  (*not* mind to close)
- Sam **suggested** go**ing** to the movies.
  (*not* suggested to go)

> Would you **mind**
> clos**ing** the door?

After **enjoy**, **mind**, and **suggest**, we use **-ing** (*not* to . . .).

Some more verbs that are followed by **-ing**:

stop	postpone	consider	admit
finish	avoid	imagine	deny
quit	risk	miss	recommend

- Suddenly everybody **stopped** talk**ing**. There was silence.
- I'll do the shopping when I've **finished** clean**ing** the apartment.
- He tried to **avoid** answer**ing** my question.
- Have you ever **considered** go**ing** to live in another country?

The negative form is **not -ing**:

- When I'm on vacation, I **enjoy not** hav**ing** to get up early.

B

We also use **-ing** after:

give up (= stop)
put off (= postpone)
go on (= continue)
keep *or* **keep on** (= do something continuously or repeatedly)

- Paula has **given up** try**ing** to lose weight.
- Jenny doesn't want to retire. She wants to **go on** work**ing**.
- You **keep** interrupt**ing** when I'm talking! *or* You **keep on** interrupt**ing** . . .

C

With some verbs you can use the structure *verb* + somebody + **-ing**:

- I can't **imagine George** rid**ing** a motorcycle.
- "Sorry to **keep you** wait**ing** so long." "That's all right."

Note the passive form (being **done/seen/kept**, etc.):

- I don't **mind being kept** waiting. (= I don't mind **people** keep**ing** me waiting.)

D

When you are talking about finished actions, you can say **having done/stolen/said**, etc.:

- They admitted **having stolen** the money.

But it is not necessary to use **having** (**done**). You can also say:

- They admitted **stealing** the money.
- I now regret **saying** (*or* **having said**) what I said.

For **regret**, see Unit 54B.

E

After some of the verbs on this page (especially **admit/deny/suggest**), you can also use **that** . . . .

- She **denied that** she had stolen the money. (*or* She **denied** steal**ing** . . .)
- Sam **suggested that** we go to the movies. (*or* Sam **suggested** go**ing** . . .)

Suggest Unit 32 *Being done (passive)* Unit 41B Verb + *to* . . . Unit 52
Verb + *to* . . . and *-ing* Units 53C, 54–56 *Regret / go on* Unit 54B *Go on / keep on* Unit 138A

Exercises

51.1 Complete each sentence with one of the following verbs (in the correct form):

~~answer~~	apply	be	forget	listen	pay
lose	make	read	try	use	write

1. He tried to avoid _answering_ my question.
2. Could you please stop _____ so much noise?
3. I enjoy _____ to music.
4. I considered _____ for the job, but in the end I decided against it.
5. Have you finished _____ the newspaper yet?
6. Let's buy a house. I don't want to go on _____ rent every month.
7. I don't mind you _____ the phone as long as you pay for all your calls.
8. My memory is getting worse. I keep _____ things.
9. I've put off _____ the letter so many times. I really have to do it today.
10. What a mean thing to do! Can you imagine anybody _____ so mean?
11. Sarah gave up _____ to find a job in this country and decided to go abroad.
12. If you invest your money in the stock market, you risk _____ it.

51.2 Complete the sentences for each situation using *-ing*.

1.
What should we do? / We could go to the movies.
She suggested _going to the movies_ .

2.
You were driving too fast. / You're right. Sorry!
She admitted _____
_____ .

3.
Let's go swimming. / Good idea!
She suggested _____
_____ .

4.
You broke my DVD player. / No, I didn't!
He denied _____
_____ .

5.
Can you wait a few minutes? / Sure, no problem.
They didn't mind _____
_____ .

51.3 Complete the sentences so that they mean the same as the first sentence. Use *-ing*.

1. She doesn't really want to retire.
   She wants to go on _working_ .
2. It's not a good idea to travel during rush hour.
   It's better to avoid _____ .
3. Should we leave tomorrow instead of today?
   Should we postpone _____ until _____ ?
4. Could you turn the radio down, please?
   Would you mind _____ ?
5. Please don't interrupt me all the time.
   Would you mind _____ ?

51.4 Use your own ideas to complete these sentences. Use *-ing*.

1. She's a very interesting person. I always enjoy _talking to her_ .
2. I'm afraid there aren't any chairs. I hope you don't mind _____ .
3. It was a beautiful day, so I suggested _____ .
4. It was very funny. I couldn't stop _____ .
5. My car isn't very reliable. It keeps _____ .

Verb + to . . . (decide to . . . / forget to . . . , etc.)

A

offer	decide	hope	deserve	promise
agree	plan	manage	afford	threaten
refuse	arrange	fail	forget	learn

After these verbs, you can use **to . . .** (*infinitive*):

- ■ It was late, so we **decided to take** a taxi home.
- ■ David was in a difficult situation, so I **agreed to help** him.
- ■ How old were you when you **learned to drive**? (*or* learned **how** to drive)
- ■ Karen **failed to make** a good impression at the job interview.

The negative is **not to . . .** :

- ■ We **decided not to go** out because of the weather.
- ■ I **promised not to be** late.

After some verbs, **to . . .** is not possible. For example, **enjoy/think/suggest**:

- ■ I **enjoy** read**ing**. (*not* enjoy to read)
- ■ Sam **suggested** go**ing** to the movies. (*not* suggested to go)
- ■ Are you **thinking of** buy**ing** a car? (*not* thinking to buy)

For *verb* + **-ing**, see Unit 51. For *verb* + *preposition* + **-ing**, see Unit 60.

B

We also use **to . . .** after:

seem	appear	tend	pretend	claim

For example:

- ■ They **seem to have** plenty of money.
- ■ I like Dan, but I think he **tends to talk** too much.
- ■ Ann **pretended not to see** me when she passed me on the street.

There is also a *continuous* infinitive (**to be** do**ing**) and a *perfect* infinitive (**to have** done):

- ■ I **pretended to be** read**ing** the newspaper. (= I pretended that I **was** read**ing**)
- ■ You **seem to have lost** weight. (= it seems that you **have lost** weight)
- ■ Joe **seems to be** enjoy**ing** his new job. (= it seems that he **is** enjoy**ing** it)

C

After **dare**, you can use a verb with or without **to**:

- ■ I wouldn't **dare to tell** him. *or* I wouldn't **dare tell** him.

D

After some verbs, you can use a question word (**what/whether/how**, etc.) + **to . . . .** We use this structure especially after:

ask	decide	know	remember	forget
learn	understand	wonder	explain	

We **asked**	how	to get	to the station.
Have you **decided**	where	to go	for your vacation?
I don't **know**	whether	to apply	for the job or not.
Do you **understand**	what	to do?	

Also: **show/tell/ask/advise/teach** somebody **what/how/where** to do something:

- ■ Can somebody **show me how to change** the film in this camera?
- ■ Ask Jack. He'll **tell you what to do**.

Verb + -ing Unit 51   **Verb + Object + to . . .** (*want*, etc.) Unit 53   **Verb + to . . . and -ing** Units 54–56

Exercises

52.1 Complete the sentences for these situations.

1. Should we get married? — Yes.

   They decided _to get married_ .

2. Please help me. — OK.

   She agreed _____ .

3. Can I carry your bags for you? — No, thanks. I can manage.

   He offered _____ .

4. Let's meet at 8:00. — OK, fine.

   They arranged _____ .

5. What's your name? — I'm not going to tell you.

   She refused _____ .

6. Please don't tell anyone. — I won't. I promise.

   She promised _____ .

52.2 Put the verb into the correct form, **to . . .** or **-ing**. (See Unit 51 for verb + **-ing**.)

1. When I'm tired, I enjoy _watching_ television. It's relaxing. (watch)
2. It was a nice day, so we decided _____ for a walk. (go)
3. There was a lot of traffic, but we managed _____ to the airport on time. (get)
4. I'm not in a hurry. I don't mind _____ . (wait)
5. They don't have much money. They can't afford _____ out very often. (eat)
6. We've got new computer software in our office. I haven't learned how _____ it yet. (use)
7. I wish that dog would stop _____ . It's driving me crazy. (bark)
8. Our neighbor threatened _____ the police if we didn't stop the noise. (call)
9. We were hungry, so I suggested _____ dinner early. (have)
10. We were all afraid to speak. Nobody dared _____ anything. (say)
11. Hurry up! I don't want to risk _____ the train. (miss)
12. I'm still looking for a job, but I hope _____ something soon. (find)

52.3 Make a new sentence using the verb in parentheses.

1. You've lost weight.   (seem)   _You seem to have lost weight._
2. Tom is worried about something. (appear) Tom appears _____
3. You know a lot of people.   (seem)   You _____
4. My English is getting better.   (seem)   _____
5. That car has broken down.   (appear) _____
6. David forgets things.   (tend)   _____
7. They have solved the problem.   (claim)   _____

52.4 Complete each sentence using **what/how/whether** + one of the following verbs:

   do   ~~get~~   **go**   **ride**   **say**   **use**

1. Do you know _how to get_ to John's house?
2. Can you show me _____ this washing machine?
3. Would you know _____ if there was a fire in the building?
4. You'll never forget _____ a bicycle once you've learned.
5. I was really astonished. I didn't know _____ .
6. I was invited to the party, but I haven't decided _____ or not.

Verb (+ Object) + to . . .
(I want you to . . . , etc.)

A

want	ask	help	expect
beg	would like	would prefer	mean (= intend)

These verbs are followed by **to . . .** (*infinitive*). The structure can be:

Verb + to . . .   or   *Verb + Object + to . . .*

- We **expected to be** late.
- **Would** you **like to go** now?
- He doesn't **want to know**.

- We **expected Dan to be** late.
- Would you **like me to go** now?
- He doesn't **want anybody to know**.

Do not say "want that":

- Do you **want me to come** with you? (*not* Do you want that I come)

After **help**, you can use the verb with or without **to**. So you can say:

- Can you help me **to move** this table? *or*   Can you help me **move** this table?

B

tell	remind	force	encourage	teach	enable
order	warn	invite	persuade	get	(= persuade, arrange for)

These verbs have the structure *verb + object + to . . .* :

- Can you **remind me to call** Ann tomorrow?
- Who **taught you to drive**?
- I didn't move the piano by myself. I **got somebody to help** me.
- Jim said the switch was dangerous and **warned me not to touch** it.

In the next example, the verb is *passive* (**I was warned / we were told**, etc.):

- **I was warned not to touch** the switch.

You cannot use **suggest** with the structure *verb + object + to . . .* :

- Jane **suggested that I ask** you for advice. (*not* Jane suggested me to ask)

C

After **advise** and **allow**, two structures are possible. Compare:

Verb + -ing (without an object)
- I wouldn't **advise stay**ing in that hotel.

- They don't **allow park**ing in front of the building.

Verb + Object + to . . .
- I wouldn't **advise anybody to stay** in that hotel.

- They don't **allow people to park** in front of the building.

Study these examples with (**be**) **allowed** (*passive*):

- Park**ing isn't allowed** in front of the building.

- You **aren't allowed to park** in front of the building.

D

Make and **let**

These verbs have the structure *verb + object + base form* (**do/open/feel**, etc.):

- I **made him promise** that he wouldn't tell anybody what happened. (*not* to promise)
- Hot weather **makes me feel** tired. (= causes me to feel tired)
- Her parents wouldn't **let her go** out alone. (= wouldn't allow her to go out)
- **Let me carry** your bag for you.

We say "**make somebody do**" (*not* to do), but the *passive* is "(**be**) **made to** do" (with **to**):

- We **were made to wait** for two hours. (= They **made us wait** . . .)

Exercises

53.1 Complete the questions. Use *do you want me to . . .* ? or *would you like me to . . .* ? with these verbs (+ any other necessary words):

~~come~~   lend   repeat   show   shut   wait

1. Do you want to go alone, or _do you want me to come with you_ ?
2. Do you have enough money, or do you want _____ ?
3. Should I leave the window open, or would you _____ ?
4. Do you know how to use the machine, or would _____ ?
5. Did you hear what I said, or do _____ ?
6. Can I go now, or do _____ ?

53.2 Complete the sentences for these situations.

1.
Lock the door.   OK.   She told _him to lock the door_ .

2.
Why don't you stay with us for a few days?   That would be nice.   They invited her _____ .

3.
Can I use your phone?   No!   She wouldn't let _____ .

4.
Be careful.   Don't worry. I will.   She warned _____ .

5.
Can you give me a hand?   Sure   He asked _____ .

53.3 Complete each second sentence so that the meaning is similar to the first sentence.

1. My father said I could use his car.   My father allowed _me to use his car._
2. I was surprised that it rained.   I didn't expect _____
3. Don't stop him from doing what he wants.   Let _____
4. He looks older when he wears glasses.   Glasses make _____
5. I think you should know the truth.   I want _____
6. Don't let me forget to call my sister.   Remind _____
7. At first I didn't want to apply for the job, but Sarah convinced me.   Sarah persuaded _____
                                                _____
8. My lawyer said I shouldn't say anything to the police.   My lawyer advised _____
                                                _____
9. I was told that I shouldn't believe everything he says.   I was warned _____
                                                _____
10. If you have a car, you are able to get around more easily.   Having a car enables _____
                                                _____

53.4 Put the verb in the right form: *-ing*, infinitive (*to do* / *to read*, etc.), or base form (*do/read*, etc.).

1. They don't allow people _to park_ in front of the building. (park)
2. I've never been to Hong Kong, but I'd like _____ there. (go)
3. I'm in a difficult position. What do you advise me _____ ? (do)
4. The movie was very sad. It made me _____ . (cry)
5. Lauren's parents always encouraged her _____ hard at school. (study)
6. I wouldn't advise _____ at that restaurant. The food is terrible. (eat)
7. She said the letter was personal and wouldn't let me _____ it. (read)
8. We are not allowed _____ personal phone calls at work. (make)
9. "I don't think Alex likes me." "What makes you _____ that?" (think)

Verb + -ing or to . . . 1 (remember/regret, etc.)

A

Some verbs are followed by **-ing**, and some are followed by **to . . . .**

Verbs usually followed by **-ing**:		
admit	finish	postpone
avoid	imagine	risk
consider	keep (on)	stop
deny	mind	suggest
enjoy		

For examples, see Unit 51.

Verbs usually followed by **to . . .** :		
afford	fail	offer
agree	forget	plan
arrange	hope	promise
decide	learn	refuse
deserve	manage	threaten

For examples, see Unit 52.

B

Some verbs can be followed by **-ing** or **to . . .** with a difference in meaning:

remember

I **remember doing** something = I did it and now I remember this.
You **remember doing** something *after* you have done it.

- I know I locked the door. I clearly **remember locking** it.
  (= I locked it, and now I remember this)
- He could **remember driving** along the road just before the accident, but he couldn't remember the accident itself.

I **remembered to do** something = I remembered that I had to do it, so I did it.
You **remember to do** something *before* you do it.

- I **remembered to lock** the door, but I forgot to shut the windows.
  (= I remembered that I had to lock it, and so I locked it)
- Please **remember to mail** the letter.
  (= don't forget to mail it)

regret

I **regret doing** something = I did it and now I'm sorry about it.

- I now **regret saying** what I said. I shouldn't have said it.
- It began to get cold and he **regretted not wearing** his coat.

I **regret to say / to tell** you **/ to inform** you = I'm sorry that I have to say (etc.):

- *(from a formal letter)* We **regret to inform** you that we cannot offer you the job.

go on

Go on doing something = continue doing the same thing:

- The president **went on talking** for hours.
- We need to change. We can't **go on living** like this.

Go on to do something = do or say something new:

- After discussing the economy, the president then **went on to talk** about foreign policy.

C

The following verbs can be followed by **-ing** or **to . . .** :
   begin   start   continue   bother

So you can say:

- It has **started raining**.   *or*   It has **started to rain**.
- Don't **bother locking** the door.   *or*   Don't **bother to lock** . . .

But normally we do not use **-ing** after **-ing**:

- It's star**ting to rain**. (*not* It's starting raining)

Verb + *-ing* Unit 51   **Verb +** *to* **. . .** Units 52–53   **Other Verbs +** *-ing* **or** *to* **. . .** Units 55–56

Exercises

54.1 Put the verb into the correct form, *-ing* or *to . . . .* Sometimes either form is possible.

1. They denied ___*stealing*___ the money. (steal)
2. I don't enjoy _____ very much. (drive)
3. I don't want _____ out tonight. I'm too tired. (go)
4. I can't afford _____ out tonight. I don't have enough money. (go)
5. Has it stopped _____ yet? (rain)
6. Our team was really unlucky yesterday. We deserved _____ the game. (win)
7. Why do you keep _____ me questions? Can't you leave me alone? (ask)
8. Please stop _____ me questions! (ask)
9. I refuse _____ any more questions. (answer)
10. One of the boys admitted _____ the window. (break)
11. The boy's father promised _____ for the window to be repaired. (pay)
12. If the company continues _____ money, the factory may be closed. (lose)
13. "Does Sarah know about the meeting?" "No, I forgot _____ her." (tell)
14. The baby began _____ in the middle of the night. (cry)
15. Julie has been sick, but now she's beginning _____ better. (get)
16. I enjoyed _____ you. I hope _____ you again soon. (meet, see)

54.2 Here is some information about Tom when he was a child.

1. He was in the hospital when he was four.   4. He went to Miami when he was eight.
2. He cried on his first day of school.   5. Once he fell into a river.
3. He said he wanted to be a doctor.   6. Once he was bitten by a dog.

He can still remember 1, 2, and 4. But he can't remember 3, 5, and 6. Write sentences beginning **He can remember . . .** or **He can't remember . . . .**

1. ___*He can remember being in the hospital when he was four.*___
2. _____
3. _____
4. _____
5. _____
6. _____

54.3 Complete each sentence with an appropriate verb in the correct form, *-ing* or *to . . . .*

1. a) Please remember ___*to lock*___ the door when you go out.
   b) *A:* You lent me some money a few months ago.
      B: I did? Are you sure? I don't remember _____ you any money.
   c) *A:* Did you remember _____ your sister?
      B: Oh no, I completely forgot. I'll call her tomorrow.
   d) When you see Amanda, remember _____ hello for me, OK?
   e) Someone must have taken my bag. I clearly remember _____ it by the window, and now it's gone.
2. a) I believe that what I said was fair. I don't regret _____ it.
   b) I knew they were in trouble, but I regret _____ I did nothing to help them.
3. a) Ben joined the company nine years ago. He became assistant manager after two years, and a few years later he went on _____ manager of the company.
   b) I can't go on _____ here anymore. I want a different job.
   c) When I came into the room, Liz was reading a newspaper. She looked up and said hello and then went on _____ her newspaper.

Verb + -ing or to . . . 2 (try/need/help)

A

Try to . . . and try -ing

Try to do = attempt to do, make an effort to do:
- I was very tired. I **tried to keep** my eyes open, but I couldn't.
- Please **try to be** quiet when you come home. Everyone will be asleep.

Try also means "do something as an experiment or test." For example:
- These cookies are delicious. You should **try** one. (= you should have one to see if you like it)
- We couldn't find anywhere to stay. We **tried** every hotel in the town, but they were all full. (= we went to every hotel to see if they had a room)

If **try** (with this meaning) is followed by a verb, we say **try -ing**:
- *A:* The photocopier doesn't seem to be working.
- *B:* **Try pressing** the green button. (= press the green button − maybe this will help to solve the problem)

Compare:
- I **tried to move** the table, but it was too heavy. (so I couldn't move it)
- I didn't like the way the furniture was arranged, so I **tried moving** the table to the other side of the room. But it still didn't look right, so I moved it back again.

B

Need to do, need to be done, and need doing

I **need to do** something = it is necessary for me to do it:
- I **need to get** more exercise.
- He **needs to work** harder if he wants to make progress.
- I don't **need to come** to the meeting, do I?

This room **needs to be cleaned up**.

Something **needs to be done** = someone needs to do it:
- My cell phone **needs to be charged**.
- Do you think my pants **need to be washed**?

Sometimes we use **need doing** instead of **need to be done**:
- My cell phone **needs charging**.
- Do you think my pants **need washing**?

C

Help and can't help

You can say **help to do** or **help do** (with or without **to**):
- Everybody **helped to clean up** after the party.   *or*
  Everybody **helped clean up** . . .
- Can you **help** me **to move** this table?   *or*
  Can you **help** me move . . .

I **can't help doing** something = I can't stop myself from doing it:
- I don't like him, but he has a lot of problems. I **can't help feeling** sorry for him.
- She tried to be serious, but she **couldn't help laughing**. (= she couldn't stop herself from laughing)
- I'm sorry I'm so nervous. I **can't help it**.
  (= I **can't help being** nervous)

Exercises

55.1 Make suggestions. Write sentences using *try* + the following suggestions:

call his office   ~~change the batteries~~   **turn it the other way**   **take an aspirin**

1. The radio isn't working. I wonder what's wrong with it.

   Have you _*tried changing the batteries?*_____

2. I can't open the door. The key won't turn.

   Try _____

3. I have a terrible headache. I wish I could get rid of it.

   Have you _____

4. I can't reach Fred. He's not at home. What should I do?

   Why don't you _____

55.2 For each picture, write a sentence with *need(s)* + one of the following verbs:

~~clean~~   cut   empty   paint   tighten

1. These pants are dirty. _*They need to be cleaned.*_ OR _*They need cleaning.*_____
2. The room doesn't look very nice. _____
3. The grass is very long. It _____
4. The screws are loose. _____
5. The garbage can is full. _____

55.3 Put the verb into the correct form.

1. a) I was very tired. I tried _*to keep*_____ (keep) my eyes open, but I couldn't.
   b) I rang the doorbell, but there was no answer. Then I tried _____ (knock) on the door, but there was still no answer.
   c) We tried _____ (put) out the fire, but we were unsuccessful. We had to call the fire department.
   d) Sue needed to borrow some money. She tried _____ (ask) Jerry, but he was short of money, too.
   e) I tried _____ (reach) the shelf, but I wasn't tall enough.
   f) Please don't bother me. I'm trying _____ (concentrate).

2. a) I need a change. I need _____ (go) away for a while.
   b) My grandmother isn't able to look after herself anymore. She needs _____ (look) after.
   c) The windows are dirty. They need _____ (wash).
   d) Your hair is getting very long. It needs _____ (cut).
   e) You don't need _____ (iron) that shirt. It doesn't need _____ (iron).

3. a) They were talking very loudly. I couldn't help _____ (overhear) them.
   b) Can you help me _____ (get) dinner ready?
   c) He looks so funny. Whenever I see him, I can't help _____ (smile).
   d) The beautiful weather helped _____ (make) it a wonderful vacation.

Verb + -ing or to . . . 3
(like / would like, etc.)

Like / love / hate

When you talk about repeated actions, you can use **-ing** or **to** . . . after these verbs.
So you can say:

- Do you **like** gett**ing** up early?   *or*   Do you **like to get** up early?
- Stephanie **hates** fly**ing**.   *or*   Stephanie **hates to fly**.
- I **love** meet**ing** people.   *or*   I **love to meet** people.
- I don't **like** be**ing** kept waiting.   *or*   . . . **like to be** kept waiting.
- I don't **like** friends call**ing** me at work.   *or*   . . . friends **to call** me at work.

but

(1) We use **-ing** (*not* **to** . . .) when we talk about a situation that already exists (or existed).

For example:
- Paul lives in Vancouver now. He **likes** liv**ing** there. (He **likes** liv**ing** in Vancouver = He lives there and he likes it)
- Do you **like** be**ing** a student? (You are a student – do you like it?)
- The office I worked at was horrible. I **hated** work**ing** there. (I worked there and I hated it)

(2) There is sometimes a difference between **I like to do** and **I like doing**:

I like doing something = I do it and I enjoy it:
- I **like** clean**ing** the kitchen. (= I enjoy it)

I like to do something = I think it is a good thing to do, but I don't necessarily enjoy it:
- It's not my favorite job, but I **like to clean** the kitchen as often as possible.

Note that **enjoy** and **mind** are always followed by **-ing** (*not* **to** . . .):
- I **enjoy** clean**ing** the kitchen. (*not* I enjoy to clean)
- I **don't mind** clean**ing** the kitchen. (*not* I don't mind to clean)

Would like / would love / would hate / would prefer

Would like / would love, etc., are usually followed by **to** . . . :
- I'**d like** (= **would** like) to go away for a few days.
- **Would** you **like to come** to dinner on Friday?
- I **wouldn't like to go** on vacation alone.
- I'**d love to meet** your family.
- **Would** you **prefer to have** dinner now or later?

Compare **I like** and **I would like** (**I'd** like):
- I **like playing** tennis. / I **like to play** tennis. (= I like it in general)
- I'**d like to play** tennis today. (= I want to play today)

Would mind is always followed by **-ing** (*not* **to** . . .):
- **Would** you **mind closing** the door, please?

I would like **to have done** something = I regret now that I didn't or couldn't do it:
- It's too bad we didn't see Johnny when we were in Nashville. I **would like to have seen** him again.
- We'**d like to have gone** on vacation, but we didn't have enough money.

You can use the same structure after **would love / would hate / would prefer**:
- Poor Tom! I **would hate to have been** in his position.
- I'**d love to have gone** to the party, but it was impossible.

Exercises

56.1 Write sentences about yourself. Say whether you like or don't like these activities.
Choose one of these verbs for each sentence:

> **like / don't like   love   hate   enjoy   don't mind**

1. (fly) _I don't like flying. OR I don't like to fly._
2. (play cards) _____
3. (be alone) _____
4. (go to museums) _____
5. (cook) _____

56.2 Make sentences from the words in parentheses. Use *-ing* or *to* . . . . Sometimes either form is possible.

1. Paul lives in Vancouver now. It's nice. He likes it.
   (he / like / live / there) _He likes living there._
2. Jane is a biology teacher. She likes her job.
   (she / like / teach / biology) She _____
3. Joe always carries his camera with him and takes a lot of photographs.
   (he / like / take / photographs) _____
4. I used to work in a supermarket. I didn't like it much.
   (I / not / like / work / there) _____
5. Rachel is studying medicine. She likes it.
   (she / like / study / medicine) _____
6. Dan is famous, but he doesn't like it.
   (he / not / like / be / famous) _____
7. Jennifer is a very cautious person. She doesn't take many risks.
   (she / not / like / take / risks) _____
8. I don't like surprises.
   (I / like / know / things / ahead of time) _____

56.3 Complete each sentence with a verb in the correct form, *-ing* or *to* . . . . In some sentences either form is possible.

1. It's good to visit other places – I enjoy __traveling__ .
2. "Would you like _____ down?"   "No, thanks, I'll stand."
3. I'm not quite ready yet. Would you mind _____ a little longer?
4. When I was a child, I hated _____ to bed early.
5. When I have to catch a plane, I'm always worried that I'll miss it. So I like
   _____ to the airport ahead of time.
6. I enjoy _____ busy. I don't like it when there's nothing to do.
7. I would love _____ to your wedding, but unfortunately I can't.
8. I don't like _____ in this part of town. I want to move somewhere else.
9. Do you have a minute? I'd like _____ to you about something.
10. When there's bad news and good news, I like _____ the bad news first.

56.4 Write sentences using *would* . . . *to have* (*done*). Use the verbs in parentheses.

1. It's too bad I couldn't go to the wedding. (like) _I would like to have gone to the wedding._
2. It's a shame I didn't see the program. (like) _____
3. I'm glad I didn't lose my watch. (hate) _____
4. It's too bad I didn't meet your parents. (love) _____
5. I'm glad I wasn't alone. (not / like) _____
6. It's a shame I couldn't travel by train. (prefer) _____

Prefer and would rather

A

Prefer to do and **prefer doing**

You can use **prefer to (do)** or **prefer –ing** to say what you prefer in general:

■ I don't like cities. I **prefer to live** in the country.   *or*   I **prefer living** in the country.

Study the differences in structure after **prefer**. We say:

	I prefer	something	**to** something else.
	I prefer	**doing** something	**to doing** something else.
but	I prefer	**to do** something	**rather than (do)** something else.

■ I **prefer** this coat **to** the coat you were wearing yesterday.
■ I **prefer driving to traveling** by train.

but

■ I **prefer to drive rather than travel** by train.
■ Ann **prefers to live** in the country **rather than** in a city.   *or*   . . . **rather than live** in a city.

B

Would prefer (I'd prefer . . .)

We use **would prefer** to say what somebody wants in a specific situation (not in general):

■ "**Would** you **prefer** tea or coffee?"   "Coffee, please."

We say "would prefer **to do**" (*not* doing):

■ "Should we take the train?"   "No, I**'d prefer to drive**." (*not* I'd prefer driving)
■ I**'d prefer to stay** at home tonight **rather than go** to the movies.

C

Would rather (I'd rather . . .)

Would rather (do) = **would prefer** (to do). We use **would rather** + *base form* (**do/have/stay**, etc.).
Compare:

■ "Should we take the train?"   { "I**'d prefer to drive**."
                                  "I**'d rather drive**." (*not* to drive)

■ "**Would** you **rather have** tea or coffee?"   "Coffee, please."

The negative is I**'d rather not** (do something):

■ I'm tired. I**'d rather not go** out tonight, if you don't mind.
■ "Do you want to go out tonight?"   "I**'d rather not**."

We say "**would rather do** something **than do** something else":

■ I**'d rather stay** at home tonight **than go** to the movies.

D

I**'d rather** you **did** something

We say "I**'d rather** you **did** something" (*not* I'd rather you do). For example:

■ "I'll fix your car tomorrow, OK?"   "I**'d rather** you **did** it today." (= I'd prefer this)
■ "Is it OK if Ben stays here?"   "I**'d rather** he **came** with us." (*not* he comes)
■ Shall I tell them, or **would** you **rather** they **didn't** know? (*not* don't know)

In this structure, we use the *past* (**did/came**, etc.), but the meaning is *not* past.
Compare:

■ I'd rather **make** dinner now.

but   I'd rather you **made** dinner now. (*not* I'd rather you make)

I**'d rather you didn't** (do something) = I'd prefer that you not do it:

■ I**'d rather you didn't tell** anyone what I said.
■ "Should I tell Stephanie?"   "I**'d rather you didn't**."

Exercises

57.1 Which do you prefer? Write sentences using *I prefer* (something) *to* (something else). Put the verb into the correct form where necessary.

1. (drive / fly)
   I prefer driving to flying.
2. (tennis / soccer)
   I prefer _____
3. (call people / send e-mails)
   I _____ to _____
4. (go to the movies / watch videos at home)
   _____

Now rewrite sentences 3 and 4 using the structure *I prefer to* (do something) *rather than* (something else).

5. (1) _I prefer to drive rather than fly._
6. (3) I prefer to _____
7. (4) _____

57.2 Write sentences using *I'd prefer* . . . or *I'd rather* . . . + the following:

eat at home	~~take a taxi~~	go alone
wait a few minutes	listen to some music	stand
go for a swim	~~wait till later~~	think about it for a while

1. Should we walk home? (prefer) _I'd prefer to take a taxi._
2. Do you want to eat now? (rather) _I'd rather wait till later._
3. Would you like to watch TV? (rather) _____
4. Do you want to go to a restaurant? (prefer) _____
5. Let's leave now. (rather) _____
6. What about a game of tennis? (rather) _____
7. I think we should decide now. (prefer) _____
8. Would you like to sit down? (rather) _____
9. Do you want me to come with you? (prefer) _____

Now use the same ideas to complete these sentences using *than* and *rather than*.

10. I'd prefer to take a taxi _rather than walk home._
11. I'd prefer to go for a swim _____
12. I'd rather eat at home _____
13. I'd prefer to think about it for a while _____
14. I'd rather listen to some music _____

57.3 Complete the sentences using *would you rather I* . . . .

1. Are you going to make dinner or _would you rather I made it_ ?
2. Are you going to tell Ann what happened or would you rather _____ ?
3. Are you going to go shopping or _____ ?
4. Are you going to call Diane or _____ ?

57.4 Complete the sentences.

1. "Should I tell Ann the news?" "No, I'd rather she _didn't_ know."
2. Do you want me to go now, or would you rather I _____ here?
3. Do you want to go out tonight or would you rather _____ at home?
4. This is a private letter addressed to me. I'd rather you _____ read it.
5. I don't really like these shoes. I'd rather they _____ a different color.
6. *A:* Do you mind if I turn on the radio?
   B: I'd rather you _____ . I'm trying to study.

Preposition (in/for/about, etc.) + -ing

If a preposition (**in/for/about**, etc.) is followed by a *verb*, the verb ends in **-ing**:

	Preposition	Verb (-ing)	
Are you interested	**in**	work**ing**	for us?
I'm not very good	**at**	learn**ing**	languages.
Sue must be fed up	**with**	study**ing**.	
What are the advantages	**of**	hav**ing**	a car?
Thanks very much	**for**	invit**ing**	me to your party.
How	**about**	meet**ing**	for lunch tomorrow?
Why don't you go out	**instead of**	sitt**ing**	at home all the time?
Carol went to work	**in spite of**	feel**ing**	sick.

You can also say "instead of **somebody** doing something," "fed up with **people** doing something," etc.:

- I'm fed up with **people** telling me what to do.

Note the use of the following prepositions + **-ing**:

before -ing and **after -ing**:

- **Before going** out, I called Sarah. (*not* Before to go out)
- What did you do **after finishing** school?

You can also say "**Before I went** out . . ." and ". . . **after you finished** school."

by -ing (to say *how* something happens):

- The burglars got into the house **by** break**ing** a window and climb**ing** in.
- You can improve your English **by** read**ing** more.
- She made herself sick **by** not eat**ing** properly.
- Many accidents are caused **by** people driv**ing** too fast.

without -ing:

- We ran 10 miles **without** stopp**ing**.
- It was a stupid thing to say. I said it **without** think**ing**.
- She needs to work **without** people disturb**ing** her. (*or* . . . **without** be**ing** disturbed.)
- I have enough problems of my own **without** hav**ing** to worry about yours.

To -ing (look forward **to** do**ing** something, etc.)

To is part of the *infinitive* (**to** do / **to** see, etc.):

- We decided **to go** out.
- Would you like **to meet** for lunch tomorrow?

But **to** is also a *preposition* (like **in/for/about/from**, etc.). For example:

- We drove from Houston **to Chicago**.
- I prefer tea **to coffee**.
- Are you looking forward **to the weekend**?

If a preposition is followed by a verb, the verb ends in **-ing**:

> **in** do**ing**   **about** meet**ing**   **without** stopp**ing** (etc.)

So, when **to** is a preposition and it is followed by a verb, you must say **to -ing**:

- I prefer driving **to** travel**ing** by train. (*not* to travel)
- Are you looking forward **to** go**ing** on vacation? (*not* looking forward to go)

Be/get used to -ing Unit 59   Verb + Preposition + *-ing* Unit 60   *While/when -ing* Unit 66B
In spite of Unit 110   Prepositions Units 118–133

Exercises

58.1 Complete the second sentence so that it means the same as the first.

1. Why is it useful to have a car?
   What are the advantages of _having a car_ ?
2. I don't intend to apply for the job.
   I have no intention of _____ .
3. Karen has a good memory for names.
   Karen is good at _____ .
4. Mark won't pass the exam. He has no chance.
   Mark has no chance of _____ .
5. Did you get into trouble because you were late?
   Did you get into trouble for _____ ?
6. We didn't eat at home. We went to a restaurant instead.
   Instead of _____ .
7. We got into the exhibition. We didn't have to wait in line.
   We got into the exhibition without _____ .
8. Our team played well, but we lost the game.
   Our team lost the game in spite of _____ .

58.2 Complete the sentences using **by -ing**. Use the following (with the verb in the correct form):

borrow too much money	~~break a window~~	drive too fast
put some pictures on the walls	stand on a chair	turn a key

1. The burglars got into the house _by breaking a window_ .
2. I was able to reach the top shelf _____ .
3. You start the engine of a car _____ .
4. Kevin got himself into financial trouble _____ .
5. You can put people's lives in danger _____ .
6. We made the room look nicer _____ .

58.3 Complete the sentences with an appropriate word. Use only one word each time.

1. We ran 10 miles without _stopping_ .
2. He left the hotel without _____ his bill.
3. It's a nice morning. How about _____ for a walk?
4. We were able to translate the letter into English without _____ a dictionary.
5. Before _____ to bed, I like to have a hot drink.
6. It was a long trip. I was very tired after _____ on a train for 36 hours.
7. I was annoyed because the decision was made without anybody _____ me.
8. After _____ the same job for 10 years, I felt I needed a change.
9. We got lost because we went straight instead of _____ left.
10. I like these pictures you took. You're good at _____ pictures.

58.4 For each situation, write a sentence with **I'm (not) looking forward to**.

1. You are going on vacation next week. How do you feel?
   I'm looking forward to going on vacation.
2. Diane is a good friend of yours and she is coming to visit you soon. So you will see her again soon. How do you feel? I'm _____
3. You are going to the dentist tomorrow. You don't enjoy going to the dentist. How do you feel?
   I'm not _____
4. Carol hates school, but she is graduating next summer. How does she feel?
   _____
5. You've arranged to play tennis tomorrow. You like tennis a lot. How do you feel?
   _____

Be/get used to something (I'm used to . . .)

A

Study this example situation:

Lisa

Lisa is American, but she lives in Tokyo. When she first drove a car in Japan, she found it very difficult because she had to drive on the left, not on the right. Driving on the left was strange and difficult for her because:

She **wasn't used to it**.
She **wasn't used to driving** on the left.

But after a lot of practice, driving on the left became less strange. So:
She **got used to driving** on the left.

Now it's no problem for Lisa:
She **is used to driving** on the left.

B

I'm used to something = it is not new or strange for me:

- Frank lives alone. He doesn't mind this because he has lived alone for 15 years. It is not strange for him. He **is used to it**. He **is used to living** alone.
- I bought some new shoes. They felt strange at first because I **wasn't used to them**.
- Our new apartment is on a very busy street. I expect we'll **get used to the noise**, but for now it's very annoying.
- Diane has a new job. She has to get up much earlier now than before – at 6:30. She finds this difficult, because she **isn't used to getting up** so early.
- Barbara's husband is often away. She doesn't mind. She **is used to him** being away.

C

After **be/get used** you cannot use the *infinitive* (**to do/to drive**, etc.). We say:

- She is used **to driving** on the left. (*not* She is used to drive)

When we say "I **am used to** something," **to** is a *preposition*, not a part of the infinitive. So we say:

- Frank is used **to living** alone. (*not* Frank is used to live)
- Lisa had to get used **to driving** on the left. (*not* get used to drive)

D

Do not confuse **I am used to doing** and **I used to do**:

I am used **to** (**doing**) something = it isn't strange or new for me:

- I **am** used **to the weather** in this country.
- I **am** used **to driving** on the left because I've lived in Japan a long time.

I used **to do** something = I did it regularly in the past but no longer do it.
You can use this only for the past, not for the present.
The structure is "I **used** to do" (*not* "I **am** used to do"):

- I **used to drive** to work every day, but these days I usually ride my bike.
- We **used to live** in a small town, but now we live in Los Angeles.

Exercises

59.1 Look again at the situation in Section A on the opposite page ("Lisa is American . . ."). The following situations are similar. Complete the sentences using *used to*.

1. Juan is Spanish and went to live in Canada. In Spain he usually had dinner late in the evening, but in Canada dinner was at 6:00. This was very early for him, and he found it very strange at first.

   When Juan first went to Canada, he __*wasn't used to having*__ dinner so early, but after a while he _____ it. Now he finds it normal.
   He _____ at 6:00.

2. Julia is a nurse. A year ago she started working nights. At first she found it hard and didn't like it.

   She _____ nights, and it took her a few months to _____ it. Now, after a year, she's pretty happy. She _____ nights.

59.2 What do you say in these situations? Use *I'm (not) used to* . . . .

1. You live alone. You don't mind this. You have always lived alone.
   Friend: Do you get a little lonely sometimes?
   You: No, __*I'm used to living alone.*__

2. You sleep on the floor. You don't mind this. You have always slept on the floor.
   Friend: Wouldn't you prefer to sleep in a bed?
   You: No, I _____

3. You have to work long hours in your job. This is not a problem for you. You have always worked long hours.
   Friend: You have to work very long hours in your job, don't you?
   You: Yes, but I don't mind that. I _____

4. You usually go to bed early. Last night you went to bed very late (for you) and as a result, you are very tired this morning.
   Friend: You look tired this morning.
   You: Yes, _____

59.3 Read the situations and complete the sentences using *get/got used to*.

1. Some friends of yours have just moved into an apartment on a busy street. It's very noisy.
   They'll have to __*get used to the noise.*__

2. Sue moved from a big house to a much smaller one. She found it strange at first.
   She had to _____ in a much smaller house.

3. The children at school got a new teacher. She was different from the teacher before her, but this wasn't a problem for the children. They soon _____

4. Some people you know from the United States are going to live in your country. What will they have to get used to?
   They'll have to _____

59.4 Complete the sentences using only one word each time (see Section C).

1. Lisa had to get used to __*driving*__ on the left.
2. We used to __*live*__ in a small town, but now we live in Los Angeles.
3. Tom used to _____ a lot of coffee. Now he prefers tea.
4. I feel very full after that meal. I'm not used to _____ so much.
5. I wouldn't like to share an office. I'm used to _____ my own office.
6. I used to _____ a car, but I sold it a few months ago.
7. When we were children, we used to _____ swimming every day.
8. There used to _____ a movie theater here, but it was torn down a few years ago.
9. I'm the boss here! I'm not used to _____ told what to do.

UNIT 60

Verb + Preposition + -ing (succeed in -ing / accuse somebody of -ing, etc.)

A

Many verbs have the structure *verb* + *preposition* (**in/for/about**, etc.) + *object*.

For example:

	Verb +	Preposition	+ Object
We **talked**	about	the problem.
You should **apologize**	for	what you said.

If the *object* is another verb, it ends in **-ing**:

	Verb +	Preposition	+ -ing (Object)
We **talked**	about	go**ing** to South America.
You should **apologize**	for	not tell**ing** the truth.

Some more verbs with this structure:

succeed (in)	Have you **succeeded**	in	find**ing** a job yet?
insist (on)	They **insisted**	on	pay**ing** for dinner.
think (of)	I'm **thinking**	of	buy**ing** a house.
dream (of)	I wouldn't **dream**	of	ask**ing** them for money.
approve (of)	He doesn't **approve**	of	swear**ing**.
decide (against)	We have **decided**	against	mov**ing** to Chicago.
feel (like)	Do you **feel**	like	go**ing** out tonight?
look forward (to)	I'm **looking forward**	to	meet**ing** her.

You can also say "approve of **somebody** doing something," "look forward to **somebody** doing something":

■ I don't approve **of people** kill**ing** animals for fun.
■ We are all looking forward **to Bob** com**ing** home.

B

The following verbs can have the structure *verb* + *object* + *preposition* + **-ing**:

	Verb +	Object +	Preposition	+ -ing (Object)
congratulate (on)	I **congratulated**	Ann	on	gett**ing** a new job.
accuse (of)	They **accused**	us	of	tell**ing** lies.
suspect (of)	Nobody **suspected**	the general	of	be**ing** a spy.
prevent (from)	What **prevented**	you	from	com**ing** to see us?
keep (from)	The noise **keeps**	me	from	fall**ing** asleep.
stop (from)	The rain didn't **stop**	us	from	enjoy**ing** our vacation.
thank (for)	I forgot to **thank**	them	for	help**ing** me.
excuse (for)	Please **excuse**	me	for	not return**ing** your call.

Some of these verbs are often used in the *passive*. For example:

■ We **were accused of** tell**ing** lies.
■ The general **was suspected of** be**ing** a spy.

Note that we say "**apologize to somebody** for . . . ":

■ I **apologized to them** for keeping them waiting. (*not* I apologized them)

Decide to . . . Unit 52A **Preposition +** *-ing* Unit 58 **Verb + Preposition** Units 129–133

Exercises

60.1 Complete each sentence using only one word.

1. Our neighbors apologized for ___*making*___ so much noise.
2. I feel lazy. I don't feel like _____ any work.
3. I wanted to go out alone, but Joe insisted on _____ with me.
4. I'm fed up with my job. I'm thinking of _____ something else.
5. We have decided against _____ a new car because we can't really afford it.
6. I hope you get in touch with me soon. I'm looking forward to _____ from you.
7. The weather was extremely bad and this kept us from _____ out.
8. The man who was arrested is suspected of _____ a false passport.
9. I think you should apologize to Sue for _____ so rude to her.
10. Some parents don't approve of their children _____ a lot of television.
11. I'm sorry I can't come to your party, but thank you very much for _____ me.

60.2 Complete each sentence using a preposition + one of the following verbs (in the correct form):

carry	cause	escape	~~go~~	interrupt
live	see	solve	spend	walk

1. Do you feel ___*like going*___ out tonight?
2. It took us a long time, but we finally succeeded _____ the problem.
3. I've always dreamed _____ in a small house by the sea.
4. The driver of the other car accused me _____ the accident.
5. There's a fence around the lawn to stop people _____ on the grass.
6. Excuse me _____ you, but may I ask you something?
7. Where are you thinking _____ your vacation this year?
8. The guards weren't able to prevent the prisoner _____ .
9. My bag wasn't very heavy, but Dave insisted _____ it for me.
10. It's too bad Paul can't come to the party. I was really looking forward _____ him.

60.3 Complete the sentences on the right.

1. You / Kevin
   It was nice of you to help me. Thanks a lot.
   Kevin thanked ___*me for helping him*___ .

2. Ann / Tom
   I'll take you to the station. I insist.
   Tom insisted _____
   _____ .

3. You / Dan
   I hear you got married. Congratulations!
   Dan congratulated me _____
   _____ .

4. Sue / Jenny
   It was nice of you to come to see me. Thank you.
   Jenny thanked _____
   _____ .

5. You / Kate
   I'm sorry I didn't call earlier.
   Kate apologized _____
   _____ .

6. You / Jane
   You're selfish.
   Jane accused _____
   _____ .

Expressions + -ing

A

When these expressions are followed by a verb, the verb ends in **-ing**:

There's no point in . . . :
- **There's no point in** hav**ing** a car if you never use it.
- **There was no point in** wait**ing** any longer, so we left.

But we usually say "**the** point **of** do**ing** something":
- **What's the point of** hav**ing** a car if you never use it?

There's no use / It's no use . . . :
- There's nothing you can do about the situation, so **there's no use** worry**ing** about it.
- *or* . . . **it's no use** worry**ing** about it.

It's (not) worth . . . :
- I live only a short walk from here, so **it's not worth** tak**ing** a taxi.
- Our flight was very early in the morning, so **it wasn't worth** go**ing** to bed.

You can say "a movie is **worth seeing**," "a book is **worth reading**," etc.:
- What was the movie like? Was it **worth seeing**?
- Thieves broke into the house but didn't take anything. There was nothing **worth stealing**.

B

Have trouble -ing, have difficulty -ing, have a problem -ing

We say "**have trouble** do**ing** something" (*not* to do):
- I **had** no **trouble** find**ing** a place to live. (*not* trouble to find)
- Did you **have** any **trouble** gett**ing** a visa?
- People often **have** a lot of **trouble** read**ing** my writing.

You can also say "have **difficulty / a problem** doing something":
- I had **difficulty** find**ing** a place to live.   *or*
  I had **a problem** find**ing** a place to live.

C

We use **-ing** after:

spend/waste (time)
- He **spent** hours try**ing** to repair the clock.
- I **waste** a lot of time daydream**ing**.

(be) **busy**
- She said she couldn't go with us. She was too **busy** do**ing** other things.

D

Go swimming / go fishing, etc.

We use **go -ing** for a number of activities (especially sports). For example, you can say:

go swimm**ing**   **go** sail**ing**   **go** fish**ing**   **go** hik**ing**   **go** ski**ing**   **go** jogg**ing**

Also **go** shopp**ing**, **go** sightsee**ing**
- How often do you **go** swimm**ing**?
- I'd like to **go** ski**ing**.
- When was the last time you **went** shopp**ing**?
- I've never **gone** sail**ing**.

Exercises

61.1 Make sentences beginning *There's no point . . . .*

1. Why have a car if you never use it?
   There's no point in having a car if you never use it.

2. Why work if you don't need money?
   _____

3. Don't try to study if you feel tired.
   _____

4. Why hurry if you've got plenty of time?
   _____

61.2 Complete the sentences on the right.

1.	Should we take a taxi home?	No, it isn't far. It's not worth _taking a taxi_ .
2.	If you need help, why don't you ask Dave?	There's no use _____ . He won't be able to do anything.
3.	I don't really want to go out tonight.	Well, stay at home! There's no point _____ _____ if you don't want to.
4.	Should I call Ann now?	No, don't waste your time _____ now. She won't be home.
5.	Are you going to complain about what happened?	No, it's not worth _____ . Nobody will do anything about it.
6.	Do you ever read newspapers?	No, I'm usually too busy _____ care of the kids.
7.	Do you want to keep these old clothes?	No, let's throw them away. They're not worth _____ .

61.3 Complete the sentences.

1. I managed to get a visa, but it was difficult.
   I had trouble _getting a visa_ .
2. I find it hard to remember people's names.
   I have a problem _____ .
3. Sarah managed to get a job without any trouble.
   She had no difficulty _____ .
4. It won't be difficult to get a ticket for the game.
   You won't have any trouble _____ .
5. Do you think it's difficult to understand him?
   Do you have a problem _____ ?

61.4 Complete the sentences. Use only one word each time.

1. I waste a lot of time _daydreaming_ .
2. Every morning I spend about an hour _____ the newspaper.
3. "What's Karen doing?" "She's going away tomorrow, so she's busy _____ ."
4. I think you waste too much time _____ television.
5. There's a beautiful view from that hill. It's worth _____ to the top.
6. There's no use _____ for the job. I know I wouldn't get it.
7. Just stay calm. There's no point in _____ angry.

61.5 Complete these sentences with the following (with the verb in the correct form):

   go riding   ~~go sailing~~   **go shopping**   **go skiing**   **go swimming**

1. Robbie lives by the ocean and he's got a boat, so he often _goes sailing_ .
2. It was a very hot day, so we _____ at the pool.
3. There's plenty of snow in the mountains, so we'll be able to _____ .
4. Michelle has two horses. She _____ regularly.
5. "Where's Dan?" "He _____ . There were a few things he needed to buy."

To . . . , for . . . , and **so that** . . . (Purpose)

A

We use **to** . . . to say why somebody does something (= the purpose of an action):

- "Why are you going out?" "**To mail** a letter."
- A friend of mine called **to invite** me to a party.
- We shouted **to warn** everybody of the danger.

We use **to** . . . to say why something exists (= its purpose):

- This fence is **to keep** people out of the yard.
- The president has a team of bodyguards **to protect** him.

B

We use **to** . . . to say what can be done or must be done with something:

- It's hard to find **a place to park** downtown. (= a place where you can park)
- Would you like **something to eat**?
- Do you have **much work to do**? (= work that you must do)
- I get lonely if there's **nobody to talk to**.
- I need **something to open** this bottle **with**.

Also **money/time/chance/opportunity/energy/courage**, etc., to (do something):

- They gave us **some money to buy** some food.
- Do you have **much opportunity to practice** your English?
- I need **a few days to think** about your proposal.

C

For . . . and **to** . . .

Compare:

for + *noun*:	**to** + *verb*:
■ I'm going to Spain **for a vacation**.	■ I'm going to Spain **to learn** Spanish. (*not* for learn, *not* for learning)
■ What would you like **for dinner**?	■ What would you like **to eat**?
■ Let's go to the pool **for a swim**.	■ Let's go to the pool **to have** a swim.

You can say "**for** (somebody) **to** (do something)":

- There weren't any chairs **for us to sit on**, so we had to sit on the floor.

You can use **for –ing** or **to** . . . to talk about the general purpose of something, or what it is generally used for:

- Do you use this brush **for** wash**ing** the dishes? (*or* . . . **to wash** the dishes?)

You can use **What . . . for**? to ask about purpose:

- **What** is this switch **for**?
- **What** did you do that **for**?

D

So that

Sometimes you have to use **so that** for purpose.

We use **so that** (*not* to . . .) especially

when the purpose is *negative* (**so that** . . . **won't/wouldn't**):

- I hurried **so that** I **wouldn't** be late. (= because I didn't want to be late)
- Leave early **so that** you **won't** (*or* **don't**) miss the bus.

with **can** and **could** (**so that** . . . **can/could**):

- She's learning English **so that** she **can** study in Canada.
- We moved to the city **so that** we **could** see our children more often.

Exercises

62.1 Choose from Box A and Box B to make a new sentence with *to* . . . .

A
1. ~~I shouted~~
2. I had to go to the bank
3. I'm saving money
4. I went into the hospital
5. I'm wearing two sweaters
6. I called the police

B
I want to keep warm
I wanted to report that my car had been stolen
I want to go to Canada
I had to have an operation
I needed to get some money
~~I wanted to warn people of the danger~~

1. _I shouted to warn people of the danger._ _____
2. I had to go to the bank _____
3. I _____
4. _____
5. _____
6. _____

62.2 Complete these sentences using appropriate verbs.

1. The president has a team of bodyguards _to protect_ him.
2. I didn't have enough time _____ the newspaper today.
3. I took a taxi home. I didn't have the energy _____ .
4. "Would you like something _____ ?" "Yes. A cup of coffee, please."
5. We need a bag _____ these things in.
6. There will be a meeting next week _____ the problem.
7. I wish we had enough money _____ another car.
8. I saw Kelly at the party, but we didn't have a chance _____ to each other.
9. I need some new clothes. I don't have anything nice _____ .
10. They've just passed their exams. They're having a party _____ .
11. I can't do all this work alone. I need somebody _____ me.

62.3 Put in *to* or *for*.

1. I'm going to Spain _for_ a vacation.
2. You need a lot of experience _____ this job.
3. You need a lot of experience _____ do this job.
4. We'll need more time _____ make a decision.
5. I went to the dentist _____ a check-up.
6. I had to put on my glasses _____ read the letter.
7. Do you have to wear glasses _____ reading?
8. I wish we had a yard _____ the children _____ play in.

62.4 Write sentences with *so that*.

1. I hurried. I didn't want to be late.
   I hurried so that I wouldn't be late.
2. I wore warm clothes. I didn't want to be cold.
   I wore _____
3. I left Dave my phone number. I wanted him to be able to contact me.
   I _____
4. We whispered. We didn't want anybody else to hear our conversation.
   _____ nobody _____
5. Please arrive early. We want to be able to start the meeting on time.
   Please _____
6. Jennifer locked the door. She didn't want to be disturbed.
   _____
7. I slowed down. I wanted the car behind me to be able to pass.
   _____

Adjective + to . . .

A

Hard to understand, etc.

Compare sentences (a) and (b):

■ Jim doesn't speak very clearly.

> (a) It is **hard to understand** him .
> (b) He is **hard to understand**.

Sentences (a) and (b) have the same meaning. Note that we say:
- ■ He is hard **to understand**. (*not* He is hard to understand him.)

You can use the same structures with:

easy	difficult	impossible	dangerous	safe	expensive
cheap	nice	good	interesting	exciting	

- ■ Do you think it is **safe** (for us) **to drink this water**?
  Do you think this water is **safe** (for us) **to drink**? (*not* to drink it)
- ■ The questions on the exam were very difficult. It was **impossible to answer them**.
  The questions on the exam were very difficult. They were **impossible to answer**.
  (*not* to answer them)
- ■ Jill has lots of interesting ideas. It's **interesting to talk** to her.
  Jill **is interesting to talk to**. (*not* to talk to her.)

You can also use this structure with *adjective + noun*:
- ■ This is a **difficult question** (for me) **to answer**. (*not* to answer it)

B

(It's) nice of (you) to . . .

You can say, "It's **nice of** somebody **to** do something":
- ■ It was **nice of you to take** me to the airport. Thank you very much.

You can use many other adjectives in this way. For example:

careless	kind	mean	considerate	foolish	stupid	generous	unfair

- ■ It's **foolish of Mary to quit** her job when she needs the money.
- ■ I think it was very **unfair of him to criticize** me.

C

I'm sorry to . . . / I was surprised to . . ., etc.

You can use *adjective + **to** . . .* to say how somebody reacts to something:
- ■ I was **sorry to hear** that your father is ill.

You can use many other adjectives in this way. For example:

happy	disappointed	glad	surprised	pleased	amazed	sad	relieved

- ■ Was Julia **surprised to see** you?
- ■ It was a long and tiring trip. We were **glad to get** home.

D

The first (person) **to know** / **the next** (train) **to arrive**

You can use **to** . . . after **the first/second/third**, etc., and also after **the last**, **the next**, **the only**:
- ■ If I have any more news, you will be **the first** (person) **to know**.
- ■ **The next** plane **to arrive** at Gate 4 will be Flight 268 from Bogotá.
- ■ Everybody was late except me. I was **the only** one **to arrive** on time.

E

You can say that something is **sure/certain/likely/bound to** happen:
- ■ Carla is a very good student. She's **bound to pass** the exam. (= she is sure to pass)
- ■ I'm **likely to get** home late tonight. (= I will probably get home late)

Exercises

63.1 (Section A) Write these sentences in another way, beginning as shown.

1. It's hard to understand him.   He _is hard to understand._
2. It's easy to use this machine.   This machine is _____
3. It was very difficult to open the window.   The window _____
4. It's impossible to translate some words.   Some words _____
5. It's expensive to maintain a car.   A _____
6. It's not safe to stand on that chair.   That _____

63.2 (Section A) Complete the second sentence. Use the adjective in parentheses. Use adjective + noun and **to** . . . as in the example.

1. I couldn't answer the question. (difficult)   It was a _difficult question to answer._
2. Everybody makes that mistake. (easy)   It's an _____
3. I like living in this place. (nice)   It's a _____
4. We enjoyed watching the game. (good)   It was a _____

63.3 (Section B) Make a new sentence beginning **It** . . . . Use one of these adjectives each time:

     careless   **inconsiderate**   ~~**kind**~~   **nice**

1. Sue has offered to help me. _It's kind of Sue to offer to help me._
2. You make the same mistake again and again.
   It _____
3. Dan and Jenny invited me to stay with them.
   _____
4. The neighbors make so much noise at night.
   _____

63.4 (Section C) Use the following words to complete these sentences:

     sorry / hear   **glad / hear**   ~~**pleased / get**~~   **surprised / see**

1. We _were pleased to get_ your letter last week.
2. I got your message. I _____ that you're doing well.
3. We _____ Paula at the party. We didn't expect her to come.
4. I _____ that your mother isn't well. I hope she gets better soon.

63.5 (Section D) Complete the second sentence using the words in parentheses + **to** . . . .

1. Nobody left before me. (the first) I was _the first person to leave._
2. Everybody else arrived before Paul.
   (the last) Paul was the _____
3. Jenny passed the exam. All the other students failed.
   (the only) Jenny was _____
4. I complained to the restaurant manager about the service. Another customer had already complained.
   (the second) I was _____
5. Neil Armstrong walked on the moon in 1969. Nobody had done this before him.
   (the first) Neil Armstrong was _____

63.6 (Section E) Complete these sentences using the words in parentheses and an appropriate verb.

1. Diane is a very good student. She _is bound to pass_ the exam. (bound)
2. I'm not surprised you're tired. After such a long trip, you _____ tired. (bound)
3. Toshi has a very bad memory. He _____ what you tell him. (sure)
4. I don't think you need an umbrella. It _____ . (not likely)
5. The holiday begins this Friday. There _____ a lot of traffic on the roads. (likely)

To . . . (afraid **to do**) and
Preposition + -ing (afraid **of** -ing)

Afraid to (do) and afraid of (do)ing

I am **afraid to do** something = I don't want to do it because it is dangerous or the result could
be bad.
We use **afraid to do** for things we do intentionally; we can choose to do them or not:

- This part of town is dangerous. People are **afraid to walk** here at night.
  (= they don't want to walk here because it is dangerous – so they don't)
- James was **afraid to tell** his parents what happened.
  (= he didn't want to tell them because he knew they would be angry/worried, etc.)

I am **afraid of** something **happening** = it is possible that something bad will happen (for
example, an accident).
We do not use **afraid of –ing** for things we do intentionally:

- The sidewalk was icy, so we walked very carefully. We were **afraid of falling**.
  (= it was possible that we would fall – *not* we were afraid to fall)
- I don't like dogs. I'm always **afraid of being bitten**. (*not* afraid to be bitten)

So, you are **afraid to do** something because you are **afraid of something happening**
as a result:

- I was **afraid to go** near the dog because I was **afraid of being** bitten.

Interested in (do)ing and interested to (do)

I'm **interested in doing** something = I'm thinking of doing it, I would like to do it:

- Let me know if you're **interested in joining** the club. (*not* to join)
- I tried to sell my car, but nobody was **interested in buying** it. (*not* to buy)

We use **interested to . . .** to say how somebody reacts to what they **hear/see/read/learn/
know/find**. For example, "I was **interested to hear** it" = I heard it and it was interesting for me:

- I was **interested to hear** that Tanya quit her job.
- Ask Mike for his opinion. I would be **interested to know** what he thinks.
  (= it would be interesting for me to know it)

This structure is the same as **surprised to . . .** / **glad to . . .**, etc. (see Unit 63C):

- I was **surprised to hear** that Tanya quit her job.

Sorry to (do) and sorry for / about (do)ing

We use **sorry to . . .** to say we regret something that happens (see Unit 63C):

- I was **sorry to hear** that Nicky lost her job. (= I was sorry when I heard that . . .)
- I've enjoyed my stay here. I'll be **sorry to leave**.

We also say **sorry to . . .** to apologize at the time we do something:

- I'm **sorry to call** you so late, but I need to ask you something.

You can use **sorry for** or **sorry about** to apologize for something you did before:

- I'm **sorry for** (*or* **about**) **shouting** at you yesterday. (*not* sorry to shout)

You can also say:

- I'm **sorry I shouted** at you yesterday.

We say:

I **want to** (do) / I'd **like to** (do)	*but*	I'm **thinking of** (do**ing**) / I **dream of** (do**ing**)
I **failed to** (do)	*but*	I **succeeded in** (do**ing**)
I **allowed** them **to** (do)	*but*	I **stopped/prevented** them **from** (do**ing**)

For examples, see Units 52–53 and 60.

Exercises

64.1 Use the words in parentheses to write sentences. Use *afraid to* . . . or *afraid of -ing*.

1. The streets are unsafe at night.
   (a lot of people / afraid / go / out) *A lot of people are afraid to go out.*
2. We walked very carefully along the icy path.
   (we / afraid / fall) *We were afraid of falling.*
3. I don't usually carry my passport with me.
   (I / afraid / lose / it) _____
4. I thought she would be angry if I told her what had happened.
   (I / afraid / tell / her) _____
5. We rushed to the station.
   (we / afraid / miss / our train) _____
6. In the middle of the film there was an especially horrifying scene.
   (we / afraid / look) _____
7. The vase was very valuable, so I held it carefully.
   (I / afraid / drop / it) _____
8. I thought the food on my plate didn't look fresh.
   a) (I / afraid / eat / it) _____
   b) (I / afraid / get / sick) _____

64.2 Complete the sentences using *in* . . . or *to* . . . . Use these verbs:

~~buy~~   get   know   look   read   start

1. I'm trying to sell my car, but nobody is interested _in buying_ it.
2. Julia is interested _____ her own business.
3. I was interested _____ your letter in the newspaper last week.
4. Ben wants to stay single. He's not interested _____ married.
5. I met Mark a few days ago. You'll be interested _____ that he's just gotten a job in Buenos Aires.
6. I don't enjoy sightseeing. I'm not interested _____ at old buildings.

64.3 Complete each sentence using *sorry for / about* . . . or *sorry to* . . . . Use the verb in parentheses.

1. I'm _sorry to call_ you so late, but I need to ask you something. (call)
2. I was _____ that you didn't get the job you applied for. (hear)
3. I'm _____ all those bad things about you. I didn't mean them. (say)
4. I'm _____ you, but do you have a pen I could borrow? (bother)
5. I'm _____ the book you lent me. I'll buy you another one. (lose)

64.4 Complete each sentence using the verb in parentheses.

1. a) We wanted _to leave_ the building. (leave)
   b) We weren't allowed _____ the building. (leave)
   c) We were prevented _____ the building. (leave)

2. a) Peter failed _____ the problem. (solve)
   b) Chris succeeded _____ the problem. (solve)

3. a) I'm thinking _____ away next week. (go)
   b) I'm hoping _____ away next week. (go)
   c) I'd like _____ away next week. (go)
   d) I'm looking forward _____ away next week. (go)

4. a) Lisa wanted _____ me lunch. (buy)
   b) Lisa promised _____ me lunch. (buy)
   c) Lisa insisted _____ me lunch. (buy)
   d) Lisa wouldn't dream _____ me lunch. (buy)

See somebody do and see somebody doing

A

Study this example situation:

Tom got into his car and drove away. You saw this. You can say:

■ I saw Tom **get** into his car and **drive** away.

In this structure we use **get/drive/do**, etc. (*not* to get / to drive / to do).

Somebody **did** something	+	I **saw** this

I **saw** somebody **do** something

Tom

B

Study this example situation:

Yesterday you saw Kate. She was waiting for a bus. You can say:

■ I saw Kate **waiting** for a bus.

In this structure we use **–ing** (**waiting/doing**, etc.):

Somebody **was doing** something	+	I **saw** this

I **saw** somebody **doing** something

Kate

C

Study the difference in meaning between the two structures:

I saw him **do** something = he **did** something *(simple past)* and I saw this. I saw the complete action from beginning to end:

■ He **fell** off the wall. I saw this. → I saw him **fall** off the wall.
■ The accident **happened**. Did you see it? → Did you see the accident **happen**?

I saw him **doing** something = he **was doing** something *(past continuous)* and I saw this. I saw him when he was in the middle of doing it. This does not mean that I saw the complete action:

■ He **was walking** along the street.
I saw this when I drove past in my car. } I saw him **walking** along the street.

Sometimes the difference is not important and you can use either form:

■ I've never seen her **dance**. *or* I've never seen her **dancing**.

D

We use these structures with **see** and **hear**, and a number of other verbs:

■ I didn't **hear** you **come** in. (you came in – I didn't hear this)
■ Liz suddenly **felt** somebody **touch** her on the shoulder.
■ Did you **notice** anyone **go** out?

■ I could **hear** it **raining**. (it was raining – I could hear it)
■ The missing children were last **seen playing** near the river.
■ **Listen to** the birds **singing**!
■ Can you **smell** something **burning**?
■ I **found** Sue in my room **reading** my letters.

Exercises

65.1 Complete the answers to the questions.

1. Did anybody go out? — I don't think so. I didn't see ___anybody go out___ .
2. Has Sarah arrived yet? — Yes, I think I heard her _____ .
3. How do you know I took the money? — I know because I saw you _____ .
4. Did the doorbell ring? — I don't think so. I didn't hear _____ .
5. Can Tom play the piano? — I've never heard _____ .
6. Did I lock the door when I went out? — Yes, I saw _____ .
7. How did the woman fall? — I don't know. I didn't see _____ .

65.2 In each of these situations you and a friend saw, heard, or smelled something. Look at the pictures and complete the sentences.

1. Look! There's Kate.
2. Look! There's Dave and Helen.
3. Look! There's Claire.
4. Listen! That's Bill!
5. Can you smell something burning? — Yes! It's our dinner.
6. Look! There's Linda.

1. ___We saw Kate waiting for a bus.___
2. We saw Dave and Helen _____
3. We saw _____ in a restaurant.
4. We heard _____
5. We could _____
6. _____

65.3 Complete these sentences. Use the following verbs (in the correct form):

climb	~~come~~	crawl	cry	explode	ride
run	say	~~sing~~	slam	sleep	tell

1. Listen to the birds ___singing___ !
2. I didn't hear you ___come___ in.
3. We listened to the old man _____ his story from beginning to end.
4. Listen! Can you hear a baby _____ ?
5. I looked out of the window and saw Dan _____ his bike along the road.
6. I thought I heard somebody _____ "Hi," so I turned around.
7. We watched two men _____ across the yard and _____ through an open window into the house.
8. Everybody heard the bomb _____ . It made a tremendous noise.
9. Oh! I can feel something _____ up my leg! It must be an insect.
10. I heard somebody _____ the door in the middle of the night. It woke me up.
11. When we got home, we found a cat _____ under the kitchen table.

-ing Phrases (**Feeling tired**, I went to bed early.)

A

Study these situations:

> Joe was playing football. He hurt his knee.
> You can say:
> - Joe hurt his knee **playing football**.
>
> You were feeling tired. So you went to bed early.
> You can say:
> - **Feeling tired**, I went to bed early.
>
> "**Playing football**" and "**feeling tired**" are **-ing** phrases.
> If the **-ing** phrase is at the beginning of the sentence (as in the second example), we write a comma (,) after it.

B

When two things happen at the same time, you can use an **-ing** phrase.
- Kate is in the kitchen **making coffee**.
  (= she is in the kitchen *and* she is making coffee)
- A man ran out of the house **shouting**.
  (= he ran out of the house *and* he was shouting)
- Do something! Don't just stand there **doing nothing**!

We also use **-ing** when one action happens during another action. We use **-ing** for the longer action.
- Joe hurt his knee **playing football**. (= while he was playing)
- Did you cut yourself **shaving**? (= while you were shaving)

You can also use **-ing** after **while** or **when**:
- Joe hurt his knee **while playing** football.
- Be careful **when crossing** the street. (= when you are crossing)

C

When one action happens before another action, we use **having** (**done**) for the first action:
- **Having found** a hotel, we looked for someplace to have dinner.
- **Having finished** her work, she went home.

You can also say **after -ing**:
- **After finishing** her work, she went home.

If one short action follows another short action, you can use the simple **-ing** form (**doing** instead of **having done**) for the first action:
- **Taking** a key out of his pocket, he opened the door.

These structures are used more in written English than in spoken English.

D

You can use an **-ing** phrase to explain something, or to say why somebody does something. The **-ing** phrase usually comes at the beginning of the sentence:
- **Feeling** tired, I went to bed early. (= because I felt tired)
- **Being** unemployed, he doesn't have much money. (= because he is unemployed)
- **Not having** a car, she has trouble getting around. (= because she doesn't have a car)
- **Having** already **seen** the movie twice, I didn't want to go again with my friends.
  (= because I had already seen it twice)

These structures are used more in written English than in spoken English.

Exercises

66.1 Choose from Box A and Box B to make sentences. Use an *-ing* phrase.

A	1. ~~Kate was in the kitchen.~~	B	She was trying not to make any noise.
	2. Diane was sitting in an armchair.		She looked at the sights and took pictures.
	3. Sue opened the door carefully.		She said she would be back in an hour.
	4. Sarah went out.		She was reading a book.
	5. Linda was in London for two years.		~~She was making coffee.~~
	6. Mary walked around the town.		She worked as a teacher.

1. *Kate was in the kitchen making coffee.* _____
2. Diane was sitting _____
3. Sue _____
4. _____
5. _____
6. _____

66.2 Make one sentence from two using an *-ing* phrase.

1. Joe was playing football. He hurt his knee. *Joe hurt his knee playing football.* _____
2. I was watching television. I fell asleep.
    I _____
3. The man slipped and fell. He was getting off a bus.
    The man _____
4. I was walking home in the rain. I got very wet.
    I _____
5. Laura was driving to work yesterday. She had an accident.
    _____
6. Two kids got lost. They were hiking in the woods.
    _____

66.3 Make sentences beginning with *Having* . . . .

1. She finished her work. Then she went home.
    Having finished her work, she went home. _____
2. We bought our tickets. Then we went into the theater.
    _____
3. They had dinner, and then they continued their trip.
    _____
4. After I'd done the shopping, I stopped for a cup of coffee.
    _____

66.4 Make sentences beginning *-ing* or *Not -ing* (like those in Section D). Sometimes you need to begin with *Having* (*done something*).

1. I felt tired. So I went to bed early.
    Feeling tired, I went to bed early.
2. I thought they might be hungry. So I offered them something to eat.
    _____
3. Sally is a vegetarian. So she doesn't eat any kind of meat.
    _____
4. I didn't know his e-mail address. So I wasn't able to contact him.
    _____
5. Sarah has traveled a lot. So she knows a lot about other countries.
    _____
6. I wasn't able to speak the local language. So I had trouble communicating.
    _____
7. We had spent nearly all our money. So we couldn't afford to stay in a hotel.
    _____

Countable and Uncountable 1

A

A noun can be *countable* or *uncountable*:

Countable	*Uncountable* 

Countable
- I eat a **banana** every day.
- I like **bananas**.

Banana is a *countable* noun.

A countable noun can be *singular* (**banana**) or *plural* (**bananas**).

We can use numbers with countable nouns. So we can say "one banana," "two bananas," etc.

Examples of nouns usually countable:
- Kate was singing **a song**.
- There's **a** nice **beach** near here.
- Do you have **a** $10 **bill**?
- It wasn't your fault. It was **an accident**.
- There are no **batteries** in the radio.
- We don't have enough **cups**.

Uncountable
- I eat **rice** every day.
- I like **rice**.

Rice is an *uncountable* noun.

An uncountable noun has only one form (**rice**).

We cannot use numbers with uncountable nouns. So we cannot say "one rice," "two rices," etc.

Examples of nouns usually uncountable:
- Kate was listening to (some) **music**.
- There's **sand** in my shoes.
- Do you have any **money**?
- It wasn't your fault. It was bad **luck**.
- There is no **electricity** in this house.
- We don't have enough **water**.

B

You can use **a/an** with singular countable nouns:

  a beach   **a student**   **an umbrella**

You cannot use singular countable nouns alone (without **a/the/my**, etc.):
- I want **a banana**. (*not* I want banana)
- There's been **an accident**.
(*not* There's been accident)

You can use *plural* countable nouns alone:
- I like **bananas**. (= bananas in general)
- **Accidents** can be prevented.

You cannot normally use **a/an** with uncountable nouns. We do not say "a sand," "a music," "a rice."
But you can often use **a . . . of**.
For example:
  a bowl of / a pound of / a grain of rice

You can use uncountable nouns alone (without **the/my/some**, etc.):
- I eat **rice** every day.
- There's **blood** on your shirt.
- Can you hear **music**?

C

You can use **some** and **any** with plural countable nouns:
- We sang **some songs**.
- Did you buy **any apples**?

We use **many** and **few** with plural countable nouns:
- We didn't take **many pictures**.
- I have a **few things** to do.

You can use **some** and **any** with uncountable nouns:
- We listened to **some music**.
- Did you buy **any** apple **juice**?

We use **much** and **little** with uncountable nouns:
- We didn't do **much shopping**.
- I have a **little work** to do.

Countable and Uncountable 2 Unit 68   *Children / the children* Unit 73   *Some* and *any* Unit 83
Many/much/few/little Unit 85

134

Exercises

67.1 Some of these sentences need *a/an*. Correct the sentences where necessary.

1. Joe goes everywhere by bike. (He doesn't have car.)   _a car._
2. Helen was listening to music when I arrived.   _OK_
3. We went to very nice restaurant last weekend.   _____
4. I brush my teeth with toothpaste.   _____
5. I use toothbrush to brush my teeth.   _____
6. Can you tell me if there's bank near here?   _____
7. My brother works for insurance company in Detroit.   _____
8. I don't like violence.   _____
9. Can you smell paint?   _____
10. When we were in Rome, we stayed in big hotel.   _____
11. We need gas. I hope we come to gas station soon.   _____
12. I wonder if you can help me. I have problem.   _____
13. I like your suggestion. It's very interesting idea.   _____
14. John has interview for job tomorrow.   _____
15. I like volleyball. It's good game.   _____
16. Liz doesn't usually wear jewelry.   _____
17. Jane was wearing beautiful necklace.   _____

67.2 Complete the sentences using the following words. Use *a/an* where necessary.

~~accident~~	blood	coat	cookie	decision	electricity
interview	key	minute	~~music~~	question	sugar

1. It wasn't your fault. It was _an accident_ .
2. Listen! Can you hear _music_ ?
3. I couldn't get into the house because I didn't have _____ .
4. It's very warm today. Why are you wearing _____ ?
5. Do you take _____ in your coffee?
6. Are you hungry? Would you like _____ with your coffee?
7. Our lives would be very difficult without _____ .
8. "I had _____ for a job yesterday." "You did? How did it go?"
9. The heart pumps _____ through the body.
10. Excuse me, but can I ask you _____ ?
11. I'm not ready yet. Can you wait _____ , please?
12. We can't delay much longer. We have to make _____ soon.

67.3 Complete the sentences using the following words. Sometimes the word needs to be plural (-s), and sometimes you need to use *a/an*.

air	day	friend	language	letter	line
meat	patience	people	~~picture~~	space	umbrella

1. I had my camera, but I didn't take any _pictures_ .
2. There are seven _____ in a week.
3. A vegetarian is a person who doesn't eat _____ .
4. Outside the movie theater, there was _____ of people waiting to see the movie.
5. I'm not very good at writing _____ .
6. Last night I went out with some _____ of mine.
7. There were very few _____ in town today. The streets were almost empty.
8. I'm going out for a walk. I need some fresh _____ .
9. Gary always wants things quickly. He doesn't have much _____ .
10. I think it's going to rain. Do you have _____ I could borrow?
11. Do you speak any foreign _____ ?
12. Our apartment is very small. We don't have much _____ .

Countable and Uncountable 2

Many nouns can be used as countable or uncountable nouns, usually with a difference in meaning. Compare:

Countable	*Uncountable*
■ Did you hear **a noise** just now? (= a specific noise)	■ I can't work here. There's too much **noise**. (*not* too many noises)
■ I bought **a paper** to read. (= a newspaper)	■ I need some **paper** to write on. (= material for writing on)
■ There's **a hair** in my soup! (= one single hair)	■ You've got very long **hair**. (*not* hairs) (= all the hair on your head)
■ You can stay with us. There is **a** spare **room**. (= a room in a house)	■ You can't sit here. There isn't any **room**. (= space)
■ I had some interesting **experiences** while I was traveling. (= things that happened to me)	■ They offered me the job because I had a lot of **experience**. (*not* experiences)
■ Enjoy your trip. Have a good **time**!	■ I can't wait. I don't have **time**.

Coffee/tea/juice/beer, etc. (drinks) are normally uncountable:
■ I don't like **coffee** very much.

But you can say **a coffee** (= a cup of coffee), **two coffees** (= two cups), etc.:
■ **Two** coffees and **an orange juice**, please.

The following nouns are usually uncountable:

advice	baggage	behavior	bread	chaos	damage
furniture	information	luck	luggage	news	permission
progress	scenery	traffic	weather	work	

You cannot use **a/an** with these nouns:
■ I'm going to buy **some bread**. *or* . . . **a loaf of bread**. (*not* a bread)
■ Enjoy your vacation! I hope you have good **weather**. (*not* a good weather)

These nouns are not usually plural (so we do not say "breads," "furnitures," etc.):
■ Where are you going to put all your **furniture**? (*not* furnitures)
■ Let me know if you need more **information**. (*not* informations)

News is uncountable, not plural:
■ The **news was** very depressing. (*not* The news were)

Travel (*noun*) means *traveling in general* (uncountable). We do not say "a travel" to mean **a trip**:
■ They spend a lot of money on **travel**.
■ We had **a** very good **trip**. (*not* a good travel)

Compare these countable and uncountable nouns:

Countable	*Uncountable*
■ I'm looking for **a job**.	■ I'm looking for **work**. (*not* a work)
■ What **a** beautiful **view**!	■ What beautiful **scenery**!
■ It's **a** nice **day** today.	■ It's nice **weather** today.
■ We had a lot of **bags** and **suitcases**.	■ We had a lot of **baggage/luggage**.
■ **These chairs** are mine.	■ **This furniture** is mine.
■ That's **a** good **suggestion**.	■ That's good **advice**.

Exercises

68.1 Which of the <u>underlined</u> parts of these sentences is correct?

1. "Did you hear ~~noise~~ / a noise just now?" "No, I didn't hear anything." (*a noise* is correct)
2. a) If you want to know the news, you can read <u>paper / a paper</u>.
   b) I want to print some documents, but the printer is out of <u>paper / papers</u>.
3. a) I thought there was somebody in the house because there was <u>light / a light</u> on inside.
   b) <u>Light / A light</u> comes from the sun.
4. a) I was in a hurry this morning. I didn't have <u>time / a time</u> for breakfast.
   b) "Did you have a good vacation?" "Yes, we had <u>wonderful time / a wonderful time</u>."
5. This is <u>nice room / a nice room</u>. Did you decorate it yourself?
6. Sue was very helpful. She gave us some very useful <u>advice / advices</u>.
7. Did you have <u>nice weather / a nice weather</u> when you were away?
8. We were very unfortunate. We had <u>bad luck / a bad luck</u>.
9. Is it difficult to find a <u>work / job</u> at this time?
10. Our <u>travel / trip</u> from Paris to Istanbul by train was very tiring.
11. When the fire alarm rang, there was <u>total chaos / a total chaos</u>.
12. I had to buy <u>a / some</u> bread because I wanted to make some sandwiches.
13. Bad news <u>don't / doesn't</u> make people happy.
14. <u>Your hair is / Your hairs are</u> too long. You should have <u>it / them</u> cut.
15. <u>The damage / The damages</u> caused by the storm will cost a lot to repair.

68.2 Complete the sentences using the following words. Use the plural (-s) where necessary.

advice	chair	experience	experience	furniture	hair
information	job	~~luggage~~	permission	progress	work

1. I didn't have much ___luggage___ – just two small bags.
2. They'll tell you all you want to know. They'll give you plenty of _____ .
3. There is room for everybody to sit down. There are plenty of _____ .
4. We have no _____ , not even a bed or a table.
5. "What does Alan look like?" "He's got a long beard and very short _____ ."
6. Carla's English is better than it was. She's made _____ .
7. Mike is unemployed. He can't find a _____ .
8. Mike is unemployed. He can't find _____ .
9. If you want to leave early, you have to ask for _____ .
10. I didn't know what to do. So I asked Chris for _____ .
11. I don't think Ann will get the job. She doesn't have enough _____ .
12. Rita has done many interesting things. She could write a book about her _____ .

68.3 What do you say in these situations? Complete each sentence using one of the words from Section B.

1. Your friends have just arrived at the station. You can't see any suitcases or bags.
   You ask them: Do ___you have any luggage_____ ?
2. You go into the tourist office. You want to know about places to see in the city.
   You say: I'd like _____ .
3. You are a student. You want your teacher to advise you about which courses to take.
   You say: Can you give me _____ ?
4. You want to watch the news on TV, but you don't know when it is on.
   You ask your friend: What time _____ ?
5. You are at the top of a mountain. You can see a very long way. It's beautiful.
   You say: It _____ , isn't it?
6. You look out the window. The weather is horrible: cold, wet, and windy.
   You say: What _____ !

Countable Nouns with **a/an** and **some**

Countable nouns can be *singular* or *plural*:

a **dog**	a **child**	the **evening**	this **party**	an **umbrella**
dogs	some **children**	the **evenings**	these **parties**	two **umbrellas**

Before singular countable nouns you can use **a/an**:
- Goodbye! Have **a** nice **evening**.
- Do you need **an umbrella**?

You cannot use singular countable nouns alone (without **a/the/my**, etc.):
- She never wears **a** hat. (*not* She never wears hat)
- Be careful of **the** dog. (*not* Be careful of dog)
- What **a** beautiful day!
- I've got **a** headache.

We use **a/an** . . . to say what kind of thing or person something/somebody is:
- That's **a nice table**.

In the plural, we use the noun alone (*not* some . . .):
- Those are **nice chairs**. (*not* some nice chairs)

Compare singular and plural:

■ A dog is **an animal**.	■ Dogs **are animals**.
■ I'm **an optimist**.	■ We're **optimists**.
■ Tim's father is **a doctor**.	■ Most of my friends are **students**.
■ Are you **a good driver**?	■ Are they **good students**?
■ Jill is **a really nice person**.	■ Jill's parents are **really nice people**.
■ What **a pretty dress**!	■ What **awful shoes**!

We say that somebody has **a long nose** / **a nice face** / **blue eyes** / **small hands**, etc.:

■ Jack has **a long nose**. (*not* the long nose)	■ Jack has **blue eyes**. (*not* the blue eyes)

Remember to use **a/an** when you say what somebody's job is:
- Sandra is **a nurse**. (*not* Sandra is nurse)
- Would you like to be **an English teacher**?

You can use **some** with plural countable nouns. We use **some** in two ways.

(1) **Some** = a number of / a few of / a pair of:
- I've seen **some** good **movies** recently. (*not* I've seen good movies)
- **Some friends** of mine are coming to stay this weekend.
- I need **some** new **sunglasses**. (= a new pair of sunglasses)

Do *not* use **some** when you are talking about things in general (see Unit 73):
- I love **bananas**. (*not* some bananas)
- My aunt is a writer. She writes **books**. (*not* some books)

Sometimes you can make sentences with or without **some** (with no difference in meaning):
- There are (**some**) eggs in the refrigerator if you're hungry.

(2) **Some** = some but not all:
- **Some children** learn very quickly. (but not all children)
- Tomorrow there will be rain in **some places**, but most of the country will be dry.

Exercises

69.1 What are these things? Use a dictionary if necessary.

1. an ant? _It's an insect._
2. ants and bees? _They're insects._
3. a cauliflower? _____
4. chess? _____
5. a violin, a trumpet, and a flute _____
_____
6. a skyscraper? _____

7. Earth, Mars, Venus, and Jupiter? _____
_____
8. a tulip? _____
9. the Nile, the Rhine, and the Mississippi?
_____
10. a pigeon, an eagle, and a crow? _____
_____

Who were these people?

11. Beethoven? _He was a composer._
12. Shakespeare? _____
_____
13. Albert Einstein? _____
_____
14. George Washington, Abraham Lincoln, and John F. Kennedy?
_____

15. Marilyn Monroe? _____
_____
16. Elvis Presley and John Lennon? _____
_____
17. Van Gogh, Renoir, and Picasso? _____
_____

69.2 Read about what these people do, and say what their jobs are. Choose from:

chef	interpreter	journalist	~~nurse~~
plumber	surgeon	travel agent	waiter

1. Sarah takes care of patients in the hospital. _She's a nurse._
2. Gary works in a restaurant. He brings the food to the tables. He _____
3. Mary arranges people's trips for them. She _____
4. Kevin works in a hospital. He operates on people. _____
5. Jonathan cooks in a restaurant. _____
6. Jane writes articles for a newspaper. _____
7. Dave installs and repairs water pipes. _____
8. Linda translates what people are saying from one language into another so that they can understand each other. _____

69.3 Put in *a/an* or *some* where necessary. If no word is necessary, leave the space empty.

1. I've seen _some_ good films recently.
2. What's wrong with you? Do you have _a_ headache?
3. I know a lot of people. Most of them are _____ students.
4. When I was _____ child, I used to be very shy.
5. Would you like to be _____ actor?
6. Do you collect _____ stamps?
7. What _____ beautiful garden!
8. _____ birds, for example, penguins cannot fly.
9. Do you enjoy going to _____ concerts?
10. I've been walking for three hours. I've got _____ sore feet.
11. I don't feel very well this morning. I've got _____ sore throat.
12. Maria speaks _____ English, but not very much.
13. It's too bad we don't have _____ camera. I'd like to take _____ picture of that house.
14. Those are _____ nice shoes. Where did you get them?
15. I'm going shopping. I want to buy _____ new shoes.
16. You need _____ visa to visit _____ countries, but not all of them.
17. Jane is _____ teacher. Her parents were _____ teachers, too.
18. I don't believe him. He's _____ liar. He's always telling _____ lies.

A/an and the

Study this example:

I had **a** sandwich and **an** apple for lunch.

The sandwich wasn't very good, but **the** apple was delicious.

John says "**a** sandwich" and "**an** apple" because this is the first time he talks about them.

John now says "**the** sandwich" and "**the** apple" because Karen knows which sandwich and which apple he means – **the** sandwich and **the** apple that he had for lunch.

John   Karen

Compare **a** and **the** in these examples:

■ **A** man and **a** woman were sitting across from me. **The** man was American, but I think **the** woman was British.

■ When we were on vacation, we stayed at **a** hotel. Sometimes we ate at **the** hotel, and sometimes we went to **a** restaurant.

We use **the** when we are thinking of one specific thing. Compare **a/an** and **the**:

■ Tim sat down on **a** chair. (perhaps one of many chairs in the room)
Tim sat down on **the** chair **nearest the door**. (a specific chair)

■ Paula is looking for **a** job. (not a specific job)
Did Paula get **the** job **she applied for**? (a specific job)

■ Do you have **a** car? (not a specific car)
I washed **the** car yesterday. (= my car)

We use **the** when it is clear in the situation which thing or person we mean. For example, in a room we talk about **the** light / **the** floor / **the** ceiling / **the** door / **the** carpet, etc.:

■ Can you turn off **the** light, please? (= the light in this room)

■ I took a taxi to **the** station. (= the station in that town)

■ *(in a store)* I'd like to speak to **the** manager, please. (= the manager of this store)

In the same way, we say (go to) **the bank**, **the post office**:

■ I have to go to **the bank** and then I'm going to **the post office**.
(The speaker is usually thinking of a specific bank or post office.)

We also say (go to) **the doctor** / **the dentist** / **the hospital**:

■ Carol isn't very well. She went to **the doctor**. (= her usual doctor)

■ Two people were taken to **the hospital** after the accident.

Compare **the** and **a**:

■ I have to go to **the bank** today.
Is there **a bank** near here?

■ I don't like going to **the dentist**.
My sister is **a dentist**.

We say "once **a** week / three times **a** day / $1.59 **a** pound," etc.:

■ "How often do you go to the movies?"   "About once **a** month."

■ "How much are those potatoes?"   "A dollar **a** pound."

■ Helen works eight hours **a** day, six days **a** week.

Exercises

70.1 Put in *a/an* or *the*.

1. This morning I bought ___*a*___ newspaper and _____ magazine. _____ newspaper is in my briefcase, but I can't remember where I put _____ magazine.
2. I saw _____ accident this morning. _____ car crashed into _____ tree. _____ driver of _____ car wasn't hurt, but _____ car was badly damaged.
3. There are two cars parked outside: _____ blue one and _____ gray one. _____ blue one belongs to my neighbors; I don't know who _____ owner of _____ gray one is.
4. My friends live in _____ old house in _____ small town. There is _____ beautiful garden behind _____ house. I would like to have _____ garden like that.

70.2 Put in *a/an* or *the*.

1. a) This house is very nice. Does it have ___*a*___ yard?
   b) It's a beautiful day. Let's sit in _____ yard.
   c) I like living in this house, but it's too bad that _____ yard is so small.
2. a) Can you recommend _____ good restaurant?
   b) We had dinner in _____ very nice restaurant.
   c) We had dinner in _____ most expensive restaurant in town.
3. a) She has _____ French name, but in fact she's English, not French.
   b) What's _____ name of that man we met yesterday?
   c) We stayed at a very nice hotel – I can't remember _____ name now.
4. a) There isn't _____ airport near where I live. _____ nearest airport is 70 miles away.
   b) Our flight was delayed. We had to wait at _____ airport for three hours.
   c) Excuse me, please. Can you tell me how to get to _____ airport?
5. a) "Are you going away next week?" "No, _____ week after next."
   b) I'm going away for _____ week in September.
   c) Gary has a part-time job. He works three mornings _____ week.

70.3 Put in *a/an* or *the* where necessary.

1. Would you like apple?   _*an apple*_
2. How often do you go to dentist? _____
3. Could you close door, please? _____
4. I'm sorry. I didn't mean to do that. It was mistake. _____
5. Excuse me, where is bus station, please? _____
6. I have problem. Can you help me? _____
7. I'm just going to post office. I won't be long. _____
8. There were no chairs, so we sat on floor. _____
9. Are you finished with book I lent you? _____
10. My sister has just gotten job at bank in Atlanta. _____
11. We live in small apartment near hospital. _____
12. There's supermarket on corner near my house. _____

70.4 Answer these questions about yourself. Where possible, use the structure in Section D (*once a week* / *three times a day*, etc.).

1. How often do you go to the movies? _*Three or four times a year.*_
2. How much does it cost to rent a car in your country? _*About $40 a day.*_
3. How often do you go to the dentist? _____
4. How often do you take a vacation? _____
5. What's the normal speed limit on highways in your country? _____
6. How much sleep do you need? _____
7. How often do you go out at night? _____
8. How much television do you watch (on average)? _____

The 1

A

We use **the** when there is only one of something:

- What is **the** longest river in **the** world? (there is only one longest river)
- **The** Earth goes around **the** sun, and **the** moon goes around **the** Earth.
- Have you ever crossed **the** equator?
- I'm going away at **the** end of this month.

Don't forget **the**:

- Paris is **the** capital of France. (*not* Paris is capital of . . .)

But we use **a/an** to say what kind of thing something is (see Unit 69B). Compare **the** and **a**:

- **The** sun is **a** star. (= one of many stars)
- **The** hotel we stayed at was **a** very nice hotel.

B

We say: **the sky / the sea / the ocean / the ground / the country / the environment**:

- We looked up at all the stars in **the sky**. (*not* in sky)
- Would you like to live in **the country**? (= not in a town or city)
- We must do more to protect **the environment**. (= the natural world around us)

But we say **space** (without **the**) when we mean "space in the universe." Compare:

- There are millions of stars **in space**. (*not* in the space)
- I tried to park my car, but **the space** was too small.

C

We use **the** before **same** (**the same**):

- Your sweater is **the same** color as mine. (*not* is same color)
- "Are these keys **the same**?" "No, they're different."

D

We say: (go to) **the movies**, **the theater**:

- I go to **the movies** a lot, but I haven't been to **the theater** in ages.

When we say **the movies** or **the theater**, we do not necessarily mean a specific theater.

We usually say **the radio**, but **television** or **TV** (without **the**). Compare:

- I listen to **the radio** a lot.   *but*   I watch **television** a lot.
- We heard the news on **the radio**. *but*   We watched the news on **TV**.

The television = the television set

- Can you turn off **the television**, please?

E

Breakfast   lunch   dinner

We do *not* normally use **the** with the names of meals (**breakfast**, **lunch**, etc.):

- What did you have for **breakfast**?
- We had **lunch** in a very nice restaurant.
- What time is **dinner**?

But we use **a** if there is an adjective before **breakfast**, **lunch**, etc.:

- We had **a** very **nice lunch**. (*not* We had very nice lunch)

F

Gate 10   Room 126, etc.

We do *not* use **the** before *noun + number*. For example, we say:

- Our plane leaves from **Gate 10**. (*not* the Gate 10)
- *(in a store)* Do you have these shoes in **size 9**? (*not* the size 9)

In the same way, we say: **Room 126** (in a hotel), **page 29** (of a book), **question 3** (on a test), **Platform 6** (at a train station), etc.

Exercises

71.1 Put in *the* or *a/an* where necessary. If no word is necessary, leave the space empty.

1. *A:* Where did you have ___—___ lunch?
   B: We went to __*a*__ restaurant.
2. *A:* Did you have _____ nice vacation?
   B: Yes, it was _____ best vacation I've ever had.
3. *A:* Where's _____ nearest drugstore?
   B: There's one on _____ next block.
4. *A:* Do you often listen to _____ radio?
   B: No. In fact, I don't have _____ radio.
5. *A:* Would you like to travel in _____ outer space?
   B: Yes, I'd love to go to _____ moon.
6. *A:* Do you go to _____ movies very often?
   B: No, not very often. But I watch a lot of movies on _____ television.
7. *A:* It was _____ nice day yesterday, wasn't it?
   B: Yes, it was beautiful. We went for a walk by _____ ocean.
8. *A:* What did you have for _____ breakfast this morning?
   B: Nothing. I never eat _____ breakfast.
9. *A:* Excuse me, where is _____ Room 225, please?
   B: It's on _____ second floor.
10. *A:* We spent all our money because we stayed at _____ most expensive hotel in town.
    B: Why didn't you stay at _____ cheaper hotel?

71.2 Put in *the* where necessary. If you don't need *the*, leave the space empty.

1. I haven't been to __*the*__ movies in ages.
2. I lay down on _____ ground and looked up at _____ sky.
3. Sarah spends most of her free time watching _____ television.
4. _____ television was on, but nobody was watching it.
5. Lisa and I arrived at _____ same time.
6. Have you had _____ dinner yet?
7. You'll find _____ information you need at _____ top of _____ page 15.
8. What's _____ capital city of Canada?

71.3 Put in *the* or *a/an* where necessary. (See Unit 70 for *a/an* and *the* if necessary.)

1. (Sun) is (star). *The sun is a star.* _____
2. Paul lives in small town in country. _____
3. Moon goes around earth every 27 days. _____
4. I'm fed up with doing same thing every day. _____
5. It was very hot day. It was hottest day of year. _____
6. I don't usually have lunch, but I always eat good breakfast. _____
7. If you live in foreign country, you should try to learn language. _____
8. We missed our train because we were waiting on wrong platform. _____
9. Next train to San Diego leaves from Platform 3. _____

71.4 Complete the sentences using the following. Use *the* where necessary.

> breakfast   ~~dinner~~   gate   Gate 21   movies   question 8   ocean

1. "Are you going out tonight?" "Yes, after __*dinner*__ ."
2. There was no wind, so _____ was very calm.
3. The test wasn't too difficult, but I couldn't answer _____ .
4. "I'm going to _____ tonight." "Really? What are you going to see?"
5. I didn't have time for _____ this morning because I was in a hurry.
6. Oh, _____ is open. I must have forgotten to close it.
7. *(airport announcement)* Flight AB123 to Tokyo is now boarding at _____ .

The 2 (school / the school, etc.)

Compare **school** and **the school**:

Claudia

Claudia is 10 years old. Every day she goes to **school**. She's at **school** now. **School** begins at 8:30 and ends at 3:00.	Today Claudia's mother wants to speak to her daughter's teacher. So she has gone to **the school** to see her. She's at **the school** now.
We say a child goes to **school** or is in **school** (as a student). We are not necessarily thinking of a specific school. We are thinking of **school** as a general idea.	Claudia's mother is not a student. She is not "in school," she doesn't "go to school." If she wants to see Claudia's teacher, she goes to **the school** (= Claudia's school, a specific school).

We use **prison/jail**, **college**, **class**, and **church** in a similar way. We do not use **the** when we are thinking of the general idea of these places and what they are used for. Compare:

- Ken's brother is in **prison** for robbery. (He is a prisoner. We are not thinking of a specific prison.)

- When I finish **high school**, I want to go to **college**.

- Mrs. Kelly goes to **church** every Sunday. (to a religious service)

- I was **in class** for five hours today. (= attending a class or classes in high school or college)

- Ken went to **the prison** to visit his brother. (He went as a visitor, not as a prisoner.)

- Dan is a student at **the college** where I used to work. (= a particular college)

- Some workmen went to **the church** to repair the roof. (not for a religious service)

- Who is the youngest student in **the class**? (= a specific group of students)

With most other places, you need **the**. For example, **the hospital**, **the bank**, **the station**. (see Units 70C and 71D)

Bed   work   home

We say **go to bed** / **be in bed**, etc. (*not* the bed):
- It's time to go to **bed** now.
- Do you ever have breakfast **in bed**?

but - I sat down on **the bed**. (a specific piece of furniture)

go to work / **be at work** / **start work** / **finish work**, etc. (*not* the work):
- Ann didn't go to **work** yesterday.
- What time do you usually finish **work**?

go home / **come home** / **arrive home** / **get home** / **be (at) home**, etc.:
- It's late. Let's go **home**.
- Will you be (at) **home** tomorrow afternoon?

Exercises

72.1 Complete each sentence using a preposition (*to/at/in*, etc.) + one of these words:

> bed   ~~college~~   home   prison   school   high school   work

1. When Julie finishes high school, she wants to study economics __*in college*__ .
2. In Mexico, children from the age of six have to go _____ .
3. Mark didn't go out last night. He stayed _____ .
4. There is a lot of traffic in the morning when everybody is going _____ .
5. Jeff hasn't graduated yet. He is still _____ .
6. Bill never gets up before 9:00. It's 8:30 now, so he is still _____ .
7. If you commit a serious crime, you could be sent _____ .

72.2 Complete the sentences with the word given (*school*, etc.). Use *the* where necessary.

1. (**school**)
   a) Every semester parents are invited to __*the school*__ to meet the teachers.
   b) Why aren't your children in __*school*__ today? Are they sick?
   c) When he was younger, Ted hated _____ .
   d) What time does _____ usually start in your country?
   e) *A:* How do your children get home from _____ ? By bus?
      B: No, they walk. _____ isn't very far away.
   f) What sort of job does Jenny want to do when she finishes _____ ?
   g) There were some people waiting outside _____ to meet their children.

2. (**college**)
   a) In your country, do many people go to _____ ?
   b) The Smiths have four children in _____ at the same time.
   c) This is only a small town, but _____ is one of the best in the country.

3. (**church**)
   a) John's mother is a regular churchgoer. She goes to _____ every Sunday.
   b) John himself doesn't go to _____ .
   c) John went to _____ to take some pictures of the building.

4. (**class**)
   a) The professor isn't in his office at this time. He's in _____ .
   b) The teacher asked _____ to turn off their cell phones.
   c) I'll get a newspaper on my way to _____ this afternoon.
   d) Not even the best student in _____ could answer the question.

5. (**prison**)
   a) In some places people are in _____ because of their political beliefs.
   b) A few days ago, the fire department was called to _____ to put out a fire.
   c) The judge decided to fine the man $500 instead of sending him to _____ .

6. (**home/work/bed**)
   a) I like to read in _____ before I go to sleep.
   b) It's nice to travel around, but there's no place like _____ !
   c) Should we meet after _____ tomorrow?
   d) If I'm feeling tired, I go to _____ early.
   e) What time do you usually start _____ in the morning?
   f) The economic situation was very bad. Many people were out of _____ .

The 3 (children / the children)

When we are talking about things or people in general, we do *not* use **the**:

- I'm afraid of **dogs**. (*not* the dogs)
  (**dogs** = dogs in general, not a specific group of dogs)
- **Doctors** are paid more than **teachers**.
- Do you collect **stamps**?
- **Crime** is a problem in most big cities. (*not* The crime)
- **Life** has changed a lot in the last 30 years. (*not* The life)
- Do you like **classical music / Chinese food / fast cars**?
- My favorite sport is **football/skiing/hockey**.
- My favorite subject at school was **history/physics/English**.

We say "**most** people / **most** books / **most** cars," etc. (*not* the most . . .):

- **Most hotels** accept credit cards. (*not* The most hotels)

We use **the** when we mean specific things or people.
Compare:

In general (without **the**)	*Specific people or things* (with **the**)
■ **Children** learn from playing. (= children in general)	■ We took **the children** to the zoo. (= a specific group, perhaps the speaker's children)
■ I couldn't live without **music**.	■ The movie wasn't very good, but I liked **the music**. (= the music in the movie)
■ All **cars** have wheels.	■ All **the cars** in this parking lot belong to people who work here.
■ **Sugar** isn't very good for you.	■ Can you pass **the sugar**, please? (= the sugar on the table)
■ Do **Americans** drink much tea? (= Americans in general)	■ Do **the Americans you know** drink tea? (= only the Americans you know, not Americans in general)

The difference between "something in general" and "something specific" is not always clear.
Compare:

In general (without **the**)	*Specific people or things* (with **the**)
■ I like working with **people**. (= people in general)	
■ I like working with **people who are lively**. (not all people, but "people who are lively" is still a general idea)	■ I like **the people I work with**. (= a specific group of people)
■ Do you like **coffee**? (= coffee in general)	
■ Do you like **strong black coffee**? (not all coffee, but "strong black coffee" is still a general idea)	■ Did you like **the coffee we had after dinner last night**? (= specific coffee)

The Units 71–72   **The + Adjective** (*the young / the English*, etc.) Unit 74

Exercises

73.1 Choose four of these things and write whether you like them or not:

    boxing   cats   fast-food restaurants   football   ~~hot weather~~
    math   opera   small children   rock music   zoos

Begin each sentence with one of these:

I like . . . / I don't like . . .   I don't mind . . .
I love . . . / I hate . . .   I'm interested in . . . / I'm not interested in . . .

1. *I don't like hot weather very much.*
2. _____
3. _____
4. _____
5. _____

73.2 Complete the sentences using the following. Use *the* where necessary.

    ~~(the) basketball~~   (the) **grass**   (the) **patience**   (the) **people**
    (the) **questions**   (the) **meat**   ~~(the) information~~   (the) **hotels**
    (the) **history**   (the) **water**   (the) **spiders**   (the) **lies**

1. My favorite sport is *basketball* .
2. *The information* we were given wasn't correct.
3. Some people are afraid of _____ .
4. A vegetarian is somebody who doesn't eat _____ .
5. The test wasn't very difficult. I answered _____ without any trouble.
6. Do you know _____ who live next door?
7. _____ is the study of the past.
8. George always tells the truth. He never tells _____ .
9. We couldn't find anywhere to stay downtown. All _____ were full.
10. _____ in the pool didn't look very clean, so we didn't go swimming.
11. Don't sit on _____ . It's wet from the rain.
12. You need _____ to teach young children.

73.3 Choose the correct form, with or without *the*.

1. I'm afraid of dogs / ~~the dogs~~. (*dogs* is correct)
2. Can you pass ~~salt~~ / the salt, please? (*the salt* is correct)
3. Apples / The apples are good for you.
4. Look at apples / the apples on that tree! They're very big.
5. Women / The women live longer than men / the men.
6. I don't drink tea / the tea. I don't like it.
7. We had a very good meal. Vegetables / The vegetables were especially good.
8. Life / The life is strange sometimes. Some very strange things happen.
9. I like skiing / the skiing, but I'm not very good at it.
10. Who are people / the people in this photograph?
11. What makes people / the people violent? What causes aggression / the aggression?
12. All books / All the books on the top shelf belong to me.
13. Don't stay in that hotel. It's very noisy and beds / the beds are very uncomfortable.
14. A pacifist is somebody who is against war / the war.
15. First World War / The First World War lasted from 1914 until 1918.
16. I'd like to go to Egypt and see Pyramids / the Pyramids.
17. Someone gave me a book about history / the history of modern art / the modern art.
18. Ron and Brenda got married, but marriage / the marriage didn't last very long.
19. Most people / The most people believe that marriage / the marriage and family life / the family life are the basis of society / the society.

The 4 (the giraffe / the telephone / the piano, etc.; the + Adjective)

A

Study these sentences:

- **The giraffe** is the tallest of all animals.
- **The bicycle** is an excellent means of transportation.
- When was **the telephone** invented?
- **The dollar** is the currency (= the money) of the United States.

In these examples, **the** . . . does not mean one specific thing.
The giraffe = a specific type of animal, not a specific giraffe.
We use **the** (+ singular countable noun) in this way to talk about
a type of animal, machine, etc.

In the same way we use **the** for musical instruments:

- Can you play **the** guitar?
- **The** piano is my favorite instrument.

Compare **a** and **the**:

- I'd like to have **a piano**.   *but*   I can't play **the piano**.
- We saw **a giraffe** at the zoo.   *but*   **The giraffe** is my favorite animal.

Note that we use **man** (= human beings in general / the human race) without **the**:

- What do you know about the origins of **man**? (*not* the man)

B

The + adjective

We use **the** + adjective (without a noun) to talk about groups of people, especially:

the young	the rich	the sick	the blind	the injured
the old	the poor	the disabled	the deaf	the dead
the elderly	the homeless	the unemployed		

The young = young people, **the rich** = rich people, etc.:

- Do you think **the rich** should pay higher taxes?
- The government has promised to provide more money to help **the homeless**.

These expressions are always *plural* in meaning. For example, you cannot say "a young" or
"the injured" for one person. You must say "**a** young **person**," "**the** injured **woman**," etc.

Note that we say "the **poor**" (*not* the poors), "the **young**" (*not* the youngs), etc.

C

The + nationality

You can use **the** + nationality adjectives that end in **–ch** or **–sh** (**the French** / **the English** /
the Spanish, etc.) The meaning is "the people of that country":

- **The French** are famous for their food. (= the people of France)

The French / **the English**, etc., are plural in meaning. We do not say "a French / an English."
You have to say **a Frenchman** / **an Englishwoman**, etc.

You can also use **the** + nationalities ending in **–ese** (**the Chinese** / **the Sudanese** /
the Japanese, etc.):

- **The Chinese** invented printing.

But these words can also be singular (**a Japan**ese, **a** Sudan**ese, a** Vietnam**ese**, etc.).
Also **a Swiss** (singular) and **the Swiss** (= the people of Switzerland)

With other nationalities, the plural noun ends in **–s**. For example:

    an Italian → Italians   **a Mexican → Mexicans**   **a Thai → Thais**

With these words (**Italians**, etc.), we do not normally use **the** to talk about the people in general.
(see Unit 73)

A/an and *the* Unit 70   *The* Units 71–73   **Names with and without** *the* Units 75–76

Exercises

74.1 Answer the questions. Choose the right answer from the column. Don't forget *the*. Use a dictionary if necessary.

1. *Animals*		2. *Birds*		3. *Inventions*		4. *Currencies*	
tiger	elephant	eagle	penguin	telephone	wheel	dollar	peso
rabbit	cheetah	swan	owl	telescope	laser	euro	rupee
giraffe	kangaroo	parrot	robin	helicopter	typewriter	ruble	yen

1. a) Which of the animals is the tallest?   *the giraffe* _____
   b) Which animal can run the fastest?   _____
   c) Which of these animals is found in Australia?   _____

2. a) Which of these birds has a long neck?   _____
   b) Which of these birds cannot fly?   _____
   c) Which bird flies at night?   _____

3. a) Which of these inventions is the oldest?   _____
   b) Which one is the most recent?   _____
   c) Which one was especially important for astronomy?   _____

4. a) What is the currency of India?   _____
   b) What is the currency of Canada?   _____
   c) And the currency of your country?   _____

74.2 Put in *the* or *a*.

1. When was __*the*__ telephone invented?
2. Can you play _____ musical instrument?
3. Jill plays _____ violin in an orchestra.
4. There was _____ piano in the corner of the room.
5. Can you play _____ piano?
6. Our society is based on _____ family.
7. Michael comes from _____ large family.
8. _____ computer has changed the way we live.

74.3 Complete these sentences using *the* + the following:

injured   poor   rich   sick   unemployed   ~~young~~

1. __*The young*__ have the future in their hands.
2. Ambulances arrived at the scene of the accident and took _____ to the hospital.
3. Life is all right if you have a job, but things are not so easy for _____ .
4. Julia has been a nurse all her life. She has spent her life caring for _____ .
5. In England, there is an old story about a man called Robin Hood. It is said that he took money from _____ and gave the money to _____ .

74.4 What do you call the people of these countries?

	one person (a/an . . .)	the people in general
1. Canada	*a Canadian*	*Canadians*
2. Germany	_____	_____
3. France	_____	_____
4. Russia	_____	_____
5. China	_____	_____
6. Brazil	_____	_____
7. Japan	_____	_____
8. and your country	_____	_____

Names with and without **the** 1

A

We do *not* use **the** with names of people (Ann, Ann Taylor, etc.). In the same way, we do *not* normally use **the** with names of places. For example:

Continents	Africa (*not* the Africa), Asia, South America
Countries, states, etc.	France (*not* the France), Japan, Brazil, Texas
Islands	Sicily, Bermuda, Vancouver Island, Cuba
Cities, towns, etc.	Cairo, New York, Bangkok
Mountains	Everest, Kilimanjaro, Fuji

But we use **the** in names with **Republic**, **Kingdom**, **States**, etc.:

the Czech **Republic**	**the** United **Kingdom** (the UK)
the Dominican **Republic**	**the** United **States** of America (the USA)

Compare:
- We visited **Canada** and **the United States**.

B

When we use **Mr./Mrs./Captain/Doctor**, etc. + a name, we do not use **the**. So we say:
  Mr. Johnson / **Doctor** Johnson / **Captain** Johnson / **President** Johnson, etc. (*not* the ...)
  Uncle Robert / **Saint** Catherine / **Princess** Anne, etc. (*not* the ...)
Compare:
- We called **the doctor**.
  We called **Doctor** Johnson. (*not* the Doctor Johnson)

We use **mount** (= mountain) and **lake** in the same way (without **the**):
  Mount Everest   **Mount** McKinley   **Lake** Superior   **Lake** Victoria (*not* the ...)
- They live near **the lake**.
  They live near **Lake Superior**. (*without* the)

C

We use **the** with the names of oceans, seas, rivers, gulfs, and canals:

the Atlantic (Ocean)	**the** Gulf of Mexico	**the** Amazon
the Indian Ocean	**the** Channel (between	**the** Nile
the Caribbean (Sea)	France and Britain)	**the** Panama Canal

We use **the** with the names of deserts:
  the Sahara (Desert)   **the** Gobi Desert

D

We use **the** with *plural* names of people and places:

People	**the** Mitchell**s** (= the Mitchell family), **the** Johnson**s**
Countries	**the** Netherland**s**, **the** Philippine**s**, **the** United State**s**
Groups of islands	**the** Bahama**s**, **the** Canarie**s**, **the** Hawaiian Islands
Mountain ranges	**the** Rocky Mountain**s** / **the** Rockie**s**, **the** Ande**s**, **the** Alps

- The highest mountain in **the Andes** is **Mount Aconcagua**.

E

We say:
  the north (of Mexico)   *but*   **northern** Mexico (*without* the)
  the southeast (of Canada) *but*   **southeastern** Canada
Compare:
- Sweden is in **northern Europe**; Spain is in **the south**.
Also **the** Middle East, **the** Far East

We also use **north/south**, etc. (without **the**) in the names of some regions and countries:

North America	**South Africa**	**southeast Texas**

Note that on maps, **the** is not usually included in the name.

Names with and without *the* 2 Unit 76

Exercises

75.1 Put in *the* where necessary. Leave the space empty if the sentence is already complete.

1. Who is _____ Doctor Johnson?
2. I was sick, so I went to see _____ doctor.
3. The most powerful person in _____ United States is _____ president.
4. _____ President Kennedy was assassinated in 1963.
5. Do you know _____ Wilsons? They're a very nice couple.
6. Do you know _____ Professor Brown's phone number?

75.2 Some of these sentences are correct, but some need *the* (sometimes more than once). Correct the sentences where necessary.

1. Everest was first climbed in 1953.   *OK*
2. Sapporo is (in north) of Japan.   *in the north of Japan*
3. Africa is much larger than Europe.   _____
4. Last year I visited Mexico and United States.   _____
5. South of India is warmer than north.   _____
6. Portugal is in western Europe.   _____
7. France and Britain are separated by Channel.   _____
8. Jim has traveled a lot in Middle East.   _____
9. Chicago is on Lake Michigan.   _____
10. Next year we're going skiing in Swiss Alps.   _____
11. UK consists of Great Britain and Northern Ireland.   _____
12. Seychelles are a group of islands in Indian Ocean.   _____
13. The highest mountain in Africa is Kilimanjaro.   _____
14. Hudson River flows into Atlantic Ocean.   _____

75.3 Here are some geography questions. Choose the right answer from one of the columns and write *the* if necessary. You do not need all the names in the columns. Use an atlas if necessary.

Continents	Countries	Oceans and seas	Mountains	Rivers and canals	
Africa	Canada	~~Atlantic Ocean~~	Alps	Amazon	Suez Canal
Asia	Denmark	Indian Ocean	Andes	Danube	Thames
Australia	Indonesia	Pacific Ocean	Himalayas	Mississippi	Volga
Europe	Sweden	Black Sea	Rockies	Nile	
North America	Thailand	Mediterranean	Urals	Panama Canal	
South America	United States	Red Sea		Rhine	

1. What do you have to cross to travel from Europe to America? *the Atlantic Ocean*
2. Where is Argentina? _____
3. What is the longest river in Africa? _____
4. Of which country is Stockholm the capital? _____
5. Of which country is Washington, D.C., the capital? _____
6. What is the name of the mountain range in the west of North America? _____
7. What is the name of the sea between Africa and Europe? _____
8. What is the smallest continent in the world? _____
9. What is the name of the ocean between North America and Asia? _____
10. What is the name of the ocean between Africa and Australia? _____
11. Which river flows through London? _____
12. Which river flows through Memphis and New Orleans? _____
13. Of which country is Bangkok the capital? _____
14. What joins the Atlantic and Pacific Oceans? _____
15. What is the longest river in South America? _____

Names with and without **the** 2

Names without **the**

We do not use **the** with names of most city streets / roads / squares / parks, etc.

Union **Street** (*not* the . . .)	Fifth **Avenue**	Central **Park**
Wilshire **Boulevard**	**Broadway**	Times **Square**

Names of important public buildings and institutions (for example, airports, stations, universities) are often two words:

Kennedy Airport   **Cambridge University**

The first word is the name of a place (Cambridge) or a person (Kennedy). These names are usually without **the**. In the same way, we say:

Penn Station (*not* the . . .)	**Boston University**	**Carnegie Hall**
Lincoln Center	**Buckingham Palace**	

Compare:

Buckingham Palace (*not* the . . .)   *but*   **the Royal Palace**

("Royal" is an adjective – it is not a name like "Buckingham.")

Most other buildings have names with **the**. For example:

Hotels/restaurants	**the** Sheraton **Hotel**, **the** Delhi **Restaurant**, **the** Holiday **Inn** (hotel)
Theaters/movie theaters	**the** Shubert **Theater**, **the** Cineplex **Odeon** (movie theater)
Museums/galleries	**the** Guggenheim **Museum**, **the** National **Gallery**
Other buildings/bridges	**the** Empire State **Building**, **the** White **House**, **the** Brooklyn **Bridge**

We often leave out the noun:

the Sheraton (Hotel)   **the Palace** (Theater)   **the Guggenheim** (Museum)

Some names are only **the** + *noun*, for example:

the Acropolis   **the Kremlin**   **the Pentagon**

Names with **of** usually have **the**. For example:

the Bank of England	**the** Museum of Modern Art
the Great Wall of China	**the** Tower of London

Note that we say:
the University of Michigan   *but*   **Michigan State University** (*without* the)

Many stores, restaurants, hotels, banks, etc., are named after the people who started them.

These names end in **-'s** or **-s**. We do not use **the** with these names:

Joe's Diner   **McDonald's**   **Macy's** (department store)

Churches are often named after saints:

St. John's Church (*not* the St. John's Church)   **St. Patrick's Cathedral**

Most newspapers and many organizations have names with **the**:

Newspapers	**the** Washington Post, **the** Financial Times, **the** Tribune
Organizations	**the** European Union, **the** BBC, **the** Red Cross

Names of companies, airlines, etc., are usually without **the**:

Fiat (*not* the Fiat)	**Sony**	**Delta Air Lines**
Coca-Cola	**Apple Computer**	**Cambridge University Press**

Exercises

76.1 Use the map to answer the questions. Write the name of the place and the street it is on.
Use *the* if necessary. (Remember that on maps we do not normally use *the*.)

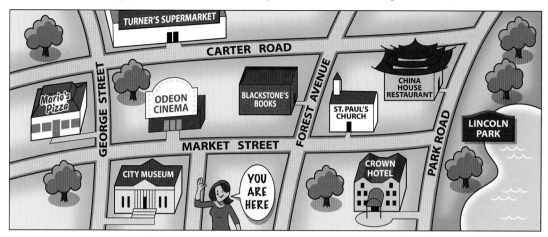

1. Is there a movie theater near here?   Yes, _the Odeon on Market Street_____ .
2. Is there a supermarket near here?   Yes, _____ on _____ .
3. Is there a hotel near here?   Yes, _____ on _____ .
4. Is there a church near here?   Yes, _____ .
5. Is there a museum near here?   Yes, _____ .
6. Is there a bookstore near here?   Yes, _____ .
7. Is there a park near here?   Yes, _____ at the end of
   _____ .
8. Is there a restaurant near here?   There are two. _____
   or _____ .

76.2 Where are the following? Use *the* where necessary.

Acropolis	**Broadway**	**Buckingham Palace**	**Eiffel Tower**
Kremlin	**White House**	**Taj Mahal**	~~**Times Square**~~

1. ___Times Square___ is in New York.
2. _____ is in Paris.
3. _____ is in Agra, India.
4. _____ is in Washington, D.C.
5. _____ is in Moscow.
6. _____ is in New York.
7. _____ is in Athens.
8. _____ is in London.

76.3 Choose the correct form, with or without *the*.

1. Have you ever been to ~~British Museum~~ / the British Museum? (*the British Museum* is correct)
2. The biggest park in New York is Central Park / the Central Park.
3. My favorite park in London is St. James's Park / the St. James's Park.
4. Ramada Inn / The Ramada Inn is on Main Street / the Main Street.
5. We flew to Mexico City from O'Hare Airport / the O'Hare Airport.
6. Frank is a student at McGill University / the McGill University.
7. If you're looking for a department store, I would recommend Harrison's / the Harrison's.
8. If you're looking for a place to have lunch, I would recommend Ship Inn / the Ship Inn.
9. Statue of Liberty / The Statue of Liberty is at the entrance to
   New York Harbor / the New York Harbor.
10. You should go to Science Museum / the Science Museum. It's very interesting.
11. John works for IBM / the IBM now. He used to work for
    General Electric / the General Electric.
12. "Which movie theater are you going to tonight?" "Classic / The Classic."
13. I'd like to go to China and see Great Wall / the Great Wall.
14. "Which newspaper do you want?" "Washington Post / The Washington Post."
15. This book is published by Cambridge University Press / the Cambridge University Press.

Singular and Plural

A Sometimes we use a *plural* noun for one thing that has two parts. For example:

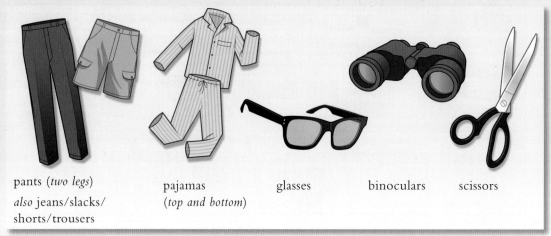

pants (*two legs*)
also jeans/slacks/
shorts/trousers

pajamas
(*top and bottom*)

glasses

binoculars

scissors

These words are plural, so they take a plural verb:

- My **pants are** too long. (*not* my pants is)

You can also use **a pair of** + these words:

- **Those are** nice **jeans**. *or* That**'s a** nice **pair of** jeans. (*not* a nice jeans)
- I need **some** new **glasses**. *or* I need **a** new **pair of** glasses.

B Some nouns end in **-ics**, but are not usually plural. For example:

economics	electronics	gymnastics	mathematics	physics	politics

- **Gymnastics** is my favorite sport. (*not* Gymnastics are)

News is not plural (see Unit 68B):

- What time **is the news** on television? (*not* are the news)

Some words ending in **-s** can be singular or plural. For example:

means	**a means** of transportation	**many means** of transportation
series	**a** television **series**	**two** television **series**
species	**a species** of bird	**200 species** of birds

C We use a plural verb with **police**:

- The **police are** investigating the murder, but **haven't** arrested anyone yet.
  (*not* The police is . . . hasn't)

Note that we say **a police officer / a policeman / a policewoman** (*not* a police).

D We do not often use the plural of **person** (persons). We normally use **people** (a plural word):

- He's **a** nice **person**. *but* They are nice **people**. (*not* nice persons)
- **Many people don't** have enough to eat. (*not* Many people doesn't)

E We think of a sum of money, a period of time, a distance, etc., as *one* thing. So we use a singular verb:

- **Twenty thousand dollars** (= it) **was** stolen in the robbery. (*not* were stolen)
- **Three years** (= it) **is** a long time to be without a job. (*not* Three years are)
- **Six miles is** a long way to walk every day.

Exercises

77.1 Complete each sentence using a word from Section A or B. Sometimes you need *a* or *some*.

1. My eyesight isn't very good. I need ___glasses___ .
2. ___A species___ is a group of animals or plants that have the same characteristics.
3. Soccer players don't wear pants when they play. They wear _____ .
4. The bicycle is _____ of transportation.
5. The bicycle and the car are _____ of transportation.
6. I want to cut this piece of material. I need _____ .
7. A friend of mine is writing _____ of articles for the local newspaper.
8. There are a lot of American TV _____ shown throughout the world.
9. While we were out walking, we saw 25 different _____ of birds.

77.2 In each example, the words on the left are connected with an activity (for example, a sport or an academic subject). Write the name of the activity. The beginning of the word is given.

1. calculate   algebra   equation   m _athematics_____
2. government   election   senator   p _____
3. finance   trade   employment   e _____
4. light   heat   gravity   ph _____
5. exercises   somersault   parallel bars gy _____
6. computer   silicon chip   video games   el _____

77.3 Choose the correct form of the verb, singular or plural.

1. Gymnastics is / ~~are~~ my favorite sport. (*is* is correct)
2. The pants you bought for me doesn't / don't fit me.
3. The police want / wants to interview two men about the robbery last week.
4. Physics was / were my best subject at school.
5. Can I borrow your scissors? Mine isn't / aren't sharp enough.
6. Fortunately the news wasn't / weren't as bad as we expected.
7. Three days isn't / aren't long enough for a good vacation.
8. I can't find my binoculars. Do you know where it is / they are?
9. It's a nice place to visit. The people is / are very friendly.
10. Does / Do the police know how the accident happened?
11. I don't like very hot weather. Ninety degrees is / are too hot for me.

77.4 Most of these sentences are wrong. Correct them where necessary.

1. (Three years are) a long time to be without a job.   *Three years is a long time*
2. The news is very depressing these days.   *OK*
3. Susan was wearing a black jeans.   _____
4. I like Matt and Jill. They're very nice persons.   _____
5. I need more than ten dollars. Ten dollars isn't enough. _____
6. I'm going to buy a new pajama.   _____
7. There was a police directing traffic on the street.   _____
8. What are the police going to do?   _____
9. This scissors isn't very sharp.   _____
10. Do you think two days are enough to see all the sights _____
    of Toronto?
11. Many people has heard about the problem.   _____

Noun + Noun (a **tennis ball** / a **headache**, etc.)

A

You can use two nouns together (*noun + noun*) to mean *one* thing/person/idea, etc. For example:

> a **tennis ball**   a **bank manager**   a **car accident**
> **income tax**   the **water temperature**

The first noun is like an adjective. It tells us what kind of thing/person/idea, etc. For example:

> a **tennis ball** = a **ball** used to play **tennis**
> a **car accident** = an **accident** that happens while driving a **car**
> **income tax** = **tax** that you pay on your **income**
> the **water temperature** = the **temperature** of the **water**
> a **Boston doctor** = a **doctor** from **Boston**
> my **life story** = the **story** of my **life**

So you can say:

> a **television** camera   a **television** program   a **television** studio   a **television** producer

(these are all different things or people to do with television)

> language **problems**   marriage **problems**   health **problems**   work **problems**

(these are all different kinds of problems)

Compare:

garden vegetables (= **vegetables** that are grown in a garden)
a **vegetable garden** (= a **garden** where vegetables are grown)

Sometimes the first word ends in **–ing**. Usually these are things used for doing something:
a **frying** pan (= a pan for frying)   a **sleeping** bag   a **swimming** pool   a **dining** room

Sometimes there are more than two nouns together:

- I waited at the **hotel reception desk**.
- We watched the **World Swimming Championships** on television.
- Everyone is talking about the **government corruption scandal**.

B

When two nouns are together like this, sometimes we write them as one word and sometimes as two separate words. For example:

a **headache**   **toothpaste**   a **weekend**   **pea soup**   a **road sign**

There are no clear rules for this. If you are not sure, write two words.

C

Note the difference between:

a **sugar bowl** (perhaps empty) and a **bowl of sugar** (= a bowl with sugar in it)
a **toolbox** (the box may be empty) and a **box of tools** (= a box full of tools)

D

When we use *noun + noun*, the first noun is like an *adjective*. It is normally singular, but the meaning is often plural. For example: a **book**store is a store where you can buy **books**, and an **apple** tree is a tree that has **apples**.
In the same way we say:

a three-**hour** trip (= a trip that takes three **hours**)   two 14-**year**-old girls (*not* years)
a 10-**dollar** bill (*not* dollars)   **a** six-**page** letter (*not* pages)
a four-**week** course (*not* weeks)   a two-**story** house (*not* stories)

Compare:

- It was **a** three-**hour** trip.   *but*   The trip took three **hours**.

-'s and of . . . Unit 79   *A week's vacation / three weeks' vacation*, etc. Unit 79E

Exercises

78.1 What do we call these things and people?

1. A ticket for a concert is __*a concert ticket*__ .
2. Problems concerning health are __*health problems*__ .
3. A magazine about computers is _____ .
4. Pictures taken on your vacation are your _____ .
5. Chocolate made with milk is _____ .
6. Somebody whose job is to inspect factories is _____ .
7. A horse that runs in races is _____ .
8. A race for horses is _____ .
9. A lawyer in Los Angeles is _____ .
10. The results of your exams are your _____ .
11. The carpet in the dining room is _____ .
12. A scandal involving an oil company is _____ .
13. A building with five stories is _____ .
14. A plan to improve traffic is _____ .
15. A course that lasts five days is _____ .
16. A question that has two parts is _____ .
17. A girl who is seven years old is _____ .

78.2 Answer the questions using two of the following words each time:

~~accident~~   belt   card   credit   editor   forecast   newspaper
number   ~~car~~   room   seat   shop   weather   window

1. This can be caused by bad driving.   __*a car accident*__
2. If you're staying at a hotel, you need to remember this.   your _____
3. You should wear this when you're in a car.   a _____
4. You can often use this to pay for things instead of cash. a _____
5. If you want to know if it's going to rain, you can
   read or listen to this.   the _____
6. This person is a top journalist.   a _____
7. You might stop to look in this when you're walking
   along a street.   a _____

78.3 Complete the sentences using the following:

15 minute(s)   six mile(s)   five day(s)   ~~10 page(s)~~
six mile(s)   two hour(s)   five course(s)   500 year(s)
60 minute(s)   20 dollar(s)   two year(s)   ~~450 page(s)~~

Sometimes you need the singular (*day/page*, etc.) and sometimes the plural
(*days/pages*, etc.).

1. It's quite a long book. There are __*450 pages*__ .
2. A few days ago I received a __*10-page*__ letter from Julia.
3. I didn't have any change. I only had a _____ bill.
4. At work in the morning I usually have a _____ break for coffee.
5. There are _____ in an hour.
6. It's only a _____ flight from New York to Montreal.
7. It was a very big meal. There were _____ .
8. Mary has just started a new job. She's got a _____ contract.
9. The oldest building in the city is the _____ castle.
10. I work _____ a week. Saturday and Sunday are free.
11. We went for a long walk in the country. We walked _____ .
12. We went for a _____ walk in the country.

-'s (your sister's name) and of . . . (the name of the book)

A

We use **-'s** (*apostrophe* + **s**) mostly for people or animals:

- **Tom's** computer isn't working. (*not* the computer of Tom)
- How old are **Chris's** children? (*not* the children of Chris)
- What's (= What is) **your sister's** name?
- What's **Tom's sister's** name?
- Be careful. Don't step on **the cat's** tail.

Note that you can use **-'s** without a noun after it:

- This isn't my book. It's **my sister's**. (= my sister's book)

We do not always use **-'s** for people. For example, we would use **of** . . . in this sentence:

- What was the name **of the man who called you**? ("the man who called you" is too long to be followed by **-'s**)

Note that we say **a woman's hat** (= a hat for a woman), **a boy's name** (= a name for a boy), **a bird's egg** (= an egg laid by a bird), etc.

B

With a *singular* noun we use **-'s**:

my **sister's** room (= **her** room – one sister)   **Mr. Carter's** house (= **his** house)

With a *plural* noun (sisters, friends, etc.) we put an apostrophe at the end of the word (**-s'**):

my sisters' room (= **their** room – *two* or *more* sisters)
the Carters' house (= **their** house – Mr. and Mrs. Carter)

If a plural noun does not end in **-s** (for example **men/women/children/people**) we use **-'s**:

the men's changing room   a **children's** book (= a book for children)

Note that you can use **-'s** after more than one noun:

Jack and Karen's wedding   **Mr. and Mrs. Carter's** house

C

For things, ideas, etc., we normally use **of** (. . . **of the book** / . . . **of the restaurant**, etc.):

the door **of the garage** (*not* the garage's door)
the name **of the book**   the owner **of the restaurant**

Sometimes the structure *noun + noun* is possible (see Unit 78):

the **garage door**   the **restaurant owner**

We say the **beginning/end/middle of** . . . , the **top/bottom of** . . . , the **front/back/side of** . . . :

the beginning of the month (*not* the month's beginning)
the top of the hill   **the back of** the car

D

You can usually use **-'s** or **of** . . . for an organization (= a group of people). So you can say:

the government's decision   *or*   the decision **of the government**
the company's success   *or*   the success **of the company**

It is also possible to use **-'s** for places. So you can say:

the city's streets   **the world's** population   **Brazil's** largest city

E

You can also use **-'s** with time expressions (**yesterday** / **next week**, etc.):

- Do you still have **yesterday's** newspaper?
- **Next week's** meeting has been canceled.

In the same way, you can say **today's** / **tomorrow's** / **tonight's** / **Monday's**, etc.

We also use **-'s** (or **-s'** with plural words) with periods of time:

- I've got **a week's** vacation starting on Monday.
- Sally needs **eight hours'** sleep a night.
- Brenda got to work 15 minutes late but lost **an hour's** pay.

The garage door (noun + noun) Unit 78   *A three-hour trip, a 10-dollar bill* Unit 78D

Exercises

79.1 In some of these sentences, it would be more natural to use -'s or -s'. Change the
underlined parts where necessary.

1. Who is the owner of this restaurant? _____OK_____
2. Where are the children of Chris? _____Chris's children_____
3. Is this the umbrella of your friend? _____
4. Write your name at the top of the page. _____
5. I've never met the daughter of Charles. _____
6. Have you met the son of Mary and Dan? _____
7. We don't know the cause of the problem. _____
8. Do we still have the newspaper of yesterday? _____
9. What's the name of this street? _____
10. What is the cost of a new computer? _____
11. The friends of your children are here. _____
12. The garden of our neighbors is very nice. _____
13. I work on the ground floor of the building. _____
14. The hair of Bill is very long. _____
15. I couldn't go to the party of Catherine. _____
16. What's the name of the woman who lives next door? _____
17. Have you seen the car of the parents of Mike? _____
18. What's the meaning of this expression? _____
19. Do you agree with the economic policy of the government? _____

79.2 What is another way of saying these things? Use -'s or -s'.

1. a hat for a woman _____a woman's hat_____
2. a name for a boy _____
3. clothes for children _____
4. a school for girls _____
5. a nest for a bird _____
6. a magazine for women _____

79.3 Read each sentence and write a new sentence beginning with the underlined words.

1. The meeting tomorrow has been canceled.
   Tomorrow's meeting has been canceled.
2. The storm last week caused a lot of damage.
   Last _____
3. The only movie theater in the town has closed down.
   The _____
4. The weather in Chicago is very changeable.
   _____
5. Tourism is the main industry in the region.
   _____

79.4 Use the information given to complete the sentences.

1. I bought groceries at the supermarket last night. They will last us for a week.
   So I bought __a week's groceries__ last night. (groceries)
2. Kim got a new car. It cost the same as her salary for a year.
   So Kim's new car cost her _____ . (salary)
3. Jim lost his job. His company gave him extra money equal to his pay for four weeks.
   So Jim got _____ when he lost his job. (pay)
4. Last night I went to bed at midnight and woke up at 5 a.m. After that I couldn't sleep.
   So I only had _____ . (sleep)
5. I haven't been able to rest all day. I haven't rested for even a minute.
   So I haven't had _____ all day. (rest)

Myself/yourself/themselves, etc.

Study this example:

Hi, I'm Steve.

Steve

Steve **introduced himself** to the other guests.
We use **myself/yourself/himself**, etc. *(reflexive pronouns)* when the *subject* and *object* are the same:

Steve	introduced	**himself**
subject		*object*

The reflexive pronouns are:

singular	my**self**	your**self** *(one person)*	him**self**/her**self**/it**self**
plural	our**selves**	your**selves** *(more than one person)*	them**selves**

- I don't want you to pay for me. **I**'ll pay for **myself**. (*not* I'll pay for me)
- Julia had a great vacation. **She** really enjoyed **herself**.
- Do **you** talk to **yourself** sometimes? *(said to one person)*
- If **you** want more to eat, help **yourselves**. *(said to more than one person)*

Compare:

- It's not our fault. **You** can't blame **us**.
- It's our own fault. **We** should blame **ourselves**.

We do not use **myself**, etc., after **feel/relax/concentrate/meet**:

- I **feel** nervous. I can't **relax**.
- You have to try and **concentrate**. (*not* concentrate yourself)
- What time should we **meet**? (*not* meet ourselves, *not* meet us)

We normally use **wash/shave/dress** *without* **myself**, etc.:

- He got up, **washed**, **shaved**, and **dressed**. (*not* washed himself, etc.)

You can also say **get dressed**. (He **got dressed**)

Compare **–selves** and **each other**:

- Kate and Joe stood in front of the mirror and looked at **themselves**.
  (= *Kate and Joe* looked at *Kate and Joe*)
- Kate looked at Joe; Joe looked at Kate. They looked at **each other**.

Themselves

Each other

You can use **one another** instead of **each other**:

- How long have you and Bill known **each other**?   *or*   . . . known **one another**?
- Sue and Ann don't like **each other**.   *or*   . . . don't like **one another**.
- Do you and Sarah live near **each other**?   *or*   . . . near **one another**?

We also use **myself/yourself**, etc., in another way. For example:

- "Who repaired your bicycle for you?"   "**I** repaired it **myself**."

I repaired it myself = I repaired it, not anybody else. Here, *myself* is used to emphasize **I** (it makes it stronger). Some more examples:

- I'm not going to do your work for you. **You** can do it **yourself**. (= you, not me)
- Let's paint the house **ourselves**. It will be much cheaper.
- The **movie itself** wasn't very good, but I loved the music.
- I don't think Sue will get the job. **Sue herself** doesn't think she'll get it.
  (*or* **Sue** doesn't think she'll get it **herself**.)

Get dressed / get married, etc. Unit 42D   *By myself / by yourself, etc.* Unit 81D

Exercises

80.1 Complete the sentences using *myself/yourself*, etc., + the following verbs
(in the correct form):

> **blame   burn   enjoy   express   hurt   ~~introduce~~   put**

1. Steve __*introduced himself*__ to the other guests at the party.
2. Bill fell down some steps, but fortunately he didn't _____ badly.
3. It isn't Sue's fault. She really shouldn't _____ .
4. Please try and understand how I feel. _____ in my position.
5. The children had a great time at the beach. They really _____ .
6. Be careful! That pan is very hot. Don't _____ .
7. Sometimes I can't say exactly what I mean. I wish I could _____ better.

80.2 Put in *myself/yourself/ourselves*, etc., or *me/you/us*, etc.

1. Julia had a great vacation. She enjoyed __*herself*__ .
2. It's not my fault. You can't blame _____ .
3. What I did was really bad. I'm ashamed of _____ .
4. We've got a problem. I hope you can help _____ .
5. "Can I have another cookie?" "Of course. Help _____ !"
6. I want you to meet Sarah. I'll introduce _____ to her.
7. Don't worry about Tom and me. We can take care of _____ .
8. I gave them a key to our house so that they could let _____ in.
9. I didn't want anybody to see the letters, so I burned _____ .

80.3 Complete these sentences. Use *myself/yourself*, etc., only where necessary. Use the
following verbs (in the correct form):

> **concentrate   defend   dry   ~~feel~~   meet   relax**

1. I was sick yesterday, but I __*feel*__ much better today.
2. She climbed out of the swimming pool and _____ with a towel.
3. I tried to study, but I couldn't _____ .
4. If somebody attacks you, you need to be able to _____ .
5. I'm going out with Chris tonight. We're _____ at 7:30.
6. You're always rushing around. Why don't you sit down and _____ ?

80.4 Complete the sentences with *-selves* or *each other*.

1. How long have you and Bill known __*each other*__ ?
2. If people work too hard, they can make _____ sick.
3. I need you and you need me. We need _____ .
4. In the U.S., friends often give _____ presents at Christmas.
5. Some people are very selfish. They think only of _____ .
6. Tracy and I don't see _____ very often these days.
7. We couldn't get back into the house. We had locked _____ out.
8. They've had an argument. They're not speaking to _____ at the moment.
9. We'd never met before, so we introduced _____ to _____ .

80.5 Complete the answers to the questions using *myself/yourself/itself*, etc.

1.	Who repaired the bicycle for you?	Nobody. I __*repaired it myself.*__ _____
2.	Who cuts Brian's hair for him?	Nobody. He cuts _____
3.	Do you want me to mail that letter for you?	No, I'll _____
4.	Who told you that Linda was getting married?	Linda _____
5.	Can you call John for me?	Why can't you _____ ?

A friend **of mine**   **My own** house   **By myself**

A

A friend of mine / a friend of Tom's, etc.

We say "a friend of **mine/yours/his/hers/ours/theirs**":

- I'm going to a wedding on Saturday. **A friend of mine** is getting married.
  (*not* a friend of me)
- We took a trip with **some friends of ours**. (*not* some friends of us)
- Michael had an argument with **a neighbor of his**.
- It was **a good idea of yours** to go to the movies.

In the same way we say "a friend **of my sister's** / (a friend) **of Tom's**," etc.:

- That woman over there is **a friend of my sister's**.
- It was **a good idea of Tom's** to go to the movies.

B

My own . . . / your own . . . , etc.

We use **my/your/his/her/its/our/their** before **own**:

> **my own** house   **your own** car   **her own** room
> (*not* an own house, an own car, etc.)

My own . . . / your own . . . , etc. = something that is only mine/yours, etc., not shared
or borrowed:

- I don't want to share a room with anybody. I want **my own room**.
- Vicky and George would like to have **their own house**.
- It's a shame that the apartment doesn't have **its own parking space**.
- It's **my own fault** that I don't have any money. I buy too many things I don't need.
- Why do you want to borrow my car? Why don't you use **your own**? (= your own car)

You can also use **own** to say that you do something yourself
instead of somebody else doing it for you. For example:

- Bill usually cuts **his own hair**. (= he cuts it himself;
  he doesn't go to a barber)
- I'd like to have a garden so that I could grow **my own
  vegetables**. (= grow them myself instead of buying
  them in stores)

Bill usually cuts **his own hair**.

C

On my own / on your own, etc. = independently

- My children are living **on their own**. (= living in their own place
  and supporting themselves)
- I traveled around Japan **on my own**. (= not on an organized tour)
- Are you raising your children **on your own**? (= without the other parent)

D

By myself / by yourself, etc.

By myself / by yourself / by themselves, etc. = alone, without other people:

- I like living **by myself**.
- "Did you go to Hawaii **by yourself**?"   "No, with a friend."
- Jack was sitting **by himself** in a corner of the café.
- Student drivers are not allowed to drive **by themselves**.

Exercises

81.1 Write new sentences with the same meaning. Change the <u>underlined</u> words and use the structure in Section A (*a friend of mine*, etc.).

1. I am meeting <u>one of my friends</u> tonight. *I'm meeting a friend of mine tonight.*
2. We met <u>one of your relatives</u>. We met a _____
3. Jason borrowed <u>one of my books</u>. Jason _____
4. Ann invited <u>some of her friends</u> to her place. Ann _____
5. We had dinner with <u>one of our neighbors</u>. _____
6. I took a trip with <u>two of my friends</u>. _____
7. Is that man <u>one of your friends</u>? _____
8. I met <u>one of Amy's friends</u> at the party. _____

81.2 Complete the sentences using *my own / your own*, etc., + the following:

~~bedroom~~   business   opinions   private beach   words

1. I share a kitchen and bathroom, but I have *my own bedroom* _____ .
2. Gary doesn't think the same as me. He's got _____ .
3. Julia is fed up with working for other people. She wants to start _____ .
4. We stayed at a luxury hotel on the ocean. The hotel had _____ .
5. On the test we had to read a story, and then write it in _____ .

81.3 Complete the sentences using *my own / your own*, etc.

1. Why do you want to borrow my car?
   Why don't you use your own car? _____
2. How can you blame me? It's not my fault.
   It's _____ .
3. She's always using my ideas.
   Why can't she use _____ ?
4. Please don't worry about my problems.
   You've got _____ .
5. I can't make his decisions for him.
   He has to make _____ .

81.4 Complete the sentences using *my own / your own*, etc. Use the following verbs:

bake   ~~cut~~   make   write

1. Bill never goes to the barber. He *cuts his own hair* _____ .
2. Mary doesn't buy many clothes. She usually _____ .
3. We don't often buy bread. We usually _____ .
4. Paul is a singer. He sings songs written by other people, but he also _____
   _____ .

81.5 Complete the sentences using *on my own / by myself*, etc.

1. Did you go to Hawaii by *yourself* ?
2. I'm glad I live with other people. I wouldn't like to live on _____ .
3. The box was too heavy for me to lift by _____ .
4. "Who was Tom with when you saw him?" "Nobody. He was by _____ ."
5. I think my brother is too young to make that decision on _____ .
6. I don't think she knows many people. When I see her, she is always by _____
7. My sister graduated from college and is living on _____ .
8. Do you like working with other people, or do you prefer working by _____ ?
9. We had no help decorating the apartment. We did it completely on _____ .
10. I went out with Sally because she didn't want to go out by _____

There . . . and It . . .

There and **it**

> There's a new restaurant on Main Street.

> Yes, I know. I went there last night. It's very good.

We use **there** when we talk about something for the first time, to say that it exists:

- ■ **There's** a new restaurant on Main Street. (*not* A new restaurant is on Main Street)
- ■ I'm sorry I'm late. **There was** a lot of traffic. (*not* It was a lot of traffic)
- ■ Things are more expensive now. **There has been** a big increase in the cost of living.

It = a specific thing, place, fact, situation, etc. (but see also section C):

- ■ We went to the new restaurant. **It's** very good. (**It** = the restaurant)
- ■ I wasn't expecting them to come. **It** was a complete surprise. (**It** = that they came)

Compare **there** and **it**:

- ■ I don't like this town. **There's** nothing to do here. **It's** a boring place.

There also means "to/at/in that place":

- ■ The new restaurant is very good. I went **there** (= to the restaurant) last night.
- ■ When we got to the party, there were already a lot of people **there** (= at the party).

You can say **there will be**, **there must be**, **there might be**, **there used to be**, etc.:

- ■ **Will there be** many people at the party?
- ■ "**Is there** a flight to Miami tonight?"   "**There might be**. I'll check."
- ■ If people drove more carefully, **there wouldn't be** so many accidents.

Also **there must have been**, **there should have been**, etc.:

- ■ There was music playing. **There must have been** somebody at home.

Compare **there** and **it**:

- ■ They live on a busy street. **There must be** a lot of noise from the traffic.
  They live on a busy main street. **It must be** very noisy.
- ■ **There used to be** a movie theater on Main Street, but it closed a few years ago.
  That building is now a supermarket. **It used to be** a movie theater.

You can also say **there is sure/certain/likely/bound** to be . . . :

- ■ **There is bound** (= sure) **to be** a flight to Miami tonight.

We also use **it** in sentences like this:

- ■ **It's** dangerous to **walk in the street**.

We do not usually say "To walk in the street is dangerous." Normally we begin with **It** . . . .

Some more examples:

- ■ **It** didn't take us long **to get here**.
- ■ **It's** too bad **(that) Sandra can't come to the party**.
- ■ Let's go. **It's** not worth **waiting any longer**.

We also use **it** to talk about distance, time, and weather:

- ■ How far is **it** from here to the airport?
- ■ What day is **it** today?
- ■ **It's** been a long time since I saw you.
- ■ **It** was windy. (*but* **There** was **a cold wind**.)

It's worth / it's no use / there's no point Unit 61A   *There is + -ing / -ed* Unit 95

Exercises

82.1 Put in *there is/was* or *it is/was*. Some sentences are questions (*is there . . . ? / is it . . . ?*, etc.) and some are negative (*isn't/wasn't*).

1. I'm sorry I'm late. <u>*There was*</u> a lot of traffic.
2. What's the new restaurant like? <u>*Is it*</u> good?
3. "_____ a bookstore near here?" "Yes, _____ one on Hill Street."
4. When we got to the movie theater, _____ a line outside. _____ a very long line, so we decided not to wait.
5. I couldn't see anything. _____ completely dark.
6. _____ trouble at the basketball game last night. They had to call the police.
7. How far _____ from Hong Kong to Taipei?
8. _____ Keith's birthday yesterday. We had a party.
9. _____ too windy to play tennis today. Let's play tomorrow instead.
10. I wanted to visit the museum, but _____ enough time.
11. "_____ time to leave?" "Yes, _____ almost midnight."
12. A few days ago _____ a storm. _____ a lot of damage.
13. _____ a beautiful day yesterday. We went on a picnic.
14. _____ anything on television, so I turned it off.
15. _____ an accident on Main Street, but _____ very serious.

82.2 Read the first sentence, and then write a sentence beginning *There . . . .*

1. The roads were busy today.   <u>*There was a lot of traffic.*</u>
2. This soup is very salty.   There _____ in the soup.
3. The box was empty.   _____ in the box.
4. The movie was very violent.   _____
5. The shopping mall was very crowded. _____
                                       _____
6. I like this town – it's lively.   _____

82.3 Complete the sentences. Use *there will be*, *there would be*, etc. Choose from:

will   might   ~~would~~   wouldn't   should   used to   (be) going to

1. If people drove more carefully, <u>*there would be*</u> fewer accidents.
2. "Do we have any eggs?" "I'm not sure. _____ some in the fridge."
3. I think everything will be OK. I don't think _____ any problems.
4. Look at the sky. _____ a storm.
5. "Is there a school in this town?" "Not now. _____ one, but it closed."
6. People drive too fast on this road. I think _____ a speed limit.
7. If people weren't aggressive, _____ any wars.

82.4 Are these sentences right or wrong? Change *it* to *there* where necessary.

1. They live on a busy street. (It must be) a lot of noise.   <u>*There must be a lot of noise.*</u>
2. Last winter it was very cold, and it was a lot of snow.   _____
3. It used to be a church here, but it was torn down.   _____
4. Why was she so unfriendly? It must have been a reason.   _____
5. It's a long way from my house to the nearest store.   _____
6. *A:* Where can we park the car?
   B: Don't worry. It's sure to be a parking lot somewhere. _____
7. After the lecture, it will be an opportunity to
   ask questions.   _____
8. I like the place where I live, but it would be nicer
   to live by the ocean.   _____
9. I was told that it would be somebody to meet me
   at the airport, but it wasn't anybody.   _____
10. The situation is still the same. It has been no change.   _____
11. I don't know who'll win, but it's sure to be a good game. _____

165

Some and any

A

In general we use **some** (*also* **somebody/someone/something**) in positive sentences and **any** (*also* **anybody**, etc.) in negative sentences:

some	any
■ We bought **some** flowers.	■ We did**n't** buy **any** flowers.
■ He's busy. He's got **some** work to do.	■ He's lazy. He **never** does **any** work.
■ There's **somebody** at the door.	■ There is**n't anybody** at the door.
■ I'm hungry. I want **something** to eat.	■ I'm not hungry. I do**n't** want **anything** to eat.

We use **any** in the following sentences because the meaning is negative:
- ■ She went out **without any** money. (= she did**n't** take **any** money with her)
- ■ He **refused** to eat **anything**. (= he did**n't** eat **anything**)
- ■ **Hardly anybody** passed the examination. (= almost **nobody** passed)

B

We use both **some** and **any** in questions. We use **some** to talk about a person or thing that we know exists or we think exists:
- ■ Are you waiting for **somebody**? (I think you are waiting for somebody)

We use **some** in questions when we offer or ask for things:
- ■ Would you like **something** to eat? (there is something to eat)
- ■ Can I have **some** sugar, please? (there is probably some sugar I can have)

But in most questions, we use **any**. We do not know if the thing or person exists:
- ■ "Do you have **any** luggage?" "No, I don't."
- ■ I can't find my bag. Has **anybody** seen it?

C

We often use **any** after **if**:
- ■ **If** there are **any** letters for me, can you send them on?
- ■ **If anyone** has any questions, I'll be glad to answer them.
- ■ Let me know **if** you need **anything**.

The following sentences have the idea of **if**:
- ■ I'm sorry for **any** trouble I've caused. (= if I have caused any trouble)
- ■ **Anyone** who wants to take the exam should tell me by Friday. (= if there is anyone)

D

We also use **any** with the meaning "it doesn't matter which":
- ■ You can take **any** bus. They all go downtown. (= it doesn't matter which bus you take)
- ■ "Sing a song." "Which song should I sing?" "**Any** song. I don't care."
  (= it doesn't matter which song)
- ■ Come and see me **anytime** you want.
- ■ "Let's go out somewhere." "Where should we go?" "**Anywhere**. It doesn't matter."
- ■ We left the door unlocked. **Anybody** could have come in.

Compare **something** and **anything**:
- ■ *A:* I'm hungry. I want **something** to eat.
  B: What would you like?
  A: I don't care. **Anything**. (= something, but it doesn't matter what)

E

Somebody/someone/anybody/anyone are singular words:
- ■ **Someone** is here to see you.

But we often use **they/them/their** after these words:
- ■ **Someone** has forgotten **their** umbrella. (= his or her umbrella)
- ■ If **anybody** wants to leave early, **they** can. (= he or she can)

Not . . . any Unit 84   *Some of / any of . . .* Unit 86   *Hardly any* Unit 99C

Exercises

83.1 Complete the sentences with *some* or *any*.

1. We didn't buy __*any*__ flowers.
2. I'm going out tonight with _____ friends of mine.
3. *A:* Have you seen _____ good movies recently?
   B: No, I haven't been to the movies in ages.
4. I didn't have _____ money, so I had to borrow _____ .
5. Can I have _____ milk in my coffee, please?
6. I was too tired to do _____ work.
7. You can cash these traveler's checks at _____ bank.
8. Can you give me _____ information about places of interest in the area?
9. With the special tourist bus pass, you can travel on _____ bus you like.
10. If there are _____ words you don't understand, use a dictionary.

83.2 Complete the sentences with *some* or *any* + *body/one/thing/where*.

1. I was too surprised to say __*anything*__ .
2. There's _____ at the door. Can you go and see who it is?
3. Does _____ mind if I open the window?
4. I wasn't feeling hungry, so I didn't eat _____ .
5. You must be hungry. Would you like _____ to eat?
6. Quick, let's go! There's _____ coming and I don't want
   _____ to see us.
7. Sarah was upset about _____ and refused to talk to _____ .
8. This machine is very easy to use. _____ can learn to use it very quickly.
9. There was hardly _____ on the beach. It was almost deserted.
10. "Do you live _____ near Jim?" "No, he lives in another part of town."
11. *A:* Where do you want to go on vacation?
    B: Let's go _____ warm and sunny.
12. They stay at home all the time. They never seem to go _____ .
13. I'm going out now. If _____ calls while I'm out, tell them I'll be
    back at 11:30.
14. Why are you looking under the bed? Did you lose _____ ?
15. _____ who saw the accident should contact the police.
16. "Can I ask you _____ ?" "Sure. What do you want to ask?"
17. Sue is very secretive. She never tells _____ . *(2 words)*

83.3 Complete the sentences. Use *any* + noun or *anybody/anyone/anything/anywhere*.

1.	Which bus do I have to catch?	__*Any bus.*__ They all go downtown.
2.	Which day should I come?	It doesn't matter. _____ .
3.	What do you want to eat?	_____ . I don't care. Whatever you have.
4.	Where should I sit?	It's up to you. You can sit _____ you like.
5.	What kind of job are you looking for?	_____ . It doesn't matter.
6.	What time should I call tomorrow?	_____ . I'll be home all day.
7.	Who should I invite to the party?	I don't care. _____ you like.
8.	Which newspaper should I buy?	_____ . Whatever they have at the store.

No/none/any   Nothing/nobody, etc.

No and none

We use **no** + noun. **No** = **not a** or **not any**:
- We had to walk home because there was **no bus**. (= there was**n't** a bus)
- Sue will have **no difficulty** finding a job. (= Sue wo**n't** have **any** difficulty . . .)
- There were **no stores** open. (= There were**n't** any stores open.)

You can use **no** + noun at the beginning of a sentence:
- **No reason** was given for the change of plan.

We use **none** without a noun:
- "How much money do you have?"   "**None**." (= no money)
- All the tickets have been sold. There are **none** left. (= no tickets left)

Or we use **none of** . . . :
- This money is all yours. **None of it** is mine.

After **none of** + plural (none of **the students**, none of **them**, etc.) the verb can be singular or plural. A plural verb is more common:
- None of the stores **were** (or **was**) open.

Nothing   nobody/no one   nowhere

You can use these negative words at the beginning of a sentence or alone (as answers to questions):
- **Nobody** (or **No one**) came to visit me while I was in the hospital.
- "What happened?"   "**Nothing**."
- "Where are you going?"   "**Nowhere**. I'm staying here."

You can also use these words after a verb, especially after **be** and **have**:
- The house is empty. There**'s no one** living there.
- We **had nothing** to eat.

Nothing/nobody, etc. = **not** + **anything/anybody**, etc.:
- I didn't say **anything**. (= I said **nothing**.)
- Jane didn't tell **anybody** about her plans. (= Jane told **nobody** . . .)
- They don't have **anywhere** to live. (= They have **nowhere** to live.)

With **nothing/nobody**, etc., do not use a negative verb (**isn't**, **didn't**, etc.):
- I **said** nothing. (not I didn't say nothing)
- Nobody **tells** me anything. (not Nobody doesn't tell me)

We also use **any/anything/anybody**, etc. (without not) to mean "it doesn't matter which/what/who" (see Unit 83D). Compare **no-** and **any-**:
- There was **no** bus, so we walked home.
  You can take **any** bus. They all go downtown. (= it doesn't matter which)
- "What do you want to eat?"   "**Nothing**. I'm not hungry."
  I'm so hungry I could eat **anything**. (= it doesn't matter what)
- The exam was extremely difficult. **Nobody** passed. (= everybody failed)
  The exam was very easy. **Anybody** could have passed. (= it doesn't matter who)

After **nobody/no one** you can use **they/them/their** (see also Unit 83E):
- **Nobody** called, did **they**? (= did he or she)
- **No one** did what I asked **them** to do. (= him or her)
- **Nobody** in the class did **their** homework. (= his or her homework)

Exercises

84.1 Complete these sentences with *no*, *none*, or *any*.

1. It was a holiday, so there were __*no*__ stores open.
2. I don't have __*any*__ money. Can you lend me some?
3. We had to walk home because there were _____ taxis.
4. We had to walk home because there weren't _____ taxis.
5. "How many eggs do we have?" " _____ . Should I go and get some?"
6. We took a few pictures, but _____ of them were very good.
7. What a stupid thing to do! _____ intelligent person would do something like that.
8. I'll try to answer _____ questions you ask me.
9. I couldn't answer _____ of the questions they asked me.
10. We canceled the party because _____ of the people we invited were able to come.
11. I tried to call Chris, but there was _____ answer.

84.2 Answer these questions using *none/nobody/no one/nothing/nowhere*.

1. What did you do? — *Nothing.* _____
2. Who were you talking to? _____
3. How much luggage do you have? _____
4. Where are you going? _____
5. How many mistakes did you make? _____
6. How much did you pay? _____

Now answer the same questions using complete sentences with *any/anybody/anything/anywhere*.

7. (1) __*I didn't do anything.*_____
8. (2) I _____
9. (3) _____
10. (4) _____
11. (5) _____
12. (6) _____

84.3 Complete these sentences with *no* or *any* + *body/one/thing/where*.

1. I don't want __*anything*__ to drink. I'm not thirsty.
2. The bus was completely empty. There was _____ on it.
3. "Where did you go for vacation?" " _____ . I stayed home."
4. I went to the mall, but I didn't buy _____ .
5. *A:* What did you buy?
   B: _____ . I couldn't find _____ I wanted.
6. The town is still the same as it was years ago. _____ has changed.
7. Have you seen my watch? I can't find it _____ .
8. There was complete silence in the room. _____ said _____ .

84.4 Choose the right word.

1. She didn't tell ~~nobody~~ / anybody about her plans. (*anybody* is correct)
2. The accident looked serious, but fortunately <u>nobody / anybody</u> was injured.
3. I looked out the window, but I couldn't see <u>no one / anyone</u>.
4. My job is very easy. <u>Nobody / Anybody</u> could do it.
5. "What's in that box?" "<u>Nothing / Anything</u>. It's empty."
6. The situation is uncertain. <u>Nothing / Anything</u> could happen.
7. I don't know <u>nothing / anything</u> about economics.

UNIT 85

Much, many, little, few, a lot, plenty

A

We use **much** and **little** with *uncountable* nouns:

much time   much luck   little energy   little money

We use **many** and **few** with *plural* nouns:

many friends   many people   few cars   few countries

B

We use **a lot of / lots of / plenty of** with both *uncountable* and *plural* nouns:

a lot of luck   lots of time   plenty of money
a lot of friends   lots of people   plenty of ideas

Plenty = more than enough:

- There's no need to hurry. We've got **plenty of time**.

C

Much is unusual in positive sentences (especially in spoken English). Compare:

- We did**n't** spend **much** money.

but   We spent **a lot of** money. (*not* We spent much money)

- Do you see David **much**?

but   I see David **a lot**. (*not* I see David much)

We use **many**, **a lot of**, and **lots of** in all kinds of sentences:

- **Many** people drive too fast.   *or*   **A lot of / Lots of** people drive too fast.
- Do you know **many** people?   *or*   Do you know **a lot of / lots of** people?
- There aren't **many** tourists here.   *or*   There aren't **a lot of** tourists here.

Note that we say **many years / many weeks / many days** (*not* a lot of . . .):

- We've lived here for **many years**. (*not* a lot of years)

D

Little and **few** (*without* a) are negative ideas (= not much / not many):

- Gary is very busy with his job. He has **little time** for other things.
  (= not much time, less time than he would like)
- Vicky doesn't like living in Paris. She has **few** friends there.
  (= not many, not as many as she would like)

You can say **very little** and **very few**:

- Gary has **very little** time for other things.
- Vicky has **very few** friends in Paris.

E

A little and **a few** have a more positive meaning.

A little = some, a small amount:

- Let's go and get something to drink. We have **a little** time before the train leaves.
  (a little time = some time, enough time to have something to drink)
- "Do you speak English?"   "**A little**." (so we can talk to each other)

A few = some, a small number:

- I enjoy my life here. I have **a few** friends, and we get together pretty often.
  (a few friends = not many but enough to have a good time)
- "When was the last time you saw Claire?"   "**A few** days ago." (= some days ago)

Compare:

- He spoke **little** English, so it was difficult to communicate with him.
- He spoke **a little** English, so we were able to communicate with him.
- She's lucky. She has **few** problems. (= not many problems)
- Things are not going so well for her. She has **a few** problems. (= some problems)

You can say **only a little** and **only a few**:

- Hurry! We have **only a little** time. (*not* only little time)
- The town was very small. There were **only a few** streets. (*not* only few streets)

Exercises

85.1 In some of these sentences *much* is incorrect or unnatural. Change *much* to *many* or *a lot (of)* where necessary. Write **OK** if the sentence is already correct.

1. We didn't spend much money. _____OK_____
2. Sue drinks (much tea). _____a lot of tea_____
3. Joe always puts much salt on his food. _____
4. We'll have to hurry. We don't have much time. _____
5. It cost much to fix the car. _____
6. Did it cost much to fix the car? _____
7. I don't know much people in this town. _____
8. I use the phone much at work. _____
9. There wasn't much traffic this morning. _____
10. You need much money to travel around the world. _____

85.2 Complete the sentences using *plenty (of)* + the following:

    hotels   money   room   things to see   ~~time~~   to learn

1. There's no need to hurry. There's _____plenty of time._____
2. He doesn't have any financial problems. He has _____
3. Come and sit with us. There's _____
4. She knows a lot, but she still has _____
5. It's an interesting town to visit. There _____
6. I'm sure we'll find somewhere to stay. _____

85.3 Put in *much/many/few/little* (one word only).

1. He isn't very popular. He has very ___few___ friends.
2. Ann is very busy these days. She has _____ free time.
3. Did you take _____ pictures when you were on vacation?
4. I'm not very busy today. I don't have _____ to do.
5. This is a very modern city. There are _____ old buildings.
6. The weather has been very dry recently. We've had very _____ rain.
7. "Do you know Boston?" "No, I haven't been there for _____ years."

85.4 Put in *a* where necessary. Write **OK** if the sentence is already complete.

1. She's lucky. She has few problems. _____OK_____
2. Things are not going so well for her. She has
   <u>few problems</u>. _____a few problems_____
3. Can you lend me <u>few dollars</u>? _____
4. There was <u>little traffic</u>, so the trip didn't take very long. _____
5. I can't give you a decision yet. I need <u>little time</u> to think. _____
6. It was a surprise that he won the match. <u>Few people</u>
   expected him to win. _____
7. I don't know much Spanish – <u>only few words</u>. _____
8. I wonder how Sam is. I haven't seen him for <u>few months</u>. _____

85.5 Put in *little / a little / few / a few*.

1. Gary is very busy with his job. He has ___little___ time for other things.
2. Listen carefully. I'm going to give you _____ advice.
3. Do you mind if I ask you _____ questions?
4. It's not a very interesting place to visit, so _____ tourists come here.
5. I don't think Jill would be a good teacher. She has _____ patience.
6. "Would you like cream in your coffee?" "Yes, please, _____ ."
7. This is a very boring place to live. There's _____ to do.
8. "Have you ever been to Paris?" "Yes, I've been there _____ times."

All / all of   most / most of   no / none of, etc.

A

all	some	any	most	much/many	little/few	no

You can use the words in the box with a noun (**some food** / **few books**, etc.):

- **All cars** have wheels.
- **Some cars** can go faster than others.
- *(on a notice)* **NO CARS**. (= no cars allowed)
- **Many people** drive too fast.
- I don't go out very often. I stay home **most days**.

You cannot say "all of cars," "some of people," etc. (see also Section B):

- **Some people** learn languages more easily than others. (*not* Some of people)

Note that we say **most** (*not* the most):

- **Most tourists** don't visit this part of town. (*not* The most tourists)

B

all	some	any	most	much/many	little/few	half	none

You can use the words in the box with **of** (**some of** / **most of**, etc.).

We use **some of** / **most of** / **none of**, etc. + **the/this/that/these/those/my** . . . , etc.

So you can say **some of the people**, **some of those people** (*but not* some of people):

- **Some of the people** I work with are not very friendly.
- **None of this money** is mine.
- Have you read **any of these books**?
- I was sick yesterday. I spent **most of the day** in bed.

You don't need **of** after **all** or **half**. So you can say:

- **All my friends** live in Los Angeles.   *or*   All **of** my friends . . .
- **Half this money** is mine.   *or*   Half **of** this money . . .

Compare:

- **All flowers** are beautiful. (= all flowers in general)
  All (**of**) **the flowers in this garden** are beautiful. (= a specific group of flowers)
- **Most problems** have a solution. (= most problems in general)
  We were able to solve **most of the problems we had**. (= a specific group of problems)

C

You can use **all of** / **some of** / **none of**, etc. + **it/us/you/them**:

- "How many of these people do you know?"   "**None of them**. / **A few of them**."
- Do **any of you** want to come to a party tonight?
- "Do you like this music?"   "**Some of it**. Not **all of it**."

We say: **all of us** / **all of you** / **half of it** / **half of them**, etc. You cannot leave out **of** before **it/us/you/them**:

- **All of us** were late. (*not* All us)
- I haven't finished the book yet. I've only read **half of it**. (*not* half it)

D

You can also use **some/most/none**, etc., alone, *without* a noun:

- Some cars have four doors and **some** have two.
- A few of the shops were open, but **most** (of them) were closed.
- Half this money is mine, and **half** (of it) is yours. (*not* the half)

Some and *any* Unit 83   *No* and *none* Unit 84   *Much/many/little/few* Unit 85
All Units 88, 107C   *All of whom* / *most of which*, etc. Unit 94B

Exercises

86.1 Put in *of* where necessary. Leave the space empty if the sentence is already complete.

1. All _____—_____ cars have wheels.
2. None __*of*__ this money is mine.
3. Some _____ movies are very violent.
4. Some _____ the movies I've seen recently have been very violent.
5. Jim has lived in Houston all _____ his life.
6. Many _____ people watch too much TV.
7. Are any _____ those letters for me?
8. Kate has lived in Miami most _____ her life.
9. Jim thinks all _____ museums are boring.
10. Most _____ days I get up before 7:00.

86.2 Choose from the list and complete the sentences. Use *of* (*some of* / *most of*, etc.) where necessary.

accidents	large cities	my dinner	my teammates
birds	her friends	my spare time	the population
~~cars~~	her opinions	the buildings	~~these books~~

1. I haven't read many __*of these books*__ .
2. All __*cars*__ have wheels.
3. I spend much _____ gardening.
4. Many _____ are caused by bad driving.
5. It's an old town. Many _____ are over 400 years old.
6. When she got married, she kept it a secret. She didn't tell any _____ .
7. Not many people live in the north of the country. Most _____ live in the south.
8. Not all _____ can fly. For example, penguins can't fly.
9. Our team played badly and lost the game. None _____ played well.
10. Julia and I have very different ideas. I don't agree with many _____ .
11. New York, like most _____ , has a traffic problem.
12. I had no appetite. I could only eat half _____ .

86.3 Use your own ideas to complete these sentences.

1. The building was damaged in the explosion. All __*the windows*__ were broken.
2. We had a very lazy vacation. We spent most of _____ on the beach.
3. I went to the movies by myself. None of _____ wanted to come.
4. The test was difficult. I could only answer half _____ .
5. Some of _____ you took at the wedding were very good.
6. *A:* Have you spent all _____ I gave you?
   B: No, there's still some left.

86.4 Complete the sentences. Use: *all of* / *some of* / *none of* + *it/them/us* (*all of it* / *some of them*, etc.)

1. These books are all Jane's. __*None of them*__ belong to me.
2. "How many of these books have you read?" " _____ . Every one."
3. We all got wet in the rain because _____ had an umbrella.
4. Some of this money is yours, and _____ is mine.
5. I asked some people for directions, but _____ was able to help me.
6. She made up the whole story from beginning to end. _____ was true.
7. Not all the tourists in the group were Spanish. _____ were French.
8. I watched most of the movie, but not _____ .

Both / both of   neither / neither of   either / either of

A

We use **both/neither/either** for two things. You can use these words with a noun
(**both books**, **neither book**, etc.).

For example, you are going out to eat. There are two possible restaurants. You say:
- **Both restaurants** are very good. (*not* The both restaurants)
- **Neither restaurant** is expensive.
- We can go to **either restaurant**. I don't care.
  (**either** = one or the other, it doesn't matter which one)

B

Both of . . . / **neither of** . . . / **either of** . . .

We use **both of / neither of / either of + the/these/my/Tom's** . . . , etc. So we say
"both of **the** restaurants," "both of **those** restaurants," etc. (*but not* both of restaurants):
- **Both of these** restaurants are very good.
- **Neither of the** restaurants we went to was (*or* were) expensive.
- I haven't been to **either of those** restaurants. (= I haven't been to one or the other)

You don't need **of** after **both**. So you can say:
- **Both my parents** are from Michigan.   *or*   Both **of** my parents . . .

You can use **both of / neither of / either of + us/you/them**:
- *(talking to two people)* Can **either of you** speak Spanish?
- I asked two people the way to the station, but **neither of them** knew.

You must say "both **of**" before **us/you/them**:
- **Both of us** were very tired. (*not* Both us were . . .)

After **neither of** . . . a *singular* or a *plural* verb is possible:
- Neither of the children **wants** (*or* **want**) to go to bed.

C

You can also use **both/neither/either** alone, *without* a noun:
- I couldn't decide which of the two shirts to buy. I liked **both**.
  (*or* I liked **both** of them.)
- "Is your friend British or American?" "**Neither**. She's Australian."
- "Do you want tea or coffee?" "**Either**. It doesn't matter."

D

You can say:

both . . . **and** . . .	■ **Both** Ann **and** Tom were late.
	■ I was **both** tired **and** hungry when I got home.
neither . . . **nor** . . .	■ **Neither** Liz **nor** Robin came to the party.
	■ She said she would contact me, but she **neither** wrote **nor** called.
either . . . **or** . . .	■ I'm not sure where he's from. He's **either** Spanish **or** Italian.
	■ **Either** you apologize, **or** I'll never speak to you again.

E

Compare **either/neither/both** (two things) and **any/none/all** (more than two):

■ There are **two** good hotels here. You could stay at **either** of them.	■ There are **many** good hotels here. You could stay at **any** of them.
■ We tried **two** hotels. **Neither** of them had any rooms. **Both** of them were full.	■ We tried **a lot of** hotels. **None** of them had any rooms. **All** of them were full.

Neither do I / I don't either Unit 49C   *Both of whom / neither of which* Unit 94B   *Both* Unit 107C

Exercises

87.1 Complete the sentences with *both/neither/either*.

1. "Do you want tea or coffee?" __*"Either.*__ It really doesn't matter."
2. "What's the date today – the 18th or the 19th?" " _____ . It's the 20th."
3. *A:* Where did you go for vacation – Florida or Puerto Rico?
   B: We went to _____ . A week in Florida and a week in Puerto Rico.
4. "When should I call you, morning or afternoon?" " _____ . I'll be home all day."
5. "Where's Kate? Is she at work or at home?" " _____ . She's out of town."

87.2 Complete the sentences with *both/neither/either*. Use *of* where necessary.

1. __*Both*__ my parents are from California.
2. To get downtown, you can take the city streets or you can take the freeway. You can go _____ way.
3. I tried to call George twice, but _____ times he was out.
4. _____ Tom's parents is American. His father is Polish, and his mother is Italian.
5. I saw an accident this morning. One car drove into the back of another. Fortunately _____ driver was injured, but _____ cars were badly damaged.
6. I have two sisters and a brother. My brother is working, but _____ my sisters are still in school.

87.3 Complete the sentences with *both/neither/either* + *of us/them*.

1. I asked two people the way to the airport, but __*neither of them*__ could help me.
2. I was invited to two parties last week, but I couldn't go to _____ .
3. There were two windows in the room. It was very warm, so I opened _____ .
4. Sarah and I play tennis together regularly, but _____ can play very well.
5. I tried two bookstores for the book I wanted, but _____ had it.

87.4 Write sentences with *both . . . and . . . / neither . . . nor . . . / either . . . or . . . .*

1. Chris was late. So was Pat. __*Both Chris and Pat were late.*__
2. He didn't write and he didn't call. __*He neither wrote nor called.*__
3. Joe is on vacation and so is Sam. _____
4. Joe doesn't have a car. Sam doesn't have one either. _____
5. Brian doesn't watch TV, and he doesn't read newspapers. _____
   _____
6. It was a boring movie. It was long, too.
   The movie _____
7. Is that man's name Richard? Or is it Robert? It's one or the other.
   That man's name _____
8. I don't have time to go on vacation. And I don't have the money.
   I have _____
9. We can leave today, or we can leave tomorrow – whichever you prefer.
   We _____

87.5 Complete the sentences with *neither/either/none/any*.

1. We tried a lot of hotels, but __*none*__ of them had any rooms.
2. I took two books with me on vacation, but I didn't read _____ of them.
3. I took five books with me on vacation, but I didn't read _____ of them.
4. There are a few stores on the next block, but _____ of them sells newspapers.
5. You can call me at _____ time during the evening. I'm always at home.
6. I can meet you next Monday or Friday. Would _____ of those days be convenient for you?
7. John and I couldn't get into the house because _____ of us had a key.

All, every, and whole

A

All and **everybody/everyone**

We do not normally use **all** to mean **everybody/everyone**:
- **Everybody** enjoyed the party. (*not* All enjoyed)

But we say **all of us/you/them** (*not* everybody of . . .):
- **All of us** enjoyed the party. (*not* Everybody of us)

B

All and **everything**

Sometimes you can use **all** or **everything**:
- I'll do **all I can** to help.   *or*   I'll do **everything I can** to help.

You can say **all I can / all you need**, etc., but we do not normally use **all** *alone*:
- He thinks he knows **everything**. (*not* he knows all)
- Our vacation was a disaster. **Everything** went wrong. (*not* All went wrong)

But you can say **all about**:
- He knows **all about** computers.

We also use **all** (*not* everything) to mean "the only thing(s)":
- **All** I've eaten today is a sandwich. (= the only thing I've eaten today)

C

Every/everybody/everyone/everything are *singular* words, so we use a *singular* verb:
- **Every seat** in the theater **was** taken.
- **Everyone has** arrived. (*not* have arrived)

But we often say **they/them/their** after **everybody/everyone**:
- **Everybody** said **they** enjoyed **themselves**. (= he or she enjoyed himself or herself)

D

Whole and **all**

Whole = complete, entire. Most often we use **whole** with *singular* nouns:
- Did you read **the whole book**? (= all of the book, not just a part of it)
- Lila has lived **her whole life** in Chile.
- I was so hungry, I ate **a whole package** of cookies. (= a complete package)

We use **the/my/her**, etc. before **whole**. Compare **whole** and **all**:
- **the whole** way / **all the** way   **her whole** life / **all her** life

We do not normally use **whole** with *uncountable* nouns. We say:
- I've spent **all the money** you gave me. (*not* the whole money)

E

Every/all/whole with time words

We use **every** to say how often something happens (**every day / every Monday / every 10 minutes / every three week**s, etc.):
- When we were on vacation, we went to the beach **every day**. (*not* all days)
- The bus service is very good. There's a bus **every 10 minutes**.
- We don't see each other very often – about **every six months**.

All day / the whole day = the complete day from beginning to end:
- We spent **all day / the whole day** at the beach.
- Dan was very quiet. He didn't say a word **all night / the whole night**.
Note that we say **all day** (*not* all the day), **all week** (*not* all the week), etc.

Compare **all the time** and **every time**:
- They never go out. They are at home **all the time**. (= always, continuously)
- **Every time** I see you, you look different. (= each time, on every occasion)

Countable and Uncountable Units 67–68   *All / all of* Unit 86   *Each and every* Unit 89
Every one Unit 89D   *All* (word order) Unit 107C

Exercises

88.1 Complete these sentences with *all*, *everything*, or *everybody* / *everyone*.

1. It was a good party. ___*Everyone*___ enjoyed it.
2. ___*All*___ I've eaten today is a sandwich.
3. _____ has their faults. Nobody is perfect.
4. Nothing has changed. _____ is the same as it was.
5. Kate told me _____ about her new job. It sounds very interesting.
6. Can _____ write their name on a piece of paper, please?
7. Why are you always thinking about money? Money isn't _____ .
8. I didn't have much money with me. _____ I had was 10 dollars.
9. When the fire alarm rang, _____ left the building immediately.
10. Sue didn't say where she was going. _____ she said was that she was going away.
11. We have completely different opinions. I disagree with _____ she says.
12. We all did well on the exam. _____ in our class passed.
13. We all did well on the exam. _____ of us passed.
14. Why are you so lazy? Why do you expect me to do _____ for you?

88.2 Write sentences with *whole*.

1. I read the book from beginning to end.
   ___*I read the whole book.*___
2. Everyone on the team played well.
   The _____
3. Paul opened a box of chocolates. When he finished eating, there were no chocolates left in the box. He ate _____
4. The police came to the house. They were looking for something. They searched everywhere, every room. They _____
5. Everyone in Dave and Jane's family plays tennis. Dave and Jane play, and so do all their children. The _____
6. Ann worked from early in the morning until late at night.
   _____
7. Jack and Lisa spent a week at the beach on vacation. It rained from the beginning of the week to the end. It _____

Now write sentences 6 and 7 again using *all* instead of *whole*.

8. (6) Ann _____
9. (7) _____

88.3 Complete these sentences using *every* with the following:

five minutes   ~~10 minutes~~   **four hours**   **six months**   **four years**

1. The bus service is very good. There's a bus ___*every 10 minutes.*___
2. Tom is sick. He has some medicine. He has to take it _____
3. The Olympic Games take place _____
4. We live near a busy airport. A plane flies over our house _____
5. It's a good idea to have a check-up with the dentist _____

88.4 Which is the correct alternative?

1. I spent ~~the whole money~~ / all the money you gave me. (*all the money* is correct)
2. Sue works every day / all days except Sunday.
3. I'm tired. I've been working hard all the day / all day.
4. It was a terrible fire. Whole building / The whole building was destroyed.
5. I've been trying to call her, but every time / all the time I call, the line is busy.
6. I don't like the weather here. It rains every time / all the time.
7. When I was on vacation, all my luggage / my whole luggage was stolen.

Each and every

Each and **every** are similar in meaning. Often it is possible to use **each** or **every**:

- **Each** time (or **Every** time) I see you, you look different.
- There's a ceiling fan in **each** room (or **every** room) of the house.

But **each** and **every** are not exactly the same. Study the difference:

We use **each** when we think of things separately, one by one.	We use **every** when we think of things as a group. The meaning is similar to **all**.
■ Study **each sentence** carefully. (= study the sentences one by one)	■ **Every sentence** must have a verb. (= all sentences in general)
each = **X + X + X + X**	every =
Each is more common for a small number:	**Every** is more common for a large number:
■ There were four books on the table. **Each book** was a different color.	■ Kate loves reading. She has read **every book** in the library. (= all the books)
■ (in a card game) At the beginning of the game, **each player** has three cards.	■ I would like to visit **every country** in the world. (= all the countries)

Each (but not **every**) can be used for two things:

- In a baseball game, **each team** has nine players. (not every team)

We use **every** (not **each**) to say how often something happens:

- "How often do you use your computer?" "**Every day**." (not Each day)
- There's a bus **every 10 minutes**. (not each 10 minutes)

Compare the structures we use with **each** and **every**:

You can use **each** with a noun:	You can use **every** with a noun:
each book **each student**	**every book** **every student**
You can use **each** alone (without a noun):	You can't use **every** alone, but you can say **every one**:
■ None of the rooms was the same. **Each** (= each room) was different.	■ A: Have you read all these books? B: Yes, **every one**.
Or you can use **each one**:	
■ **Each one** was different.	
You can say **each of** (**the . . . / these . . .**, **them**, etc.):	You can say **every one of** . . . (but not every of):
■ Read **each of these** sentences carefully.	■ I've read **every one of those** books. (not every of those books)
■ **Each of the** books is a different color.	■ I've read **every one of them**.
■ **Each of them** is a different color.	

You can also use **each** in the middle or at the end of a sentence. For example:

- The students were **each** given a book. (= Each student was given a book)
- These oranges cost 75 cents **each**.

Everyone and **every one**

Everyone (one word) is only for people (= everybody).

Every one (two words) is for things or people and is similar to **each one** (see Section B).

- **Everyone** enjoyed the party. (= **Everybody** . . .)
- Sarah is invited to lots of parties and she goes to **every one**. (= to **every party**)

Exercises

89.1 Look at the pictures and complete the sentences with *each* or *every*.

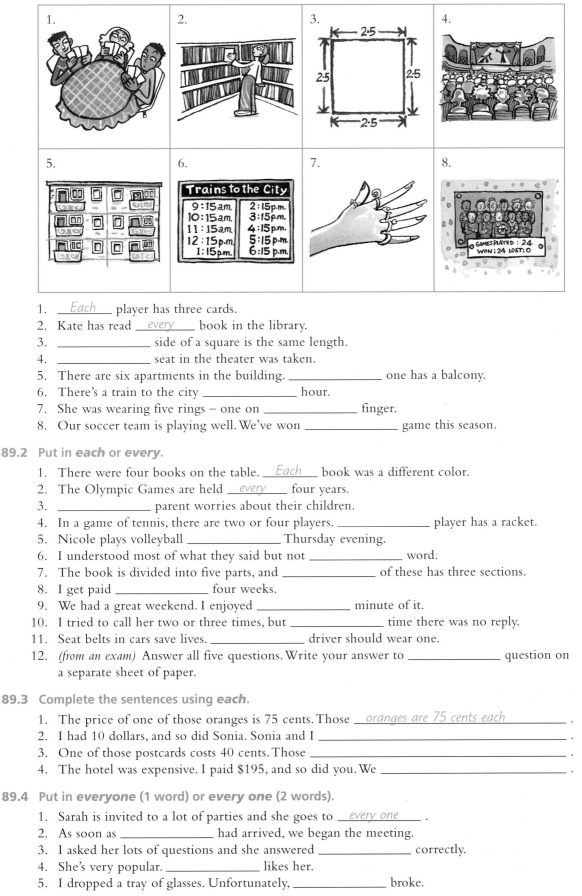

1. __Each__ player has three cards.
2. Kate has read __every__ book in the library.
3. _____ side of a square is the same length.
4. _____ seat in the theater was taken.
5. There are six apartments in the building. _____ one has a balcony.
6. There's a train to the city _____ hour.
7. She was wearing five rings – one on _____ finger.
8. Our soccer team is playing well. We've won _____ game this season.

89.2 Put in *each* or *every*.

1. There were four books on the table. __Each__ book was a different color.
2. The Olympic Games are held __every__ four years.
3. _____ parent worries about their children.
4. In a game of tennis, there are two or four players. _____ player has a racket.
5. Nicole plays volleyball _____ Thursday evening.
6. I understood most of what they said but not _____ word.
7. The book is divided into five parts, and _____ of these has three sections.
8. I get paid _____ four weeks.
9. We had a great weekend. I enjoyed _____ minute of it.
10. I tried to call her two or three times, but _____ time there was no reply.
11. Seat belts in cars save lives. _____ driver should wear one.
12. *(from an exam)* Answer all five questions. Write your answer to _____ question on a separate sheet of paper.

89.3 Complete the sentences using *each*.

1. The price of one of those oranges is 75 cents. Those _oranges are 75 cents each_____ .
2. I had 10 dollars, and so did Sonia. Sonia and I _____ .
3. One of those postcards costs 40 cents. Those _____ .
4. The hotel was expensive. I paid $195, and so did you. We _____ .

89.4 Put in *everyone* (1 word) or *every one* (2 words).

1. Sarah is invited to a lot of parties and she goes to _every one_____ .
2. As soon as _____ had arrived, we began the meeting.
3. I asked her lots of questions and she answered _____ correctly.
4. She's very popular. _____ likes her.
5. I dropped a tray of glasses. Unfortunately, _____ broke.

Relative Clauses 1:
Clauses with **who/that/which**

A Look at this example sentence:

The woman ⎡who lives next door⎤ is a doctor.

└─── *relative clause* ───┘

A *clause* is part of a sentence. A *relative clause* tells us which person or thing (or what kind of person or thing) the speaker means:

■ The woman **who lives next door** . . .   ("who lives next door" tells us which woman)
■ People **who live in the country** . . .   ("who live in the country" tells us what kind of people)

We use **who** in a relative clause when we are talking about people (not things):

> the woman – she lives next door – is a doctor
> ↓
> → The woman **who lives next door** is a doctor.
>
> we know a lot of people – they live in the country
> ↓
> → We know a lot of people **who live in the country**.

■ An architect is someone **who designs buildings**.
■ What was the name of the person **who called you**?
■ Anyone **who wants to apply for the job** must do so by Friday.

You can also use **that** (instead of **who**), but you can't use **which** for people:

■ The woman **that lives next door** is a doctor. (*not* the woman **which**)

Sometimes you must use **who** (*not* that) for people – see Unit 93.

B When we are talking about things, we use **that** or **which** (*not* who) in a relative clause:

> where is the cheese? – it was in the refrigerator
> ↓
> → Where is the cheese ⎰ **that** ⎱ **was in the refrigerator**?
>   ⎱ **which** ⎰

■ I don't like stories **that have unhappy endings**. (*or* stories **which** have . . .)
■ Barbara works for a company **that makes furniture**.
   (*or* a company **which** makes furniture)
■ The machine **that broke down** is working again now.
   (*or* The machine **which** broke down)

That is more common than **which**, but sometimes you must use **which** – see Unit 93.

C **What** = "the thing(s) that." Compare **what** and **that**:

■ **What** happened was my fault. (= the thing that happened)
■ Everything **that happened** was my fault. (*not* Everything what happened)
■ The machine **that broke down** is now working again.
   (*not* The machine what broke down)

D Remember that in relative clauses we use **who/that/which**, not **he/she/they/it**:

■ I've never spoken to the woman **who lives** next door. (*not* the woman she lives)

Exercises

90.1 In this exercise you have to explain what some words mean. Choose the right meaning from the box, and then write a sentence with *who*. Use a dictionary if necessary.

he/she	steals from a store ~~designs buildings~~ doesn't believe in God is not brave	he/she	buys something from a store pays rent to live in a room or apartment breaks into a house to steal things expects the worst to happen

1. (an architect) _An architect is someone who designs buildings._
2. (a burglar) A burglar is someone _____
3. (a customer) _____
4. (a shoplifter) _____
5. (a coward) _____
6. (an atheist) _____
7. (a pessimist) _____
8. (a tenant) _____

90.2 Make one sentence from two. Use *who/that/which*.

1. A girl was injured in the accident. She is now in the hospital.
   The girl who was injured in the accident is now in the hospital.
2. A waitress served us. She was impolite and impatient.
   The _____
3. A building was destroyed in the fire. It has now been rebuilt.
   The _____
4. Some people were arrested. They have now been released.
   The _____
5. A bus goes to the airport. It runs every half hour.
   The _____

90.3 Complete the sentences. Choose the best ending from the box and change it into a relative clause.

he invented the telephone	~~it makes furniture~~
she runs away from home	it gives you the meanings of words
they stole my car	it can support life
they were on the wall	it cannot be explained

1. Barbara works for a company _that makes furniture_ .
2. The book is about a girl _____ .
3. What happened to the pictures _____ ?
4. A mystery is something _____ .
5. The police have caught the men _____ .
6. A dictionary is a book _____ .
7. Alexander Bell was the man _____ .
8. It seems that Earth is the only planet _____ .

90.4 Are these sentences right or wrong? Correct them where necessary.

1. I don't like stories who have unhappy endings. _stories that have_
2. What was the name of the person who called you? _OK_
3. Where's the nearest shop who sells newspapers? _____
4. The driver which caused the accident was fined $500. _____
5. Do you know the person that took these photographs? _____
6. We live in a world what is changing all the time. _____
7. Dan said some things about me that were not true. _____
8. What was the name of the horse it won the race? _____

Relative Clauses 2:
Clauses with and without **who/that/which**

Look at these example sentences from Unit 90:

- The woman **who lives next door** is a doctor. (*or* The woman **that** lives . . .)

  The woman lives next door.   **who** (= the woman) is the *subject*

- Where is the cheese **that was in the refrigerator**? (*or* the cheese **which** was . . .)

  The cheese was in the refrigerator.   **that** (= the cheese) is the *subject*

You must use **who/that/which** when it is the subject of the relative clause. You cannot say
"The woman lives next door is a doctor" or "Where is the cheese was in the refrigerator?"

Sometimes **who/that/which** is the *object* of the verb. For example:

- The woman **who I wanted to see** was away on vacation.

  I wanted to see the **woman**.   **who** = the woman = *object*
                                     I is the *subject*

- Have you found the keys **that you lost**?

  You lost the keys.   **that** = the keys = *object*
                        You is the *subject*

When **who/that/which** is the *object*, you can leave it out. So you can say:
- The **woman I wanted to see** was away.   *or*   The woman **who** I wanted to see . . .
- Have you found **the keys you lost**?   *or*   . . . the keys **that** you lost?
- **The dress Ann bought** doesn't fit her very well.   *or*   The dress **that** Ann bought . . .
- Is there **anything I can do**?   *or*   . . . anything **that** I can do?

Note that we say:
  the keys you lost (*not* the keys you lost them)
  the dress Ann bought (*not* the dress Ann bought it)

Note the position of prepositions (**in/to/for**, etc.) in relative clauses:

  Tom is talking **to** a woman – do you know her?

  → Do you know the woman (who/that) **Tom is talking to**?

  I slept **in** a bed last night – it wasn't very comfortable

  → The bed (that/which) **I slept in last night** wasn't very comfortable.

- Are these the books **you were looking for**?   *or*   . . . the books **that/which** you were . . .
- The woman **he fell in love with** left him after a month.   *or*   The woman **who/that** he . . .
- The man **I was sitting next to on the plane** talked all the time.   *or*
  The man **who/that** I was sitting next to . . .

Note that we say:
  the books you were looking for (*not* the books you were looking for them)

You cannot use **what** in sentences like these (see also Unit 90C):
- Everything **(that) they said** was true. (*not* Everything what they said)
- I gave her all the money **(that) I had**. (*not* all the money what I had)

What = "the thing(s) that":
- Did you hear **what they said**? (= the things that they said)

Exercises

91.1 In some of these sentences you need *who* or *that*. Correct the sentences where necessary.

1. (The woman lives next door) is a doctor   *The woman who lives next door*
2. Have you found the keys you lost?   *OK*
3. The people we met last night were very nice.   _____
4. The people work in the office are very nice.   _____
5. The people I work with are very nice.   _____
6. What have you done with the money I gave you?   _____
7. What happened to the money was on the table?   _____
8. What's the worst film you've ever seen?   _____
9. What's the best thing it has ever happened to you?   _____

91.2 What do you say in these situations? Complete each sentence with a relative clause.

1. Your friend lost some keys. You want to know if he has found them. You say:
   Have you found the keys ___*you lost*_____ ?
2. A friend is wearing a dress. You like it. You tell her:
   I like the dress _____ .
3. A friend is going to see a movie. You want to know the name of the movie. You say:
   What's the name of the movie _____ ?
4. You wanted to visit a museum. It was closed when you got there. You tell a friend:
   The museum _____ was closed when we got there.
5. You invited some people to your party. Some of them couldn't come. You tell someone:
   Some of the people _____ couldn't come.
6. Your friend had to do some work. You want to know if she has finished. You say:
   Have you finished the work _____ ?
7. You rented a car. It broke down after a few miles. You tell a friend:
   The car _____ broke down after a few miles.
8. You stayed at a hotel. Tom had recommended it to you. You tell a friend:
   We stayed at a hotel _____ .

91.3 Complete each sentence using a relative clause with a preposition. Choose from the box.

we went to a party last night	you can rely on Brian	we were invited to a wedding
I work with some people	I applied for a job	you told me about a hotel
~~you were looking for some books~~	I saw you with a man	

1. Are these the books ___*you were looking for*_____ ?
2. Unfortunately we couldn't go to the wedding _____ .
3. I enjoy my job. I like the people _____ .
4. What's the name of that hotel _____ .
5. The party _____ wasn't very much fun.
6. I didn't get the job _____ .
7. Brian is a good person to know. He's somebody _____ .
8. Who was that man _____ in the restaurant?

91.4 Put in *that* or *what* where necessary. If the sentence is already complete, leave the space empty.

1. I gave her all the money ___—___ I had. (all the money **that** I had *is also correct*)
2. Did you hear ___*what*___ they said?
3. They give their children everything _____ they want.
4. Tell me _____ you want, and I'll try to get it for you.
5. Why do you blame me for everything _____ goes wrong?
6. I won't be able to do much, but I'll do _____ I can.
7. I won't be able to do much, but I'll do the best _____ I can.
8. I don't agree with _____ you've just said.
9. I don't trust him. I don't believe anything _____ he says.

Relative Clauses 3: **whose/whom/where**

Whose

We use **whose** in relative clauses instead of **his/her/their**:

> we saw some people – their car had broken down
>
> → We saw some people **whose car had broken down**.

We use **whose** mostly for people:

- A widow is a woman **whose husband is dead**. (**her** husband is dead)
- What's the name of the man **whose car you borrowed**? (you borrowed **his** car)
- I met someone **whose brother I went to school with**.
  (I went to school with **his/her** brother)

Compare **who** and **whose**:

- I met a man **who** knows you. (**he** knows you)
- I met a man **whose sister** knows you. (**his sister** knows you)

Whom

Whom is possible instead of **who** when it is the *object* of the verb in the relative clause (like the sentences in Unit 91B):

- The woman **whom I wanted to see** was away on vacation. (I wanted to see **her**)

You can also use **whom** with a preposition (**to whom** / **from whom** / **with whom**, etc.):

- The people **with whom I work** are very nice. (I work **with them**)

But we do not often use **whom** in spoken English. We usually prefer **who** or **that**, or nothing (see Unit 91). So we usually say:

- The woman **I wanted to see** . . . *or* The woman **who/that** I wanted to see . . .
- The people **I work with** . . . *or* The people **who/that** I work with . . .

Where

You can use **where** in a relative clause to talk about a place:

> the restaurant – we had dinner there – it was near the airport
>
> → The restaurant **where we had dinner** was near the airport.

- I recently went back to **the town where I grew up**.
  (*or* . . . the town I grew up in *or* . . . the town **that** I grew up in)
- I would like to live in **a place where there is plenty of sunshine**.

We say:

the day / the year / the time, etc. $\begin{cases} \text{something happens} & or \\ \textbf{that } \text{something happens} \end{cases}$

- Do you remember **the day (that) we went to the zoo**?
- **The last time (that) I saw her**, she looked fine.
- I haven't seen them since **the year (that) they got married**.

We say:

the reason $\begin{cases} \text{something happens} & or \\ \textbf{that/why } \text{something happens} \end{cases}$

- **The reason I'm calling you** is to ask your advice.
  (*or* The reason **that** I'm calling / The reason **why** I'm calling)

Relative Clauses 1–2 Units 90–91 **Relative Clauses 4–5** Units 93–94 *Whom* Unit 94

Exercises

92.1 You met these people at a party:

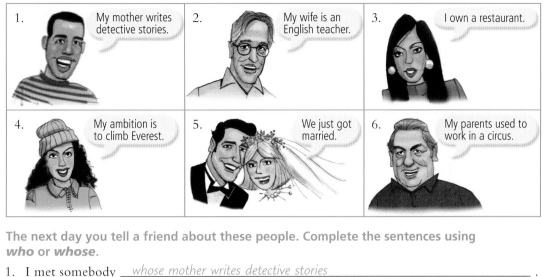

1. My mother writes detective stories.
2. My wife is an English teacher.
3. I own a restaurant.
4. My ambition is to climb Everest.
5. We just got married.
6. My parents used to work in a circus.

The next day you tell a friend about these people. Complete the sentences using
who or *whose*.

1. I met somebody *whose mother writes detective stories* .
2. I met a man _____ .
3. I met a woman _____ .
4. I met somebody _____ .
5. I met a couple _____ .
6. I met somebody _____ .

92.2 Read the situations and complete the sentences using *where*.

1. You grew up in a small town. You went back there recently. You tell someone this.
   I recently went back to the small town *where I grew up* .
2. You want to buy some postcards. You ask a friend where you can do this.
   Is there someplace near here _____ ?
3. You work in a factory. The factory is going to close down next month. You tell a friend:
   The factory _____ is going to close down next month.
4. Sue is staying at a hotel. You want to know the name of the hotel. You ask a friend:
   Do you know the name of the hotel _____ ?
5. You play baseball in a park on Sundays. You show a friend the park. You say:
   This is the park _____ on Sundays.

92.3 Complete each sentence using *who/whom/whose/where*.

1. What's the name of the man *whose* car you borrowed?
2. A cemetery is a place _____ people are buried.
3. A pacifist is a person _____ believes that all wars are wrong.
4. An orphan is a child _____ parents are dead.
5. What was the name of the person to _____ you spoke on the phone?
6. The place _____ we spent our vacation was really beautiful.
7. This school is only for children _____ first language is not English.
8. The woman with _____ he fell in love left him after a month.

92.4 Use your own ideas to complete these sentences. See Sections D and E.

1. I'll always remember the day *I first met you* .
2. I'll never forget the time _____ .
3. The reason _____ was that I didn't know your address.
4. Unfortunately I wasn't at home the evening _____ .
5. The reason _____ is that they don't need one.
6. _____ was the year _____ .

Relative Clauses 4:
Extra Information Clauses (1)

A

There are two types of *relative clauses*. In these examples, the relative clauses are <u>underlined</u>.
Compare:

Type 1	*Type 2*
■ The woman <u>who lives next door</u> is a doctor.	■ My brother Jim, <u>who lives in Houston,</u> is a doctor.
■ Barbara works for a company <u>that makes furniture</u>.	■ Brad told me about his new job, <u>which he's enjoying a lot</u>.
■ We stayed at the hotel <u>(that) you recommended</u>.	■ We stayed at the Grand Hotel, <u>which a friend of ours recommended</u>.

In these examples, the relative clause tells you which person or thing (or what kind of person or thing) the speaker means:	In these examples, the relative clauses do not tell you which person or thing the speaker means. We already know which thing or person is meant: "My brother Jim," "Brad's new job," and "the Grand Hotel."
"The woman **who lives next door**" tells us *which* woman.	
"A company **that makes furniture**" tells us *what kind* of company.	
"The hotel (**that**) **you recommended**" tells us *which* hotel.	The relative clauses in these sentences give us *extra information* about the person or thing.

We do not use commas (,) with these clauses:	We use commas (,) with these clauses:
■ People <u>who come from Texas love football</u>.	■ My English teacher, <u>who comes from Texas</u>, loves computers.

B

In both types of relative clauses we use **who** for people and **which** for things. But:

Type 1	*Type 2*
You can use **that**:	You cannot use **that**:
■ Do you know anyone **who/that** speaks French and Italian?	■ John, **who** (*not* that) speaks French and Italian, works as a tour guide.
■ Barbara works for a company **which/that** makes furniture.	■ Brad told me about his new job, **which** (*not* that) he's enjoying a lot.
You can leave out **who/which/that** when it is the object (see Unit 91):	You cannot leave out **who** or **which**:
■ We stayed at the hotel (that/which) you recommended.	■ We stayed at the Grand Hotel, **which** a friend of ours recommended.
■ This morning I met somebody (who/that) I hadn't seen for ages.	■ This morning I met Chris, **who** I hadn't seen for ages.
We do not often use **whom** in this type of clause (see Unit 92B).	You can use **whom** for people (when it is the object):
	■ This morning I met Chris, **whom** I hadn't seen for ages.

In both types of relative clauses you can use **whose** and **where**:

■ We met some people **whose** car had broken down.	■ Amy, **whose** car had broken down, was in a very bad mood.
■ What's the name of the place **where** you spent your vacation?	■ Mrs. Bond is spending a few weeks in Sweden, **where** her daughter lives.

Exercises

93.1 Make one sentence from two. Use the sentence in parentheses to make a relative clause (Type 2). You will need to use *who(m)*/*whose*/*which*/*where*.

1. Ann is very friendly. (She lives next door.)
   Ann, who lives next door, is very friendly.
2. We stayed at the Grand Hotel. (A friend of ours had recommended it.)
   We stayed at the Grand Hotel, which a friend of ours had recommended.
3. We often go to visit our friends in New York. (It is not very far away.)
   _____
4. I went to see the doctor. (He told me to rest for a few days.)
   _____
5. John is one of my closest friends. (I have known him for a very long time.)
   John, _____
6. Sheila is away from home a lot. (Her job involves a lot of travel.)
   _____
7. The new stadium will be opened next month. (It can hold 90,000 people.)
   _____
8. Alaska is the largest state in the United States. (My brother lives there.)
   _____
9. A friend of mine helped me to get a job. (His father is the manager of a company.)
   _____

93.2 Read the information and complete each sentence. Use a relative clause of Type 1 or Type 2. Use commas where necessary.

1. There's a woman living next door to me. She's a doctor.
   The woman _who lives next door to me is a doctor._
2. I have a brother named Jim. He lives in Houston. He's a doctor.
   My brother Jim, _who lives in Houston, is a doctor._
3. There was a strike at the car factory. It began 10 days ago. It is now over.
   The strike at the car factory _____
4. I was looking for a book this morning. I've found it now.
   I've found _____
5. London was once the largest city in the world, but the population is now decreasing.
   The population of London, _____
6. A job was advertised. A lot of people applied for it. Few of them had the necessary qualifications. Few of _____
7. Amanda has a son. She showed me a picture of him. He's a police officer.
   Amanda showed me _____

93.3 Correct the sentences that are wrong and put in commas where necessary. If the sentence is correct, write "OK."

1. Brad told me about his (new job that) he's enjoying a lot.
   Brad told me about his new job, which he's enjoying a lot.
2. My office that is on the second floor is very small.
   _____
3. The office I'm using these days is very small.
   _____
4. Ben's father that used to be a teacher now works for a TV company.
   _____
5. The doctor that examined me couldn't find anything wrong.
   _____
6. The sun that is one of millions of stars in the universe provides us with heat and light.
   _____

Relative Clauses 5:
Extra Information Clauses (2)

A

Prepositions + **whom/which**

You can use a *preposition* before **whom** (for people) and **which** (for things). So you can say:
to whom / with whom / about which / without which, etc.:

- Mr. Carter, **to whom** I spoke at the meeting, is very interested in our plan.
- Fortunately we had a map, **without which** we would have gotten lost.

In spoken English, we usually keep the preposition after the verb in the relative clause. When
we do this, we normally use **who** (*not* whom) for people:

- This is my friend from Canada, **who** I was telling you **about**.
- Yesterday we visited the City Museum, **which** I'd never been **to** before.

B

All of / most of, etc. + **whom / which**

Study these examples:

> Mary has three brothers. All of them are married. *(2 sentences)*
>
> → Mary has three brothers, **all of whom** are married. *(1 sentence)*
>
> They asked me a lot of questions. I couldn't answer most of them . *(2 sentences)*
>
> → They asked me a lot of questions, **most of which** I couldn't answer. *(1 sentence)*

In the same way you can say:

none of / neither of / any of / either of
some of / many of / much of / (a) few of   } + **whom** (people)
both of / half of / each of / one of / two of (etc.)   + **which** (things)

- Tom tried on three jackets, **none of which** fit him.
- Two men, **neither of whom** I had ever seen before, came into the office.
- They have three cars, **two of which** they rarely use.
- Sue has a lot of friends, **many of whom** she went to school with.

You can also say **the cause of which / the name of which**, etc.:

- The building was destroyed in a fire, **the cause of which** was never established.
- We stayed at a beautiful hotel, **the name of which** I can't remember now.

C

Which (*not* what)

Study this example:

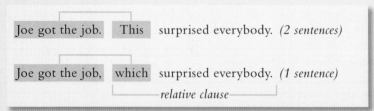

> Joe got the job.   This   surprised everybody. *(2 sentences)*
>
> Joe got the job,   which   surprised everybody. *(1 sentence)*
> ————relative clause————

In this example, **which** = the fact that he got the job. You must use **which** (*not* what) in
sentences like these:

- Sarah couldn't meet us, **which** was a shame. (*not* what was a shame)
- The weather was good, **which** we hadn't expected. (*not* what we hadn't expected)

For **what**, see Units 90C and 91D.

Exercises

94.1 Write the relative clauses in a more formal way using a preposition + *whom*/*which*.

1. Yesterday we visited the City Museum, which I'd never been to before.
   Yesterday we visited the City Museum, _to which I'd never been before_ .
2. My brother showed us his new car, which he's very proud of.
   My brother showed us his new car, _____ .
3. This is a picture of our friends Chris and Sam, who we went on vacation with.
   This is a picture of our friends Chris and Sam, _____ .
4. The wedding, which only members of the family were invited to, took place on Friday.
   The wedding, _____ ,
   took place on Friday.

94.2 Use the information in the first sentence to complete the second sentence. Use *all of* / *most of*, etc. or *the . . . of* + *whom*/*which*.

1. All of Mary's brothers are married.
   Mary has three brothers, _all of whom are married_ .
2. Most of the information we were given was useless.
   We were given a lot of information, _____ .
3. Jane has received neither of the letters I sent her.
   I sent Jane two letters, _____ .
4. None of the ten people who applied for the job was suitable.
   Ten people applied for the job, _____ .
5. Kate hardly ever uses one of her computers.
   Kate has got two computers, _____ .
6. Mike gave half of the $50,000 he won to his parents.
   Mike won $50,000, _____ .
7. Both of Julia's sisters are teachers.
   Julia has two sisters, _____ .
8. I went to a party – I knew only a few of the people there.
   There were a lot of people at the party, _____ .
9. The sides of the road we drove along were lined with trees.
   We drove along the road, the _____ .
10. The aim of the company's new business plan is to save money.
    The company has a new business plan, _____ .

94.3 Join sentences from the boxes to make new sentences. Use *which*.

1. ~~Laura couldn't come to the party.~~
2. Jane doesn't have a phone.
3. Neil has passed his exams.
4. Our flight was delayed.
5. Kate offered to let me stay at her house.
6. The street I live on is very noisy at night.
7. Our car has broken down.

This was very nice of her.
This means we can't take our trip tomorrow.
This makes it difficult to contact her.
This makes it difficult to sleep sometimes.
~~This was a shame.~~
This is good news.
This meant we had to wait three hours at the airport.

1. Laura couldn't come to the party, _which was a shame._
2. Jane _____
3. _____
4. _____
5. _____
6. _____
7. _____

-ing and -ed Phrases (the woman talking to Tom, the boy injured in the accident)

A

A *phrase* is a part of a sentence. Some phrases begin with **-ing** or **-ed**. For example:

Do you know the woman **talking to Tom**?
└─ **-ing** *phrase* ─┘

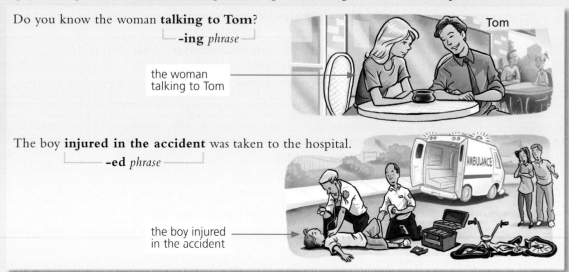

the woman talking to Tom

Tom

The boy **injured in the accident** was taken to the hospital.
└─── **-ed** *phrase* ───┘

the boy injured in the accident

B

We use **-ing** phrases to say what somebody (or something) is (or was) doing at a particular time:

- Do you know the woman **talking to Tom**? (the woman **is talking** to Tom)
- Police **investigating the crime** are looking for three men. (police **are investigating** the crime)
- Who were those people **waiting outside**? (they **were waiting**)
- I was awakened by a bell **ringing**. (a bell **was ringing**)

You can also use an **-ing** phrase to say what happens all the time, not just at a particular time. For example:

- The road **connecting the two towns** is very narrow.
  (the road **connects** the two towns)
- I have a large bedroom **overlooking the garden**.
  (the room **overlooks** the garden)
- Can you think of the name of a flower **beginning with "t"**?
  (the name **begins** with "t")

C

-ed phrases have a *passive* meaning:

- The boy **injured in the accident** was taken to the hospital.
  (he **was injured** in the accident)
- George showed me some pictures **painted by his father**.
  (they **had been painted** by his father)

Injured and **painted** are *past participles*. Note that many past participles are irregular and do not end in **-ed** (**stolen/made/written**, etc.):

- The police never found the money **stolen in the robbery**.
- Most of the goods **made in this factory** are exported.

You can use **left** in this way, with the meaning "not used, still there":

- We've eaten almost all the chocolates. There are only a few **left**.

D

We often use **-ing** and **-ed** phrases after **there is / there was**, etc.:

- **There were** some children **swimming** in the river.
- **Is there** anybody **waiting**?
- **There was** a big red car **parked** outside the house.

See/hear somebody doing something Unit 65   *-ing Phrases* Unit 66   *There (is)* Unit 82
Irregular Past Participles (*made/stolen*, etc.) Appendix 1

Exercises

95.1 Make one sentence from two. Complete the sentences with an *-ing* phrase.

1. A bell was ringing. I was awakened by it.
   I was awakened by __*a bell ringing*__ .
2. A man was sitting next to me on the plane. I didn't talk much to him.
   I didn't talk much to the _____ .
3. A taxi was taking us to the airport. It broke down.
   The _____ broke down.
4. There's a path at the end of this street. The path leads to the river.
   At the end of the street there's a _____ .
5. A factory has just opened in town. It employs 500 people.
   A _____ has just opened in town.
6. The company sent me a brochure. It contained the information I needed.
   The company sent me _____ .

95.2 Make one sentence from two, beginning as shown. Each time make an *-ed* phrase.

1. A boy was injured in the accident. He was taken to the hospital.
   The boy __*injured in the accident*__ was taken to the hospital.
2. A gate was damaged in the storm. It has now been repaired.
   The gate _____ has now been repaired.
3. A number of suggestions were made at the meeting. Most of them were not very practical.
   Most of the _____ were not very practical.
4. Some paintings were stolen from the museum. They haven't been found yet.
   The _____ haven't been found yet.
5. A man was arrested by the police. What was his name?
   What was the name of _____ ?

95.3 Complete the sentences using the following verbs in the correct form:

> blow   drive   ~~invite~~   live   name   offer   read   ~~ring~~   sell   sit

1. I was awakened by a bell __*ringing*__ .
2. Some of the people __*invited*__ to the party can't come.
3. Life must be very unpleasant for people _____ near busy airports.
4. A few days after the interview, I received a letter _____ me the job.
5. Somebody _____ Jack phoned while you were out.
6. There was a tree _____ down in the storm last night.
7. The waiting room was empty except for a young man _____ by the
   window _____ a magazine.
8. Look! The man _____ the red car almost hit the person
   _____ newspapers on the street corner.

95.4 Use the words in parentheses to make sentences using *There is / There was*, etc.

1. That house is empty. (nobody / live / in it) __*There's nobody living in it.*__
2. The accident wasn't serious. (nobody / injure) __*There was nobody injured.*__
3. I can hear footsteps. (somebody / come)
   There _____
4. The train was full. (a lot of people / travel)
   _____
5. We were the only guests at the hotel. (nobody else / stay there)
   _____
6. The piece of paper was blank. (nothing / write / on it)
   _____
7. The school offers English courses in the evening. (a new course / begin / next Monday)
   _____

Adjectives Ending in -ing and -ed (boring/bored, etc.)

A

There are many adjectives ending in **-ing** and **-ed**, for example: **boring** and **bored**.

bored

boring

Jane has been doing the same job for a very long time. Every day she does exactly the same thing again and again. She doesn't enjoy her job any more and would like to do something different.

Jane's job is **boring**.

Jane is **bored** (with her job).

Somebody is **bored** if something (or somebody else) is **boring**. Or, if something is **boring**, it makes you **bored**. So:

- Jane is **bored** because her job is **boring**.
- Jane's job is **boring**, so Jane is **bored**. (*not* Jane is boring)

If a person is **boring**, this means that they make other people **bored**:

- George always talks about the same things. He's really **boring**.

B

Compare adjectives ending in **-ing** and **-ed**:

- My job is {
  boring.
  interesting.
  tiring.
  satisfying.
  depressing. (etc.)
}

- I'm **bored** with my job.
- I'm not **interested** in my job any more.
- I get very **tired** doing my job.
- I'm not **satisfied** with my job.
- My job makes me **depressed**. (etc.)

In these examples, the **-ing** adjective tells you about the job.

In these examples, the **-ed** adjective tells you how somebody feels (about the job).

Compare these examples:

interesting
- Julia thinks politics is **interesting**.
- Did you meet anyone **interesting** at the party?

interested
- Julia is **interested** in politics.
  (*not* interesting in politics)
- Are you **interested** in buying a car? I'm trying to sell mine.

surprising
- It was **surprising** that he passed the exam.

surprised
- Everybody was **surprised** that he passed the exam.

disappointing
- The movie was **disappointing**. We expected it to be much better.

disappointed
- We were **disappointed** with the movie. We expected it to be much better.

shocking
- The news was **shocking**.

shocked
- I was **shocked** when I heard the news.

Exercises

96.1 Complete the sentences for each situation. Use the word in parentheses + *-ing* or *-ed*.

1. The movie wasn't as good as we had expected. (disappoint-)
   a) The movie was __*disappointing*__ .
   b) We were __*disappointed*__ with the movie.

2. Diana teaches young children. It's a very hard job, but she enjoys it. (exhaust-)
   a) She enjoys her job, but it's often _____ .
   b) At the end of a day's work, she is often _____ .

3. It's been raining all day. I hate this weather. (depress-)
   a) This weather is _____ .
   b) This weather makes me _____ .
   c) It's silly to get _____ because of the weather.

4. Claire is going to Mexico next month. She has never been there before. (excit-)
   a) It will be an _____ experience for her.
   b) Going to new places is always _____ .
   c) She is really _____ about going to Mexico.

96.2 Choose the correct word.

1. I was ~~disappointing~~ / disappointed with the movie. I had expected it to be better. (*disappointed* is correct)
2. Are you interesting / interested in tennis?
3. The tennis match was very exciting / excited. I had a great time.
4. It's sometimes embarrassing / embarrassed when you have to ask people for money.
5. Do you get embarrassing / embarrassed easily?
6. I never expected to get the job. I was really amazing / amazed when it was offered to me.
7. She has learned really fast. She has made astonishing / astonished progress.
8. I didn't find the situation funny. I was not amusing / amused.
9. It was a really terrifying / terrified experience. Everybody was very shocking / shocked.
10. Why do you always look so boring / bored? Is your life really so boring / bored?
11. He's one of the most boring / bored people I've ever met. He never stops talking and he never says anything interesting / interested.

96.3 Complete each sentence using a word from the list.

amusing/amused	annoying/annoyed	boring/bored
confusing/confused	disgusting/disgusted	exciting/excited
exhausting/exhausted	interesting/interested	~~surprising~~ /surprised

1. He works very hard. It's not __*surprising*__ that he's always tired.
2. I don't have anything to do. I'm _____ .
3. The teacher's explanation was _____ . Most of the students didn't understand it.
4. The kitchen hadn't been cleaned in ages. It was really _____ .
5. I seldom go to art galleries. I'm not particularly _____ in art.
6. You don't have to get _____ just because I'm a few minutes late.
7. The lecture was _____ . I fell asleep.
8. I've been working very hard all day and now I'm _____ .
9. I'm starting a new job next week. I'm very _____ about it.
10. Tom is very good at telling funny stories. He can be very _____ .
11. Liz is a very _____ person. She knows a lot, she's traveled a lot, and she's done lots of different things.

Adjectives: a **nice new** house, you look **tired**

A

Sometimes we use two or more *adjectives* together:

- My brother lives in a **nice new** house.
- There was a **beautiful large round wooden** table in the kitchen.

Adjectives like **new/large/round/wooden** are *fact* adjectives. They give us factual information about age, size, color, etc.

Adjectives like **nice/beautiful** are *opinion* adjectives. They tell us what somebody thinks of something or somebody.

Opinion adjectives usually go before fact adjectives.

	Opinion	*Fact*	
a	**nice**	**long**	summer vacation
an	**interesting**	**young**	man
a	**delicious**	**hot**	vegetable soup
a	**beautiful**	**large round wooden**	table

B

Sometimes we use two or more fact adjectives together. Usually (but not always) we put fact adjectives in this order:

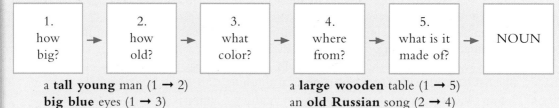

1. how big? → 2. how old? → 3. what color? → 4. where from? → 5. what is it made of? → NOUN

    a **tall young** man (1 → 2)   a **large wooden** table (1 → 5)
    big blue eyes (1 → 3)   an **old Russian** song (2 → 4)
    a **small black plastic** bag (1 → 3 → 5)   an **old white cotton** shirt (2 → 3 → 5)

Adjectives of size and length (**big/small/tall/short/long**, etc.) usually go before adjectives of shape and width (**round/fat/thin/slim/wide**, etc.):

    a **large round** table   a **tall thin** girl   a **long narrow** street

When there are two or more color adjectives, we use **and**:

    a **black and white** dress   a **red, white, and green** flag

This does not usually happen with other adjectives before a noun:

    a **long black** dress (*not* a long and black dress)

C

We use adjectives after **be/get/become/seem**:

- **Be careful**!
- **I'm tired** and **I'm getting hungry**.
- As the movie went on, it **became** more and more **boring**.
- Your friend **seems** very **nice**.

We also use adjectives to say how somebody/something looks, feels, sounds, tastes, or smells:

- You **look tired**. / I **feel tired**. / She **sounds tired**.
- The dinner **smells good**.
- This milk **tastes** a little **strange**.

But to say *how* somebody does something you must use an *adverb* (see Units 98–99):

- Drive **carefully**! (*not* Drive careful)
- Susan plays the piano very **well**. (*not* plays . . . very good)

D

We say "the **first two** days / the **next few** weeks / the **last 10** minutes," etc.:

- I didn't enjoy the **first two** days of the course. (*not* the two first days)
- They'll be away for the **next few** weeks. (*not* the few next weeks)

Adverbs Units 98-99   **Comparison (*cheaper*, etc.)** Units 102–104   **Superlatives (*cheapest*, etc.)** Unit 105

Exercises

97.1 Put the adjectives in parentheses in the correct position.

1. a beautiful table (wooden / round) _a beautiful round wooden table_
2. an unusual ring (gold) _____
3. an old house (beautiful) _____
4. black gloves (leather) _____
5. an Italian film (old) _____
6. a long face (thin) _____
7. big clouds (black) _____
8. a sunny day (lovely) _____
9. an ugly dress (yellow) _____
10. a wide avenue (long) _____
11. a red car (old / little) _____
12. a new sweater (green / nice) _____
13. a metal box (black / small) _____
14. a big cat (fat / black) _____
15. a little country inn (old / charming) _____
16. long hair (black / beautiful) _____
17. an old painting (interesting / French) _____
18. an enormous umbrella (red / yellow) _____

97.2 Complete each sentence with a verb (in the correct form) and an adjective from the boxes.

feel	look	~~seem~~		awful	fine	interesting
smell	sound	taste		nice	~~upset~~	wet

1. Helen _seemed upset_ this morning. Do you know what was wrong?
2. I can't eat this. I just tried it and it _____ .
3. I was sick yesterday, but I _____ today.
4. What beautiful flowers! They _____ , too.
5. You _____ . Have you been out in the rain?
6. Jim was telling me about his new job. It _____ – much better than his old job.

97.3 Put in the correct word.

1. This milk tastes _strange_ . (strange / strangely)
2. I always feel _____ when the sun is shining. (happy / happily)
3. The children were playing _____ in the yard. (happy / happily)
4. The man became _____ when the manager of the restaurant asked him to leave. (violent / violently)
5. You look _____ ! Are you all right? (terrible / terribly)
6. There's no point in doing a job if you don't do it _____ . (proper / properly)
7. The soup tastes _____ . (good / well)
8. Hurry up! You're always so _____ . (slow / slowly)

97.4 Write the following in another way using *the first* . . . / *the next* . . . / *the last* . . . .

1. the first day and the second day of the course _the first two days of the course_
2. next week and the week after _the next two weeks_
3. yesterday and the day before yesterday _____
4. the first week and the second week of May _____
5. tomorrow and a few days after that _____
6. questions 1, 2, and 3 on the exam _____
7. next year and the year after _____
8. the last day of our vacation and the two days before that _____

Adjectives and Adverbs 1
(quick/quickly)

A

Look at these examples:
- Our vacation was too short – the time passed very **quickly**.
- Two people were **seriously** injured in the accident.

Quickly and **seriously** are *adverbs*. Many adverbs are formed from an adjective + **-ly**:

adjective:	quick	serious	careful	quiet	heavy	bad
adverb:	quick**ly**	seriou**sly**	careful**ly**	quiet**ly**	heavi**ly**	bad**ly**

For spelling, see Appendix 6.

Not all words ending in **-ly** are adverbs. Some *adjectives* end in **-ly**, too, for example:
friendly   lively   elderly   lonely   silly   lovely

B

Adjective or *adverb*?

Adjectives (**quick/careful**, etc.) tell us about a *noun* (somebody or something). We use adjectives before nouns:	Adverbs (**quickly/carefully**, etc.) tell us about a *verb* (*how* somebody does something or *how* something happens):
■ Tom is a **careful driver**. (*not* a carefully driver) ■ We didn't go out because of the **heavy rain**.	■ Tom **drove carefully** along the narrow road. (*not* drove careful) ■ We didn't go out because it was **raining heavily**. (*not* raining heavy)

Compare:

■ She speaks **perfect English**. *adjective + noun*	■ She **speaks** English **perfectly**. *verb + noun + adverb*

We also use adjectives after some verbs, especially **be**, and also **look/feel/sound**, etc.
Compare:

■ Please **be quiet**. ■ I was disappointed that my exam results **were** so **bad**. ■ Why do you always **look** so **serious**? ■ I **feel happy**.	■ Please **speak quietly**. ■ I was unhappy that I **did** so **badly** on the exam. (*not* did so bad) ■ Why do you never **take** me **seriously**? ■ The children were **playing happily**.

C

We also use adverbs before *adjectives* and *other adverbs*. For example:
reasonably cheap   (*adverb + adjective*)
terribly sorry   (*adverb + adjective*)
incredibly quickly   (*adverb + adverb*)

- It's a **reasonably cheap** restaurant, and the food is **extremely good**.
- I'm **terribly sorry**. I didn't mean to push you. (*not* terrible sorry)
- Maria learns languages **incredibly quickly**.
- The test was **surprisingly easy**.

You can also use an adverb before a *past participle* (**injured/organized/written**, etc.):
- Two people were **seriously injured** in the accident. (*not* serious injured)
- The conference was very **badly organized**.

Adjectives after *be/look/feel*, etc. Unit 97C   **Adjectives and Adverbs 2** Unit 99

Exercises

98.1 Complete each sentence with an adverb. The first letters of the adverb are given.

1. We didn't go out because it was raining he_avily___ .
2. Our team lost the game because we played very ba_____ .
3. I had little trouble finding a place to live. I found an apartment quite ea_____ .
4. We had to wait for a long time, but we didn't complain. We waited pat_____ .
5. Nobody knew Steve was coming to see us. He arrived unex_____ .
6. Mike stays in shape by playing tennis reg_____ .
7. I don't speak French very well, but I can understand per_____ if people speak sl_____ and cl_____ .

98.2 Put in the correct word.

1. Two people were __seriously_____ injured in the accident. (serious / seriously)
2. The driver of the car had __serious_____ injuries. (serious / seriously)
3. I think you behaved very _____ . (selfish / selfishly)
4. Kelly is _____ upset about losing her job. (terrible / terribly)
5. There was a _____ change in the weather. (sudden / suddenly)
6. Everybody at the party was _____ dressed. (colorful / colorfully)
7. Linda likes wearing _____ clothes. (colorful / colorfully)
8. Liz fell and hurt herself really _____ . (bad / badly)
9. These pants are already coming apart. They're _____ made. (bad / badly)
10. Don't go up that ladder. It doesn't look _____ . (safe / safely)

98.3 Complete each sentence using a word from the box. Sometimes you need the adjective (**careful**, etc.) and sometimes the adverb (**carefully**, etc.).

careful(ly)	complete(ly)	continuous(ly)	financial(ly)	fluent(ly)
happy / happily	nervous(ly)	perfect(ly)	~~quick(ly)~~	special(ly)

1. Our vacation was too short. The time passed very __quickly___ .
2. Tom doesn't take risks when he's driving. He's always _____ .
3. Sue works _____ . She never seems to stop.
4. Amy and Eric are very _____ married.
5. Nicole's English is very _____ although she makes a lot of mistakes.
6. I cooked this meal _____ for you, so I hope you like it.
7. Everything was very quiet. There was _____ silence.
8. I tried on the shoes and they fit me _____ .
9. Do you usually feel _____ before exams?
10. I'd like to buy a car, but it's _____ impossible for me at this time.

98.4 Choose two words (one from each box) to complete each sentence.

absolutely	badly	completely	changed	~~cheap~~	damaged
~~reasonably~~	seriously	slightly	enormous	ill	long
unnecessarily	unusually		planned	quiet	

1. I thought the restaurant would be expensive, but it was __reasonably cheap____ .
2. Steve's mother is _____ in the hospital.
3. What a big house! It's _____ .
4. It wasn't a serious accident. The car was only _____ .
5. The children are normally very lively, but they're _____ today.
6. When I returned home after 20 years, everything had _____ .
7. The movie was _____ . It could have been much shorter.
8. A lot went wrong during our vacation because it was _____ .

Adjectives and Adverbs 2
(well/fast/late, hard/hardly)

A Good/well

Good is an *adjective*. The *adverb* is **well**:

- Your English is **good**.   *but*   You **speak** English **well**.
- Susan is a **good** pianist.   *but*   Susan **plays** the piano **well**.

We use **well** (*not* good) with *past participles* (**dressed/known**, etc.):

well dressed   well known   well educated   well paid

- Gary's father is a **well known** writer.

But **well** is also an adjective with the meaning "in good health":

- "How are you today?"   "I'm very **well**, thanks."

B Fast/hard/late

These words are both adjectives and adverbs:

Adjective	*Adverb*
■ Jack is a very **fast runner**.	■ Jack can **run** very **fast**.
■ Kate is a **hard worker**.	■ Kate **works hard**. (*not* works hardly)
■ I **was late**.	■ I **got up late** this morning.

Lately = recently:

- Have you seen Tom **lately**?

C Hardly

Hardly = very little, almost not. Study these examples:

- Sarah wasn't very friendly at the party. She **hardly** spoke to me.
  (= she spoke to me very little, almost not at all)
- We've only met once or twice. We **hardly** know each other.

Hard and **hardly** are different. Compare:

- He tried **hard** to find a job, but he had no luck. (= he tried a lot, with a lot of effort)
- I'm not surprised he didn't find a job. He **hardly** tried to find one. (= he tried very little)

You can use **hardly** + **any/anybody/anyone/anything/anywhere**:

- *A:* How much money have we got?
  B: **Hardly any**. (= very little, almost none)
- These two cameras are very similar. There's **hardly any** difference between them.
- The results of the test were very bad. **Hardly anybody** in our class passed. (= very few students passed)

Note that you can say:

- She said **hardly anything**.   *or*   She **hardly** said **anything**.
- We've got **hardly any** money.   *or*   We've **hardly** got any **money**.

There's **hardly anything** in the fridge.

I **can hardly** do something = it's very difficult for me, almost impossible:

- Your writing is terrible. I **can hardly** read it. (= it is almost impossible to read it)
- My leg was hurting me. I **could hardly** walk.

Hardly ever = almost never:

- I'm nearly always at home at night. I **hardly ever** go out.

Hardly also means "certainly not." For example:

- It's **hardly surprising** that you're tired. You haven't slept for three days. (= it's certainly not surprising)
- The situation is serious, but it's **hardly a crisis**. (= it's certainly not a crisis)

Exercises

UNIT 99

99.1 Put in *good* or *well*.

1. I play tennis but I'm not very __good__ .
2. Your test results were very _____ .
3. You did _____ on the test.
4. The weather was _____ while we were on vacation.
5. I didn't sleep _____ last night.
6. Jason speaks Spanish very _____ .
7. Jason's Spanish is very _____ .
8. Our new business isn't doing very _____ at the moment.
9. I like your jacket. It looks _____ on you.
10. I've met her a few times, but I don't know her _____ .

99.2 Complete these sentences using *well* + the following words:

~~behaved~~ dressed informed known maintained paid written

1. The children were very good. They were __well behaved__ .
2. I'm surprised you haven't heard of her. She is quite _____ .
3. Our neighbors' yard is neat and clean. It is very _____ .
4. I enjoyed the book you lent me. It's a great story, and it's very _____ .
5. Tania knows a lot about many things. She is very _____ .
6. Mark always wears nice clothes. He is always _____ .
7. Jane has a lot of responsibility in her job, but she isn't very _____ .

99.3 Are the underlined words right or wrong? Correct them where necessary.

1. I'm tired because I've been working <u>hard</u>.   __OK__
2. I tried <u>hard</u> to remember her name, but I couldn't.   _____
3. This coat is practically unused. I've <u>hardly</u> worn it. _____
4. Judy is a good tennis player. She hits the ball <u>hardly</u>. _____
5. Don't walk so <u>fast</u>! I can't keep up with you.   _____
6. I had plenty of time, so I was walking <u>slow</u>.   _____

99.4 Complete the sentences. Use *hardly* + the following verbs (in the correct form):

change hear ~~know~~ recognize say sleep speak

1. Scott and Amy have only met once before. They __hardly know__ each other.
2. You're speaking very quietly. I can _____ you.
3. I'm very tired this morning. I _____ last night.
4. We were so shocked when we heard the news, we could _____ .
5. Kate was very quiet this evening. She _____ a word.
6. You look the same now as you looked 15 years ago. You've _____ .
7. I met Dave a few days ago. I hadn't seen him for a long time and he looks very different now. I _____ him.

99.5 Complete these sentences with *hardly* + *any/anybody/anything/anywhere/ever*.

1. I'll have to go shopping. There's __hardly anything__ to eat.
2. It was a very warm day. There was _____ wind.
3. "Do you know much about computers?" "No, _____ ."
4. The hotel was almost empty. There was _____ staying there.
5. I listen to the radio a lot, but I _____ watch television.
6. Our new boss is not very popular. _____ likes her.
7. It was very crowded in the room. There was _____ to sit.
8. We used to be good friends, but we _____ see each other now.
9. It was nice driving this morning. There was _____ traffic.
10. I hate this town. There's _____ to do and _____ to go.

Additional Exercise 31 (page 314)   199

UNIT 100

So and such

A

Compare **so** and **such**:

We use **so** + *adjective/adverb*:	We use **such** + *noun*:
so stupid **so quick**	**such a story** **such people**
so nice **so quickly**	We also use **such** + *adjective* + *noun*:
	such a stupid **story** **such** nice **people**

- I didn't like the book. The story was **so stupid**.
- I like Liz and Joe. They are **so nice**.

- I didn't like the book. It was **such** a stupid **story**. (*not* a so stupid story)
- I like Liz and Joe. They are **such nice people**. (*not* so nice people)

We say **such a** . . . (*not* a such):
- **such a** big **dog** (*not* a such big dog)

B

So and **such** make the meaning of an adjective (or adverb) stronger:

- It's a beautiful day, isn't it? It's **so warm**. (= really warm)
- It's difficult to understand him because he talks **so quietly**.

You can use **so** . . . **that**:
- The book was **so good that** I couldn't put it down.
- I was **so tired that** I fell asleep in the armchair.

We usually leave out **that**:
- I was **so tired** I fell asleep.

- It was a great holiday. We had **such a good time**. (= a really good time)

You can use **such** . . . **that**:
- It was **such a good book that** I couldn't put it down.
- It was **such nice weather that** we spent the whole day on the beach.

We usually leave out **that**:
- It was **such nice weather** we spent . . .

C

We also use **so** and **such** with the meaning "like this":

- Somebody told me the house was built 100 years ago. I didn't realize it was **so old**. (= as old as it is)
- I'm tired because I got up at six. I don't usually get up **so early**.
- I expected the weather to be cooler. I'm surprised it is **so warm**.

- I didn't realize it was **such an old house**.
- You know it's not true. How can you say **such a thing**?

Note the expression **no such** . . . :
- You won't find the word 'blid' in the dictionary. There's **no such word**. (= this word does not exist)

D

Compare:

so long
- I haven't seen her for **so long** I've forgotten what she looks like.

so far
- I didn't know it was **so far**.

so much, so many
- I'm sorry I'm late – there was **so much** traffic.

such a long time
- I haven't seen her for **such a long time**. (*not* so long time)

such a long way
- I didn't know it was **such a long way**.

such a lot (of)
- I'm sorry I'm late – there was **such a lot** of traffic.

200   *Not so . . . as* Unit 104A   *Such as* Unit 114B

Exercises

100.1 Put in *so*, *such*, or *such a*.

1. It's difficult to understand him because he speaks ___so___ quietly.
2. I like Liz and Joe. They're ___such___ nice people.
3. It was a great vacation. We had ___such a___ good time.
4. I was surprised that he looked _____ good after his recent illness.
5. Everything is _____ expensive these days, isn't it?
6. The weather is beautiful, isn't it? I didn't expect it to be _____ nice day.
7. I have to go. I didn't realize it was _____ late.
8. He always looks good. He wears _____ nice clothes.
9. It was _____ boring movie that I fell asleep while I was watching it.
10. I couldn't believe the news. It was _____ shock.
11. I think she works too hard. She looks _____ tired all the time.
12. The food at the hotel was _____ awful. I've never eaten _____ awful food.
13. They've got _____ much money that they don't know what to do with it.
14. I didn't realize you lived _____ long way from downtown.
15. The party was really great. It was _____ shame you couldn't come.

100.2 Make one sentence from two. Use *so* or *such*.

1. ~~She worked hard.~~	You could hear it from miles away.
2. ~~It was a beautiful day.~~	You would think it was her native language.
3. I was tired.	We spent the whole day indoors.
4. We had a good time on vacation.	~~She made herself sick.~~
5. She speaks English well.	I couldn't keep my eyes open.
6. I've got a lot to do.	I didn't eat anything else for the rest of the day.
7. The music was loud.	~~We decided to go to the beach.~~
8. I had a big breakfast.	I didn't know what to say.
9. It was terrible weather.	I don't know where to begin.
10. I was surprised.	We didn't want to come home.

1. _She worked so hard (that) she made herself sick._
2. _It was such a beautiful day (that) we decided to go to the beach._
3. I was _____
4. _____
5. _____
6. _____
7. _____
8. _____
9. _____
10. _____

100.3 Use your own ideas to complete these pairs of sentences.

1. a) We enjoyed our vacation. It was so ___relaxing___ .
   b) We enjoyed our vacation. We had such ___a good time___ .

2. a) I like Catherine. She's so _____ .
   b) I like Catherine. She's such _____ .

3. a) I like New York. It's so _____ .
   b) I like New York. It's such _____ .

4. a) I wouldn't like to be a teacher. It's so _____ .
   b) I wouldn't like to be a teacher. It's such _____ .

5. a) It's great to see you again! I haven't seen you for so _____ .
   b) It's great to see you again! I haven't seen you for such _____ .

Enough and too

A

Enough goes *after* adjectives and adverbs:

- I can't run very far. I'm not **fit enough**. (*not* enough fit)
- Let's go. We've waited **long enough**.
- Is Joe going to apply for the job? Is he **experienced enough**?

Compare **too . . .** and **not . . . enough**:

- You never stop working. You work **too hard**.
  (= more than is necessary)
- You're lazy. You do**n't** work **hard enough**.
  (= less than is necessary)

I'm not **fit enough**.

B

Enough normally goes *before* nouns:

- I can't run very far. I don't have **enough energy**. (*not* energy enough)
- Is Joe going to apply for the job? Does he have **enough experience**?
- We've got **enough money**. We don't need any more.
- Some of us had to sit on the floor because there weren't **enough chairs**.

Note that we say:

- We didn't have **enough time**. (*not* the time wasn't enough)
- There is **enough money**. (*not* the money is enough)

You can use **enough** alone (without a noun):

- We don't need any more money. We've got **enough**.

Compare **too much/many** and **enough**:

- There's **too much** furniture in this room. There's not **enough space**.
- There were **too many people** and not **enough chairs**.

C

We say **enough/too . . . for** somebody/something:

- We don't have **enough** money **for a vacation**.
- Is Joe experienced **enough for the job**?
- This shirt is **too big for me**. I need a smaller size.

But we say **enough/too . . . to** do something (*not* for doing). For example:

- We don't have **enough money to go** on vacation. (*not* for going)
- Is Joe **experienced enough to do** the job?
- They're **too young to get** married. / They're not **old enough to get** married.
- Let's take a taxi. It's **too far to walk** home from here.
- The bridge is just **wide enough** for two cars **to pass** each other.

D

We say:

	The food was very hot. We couldn't eat **it**.
and	The food was so hot that we couldn't eat **it**.
but	The food was **too hot to eat**. (*without* it)

Some more examples like this:

- These boxes are **too heavy to carry**.
  (*not* too heavy to carry them)
- The wallet was **too big to put** in my pocket.
  (*not* too big to put it)
- This chair isn't **strong enough to stand** on.
  (*not* strong enough to stand on it)

To . . . and *for . . .* (purpose) **Unit 62**   Adjective + *to . . .* (*difficult to understand*, etc.) **Unit 63**

Exercises

101.1 Complete the sentences using *enough* + the following words:

> big   ~~chairs~~   cups   ~~fit~~   milk   money
> qualified   room   time   warm   well

1. I can't run very far. I'm not __*fit enough*__ .
2. Some of us had to sit on the floor because there weren't __*enough chairs*__ .
3. I'd like to buy a car, but I don't have _____ right now.
4. Do you have _____ in your coffee, or would you like some more?
5. Are you _____ ? Or should I turn up the heat?
6. It's only a small car. There isn't _____ for all of us.
7. Steve didn't feel _____ to go to work this morning.
8. I enjoyed my trip to Paris, but there wasn't _____ to do everything I wanted.
9. Do you think I am _____ to apply for the job?
10. Try this jacket on and see if it's _____ for you.
11. There weren't _____ for everybody to have coffee at the same time.

101.2 Complete the answers to the questions. Use *too* or *enough* + the word(s) in parentheses.

1. Are they going to get married? — (old) No, they're not __*old enough to*__ __*get married*__ .
2. I need to talk to you about something. — (busy) Well, I'm afraid I'm _____ to you now.
3. Let's go to the movies. — (late) No, it's _____ to the movies.
4. Why don't we sit outside? — (warm) It's not _____ outside.
5. Would you like to be a politician? — (shy) No, I'm _____ a politician.
6. Would you like to be a teacher? — (patience) No, I don't have _____ a teacher.
7. Did you hear what he was saying? — (far away) No, we were _____ what he was saying.
8. Can he read a newspaper in English? — (English) No, he doesn't know _____ a newspaper.

101.3 Make one sentence from two. Complete the new sentence using *too* or *enough*.

1. We couldn't carry the boxes. They were too heavy.
   *The boxes were too heavy to carry.*
2. I can't drink this coffee. It's too hot.
   This coffee is _____
3. Nobody could move the piano. It was too heavy.
   The piano _____
4. Don't eat these apples. They're not ripe enough.
   These apples _____
5. I can't explain the situation. It is too complicated.
   The situation _____
6. We couldn't climb over the wall. It was too high.
   The wall _____
7. Three people can't sit on this sofa. It isn't big enough.
   This sofa _____
8. You can't see some things without a microscope. They are too small.
   Some _____

Comparison 1
(cheaper, more expensive, etc.)

A

Study these examples:

> Should I drive or take the train?
>> You should drive. It's **cheaper**.
>> Don't take the train. It's **more expensive**.
> **Cheaper** and **more expensive** are *comparative* forms.

After comparatives you can use **than** (see Unit 104):

- ■ It's **cheaper** to go by car **than** by train.
- ■ Going by train is **more expensive than** going by car.

B

The comparative form is **–er** or **more** . . .

We use **–er** for short words (one syllable): cheap → cheap**er** fast → fast**er** large → larg**er** thin → thin**ner** We also use **–er** for two-syllable words that end in **–y** (**–y → ier**): luck**y** → luck**ier** earl**y** → earl**ier** eas**y** → eas**ier** prett**y** → prett**ier** For spelling, see Appendix 6.	We use **more** . . . for longer words (two syllables or more): **more serious** **more often** **more expensive** **more comfortable** We also use **more** . . . for adverbs that end in **–ly**: **more slowly** **more seriously** **more quietly** **more carefully**

Compare these examples:

■ You're **older** than me. ■ The test was pretty easy – **easier** than I expected. ■ Can you walk a little **faster**? ■ I'd like to have a **bigger** car. ■ Last night I went to bed **earlier** than usual.	■ You're **more patient** than me. ■ The test was pretty difficult – **more difficult** than I expected. ■ Can you walk a little **more slowly**? ■ I'd like to have a **more reliable** car. ■ I don't play tennis much these days. I used to play **more often**.

You can use **–er** *or* **more** . . . with some two-syllable adjectives, especially:

> clever   narrow   quiet   shallow   simple

- ■ It's too noisy here. Can we go somewhere **quieter** / **more quiet**?

C

A few adjectives and adverbs have irregular comparative forms:

good/well → better

- ■ The yard looks **better** since you cleaned it up.
- ■ I know him **well** – probably **better** than anybody else knows him.

bad/badly → worse:

- ■ "How is your headache? Better?" "No, it's **worse**."
- ■ He did very badly on the test – **worse** than expected.

far → farther (*or* **further**):

- ■ "It's a long walk from here to the park – **farther** than I thought. (*or* **further** than)

Further (*but not* farther) can also mean "more" or "additional":

- ■ Let me know if you hear any **further** news. (= any more news)

Exercises

102.1 Complete the sentences using a comparative form (*older* / *more important*, etc.).

1. It's too noisy here. Can we go somewhere __*quieter*__ ?
2. This coffee is very weak. I like it a little _____ .
3. The hotel was surprisingly big. I expected it to be _____ .
4. The hotel was surprisingly cheap. I expected it to be _____ .
5. The weather is too cold here. I'd like to live somewhere _____ .
6. My job is kind of boring sometimes. I'd like to do something _____ .
7. It's too bad you live so far away. I wish you lived _____ .
8. I was surprised how easy it was to use the computer. I thought it would be

   _____ .
9. Your work isn't very good. I'm sure you can do _____ .
10. Don't worry. The situation isn't so bad. It could be _____ .
11. I was surprised we got here so quickly. I expected the trip to take _____ .
12. You're talking very loudly. Can you speak a little _____ ?
13. You hardly ever call me. Why don't you call me _____ ?
14. You're standing too close to the camera. Can you move a little _____ away?
15. You were a little depressed yesterday, but you look _____ today.

102.2 Complete the sentences. Each time use the comparative form of one of the words in the list.
Use *than* where necessary.

big	crowded	~~early~~	easily	high	important
interested	peaceful	~~reliable~~	serious	simple	thin

1. I was feeling tired last night, so I went to bed __*earlier than*__ usual.
2. I'd like to have a __*more reliable*__ car. Mine keeps breaking down.
3. Unfortunately, her illness was _____ we thought at first.
4. You look _____ . Have you lost weight?
5. I want a _____ apartment. We don't have enough space here.
6. He doesn't study very hard. He's _____ in having a good time.
7. Health and happiness are _____ money.
8. The instructions were very complicated. They could have been _____ .
9. There were a lot of people on the bus. It was _____ usual.
10. I like living in the country. It's _____ living in a city.
11. You'll find your way around the city _____ if you have a good map.
12. In some parts of the country, prices are _____ in others.

102.3 Read the situations and complete the sentences. Use a comparative form (*-er* or *more* . . .).

1. Yesterday the temperature was 6 degrees. Today it is only 3 degrees.
   It's __*colder today than it was yesterday*__ .
2. The trip takes four hours by car and five hours by train.
   It takes _____ .
3. Dave and I went for a run. I ran five miles. Dave stopped after three.
   I ran _____ .
4. Chris and Joe both did badly on the test. Chris got a C, but Joe only got a C–.
   Joe did _____ .
5. I expected my friends to arrive at about 4:00. In fact they arrived at 2:30.
   My friends _____ .
6. You can go by bus or by train. The buses run every 30 minutes. The trains run every hour.
   The buses _____ .
7. We were very busy at work today. We're not usually so busy.
   We _____ .

Comparison 2 (much better / any better / better and better / the sooner the better)

A | Before comparatives you can use:

| much | a lot | far (= a lot) | a bit | a little | slightly (= a little) |

- Let's drive. It's **much cheaper**. (*or* **a lot cheaper**)
- "How do you feel?" "**Much better**, thanks."
- Don't go by train. It's **a lot more expensive**. (*or* **much more expensive**)
- Could you speak **a bit more slowly**? (*or* **a little more slowly**)
- This bag is **slightly heavier** than the other one.
- Her illness was **far more serious** than we thought at first.
  (*or* **much more serious** / **a lot more serious**)

B | You can use **any** and **no** + comparative (**any longer** / **no bigger**, etc.):
- I've waited long enough. I'm not waiting **any longer**. (= not even a little longer)
- We expected their house to be very big, but it's **no bigger** than ours. *or*
  . . . it is**n't any bigger** than ours. (= not even a little bigger)
- How do you feel now? Do you feel **any better**?
- This hotel is better than the other one, and it's **no more expensive**.

C | Better and better / more and more, etc.

We repeat comparatives (**better and better**, etc.) to say that something is changing continuously:
- Your English is improving. It's getting **better and better**.
- The city is growing fast. It's getting **bigger and bigger**.
- Cathy got **more and more bored** in her job. In the end, she quit.
- These days **more and more** people are learning English.

D | The sooner the better

You can say **the** (sooner/bigger/more, etc.) **the better**:
- "What time should we leave?" "**The sooner the better**." (= as soon as possible)
- *A:* What sort of box do you want? A big one?
  B: Yes, **the bigger the better**. (= as big as possible)
- When you're traveling, **the less luggage** you have **the better**.

We also use **the** . . . **the** . . . to say that one thing depends on another thing:
- **The warmer** the weather, **the better** I feel. (= if the weather is warmer, I feel better)
- **The sooner** we leave, **the earlier** we will arrive.
- **The younger** you are, **the easier** it is to learn.
- **The more expensive** the hotel, **the better** the service.
- **The more electricity** you use, **the higher** your bill will be.
- **The more** I thought about the plan, **the less** I liked it.

E | **Older** and **elder**

The comparative of **old** is **older**:
- David looks **older** than he really is.

You can use **elder** (*or* **older**) when you talk about people in a family. You can say
(**my/your**, etc.) **elder sister/brother/daughter/son**:
- **My elder sister** is a TV producer. (*or* My **older** sister . . .)

We say "my **elder sister**," but we do not say that somebody is elder:
- My sister is **older** than me. (*not* elder than me)

Any/no Unit 84   **Comparison 1, 3** Units 102, 104   *Eldest* Unit 105D   *Even* + **Comparative** Unit 109C

Exercises

103.1 Use the words in parentheses to complete the sentences. Use *much* / *a little*, etc. +
a comparative form. Use *than* where necessary.

1. Her illness was _much more serious than_ we thought at first. (much / serious)
2. This bag is too small. I need something _____ . (much / big)
3. I'm afraid the problem is _____ it seems. (much / complicated)
4. It was very hot yesterday. Today it's _____ . (a little / cool)
5. I enjoyed our visit to the museum. It was _____ I expected.
   (far / interesting)
6. You're driving too fast. Can you drive _____ ? (a little / slowly)
7. It's _____ to learn a foreign language in a country where it is
   spoken. (a lot / easy)
8. I thought she was younger than me, but in fact she's _____ .
   (slightly / old)

103.2 Complete the sentences using *any* / *no* + a comparative. Use *than* where necessary.

1. I've waited long enough. I'm not waiting _any longer_ .
2. I'm sorry I'm a little late, but I couldn't get here _____ .
3. This store isn't expensive. The prices are _____ anywhere else.
4. I need to stop for a rest. I can't walk _____ .
5. The traffic isn't particularly bad today. It's _____ usual.

103.3 Complete the sentences using the structure in Section C (. . . *and* . . .).

1. Cathy got _more and more bored_ in her job. In the end she quit. (bored)
2. That hole in your sweater is getting _____ . (big)
3. My bags seemed to get _____ as I carried them. (heavy)
4. As I waited for my interview, I became _____ . (nervous)
5. As the day went on, the weather got _____ . (bad)
6. Health care is becoming _____ . (expensive)
7. Since Anna went to Canada, her English has gotten _____ . (good)
8. As the conversation went on, Paul became _____ . (talkative)

103.4 These sentences are like those in Section D. Use the words in parentheses (in the correct form) to
complete the sentences.

1. I like warm weather.
   The warmer the weather, _the better I feel_ . (feel)
2. I didn't really like him when we first met.
   But the more I got to know him, _____ . (like)
3. If you're in business, you want to make a profit.
   The more goods you sell, _____ . (profit)
4. It's hard to concentrate when you're tired.
   The more tired you are, _____ . (hard)
5. Kate had to wait a very long time.
   The longer she waited, _____ . (impatient / become)

103.5 Which is correct, *older* or *elder*? Or both of them?

1. My <u>older</u> ✓ / <u>elder</u> ✓ sister is a TV producer. (*older* and *elder* are both correct)
2. I'm surprised Diane is only 25. I thought she was <u>older / elder</u>.
3. Jane's younger sister is still in school. Her <u>older / elder</u> sister is a nurse.
4. Martin is <u>older / elder</u> than his brother.

Comparison 3 (as . . . as / than)

A

Study this example situation:

Sarah   Eric   David

Sarah, Eric, and David are all very rich.
Sarah has $20 million, Eric has $15 million,
and David has $10 million. So:

Eric is rich.
He is **richer than** David.
But he is**n't as rich as** Sarah.
(= Sarah is **richer than** he is)

Some more examples of **not as . . . (as)**:

- ■ Richard is**n't as old as** he looks. (= he looks **older than** he is)
- ■ The shopping mall was**n't as crowded as** usual. (= it is usually **more crowded**)
- ■ Jenny did**n't** do **as well** on the test **as** she had hoped.
  (= she had hoped to do **better**)
- ■ The weather is better today. It's **not as cold**. (= yesterday was **colder**)
- ■ I do**n't** know **as many** people **as** you do. (= you know **more** people)
- ■ *A:* How much did it cost? Fifty dollars?
  B: No, **not as much as** that. (= less than fifty dollars)

You can also say **not so . . . (as)**:

- ■ It's not warm, but it is**n't so** cold **as** yesterday. (= it is**n't as** cold **as** . . .)

Less . . . than is similar to **not as . . . as**:

- ■ I spent **less money than** you. (= I did**n't** spend **as** much money **as** you)
- ■ The shopping mall was **less crowded than** usual. (= it was**n't as** crowded **as** usual)
- ■ Ted talks **less than** his brother. (= he does**n't** talk **as** much **as** his brother does)

B

We also use **as . . . as** (*but not* so . . . as) in positive sentences and in questions:

- ■ I'm sorry I'm late. I got here **as fast as** I could.
- ■ There's plenty of food. You can have **as much as** you want.
- ■ Let's walk. It's **just as quick as** taking the bus.
- ■ Can you send me the money **as soon as possible**, please?

Also **twice as . . . as, three times as . . . as**, etc.:

- ■ Gas is **twice as expensive as** it was a few years ago.
- ■ Their house is about **three times as big as** ours.

C

We say **the same as** (*not* the same like):

- ■ Ann's salary is **the same as** mine.   *or*   Ann gets **the same** salary **as** me.
- ■ David is **the same** age **as** James.
- ■ "What would you like to drink?"   "I'll have **the same as** you."

D

Than me / than I am, etc.

You can say:

- ■ You're taller **than I am**.   *or*   You're taller **than me**.
  (*not usually* You're taller than I)
- ■ He's not as clever **as she is**.   *or*   He's not as clever **as her**.
- ■ They have more money **than we do**.   *or*   They have more money **than us**.
- ■ I can't run as fast as **he can**.   *or*   I can't run as fast **as him**.

Exercises

104.1 Complete the sentences using *as ... as*.

1. I'm pretty tall, but you are taller. I'm not _as tall as you_____ .
2. My salary is high, but yours is higher.
   My salary isn't _____ .
3. You know a little about cars, but I know more.
   You don't _____ .
4. It's still cold, but it was colder yesterday.
   It isn't _____ .
5. I still feel tired, but I felt a lot more tired yesterday.
   I don't _____ .
6. Our neighbors have lived here quite a while, but we've lived here longer.
   Our neighbors haven't _____ .
7. I was a little nervous before the interview, but usually I'm a lot more nervous.
   I wasn't _____ .

104.2 Write a new sentence with the same meaning.

1. Jack is younger than he looks. Jack isn't _as old as he looks_____ .
2. I didn't spend as much money as you. You _spent more money than me_____ .
3. The station was closer than I thought. The station wasn't _____ .
4. The meal didn't cost as much as I expected. The meal cost _____ .
5. I go out less than I used to. I don't _____ .
6. Karen's hair isn't as long as it used to be. Karen used to _____ .
7. I know them better than you do. You don't _____ .
8. There are fewer people at this meeting than at the last one.
   There aren't _____ .

104.3 Complete the sentences using *as ... as* + the following:

bad	comfortable	~~fast~~	long	often
quietly	well qualified	well	soon	

1. I'm sorry I'm late. I got here _as fast as___ I could.
2. It was a difficult question. I answered it _____ I could.
3. "How long can I stay with you?" "You can stay _____ you like."
4. I need the information quickly, so let me know _____ possible.
5. I like to stay in shape, so I go swimming _____ I can.
6. I didn't want to wake anybody, so I came in _____ I could.

In the following sentences use *just as ... as*.

7. I'm going to sleep on the floor. It's _____ the bed.
8. Why did he get the job rather than me? I'm _____ him.
9. At first I thought he was nice, but really he's _____
   everybody else.

104.4 Write sentences using *the same as*.

1. David and James are both 22 years old. David _is the same age as James_____ .
2. You and I both have dark brown hair. Your hair _____ .
3. I arrived at 10:25 and so did you. I _____ .
4. My birthday is April 5. Tom's birthday is April 5, too. My _____ .

104.5 Complete the sentences with *than ...* or *as ....*

1. I can't reach as high as you. You are taller _than me___ .
2. He doesn't know much. I know more _____ .
3. I don't work especially hard. Most people work as hard _____ .
4. We were very surprised. Nobody was more surprised _____ .
5. She's not a very good player. I'm a better player _____ .
6. They've been very lucky. I wish we were as lucky _____ .

Superlatives
(the longest / the most enjoyable, etc.)

A

Study these examples:

> What is **the longest river** in the world?
> What was **the most enjoyable** vacation you've ever taken?
>
> **Longest** and **most enjoyable** are *superlative* forms.

B

The superlative form is **-est** or **most** . . . . In general, we use **-est** for short words and **most** . . .
for longer words. The rules are the same as those for the comparative – see Unit 102.

	long → long**est**	hot → hot**test**	easy → easi**est**	hard → hard**est**
but	**most** famous	**most** boring	**most** difficult	**most** expensive

A few adjectives are irregular:

good → **best**   bad → **worst**   far → **farthest/furthest**

For spelling, see Appendix 6.

C

We normally use **the** before a superlative (**the** longest / **the** most famous, etc.):
- Yesterday was **the hottest** day of the year.
- The film was really boring. It was **the most boring** film I've ever seen.
- She is a really nice person – one of **the nicest** people I know.
- Why does he always come to see me at **the worst** possible time?

> Compare superlative and comparative:
> - This hotel is **the cheapest** in town. *(superlative)*
>   This hotel is **cheaper** than all the others in town. *(comparative)*
> - He's **the most patient** person I've ever met.
>   He's much **more patient** than I am.

D

Oldest and **eldest**

The superlative of **old** is **oldest**:
- That church is **the oldest** building in the town. (*not* the eldest)

We use **eldest** (*or* **oldest**) when we are talking about people in a family:
- **My eldest son** is 13 years old. (*or* My **oldest** son)
- Are you **the eldest** in your family? (*or* the **oldest**)

E

After superlatives we normally use **in** with places:
- What's the longest river **in the world**? (*not* of the world)
- We had a nice room. It was one of the best **in the hotel**. (*not* of the hotel)

We also use **in** for organizations and groups of people (a class / a company, etc.):
- Who is the youngest student **in the class**? (*not* of the class)

For a period of time, we normally use **of**:
- What was the happiest day **of your life**?
- Yesterday was the hottest day **of the year**.

F

We often use the *present perfect* (I **have done**) after a superlative (see also Unit 7B):
- What's **the most important** decision you**'ve** ever **had** to make?
- That was **the best** vacation I**'ve taken** for a long time.

Comparison (*cheaper / more expensive*, etc.) Units 102–104   *Elder* Unit 103E

Exercises

105.1 Complete the sentences. Use a superlative (*-est* or *most* . . .) + a preposition (*of* or *in*).

1. It's a very good room. It _is the best room in_ the hotel.
2. It's a very cheap restaurant. It's _____ town.
3. It was a very happy day. It was _____ my life.
4. She's a very intelligent student. She _____ the class.
5. It's a very valuable painting. It _____ the gallery.
6. Spring is a very busy time for me. It _____ the year.

In the following sentences use ***one of*** + a superlative + a preposition.

7. It's a very good room. It _is one of the best rooms in_ the hotel.
8. He's a very rich man. He's one _____ the world.
9. It's a very old house. It _____ the city.
10. It's a very good college. It _____ the state.
11. It was a very bad experience. It _____ my life.
12. He's a very dangerous criminal. He _____ the country.

105.2 Complete the sentences. Use a superlative (*-est* or *most* . . .) or a comparative (*-er* or *more* . . .).

1. We stayed at _the cheapest_ hotel in town. (cheap)
2. Our hotel was _cheaper_ than all the others in town. (cheap)
3. The United States is very large, but Canada is _____ . (large)
4. What's _____ country in the world? (small)
5. I wasn't feeling well yesterday, but I feel a little _____ today. (good)
6. It was an awful day. It was _____ day of my life. (bad)
7. What is _____ sport in your country? (popular)
8. Everest is _____ mountain in the world. It is _____ than any other mountain. (high)
9. We had a great vacation. It was one of _____ vacations we've ever taken. (enjoyable)
10. I prefer this chair to the other one. It's _____ . (comfortable)
11. What's _____ way to get to the station? (quick)
12. Sue and Kevin have three daughters. _____ is 14 years old. (old)

105.3 What do you say in these situations? Use a superlative + ***ever***. Use the words in parentheses (in the correct form).

1. You've just been to the movies. The movie was extremely boring. You tell your friend:
   (boring / movie / see) That's _the most boring movie I've ever seen_ .
2. Your friend has just told you a joke, which you think is very funny. You say:
   (funny / joke / hear) That's _____ .
3. You're drinking coffee with a friend. It's really good coffee. You say:
   (good / coffee / taste) This _____ .
4. You are talking to a friend about Mary. Mary is very generous. You tell your friend about her: (generous / person / meet) She _____ .
5. You have just run 10 miles. You've never run farther than this. You say to your friend:
   (far / run) That _____ .
6. You decided to quit your job. Now you think this was a bad mistake. You say to your friend: (bad / mistake / make) It _____ .
7. Your friend meets a lot of people, some of them famous. You ask your friend:
   (famous / person / meet?) Who _____ ?

Word Order 1:
Verb + Object; Place and Time

A

Verb + object

The *verb* and the *object* normally go together. We do not usually put other words between them:

	Verb +	*Object*	
I	**like**	**my job**	very much. (*not* I like very much my job)
Did you	**see**	**your friends**	yesterday?
Ann often	**plays**	**tennis**.	

Study these examples. The verb and the object go together each time:

■ Do you **eat meat** every day? (*not* Do you eat every day meat?)

■ Everybody **enjoyed the party** very much. (*not* enjoyed very much the party)

■ Our guide **spoke English** fluently. (*not* spoke fluently English)

■ I lost all my money, and I also **lost my passport** . (*not* I lost also my passport)

■ At the end of the block, you'll **see a supermarket** on your left.
(*not* see on your left a supermarket)

B

Place and time

Usually the *verb* and the place (where?) go together:
go home   live in a city   walk to work, etc.

If the verb has an *object*, the place comes after the *verb + object*:
take somebody home   meet a friend on the street

Time (when? / how often? / how long?) usually goes after *place*:

	Place	+	*Time*
Tom walks	**to work**		**every morning**. (*not* every morning to work)
Sam has been	**in Canada**		**since April**.
We arrived	**at the airport**		**early**.

Study these examples. *Time* goes after *place*:

■ I'm going **to Paris on Monday** . (*not* I'm going on Monday to Paris)

■ They have lived **in the same house for a long time** .

■ Don't be late. Make sure you're **here by 8:00** .

■ Sarah gave me a ride **home after the party** .

■ You really shouldn't go **to bed so late** .

It is often possible to put *time* at the beginning of the sentence:
■ **On Monday** I'm going to Paris.
■ **Every morning** Tom walks to work.

Some time words (for example, **always/never/often**) usually go with the verb in the middle of the sentence. See Unit 107.

Word Order in Questions Units 47–48   **Adjective Order** Unit 97   **Word Order 2** Unit 107

Exercises

106.1 Is the word order right or wrong? Correct the sentences where necessary.

1. Everybody enjoyed the party very much.   _OK_
2. Tom walks (every morning to work).   _Tom walks to work every morning._
3. Jim doesn't like very much basketball.   _____
4. I drink three or four cups of coffee
   every morning.   _____
5. I ate quickly my breakfast and went out.   _____
6. Are you going to invite to the party a lot
   of people?   _____
7. I called Tom immediately after hearing
   the news.   _____
8. Did you go late to bed last night?   _____
9. Did you learn a lot of things at school today?   _____
10. I met on my way home a friend of mine.   _____

106.2 Put the parts of the sentence in the correct order.

1. (the party / very much / everybody enjoyed) _Everybody enjoyed the party very much._
2. (we won / easily / the game) _____
3. (quietly / the door / I closed) _____
4. (Diane / quite well / speaks / Chinese) _____
5. (Tim / all the time / TV / watches) _____
6. (again / please don't ask / that question)
   _____
7. (golf / every weekend / does Ken play / ?)
   _____
8. (some money / I borrowed / from a friend of mine)

106.3 Complete the sentences. Put the parts in the correct order.

1. (for a long time / have lived / in the same house)
   They _have lived in the same house for a long time_ .
2. (to the supermarket / every Friday / go)
   I _____ .
3. (home / did you come / so late)
   Why _____ ?
4. (her children / takes / every day / to school)
   Sarah _____ .
5. (been / recently / to the movies)
   I haven't _____ .
6. (at the top of the page / your name / write)
   Please _____ .
7. (her name / after a few minutes / remembered)
   I _____ .
8. (around the town / all morning / walked)
   We _____ .
9. (on Saturday night / didn't see you / at the party)
   I _____ .
10. (some interesting books / found / in the library)
    We _____ .
11. (her umbrella / last night / in a restaurant / left)
    Jackie _____ .
12. (across from the park / a new hotel / are building)
    They _____ .

Word Order 2:
Adverbs with the Verb

A Some *adverbs* (for example, **always/also/probably**) go with the verb in the middle of a sentence:
- Helen **always drives** to work.
- We were feeling very tired, and we **were also** hungry.
- The concert **will probably be** canceled.

B Study these rules for the position of adverbs in the middle of a sentence. (They are only general rules, so there are exceptions.)

(1) If the verb is one word (**drives/fell/cooked**, etc.), the adverb usually goes *before* the verb:

	Adverb	*Verb*	
Helen	**always**	**drives**	to work.
I	**almost**	**fell**	as I was going down the stairs.

- I cleaned the house and **also cooked** dinner. (*not* cooked also)
- Lucy **hardly ever watches** television and **rarely reads** newspapers.
- "Should I give you my address?"   "No, I **already have** it."

Note that these adverbs (**always/often/also**, etc.) go before **have to** ...:
- Joe never calls me. I **always have to** call him. (*not* I have always to call)

(2) But adverbs go *after* **am/is/are/was/were**:
- We were feeling very tired, and we **were also** hungry.
- Why are you always late? You**'re never** on time.
- The traffic **isn't usually** as bad as it was this morning.

(3) If the verb is two or more words (for example, **can remember / doesn't eat / will be canceled**), the adverb usually goes *after the first verb* (**can/doesn't/will**, etc.):

	Verb 1	*Adverb*	*Verb 2*	
I	**can**	**never**	**remember**	her name.
Claire	**doesn't**	**often**	**eat**	meat.
	Are you	**definitely**	**going**	to the party tomorrow?
The concert	**will**	**probably**	**be**	canceled.

- You **have always been** very kind to me.
- Jack can't cook. He **can't even boil** an egg.
- **Do** you **still work** for the same company?
- The house **was only built** a year ago, and it**'s already falling** down.

Note that **probably** goes before a negative (**isn't/won't** etc.). So we say:
- I **probably won't** see you.   *or*   I will **probably not** see you. (*not* I won't probably)

C We also use **all** and **both** in these positions:
- We **all felt** sick after we ate. (*not* we felt all sick)
- My parents **are both** teachers. (*not* my parents both are teachers)
- Sarah and Jane **have both applied** for the job.
- We **are all going** out tonight.

D Sometimes we use **is/will/did**, etc. instead of repeating part of a sentence (see Unit 49).
Note the position of **always/never**, etc. in these sentences:
- He always says he won't be late, but he **always is**. (= he **is always** late)
- I've never done it, and I **never will**. (= I **will never** do it)

We normally put **always/never**, etc. before the verb in sentences like these.

Exercises

107.1 Are the <u>underlined</u> words in the right position or not? Correct the sentences where necessary.

1. Helen drives <u>always</u> to work.   *Helen always drives to work.*
2. I cleaned the house and <u>also</u> cooked dinner.   *OK*
3. I take <u>usually</u> a shower in the morning. _____
4. We <u>soon</u> found the solution to the problem. _____
5. Steve gets <u>hardly ever</u> angry. _____
6. I did some shopping, and I went <u>also</u> to the bank. _____
7. Jane has <u>always</u> to hurry in the morning. _____
8. We <u>all</u> were tired, so we <u>all</u> fell asleep. _____
9. She <u>always</u> says she'll call me, but she <u>never</u> does. _____

107.2 Rewrite the sentences to include the word in parentheses.

1. Claire doesn't eat meat. (often)   *Claire doesn't often eat meat.*
2. a) We were on vacation in Spain. (all) _____
   b) We were staying at the same hotel. (all) _____
   c) We enjoyed ourselves. (all) _____
3. Catherine is very generous. (always) _____
4. I don't have to work on Saturdays. (usually) _____
5. Do you watch TV in the evenings? (always) _____
6. Josh is studying Spanish, and he is studying Japanese. (also)
   Josh is studying Spanish, and he _____
7. a) The new hotel is very expensive. (probably) _____
   b) It costs a lot to stay there. (probably) _____
8. a) I can help you. (probably) _____
   b) I can't help you. (probably) _____

107.3 Complete the sentences. Use the words in parentheses in the correct order.

1. I _*can never remember*_ her name. (remember / never / can)
2. I _____ sugar in my coffee. (take / usually)
3. I _____ hungry when I get home from work. (am / usually)
4. *A:* Where's Joe?
   B: He _____ home early. (gone / has / probably)
5. Mark and Diane _____ in Texas. (both / were / born)
6. Liz is a good pianist. She _____ very well.
   (sing / also / can)
7. Our cat _____ under the bed. (often / sleeps)
8. They live on the same street as me, but I _____ to them.
   (never / have / spoken)
9. We _____ a long time for the bus.
   (have / always / to wait)
10. My eyesight isn't very good. I _____ with glasses.
    (read / can / only)
11. I _____ early tomorrow. (probably / leaving / will / be)
12. I'm afraid I _____ able to come to the party.
    (probably / be / won't)
13. It's hard to contact Sue. Her cell phone _____ on when I
    call her. (is / hardly ever)
14. We _____ in the same place. We haven't moved.
    (still / are / living)
15. If we hadn't taken the same train, we _____ each other.
    (never / met / would / have)
16. *A:* Are you tired?
    B: Yes, I _____ at this time of day. (am / always)

Still, yet, and already
Anymore / any longer / no longer

A

Still

We use **still** to say that a situation or action is continuing. It hasn't changed or stopped:

- It's 10:00 and Joe is **still** in bed.
- When I went to bed, Chris was **still** working.
- Do you **still** want to go to the party, or have you changed your mind?

Still usually goes in the middle of the sentence with the verb (see Unit 107).

B

Anymore / any longer / no longer

We use **not . . . anymore** or **not . . . any longer** to say that a situation has changed.
Anymore and **any longer** go at the end of a sentence:

- Lucy does**n't** work here **anymore** (*or* **any longer**). She left last month.
  (*not* Lucy doesn't still work here.)
- We used to be good friends, but we are**n't** anymore (*or* **any longer**).

You can also use **no longer**. **No longer** goes in the middle of the sentence:

- Lucy **no longer** works here.

Note that we do not normally use **no more** in this way:

- We are **no longer** friends. (*not* We are no more friends.)

Compare **still** and **not . . . anymore**:

- Sally **still** works here, but Ann does**n't** work here **anymore**.

C

Yet

Yet = until now. We use **yet** mainly in negative sentences (**He isn't** here **yet**) and questions
(**Is he** here **yet**?). **Yet** shows that the speaker is expecting something to happen.

Yet usually goes at the end of a sentence:

- It's 10:00 and Joe **isn't** here **yet**.
- **Have** you **met** your new neighbors **yet**?
- "Where are you going for vacation?" "We **don't** know **yet**."

We often use **yet** with the *present perfect* (**Have** you **met** . . . **yet**?). See Unit 8D.

Compare **yet** and **still**:

- Mike lost his job six months ago and **is still** unemployed.
  Mike lost his job six months ago and **hasn't found** another job **yet**.
- **Is** it **still** raining?
  Has it **stopped** raining **yet**?

Still is also possible in *negative* sentences (before the negative):

- She said she would be here an hour ago, and she **still** has**n't** come.

This is similar to "she hasn't come **yet**." But **still . . . not** shows a stronger feeling of surprise
or impatience. Compare:

- I wrote to him last week. He has**n't** replied **yet**. (but I expect he will reply soon)
- I wrote to him months ago and he **still** has**n't** replied. (he should have replied before now)

D

Already

We use **already** to say that something happened sooner than expected. **Already** usually goes
in the middle of a sentence (see Unit 107):

- "What time is Sue leaving?" "She has **already** left." (= sooner than you expected)
- Should I tell Joe what happened, or does he **already** know?
- I've just had lunch, and I'm **already** hungry.

Present Perfect + *already* **/** *yet* Unit 8D   **Word Order** Unit 107

Exercises

108.1 Compare what Paul said a few years ago with what he says now. Some things are the same as before, and some things have changed. Write sentences with *still* and *anymore*.

I travel a lot.
I work in a store.
I write poems.
I want to be a teacher.
I'm interested in politics.
I'm single.
I go fishing a lot.

Paul a few years ago

I travel a lot.
I work in a hospital.
I gave up writing poems.
I want to be a teacher.
I'm not interested in politics.
I'm single.
I haven't been fishing in years.

Paul now

1. (travel) _He still travels a lot._
2. (store) _He doesn't work in a store anymore._
3. (poems) He _____
4. (teacher) _____

5. (politics) _____
    _____
6. (single) _____
7. (fishing) _____
8. (beard) _____

Now write three sentences about Paul using *no longer*.

9. _He no longer works in a store._
10. _____

11. _____
12. _____

108.2 For each sentence (with *still*) write a sentence with a similar meaning using *not . . . yet* + one of the following verbs:

    decide   find   finish   leave   ~~stop~~   take off   wake up

1. It's still raining. _It hasn't stopped raining yet_ .
2. Gary is still here. He _____ .
3. They're still repairing the road. They _____ .
4. The children are still asleep. _____ .
5. Is Ann still looking for a place to live? _____ ?
6. I'm still wondering what to do. _____ .
7. The plane is still waiting on the runway. _____ .

108.3 Put *still*, *yet*, *already*, or *anymore* in the underlined sentence (or part of the sentence). Study the examples carefully.

1. Mike lost his job a year ago, and <u>he is unemployed</u>. _he is still unemployed_
2. Should I tell Joe what happened, or <u>does he know</u>? _does he already know_
3. I'm hungry. <u>Is dinner ready</u>? _Is dinner ready yet_
4. I was hungry earlier, but <u>I'm not hungry</u>. _I'm not hungry anymore_
5. Can we wait a few minutes? <u>I don't want to go out</u>. _____
6. Jenny used to work at the airport, but <u>she doesn't work there</u>. _____
7. I used to live in Tokyo. <u>I have a lot of friends there</u>. _____
8. "Let me introduce you to Jim." "You don't have to. <u>We've met</u>." _____
9. <u>Do you live in the same place</u>, or have you moved? _____
10. Would you like to eat with us, or <u>have you eaten</u>? _____
11. "Where's John?" "<u>He's not here</u>. He'll be here soon." _____
12. Tim said he'd be here at 8:30. It's 9:00 now, and <u>he isn't here</u>. _____
13. Do you want to join the club, or <u>are you a member</u>? _____
14. It happened a long time ago, but <u>I can remember it very clearly</u>. _____
15. I've put on weight. <u>These pants don't fit me</u>. _____
16. "<u>Have you finished with the paper</u>?" "No, <u>I'm reading it</u>." _____

Even

Study this example situation:

Tina loves watching television.

She has a TV set in every room of
the house – **even** the bathroom.

We use **even** to say that something is
unusual or surprising. It is unusual to
have a TV set in the bathroom.

Some more examples:

- These pictures are really awful. **Even I** could take better pictures than these.
  (and I'm certainly not a good photographer)
- He always wears a coat – **even in hot weather**.
- Nobody would help her – **not even her best friend**.
- *or* **Not even** her best friend would help her.

Very often we use **even** with the verb in the middle of a sentence (see Unit 107):

- Sue has traveled all over the world. She has **even** been to the Antarctic.
  (It's especially unusual to go to the Antarctic, so she must have traveled a lot.)
- They are very rich. They **even** have their own private jet.

Study these examples with **not even**:

- I can't cook. I ca**n't even** boil an egg. (and boiling an egg is very easy)
- They weren't very friendly to us. They did**n't even** say hello.
- Jenny is in great shape. She's just run five miles, and she's **not even** out of breath.

You can use **even** + *comparative* (**cheaper** / **more expensive**, etc.):

- I got up very early, but Jack got up **even earlier**.
- I knew I didn't have much money, but I have **even less** than I thought.
- We were surprised to get a letter from her. We were **even more surprised** when she
  came to see us a few days later.

Even though / even when / even if

You can use **even though** / **even when** / **even if** + *subject* + *verb*:

- **Even though she can't drive**, she bought a car.

  subject + verb
- He never shouts, **even when he's** angry.
- I'll probably see you tomorrow. But **even if I don't see** you tomorrow, I'm sure we'll
  see each other before the weekend.

You cannot use **even** in this way (+ *subject* + *verb*). We say:

- **Even though she can't drive**, she bought a car. (*not* Even she can't drive)
- I can't reach the shelf **even if I stand** on a chair. (*not* even I stand)

Compare **even if** and **if**:

- We're going to the beach tomorrow. It doesn't matter what the weather is like.
  We're going **even if** it's raining.
- We want to go to the beach tomorrow, but we won't go **if** it's raining.

If and *when* Unit 24D   *Though / even though* Unit 110E

Exercises

109.1 Julie, Sarah, and Amanda are three friends who went on vacation together. Use the information given about them to complete the sentences using *even* or *not even*.

Julie 	Sarah	Amanda
is usually happy	doesn't really like art	is almost always late
is usually on time	is usually miserable	is a good photographer
likes getting up early	usually hates hotels	loves staying at hotels
is very interested in art	doesn't have a camera	isn't good at getting up early

1. They stayed at a hotel. Everybody liked it, _even Sarah_ .
2. They arranged to meet. They all arrived on time, _____ .
3. They went to an art gallery. Nobody enjoyed it, _____ .
4. Yesterday they had to get up early. They all managed to do this, _____ .
5. They were together yesterday. They were all in a good mood, _____ .
6. None of them took any pictures, _____ .

109.2 Make sentences with *even*. Use the words in parentheses.

1. Sue has been all over the world. (the Antarctic) _She has even been to the Antarctic._
2. We painted the whole room. (the floor) We _____
3. Rachel has met lots of famous people. (the president)
   She _____
4. You could hear the noise from a long way away. (from two blocks away)
   You _____

In the following sentences you have to use *not . . . even*.

5. They didn't say anything to us. (hello) _They didn't even say hello._
6. I can't remember anything about her. (her name)
   I _____
7. There isn't anything to do in this town. (a movie theater)
   _____
8. He didn't tell anybody where he was going. (his wife)
   _____
9. I don't know anyone on my street. (the people next door)
   _____

109.3 Complete the sentences using *even* + comparative.

1. It was very hot yesterday, but today it's _even hotter_ .
2. The church is 200 years old, but the house next to it is _____ .
3. That's a very good idea, but I've got an _____ one.
4. The first question was very difficult to answer. The second one was _____ .
5. I did very badly on the test, but most of my friends did _____ .
6. Neither of us was hungry. I ate very little, and my friend ate _____ .

109.4 Put in *if, even, even if,* or *even though*.

1. _Even though_ she can't drive, she bought a car.
2. The bus leaves in five minutes, but we can still catch it _____ we run.
3. The bus leaves in two minutes. We won't catch it now _____ we run.
4. His Spanish isn't very good – _____ after three years in Mexico.
5. His Spanish isn't very good _____ he's lived in Mexico for three years.
6. _____ with the heat on, it was very cold in the house.
7. I couldn't sleep _____ I was very tired.
8. I won't forgive them for what they did _____ they apologize.
9. _____ I hadn't eaten anything for 24 hours, I wasn't hungry.

Although / though / even though / in spite of / despite

A Study this example situation:

Last year Paul and Joanne spent their vacation at the beach. It rained a lot, but they had a good time.

You can say:
Although it rained a lot, they had a good time.
(= It rained a lot, *but* they . . .)
or
In spite of
Despite } **the rain**, they had a good time.

B After **although** we use a *subject + verb*:
- **Although it rained** a lot, we enjoyed our vacation.
- I didn't get the job **although I was** well qualified.

Compare the meaning of **although** and **because**:
- We went out **although** it was raining.
- We didn't go out **because** it was raining.

C After **in spite of** or **despite**, we use a *noun*, a *pronoun* (**this/that/what**, etc.), or **-ing**:
- **In spite of the rain**, we enjoyed our vacation.
- I didn't get the job **in spite of being** well qualified.
- She wasn't feeling well, but **in spite of this** she went to work.
- **In spite of what** I said yesterday, I still love you.

Despite is the same as **in spite of**. We say **in spite of** but **despite** (*without* of):
- She felt sick, but **despite this** she went to work. (*not* despite of this)

You can say **in spite of the fact (that)** . . . and **despite the fact (that)** . . . :
- I didn't get the job { **in spite of the fact (that)** **despite the fact (that)** } I was well qualified.

Compare **in spite of** and **because of**:
- We went out **in spite of the rain**. (*or* . . . **despite the rain**.)
- We didn't go out **because of the rain**.

D Compare **although** and **in spite of** / **despite**:
- **Although the traffic was** bad, **In spite of the traffic**, } we arrived on time. (*not* In spite of the traffic was bad)

- I couldn't sleep { **although I was** very tired. **despite being** very tired. } (*not* despite I was tired)

E Sometimes we use **though** instead of **although**:
- I didn't get the job **though** I was well qualified.

In spoken English we often use **though** at the end of a sentence:
- The house isn't very nice. I like the garden, **though**. (= but I like the garden)
- I see them every day. I've never spoken to them, **though**.
  (= but I've never spoken to them)

Even though (*but not* "even" alone) is a stronger form of **although**:
- **Even though** I was really tired, I couldn't sleep. (*not* Even I was really tired . . .)

Exercises

110.1 Complete the sentences. Use *although* + a sentence from the box.

I didn't speak the language	~~he has a very important job~~
I had never seen her before	we don't like them very much
it was quite cold	the heat was on
I'd met her twice before	we've known each other a long time

1. _Although he has a very important job_ , he isn't particularly well paid.
2. _____ , I recognized her from a photograph.
3. She wasn't wearing a coat _____ .
4. We thought we'd better invite them to the party _____ .
5. _____ , I managed to make myself understood.
6. _____ , the room wasn't warm.
7. I didn't recognize her _____ .
8. We're not very good friends _____ .

110.2 Complete the sentences with *although* / *in spite of* / *because* / *because of*.

1. _Although_ it rained a lot, we enjoyed our vacation.
2. a) _____ all our careful plans, a lot of things went wrong.
   b) _____ we had planned everything carefully, a lot of things
      went wrong.
3. a) I went home early _____ I wasn't feeling well.
   b) I went to work the next day _____ I was still feeling sick.
4. a) She only accepted the job _____ the salary, which was very high.
   b) She accepted the job _____ the salary, which was rather low.
5. a) I managed to get to sleep _____ there was a lot of noise.
   b) I couldn't get to sleep _____ the noise.

Use your own ideas to complete the following sentences:

6. a) He passed the exam although _____ .
   b) He passed the exam because _____ .
7. a) I didn't eat anything although _____ .
   b) I didn't eat anything in spite of _____ .

110.3 Make one sentence from two. Use the word(s) in parentheses in your sentences.

1. I couldn't sleep. I was very tired. (despite)
   I couldn't sleep despite being very tired.
2. They have very little money. They are happy. (in spite of)
   In spite _____
3. My foot was injured. I managed to walk to the nearest town. (although)
   _____
4. I enjoyed the movie. The story was silly. (in spite of)
   _____
5. We live on the same street. We hardly ever see each other. (despite)
   _____
6. I got very wet in the rain. I was only out for five minutes. (even though)
   _____

110.4 Use the words in parentheses to make a sentence with *though* at the end.

1. The house isn't very nice. (like / yard) _I like the yard, though._
2. It's warm today. (very windy) _____
3. We didn't like the food. (ate) _____
4. Liz is very nice. (don't like / husband) I _____

In case

Study this example situation:

Your car should have a spare tire because it is possible you will have a flat tire.

Your car should have a spare tire **in case** you have a flat tire.

In case you have a flat tire = because it is possible you will have a flat tire.

Some more examples of **in case**:

- I'll leave my cell phone on **in case Jane calls**. (= because it is possible she will call)
- I'll draw a map for you **in case you can't find our house**. (= because it is possible you won't be able to find it)
- I'll remind them about the meeting **in case they've forgotten**. (= because it is possible they have forgotten)

We use **just in case** for a smaller possibility:

- I don't think it will rain, but I'll take an umbrella **just in case**. (= **just in case** it rains)

Do not use **will** after **in case**. Use a present tense for the future (see Unit 24):

- I'll leave my phone on **in case** Jane **calls**. (*not* in case Jane will call)

In case is not the same as **if**. We use **in case** to say *why* somebody does (or doesn't do) something. You do something *now* **in case** something happens *later*.

Compare:

in case	if
■ We'll buy some more food **in case** Tom comes. (= Maybe Tom will come; we'll buy some more food now, whether he comes or not; then we'll *already* have the food *if* he comes.)	■ We'll buy some more food **if** Tom comes. (= Maybe Tom will come; if he comes, we'll buy some more food; if he doesn't come, we won't buy any more food.)
■ I'll give you my phone number **in case** you need to contact me.	■ You can call me at the hotel **if** you need to contact me.
■ You should register your bike **in case** it is stolen.	■ You should inform the police **if** your bike is stolen.

You can use **in case** + *past* to say why somebody did something:

- I left my phone on **in case Jane called**.
  (= because it was possible that Jane would call)
- I drew a map for Sarah **in case** she **couldn't** find the house.
- We rang the doorbell again **in case** they **hadn't** heard it the first time.

In case of is not the same as **in case**. **In case of** . . . = if there is . . . (especially on signs, etc.):

- **In case of fire**, please leave the building as quickly as possible. (= if there is a fire)
- **In case of emergency**, call this number. (= if there is an emergency)

Exercises

111.1 Barbara is going for a long walk in the country. You think she should take:

~~some chocolate~~   a map   a raincoat   her camera   some water

You think she should take these things because:

it's possible she'll get lost perhaps she'll be thirsty she might want to take some pictures	~~she might get hungry~~ maybe it will rain

What do you say to Barbara? Write sentences with *in case*.

1. _Take some chocolate with you in case you get hungry._
2. Take _____
3. _____
4. _____
5. _____

111.2 What do you say in these situations? Use *in case*.

1. It's possible that Mary will need to contact you, so you give her your phone number.
   You say: Here's my phone number _in case you need to contact me_ .
2. A friend of yours is going away for a long time. Maybe you won't see her again before she goes, so you decide to say goodbye now.
   You say: I'll say goodbye now _____ .
3. You are shopping in a supermarket with a friend. You think you have everything you need, but perhaps you've forgotten something. Your friend has the list. You ask her to check it.
   You say: Can you _____ ?
4. You are giving a friend some advice about using a computer. You think he should back up (= copy) his files because the computer might crash (and he would lose all his data).
   You say: You should back up _____ .

111.3 Write sentences with *in case*.

1. There was a possibility that Jane would call. So I left my phone switched on.
   I left _my phone switched on in case Jane called_ .
2. Mike thought that he might forget the name of the book. So he wrote it down.
   He wrote down _____ .
3. I thought my parents might be worried about me. So I called them.
   I called _____ .
4. I sent an e-mail to Liz, but I didn't get an answer. So I sent another e-mail because I thought that maybe she hadn't received the first one.
   I sent _____ .
5. I met some people when I was on vacation in France. They said they might come to New York one day. I live in New York, so I gave them my address.
   I gave _____ .

111.4 Put in *in case* or *if*.

1. I'll draw a map for you _in case_ you can't find our house.
2. You should tell the police _if_ you have any information about the crime.
3. I hope you'll come to Chicago sometime. _____ you come, you can stay with us.
4. This letter is for Susan. Can you give it to her _____ you see her?
5. Write your name and address on your bag _____ you lose it.
6. Go to the Lost and Found office _____ you lose your bag.
7. The burglar alarm will ring _____ somebody tries to break into the house.
8. You should lock your bike to something _____ somebody tries to steal it.
9. I was advised to get insurance _____ I needed medical treatment while I was abroad.

Unless   As long as   Provided/providing

A

Unless

Study this example situation:

The club is for members only.

You can't go in **unless you are a member**.

This means:
You can't go in *except if* you are a member.
or
You can go in *only if* you are a member.

Unless = except if.

Some more examples of **unless**:

- ■ I'll see you tomorrow **unless I have to work late**. (= except if I have to work late)
- ■ There are no buses to the beach. **Unless you have a car**, it's difficult to get there. (= except if you have a car)
- ■ "Should I tell Liz what happened?"   "**Not unless she asks you**." (= only if she asks you)
- ■ Sally hates to complain. She wouldn't complain about something **unless it was really bad**. (= except if it was really bad)
- ■ We can take a taxi to the restaurant – **unless you'd prefer to walk**. (= except if you'd prefer to walk)

Instead of **unless**, it is often possible to say **if . . . not**:

- ■ **Unless we leave now**, we'll be late.   *or*   **If we don't leave now**, we'll . . .

B

As long as, etc.

as long as *or* **so long as**
provided (**that**) *or* **providing** (**that**) } All these expressions mean "if" or "on condition that."

For example:

- ■ You can borrow my car { **as long as** / **so long as** } you promise not to drive too fast.

  (= you can borrow my car, but you must promise not to drive too fast – this is a condition)

- ■ Traveling by car is convenient { **provided** (**that**) / **providing** (**that**) } you have somewhere to park.

  (= but only if you have somewhere to park)

- ■ **Providing** (**that**) / **Provided** (**that**) } the room is clean, I don't care which hotel we stay at.

  (= the room must be clean – otherwise, I don't care)

C

When you are talking about the future, do *not* use **will** after **unless / as long as / so long as / provided / providing**. Use a *present* tense (see Unit 24A):

- ■ I'm not going out **unless** it **stops** raining. (*not* unless it will stop)
- ■ **Providing** the weather is good, we're going on a picnic. (*not* providing the weather will be good)

If Units 24, 36–38

Exercises

112.1 Write a new sentence with the same meaning. Use *unless* in your sentence.

1. You need to try a little harder, or you won't pass the exam.
   You won't pass the exam unless you try a little harder.

2. Listen carefully, or you won't know what to do.
   You won't know what to do _____

3. She has to apologize to me, or I'll never speak to her again.
   _____

4. You have to speak very slowly, or he won't be able to understand you.
   _____

5. Business has got to improve soon, or the company will have to close.
   _____

112.2 Write sentences with *unless*.

1. The club isn't open to everyone. You are allowed in only if you're a member.
   You aren't allowed in the club unless you're a member.

2. I don't want to go to the party alone. I'm going only if you go, too.
   I'm not going _____

3. Don't worry about the dog. It will attack you only if you move suddenly.
   The dog _____

4. Ben isn't very talkative. He'll speak to you only if you ask him something.
   Ben _____

5. The doctor will see you only if it's an emergency.
   The doctor _____

112.3 Choose the correct word or expression for each sentence.

1. You can borrow my car ~~unless~~ / as long as you promise not to drive too fast.
   (*as long as* is correct)
2. I'm playing tennis tomorrow <u>unless</u> / providing it rains.
3. I'm playing tennis tomorrow unless / <u>providing</u> it doesn't rain.
4. I don't mind if you come home late unless / <u>as long as</u> you come in quietly.
5. I'm going now <u>unless</u> / provided you want me to stay.
6. I don't watch TV unless / <u>as long as</u> I've got nothing else to do.
7. Children are allowed to use the swimming pool unless / <u>provided</u> they are with an adult.
8. <u>Unless</u> / Provided they are with an adult, children are not allowed to use the
   swimming pool.
9. We can sit here in the corner unless / <u>as long as</u> you'd rather sit over there
   by the window.
10. *A:* Our vacation cost a lot of money.
    B: Did it? Well, that doesn't matter unless / <u>as long as</u> you had a good time.

112.4 Use your own ideas to complete these sentences.

1. We'll be late unless _*we take a taxi*_ .
2. I like hot weather as long as _____ .
3. It takes Kate about 20 minutes to drive to work provided _____ .
4. I don't mind walking home as long as _____ .
5. I like to walk to work in the morning unless _____ .
6. We can meet tomorrow unless _____ .
7. You can borrow the money providing _____ .
8. You won't achieve anything unless _____ .

As (= at the same time) and as (= because)

A

As = at the same time as

You can use **as** when two things happen at the same time:
- We all waved goodbye to Liz **as** she drove away.
  (we **waved** and she **drove** away at the same time)
- I watched her **as** she opened the letter.
- **As** I walked along the street, I looked in the store windows.
- Can you turn off the light **as** you go out, please?

Bye!

Liz

Or you can say that something happened **as you were doing** something else (in the middle of doing something else):
- Jill slipped **as she was getting off** the bus.
- We met Paul **as we were leaving** the hotel.

For the *past continuous* (**was getting** / **were going**, etc.), see Unit 6.

You can also use **just as** (= exactly at that moment):
- **Just as** I sat down, the phone rang.
- I had to leave **just as** the conversation was getting interesting.

We also use **as** when two things happen together in a longer period of time:

- **As** the day went on, the weather got worse.
- I began to enjoy the job more **as** I got used to it.

the day went on

the weather got worse

As the day went on, the weather got worse.

Compare **as** and **when**:

We use **as** only if two things happen at the same time.	Use **when** (*not* as) if one thing happens after another.
■ **As we walked home**, we talked about what we would have for dinner. (= at the same time)	■ **When we got home**, we started cooking dinner. (*not* As we got home)

B

As = because

As sometimes means "because":
- **As it was a national holiday** last Thursday, all the banks were closed.
  (= because it was a national holiday)
- The thief was difficult to identify **as he was wearing a mask** during the robbery.

We also use **since** in this way:
- **Since it was a national holiday** last Thursday, all the banks were closed.
- The thief was difficult to identify **since he was wearing a mask** during the robbery.

Compare **as** with **when**:

■ I couldn't contact David **as he was on a business trip**, and he doesn't have a cell phone. (= because he was on a trip)	■ David's passport was stolen **when he was on a business trip**. (= during the time he was away)
■ **As they lived near us**, we used to see them pretty often. (= because they lived near us)	■ **When they lived near us**, we used to see them pretty often. (= at the time they lived near us)

As . . . as Unit 104   *Like* and *as* Unit 114   *As if* Unit 115

Exercises

113.1 (Section A) Use *as* to join sentences from the boxes.

1. ~~we all waved goodbye to Liz~~	we were driving along the road
2. we all smiled	I was taking a hot dish out of the oven
3. I burned myself	~~she drove away~~
4. the crowd cheered	we posed for the photograph
5. a dog ran out in front of the car	the two teams ran onto the field

1. *We all waved goodbye to Liz as she drove away.* _____
2. _____
3. _____
4. _____
5. _____

113.2 What does *as* mean in these sentences?

	because	at the same time as
1. **As** they live near me, I see them fairly often.	✓	
2. Jill slipped **as** she was getting off the bus.		✓
3. **As** I was tired, I went to bed early.		
4. Unfortunately, **as** I was parking the car, I hit the car behind me.		
5. **As** we climbed the hill, we got more and more tired.		
6. We decided to go out to eat **as** we had no food at home.		
7. **As** we don't use the car very often, we've decided to sell it.		

Find the sentences where *as* means "because." Rewrite these sentences with *since*.

8. *Since they live near me, I see them fairly often.* _____
9. _____
10. _____
11. _____

113.3 In some of these sentences, you need *when* (not *as*). Correct the sentences where necessary.

1. Maria got married (as she was 22).   *when she was 22*
2. As the day went on, the weather got worse.   *OK*
3. He dropped the glass as he was taking it out of the cabinet.   _____
4. My camera was stolen as I was asleep on the beach.   _____
5. As I finished high school, I went into the army.   _____
6. The train slowed down as it approached the station.   _____
7. I used to live near the ocean as I was a child.   _____

113.4 Use your own ideas to complete these sentences.

1. I saw you as _____
2. It started to rain just as _____
3. As I didn't have enough money for a taxi, _____
4. Just as I took the photograph, _____

Like and as

Like = "similar to," "the same as." You cannot use **as** in this way:
- What a beautiful house! It's **like a palace**. (*not* as a palace)
- "What does Sandra do?" "She's a teacher, **like me**." (*not* as me)
- Be careful! The floor has been polished. It's **like walking on ice**. (*not* as walking)
- It's raining again. I hate weather **like this**. (*not* as this)

In these sentences, **like** is a *preposition*. So it is followed by a *noun* (like **a palace**),
a *pronoun* (like **me** / like **this**), or **–ing** (like walk**ing**).

You can also say ". . . **like** (somebody/something) do**ing** something":
- "What's that noise?" "It sounds **like a baby** cry**ing**."

Sometimes **like** = for example:
- Some sports, **like** race-car driving, can be dangerous.

You can also use **such as** (= for example):
- Some sports, **such as** race-car driving, can be dangerous.

As = in the same way as, or in the same condition as. We use **as** before *subject + verb*:
- I didn't move anything. I left everything **as it was**.
- You should have done it **as I showed you**. (= the way I showed you)

Like is also possible in informal spoken English:
- I left everything **like it was**.

Compare **as** and **like**:
- You should have done it **as I showed you**. (*or* **like I showed you**)
- You should have done it **like this**. (*not* as this)

Note that we say **as usual** / **as always**:
- You're late **as usual**.
- **As always**, Nick was the first to complain.

Sometimes **as** *(+ subject + verb)* has other meanings. For example, after **do**:
- You can do **as you like**. (= do what you like)
- They did **as they promised**. (= They did what they promised)

We also say **as you know** / **as I said** / **as she expected** / **as I thought**, etc.:
- **As you know**, it's Emma's birthday next week. (= you know this already)
- Ann failed her driving test, **as she expected**. (= she expected this before)

Like is not common in these expressions, except with **say** (**like I said**):
- **As I said** yesterday, I'm sure we can solve the problem. *or* **Like I said** yesterday . . .

As can also be a *preposition*, but the meaning is different from **like**. Compare:

■ Brenda Casey is the manager of a company. **As the manager**, she has to make many important decisions. (**As** the manager = in her position as the manager)	■ Mary Stone is the assistant manager. **Like the manager** (Brenda Casey), she also has to make important decisions. (**Like** the manager = similar to the manager)

As *(preposition)* = in the position of, in the form of, etc.:
- A few years ago I worked **as a taxi driver**. (*not* like a taxi driver)
- We don't have a car, so we use the garage **as a workshop**.
- Many words, for example "work" and "rain," can be used **as verbs or nouns**.
- New York is all right **as a place to visit**, but I wouldn't like to live there.
- The news of the tragedy came **as a great shock**.

As . . . as **Unit 104**   *As (= at the same time as / because)* **Unit 113**   *As if* **Unit 115**

Exercises

114.1 In some of these sentences, you need *like* (not *as*). Correct the sentences where necessary.

1. It's raining again. I hate (weather as this).   _weather like this_
2. Ann failed her driving test, as she expected.   _OK_
3. Do you think Carol looks as her mother?   _____
4. Tim gets on my nerves. I can't stand people as him.   _____
5. Why didn't you do it as I told you to do it?   _____
6. Brian is a student, as most of his friends.   _____
7. You never listen. Talking to you is as talking to the wall.   _____
8. As I said yesterday, I'm thinking of changing my job.   _____
9. Tom's idea seemed to be a good one, so we did as he suggested.   _____
10. I'll call you tomorrow as usual, OK?   _____
11. Suddenly there was a terrible noise. It was as a bomb exploding.   _____
12. She's a very good swimmer. She swims as a fish.   _____

114.2 Complete the sentences using *like* or *as* + the following:

| a beginner | blocks of ice | ~~a palace~~ | a birthday present |
| a child | a church | winter | a tour guide |

1. This house is beautiful. It's _like a palace_ .
2. My feet are really cold. They're _____ .
3. I've been playing tennis for years, but I still play _____ .
4. Margaret once had a part-time job _____ .
5. I wonder what that building with the tower is. It looks _____ .
6. My brother gave me this watch _____ a long time ago.
7. It's very cold for the middle of summer. It's _____ .
8. He's 22 years old, but he sometimes behaves _____ .

114.3 Put in *like* or *as*. Sometimes either word is possible.

1. We heard a noise _like_ a baby crying.
2. Your English is very fluent. I wish I could speak _____ you.
3. Don't take my advice if you don't want to. You can do _____ you like.
4. You waste too much time doing things _____ sitting in cafés all day.
5. I wish I had a car _____ yours.
6. You don't need to change your clothes. You can go out _____ you are.
7. My neighbor's house is full of lots of interesting things. It's _____ a museum.
8. We saw Kevin last night. He was very cheerful, _____ always.
9. Sally has been working _____ a waitress for the last two months.
10. While we were on vacation, we spent most of our time doing active things _____ sailing, water skiing, and swimming.
11. You're different from the other people I know. I don't know anyone _____ you.
12. We don't need all the bedrooms in the house, so we use one of them _____ a study.
13. The news that Sue and Gary were getting married came _____ a complete surprise to me.
14. _____ her father, Catherine has a very good voice.
15. At the moment I've got a temporary job in a bookstore. It's OK _____ a temporary job, but I wouldn't like to do it permanently.
16. _____ you can imagine, we were very tired after such a long trip.
17. This tea is awful. It tastes _____ water.
18. I think I preferred this room _____ it was, before we decorated it.

Like / as if / as though

You can use **like** to say how somebody or something **looks/sounds/feels**:

■ That house **looks like** it's going to fall down.
■ Helen **sounded like** she had a cold, didn't she?
■ I've just come back from vacation, but I feel very tired. I don't **feel like** I just had a vacation.

We also use **as if** and **as though** in all these examples:

■ That house looks **as if** it's going to fall down.
■ I don't feel **as though** I just had a vacation.

Like is more common in spoken English.

Compare:

■ You look **tired**. (**look** + *adjective*)
■ You look $\begin{Bmatrix} \textbf{like} \\ \textbf{as if} \end{Bmatrix}$ **you didn't sleep** last night.

(**look like** / **as if** + *subject* + *verb*)

You can say: **It looks like . . . / It sounds like . . .**

■ Sandra is very late, isn't she? **It looks like** she isn't coming.
■ We took an umbrella because **it looked like** it was going to rain.
■ Do you hear that music next door? **It sounds like** they're having a party.

You can also use **as if** or **as though**:

■ It looks **as if** she isn't coming.
■ It looks **as though** she isn't coming.

It sounds like they're having a party next door.

You can use **like** / **as if** / **as though** with other verbs to say how somebody does something:

■ He **ran like** he was running for his life.
■ After the interruption, the speaker **went on talking as if** nothing had happened.
■ When I told them my plan, they **looked at me as though** I was crazy.

After **as if**, we sometimes use the *past* when we are talking about the *present*. For example:

■ I don't like Tim. He talks **as if** he **knew** everything.

The meaning is not past in this sentence. We use the past (as if he **knew**) because the idea is not real: Tim does *not* know everything. We use the past in the same way in **if** sentences and after **wish** (see Unit 37).

Some more examples:

■ She's always asking me to do things for her – **as if I didn't** have enough to do already. (I *do* have enough to do)
■ Gary's only 40. Why do you talk about him **as if he was** an old man? (he isn't an old man)

When you use the past in this way, you can use **were** instead of **was**:

■ Why do you talk about him **as if he were** (or **was**) an old man?
■ They treat me **as if I were** (or **was**) their own son. (I'm not their son)

If I was / were Unit 37C   *Look / sound* etc. + adjective Unit 97C   *Like and as* Unit 114

Exercises

115.1 What do you say in these situations? Use *look/sound/feel* + *like* . . . . Use the words in parentheses to make your sentence.

1. You meet Bill. He has a black eye and some bandages on his face. (be / a fight)
   You say to him:
   You look like you've been in a fight.

2. Christine comes into the room. She looks absolutely terrified. (see / a ghost)
   You say to her: What's the matter? You _____

3. Joe is on vacation. He's talking to you on the phone and sounds very happy. (enjoy / yourself)
   You say to him: You _____

4. You have just run a mile. You are absolutely exhausted. (run / a marathon)
   You say to a friend: I _____

115.2 Make sentences beginning *It looks like* . . . / *It sounds like* . . . .

you should see a doctor	there's been an accident	they are having an argument
it's going to rain	~~she isn't coming~~	we'll have to walk

1. Sandra said she would be here an hour ago.
   You say: _It looks like she isn't coming._

2. The sky is full of black clouds.
   You say: It _____

3. You hear two people shouting at each other next door.
   You say: _____

4. You see an ambulance, some police officers, and two damaged cars at the side of the road.
   You say: _____

5. You and a friend have just missed the last bus home.
   You say: _____

6. Dave isn't feeling well. He tells you all about it.
   You say: _____

115.3 Complete the sentences with *as if*. Choose from the box, putting the verbs in the correct form.

she / enjoy / it	I / go / be sick	not / eat / for a week
~~he / need / a good rest~~	she / hurt / her leg	he / mean / what he / say
I / not / exist	she / not / want / come	

1. Mark looks very tired. He looks _as if he needs a good rest_ .
2. I don't think Paul was joking. He looked _____ .
3. What's the matter with Liz? She's walking _____ .
4. Peter was extremely hungry and ate his dinner very quickly.
   He ate _____ .
5. Carol had a bored expression on her face during the concert.
   She didn't look _____ .
6. I've just eaten too many chocolates. Now I don't feel well.
   I feel _____ .
7. I called Liz and invited her to the party, but she wasn't very enthusiastic about it.
   She sounded _____ .
8. I went into the office, but nobody spoke to me or looked at me.
   Everybody ignored me _____ .

115.4 These sentences are like the ones in Section D. Complete each sentence using *as if*.

1. Brian is a terrible driver. He drives _as if he were_ the only driver on the road.
2. I'm 20 years old, so please don't talk to me _____ I _____ a child.
3. Steve has never met Maria, but he talks about her _____ his best friend.
4. It was a long time ago that we first met, but I remember it _____ yesterday.

For, during, and while

For and **during**

We use **for** + a period of time to say how long something goes on:
for **two hours**   for **a week**   for **ages**

- We watched television **for two hours** last night.
- Diane is going away **for a week** in September.
- Where have you been? I've been waiting **for ages**.
- Are you going away **for the weekend**?

We use **during** + *noun* to say when something happens (*not* how long):
during **the movie**   during **our vacation**   during **the night**

- I fell asleep **during the movie**.
- We met some really nice people **during our vacation**.
- The ground is wet. It must have rained **during the night**.

With "time words" (for example: **the morning / the afternoon / the summer**), you can
usually say **in** or **during**:

- It must have rained **in the night**. (*or* **during the night**)
- I'll call you sometime **during the afternoon**. (*or* **in the afternoon**)

You cannot use **during** to say how long something goes on:

- It rained **for** three days without stopping. (*not* during three days)

Compare **during** and **for**:

- I fell asleep **during the movie**. I was asleep **for half an hour**.

During and **while**

Compare:

We use **during** + *noun*:	We use **while** + *subject* + *verb*:

■ I fell asleep **during the movie**.
    └ *noun*
	■ I fell asleep **while I was watching TV**.
	    └ *subject + verb*

■ We met a lot of interesting people **during our vacation**.	■ We met a lot of interesting people **while we were on vacation**.
■ Robert suddenly began to feel sick **during the exam**.	■ Robert suddenly began to feel sick **while he was taking the exam**.

Some more examples of **while**:

- We saw Claire **while we were waiting** for the bus.
- **While you were** out, there was a phone call for you.
- Chris read a book **while I watched** TV.

When you are talking about the future, use the *present* (*not* will) after **while**:

- I'll be in Toronto next week. I hope to see Tom **while I'm** there.
  (*not* while I will be there)
- What are you going to do **while** you **are** waiting? (*not* while you will be waiting)

See also Unit 24.

Exercises

116.1 Put in *for* or *during*.

1. It rained __*for*__ three days without stopping.
2. I fell asleep __*during*__ the movie.
3. I went to the theater last night. I met Sue _____ the intermission.
4. Matt hasn't lived in the United States all his life. He lived in Brazil _____ four years.
5. Production at the factory was seriously affected _____ the strike.
6. I felt really sick last week. I could hardly eat anything _____ three days.
7. I waited for you _____ half an hour and decided that you weren't coming.
8. Sarah was very angry with me. She didn't speak to me _____ a week.
9. We usually go out on weekends, but we don't often go out _____ the week.
10. Jack started a new job a few weeks ago. Before that he was out of work _____ six months.
11. I need a change. I think I'll go away _____ a few days.
12. The president gave a long speech. She spoke _____ two hours.
13. We were hungry when we arrived. We hadn't had anything to eat _____ the trip.
14. We were hungry when we arrived. We hadn't had anything to eat _____ eight hours.

116.2 Put in *during* or *while*.

1. We met a lot of interesting people __*while*__ we were on vacation.
2. We met a lot of interesting people __*during*__ our vacation.
3. I met Mike _____ I was shopping.
4. _____ I was on vacation, I didn't read any newspapers or watch TV.
5. _____ our stay in Paris, we visited a lot of museums and galleries.
6. The phone rang three times _____ we were having dinner.
7. The phone rang three times _____ the night.
8. I had been away for many years. _____ that time, many things had changed.
9. What did they say about me _____ I was out of the room?
10. I went out for dinner last night. Unfortunately, I began to feel sick _____ the meal and had to go home.
11. Please don't interrupt me _____ I'm speaking.
12. There were many interruptions _____ the president's speech.
13. Can you set the table _____ I get dinner ready?
14. We were hungry when we arrived. We hadn't had anything to eat _____ we were traveling.

116.3 Use your own ideas to complete these sentences.

1. I fell asleep while __*I was watching television.*__
2. I fell asleep during __*the movie.*__
3. I hurt my arm while _____
4. Can you wait here while _____
5. Most of the students looked bored during _____
6. I was asked a lot of questions during _____
7. Don't open the car door while _____
8. The lights suddenly went out while _____
9. It started to rain during _____
10. It started to rain while _____

By and **until**   **By the time** . . .

A

By (+ a time) = no later than:

- I sent the letter to them today, so they should receive it **by Monday**.
  (= on or before Monday, no later than Monday)

- We'd better hurry. We have to be home **by 5:00**.
  (= at or before 5:00, no later than 5:00)

- Where's Sue? She should be here **by now**.
  (= now or before now – so she should have arrived already)

This milk should be sold **by August 14**.

B

We use **until** (*or* **till**) to say *how long* a situation continues:

- "Shall we go now?" "No, let's wait **until** (*or* **till**) it stops raining."

- I couldn't get up this morning. { I stayed in bed **until** half past ten.
  I didn't get up **until** half past ten.

Compare **until** and **by**:

Something *continues* **until** a time in the future:	Something *happens* **by** a time in the future:
■ Fred **will be away until** Monday. (so he'll be back *on* Monday)	■ Fred **will be back by** Monday. (= he'll be back no later than Monday)
■ **I'll be working until** 11:30. (so I'll stop working *at* 11:30)	■ **I'll have finished my work by** 11:30. (= I'll finish my work no later than 11:30)

C

You can say "**by the time** something happens." Study these examples:

- It's too late to go to the bank now. **By the time we get there**, it will be closed.
  (= the bank will close between now and the time we get there)

- *(from a postcard)* Our vacation ends tomorrow. So **by the time you receive this postcard**, I'll be back home.
  (= I will arrive home between tomorrow and the time you receive this postcard)

- Hurry up! **By the time we get to the theater**, the play will already have started.

You can say "**by the time** something happened" (for the past):

- Karen's car broke down on the way to the party last night. **By the time she arrived**, most of the other guests had left.
  (= It took her a long time to get to the party and most of the guests left during this time)

- I had a lot of work to do last night. I was very tired **by the time I finished**.
  (= It took me a long time to do the work, and I became more and more tired during this time)

- We went to the theater last night. It took us a long time to find a place to park. **By the time we got to the theater**, the play had already started.

Also **by then** *or* **by that time**:

- Karen finally arrived at the party at midnight, but **by then** (*or* **by that time**), most of the guests had left.

Exercises

117.1 Make sentences with *by*.

1. We have to be home no later than 5:00.
   <u>*We have to be home by 5:00.*</u>
2. I have to be at the airport no later than 8:30.
   I have to be at the airport _____
3. Let me know no later than Saturday whether you can come to the party.
   Let me know _____
4. Please make sure that you're here no later than 2:00.
   Please make sure that _____
5. If we leave now, we should arrive no later than lunchtime.
   If we leave now, _____

117.2 Put in *by* or *until*.

1. Fred is out of town. He'll be away <u>*until*</u> Monday.
2. Sorry, but I have to go. I have to be home _____ 5:00.
3. I've been offered a job. I haven't decided yet whether to accept it or not.
   I have to decide _____ Friday.
4. I think I'll wait _____ Thursday before making a decision.
5. It's too late to go shopping. The stores are open only _____ 5:30 today.
   They'll be closed _____ now.
6. I'd better pay the phone bill. It has to be paid _____ tomorrow.
7. Don't pay the bill today. Wait _____ tomorrow.
8. *A:* Have you finished redecorating your house?
   B: Not yet. We hope to finish _____ the end of the week.
9. *A:* I'm going out now. I'll be back at about 10:30. Will you still be here?
   B: I don't think so. I'll probably have left _____ then.
10. I'm moving into my new apartment next week. I'm staying with a friend
    _____ then.
11. I've got a lot of work to do. _____ the time I finish, it will be time to go to bed.
12. If you want to take the exam, you have to register _____ April 3.

117.3 Use your own ideas to complete these sentences. Use *by* or *until*.

1. Fred is out of town at the moment. He'll be away <u>*until Monday*</u> .
2. Fred is out of town at the moment. He'll be back <u>*by Monday*</u> .
3. I'm going out. I won't be very long. Wait here _____ .
4. I'm going out to buy a few things. It's 4:30 now. I won't be long. I'll be back _____ .
5. If you want to apply for the job, your application must be received _____ .
6. Last night I watched TV _____ .

117.4 Read the situations and complete the sentences using *By the time* . . . .

1. I was invited to a party, but I got there much later than I intended.
   <u>*By the time I got to the party*</u> , most of the other guests had left.
2. I wanted to catch a train, but it took me longer than expected to get to the station.
   _____ , my train had already left.
3. I intended to go shopping after finishing work. But I finished much later than expected.
   _____ , it was too late to go shopping.
4. I saw two men who looked as if they were trying to steal a car. I called the police, but it was some time before they arrived.
   _____ , the two men had disappeared.
5. We climbed a mountain, and it took us a very long time to get to the top. There wasn't much time to enjoy the view.
   _____ , we had to come down again.

At/on/in (Time)

A

Compare **at**, **on**, and **in**:
- They arrived **at 5:00**.
- They arrived **on Friday**.
- They arrived **in October**. / They arrived **in 1968**.

We use:

at for the time of day:
> **at 5:00**   **at 11:45**   **at midnight**   **at lunchtime**   **at sunset**, etc.

on for days and dates:
> **on Friday / on Fridays**   **on May 16, 1999**   **on Christmas Day**   **on my birthday**
> *also* **on the weekend, on weekends**

in for longer periods (for example, months/years/seasons):
> **in October**   **in 1988**   **in the 18th century**   **in the past**
> **in (the) winter**   **in the 1990s**   **in the Middle Ages**   **in the future**

B

We use **at** in these expressions:

at night	I don't like going out **at night**.
at Christmas	Do you give each other presents **at Christmas**?
at this time / at the moment	Mr. Brown is busy **at this time / at the moment**.
at the same time	Liz and I arrived **at the same time**.

C

We say:

in the morning(s)	*but*	**on Friday morning(s)**
in the afternoon(s)		**on Sunday afternoon(s)**
in the evening(s)		**on Monday evening(s)**, etc.

- I'll see you **in the morning**.
- Do you work **in the evenings**?
- I'll see you **on Friday morning**.
- Do you work **on Saturday evenings**?

D

We do not use **at/on/in** before **last/next/this/every**:
- I'll see you **next Friday**. (*not* on next Friday)
- They got married **last March**.

In spoken English, we often leave out **on** before days (**Sunday**) and dates (**March 12**, etc.).
So you can say:
- I'll see you **on Friday**.   *or*   I'll see you **Friday**.
- She works **on Saturday** mornings.   *or*   She works **Saturday** mornings.
- They got married **on March 12**.   *or*   They got married **March 12**.

E

In a few minutes / in six months, etc.
- The train will be leaving **in a few minutes**. (= a few minutes from now)
- Andy has left town. He'll be back **in a week**. (= a week from now)
- She'll be here **in a moment**. (= a moment from now)

You can also say "in six months' **time**," "in a week's **time**," etc.:
- They're getting married **in six months' time**.   *or*   . . . **in six months**.

We also use **in** . . . to say how long it takes to do something:
- I learned to drive **in four weeks**. (= it took me four weeks to learn)

On/in time, at/in the end Unit 119   *In/at/on (Position)* Units 120–122   *In/at/on (Other Uses)* Unit 124
British English Appendix 7

Exercises

118.1 Complete the sentences. Use *at*, *on*, or *in* + the following:

the evening	about 20 minutes	~~1492~~	the same time
the moment	July 21, 1969	the 1920s	night
Saturdays	the Middle Ages	11 seconds	

1. Columbus made his first voyage from Europe to America __*in 1492*__ .
2. If the sky is clear, you can see the stars _____ .
3. After working hard during the day, I like to relax _____ .
4. Neil Armstrong was the first man to walk on the moon _____ .
5. It's difficult to listen if everyone is speaking _____ .
6. Jazz became popular in the United States _____ .
7. I'm just going out to the store. I'll be back _____ .
8. *(on the phone)* "Can I speak to Dan?" "I'm sorry, but he's not here _____ ."
9. Many of Europe's great cathedrals were built _____ .
10. Bob is a very fast runner. He can run 100 meters _____ .
11. Liz works from Monday to Friday. Sometimes she also works _____ .

118.2 Put in *at*, *on*, or *in*.

1. Mozart was born in Salzburg __*in*__ 1756.
2. "Have you seen Kate recently?" "Yes, I saw her _____ Tuesday."
3. The price of electricity is going up _____ October.
4. _____ weekends, we often go for long walks in the country.
5. I've been invited to a wedding _____ February 14.
6. Henry is 63. He'll be retiring from his job _____ two years.
7. I'm busy right now, but I'll be with you _____ a moment.
8. Jenny's brother is an engineer, but he doesn't have a job _____ the moment.
9. There are usually a lot of parties _____ New Year's Eve.
10. I don't like driving _____ night.
11. My car is being repaired. It will be ready _____ two hours.
12. The telephone and the doorbell rang _____ the same time.
13. Mary and David always go out for dinner _____ their wedding anniversary.
14. It was a short book and easy to read. I read it _____ a day.
15. _____ Saturday night I went to bed _____ midnight.
16. We traveled overnight to Paris and arrived _____ 5:00 _____ the morning.
17. The course begins _____ January 7 and ends sometime _____ April.
18. I might not be at home _____ Tuesday morning, but I'll be there _____ the afternoon.

118.3 Which is correct: (a), (b), or both of them?

1. a) I'll see you on Friday. b) I'll see you Friday. __*both*__
2. a) I'll see you on next Friday. b) I'll see you next Friday. __*b*__
3. a) Paul got married in April. b) Paul got married April. _____
4. a) They never go out on Sunday evenings. b) They never go out Sunday evenings. _____
5. a) We usually take a short vacation on Christmas. b) We usually take a short vacation at Christmas. _____
6. a) What are you doing the weekend? b) What are you doing on the weekend? _____
7. a) Will you be here on Tuesday? b) Will you be here Tuesday? _____
8. a) We were sick at the same time. b) We were sick in the same time. _____
9. a) Sue got married at May 18, 2002. b) Sue got married on May 18, 2002. _____
10. a) He finished school last June. b) He finished school in last June. _____

On time and in time
At the end and in the end

A

On time and in time

On time = punctual, not late. If something happens **on time**, it happens at the time that was planned:

- The 11:45 train left **on time**. (= it left at 11:45)
- "I'll meet you at 7:30." "OK, but please be **on time**." (= don't be late, be there at 7:30)
- The conference was well organized. Everything began and ended **on time**.

The opposite of **on time** is **late**:

- Be **on time**. Don't be **late**.

In time (for something / to do something) = soon enough:

- Will you be home **in time for dinner**? (= soon enough for dinner)
- I've sent Jill a birthday present. I hope it arrives **in time** (for her birthday).
  (= on or before her birthday)
- I'm in a hurry. I want to be home **in time to see** the game on television.
  (= soon enough to see the game)

The opposite of **in time** is **too late**:

- I got home **too late** to see the game on television.

You can say **just in time** (= almost too late):

- We got to the station **just in time** for our train.
- A child ran into the street in front of the car – I managed to stop **just in time**.

B

At the end and in the end

At the end (of something) = at the time when something ends. For example:

at the end of the month	at the end of January	at the end of the game
at the end of the movie	at the end of the course	at the end of the concert

- I'm going away **at the end of January** / **at the end of the month**.
- **At the end of the concert**, there was great applause.
- The players shook hands **at the end of the game**.

You cannot say "**in** the end of . . ." So you cannot say "in the end of January" or "in the end of the concert."

The opposite of **at the end** (of . . .) is **at the beginning** (of . . .):

- I'm going away **at the beginning of January**. (*not* in the beginning)

In the end = finally

We use **in the end** when we say what the final result of a situation was:

- We had a lot of problems with our car. We sold it **in the end**. (= finally we sold it)
- He got angrier and angrier. **In the end** he just walked out of the room.
- Alan couldn't decide where to go on vacation. He didn't go anywhere **in the end**.
  (*not* at the end)

The opposite of **in the end** is usually **at first**:

- **At first** we didn't get along very well, but **in the end** we became good friends.

Exercises

119.1 Complete the sentences with *on time* or *in time*.

1. The bus was late this morning, but it's usually ___on time___ .
2. The movie was supposed to start at 8:30, but it didn't begin _____ .
3. I like to get up _____ to have a big breakfast before going to work.
4. We want to start the meeting _____ , so please don't be late.
5. I just washed this shirt. I want to wear it tonight, so I hope it will dry _____ .
6. The train service isn't very good. The trains are seldom _____ .
7. I nearly missed my flight this morning. I got to the airport just _____ .
8. I almost forgot that it was Joe's birthday. Fortunately I remembered _____ .
9. Why aren't you ever _____ ? You always keep everybody waiting.

119.2 Read the situations and make sentences using *just in time*.

1. A child ran into the street in front of your car. You saw the child at the last moment.
   (manage / stop) ___I managed to stop just in time.___
2. You were walking home. Just after you got home, it started to rain very heavily.
   (get / home) I _____
3. Tim was going to sit on the chair you had just painted. You said, "Don't sit on that chair!"
   so he didn't. (stop / him) I _____
4. You and a friend went to the movies. You were late, and you thought you would miss the
   beginning of the film. But the film began just as you sat down in the theater.
   (get / theater / beginning of the film)
   We _____

119.3 Complete the sentences using *at the end* + the following:

   the course   ~~the game~~   **the interview**   **the month**   **the race**

1. The players shook hands ___at the end of the game___ .
2. I usually get paid _____ .
3. The students had a party _____ .
4. Two of the runners collapsed _____ .
5. To my surprise, I was offered the job _____ .

119.4 Write sentences with *In the end*. Use the verbs in parentheses.

1. We had a lot of problems with our car.
   (sell) ___In the end we sold it.___
2. Judy got more and more fed up with her job.
   (resign) _____
3. I tried to learn German, but I found it too difficult.
   (give up) _____
4. We couldn't decide whether to go to the party or not.
   (not / go) _____

119.5 Put in *at* or *in*.

1. I'm going away ___at___ the end of the month.
2. It took me a long time to find a job. _____ the end I got a job in a hotel.
3. Are you going away _____ the beginning of August or _____ the end?
4. I couldn't decide what to buy Laura for her birthday. I didn't buy her anything _____
   the end.
5. We waited ages for a taxi. We gave up _____ the end and walked home.
6. I'll be moving to a new address _____ the end of September.
7. We had a few problems at first, but _____ the end everything was OK.
8. I'm going away _____ the end of this week.
9. *A:* I didn't know what to do.
   B: Yes, you were in a difficult position. What did you do _____ the end?

In/at/on (Position) 1

A   In

in a room   **in** a garden   **in** a pool
in a building   **in** a town/city   **in** an ocean
in a box   **in** a country   **in** a river

- There's somebody **in the room** / **in the building** / **in the garden**.
- What do you have **in your hand** / **in your mouth**?
- When we were **in Chile**, we spent a few days **in Santiago**.
- I have a friend who lives **in a small village in the mountains**.
- There were some people swimming **in the pool** / **in the ocean** / **in the river**.

B   At

at the bus stop   **at** the door   **at** the intersection   **at** the front desk

- Do you know that man standing **at the bus stop** / **at the door** / **at the window**?
- Turn left **at the traffic light** / **at the church** / **at the intersection**.
- We have to get off the bus **at the next stop**.
- When you leave the hotel, please leave your key **at the front desk**.

C   On

on the ceiling
on the door
on the table
on her nose
on the wall   **on** the floor
on a page
on an island

- I sat **on the floor** / **on the ground** / **on the grass** / **on the beach** / **on a chair**.
- There's a dirty mark **on the wall** / **on the ceiling** / **on your nose** / **on your shirt**.
- Have you seen the notice **on the bulletin board** / **on the door**?
- You'll find the listings of TV programs **on page 7** (of the newspaper).
- The hotel is **on a small island** in the middle of the lake.

D

Compare **in** and **at**:

- There were a lot of people **in the store**. It was very crowded.
  Go along this road, then turn left **at the store**.
- I'll meet you **in the hotel lobby**.
  I'll meet you **at the entrance to the hotel**.

Compare **in** and **on**:

- There is some water **in the bottle**.
  There is a label **on the bottle**.

Compare **at** and **on**:

- There is somebody **at the door**. Should I go and see who it is?
  There is a sign **on the door**. It says "Do not disturb."

in the bottle

on the bottle

Exercises

120.1 Answer the questions about the pictures. Use *in*, *at*, or *on* with the words below the pictures.

1. (bottle)	2. (arm)	3. (traffic light)	4. (door)
5. (wall)	6. (Paris)	7. (front desk)	8. (beach)

1. Where's the label?   _On the bottle._
2. Where's the butterfly?   _____
3. Where is the car waiting?   _____
4. a) Where's the sign?   _____
   b) Where's the key?   _____
5. Where are the shelves?   _____
6. Where's the Eiffel Tower?   _____
7. a) Where's the man standing?   _____
   b) Where's the telephone?   _____
8. Where are the children playing?   _____

120.2 Complete the sentences. Use *in*, *at*, or *on* + the following:

the window	**your coffee**	**the mountains**	**that tree**
my guitar	~~the river~~	**the island**	**the next gas station**

1. Look at those people swimming ___*in the river*___ .
2. One of the strings _____ is broken.
3. There's something wrong with the car. We'd better stop _____ .
4. Would you like sugar _____ ?
5. The leaves _____ are a beautiful color.
6. Last year we had a wonderful ski trip _____ .
7. There's nobody living _____ . It's uninhabited.
8. He spends most of the day sitting _____ and looking outside.

120.3 Complete the sentences with *in*, *at*, or *on*.

1. There was a long line of people ___*at*___ the bus stop.
2. Nicole was wearing a silver ring _____ her little finger.
3. There was an accident _____ the intersection this morning.
4. I wasn't sure whether I had come to the right office. There was no name _____ the door.
5. There are some beautiful trees _____ the park.
6. You'll find the sports results _____ the back page of the newspaper.
7. I wouldn't like an office job. I couldn't spend the whole day sitting _____ a desk.
8. My brother lives _____ a small town _____ eastern Tennessee.
9. The man the police are looking for has a scar _____ his right cheek.
10. The headquarters of the company are _____ Tokyo.
11. I like that picture hanging _____ the wall _____ the kitchen.
12. If you come here by bus, get off _____ the stop after the traffic light.

In/at/on (Position) 2

A

We say that somebody/something is:

in a row

in a line / in a row	**in bed**
in the sky / in the world	**in the country / in the countryside**
in an office / in a department	**in a photograph / in a picture**
in a book / in a (news)paper / in a magazine / in a letter	

- When I go to the movies, I like to sit **in the front row**.
- I just started working **in the sales department**.
- Who is the woman **in that photo**?
- Have you seen this picture **in today's paper**?

in the front

in the back

We say **in the front** / **in the back** of a car / building / theater / group of people, etc.

- I was sitting **in the back** (of the car) when we crashed.
- Let's sit **in the front** (of the movie theater).
- John was standing **in the back** of the crowd.

B

on the left / on the right	**on the left-hand side / right-hand side**
on the ground floor / on the first floor / on the second floor, etc.	
on a map / on a menu / on a list	
on a farm / on a ranch	

- In Britain they drive **on the left**. (*or* . . . **on the left-hand side**.)
- Our apartment is **on the second floor** of the building.
- Here's a shopping list. Don't buy anything that's not **on the list**.
- Have you ever worked **on a farm**? It's a lot like working **on a ranch**.

We say that a place is **on a river** / **on a street** / **on a road** / **on the coast**:

- Washington, D.C., is **on the East Coast** of the United States, **on the Potomac River**.
- I live **on Main Street**. My brother lives **on Elm**. (= on Elm Street)

Also **on the way**:

- We stopped at a small town **on the way** to Atlanta.

on the front / **on the back** of the letter / piece of paper / photo, etc.

- I wrote the date **on the back** of the photo.

C

at the top (of) / **at the bottom** (of) / **at the end** (of)

- Write your name **at the top of the page**.   **at** the top (of the page)
- Jane's house is **at the other end of the street**.

at the bottom (of the page)

D

in the corner of a room

- The television is **in the corner** of the room.

at the corner *or* **on the corner** of a street

- There is a mailbox **at/on the corner** of the street.

in the corner   **at/on** the corner

In the world Unit 105E   *In/at/on* (Position) Units 120, 122   British English Appendix 7

Exercises

121.1 Answer the questions about the pictures. Use *in*, *at*, or *on* with the words below the pictures.

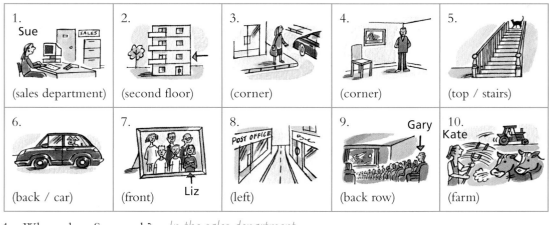

| 1. Sue (sales department) | 2. (second floor) | 3. (corner) | 4. (corner) | 5. (top / stairs) |
| 6. (back / car) | 7. (front) Liz | 8. (left) | 9. Gary (back row) | 10. Kate (farm) |

1. Where does Sue work? _In the sales department._
2. Sue lives in this building. Where's her apartment exactly? _____
3. Where is the woman standing? _____
4. Where is the man standing? _____
5. Where's the cat? _____
6. Where's the dog? _____
7. Liz is in this group of people. Where is she? _____
8. Where's the post office? _____
9. Gary is at the movies. Where is he sitting? _____
10. Where does Kate work? _____

121.2 Complete the sentences. Use *in*, *at*, or *on* + the following:

| the West Coast | the world | the back of the class | ~~the sky~~ |
| the front row | the right | the back of this card | the way to work |

1. It was a lovely day. There wasn't a cloud _in the sky_ .
2. In most countries people drive _____ .
3. What is the tallest building _____ ?
4. I usually buy a newspaper _____ in the morning.
5. San Francisco is _____ of the United States.
6. We went to the theater last night. We had seats _____ .
7. I couldn't hear the teacher. She spoke quietly and I was sitting _____ .
8. I don't have your address. Could you write it _____ ?

121.3 Complete the sentences with *in*, *at*, or *on*.

1. Write your name _at_ the top of the page.
2. Is your sister _____ this photo? I don't recognize her.
3. I didn't feel very well when I woke up, so I stayed _____ bed.
4. We normally use the front entrance to the building, but there's another one _____ the back.
5. Is there anything interesting _____ the paper today?
6. There was a list of names, but my name wasn't _____ the list.
7. _____ the end of the block, there is a small store. You'll see it _____ the corner.
8. I love to look up at the stars _____ the sky at night.
9. When I'm a passenger in a car, I prefer to sit _____ the front.
10. It's a very small town. You probably won't find it _____ your map.
11. Joe works _____ the furniture department of a large store.
12. Paris is _____ the Seine River.
13. I don't like cities. I'd rather live _____ the country.
14. My office is _____ the top floor. It's _____ the left as you come out of the elevator.

In/at/on (Position) 3

A

At home / in the hospital, etc.

We say that somebody is **at home / at work**:

- I'll be **at work** until 5:30, but I'll be **at home** all evening.

You can also say **be/stay home** (without **at**):

- You can stop by anytime. I'll **be home** all evening.

We say that somebody is **in the hospital / in prison / in jail**:

- Ann's mother is **in the hospital**.

You can be **at** or **in school/college**. Use **at school/college** to say where someone is:

- Kim is not living at home. She's away **at college**.

But use **in school/college** to say what someone is doing:

- Amy works at a bank and her brother is **in medical school**. (= he's studying medicine)

B

At a party / at a concert, etc.

We say that somebody is **at** an event (**at a party / at a conference**, etc.):

- Were there many people **at the party / at the meeting / at the wedding**?
- I saw Steve **at a tennis match / at a concert** on Saturday.

C

In and **at** for buildings

You can often use **in** or **at** with buildings. For example, you can eat **in a restaurant** or **at a restaurant**; you can buy something **in a supermarket** or **at a supermarket**. We usually say **at** when we say where an event takes place (for example, a concert, a movie, a party, a meeting):

- We went to a concert **at Lincoln Center**.
- The meeting took place **at the company's headquarters** in New York.

We say **at the station / at the airport**:

- Don't meet me **at the station**. I can get a taxi.

We say **at** somebody's house:

- I was **at Sue's house** last night. *or* I was **at Sue's** last night.

Also **at the doctor's**, **at the hairdresser's**, etc.

We use **in** when we are thinking about the building itself. Compare:

- We had dinner **at the hotel**. *but*
  All the rooms **in the hotel** have air conditioning. (*not* at the hotel)
- I was **at Sue's** (**house**) last night. *but*
  It's always cold **in Sue's house**. The heating doesn't work very well. (*not* at Sue's house)

D

In and **at** for towns, etc.

We normally use **in** with cities, towns, and villages:

- Sam's parents live **in St. Louis**. (*not* at St. Louis)
- The Louvre is a famous art museum **in Paris**. (*not* at Paris)

But you can use **at** *or* **in** when you think of the place as a point or station on a trip:

- Does this train stop **at** (*or* **in**) **Denver**? (= at the Denver station)
- We stopped **at** (*or* **in**) a small **town** on the way to Denver.

E

On a bus / in a car, etc.

We usually say **on a bus / on a train / on a plane / on a ship** *but* **in a car / in a taxi**:

- **The bus** was very full. There were too many people **on it**.
- Mary arrived **in a taxi**.

We say **on a bike** (= bicycle) / **on a motorcycle** / **on a horse**:

- Jane passed me **on her bike**.

At school / in prison, etc. Unit 72 *In/at/on* (Position) Units 120–121 *To/at/in/into* Unit 123
By car / by bike, etc. Unit 125B

Exercises

122.1 Complete the sentences about the pictures. Use *in*, *at*, or *on* with the words below the pictures.

1. AIRPORT CAR RENTALS
(the airport)

2. Dave
(a train)

3. CONFERENCE
Karen
(a conference)

4. Martin
(the hospital)

5. Judy
(the hairdresser's)

6. Gary
(his bike)

7. (New York)

8. THE FORD THEATER
(the Ford Theater)

1. You can rent a car __*at the airport*__ .
2. Dave is _____ .
3. Karen is _____ .
4. Martin is _____ .
5. Judy is _____ .
6. I saw Gary _____ .
7. We spent a few days _____ .
8. We went to a show _____ .

122.2 Complete the sentences. Use *in*, *at*, or *on* + the following:

the plane	the hospital	a taxi	~~the station~~	the party
the gym	school	prison	the airport	

1. My train arrives at 11:30. Can you meet me __*at the station*__ ?
2. We walked to the restaurant, but we went home _____ .
3. Did you have a good time _____ ? I heard it was a lot of fun.
4. I enjoyed the flight, but the food _____ wasn't very good.
5. *A:* What does your sister do? Does she have a job?
   B: No, she's only 16. She's still _____ .
6. I play basketball _____ on Friday evenings.
7. A friend of mine was injured in an accident a few days ago. She's still _____ .
8. Our flight was delayed. We had to wait _____ for four hours.
9. Some people are _____ for crimes that they did not commit.

122.3 Complete the sentences with *in*, *at*, or *on*.

1. We went to a concert __*at*__ Lincoln Center.
2. It was a very slow train. It stopped _____ every station.
3. My parents live _____ a suburb of Chicago.
4. I haven't seen Kate for some time. I last saw her _____ David's wedding.
5. We stayed _____ a very nice hotel when we were _____ Amsterdam.
6. There were 50 rooms _____ the hotel.
7. I don't know where my umbrella is. Maybe I left it _____ the bus.
8. I wasn't home when you called. I was _____ my sister's house.
9. There must be somebody _____ the house. The lights are on.
10. The exhibition _____ the Museum of Modern Art closed on Saturday.
11. Should we go _____ your car or mine?
12. What are you doing _____ home? I expected you to be _____ work.
13. "Did you like the movie?" "Yes, but it was too hot _____ the theater."
14. Paul lives _____ Boston. He's a student _____ Boston University.

To/at/in/into

A

We say **go/come/travel**, etc., **to** a place or event. For example:

go to China	**go to** bed	**come to** my house
go back to Italy	**go to** the bank	**be taken to** the hospital
return to Boston	**go to** a concert	**be sent to** prison
welcome (somebody) **to** (a place)		**drive to** the airport

TO

- When are your friends **going back to** Italy? (*not* going back in Italy)
- Three people were injured in the accident and **taken to** the hospital.
- **Welcome to** our country! (*not* Welcome in)

In the same way we say a **trip to** / a **visit to** / on **my way to** . . ., etc.:
- Did you enjoy **your trip to** Paris / **your visit to** the zoo?

Compare **to** (for *movement*) and **in/at** (for *position*):
- They are **going to** France.   *but*   They **live in** France.
- Can you **come to** the party?   *but*   I'll see **you at** the party.

B

Been to

We say "**been to** (a place)":
- I've **been to Italy** four times, but I've never **been to Rome**.
- Amanda has never **been to a hockey game** in her life.

C

Get and **arrive**

We say **get to** (a place):
- What time did they **get to London** / **get to work** / **get to the party** / **get to the hotel**?

But we say **arrive in** . . . or **arrive at** . . . (*not* arrive to).
We say **arrive in** a town or country:
- They **arrived in Rio de Janeiro** / **in Brazil** a week ago.

For other places (buildings, etc.) or events, we say **arrive at**:
- When did they **arrive at the hotel** / **at the airport** / **at the party**?

D

Home

We say **go home** / **come home** / **get home** / **arrive home** / **on the way home**, etc.
(no preposition).

We do not say "to home":
- I'm tired. Let's **go home** now. (*not* go to home)
- I met Linda **on my way home**. (*not* my way to home)

E

Into

Go into, **get into** . . ., etc. = enter (a room / a building / a car, etc.):
- I opened the door, **went into** the room, and sat down.
- A bird **flew into** the kitchen through the window.

INTO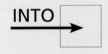

With some verbs (especially **go/get/put**) we often use **in** (instead of **into**):
- She **got in** the car and drove away. (*or* She **got into** the car . . .)
- I read the letter and **put it** back **in the envelope**.

The opposite of **into** is **out of**:
- She **got out of** the car and **went into** a shop.

We usually say **get on/off** a bus / a train / a plane (*not usually* get into/out of):
- She **got on the** bus and I never saw her again.

Been to Unit 7   *In/at/on* (Position) Units 120–122   *At home* Unit 122A   *Into* and *in* Unit 135A

Exercises

123.1 Put in *to/at/in/into* where necessary. If no preposition is necessary, leave the space empty.

1. Three people were taken __to__ the hospital after the accident.
2. I met Kate on my way ___—___ home. *(no preposition)*
3. We left our luggage _____ the hotel and went to find something to eat.
4. Should we take a taxi _____ the station, or should we walk?
5. I have to go _____ the bank today to change some money.
6. The Mississippi River flows _____ the Gulf of Mexico.
7. "Do you have your camera?" "No, I left it _____ home."
8. Have you ever been _____ China?
9. I had lost my key, but I managed to climb _____ the house through a window.
10. We got stuck in a traffic jam on our way _____ the airport.
11. We had lunch _____ the airport while we were waiting for our plane.
12. Welcome _____ the hotel. We hope you enjoy your stay here.
13. I got a flat tire, so I turned _____ a parking lot to change it.
14. Did you enjoy your visit _____ the zoo?
15. I'm tired. As soon as I get _____ home, I'm going _____ bed.
16. Marcel is French. He has just returned _____ France after two years _____ Brazil.
17. Carl was born _____ Chicago, but his family moved _____ New York when he was three. He still lives _____ New York.

123.2 Have you been to these places? If so, how many times? Choose three of the places and write a sentence using *been to*.

Australia   Hong Kong   Mexico   Paris   Thailand   Tokyo   Washington, D.C.

1. *(example answers)* __I've never been to Australia. / I've been to Thailand once.__
2. _____
3. _____
4. _____

123.3 Put in *to/at/in* where necessary. If no preposition is necessary, leave the space empty.

1. What time does this bus get __to__ Vancouver?
2. What time does this bus arrive _____ Vancouver?
3. What time did you get _____ home last night?
4. What time do you usually arrive _____ work in the morning?
5. When we got _____ the theater, there was a long line outside.
6. I arrived _____ home feeling very tired.

123.4 Write sentences using *got + into / out of / on / off*.

1. You were walking home. A friend passed you in her car. She saw you, stopped, and offered you a ride. She opened the door. What did you do? __I got into the car.__
2. You were waiting for the bus. At last your bus came. The doors opened. What did you do then? I _____
3. You drove home in your car. You stopped outside your house and parked the car. What did you do then? _____
4. You were traveling by train to Chicago. When the train got to Chicago, what did you do? _____
5. You needed a taxi. After a few minutes a taxi stopped for you. You opened the door. What did you do then? _____
6. You were traveling by air. At the end of your flight, your plane landed at the airport and stopped. The doors were opened. You took your bag and stood up. What did you do then? _____

In/at/on (Other Uses)

A

Expressions with **in**

in the rain / **in the sun** (= sunshine) / **in the shade** / **in the dark** / **in bad weather**, etc.
- We sat **in the shade**. It was too hot to sit **in the sun**.
- Don't go out **in the rain**. Wait until it stops.

(write) **in ink** / **in pen** / **in pencil**
- When you take the exam, you're not allowed to write **in pencil**.

Also (write) **in words** / **in numbers** / **in capital letters**, etc.
- Please write your name **in capital letters**.
- Write the story **in your own words**. (= don't copy somebody else)

(be/fall) **in love** (**with** somebody)
- Have you ever been **in love with** anybody?

in (my) **opinion**
- **In my opinion**, the movie wasn't very good.

B

At the age of . . . , etc.

We say **at the age of 16** / **at 120 miles an hour** / **at 100 degrees**, etc.:
- Tracy left school **at 16**.   *or*   . . . **at the age of 16**.
- The train was traveling **at 120 miles an hour**.
- Water boils **at 100 degrees Celsius**.

We are now flying **at a speed of** 500 miles per hour **at an altitude of** 30,000 feet.

C

On vacation / **on a tour**, etc.

We say: (be/go) **on vacation** / **on business** / **on a trip** / **on a tour** / **on a cruise**, etc.
- I'm going **on vacation** next week.
- Emma's away **on business** at this time.
- One day I'd like to go **on a world tour**.

You can also say "go to a place **for vacation**":
- Steve has gone to France **for vacation**.

D

Other expressions with **on**

on television / **on the radio**
- I didn't watch the news **on television**, but I heard it **on the radio**.

on the phone/telephone
- I've never met her, but I've spoken to her **on the phone** a few times.

(be/go) **on strike**
- There are no trains today. The railroad workers are **on strike**.

(be/go) **on a diet**
- I've put on a lot of weight. I'll have to go **on a diet**.

(be) **on fire**
- Look! That car is **on fire**.

on the whole (= in general)
- Sometimes I have problems at work, but **on the whole** I enjoy my job.

on purpose (= intentionally)
- I'm sorry. I didn't mean to annoy you. I didn't do it **on purpose**.

Exercises

124.1 Complete the sentences using *in* + the following:

> capital letters   cold weather   love   my opinion
> pencil   ~~the rain~~   the shade

1. Don't go out __*in the rain*__ . Wait until it stops.
2. Matt likes to keep warm, so he doesn't go out much _____ .
3. If you write _____ and make a mistake, you can erase it and correct it.
4. They fell _____ almost immediately and were married a few weeks later.
5. Please write your address clearly, preferably _____ .
6. It's too hot in the sun. I'm going to sit _____ .
7. Ann thought the restaurant was OK, but _____ it wasn't very good.

124.2 Complete the sentences using *on* + the following:

> business   ~~fire~~   purpose   television   vacation
> a diet   the phone   strike   a tour   the whole

1. Look! That car is __*on fire*__ ! Somebody call the fire department.
2. Workers at the factory have gone _____ for better pay and conditions.
3. Soon after we arrived, we were taken _____ of the city.
4. I feel lazy tonight. Is there anything worth watching _____ ?
5. I'm sorry. It was an accident. I didn't do it _____ .
6. Richard has put on a lot of weight recently. I think he should go _____ .
7. Jane's job involves a lot of traveling. She is out of town a lot _____ .
8. *A:* I'm going _____ next week.
   B: Where are you going? Somewhere nice?
9. *A:* Is Sarah here?
   B: Yes, but she's _____ at the moment. She won't be long.
10. *A:* How did your exams go?
    B: Well, there were some difficult questions, but _____ they were OK.

124.3 Complete the sentences with *on*, *in*, *at*, or *for*.

1. Water boils __*at*__ 100 degrees Celsius.
2. When I was 14, I went _____ a trip to Mexico organized by my school.
3. There was panic when people realized that the building was _____ fire.
4. Julia's grandmother died recently _____ the age of 79.
5. Can you turn the light on, please? I don't want to sit _____ the dark.
6. We didn't go _____ vacation last year. We stayed at home.
7. I'm going to Miami _____ a short vacation next month.
8. I won't be here next week. I'll be _____ vacation.
9. Technology has developed _____ great speed.
10. Allan got married _____ 17, which is really young to get married.
11. I heard an interesting program _____ the radio this morning.
12. _____ my opinion, violent films should not be shown _____ television.
13. I wouldn't want to go _____ a cruise. I think I'd get bored.
14. I can't eat a lot. I'm supposed to be _____ a diet.
15. I wouldn't want his job. He spends most of his time talking _____ the phone.
16. The earth travels around the sun _____ a speed of 67,000 miles an hour.
17. "Did you enjoy your vacation?" "Not every minute, but _____ the whole, yes."
18. When you write a check, you have to write the amount _____ words and figures.

By

We use **by** in many expressions to say how we do something. For example, you can:

send something **by mail**	contact somebody **by phone** / **by e-mail** / **by fax**
do something **by hand**	pay **by check** / **by credit card**

- Can I pay **by credit card**?
- You can contact me **by phone**, **by fax**, or **by e-mail**.

But we say **pay cash** or **pay in cash** (*not* by cash).

We also say **by mistake** / **by accident** / **by chance**:

- We hadn't arranged to meet. We met **by chance**.

But we say "do something **on purpose**" (= you mean to do it):

- I didn't do it **on purpose**. It was an accident.

Note that we say **by chance**, **by check**, etc. (*not* by the chance / by a check). In these expressions we use **by** + *noun* without "the" or "a."

B

In the same way, we use **by** . . . to say how somebody travels:

by car / **by train** / **by plane** / **by boat** / **by ship** / **by bus** / **by bike**, etc.
by road / **by rail** / **by air** / **by sea** / **by subway**

- Joanne usually goes to work **by bus**.
- Do you prefer to travel **by plane** or **by train**?

But we say **on foot**:

- Did you come here **by car** or **on foot**?

You cannot use **by** if you say **my car** / **the train** / **a taxi**, etc. We use **by** + *noun* without "a/the/my," etc. We say:

by car	*but*	**in my** car (*not* by my car)
by train	*but*	**on the** train (*not* by the train)

We use **in** for cars and taxis:

- They didn't come **in their car**. They came **in a taxi**.

We use **on** for bicycles and public transportation (buses, trains, etc.):

- We came **on the 6:45 train**.

C

We say that "something is done **by** somebody/something" (*passive*):

- Have you ever been bitten **by a dog**?
- The program was watched **by millions of people**.

Compare **by** and **with**:

- The door must have been opened **with a key**. (*not* by a key)
  (= somebody used a key to open it)
- The door must have been opened **by somebody** with a key.

We say "a play **by Shakespeare**" / "a painting **by Rembrandt**" / "a novel **by Tolstoy**," etc.:

- Have you read anything **by** Ernest Hemingway?

D

By also means "next to / beside":

- Come and sit **by me**. (= beside me)
- "Where's the light switch?" "**By the door**."

light switch

E

Note the following use of **by**:

- Claire's salary has just gone up **from** $3,000 a month **to** $3,300. So it has increased **by $300** / **by 10 percent**.
- Carl and Mike ran a 100-meter race. Carl won **by** about **three meters**.

New Salary ——— $3,300/month
salary increased **by $300**
Old Salary ——— $3,000/month

Passive + *by* Unit 40B   *By* + *-ing* Unit 58B   *By myself* Unit 81D   *By* (Time) Unit 117

Exercises

UNIT **125**

125.1 Complete the sentences using *by* + the following:

~~chance~~   credit card   hand   mistake   satellite

1. We hadn't arranged to meet. We met _by chance_ .
2. I didn't mean to take your umbrella. I took it _____ .
3. Don't put the sweater in the washing machine. It has to be washed _____ .
4. I don't need cash. I can pay the bill _____ .
5. The two cities were connected _____ for a television program.

125.2 Put in *by*, *in*, or *on*.

1. Joanne usually goes to work _by_ bus.
2. I saw Jane this morning. She was _____ the bus.
3. How did you get here? Did you come _____ train?
4. I decided not to go _____ car. I went _____ my bike instead.
5. I didn't feel like walking home, so I came home _____ a taxi.
6. Sorry we're late. We missed the bus, so we had to come _____ foot.
7. How long does it take to cross the Atlantic _____ ship?

125.3 Write three sentences like the examples. Write about a song, a painting, a movie, a book, etc.

1. _War and Peace is a book by Tolstoy._
2. _Romeo and Juliet is a play by Shakespeare._
3. _____
4. _____
5. _____

125.4 Put in *by*, *in*, *on*, or *with*.

1. Have you ever been bitten _by_ a dog?
2. The plane was badly damaged _____ lightning.
3. We managed to put the fire out _____ a fire extinguisher.
4. Who is that man standing _____ the window?
5. These photos were taken _____ a friend of mine.
6. I don't mind going _____ car, but I don't want to go _____ your car.
7. There was a small table _____ the bed _____ a lamp and a clock _____ it.

125.5 All these sentences have a mistake. Correct them.

1. Did you come here (by Kate's car) or yours?   _in Kate's car_
2. I don't like traveling on bus.   _____
3. These photographs were taken by a very good camera. _____
4. I know this music is from Beethoven, but I can't   _____
   remember what it's called.
5. I couldn't pay by cash – I didn't have any money on me. _____
6. We lost the game only because of a mistake of one of _____
   our players.

125.6 Complete the sentences using *by*.

1. Claire's salary was $2,000 a month. Now it is $2,200.
   Her salary _has increased by $200 a month._
2. My daily newspaper used to cost a dollar. Starting today, it will cost $1.25.
   The price has gone up _____
3. There was an election. Helen won. She got 25 votes and Norman got 23.
   Helen won _____
4. I went to Kate's house to see her, but she had gone out five minutes before I arrived.
   I missed _____

Additional Exercise 34 (pages 315–316)   251

Noun + Preposition
(reason for, cause of, etc.)

A   *Noun +* **for** ...

a **check FOR** (a sum of money)
- They sent me **a check for** $200.

a **demand** / a **need FOR** ...
- The company closed down because there wasn't enough **demand for** its product.
- There's no excuse for behavior like that. There's no **need for** it.

a **reason FOR** ...
- The train was late, but nobody knew the **reason for** the delay. (*not* reason of)

B   *Noun +* **of** ...

an **advantage** / a **disadvantage OF** ...
- The **advantage of living alone** is that you can do what you like.

but **there is** an advantage **to** (*or* **in**) doing something
- **There are** many advantages **to** living alone. (*or* ... **in** living alone)

a **cause OF** ...
- The **cause of** the explosion is unknown.

a **photo** / a **picture** / a **map** / a **plan** / a **drawing**, etc. **OF** ...
- Rachel showed me some **photos of** her family.
- I had a **map of** the town, so I was able to find my way around.

C   *Noun +* **in** ...

an **increase** / a **decrease** / a **rise** / a **drop IN** (prices, etc.)
- There has been an **increase in** the number of traffic accidents recently.
- Last year was a bad one for the company. There was a big **drop in** sales.

D   *Noun +* **to** ... / **toward** ...

damage TO ...
- The accident was my fault, so I had to pay for the **damage to** the other car.

an **invitation TO** ... (a party / a wedding, etc.)
- Did you get an **invitation to** the party?

a **solution TO** (a problem) / a **key TO** (a door) / an **answer TO** (a question) /
a **reply TO** (a letter) / a **reaction TO** ...
- I hope we find a **solution to** the problem. (*not* a solution of the problem)
- I was surprised at her **reaction to** my suggestion.

an **attitude TOWARD** ...
- His **attitude toward** his job is very negative.

E   *Noun +* **with** ... / **between** ...

a **relationship** / a **connection** / **contact WITH** ...
- Do you have a good **relationship with** your parents?
- The police want to question a man in **connection with** the robbery.

but a **relationship** / a **connection** / **contact** / a **difference BETWEEN** two things
or people
- The police believe that there is no **connection between** the two crimes.
- There are some **differences between** British and American English.

Exercises

126.1 Complete the second sentence so that it has the same meaning as the first.

1. What caused the explosion?
   What was the cause __*of the explosion*_____ ?
2. We're trying to solve the problem.
   We're trying to find a solution _____ .
3. Sue gets along well with her brother.
   Sue has a good relationship _____ .
4. The cost of living has gone up a lot.
   There has been a big increase _____ .
5. I don't know how to answer your question.
   I can't think of an answer _____ .
6. I don't think that a new road is necessary.
   I don't think there is any need _____ .
7. I think that working at home has many advantages.
   I think that there are many advantages _____ .
8. The number of people without jobs fell last month.
   Last month there was a drop _____ .
9. Nobody wants to buy shoes like these anymore.
   There is no demand _____ .
10. In what way is your job different from mine?
    What is the difference _____ ?

126.2 Complete the sentences using the following nouns + the correct preposition:

> cause   connection   contact   damage   invitation
> key   ~~map~~   pictures   reason   reply

1. On the wall there were some pictures and a __*map of*___ the world.
2. Thank you for the _____ your party next week.
3. Since she left home two years ago, Sofia has had little _____ her family.
4. I can't open this door. Do you have a _____ the other door?
5. The _____ the fire at the hotel last night is still unknown.
6. I e-mailed Jim last week, but I still haven't received a _____ my message.
7. The two companies are completely independent. There is no _____ them.
8. Jane showed me some old _____ the city the way it looked 100 years ago.
9. Carol has decided to quit her job. I don't know her _____ doing this.
10. It wasn't a bad accident. The _____ the car wasn't serious.

126.3 Complete the sentences with the correct preposition.

1. There are some differences __*between*___ British and American English.
2. Money isn't the solution _____ every problem.
3. There has been an increase _____ the amount of traffic using this road.
4. When I opened the envelope, I was delighted to find a check _____ $500.
5. The advantage _____ having a car is that you don't have to rely on public transportation.
6. There are many advantages _____ being able to speak a foreign language.
7. Everything can be explained. There's a reason _____ everything.
8. When Paul left home, his attitude _____ his parents seemed to change.
9. Ben and I used to be good friends, but I don't have much contact _____ him now.
10. There has been a sharp rise _____ property values in the past few years.
11. What was Ann's reaction _____ the news?
12. If I give you the camera, can you take a picture _____ me?
13. The company has rejected the workers' demands _____ an increase _____ pay.
14. What was the answer _____ question 3 on the test?
15. The fact that Jane was offered a job has no connection _____ the fact that she is a friend of the managing director.

Adjective + Preposition 1

A

It was **nice of** you to . . .

> **nice / kind / good / generous / polite / stupid / silly**, etc. **OF** somebody (to do something)
> - Thank you. It was very **kind of** you to help me.
> - It is **stupid of** me to go out without a coat in such cold weather.
>
> *but* (be) **nice / kind / good / generous / polite / rude / friendly / cruel**, etc. **TO** somebody
> - They have always been very **nice to** me. (*not* with me)
> - Why were you so **unfriendly to** Lucy?

B

Adjective + **about** / **with** / **at**

> **furious / angry / mad / upset ABOUT** something
> - Max is really **angry about** what his brother said.
>
> | | | |
> |---|---|---|
> | **mad** | **AT** | |
> | **upset** | **WITH** | } somebody **FOR** doing something |
> | **furious / angry** | **AT / WITH** | |
>
> - My parents are **mad at** me **for** disobeying them.
> - Are you **upset with** me **for** being late?
> - Pat's **furious with** me **for** telling her secret. (*or* **furious at** me)
>
> **excited / worried / upset / nervous / happy**, etc. **ABOUT** a situation
> - Are you **excited about** going away next week?
> - Lisa is **upset about** not being invited to the party.
>
> **delighted / pleased / satisfied / happy / disappointed WITH** something you receive,
> or the result of something
> - I was very **pleased with** the present you gave me.
> - Were you **happy with** your exam results?

C

Adjective + **at** / **by** / **with**

> **surprised / shocked / amazed / astonished AT / BY** something
> - Everybody was **surprised AT** (*or* **BY**) the news.
> - I hope you weren't **shocked BY** (*or* **AT**) what I said.
>
> **impressed WITH / BY** somebody/something
> - I'm very **impressed with** (*or* **by**) her English. It's very good.
>
> **fed up / bored WITH** something
> - I don't enjoy my job any more. I'm **fed up with** it. / I'm **bored with** it.

D

Sorry about / for

> **sorry ABOUT** a situation or something that happened
> - I'm **sorry about** the mess. I'll clean it up later.
> - We're all **sorry about** Julie losing her job.
>
> **sorry FOR / ABOUT** something you did
> - Alex is very **sorry for** what he said. (*or* **sorry about** what he said)
> - I'm **sorry for** shouting at you yesterday. (*or* **sorry about** shouting)
> You can also say "I'm sorry I (did something)":
> - I'm **sorry I shouted** at you yesterday.
>
> **feel / be sorry FOR** somebody who is in a bad situation
> - I **feel sorry for** Matt. He's had a lot of bad luck. (*not* I feel sorry about Matt)

Preposition + *-ing* Unit 58   Adjective + *to* Unit 63   *Sorry to . . . / sorry for . . .* Unit 64C
Adjective + Preposition 2 Unit 128

Exercises

127.1 Write sentences using *nice of . . . , kind of . . . ,* etc.

1. I went out in the cold without a coat. (silly) _That was silly of you._
2. Sue offered to drive me to the airport. (nice) That was _____ her.
3. I needed money and Tom gave me some. (generous) That _____
   _____
4. They didn't invite us to their party. (not very nice) That _____
   _____
5. Can I help you with your luggage? (very kind) _____ you.
6. Kevin didn't thank me for the present. (not very polite) _____
   _____
7. They've had an argument and now they refuse to speak to each other. (a little childish) _____
   _____

127.2 Complete the sentences using the following adjectives + the correct preposition:

> astonished   bored   ~~excited~~   impressed   kind   nervous   sorry   upset

1. Are you _excited about_ going away next week?
2. Thank you for all your help. You've been very _____ me.
3. I wouldn't want to be in her position. I feel _____ her.
4. I'm really _____ taking my driver's test. I hope I don't fail.
5. Why do you always get so _____ things that don't matter?
6. I wasn't very _____ the service at the restaurant. We had to wait ages before our food arrived.
7. Ben isn't very happy at college. He says he's _____ the classes he's taking.
8. I had never seen so many people before. I was _____ the crowds.

127.3 Put in the correct preposition.

1. I was delighted _with_ the present you gave me.
2. It was very nice _____ you to do my shopping for me. Thank you very much.
3. Why are you always so rude _____ your parents? Can't you be nice _____ them?
4. It was careless _____ you to leave the door unlocked when you went out.
5. They didn't reply to our letter, which wasn't very polite _____ them.
6. We always have the same food every day. I'm fed up _____ it.
7. I can't understand people who are cruel _____ animals.
8. We enjoyed our vacation, but we were a little disappointed _____ the hotel.
9. I was surprised _____ the way he behaved. It was completely out of character.
10. I've been trying to learn Spanish, but I'm not very satisfied _____ my progress.
11. Linda doesn't look very well. I'm worried _____ her.
12. Are you angry _____ what happened?
13. I'm sorry _____ what I did. I hope you're not mad _____ me.
14. The people next door are furious _____ us _____ making so much noise last night.
15. Jill starts her new job next week. She's quite excited _____ it.
16. I'm sorry _____ the smell of paint in this room. I'm redecorating it.
17. I was shocked _____ what I saw. I'd never seen anything like it before.
18. The man we interviewed for the job was intelligent, but we weren't very impressed _____ his appearance.
19. Are you still upset _____ what I said to you yesterday?
20. He said he was sorry _____ the situation, but there was nothing he could do.
21. I felt sorry _____ the children when we went on vacation. It rained every day and they had to spend most of the time indoors.

Adjective + Preposition 2

Adjective + **of** (1)

> **afraid / frightened / terrified / scared OF . . .**
> - "Are you **afraid of** spiders?"   "Yes, I'm **terrified of** them."
>
> **fond / proud / ashamed / jealous / envious OF . . .**
> - Why are you always so **jealous of** other people?
>
> **suspicious / critical / tolerant OF . . .**
> - He didn't trust me. He was **suspicious of** my intentions.

Adjective + **of** (2)

> **aware / conscious OF . . .**
> - "Did you know he was married?"   "No, I wasn't **aware of** that."
>
> **capable / incapable OF . . .**
> - I'm sure you are **capable of** passing the exam.
>
> **full / short OF . . .**
> - The letter I wrote was **full of** mistakes. (*not* full with)
> - I'm a little **short of** money. Can you lend me some?
>
> **typical OF . . .**
> - He's late again. It's **typical of** him to keep everybody waiting.
>
> **tired / sick OF . . .**
> - Come on, let's go! I'm **tired of** waiting. (= I've had enough of waiting)
>
> **certain / sure OF** *or* **ABOUT . . .**
> - I think she's arriving tonight, but I'm not **sure of** that.   *or*   . . . sure **about** that.

Adjective + **at / to / from / in / on / with / for**

> **good / bad / excellent / better / hopeless**, etc. **AT . . .**
> - I'm not very **good at** repairing things. (*not* good in repairing things)
>
> **married / engaged TO . . .**
> - Linda is **married to** an American. (*not* married with)
> *but*   Linda is married **with three children**. (= she is married and has three children)
>
> **similar TO . . .**
> - Your writing is **similar to** mine.
>
> **different FROM** *or* **different THAN . . .**
> - The film was **different from** what I'd expected. (*or* **different than** what I'd expected)
>
> **interested IN . . .**
> - Are you **interested in** art?
>
> **dependent ON . . .** (*but* **independent OF . . .**)
> - I don't want to be **dependent on** anybody.
>
> **crowded WITH** (people, etc.)
> - The streets were **crowded with** tourists. (*but* **full of** tourists)
>
> **famous FOR . . .**
> - The Italian city of Florence is **famous for** its art treasures.
>
> **responsible FOR . . .**
> - Who was **responsible for** all that noise last night?

Preposition + *-ing* Unit 58   *Afraid of/to* . . . Unit 64A   **Adjective + Preposition 1** Unit 127
British English Appendix 7

256

Exercises

128.1 Complete the second sentence so that it has the same meaning as the first.

1. There were lots of tourists in the streets.   The streets were crowded ___with tourists___ .
2. There was a lot of furniture in the room.   The room was full _____ .
3. Who made this mess?   Who is responsible _____ ?
4. We don't have enough time.   We're a little short _____ .
5. I'm not a very good tennis player.   I'm not very good _____ .
6. Catherine's husband is Russian.   Catherine is married _____ .
7. I don't trust Robert.   I'm suspicious _____ .
8. My problem is not the same as yours.   My problem is different _____ .

128.2 Complete the sentences using the following adjectives + the correct preposition:

afraid   different   interested   proud   responsible   similar   ~~sure~~

1. I think she's arriving tonight, but I'm not ___sure of___ that.
2. Your camera is _____ mine, but it isn't exactly the same.
3. Don't worry. I'll take care of you. There's nothing to be _____ .
4. I never watch the news on television. I'm not _____ the news.
5. The editor is the person who is _____ what appears in a newspaper.
6. Sarah loves gardening. She's very _____ her garden and loves showing it to visitors.
7. I was surprised when I met Lisa for the first time. She was _____ what I expected.

128.3 Put in the correct preposition.

1. The letter I wrote was full __of__ mistakes.
2. My hometown is not an especially interesting place. It's not famous _____ anything.
3. Kate is very fond _____ her younger brother.
4. I don't like climbing ladders. I'm scared _____ heights.
5. You look bored. You don't seem interested _____ what I'm saying.
6. Did you know that Liz is engaged _____ a friend of mine?
7. I'm not ashamed _____ what I did. In fact I'm quite proud _____ it.
8. Mark has no money of his own. He's totally dependent _____ his parents.
9. These days everybody is aware _____ the dangers of smoking.
10. The station platform was crowded _____ people waiting for the train.
11. Sue is much more successful than I am. Sometimes I feel a little jealous _____ her.
12. I'm tired _____ doing the same thing every day. I need a change.
13. Do you know anyone who might be interested _____ buying an old car?
14. We've got plenty to eat. The fridge is full _____ food.
15. She is a very honest person. I don't think she is capable _____ telling a lie.
16. Helen works hard and she's extremely good _____ her job.
17. I'm not surprised he changed his mind at the last minute. That's typical _____ him.
18. The woman Sam is married _____ runs a software business.
19. We're short _____ staff in our office at the moment. We need more people to do the work.

128.4 Write sentences about yourself. Are you good at these things or not? Use the following:

good   pretty good   not very good   hopeless

1. (repairing things) ___I'm not very good at repairing things.___
2. (telling jokes) _____
3. (mathematics) _____
4. (remembering names) _____

Verb + Preposition 1   to and at

A

Verb + **to**

talk / speak TO somebody (**with** is also possible but less common)
- ■ Who was that man you were **talking to**?

listen TO . . .
- ■ We spent the evening **listening to** music. (*not* listening music)

apologize TO somebody (for . . .)
- ■ They **apologized to me** for what happened. (*not* They apologized me)

explain something **TO** somebody
- ■ Can you **explain** this word **to me**? (*not* explain me this word)

explain / describe (**to** somebody) what/how/why . . .
- ■ I **explained to them** why I was worried. (*not* I explained them)
- ■ Let me **describe to you** what I saw. (*not* Let me describe you)

B

We do not use **to** with these verbs:

call / phone / telephone somebody
- ■ Did you **call your father** yesterday? (*not* call to your father)

answer somebody/something
- ■ He refused to **answer my question**. (*not* answer to my question)

ask somebody
- ■ Can I **ask you** a question? (*not* ask to you)

thank somebody (for something)
- ■ He **thanked me** for helping him. (*not* He thanked to me)

C

Verb + **at**

look / stare / glance AT . . . , **have a look / take a look AT** . . .
- ■ Why are you **looking at** me like that?

laugh AT . . .
- ■ I look stupid with this haircut. Everybody will **laugh at** me.

aim / point (something) **AT** . . . , **shoot / fire** (a gun) **AT** . . .
- ■ Don't **point** that knife **at** me. It's dangerous.
- ■ We saw someone with a gun **shooting at** birds, but he didn't hit any.

D

Some verbs can be followed by **at** or **to**, with a difference in meaning. For example:

shout AT somebody (when you are angry)
- ■ He got very angry and started **shouting at** me.

shout TO somebody (so that they can hear you)
- ■ He **shouted to** me from the other side of the street.

throw something **AT** somebody/something (in order to hit them)
- ■ Somebody **threw** an egg **at** the politician.

throw something **TO** somebody (for somebody to catch)
- ■ Lisa shouted "Catch!" and **threw** the keys **to** me from the window.

Verb + Preposition 2–4 Units 130–132   *Ask for* Unit 130C   *Apologize for / thank somebody for* Unit 132B
Other Verbs + *to* Unit 133D   **British English** Appendix 7

Exercises

129.1 You ask somebody to explain things that you don't understand. Write questions beginning *Can you explain . . . ?*

1. (I don't understand this word.)
   Can you explain this word to me?
2. (I don't understand what you mean.)
   Can you explain to me what you mean?
3. (I don't understand this question.)
   Can you explain _____
4. (I don't understand the problem.)
   Can _____
5. (I don't understand how this machine works.)
   _____
6. (I don't understand what I have to do.)
   _____

129.2 Put in *to* where necessary. If the sentence is already complete, leave the space empty.

1. I know who she is, but I've never spoken __*to*__ her.
2. Why didn't you answer __−__ my letter?
3. I like to listen _____ the radio while I'm having breakfast.
4. We'd better call _____ the restaurant to reserve a table.
5. "Did Mike apologize _____ you?" "Yes, he said he was very sorry."
6. I explained _____ everybody the reasons for my decision.
7. I thanked _____ everybody for all the help they had given me.
8. Ask me what you like, and I'll try and answer _____ your questions.
9. Mike described _____ me exactly what happened.
10. Karen won't be able to help you, so there's no point in asking _____ her.

129.3 Complete the sentences. Use the following verbs (in the correct form) + the correct preposition:

~~explain~~   glance   ~~laugh~~   listen   point   speak   throw   throw

1. I look stupid with this haircut. Everybody will __*laugh at*__ me.
2. I don't understand this. Can you __*explain*__ it __*to*__ me?
3. Sue and Kevin had an argument and now they're not _____ each other.
4. Be careful with those scissors! Don't _____ them _____ me!
5. I _____ my watch to see what time it was.
6. Please _____ me! I've got something important to tell you.
7. Don't _____ stones _____ the birds! It's cruel.
8. If you don't want that sandwich, _____ it _____ the birds. They'll eat it.

129.4 Put in *to* or *at*.

1. Lisa shouted, "Catch!" and threw the keys __*to*__ me from the window.
2. Look _____ these flowers. Aren't they pretty?
3. Please don't shout _____ me! Try to calm down.
4. I saw Sue as I was riding along the road. I shouted _____ her, but she didn't hear me.
5. Don't listen _____ what he says. He doesn't know what he's talking about.
6. What's so funny? What are you laughing _____ ?
7. Do you think I could have a look _____ your magazine, please?
8. I'm a little lonely. I need somebody to talk _____ .
9. She was so angry she threw a book _____ the wall.
10. The woman sitting opposite me on the train kept staring _____ me.
11. Can I speak _____ you a moment? There's something I want to ask you.

A   Verb + about

talk / read / know ABOUT ..., **tell** somebody **ABOUT** ...
- We **talked about** a lot of things at the meeting.

have a discussion ABOUT something, *but* **discuss** something (no preposition)
- We **had a discussion about** what we should do.
- We **discussed** a lot of things at the meeting. (*not* discussed about)

do something **ABOUT** something = *do something to improve a bad situation*
- If you're worried about the problem, you should **do** something **about** it.

B   Care about, care for, and take care of

care ABOUT somebody/something = *think that somebody/something is important*
- He's very selfish. He doesn't **care about** other people.

We say **care what/where/how** ..., etc. (*without* about)
- You can do what you like. I don't **care what** you do.

care FOR somebody/something
(1) = *like something* (usually in questions and negative sentences)
- Would you **care for** a cup of coffee? (= Would you like ... ?)
- I don't **care for** very hot weather. (= I don't like ...)
(2) = *make sure somebody is safe and well*
- Alan is 85 and lives alone. He needs somebody to **care for** him.

take care OF ... = *make sure somebody/something stays safe or in good condition, take responsibility for something*
- John gave up his job to **take care of** his elderly parents.
- I'll **take care of** all the travel arrangements – you don't need to do anything.

C   Verb + for

ask (somebody) **FOR** ...
- I wrote to the company **asking** them **for** more information about the job.
but "I **asked** him **the way** to ...," "She **asked** me **my name**." (no preposition)

apply (**TO** a person, a company, etc.) **FOR** a job, etc.
- I think you'd be good at this job. Why don't you **apply for** it?

wait FOR ...
- Don't **wait for** me. I'll join you later.
- I'm not going out yet. I'm **waiting for** the rain to stop.

search (a person / a place / a bag, etc.) **FOR** ...
- I've **searched** the house **for** my keys, but I still can't find them.

leave (a place) **FOR** another place
- I haven't seen her since she **left** (home) **for** the office this morning. (*not* left to the office)

D   Look for and look after

look FOR ... = *search for, try to find*
- I've lost my keys. Can you help me **look for** them?

look AFTER ... = *take care of*
- Alan is 85 and lives alone. He needs somebody to **look after** him. (*not* look for)
- You can borrow this book if you promise to **look after** it.

Exercises

130.1 Put in the correct preposition. If no preposition is necessary, leave the space empty.

1. I'm not going out yet. I'm waiting __*for*__ the rain to stop.
2. I couldn't find the street I was looking for, so I stopped someone to ask _____ directions.
3. I've applied _____ a job at the factory. I don't know if I'll get it.
4. I've applied _____ three colleges. I hope one of them accepts me.
5. I've searched everywhere _____ John, but I haven't been able to find him.
6. I don't want to talk _____ what happened last night. Let's forget it.
7. I don't want to discuss _____ what happened last night. Let's forget it.
8. We had an interesting discussion _____ the problem, but we didn't reach a decision.
9. We discussed _____ the problem, but we didn't reach a decision.
10. I don't want to go out yet. I'm waiting _____ the mail to arrive.
11. Ken and Sonia are touring Italy. They're in Rome right now, but tomorrow they leave _____ Venice.
12. The roof of the house is in very bad condition. I think we ought to do something _____ it.
13. We waited _____ Steve for half an hour, but he never came.
14. Tomorrow morning I have to catch a plane. I'm leaving my house _____ the airport at 7:30.

130.2 Complete the sentences with the following verbs (in the correct form) + preposition:

> **apply   ask   do   leave   look   ~~search~~   talk   wait**

1. Police are __*searching for*__ the man who escaped from prison.
2. We're still _____ a reply to our letter. We haven't heard anything yet.
3. I think Ben likes his job, but he doesn't _____ it much.
4. When I'd finished my meal, I _____ the waiter _____ the check.
5. Cathy is unemployed. She has _____ several jobs, but she hasn't had any luck.
6. If something is wrong, why don't you _____ something _____ it?
7. Linda's car is very old, but it's in excellent condition. She _____ it very well.
8. Diane is from Boston, but now she lives in Paris. She _____ Boston _____ Paris when she was 19.

130.3 Put in the correct preposition after *care*. If no preposition is necessary, leave the space empty.

1. He's very selfish. He doesn't care __*about*__ other people.
2. Are you hungry? Would you care _____ something to eat?
3. She doesn't care _____ the exam. She doesn't care whether she passes or fails.
4. Please let me borrow your camera. I promise I'll take good care _____ it.
5. "Do you like this coat?" "Not really. I don't care _____ the color."
6. Don't worry about the shopping. I'll take care _____ that.
7. I want to have a nice vacation. I don't care _____ the cost.
8. I want to have a nice vacation. I don't care _____ how much it costs.

130.4 Complete the sentences with *look for* or *look after*. Use the correct form of *look* (*looks/looked/looking*).

1. I __*looked for*__ my keys, but I couldn't find them anywhere.
2. Kate is _____ a job. I hope she finds one soon.
3. Who _____ you when you were sick?
4. I'm _____ Elizabeth. Have you seen her?
5. The parking lot was full, so we had to _____ somewhere else to park.
6. A babysitter is somebody who _____ other people's children.

Verb + Preposition 3   **about** and **of**

A

dream ABOUT . . . (when you are asleep)
- I **dreamed about** you last night.

dream OF/ABOUT being something / doing something = *imagine*
- Do you **dream of/about** being rich and famous?

(I) **wouldn't dream OF** doing something = *I would never do it*
- "Don't tell anyone what I said." "No, I **wouldn't dream of** it." (= I would never do it)

B

hear ABOUT . . . = *be told about something*
- Did you **hear about** what happened at the club on Saturday night?

hear OF . . . = *know that somebody/something exists*
- "Who is Tom Hart?" "I have no idea. I've never **heard of** him." (*not* heard from him)

hear FROM . . . = *receive a letter, phone call, or message from somebody*
- "Have you **heard from** Jane recently?" "Yes, she called a few days ago."

C

think ABOUT . . . and **think OF** . . .

When you **think ABOUT** something, you consider it, you concentrate your mind on it:
- I've **thought about** what you said, and I've decided to take your advice.
- "Will you lend me the money?" "I'll **think about** it."

When you **think OF** something, the idea comes to your mind:
- He told me his name, but I can't **think of** it now. (*not* think about it)
- That's a good idea. Why didn't I **think of** that? (*not* think about that)
We also use **think of** when we ask or give an opinion:
- "What did you **think of** the film?" "I didn't **think** much **of** it." (= I didn't like it much)

The difference is sometimes very small and you can use **of** or **about**:
- When I'm alone, I often **think of** (*or* about) you.
You can say **think of** *or* **think about** doing something (for possible future actions):
- My sister is **thinking of** (*or* about) going to Canada. (= she is considering it)

D

remind somebody **ABOUT** . . . = *tell somebody not to forget*
- I'm glad you **reminded** me **about** the meeting. I had completely forgotten about it.

remind somebody **OF** . . . = *cause somebody to remember*
- This house **reminds** me **of** the one I lived in when I was a child.
- Look at this picture of Richard. Who does he **remind** you **of**?

E

complain (**TO** somebody) **ABOUT** . . . = *say that you are not satisfied*
- We **complained to** the manager of the restaurant **about** the food.

complain OF a pain, an illness, etc. = *say that you have a pain, etc.*
- We called the doctor because George was **complaining of** a pain in his stomach.

F

warn somebody **ABOUT** a person or thing which is bad, dangerous, unusual, etc.
- I knew he was a strange person. I had been **warned about** him. (*not* warned of him)
- Vicky **warned** me **about** the traffic. She said it would be bad.

warn somebody **ABOUT/OF** a danger, something bad which might happen later
- Scientists have **warned** us **about/of** the effects of global warming.

Exercises

131.1 Put in the correct preposition.

1. Did you hear __*about*__ what happened at the party on Saturday?
2. "I had a strange dream last night." "Did you? What did you dream _____ ?"
3. Our neighbors complained _____ us _____ the noise we made last night.
4. Kevin was complaining _____ pains in his chest, so he went to the doctor.
5. I love this music. It reminds me _____ a warm day in spring.
6. He loves his job. He thinks _____ his job all the time, he dreams _____ it, he talks _____ it, and I'm sick of hearing _____ it.
7. I tried to remember the name of the book, but I couldn't think _____ it.
8. Jackie warned me _____ the water. She said it wasn't safe to drink.
9. We warned our children _____ the dangers of playing in the street.

131.2 Complete the sentences using the following verbs (in the correct form) + the correct preposition:

complain   dream   hear   remind   remind   ~~think~~   think   warn

1. That's a good idea. Why didn't I __*think of*__ that?
2. Bill is never satisfied. He is always _____ something.
3. I can't make a decision yet. I need time to _____ your proposal.
4. Before you go into the house, I should _____ you _____ the dog. He is very aggressive sometimes, so be careful.
5. She's not a well-known singer. Not many people have _____ her.
6. *A:* You wouldn't leave without telling me, would you?
   B: Of course not. I wouldn't _____ it.
7. I would have forgotten my appointment if Jane hadn't _____ me _____ it.
8. Do you see that man over there? Does he _____ you _____ anybody you know?

131.3 Complete the sentences using *hear* or *heard* + the correct preposition (*about/of/from*).

1. I've never __*heard of*__ Tom Hart. Who is he?
2. "Did you _____ the accident last night?" "Yes, Vicky told me."
3. Jill used to call quite often, but I haven't _____ her for a long time now.
4. *A:* Have you _____ a writer called William Hudson?
   B: No, I don't think so. What sort of writer is he?
5. Thank you for your letter. It was good to _____ you again.
6. "Do you want to _____ our vacation?" "Not now. Tell me later."
7. I live in a small town in Texas. You've probably never _____ it.

131.4 Complete the sentences using *think about* or *think of*. Sometimes both *about* and *of* are possible. Use the correct form of *think* (*think/thinking/thought*).

1. You look serious. What are you __*thinking about*__ ?
2. I like to have time to make decisions. I like to _____ things carefully.
3. I don't know what to get Sarah for her birthday. Can you _____ anything?
4. *A:* I've finished reading the book you lent me.
   B: You have? What did you _____ it? Did you like it?
5. We're _____ going out for dinner tonight. Would you like to come?
6. I don't really want to go out with Tom tonight. I'll have to _____ an excuse.
7. When I was offered the job, I didn't accept immediately. I went away and _____ it for a while. In the end I decided to take the job.
8. I don't _____ much _____ this coffee. It's like water.
9. Carol is very homesick. She's always _____ her family back home.

Verb + Preposition 4   of/for/from/on

A   *Verb* + **of**

accuse / **suspect** somebody **OF** . . .
- Sue **accused** me **of** being selfish.
- Some students were **suspected of** cheating on the exam.

approve / **disapprove OF** . . .
- His parents don't **approve of** what he does, but they can't stop him.

die OF (*or* **FROM**) an illness, etc.
- "What did he **die of**?" "A heart attack."

consist OF . . .
- We had an enormous meal. It **consisted of** seven courses.

B   *Verb* + **for**

pay (somebody) **FOR** . . .
- I didn't have enough money to **pay for** the meal. (*not* pay the meal)
but   **pay** a bill / a fine / tax / rent / a sum of money, etc. (no preposition)
- I didn't have enough money to **pay the rent**.

thank / **forgive** somebody **FOR** . . .
- I'll never **forgive** them **for** what they did.

apologize (to somebody) **FOR** . . .
- When I realized I was wrong, I **apologized** (to them) **for** my mistake.

blame somebody/something **FOR** . . . , somebody is **to blame FOR** . . .
- Everybody **blamed** me **for** the accident.
- Everybody said that I was **to blame for** the accident.

blame (a problem, etc.) **ON** . . .
- Everybody **blamed** the accident **on** me.

C   *Verb* + **from**

suffer FROM an illness, etc.
- The number of people **suffering from** heart disease has increased.

protect somebody/something **FROM** (*or* **AGAINST**) . . .
- Sunblock **protects** the skin **from** the sun. (*or* . . . **against** the sun.)

D   *Verb* + **on**

depend / **rely ON** . . .
- "What time will you be home?" "I don't know. It **depends on** the traffic."
- You can **rely on** Jill. She always keeps her promises.
You can use **depend** + **when/where/how**, etc. with or without **on**:
- "Are you going to buy it?" "It **depends how** much it is." (*or* It depends **on** how much)

live ON money/food
- Michael's salary is very low. It isn't enough to **live on**.

congratulate / **compliment** somebody **ON** . . .
- I **congratulated** her **on** being admitted to law school.

Exercises

132.1 Complete the second sentence so that it means the same as the first.

1. Sue said I was selfish.
   Sue accused me __*of being selfish*__ .
2. The misunderstanding was my fault, so I apologized.
   I apologized _____ .
3. Jane won the tournament, so I congratulated her.
   I congratulated Jane _____ .
4. He has enemies, but he has a bodyguard to protect him.
   He has a bodyguard to protect him _____ .
5. There are nine players on a baseball team.
   A baseball team consists _____ .
6. Sandra eats only bread and eggs.
   She lives _____ .

132.2 Complete the second sentence using *for* or *on*. These sentences all have *blame*.

1. Liz said that what happened was Joe's fault.
   Liz blamed Joe __*for what happened*__ .
2. You always say everything is my fault.
   You always blame me _____ .
3. Do you think the economic crisis is the fault of the government?
   Do you blame the government _____ ?
4. I think the increase in violent crime is the fault of television.
   I blame the increase in violent crime _____ .

   Now rewrite sentences 3 and 4 using *to blame for*.

5. (3.) Do you think the government _____ ?
6. (4.) I think that _____ .

132.3 Complete the sentences using the following verbs (in the correct form) + the correct preposition:

   accuse   apologize   ~~approve~~   congratulate   depend   live   pay

1. His parents don't __*approve of*__ what he does, but they can't stop him.
2. When you went to the theater with Paul, who _____ the tickets?
3. It's a terrible feeling when you are _____ something you didn't do.
4. *A:* Are you going to the beach tomorrow?
   B: I hope so. It _____ the weather.
5. Things are very cheap there. You can _____ very little money.
6. When I saw David, I _____ him _____ passing his driving test.
7. You were very rude to Liz. Don't you think you should _____ her?

132.4 Put in the correct preposition. If no preposition is necessary, leave the space empty.

1. Some students were suspected __*of*__ cheating on the exam.
2. Sally is often sick. She suffers _____ very bad headaches.
3. You know that you can rely _____ me if you ever need any help.
4. It is terrible that some people are dying _____ hunger while others eat too much.
5. Are you going to apologize _____ what you did?
6. The accident was my fault, so I had to pay _____ the repairs.
7. I didn't have enough money to pay _____ the bill.
8. I complimented her _____ her English. She spoke very fluently, and her pronunciation was excellent.
9. She doesn't have a job. She depends _____ her parents for money.
10. I don't know whether I'll go out tonight. It depends _____ how I feel.
11. They wore warm clothes to protect themselves _____ the cold.
12. Cake consists mainly _____ sugar, flour, and butter.

Verb + Preposition 5   in/into/with/to/on

Verb + in

believe IN . . .
- Do you **believe in** God? (= Do you believe that God exists?)
- I **believe in** saying what I think. (= I believe it is right to say what I think)

but **believe** something (= believe it is true), **believe** somebody (= believe they are telling the truth)
- The story can't be true. I don't **believe it**. (*not* believe in it)

specialize IN . . .
- Helen is a lawyer. She **specializes in** corporate law.

succeed IN . . .
- I hope you **succeed in** finding the job you want.

Verb + into

break INTO . . .
- Our house was **broken into** a few days ago, but nothing was stolen.

crash / drive / bump / run INTO . . .
- He lost control of the car and **crashed into** a wall.

divide / cut / split something **INTO** two or more parts
- The book is **divided into** three parts.

translate a book, etc., **FROM** one language **INTO** another
- Ernest Hemingway's books have been **translated into** many languages.

Verb + with

collide WITH . . .
- There was an accident this morning. A bus **collided with** a car.

fill something **WITH . . .** (*but* **full of . . .** – see Unit 128B)
- Take this pot and **fill** it **with** water.

provide / supply somebody **WITH . . .**
- The school **provides** all its students **with** books.

Verb + to

happen TO . . .
- What **happened to** that gold watch you used to have? (= where is it now?)

invite somebody **TO** a party / a wedding, etc.
- They only **invited** a few people **to** their wedding.

prefer one thing/person **TO** another
- I **prefer** tea **to** coffee.

Verb + on

concentrate ON . . .
- Don't look out the window. **Concentrate on** your work.

insist ON . . .
- I wanted to go alone, but some friends of mine **insisted on** coming with me.

spend (money) **ON . . .**
- How much do you **spend on** food each week?

Verb + Preposition + *-ing* Unit 60   **Other Verbs +** *to* Unit 129   **Other Verbs +** *on* Unit 132D

Exercises

133.1 Complete the second sentence so that it means the same as the first.

1. There was a collision between a bus and a car.
   A bus collided __*with a car*_____ .
2. I don't mind big cities, but I prefer small towns.
   I prefer _____ .
3. I got all the information I needed from Jane.
   Jane provided me _____ .
4. This morning I bought a pair of shoes, which cost $70.
   This morning I spent _____ .

133.2 Complete the sentences using the following verbs (in the correct form) + the correct preposition:

> **believe   concentrate   divide   drive   fill   happen   ~~insist~~   invite   succeed**

1. I wanted to go alone, but Sue __*insisted on*___ coming with me.
2. I haven't seen Mike for ages. I wonder what has _____ him.
3. We've been _____ the party, but unfortunately we can't go.
4. It's a very large house. It's _____ four apartments.
5. I don't _____ ghosts. I think people only imagine that they see them.
6. Steve gave me an empty bucket and told me to _____ it _____ water.
7. I was driving along when the car in front of me stopped suddenly. Unfortunately I couldn't stop in time and _____ the back of it.
8. Don't try and do two things together. _____ one thing at a time.
9. It wasn't easy, but in the end we _____ finding a solution to the problem.

133.3 Put in the correct preposition. If the sentence is already complete, leave the space empty.

1. The school provides all its students __*with*___ books.
2. A strange thing happened _____ me a few days ago.
3. Mark decided to give up sports so that he could concentrate _____ his studies.
4. I don't believe _____ working very hard. It's not worth it.
5. My present job isn't wonderful, but I prefer it _____ what I did before.
6. I hope you succeed _____ getting what you want.
7. As I was coming out of the room, I collided _____ somebody who was coming in.
8. There was an awful noise as the car crashed _____ a tree.
9. Patrick is a photographer. He specializes _____ sports photography.
10. Do you spend much money _____ clothes?
11. The country is divided _____ six regions.
12. I prefer traveling by train _____ driving. It's much more pleasant.
13. I was amazed when Joe walked into the room. I couldn't believe _____ it.
14. Somebody broke _____ my car and stole the radio.
15. I was very cold, but Tom insisted _____ keeping the window open.
16. Some words are difficult to translate _____ one language _____ another.
17. What happened _____ the money I lent you? What did you spend it _____ ?
18. The teacher decided to split the class _____ four groups.
19. I filled the tank, but unfortunately I filled it _____ the wrong kind of gas.

133.4 Use your own ideas to complete these sentences. Use a preposition.

1. I wanted to go out alone, but my friend insisted __*on coming with me*_____ .
2. I spend a lot of money _____ .
3. I saw the accident. The car crashed _____ .
4. Chris prefers basketball _____ .
5. Shakespeare's plays have been translated _____ .

Phrasal Verbs 1   Introduction

A

We often use verbs with the following words:

in	on	up	away	around	about	over	by
out	off	down	back	through	along	forward	

So you can say **look out** / **get on** / **take off** / **run away**, etc. These are *phrasal verbs*.

We often use **on/off/out**, etc. with verbs of movement. For example:

get on	■	The bus was full. We couldn't **get on**.
drive off	■	A woman got into the car and **drove off**.
come back	■	Sally is leaving tomorrow and **coming back** on Saturday.
turn around	■	When I touched him on the shoulder, he **turned around**.

But often the second word (**on/off/out**, etc.) gives a special meaning to the verb. For example:

break down	■	Sorry I'm late. The car **broke down**. (= the engine stopped working)
take off	■	It was my first flight. I was nervous as the plane **took off**. (= went into the air)
run out	■	We don't have any more milk. We **ran out**. (= used it all)
get along	■	My brother and I **get along** well. (= are friendly with each other)
get by	■	My French isn't very good, but it's enough to **get by**. (= manage)

For more phrasal verbs, see Units 135–142.

B

Sometimes a phrasal verb is followed by a *preposition*. For example:

Phrasal Verb	*Preposition*		
run away	from	■	Why did you **run away from** me?
keep up	with	■	You're walking too fast. I can't **keep up with** you.
look up	at	■	We **looked up at** the plane as it flew above us.
look forward	to	■	Are you **looking forward to** the weekend?
get along	with	■	Do you **get along with** your boss?

C

Sometimes a phrasal verb has an *object*. Usually there are two possible positions for the object. So you can say:

I **turned on** the light.   *or*   I **turned** the light **on**.
     object   *object*

If the object is a *pronoun* (**it/them/me/him**, etc.), only one position is possible:

I **turned** it **on**. (*not* I turned on it)

Some more examples:

■ Could you { **fill out** this form? / **fill** this form **out**? }

but   They gave me a form and told me to **fill it out**. (*not* fill out it)

■ Don't { **throw away** this postcard. / **throw** this postcard **away**. }

but   I want to keep this postcard, so don't **throw it away**. (*not* throw away it)

■ I'm going to { **take off** my shoes. / **take** my shoes **off**. }

but   These shoes are uncomfortable. I'm going to **take them off**. (*not* take off them)

■ Don't { **wake up** the baby. / **wake** the baby **up**. }

but   The baby is asleep. Don't **wake her up**. (*not* wake up her)

Exercises

134.1 Complete each sentence using a verb from A (in the correct form) + a word from B. You can use a word more than once.

A **fly   get   go   look   run   sit**   B **around   away   by   down   on   out   up**

1. The bus was full. We couldn't __get on__ .
2. I've been standing for the last two hours. I'm going to _____ for a bit.
3. A cat tried to catch the bird, but the bird _____ just in time.
4. We were trapped in the building. We couldn't _____ .
5. "Did you get fish at the store?" "I couldn't. They had _____ ."
6. "Do you speak German?" "Not very well, but I can _____ ."
7. The cost of living is higher now. Prices have _____ a lot.
8. I thought there was somebody behind me, but when I _____ , there was nobody there.

134.2 Complete the sentences using a word from A and a word from B. You can use a word more than once.

A **along   away   back   forward   in   up**   B **at   through   to   with**

1. You're walking too fast. I can't keep __up with__ you.
2. My vacation is nearly over. Next week I'll be _____ work.
3. We went _____ the top floor of the building to admire the view.
4. Are you looking _____ the party next week?
5. There was a bank robbery last week. The robbers got _____ $50,000.
6. I love to look _____ the stars in the sky at night.
7. I was sitting in the kitchen when suddenly a bird flew _____ the open window.
8. "Why did Sally quit her job?" "She didn't get _____ her co-workers."

134.3 Complete the sentences using the following verbs + *it/them/me*:

   ~~fill out~~   get out   give back   turn on   take off   wake up

1. They gave me a form and told me to __fill it out__ .
2. I'm going to bed now. Can you _____ at 6:30?
3. I've got something in my eye and I can't _____ .
4. I don't like it when people borrow things and don't _____ .
5. I want to use the heater. How do I _____ ?
6. My shoes are dirty. I'd better _____ before going into the house.

134.4 Use your own ideas to complete the sentences. Use a noun (*this newspaper*, etc.) or a pronoun (*it/them*, etc.) + the word in parentheses (*away/up*, etc.).

1. Don't throw __away this newspaper__ . I want to read it. (away)
2. "Do you want this postcard?" "No, you can throw __it away__ ." (away)
3. I borrowed these books from the library. I have to take _____ tomorrow. (back)
4. We can turn _____ . Nobody is watching it. (off)
5. *A*: How did the vase get broken?
   B: Unfortunately, I knocked _____ while I was cleaning. (over)
6. Shh! My mother is asleep. I don't want to wake_____ . (up)
7. It's pretty cold. You should put _____ if you're going out. (on)
8. It was only a small fire. I was able to put _____ easily. (out)
9. I took _____ because they were uncomfortable and my feet were hurting. (off)
10. It's a little dark in this room. Should I turn _____ ? (on)

Phrasal Verbs 2   in/out

A

Compare **in** and **out**:

in = into a room, a building, a car, etc.
- How did the thieves **get in**?
- Here's a key, so you can **let yourself in**.
- Sally walked up to the edge of the pool and **dived in**. (= into the water)
- I've got a new apartment. I'm **moving in** on Friday.
- As soon as I got to the airport, I **checked in**.

In the same way, you can say **go in**, **come in**, **walk in**, **break in**, etc.

Compare **in** and **into**:
- I'm moving **in** next week.
- I'm moving **into my new apartment** on Friday.

out = out of a room, a building, a car, etc.
- He just stood up and **walked out**.
- I had no key, so I was **locked out**.
- She swam up and down the pool, and then **climbed out**.
- Tim opened the window and **looked out**.
- *(at a hotel)* What time do we have to **check out**?

In the same way you can say **go out**, **get out**, **move out**, **let** somebody **out**, etc.

Compare **out** and **out of**:
- He walked **out**.
- He walked **out of the room**.

B

Other verbs + **in**

drop in = *visit somebody for a short time*
- I **dropped in** to see Chris on my way home.

join in = *take part in an activity that is already going on*
- We're playing a game. Why don't you **join in**?

plug in an electrical machine = *connect it to the electricity supply*
- The fridge isn't working because you haven't **plugged** it **in**.

hand in / turn in homework, a report, a resignation, etc. = *give something written to a teacher, boss, etc.*
- Your report is due this week. Please **hand** it **in** by Friday at 3 p.m.

fit in = *feel you belong or are accepted by a group*
- Some children have trouble **fitting in** at a new school.

plug in

C

Other verbs + **out**

eat out = *eat at a restaurant, not at home*
- There wasn't anything to eat at home, so we decided to **eat out**.

drop out of college / school / a course / a race = *stop before you have completely finished a course/race, etc.*
- Gary went to college but **dropped out** after a year.

get out of something that you arranged to do = *avoid doing it*
- I promised I'd go to the wedding. I don't want to go, but I can't **get out** of it now.

cut something **out** (of a newspaper, etc.)
- There was a beautiful picture in the magazine, so I **cut** it **out** and kept it.

leave something **out** = *omit it, not include it*
- In the sentence "She said that she was sick," you can **leave out** the word "that."

fill out a form, a questionnaire, etc. = *write the necessary information on a form*
- I have to **fill out** this application by the end of the week.

Exercises

135.1 Complete each sentence using a verb in the correct form.

1. Here's a key so that you can ___let___ yourself in.
2. Liz doesn't like cooking, so she _____ out a lot.
3. Eva isn't living in this apartment anymore. She _____ out a few weeks ago.
4. If you're in our part of town, you should _____ in and see us.
5. When I _____ in at the airport, I was told my flight was delayed.
6. There were some advertisements in the paper that I wanted to keep, so I _____ them out.
7. I wanted to iron some clothes, but there was nowhere to _____ the iron in.
8. Everyone else at the party was dressed up. In my jeans, I didn't _____ in.
9. Throw this away. I don't have time to _____ out useless questionnaires.
10. Sue is going to _____ in her essay a week early in order to be free next weekend.
11. Soup isn't very tasty if you _____ out the salt.
12. Paul started taking a Spanish class, but he _____ out after a few weeks.

135.2 Complete the sentences with *in*, *into*, *out*, or *out of*.

1. I've got a new apartment. I'm moving __in__ on Friday.
2. We checked _____ the hotel as soon as we arrived.
3. As soon as we arrived at the hotel, we checked _____ .
4. The car stopped and the driver got _____ .
5. Thieves broke _____ the house while we were away.
6. Why did Sarah drop _____ college? Did she fail her exams?

135.3 Complete each sentence using a verb + *in* or *out (of)*.

1. Sally walked to the edge of the pool, ___dived in___ , and swam to the other end.
2. Not all the runners finished the race. Three of them _____ .
3. I went to see Joe and Sue in their new house. They _____ last week.
4. I've told you everything you need to know. I don't think I've _____ anything.
5. Some people in the crowd started singing. Then a few more people _____ , and soon everybody was singing.
6. We go to restaurants a lot. We like _____ .
7. Sam is still new at the job, but his co-workers already like him. Everyone agrees that he _____ well.
8. I _____ to see Laura a few days ago. She was fine.
9. *A:* Can we meet tomorrow morning at 10:00?
   B: Probably. I'm supposed to go to another meeting, but I think I can _____ it.

135.4 Complete the sentences. Use the word in parentheses in the correct form.

1. *A:* The fridge isn't working.
   B: That's because you haven't ___plugged it in___ . (plug)
2. *A:* What do I have to do with these forms?
   B: _____ and send them to this address. (fill)
3. *A:* Your book report is better than mine, but you got a lower grade.
   B: That's because I _____ late. (hand)
4. *A:* Don't you usually put nuts in these cookies?
   B: This time I _____ because Jill is allergic to them. (leave)
5. *A:* Have you been to that new club on Bridge Street?
   B: We wanted to go there a few nights ago, but the doorman wouldn't _____ because we weren't members. (let)

Phrasal Verbs 3   out

A

out = not burning, not shining

go out	■ Suddenly all the lights in the building **went out**.
put out a fire / a cigarette / a light	■ We managed to **put** the fire **out**.
turn out a light	■ I **turned** the lights **out** before leaving.
blow out a candle	■ We don't need the candle. You can **blow it out**.

B

work out

work out = *do physical exercises*
- ■ Rachel **works out** at the gym three times a week.

work out = *develop, progress*
- ■ Good luck for the future. I hope everything **works out** well for you.
- ■ *A:* Why did James leave the company?
  B: Things didn't **work out**. (= things didn't work out well)

work out a problem / difficulties, etc. = *solve, put right*
- ■ The family has been having some problems, but I'm sure they'll **work** things **out**.

work out a plan / an agreement / a contract, etc. = *produce a plan, etc.*
- ■ The two sides in the conflict are trying to **work out** a peace plan.

C

Other verbs + **out**

carry out an order / an experiment / a survey / an investigation / a plan, etc.
- ■ Soldiers are expected to **carry out** orders.
- ■ An investigation into the accident will be **carried out** as soon as possible.

figure out something/somebody = *understand*
- ■ Can you help me **figure out** why my answer to this math problem is wrong?
- ■ Why did Erica do that? I can't **figure** her **out**.

find out that/what/when . . . , etc., **find out about** something = *get information*
- ■ The police never **found out** who committed the murder.
- ■ I just **found out** that it's Helen's birthday today.
- ■ I went online to **find out about** hotels in the town.

hand/**give** things **out** = *give to each person*
- ■ At the end of the lecture, the speaker **handed out** information sheets to the audience.

point something **out** (**to** somebody) = *draw attention to something*
- ■ As we drove through the city, our guide **pointed out** all the sights.
- ■ I didn't realize I'd made a mistake until somebody **pointed** it **out to** me.

run out (**of** something) = *use all of something*
- ■ We **ran out of** gas on the freeway. (= we used all our gas)

turn out to be . . . / **turn out** good/nice, etc. / **turn out** that . . .
- ■ Nobody believed Paul at first, but he **turned out** to be right.
  (= it became clear in the end that he was right)
- ■ The weather wasn't so good in the morning, but it **turned out** nice later.
- ■ I thought they knew each other, but it **turned out** that they'd never met.

try out a machine, a system, a new idea, etc. = *test it to see if it is OK*
- ■ The company is **trying out** a new computer system at the moment.

Exercises

136.1 Which words can go together? Choose from the list.

> a candle   a campfire   ~~a light~~   a problem   a mistake   a new product   an order

1. turn out _a light_
2. point out _____
3. blow out _____
4. carry out _____

5. put out _____
6. try out _____
7. work out _____

136.2 Complete each sentence using a verb + *out*.

1. The company is __*trying out*__ a new computer system at the moment.
2. Steve is in shape. He plays a lot of sports and _____ regularly.
3. The road will be closed for two days next week while repairs are _____ .
4. We didn't manage to discuss everything at the meeting. We _____ of time.
5. My father helped me _____ a plan to save money.
6. I called the station to _____ what time the train arrived.
7. The new drug will be _____ on a small group of patients.
8. I thought the two books were the same until a friend of mine _____ the difference.
9. They got married a few years ago, but it didn't _____ , and they separated.
10. There was a power outage and all the lights _____ .
11. We thought she was American at first, but she _____ to be Swedish.
12. I haven't been able to _____ how the water is getting into the house.
13. I haven't applied for the job yet. I want to _____ more about the company first.
14. It took the fire department two hours to _____ the fire.

136.3 For each picture, complete the sentence using a verb + *out*.

1. *8:01 p.m.*   *8:02 p.m.*
The lights have _gone out_ .

2. The man with a beard is _____ _____ leaflets.

3. *earlier*   *now*
The weather has _____ _____ .

4. Sally   Kim
Sally and Kim are _____ _____ at the gym.

5. Joe
Joe has _____ of water.

6. Lisa
Lisa is trying to _____ how to _____ .

136.4 Complete the sentences. Each time use a verb + *out*.

1. *A:* Do we still need the candle?
   B: No, you can __*blow it out*__ .
2. *A:* This recipe looks interesting.
   B: Yes, let's _____
3. *A:* Jason is strange. I'm not sure I like him.
   B: I agree. I can't _____
4. *A:* You realize that tomorrow's a holiday, don't you?
   B: No, I completely forgot. Thanks for _____ to me.

Phrasal Verbs 4   on/off (1)

A   **on** and **off** for lights, machines, etc.

> We say: the light **is on** / **put** the light **on** / **leave** the light **on**, etc.
>   **turn** the light **on/off**   *or*   **shut** the light **off**
> ■   Should I **leave** the lights **on** or **turn** them **off**?
> ■   "**Is** the heat **on**?" "No, I **shut** it **off**."
> ■   Who **left** the computer **on**?
>
> *Also* **put on** some music / a CD / a DVD, etc.
> ■   "What's this CD like?" "It's great. Should I **put** it **on**?"

B   **on** and **off** for events, etc.

> **go on** = *happen*
> ■   What's all that noise? What's **going on**? (= what's happening)
> **call** something **off** = *cancel it*
> ■   The open air concert had to be **called off** because of the weather.
> **put** something **off**, **put off** doing something = *delay it*
> ■   The wedding has been **put off** until January.
> ■   We can't **put off** making a decision. We have to decide now.

C   **on** and **off** for clothes, etc.

> **put on** clothes, glasses, makeup, a seat belt, etc.
> ■   My hands were cold, so I **put** my gloves **on**.
> *Also* **put on** weight = *get heavier*
> ■   I've **put on** five pounds in the last month.
> **try on** clothes (to see if they fit)
> ■   I **tried on** a jacket in the store, but it didn't fit me very well.
> **have** something **on** = *be wearing (clothes, jewelery, perfume, etc.)*
> ■   I like the perfume you **had on** yesterday.
> **take off** clothes, glasses, etc.
> ■   It was warm, so I **took off** my jacket.

D   **off** = away from a person or place

> **be off** (to a place)
> ■   Tomorrow I**'m off** to Paris / I**'m off** to the store.
>   (= I'm going to Paris / I'm going shopping)
> **walk off** / **run off** / **drive off** / **ride off** / **go off** (similar to **walk away** / **run away**, etc.)
> ■   Diane got on her bike and **rode off**.
> ■   Mark left home at the age of 18 and **went off** to Canada.
> **take off** = *leave the ground (for planes)*
> ■   After a long delay the plane finally **took off**.
> **see** somebody **off** = *go with them to the airport/station to say goodbye*
> ■   Helen was going away. We went to the station with her to **see her off**.

Exercises

137.1 Complete the sentences using **put on** + the following:

~~a CD~~   a DVD   the heat   the light   the radio

1. I wanted to listen to some music, so I ___put a CD on___ .
2. It was getting cold, so I _____ .
3. I wanted to hear the news, so I _____ .
4. It was getting dark, so I _____ .
5. I wanted to watch a movie, so I _____ .

137.2 Complete the sentences. Each time use a verb + **on** or **off**.

1. It was warm, so I ___took off___ my jacket.
2. What are all these people doing? What's _____ ?
3. The weather was too bad for the plane to _____ , so the flight was delayed.
4. I didn't want to be disturbed, so I _____ my cell phone.
5. Rachel got into her car and _____ at high speed.
6. Tim has _____ weight since I last saw him. He used to be quite thin.
7. The clothes Bill _____ weren't warm enough so he borrowed my jacket.
8. Don't _____ until tomorrow what you can do today.
9. There was going to be a strike by bus drivers, but now they have been offered more money and the strike has been _____ .
10. Are you cold? Should I get you a sweater to _____ ?
11. When I go away, I prefer to be alone at the station or airport. I don't like it when people come to _____ me _____ .

137.3 Look at the pictures and complete the sentences.

1. Her hands were cold, so she ___put her gloves on___ .

2. The plane _____ at 10:55.

3. Maria _____ , but it was too big for her.

4. The game _____ because of the weather.

5. Bye!
   Mark
   Mark's parents went to the airport to _____ .

6. He took his sunglasses out of his pocket and _____ .

A   Verb + **on** = continue doing something

drive on / **walk on** / **play on** = *continue walking/driving/playing, etc.*
- Should we stop at this gas station or should we **drive on** to the next one?

go on = *continue*
- The party **went on** until 4 o'clock in the morning.

go on doing something = *continue doing something*
- We can't **go on** spending money like this. We'll have nothing left soon.

Also **go on with** something
- Don't let me disturb you. Please **go on with** what you were doing.

keep on doing something = *do it continuously or repeatedly*
- He **keeps on** criticizing me. I'm really tired of it!

drag on = *continue for too long*
- Let's make a decision now. I don't want this problem to **drag on**.

B   Other verbs + **on**

hold on / **hang on** = *wait*
- (on the phone) **Hold on** a minute. I'll see if Max is home.

move on = *start a new activity, start talking about a new topic*
- (in a lecture) That's enough about the political situation. Let's **move on** to the economy.

take on a job / extra work / a responsibility = *accept it and do what is necessary*
- When Sally was sick, a friend **took on** her work at the office.

C   Verb + **off**

doze off / **drop off** / **nod off** = *fall asleep*
- The lecture wasn't very interesting. In fact, I **dozed off** in the middle of it.

drop somebody/something **off** = *take to a place by car and leave there*
- Sue **drops** her children **off** at school before she goes to work every morning.

go off = *explode*
- A bomb **went off** in a hotel downtown, but fortunately nobody was hurt.

Also an alarm can **go off** (= *ring*)
- Did you hear the alarm **go off**?

lay someone **off** = *stop employing someone because there isn't enough work*
- My brother was **laid off** two months ago and still hasn't found another job.

rip somebody **off** = *cheat somebody (informal)*
- Did you really pay $2,000 for that painting? I think you were **ripped off**. (= you paid too much)

show off = *try to impress people with your ability, your knowledge, etc.*
- Look at that boy on the bike riding with no hands. He's just **showing off**.

tell somebody **off** = *speak angrily to somebody because they did something wrong*
- Claire's mother **told** her **off** for wearing dirty shoes in the house.

Exercises

138.1 Change the <u>underlined</u> words. Keep the same meaning, but use a verb + **on** or **off**.

1. Did you hear the bomb <u>explode</u>?
   Did you hear the bomb ___go off___ ?
2. The meeting <u>continued</u> longer than I expected.
   The meeting _____ longer than I expected.
3. We didn't stop to rest. We <u>continued walking</u>.
   We didn't stop to rest. We _____ .
4. I <u>fell asleep</u> while I was watching TV.
   I _____ while I was watching TV.
5. Gary doesn't want to retire. He wants to <u>continue working</u>.
   Gary doesn't want to retire. He wants to _____ .
6. The fire alarm <u>rang</u> in the middle of the night.
   The fire alarm _____ in the middle of the night.
7. Martin <u>calls me continuously</u>. It's very annoying.
   Martin _____ . It's very annoying.

138.2 Complete each sentence using a verb + **on** or **off**.

1. We can't __go on__ spending money like this. We'll have nothing left soon.
2. I was standing by the car when suddenly the alarm _____ .
3. I _____ my clothes at the laundry and then I went shopping.
4. *A:* Michael seems very busy at the office these days.
   B: Yes, he has _____ too much extra work, I think.
5. Bill paid too much for the car he bought. I think he was _____ .
6. As time _____ , I feel less and less upset about what happened.
7. I was very tired at work today. I nearly _____ at my desk a couple of times.
8. Ben was _____ by his boss for being late for work repeatedly.
9. If business doesn't improve, my company may have to _____ some employees.
10. There was a very loud noise. It sounded like a bomb _____ .
11. I _____ making the same mistake. It's very frustrating.
12. Please _____ with what you were saying. I'm sorry I interrupted you.
13. Peter is always trying to impress people. He's always _____ .
14. "Are you ready to go yet?" "Almost. Can you _____ just a while longer?"

138.3 Complete the sentences. Use the following verbs (in the correct form) + **on** or **off**. Sometimes you will need other words as well.

> drag   go   go   ~~hold~~   lay   move   rip   tell

1. *A: (on the phone)* May I speak to Mrs. Jones?
   B: __Hold on__ a second. I'll get her for you.
2. *A:* Are you still working on that project? I can't believe it isn't finished.
   B: I know. I'm fed up with it. It's really _____ .
3. *A:* We took a taxi to the airport. It cost forty dollars.
   B: Forty dollars! Normally it costs about twenty dollars. You _____ .
4. *A:* Why were you late for work this morning?
   B: I overslept. My alarm clock didn't _____ .
5. *A:* Have we discussed this point enough?
   B: I think so. Let's _____ to the next point on our agenda.
6. *A:* There won't be any more interruptions. I've turned off my phone.
   B: Good. Let's _____ what we were doing.
7. *A:* Some children at the next table in the restaurant were behaving very badly.
   B: Why didn't their parents _____ ?
8. *A:* Why did Paul quit his job?
   B: He didn't quit. He was _____ .

Phrasal Verbs 6   **up/down**

A

Compare **up** and **down**:

put something **up** (on a wall, etc.)
- I **put** some pictures **up** on the wall.

pick something **up**
- There was a letter on the floor. I **picked** it **up** and looked at it.

stand up
- Alan **stood up** and walked out.

turn something **up**
- I can't hear the TV. Can you **turn** it **up** a little?

take something **down** (from a wall, etc.)
- I didn't like the picture, so I **took** it **down**.

put something **down**
- I stopped writing and **put down** my pen.

sit down / bend down / lie down
- I **bent down** to tie my shoes.

turn something **down**
- The oven is too hot. **Turn** it **down** to 325 degrees.

B

Tear down, **cut down**, etc.

tear down a building / **cut down** a tree / **blow** something **down**
- Some old houses were **torn down** to make room for the new shopping mall.
- *A:* Why did you **cut down** the tree in your yard?
  B: I didn't. It was **blown down** in the storm last week.

burn down = *be destroyed by fire*
- They were able to put out the fire before the house **burned down**.

C

Down = becoming or having less

slow down = *go more slowly*
- You're driving too fast. **Slow down**.

calm somebody **down** = *become calmer, make somebody calmer*
- **Calm down**. There's no point in getting mad.

cut down (**on** something) = *eat, drink, or do something less often*
- I'm trying to **cut down on** coffee. I drink too much of it.

D

Other verbs + **down**

break down = *stop working (for machines, cars)*
- The car **broke down** and I had to call for help.

Also discussions, talks, etc. can **break down** (= *fail*)
- Talks between the two groups **broke down** without a solution being reached. (= the talks failed)

close down = *stop doing business*
- There used to be a shop on this street; it **closed down** a few years ago.

let somebody **down** = *disappoint somebody because you didn't do what they hoped*
- You can always rely on Pete. He'll never **let** you **down**.

turn somebody/something **down** = *refuse an application, an offer, etc.*
- I applied for several jobs, but I was **turned down** for all of them.
- Rachel was offered the job, but she decided to **turn** it **down**.

write something **down** = *write something on paper because you may need the information later*
- I can't remember Tim's address. I **wrote** it **down**, but I can't find it.

Exercises

139.1 Complete the sentences. Use the following verbs (in the correct form) + *up* or *down*:

calm   let   put   ~~take~~   turn   turn

1. I don't like this picture on the wall. I'm going to ___take it down___ .
2. The music is too loud. Can you _____ ?
3. David was very angry. I tried to _____ .
4. I've bought some new curtains. Can you help me _____ ?
5. I promised I would help Anna. I don't want to _____ .
6. I was offered the job, but I decided I didn't want it. So I _____ .

139.2 For each picture, complete the sentences using a verb + *up* or *down*. In most sentences, you will need other words as well.

1. | 2. before   now | 3. | 4.
5. BUS STOP | 6. | 7. Sarah 555-3521 | 8. Liz

1. There used to be a tree in front of the house, but we ___cut it down___ .
2. There used to be some shelves on the wall, but I _____ .
3. The ceiling was so low, he couldn't _____ straight.
4. She couldn't hear the radio very well, so she _____ .
5. While they were waiting for the bus, they _____ on the ground.
6. A lot of trees _____ in the storm last week.
7. Sarah gave me her phone number. I _____ on a piece of paper.
8. Liz dropped her keys, so she _____ and _____ .

139.3 Complete each sentence using a verb (in the correct form) + *down*.

1. I stopped writing and ___put down___ my pen.
2. I was really upset. It took me a long time to _____ .
3. The train _____ as it approached the station.
4. Sarah applied for medical school, but she _____ .
5. Our car is very reliable. It has never _____ .
6. I need to spend less money. I'm going to _____ on things I don't really need.
7. I didn't play very well. I felt that I had _____ the other players on the team.
8. The shop _____ because it was losing money.
9. This is a very ugly building. Many people would like it to _____ .
10. I don't understand why you _____ the chance to work abroad for a year. It would have been a great experience.
11. Unfortunately, the house _____ before the fire department got there, but no one was hurt.
12. The strike is going to continue. Talks between the two sides have _____ without agreement.

Phrasal Verbs 7   up (1)

A

go up / **come up** / **walk up** (**to** . . .) = *approach*
- A man **came up to** me in the street and asked me for money.

catch up (**with** somebody) = *move faster than somebody in front of you so that you reach them*
- I'm not ready to go yet. You go on and I'll **catch up with** you.

keep up (**with** somebody) = *continue at the same speed or level*
- You're walking too fast. I can't **keep up** (**with** you).
- You're doing well. **Keep** it **up**!

B

set up an organization, a company, a business, a system, a Web site, etc. = *start it*
- The government has **set up** a committee to investigate the problem.

take up a hobby, a sport, an activity, etc. = *start doing it*
- Laura **took up** photography a few years ago. She takes really good pictures.

C

grow up = *become an adult*
- Sara was born in Mexico but **grew up** in the United States.

bring up a child = *raise, look after a child*
- Her parents died when she was a child, so she was **brought up** by her grandparents.

D

back up

back someone **up** = *support someone*
- Will you **back** me **up** if I tell the police what happened? (= say I'm telling the truth)

back up computer files = *make a copy*
- You've spent a long time on that document; you'd better **back up** your files.

back up a car = *go backward*
- I couldn't turn around in the narrow street. I had to **back** the car **up** for a block.

Also traffic can **back up** (= stop moving)
- Cars are **backed up** for a mile at the entrance to the stadium.

E

end up somewhere, **end up** doing something, etc.
- There was a fight in the street and three men **ended up** in the hospital.
  (= that's what happened to these men in the end)
- I couldn't find a hotel and **ended up** sleeping on a bench at the station.
  (= that's what happened to me in the end)

give up = *stop trying*, **give** something **up** = *stop doing it*
- Don't **give up**. Keep trying!
- Ted failed his driving test at age 80, so he had to **give up** driving. (= stop doing it)

make up something / be **made up of** something
- Children under 16 **make up** half the population of the city.
  (= half the population are children under 16)
- Air is **made up** mainly **of** nitrogen and oxygen. (= air consists of . . .)

take up space or time = *use space or time*
- Most of the space in the room was **taken up** by a large table.

turn up / **show up** = *arrive, appear*
- We arranged to meet Dave last night, but he didn't **turn up**.

use something **up** = *use all of it so that nothing is left*
- I'm going to make some soup. I want to **use up** the vegetables I have.

Exercises

140.1 Look at the pictures and complete the sentences. Use <u>three</u> words each time, including a verb from Section A.

1.

   Can you tell me . . .?

   A man __*came up to*__ me in the street and asked me the way to the station.

2.

   Sue

   Sue _____ the front door of the house and rang the doorbell.

3. Tom   Tom

   Tom was a long way behind the other runners, but he managed to _____ them.

4. Tanya

   Paul

   Tanya was running too fast for Paul. He couldn't _____ her.

140.2 Complete the sentences. Use the following verbs (in the correct form) + **up**:

back   ~~end~~   end   give   give   grow   make   take   take   turn   use

1. I couldn't find a hotel and __*ended up*__ sleeping on a bench at the station.
2. I'm feeling very tired now. I've _____ all my energy.
3. I hadn't _____ my files and my computer crashed. I lost everything I was working on.
4. People often ask children what they want to be when they _____ .
5. We invited Tim to the party, but he didn't _____ .
6. Two years ago Mark _____ his studies to be a professional basketball player.
7. *A:* Do you play any sports?
   B: Not right now, but I'm thinking of _____ tennis.
8. You don't have enough determination. You _____ too easily.
9. Karen traveled a lot for a few years and _____ in Canada, where she still lives.
10. I do a lot of gardening. It _____ most of my free time.
11. There are two universities in the city, and students _____ 20 percent of the population.

140.3 Complete the sentences. Use the following verbs + **up** (with any other necessary words):

back   back   bring   ~~catch~~   ~~give~~   go   keep   keep   make   set

1. Sue was on the volleyball team, but she got injured and had to __*give it up*__ .
2. I'm not ready yet. You go on and I'll __*catch up with*__ you.
3. Helen has her own Web site. A friend of hers helped her to _____ .
4. Steven is having problems at school. He can't _____ the rest of the class.
5. Although I _____ in the country, I have always preferred cities.
6. Our team started the game well, but we couldn't _____ , and in the end we lost.
7. Traffic has been _____ on this road for an hour. Is there another way to go?
8. I saw Mike at the party, so I _____ him and said hello.
9. When I was on my trip, I joined a tour group. The group _____ two Americans, three Germans, five Italians, and myself.
10. "I agree with your solution and will give you my support." "Thanks for _____ ."

Phrasal Verbs 8 up (2)

A

bring up a topic, etc. = *introduce it in a conversation*
- I don't want to hear any more about this issue. Please don't **bring** it **up** again.

come up = *be introduced in a conversation*
- Some interesting issues **came up** in our discussion yesterday.

come up with an idea, a suggestion, etc. = *produce an idea*
- Sarah is very creative. She's always **coming up with** new ideas.

make something **up** = *invent something that is not true*
- What Kevin told you about himself wasn't true. He **made** it all **up**.

B

cheer up = *be happier*, **cheer** somebody **up** = *make somebody feel happier*
- You look so sad! **Cheer up**!
- Helen is depressed these days. What can we do to **cheer** her **up**?

save up for something / to do something = *save money to buy something*
- Dan is **saving up** for a trip around the world.

clear up = *become bright (for weather)*
- It was raining when I got up, but it **cleared up** during the morning.

C

blow up = *explode*, **blow** something **up** = *destroy it with a bomb, etc.*
- The engine caught fire and **blew up**.
- The bridge was **blown up** during the war.

tear something **up** = *tear it into pieces*
- I didn't read the letter. I just **tore** it **up** and threw it away.

beat somebody **up** = *hit someone repeatedly so that they are badly hurt*
- A friend of mine was attacked and **beaten up** a few days ago. He was badly hurt and had to go to the hospital.

D

break up / split up (with somebody) = *separate*
- I'm surprised to hear that Sue and Paul have **split up**. They seemed very happy together the last time I saw them.

clean something **up** = *make it clean, neat, etc.*
- Look at this mess! Who is going to **clean** it **up**?

fix up a building, a room, a car, etc. = *repair and improve it*
- I love how you've **fixed up** this room. It looks so much nicer.

look something **up** in a dictionary/encyclopedia, etc.
- If you don't know the meaning of a word, you can **look** it **up** in a dictionary.

put up with something = *tolerate it*
- We live on a busy road, so we have to **put up with** a lot of noise from the traffic.

hold up a person, a plan, etc. = *delay*
- Don't wait for me. I don't want to **hold** you **up**.
- Plans to build a new factory have been **held up** because of the company's financial problems.

mix up people/things, **get** people/things **mixed up** = *you think one is the other*
- The two brothers look very similar. Many people **mix** them **up**.
  (*or* . . . **get** them **mixed up**)

Exercises

141.1 Which goes with which?

1. I'm going to tear up	A a new camera
2. Jane came up with	B a lot of bad weather
3. Paul is always making up	C the two medicines
4. Be careful not to mix up	D an interesting suggestion
5. I don't think you should bring up	E excuses
6. I'm saving up for	F ~~the letter~~
7. We had to put up with	G that subject

1. _F_
2. _____
3. _____
4. _____
5. _____
6. _____
7. _____

141.2 Look at the pictures and complete the sentences. You will need two or three words each time.

1. *this morning* / *now*
The weather was horrible this morning, but it's ___cleared up___ now.

2. Linda / Sorry I'm late.
Linda was late because she was _____ by the traffic.

3. They bought an old house and _____ _____. It's really nice now.

4. Pete / Come out to dinner with us!
Pete was really depressed. We took him out for dinner to _____ .

141.3 Complete the sentences. Each time use a verb (in the correct form) + **up**. Sometimes you will need other words as well.

1. I love how you've ___fixed up___ this room. It looks so much nicer.
2. The ship _____ and sank. The cause of the explosion was never discovered.
3. Two men have been arrested after a man was _____ outside a restaurant last night. The injured man was taken to the hospital.
4. "Is Robert still going out with Tina?" "No, they've _____ ."
5. An interesting question _____ in class today.
6. The weather is terrible this morning, isn't it? I hope it _____ later.
7. I wanted to call Chris, but I dialed Laura's number by mistake. I got their phone numbers _____ .

141.4 Complete the sentences. Each time use a verb + **up**. Sometimes you will need other words as well.

1. Don't wait for me. I don't want to ___hold you up___ .
2. I don't know what this word means. I'll have to _____ .
3. There's nothing we can do about the problem. We'll just have to _____ it.
4. "Was that story true?" "No, I _____ ."
5. I think we should follow Tom's suggestion. Nobody has _____ a better plan.
6. I hate this photo of me. I'm going to _____ .
7. I'm trying to spend less money these days. I'm _____ a trip to Australia.
8. After the party, my place was a mess. Some friends helped me _____ .

Phrasal Verbs 9   away/back

A

Compare **away** and **back**:

away = away from home
- We're **going away** on a trip today.

away = away from a place, a person, etc.
- The woman got into her car and **drove away**.
- I tried to take a picture of the bird, but it **flew away**.
- I dropped the ticket and it **blew away** in the wind.
- The police searched the house and **took away** a computer.

In the same way you can say:
walk away, **run away**, **look away**, etc.

back = back home
- We'll **be back** in three weeks.

back = back to a place, a person, etc.
- *A:* I'm going out now.
  B: What time will you **be back**?
- After eating at a restaurant, we **walked back** to our hotel.
- I've still got Jane's keys. I forgot to **give** them **back** to her.
- When you're finished with that book, can you **put** it **back** on the shelf?

In the same way you can say:
go back, **come back**, **get back**,
take something **back**, etc.

B

Other verbs + **away**

get away = *escape, leave with difficulty*
- We tried to catch the thief, but he managed to **get away**.

get away with something = *do something wrong without being caught*
- I parked in a no-parking zone, but I **got away with** it.

keep away (**from** . . .) = *don't go near*
- **Keep away from** the edge of the pool. You might fall in.

give something **away** = *give it to somebody else because you don't want it any more*
- "Did you sell your old computer?"   "No, I **gave** it **away**."

put something **away** = *put it in the place where it is kept, usually out of sight*
- When the children had finished playing with their toys, they **put** them **away**.

throw something **away** = *put it in the garbage*
- I kept the letter, but I **threw away** the envelope.

C

Other verbs + **back**

wave back / **smile back** / **shout back** / **write back** / **hit** somebody **back**
- I waved to her and she **waved back**.

call/phone (somebody) **back** = *return a phone call*
- I can't talk to you now. I'll **call** you **back** in 10 minutes.

get back to somebody = *reply to them by phone, etc.*
- I sent him an e-mail, but he never **got back to** me.

look back (**on** something) = *think about what happened in the past*
- My first job was at a travel agency. I didn't like it very much at the time but, **looking back on** it, I learned a lot, and it was a very useful experience.

pay back money, **pay** somebody **back**
- If you borrow money, you have to **pay** it **back**.
- Thanks for lending me the money. I'll **pay** you **back** next week.

Phrasal Verbs 1 (Introduction) Unit 134

Exercises

142.1 Complete each sentence using a verb in the correct form.

1. The woman got into her car and __drove__ away.
2. Here's the money you need. _____ me back when you can.
3. Don't _____ that box away. It could be useful.
4. Jane doesn't do anything at work. I don't know how she _____ away with it.
5. I'm going out now. I'll _____ back at about 10:30.
6. You should think more about the future; don't _____ back all the time.
7. Gary is very generous. He won some money in the lottery and _____ it all away.
8. I'll _____ back to you as soon as I have the information you need.

142.2 Complete the sentences. Each time use a verb + *away* or *back*.

1. I was away all day yesterday. I __got back__ very late.
2. I haven't seen our neighbors for a while. I think they must _____ .
3. "I'm going out now." "OK. What time will you _____ ?"
4. A man was trying to break into a car. When he saw me, he _____ .
5. I smiled at him, but he didn't _____ .
6. If you cheat on the exam, you might _____ with it. But you might get caught.
7. Be careful! That's an electric fence. _____ from it.

142.3 Look at the pictures and complete the sentences.

1.  She waved to him, and he __waved back__ .	2.  It was windy. I dropped a $20 bill and it _____ .	3. Sue  Sue opened the letter, read it, and _____ in the envelope.
4.  He tried to talk to her, but she just _____ .	5. Ellie Ben  Ellie threw the ball to Ben, and he _____ .	6.  His shoes were worn out, so he _____ .

142.4 Complete the sentences. Use the verb in parentheses + *away* or *back*.

1. *A:* Do you still have my keys?
   B: No. Don't you remember? I __gave them back__ to you yesterday. (give)
2. *A:* Do you want this magazine?
   B: No, I'm finished with it. You can _____ . (throw)
3. *A:* How are your new jeans? Do they fit you OK?
   B: No, I'm going to _____ to the shop. (take)
4. *A:* Here's the money you asked me to lend you.
   B: Thanks. I'll _____ as soon as I can. (pay)
5. *A:* What happened to all the books you used to have?
   B: I didn't want them any more, so I _____ . (give)
6. *A:* Did you call Sarah?
   B: She wasn't there. I left a message asking her to _____ . (call)

APPENDIX 1
Regular and Irregular Verbs

1.1 Regular Verbs

If a verb is *regular*, the *simple past* and *past participle* end in **-ed**. For example:

Base	clean	finish	use	paint	stop	carry
Simple Past / *Past Participle*	cleaned	finished	used	painted	stopped	carried

For spelling rules, see Appendix 6.

For the *simple past* (I **cleaned** / they **finished** / she **carried**, etc.), see Unit 5.

We use the *past participle* to make the perfect tenses and all the passive forms.

Perfect tenses (**have/has/had** cleaned):
- ◼ I **have cleaned** the windows. (*present perfect* – see Units 7–9)
- ◼ They were still working. They **hadn't finished**. (*past perfect* – see Unit 14)

Passive (**is** clean**ed** / **was** clean**ed**, etc.):
- ◼ He **was carried** out of the room. (*simple past passive*) ⎱ see Units 40–42
- ◼ This gate **has** just **been painted**. (*present perfect passive*) ⎰

1.2 Irregular Verbs

When the simple past and past participle do *not* end in **-ed** (for example, **I saw / I have seen**), the verb is *irregular*.

With some irregular verbs, all three forms (*base, simple past,* and *past participle*) are the same. For example, **hit**:
- ◼ Don't **hit** me. *(base)*
- ◼ Somebody **hit** me as I came into the room. *(simple past)*
- ◼ I've never **hit** anybody in my life. *(past participle – present perfect)*
- ◼ George was **hit** on the head by a stone. *(past participle – passive)*

With other irregular verbs, the simple past is the same as the past participle (but different from the base form). For example, **tell → told**:
- ◼ Can you **tell** me what to do? *(base)*
- ◼ She **told** me to come back the next day. *(simple past)*
- ◼ Have you **told** anybody about your new job? *(past participle – present perfect)*
- ◼ I was **told** to come back the next day. *(past participle – passive)*

With other irregular verbs, all three forms are different. For example, **wake → woke/woken**:
- ◼ I'll **wake** you up. *(base)*
- ◼ I **woke** up in the middle of the night. *(simple past)*
- ◼ The baby has **woken** up. *(past participle – present perfect)*
- ◼ I was **woken** up by a loud noise. *(past participle – passive)*

1.3 List of Irregular Verbs

Base Form	Simple Past	Past Participle	Base Form	Simple Past	Past Participle
be	was/were	been	**blow**	blew	blown
beat	beat	beaten	**break**	broke	broken
become	became	become	**bring**	brought	brought
begin	began	begun	**broadcast**	broadcast	broadcast
bend	bent	bent	**build**	built	built
bet	bet	bet	**burst**	burst	burst
bite	bit	bitten	**buy**	bought	bought

Base Form	Simple Past	Past Participle
catch	caught	caught
choose	chose	chosen
come	came	come
cost	cost	cost
creep	crept	crept
cut	cut	cut
deal	dealt	dealt
dig	dug	dug
do	did	done
draw	drew	drawn
drink	drank	drunk
drive	drove	driven
eat	ate	eaten
fall	fell	fallen
feed	fed	fed
feel	felt	felt
fight	fought	fought
find	found	found
fit	fit	fit
flee	fled	fled
fly	flew	flown
forbid	forbade	forbidden
forget	forgot	forgotten
forgive	forgave	forgiven
freeze	froze	frozen
get	got	gotten
give	gave	given
go	went	gone
grow	grew	grown
hang	hung	hung
have	had	had
hear	heard	heard
hide	hid	hidden
hit	hit	hit
hold	held	held
hurt	hurt	hurt
keep	kept	kept
kneel	knelt	knelt
know	knew	known
lay	laid	laid
lead	led	led
leave	left	left
lend	lent	lent
let	let	let
lie	lay	lain
light	lit/lighted	lit/lighted
lose	lost	lost
make	made	made
mean	meant	meant
meet	met	met
pay	paid	paid
put	put	put

Base Form	Simple Past	Past Participle
quit	quit	quit
read	read [red]★	read [red]★
ride	rode	ridden
ring	rang	rung
rise	rose	risen
run	ran	run
say	said	said
see	saw	seen
seek	sought	sought
sell	sold	sold
send	sent	sent
set	set	set
sew	sewed	sewn/sewed
shake	shook	shaken
shine	shone/shined	shone/shined
shoot	shot	shot
show	showed	shown/showed
shrink	shrank	shrunk
shut	shut	shut
sing	sang	sung
sink	sank	sunk
sit	sat	sat
sleep	slept	slept
slide	slid	slid
speak	spoke	spoken
spend	spent	spent
spit	spit/spat	spit/spat
split	split	split
spread	spread	spread
spring	sprang	sprung
stand	stood	stood
steal	stole	stolen
stick	stuck	stuck
sting	stung	stung
stink	stank	stunk
strike	struck	struck
swear	swore	sworn
sweep	swept	swept
swim	swam	swum
swing	swung	swung
take	took	taken
teach	taught	taught
tear	tore	torn
tell	told	told
think	thought	thought
throw	threw	thrown
understand	understood	understood
wake	woke	woken
wear	wore	worn
weep	wept	wept
win	won	won
write	wrote	written

★ *pronunciation*

Present and Past Tenses

	Simple	Continuous
Present	**I do** *simple present* (→ Units 2–4) ■ Ann often **plays** tennis. ■ I **work** in a bank, but I **don't enjoy** it much. ■ **Do** you **like** parties? ■ It **doesn't rain** so much in summer.	**I am doing** *present continuous* (→ Units 1, 3–4) ■ "Where's Ann?" "She**'s playing** tennis." ■ Please don't disturb me now. I**'m working**. ■ Hello. **Are** you **enjoying** the party? ■ It **isn't raining** right now.
Present Perfect	**I have done** *present perfect simple* (→ Units 7–9, 11–13) ■ Ann **has played** tennis many times. ■ Where's Tom? **Have** you **seen** him this morning? ■ How long **have** you and Chris **known** each other? ■ *A:* Is it still raining? *B:* No, it **has stopped**. ■ I'm hungry. I **haven't eaten** anything since breakfast.	**I have been doing** *present perfect continuous* (→ Units 10–13) ■ Ann is tired. She **has been playing** tennis. ■ You're out of breath. **Have** you **been running**? ■ How long **have** you **been studying** English? ■ It's still raining. It **has been raining** all day. ■ I **haven't been feeling** well recently. Maybe I should go to the doctor.
Past	**I did** *simple past* (→ Units 5–6, 8–9) ■ Ann **played** tennis yesterday afternoon. ■ I **lost** my key a few days ago. ■ There was a movie on TV last night, but we **didn't watch** it. ■ What **did** you **do** when you finished work yesterday?	**I was doing** *past continuous* (→ Unit 6) ■ I saw Ann at the park yesterday. She **was playing** tennis. ■ I dropped my key when I **was trying** to open the door. ■ The television was on, but we **weren't watching** it. ■ What **were** you **doing** at this time yesterday?
Past Perfect	**I had done** *past perfect* (→ Unit 14) ■ It wasn't her first game of tennis. She **had played** many times before. ■ They couldn't get into the house because they **had lost** the key. ■ The house was dirty because I **hadn't cleaned** it for weeks.	**I had been doing** *past perfect continuous* (→ Unit 15) ■ Ann was tired last night because she **had been playing** tennis in the afternoon. ■ George decided to go to the doctor because he **hadn't been feeling** well.

For the passive, see Units 40–42.

The Future

3.1   List of future forms

▨ I**'m leaving** tomorrow.	*Present Continuous*	(Unit 18A)
▨ My train **leaves** at 9:30.	*Simple Present*	(Unit 18B)
▨ I**'m going to leave** tomorrow.	(**be**) **going to**	(Units 19, 22)
▨ I**'ll leave** tomorrow.	**will**	(Units 20–22)
▨ I**'ll be leaving** tomorrow.	*Future Continuous*	(Unit 23)
▨ I**'ll have left** by this time tomorrow.	*Future Perfect*	(Unit 23)
▨ I hope to see you before I **leave** tomorrow.	*Simple Present*	(Unit 24)

3.2   Future actions

We use the present continuous (I**'m doing**) for arrangements:
- I**'m leaving** tomorrow. I've got my plane ticket. (already planned and arranged)
- "When **are** they **getting** married?"   "On July 24."

We use the simple present (I **leave** / it **leaves**, etc.) for schedules, programs, etc.:
- My train **leaves** at 11:30. (according to the schedule)
- What time **does** the movie **start**?

We use (**be**) **going to . . .** to say what somebody has already decided to do:
- I've decided not to stay here any longer. I**'m going to leave** tomorrow.   *or*
  I**'m leaving** tomorrow.
- "Your shoes are dirty."   "Yes, I know. I**'m going to clean** them."

We use **will** (**'ll**) when we decide or agree to do something at the time of speaking:
- *A:* I don't want you to stay here any longer.
  B: OK. I**'ll leave** tomorrow. (B decides this at the time of speaking)
- That bag looks heavy. I**'ll help** you with it.
- I **won't tell** anybody what happened. I promise. (**won't** = **will not**)

3.3   Future happenings and situations

Most often we use **will** to talk about future happenings (something **will happen**) or
situations (something **will be**):
- I don't think John is happy at work. I think he**'ll leave** soon.
- This time next year I**'ll be** in Japan. Where **will** you **be**?

We use (**be**) **going to** when the situation *now* shows what **is going to happen** *in the future*:
- Look at those black clouds. It**'s going to rain**. (you can see the clouds *now*)

3.4   Future continuous and future perfect

Will be (do)**ing** = will be in the middle of (doing something):
- This time next week I'll be on vacation. I**'ll be lying** on a beach or **swimming**
  in the ocean.

We also use **will be –ing** for future actions (see Unit 23C):
- What time **will** you **be leaving** tomorrow?

We use **will have** (**done**) to say that something will already be complete before a time
in the future:
- I won't be here this time tomorrow. I**'ll have** already **left**.

3.5   We use the *present* (*not* will) after *when/if/while/before*, etc. (see Unit 24):

- I hope to see you **before** I **leave** tomorrow. (*not* before I will leave)
- **When** you **are** in New York again, come and see us. (*not* When you will be)
- **If** we **don't hurry**, we'll be late.

APPENDIX 4
Modal Verbs (can/could/will/would, etc.)

This appendix is a summary of modal verbs. For more information, see Units 25–35.

4.1 Compare *can*/*could*, etc., for actions:

can	■ I **can go** out tonight. (= there is nothing to stop me)
	■ I **can't go** out tonight.
could	■ I **could go** out tonight, but I don't feel like it.
	■ I **couldn't go** out last night. (= I wasn't able)
can *or* may	■ $\left.\begin{array}{l}\textbf{Can}\\\textbf{May}\end{array}\right\}$ I **go** out tonight? (= do you allow me)
will/won't	■ I think I**'ll go** out tonight.
	■ I promise I **won't go** out.
would	■ I **would go** out tonight, but I have too much to do.
	■ I promised I **wouldn't go** out.
should/shall	■ **Should** we **go** out tonight? (*or* **Shall** we . . .) (= do you think it is a good idea?)
should *or* ought to	■ I $\left\{\begin{array}{l}\textbf{should}\\\textbf{ought to}\end{array}\right\}$ **go** out tonight. (= it would be a good thing to do)

Compare **could have . . .** / **would have . . .** , etc.:

could	■ I **could have gone** out last night, but I decided to stay at home.
would	■ I **would have gone** out last night, but I had too much to do.
should	■ I **should have gone** out last night. I'm sorry I didn't.

4.2 We use *will*/*would*/*may*, etc., to say whether something is possible, impossible, probable, certain, etc. Compare:

will	■ "What time **will** she **be** here?" "She**'ll be** here soon."
would	■ She **would be** here now, but she's been delayed.
should *or* ought to	■ She $\left\{\begin{array}{l}\textbf{should}\\\textbf{ought to}\end{array}\right\}$ **be** here soon. (= I expect she will be here soon)
may *or* might *or* could	■ She $\left\{\begin{array}{l}\textbf{may}\\\textbf{might}\\\textbf{could}\end{array}\right\}$ **be** here now. I'm not sure. (= it's possible that she is here)
must	■ She **must be** here. I saw her come in.
	■ She **must not be** here. I've looked everywhere for her.
can't	■ She **can't be** here. I know for sure she is away on vacation.

Compare **would have . . .** / **should have . . .** , etc.:

will	■ She **will have arrived** by now. (= before now)
would	■ She **would have arrived** earlier, but she was delayed.
should	■ I wonder where she is. She **should have arrived** by now.
may *or* might *or* could	■ She $\left\{\begin{array}{l}\textbf{may}\\\textbf{might}\\\textbf{could}\end{array}\right\}$ **have arrived**. I'm not sure. (= it's possible that she has arrived)
must	■ She **must have arrived** by now. (= I'm sure – there is no other possibility)
couldn't	■ She **couldn't have arrived** yet. It's much too early. (= it's impossible)

Short forms (**I'm/you've/didn't**, etc.)

5.1 In spoken English we usually say **I'm** / **you've** / **didn't**, etc. (*short forms* or *contractions*) rather than **I am** / **you have** / **did not**, etc. We also use these short forms in informal writing (for example, a letter or message to a friend), but not in formal written English (for example, essays for school or business reports).

When we write short forms, we use an *apostrophe* (') for the missing letter(s):

I'm = I <u>am</u>   you've = you <u>have</u>   didn't = did n<u>o</u>t

5.2 List of short forms

'm = am	**I'm**						
's = is *or* has		he**'s**	she**'s**	it**'s**			
're = are					you**'re**	we**'re**	they**'re**
've = have	**I've**				you**'ve**	we**'ve**	they**'ve**
'll = will	**I'll**	he**'ll**	she**'ll**		you**'ll**	we**'ll**	they**'ll**
'd = would *or* had	**I'd**	he**'d**	she**'d**		you**'d**	we**'d**	they**'d**

's can be **is** or **has**:
- She**'s** sick. (= She **is** sick.)
- She**'s** gone away. (= She **has** gone)

but let**'s** = **let us**:
- Let**'s** go now. (= Let **us** go)

'd can be **would** or **had**:
- I**'d** see a doctor if I were you. (= I **would** see)
- I**'d** never seen her before. (= I **had** never seen)

We use some of these short forms (especially **'s**) after question words (**who/what**, etc.) and after **that/there/here**:

who**'s**   what**'s**   where**'s**   how**'s**   that**'s**   there**'s**   here**'s**   who**'ll**   there**'ll**   who**'d**
- Who**'s** that woman over there? (= who **is**)
- What**'s** happened? (= what **has**)
- Do you think there**'ll** be many people at the party? (= there **will**)

We also use short forms (especially **'s**) after a noun:
- Catherine**'s** going out tonight. (= Catherine **is**)
- My best friend**'s** just gotten married. (= My best friend **has**)

You cannot use **'m** / **'s** / **'re** / **'ve** / **'ll** / **'d** at the end of a sentence (because the verb is stressed in this position):
- "Are you tired?" "Yes, I **am**." (*not* Yes, I'm.)
- Do you know where she **is**? (*not* Do you know where she's?)

5.3 Negative short forms

isn't	(= is not)	**don't**	(= do not)	**haven't**	(= have not)
aren't	(= are not)	**doesn't**	(= does not)	**hasn't**	(= has not)
wasn't	(= was not)	**didn't**	(= did not)	**hadn't**	(= had not)
weren't	(= were not)				

can't	(= cannot)	**couldn't**	(= could not)
won't	(= will not)	**wouldn't**	(= would not)
		shouldn't	(= should not)

Negative short forms for **is** and **are** can be:

he **isn't** / she **isn't** / it **isn't**   *or*   he**'s** not / she**'s** not / it**'s** not

you **aren't** / we **aren't** / they **aren't**   *or*   you**'re** not / we**'re** not / they**'re** not

APPENDIX 6
Spelling

6.1   Nouns, verbs, and adjectives can have the following endings:

noun + **-s/-es** *(plural)*	book**s**	idea**s**	match**es**
verb + **-s/-es** (after **he/she/it**)	work**s**	enjoy**s**	wash**es**
verb + **-ing**	work**ing**	enjoy**ing**	wash**ing**
verb + **-ed**	work**ed**	enjoy**ed**	wash**ed**
adjective + **-er** *(comparative)*	cheap**er**	quick**er**	bright**er**
adjective + **-est** *(superlative)*	cheap**est**	quick**est**	bright**est**
adjective + **-ly** *(adverb)*	cheap**ly**	quick**ly**	bright**ly**

When we use these endings, there are sometimes changes in spelling. These changes are listed below.

6.2   **Nouns and verbs + -s/-es**

The ending is **-es** when the word ends in **-s/-ss/-sh/-ch/-x**:

bu**s**/bus**es**   mi**ss**/miss**es**   wa**sh**/wash**es**

mat**ch**/match**es**   sear**ch**/search**es**   bo**x**/box**es**

Note also:

potat**o**/potato**es**   tomat**o**/tomato**es**

d**o**/do**es**   g**o**/go**es**

6.3   **Words ending in -y (baby, carry, easy, etc.)**

If a word ends in a *consonant** + **-y** (**-by/-ry/-sy/-vy**, etc.)

y changes to **ie** before the ending **-s**:
   bab**y**/bab**ies**   stor**y**/stor**ies**   countr**y**/countr**ies**   secretar**y**/secretar**ies**
   hurr**y**/hurr**ies**   stud**y**/stud**ies**   appl**y**/appl**ies**   tr**y**/tr**ies**

y changes to **i** before the ending **-ed**:
   hurr**y**/hurr**ied**   stud**y**/stud**ied**   appl**y**/appl**ied**   tr**y**/tr**ied**

y changes to **i** before the endings **-er** and **-est**:
   eas**y**/eas**ier**/eas**iest**   heav**y**/heav**ier**/heav**iest**   luck**y**/luck**ier**/luck**iest**

y changes to **i** before the ending **-ly**:
   eas**y**/eas**ily**   heav**y**/heav**ily**   temporar**y**/temporar**ily**

y does *not* change before **-ing**:
   hurry**ing**   study**ing**   apply**ing**   try**ing**

y does *not* change if the word ends in a *vowel** + **-y** (**-ay/-ey/-oy/-uy**):
   pl**ay**/pl**ays**/pl**ayed**   monk**ey**/monk**eys**   enj**oy**/enj**oys**/enj**oyed**   b**uy**/b**uys**

An exception is: d**ay**/d**aily**

Note also: p**ay**/p**aid**   l**ay**/l**aid**   s**ay**/s**aid**

6.4   **Verbs ending in -ie (die, lie, tie)**

If a verb ends in **-ie**, **ie** changes to **y** before the ending **-ing**:

d**ie**/d**ying**   l**ie**/l**ying**   t**ie**/t**ying**

---

* a e i o u are *vowel* letters.
The other letters (**b c d f g**, etc.) are *consonant* letters.

6.5   Words ending in -e (hop**e**, danc**e**, wid**e**, etc.)

Verbs

If a verb ends in **-e**, we leave out **e** before the ending **–ing**:

    hop**e**/hop**ing**   smil**e**/smil**ing**   danc**e**/danc**ing**   confus**e**/confus**ing**

Exceptions are **be/being**

and verbs ending in **-ee**:   s**ee**/s**eeing**   agr**ee**/agr**eeing**

If a verb ends in **-e**, we add **–d** for the past (of regular verbs):

    hop**e**/hop**ed**   smil**e**/smil**ed**   danc**e**/danc**ed**   confus**e**/confus**ed**

Adjectives and adverbs

If an adjective ends in **-e**, we add **–r** and **–st** for the comparative and superlative:

    wid**e**/wid**er**/wid**est**   lat**e**/lat**er**/lat**est**   larg**e**/larg**er**/larg**est**

If an adjective ends in **-e**, we *keep* **e** before **–ly** in the adverb:

    polit**e**/polit**ely**   extrem**e**/extrem**ely**   absolut**e**/absolut**ely**

If an adjective ends in **-le** (sim**ple**, terri**ble**, etc.), the adverb ending is **–ply**, **–bly**, etc.:

    sim**ple**/sim**ply**   terri**ble**/terri**bly**   reasona**ble**/reasona**bly**

6.6   Doubling consonants (stop/stopping/stopped, wet/wetter/wettest, etc.)

Sometimes a word ends in *vowel + consonant*. For example:

    st**op**   pl**an**   r**ub**   b**ig**   w**et**   th**in**   pref**er**   regr**et**

Before the endings **–ing/–ed/–er/–est**, we double the consonant at the end. So **p → pp**, **n → nn**, etc. For example:

sto**p**	p **→ pp**	sto**pp**ing	sto**pp**ed
pla**n**	n **→ nn**	pla**nn**ing	pla**nn**ed
ru**b**	b **→ bb**	ru**bb**ing	ru**bb**ed
bi**g**	g **→ gg**	bi**gg**er	bi**gg**est
we**t**	t **→ tt**	we**tt**er	we**tt**est
thi**n**	n **→ nn**	thi**nn**er	thi**nn**est

If the word has more than one syllable (**prefer**, **begin**, etc.), we double the consonant at the end *only if the final syllable is stressed*:

    preFER / prefe**rr**ing / prefe**rr**ed   perMIT / permi**tt**ing / permi**tt**ed

    reGRET / regre**tt**ing / regre**tt**ed   beGIN / begi**nn**ing

If the final syllable is not stressed, we do *not* double the final consonant:

    VISit / visi**t**ing / visi**t**ed   deVELop / develo**p**ing / develo**p**ed

    HAPpen / happe**n**ing / happe**n**ed   reMEMber / remembe**r**ing / remembe**r**ed

For British spelling, see Appendix 7.

Note that

we do *not* double the final consonant if the word ends in *two* consonants (**-rt**, **-lp**, **-ng**, etc.):

    sta**rt** / starting / started   he**lp** / helping / helped   lo**ng** / longer / longest

we do *not* double the final consonant if there are *two* vowel letters before it (**-oil**, **-eed**, etc.):

    b**oil** / boiling / boiled   n**eed** / needing / needed   expl**ain** / explaining / explained

    ch**eap** / cheaper / cheapest   l**oud** / louder / loudest   qu**iet** / quieter / quietest

we do *not* double **y** or **w** at the end of words. (At the end of words **y** and **w** are not consonants.)

    sta**y** / staying / stayed   gro**w** / growing   ne**w** / newer / newest

There are a few grammatical differences between North American English and British English.

Unit	NORTH AMERICAN	BRITISH
8A–C	The *simple past* or *present perfect* can be used for new or recent happenings: ■ I **lost** my keys. **Did** you **see** them? *or* I'**ve lost** my keys. **Have** you **seen** them? ■ Sally isn't here. { She **went** out. / She'**s gone** out. The *simple past* or *present perfect* can be used with **just**, **already**, and **yet**: ■ I'm not hungry. { I **just had** lunch. / I'**ve just had** lunch. ■ *A:* What time is Mark leaving? *B:* { He **already left**. / He **has already left**. ■ **Did** you **finish** your work **yet**? *or* **Have** you **finished** your work **yet**?	The *present perfect* is more common for new or recent happenings: ■ I'**ve lost** my keys. **Have** you **seen** them? ■ Sally isn't here. She'**s gone** out. The *present perfect* is more common with **just**, **already**, and **yet**: ■ I'm not hungry. I'**ve just had** lunch. ■ *A:* What time is Mark leaving? *B:* He **has already left**. ■ **Have** you **finished** your work **yet**?
27	North American speakers use **must not** to say they feel sure something is not true: ■ Their car isn't outside their house. They **must not** be at home. ■ She walked past me without speaking. She **must not** have seen me.	British speakers usually use **can't** in these situations: ■ Their car isn't outside their house. They **can't** be at home. ■ She walked past me without speaking. She **can't** have seen me.
32	After **demand**, **insist**, etc., North American speakers use the *subjunctive*: ■ I **insisted** he **have** dinner with us.	British speakers more often use **should**, or the *simple present/past*: ■ I **insisted** that he **should have** dinner with us. *or* I **insisted** that he **had** dinner with us.
49B	North American speakers generally use **You have?** / **She isn't?**, etc.: ■ *A:* Liz isn't feeling very well today. *B:* **She isn't?** What's wrong with her?	British speakers generally use **Have you?** / **Isn't she?**, etc.: ■ *A:* Liz isn't feeling very well today. *B:* **Isn't she?** What's wrong with her?
70C, 122A	to/in **the hospital** ■ Two people were taken to **the hospital** after the accident.	to/in **hospital** (without **the**) ■ Two people were taken to **hospital** after the accident.
118A	**on the weekend** / **on weekends** ■ Will you be here **on the weekend**?	**at the weekend** / **at weekends** ■ Will you be here **at the weekend**?
121A	**in** the front / **in** the back (a group, etc.) ■ Let's sit **in** the front (of the movie theater).	**at** the front / **at** the back (a group, etc.) ■ Let's sit **at** the front (of the cinema).

Unit	NORTH AMERICAN	BRITISH
128	**different from** or **different than** ■ It was **different from/than** what I'd expected.	**different from** or **different to** ■ It was **different from/to** what I'd expected.
134A	American speakers use **around** (not usually "round"): ■ He turned **around**.	British speakers use both **round** and **around**: ■ He turned **round**. *or* He turned **around**.
134A–B	**get along** (**with** somebody) ■ Do you **get along with** your boss?	**get on** *or* **get along** (**with** somebody) ■ Do you **get on with** your boss? *or* . . . **get along with** your boss?
134C, 135C	**fill out** (a form, etc.) ■ Could you **fill out** this form?	**fill in** *or* **fill out** (a form, etc.) ■ Could you **fill in** this form? *or* . . . **fill out** this form?
139B	**tear down** (a building) ■ Some old houses were **torn down** to make room for a new shopping mall.	**knock down** (a building) ■ Some old houses were **knocked down** to make room for a new shopping mall.
141D	**fix up** (a house, etc.) ■ That old house looks great now that it has been **fixed up**.	**do up** (a house, etc.) ■ That old house looks great now that it has been **done up**.

Appendix	NORTH AMERICAN	BRITISH
1.3	The following verbs are regular in North American English: **burn** → burned **dream** → dreamed **lean** → leaned **learn** → learned **smell** → smelled **spell** → spelled **spill** → spilled **spoil** → spoiled The past participle of **get** is **gotten**: ■ Your English has **gotten** much better. (= has become much better) **Have got** (*not* gotten) means the same as **have**: ■ I**'ve got** two brothers. (= I have two brothers.)	In British English, these verbs can be regular or irregular: **burn** → burned *or* burnt **dream** → dreamed *or* dreamt **lean** → leaned *or* leant **learn** → learned *or* learnt **smell** → smelled *or* smelt **spell** → spelled *or* spelt **spill** → spilled *or* spilt **spoil** → spoiled *or* spoilt The past participle of **get** is **got**: ■ Your English has **got** much better. **Have got** = have (as in North American English): ■ I**'ve got** two brothers.
6.6	North American spelling: travel → traveling, traveled cancel → canceling, canceled	British spelling: travel → travelling, travelled cancel → cancelling, cancelled

Additional Exercises

These exercises are divided into the following sections:

Present and Past   Units 1–6, Appendix 2

1 Put the verb into the correct form: simple present (***I do***), present continuous (***I am doing***), simple past (***I did***), or past continuous (***I was doing***).

1. We can go out now. It __*isn't raining*__ (not / rain) anymore.
2. Catherine __*was waiting*__ (wait) for me when I __*arrived*__ (arrive).
3. I _____ (get) hungry. Let's go and have something to eat.
4. What _____ (you / do) in your spare time? Do you have any hobbies?
5. The weather was horrible when we _____ (arrive). It was cold and it
   _____ (rain) hard.
6. Louise usually _____ (call) me on Fridays, but she _____
   (not / call) last Friday.
7. *A:* The last time I saw you, you _____ (think) of moving to a new apartment.
   B: That's right, but in the end I _____ (decide) to stay where I was.
8. Why _____ (you / look) at me like that? What's the matter?
9. It's usually dry here at this time of the year. It _____ (not / rain) much.
10. The phone _____ (ring) three times while we _____ (have)
    dinner last night.
11. Linda was busy when we _____ (go) to see her yesterday. She
    _____ (study) for an exam. We _____ (not / want) to bother
    her, so we _____ (not / stay) very long.
12. When I _____ (tell) Tom the news, he _____ (not / believe) me at
    first. He _____ (think) that I _____ (joke).

2   Which is correct?

1. Everything is going well. We ~~didn't have~~ / <u>haven't had</u> any problems so far. (*haven't had* is correct)
2. Lisa <u>didn't go / hasn't gone</u> to work yesterday. She wasn't feeling well.
3. Look! That man over there <u>wears / is wearing</u> the same sweater as you.
4. I <u>went / have been</u> to New Zealand last year.
5. I <u>didn't hear / haven't heard</u> from Ann in the last few days. I wonder why.
6. I wonder why Jim <u>is / is being</u> so nice to me today. He isn't usually like that.
7. Jane had a book open in front of her, but she <u>didn't read / wasn't reading</u> it.
8. I wasn't very busy. I <u>didn't have / wasn't having</u> much to do.
9. <u>It begins / It's beginning</u> to get dark. Should I turn on the light?
10. After finishing high school, Tim <u>got / has got</u> a job in a factory.
11. When Sue heard the news, she <u>wasn't / hasn't been</u> very pleased.
12. This is a nice restaurant, isn't it? Is this the first time <u>you are / you've been</u> here?
13. I need a new job. <u>I'm doing / I've been doing</u> the same job for too long.
14. "Anna has gone out." "She has? What time <u>did she go / has she gone</u>?"
15. "You look tired." "Yes, <u>I've played / I've been playing</u> basketball."
16. Where <u>are you coming / do you come</u> from? Are you Australian?
17. I'd like to see Tina again. It's been a long time <u>since I saw her / that I didn't see her</u>.
18. Robert and Maria have been married <u>since 20 years / for 20 years</u>.

3   Complete each question using an appropriate verb.

1. *A:* I'm looking for Paul. <u>*Have you seen*</u> him?
   B: Yes, he was here a minute ago.
2. *A:* Why <u>*did you go*</u> to bed so early last night?
   B: Because I was very tired.
3. *A:* Where _____ ?
   B: To the post office. I want to mail these letters. I'll be back in a few minutes.
4. *A:* _____ television every night?
   B: No, only if there's something special on.
5. *A:* Your house is very beautiful. How long _____ here?
   B: Almost 10 years.
6. *A:* How was your vacation? _____ a nice time?
   B: Yes, thanks. It was great.
7. *A:* _____ Julie recently?
   B: Yes, we had lunch together a few days ago.
8. *A:* Can you describe the woman you saw? What _____ ?
   B: A red sweater and black jeans.
9. *A:* I'm sorry to keep you waiting. _____ long?
   B: No, only about 10 minutes.
10. *A:* How long _____ you to get to work in the morning?
    B: Usually about 45 minutes. It depends on the traffic.
11. *A:* _____ a horse before?
    B: No, this is the first time.
12. *A:* _____ to Mexico?
    B: No, never, but I went to Costa Rica a few years ago.

4 Use your own ideas to complete B's sentences.

1. *A:* What's the new restaurant like? Is it good?
   B: I have no idea. ___I've never been_____ there.
2. *A:* How well do you know Bill?
   B: Very well. We _____ since we were children.
3. *A:* Did you enjoy your vacation?
   B: Yes, it was fantastic. It's the best vacation _____ .
4. *A:* Is David still here?
   B: No, I'm afraid he isn't. _____ about 10 minutes ago.
5. *A:* I like your suit. I haven't seen it before.
   B: It's new. It's the first time _____ .
6. *A:* How did you cut your knee?
   B: I slipped and fell while _____ tennis.
7. *A:* Do you ever go swimming?
   B: Not these days. I haven't _____ a long time.
8. *A:* How often do you go to the movies?
   B: Hardly ever. It's been almost a year _____ to the movies.
9. *A:* I've bought some new shoes. Do you like them?
   B: Yes, they're very nice. Where _____ them?

Present and Past   Units 1–15, 107, Appendix 2

5 Put the verb into the correct form: simple past (*I did*), past continuous (*I was doing*), past
perfect (*I had done*), or past perfect continuous (*I had been doing*).

1.

Yesterday afternoon Sarah ___went___ (go) to the station to meet Paul. When she
_____ (get) there, Paul _____ (already / wait)
for her. His train _____ (arrive) early.

2.

When I got home, Bill _____ (lie) on the sofa. The television was on,
but he _____ (not / watch) it. He _____ (fall)
asleep and _____ (snore) loudly. I _____ (turn)
the television off and just then he _____ (wake) up.

3.

Last night I _____ (just / go) to bed and _____ (read) a book when suddenly I _____ (hear) a noise. I _____ (get) up to see what it was, but I _____ (not / see) anything, so I _____ (go) back to bed.

4.

Lisa had to go to Tokyo last week, but she almost _____ (miss) the plane. She _____ (stand) in line at the check-in counter when she suddenly _____ (realize) that she _____ (leave) her passport at home. Fortunately she lives near the airport, so she _____ (have) time to take a taxi home to get it. She _____ (get) back to the airport just in time for her flight.

5.

I _____ (meet) Peter and Lucy yesterday as I _____ (walk) through the park. They _____ (be) to the Sports Center where they _____ (play) tennis. They _____ (go) to a café and _____ (invite) me to join them, but I _____ (arrange) to meet another friend and _____ (not / have) time.

6 Make sentences from the words in parentheses. Put the verb into the correct form: present perfect (**I have done**), present perfect continuous (**I have been doing**), past perfect (**I had done**), or past perfect continuous (**I had been doing**).

1. Amanda is sitting on the ground. She's out of breath.
   (she / run) _She has been running._

2. Where's my bag? I left it under this chair.
   (somebody / take / it) _____

3. We were all surprised when Jenny and Andy got married last year.
   (they / only / know / each other / a few weeks)
   _____

4. It's still raining. I wish it would stop.
   (it / rain / all day) _____

5. Suddenly I woke up. I was confused and didn't know where I was.
   (I / dream) _____

ADDITIONAL EXERCISES 299

6. I wasn't hungry at lunchtime, so I didn't have anything to eat.
   (I / have / a big breakfast) _____
7. Every year Robert and Tina spend a few days at the same hotel in Hawaii.
   (they / go / there for years) _____
8. I've got a headache.
   (I / have / it / since I got up) _____
9. Next week Gary is going to run in a marathon.
   (he / train / very hard for it) _____

7 **Put the verb into the correct form.**

Julia and Kevin are old friends. They meet by chance at the train station.

Julia: Hello, Kevin. (1) _____ (I / not / see)
you in ages. How are you?

Kevin: I'm fine. How about you?
(2) _____ (you / look) good.

Julia: Thanks. So, (3) _____ (you / go) somewhere or
(4) _____ (you / meet) somebody?

Kevin: (5) _____ (I / go) to New York for a business meeting.

Julia: Oh. (6) _____ (you / travel / a lot) on business?

Kevin: Fairly often, yes. And you? Where (7) _____ (you / go)?

Julia: Nowhere. (8) _____ (I / meet) a friend. Unfortunately,
her train (9) _____ (be) delayed – (10) _____
(I / wait) here for nearly an hour.

Kevin: How are your children?

Julia: They're all fine, thanks. The youngest (11) _____ (just / start)
school.

Kevin: How (12) _____ (she / do)?
(13) _____ (she / like) it?

Julia: Yes, (14) _____ (she / think) it's great.

Kevin: (15) _____ (you / work) these days? The last time I
(16) _____ (speak) to you, (17) _____
(you / work) in a travel agency.

Julia: That's right. Unfortunately, the company (18) _____ (go) out
of business a couple of months after (19) _____ (I / start)
work there, so (20) _____ (I / lose) my job.

Kevin: And (21) _____ (you / not / have) a job since then?

Julia: Not a permanent job. (22) _____ (I / have) a few temporary
jobs. By the way, (23) _____ (you / see) Joe recently?

Kevin: Joe? He's in Canada.

Julia: Really? How long (24) _____ (he / be) in Canada?

Kevin: About a year now. (25) _____ (I / see) him a few days before
(26) _____ (he / leave). (27) _____ (he / be)
unemployed for months, so (28) _____ (he / decide) to try his
luck somewhere else. (29) _____ (he / really / look forward)
to going.

Julia: So, what (30) _____ (he / do) there?

Kevin: I have no idea. (31) _____ (I / not / hear) from him since
(32) _____ (he / leave). Anyway, I have to go – my train is
here. It was really nice to see you again.

Julia: You, too. Bye. Have a good trip.

Kevin: Thanks. Bye.

8 Put the verb into the most appropriate form.

1. Who _____ (invent) the bicycle?
2. "Do you still have that class on Wednesdays?" "No, _____ (it / end)."
3. I was the last to leave the office last night. Everybody else _____ (go) home when I _____ (leave).
4. What _____ (you / do) last weekend? _____ (you / go) away?
5. I like your car. How long _____ (you / have) it?
6. It's a shame the trip was canceled. I _____ (look) forward to it.
7. Jane is an experienced teacher. _____ (she / teach) for 15 years.
8. _____ (I / buy) a new jacket last week, but _____ (I / not / wear) it yet.
9. A few days ago _____ (I / see) a man at a party whose face _____ (be) very familiar. At first I couldn't think where _____ (I / see) him before. Then suddenly _____ (I / remember) who _____ (he / be).
10. _____ (you / hear) of Agatha Christie? _____ (she / be) a writer who _____ (die) in 1976. _____ (she / write) more than 70 detective novels. _____ (you / read) any of them?
11. *A:* What _____ (this word / mean)?
    B: I have no idea. _____ (I / never / see) it before. Look it up in the dictionary.
12. *A:* _____ (you / get) to the theater in time for the play last night?
    B: No, we were late. By the time we got there, _____ (it / already / begin).
13. I went to Sarah's room and _____ (knock) on the door, but there _____ (be) no answer. Either _____ (she / go) out or _____ (she / not / want) to see anyone.
14. Patrick asked me how to use the photocopier. _____ (he / never / use) it before, so _____ (he / not / know) what to do.
15. Liz _____ (go) for a swim after work yesterday. _____ (she / need) some exercise because _____ (she / sit) in an office all day in front of a computer.

Past Continuous and *used to*   Units 6, 17

9 Complete the sentences using the past continuous (*was/were -ing*) or *used to . . . .* Use the verb in parentheses.

1. I haven't been to the movies in ages now. We _*used to go*_ a lot. (go)
2. Ann didn't see me wave to her. She _*was looking*_ in the other direction. (look)
3. I _____ a lot, but I don't use my car very much these days. (drive)
4. I asked the taxi driver to slow down. She _____ too fast. (drive)
5. Rosemary and Jonathan met for the first time when they _____ at the same bank. (work)
6. When I was a child, I _____ a lot of bad dreams. (have)
7. I wonder what Joe is doing these days. He _____ in Spain when I last heard from him. (live)
8. "Where were you yesterday afternoon?" "I _____ volleyball." (play)
9. "Do you play any sports?" "Not these days, but I _____ volleyball." (play)
10. George looked very nice at the party. He _____ a very stylish suit. (wear)

10 What do you say to your friend in these situations? Use the words given in parentheses. Use the present continuous (*I am doing*), *going to*, or *will* (*I'll*).

1. You have made all your vacation plans. Your destination is Jamaica.
   Friend: Have you decided where you're going on vacation yet?
   You: ___I am going to Jamaica.___ (I / go)
2. You have made an appointment with the dentist for Friday morning.
   Friend: Do you want to get together on Friday morning?
   You: I can't on Friday. _____ (I / go)
3. You and some friends are planning a vacation in Mexico. You have decided to rent a car, but you haven't arranged this yet.
   Friend: How do you plan to travel around Mexico? By bus?
   You: No, _____ (we / rent)
4. Your friend has two young children. She wants to go out tomorrow night. You offer to take care of the children.
   Friend: I want to go out tomorrow night, but I don't have a babysitter.
   You: That's no problem. _____ (I / take care of)
5. You have already arranged to have lunch with Sue tomorrow.
   Friend: Are you free at lunchtime tomorrow?
   You: No, _____ (have lunch)
6. You are in a restaurant. You and your friend are looking at the menu. Maybe your friend has decided what to have. You ask her/him.
   You: What _____ ? (you / have)
   Friend: I don't know. I can't make up my mind.
7. You and a friend are reading. It's getting dark, and your friend is having trouble reading. You decide to turn on the light.
   Friend: It's getting dark, isn't it? It's difficult to read.
   You: Yes. _____ (I / turn on)
8. You and a friend are reading. It's getting dark and you decide to turn on the light. You stand up and walk toward the light switch.
   Friend: What are you doing?
   You: _____ (I / turn on)

11 Put the verb into the most appropriate form. Use a present tense (simple or continuous), *will* (*I'll*), or *shall*/*should*.

Conversation 1 *(in the morning)*

Jenny: (1) ___Are you doing___ (you / do) anything tomorrow night, Helen?
Helen: No, why?
Jenny: Well, do you feel like going to the movies? *Strangers on a Plane* is playing. I want to see it, but I don't want to go alone.
Helen: OK, (2) _____ (I / go) with you. What time
   (3) _____ (we / meet)?
Jenny: Well, the movie (4) _____ (start) at 8:45, so
   (5) _____ (I / meet) you at about 8:30 outside the theater, OK?
Helen: Fine. (6) _____ (I / see) Tina later on tonight.
   (7) _____ (I / ask) her if she wants to come, too?
Jenny: Yes, why don't you? (8) _____ (I / see) you tomorrow then. Bye.

Conversation 2 *(later the same day)*

Helen: Jenny and I (9) _____ (go) to the movies tomorrow
   night to see *Strangers on a Plane*. Why don't you come with us?
Tina: I'd love to come. What time (10) _____ (the movie / start)?
Helen: 8:45.
Tina: (11) _____ (you / meet) outside the theater?
Helen: Yes, at 8:30. Is that OK for you?
Tina: Yes, (12) _____ (I / be) there at 8:30.

12 **Put the verb into the most appropriate form. Sometimes there is more than one possibility.**

1. *A has decided to learn a language.*
   A: I've decided to try and learn a foreign language.
   B: You have? Which language (1) __are you going to learn__ (you / learn)?
   A: Spanish.
   B: (2) _____ (you / take) a class?
   A: Yes, (3) _____ (it / start) next week.
   B: That's great. I'm sure (4) _____ (you / enjoy) it.
   A: I hope so. But I think (5) _____ (it / be) a lot of work.

2. *A wants to know about B's vacation plans.*
   A: I hear (1) _____ (you / go) on vacation soon.
   B: That's right. (2) _____ (we / go) to Brazil.
   A: I hope (3) _____ (you / have) a nice time.
   B: Thanks. (4) _____ (I / send) you a postcard and
       (5) _____ (I / get) in touch with you when
       (6) _____ (I / get) back.

3. *A invites B to a party.*
   A: (1) _____ (I / have) a party next Saturday. Can you come?
   B: On Saturday? I'm not sure. Some friends of mine (2) _____ (come) to
       stay with me next week, but I think (3) _____ (they / leave) by
       Saturday. But if (4) _____ (they / be) still here,
       (5) _____ (I / not / be) able to come to the party.
   A: OK. Well, tell me as soon as (6) _____ (you / know).
   B: All right. (7) _____ (I / call) you during the week.

4. *A and B are two secret agents arranging a meeting. They are talking on the phone.*
   A: Well, what time (1) _____ (we / meet)?
   B: Come to the café by the station at 4:00.
       (2) _____ (I / wait) for you
       when (3) _____ (you / arrive).
       (4) _____ (I / sit) by the window
       and (5) _____ (I / wear) a bright green sweater.
   A: OK. (6) _____ (Agent 307 / come), too?
   B: No, she can't come.
   A: Oh. (7) _____ (I / bring) the documents?
   B: Yes. (8) _____ (I / explain) everything when
       (9) _____ (I / see) you. And don't be late.
   A: OK. (10) _____ (I / try) to be on time.

13 Put the verb into the correct form. Choose from the following:

present continuous (**I am doing**)	**will ('ll) / won't**
simple present (**I do**)	**will be doing**
going to (**I'm going to do**)	**should / shall**

1. I'm a little hungry. I think _____ (I / have) something to eat.
2. Why are you putting on your coat? _____ (you / go) somewhere?
3. What time _____ (I / call) you tonight? About 7:30?
4. Look! That plane is flying toward the airport. _____ (it / land).
5. We have to do something soon before _____ (it / be) too late.
6. I'm sorry you've decided to leave the company. _____ (I / miss) you
   when _____ (you / go).
7. _____ (I / give) you my address? If _____
   (I / give) you my address, _____ (you / send) me a postcard?
8. Are you still watching that TV program? What time _____ (it / end)?
9. _____ (I / go) to Chicago next weekend for a wedding.
   My sister _____ (get) married.
10. I'm not ready yet. _____ (I / tell) you when _____
    (I / be) ready. I promise _____ (I / not / be) very long.
11. *A:* Where are you going?
    B: To the hairdresser. _____ (I / have) my hair cut.
12. She was very rude to me. I refuse to speak to her again until _____
    (she / apologize).
13. I wonder where _____ (we / live) 10 years from now?
14. What do you plan to do when _____ (you / finish) college?

Past, Present, and Future   Units 1–24

14 Use your own ideas to complete B's sentences.

1. *A:* How did the accident happen?
   B: I _was going_ too fast and couldn't stop in time.
2. *A:* Is that a new camera?
   B: No, I _____ it a long time.
3. *A:* Is that a new computer?
   B: Yes, I _____ it a few weeks ago.
4. *A:* I can't talk to you right now. You can see I'm very busy.
   B: OK. I _____ back in about half an hour.
5. *A:* This is a nice restaurant. Do you come here often?
   B: No, it's the first time I _____ here.
6. *A:* Do you play any sports?
   B: No, I _____ tennis, but I gave it up.
7. *A:* I'm sorry I'm late.
   B: That's OK. I _____ long.
8. *A:* When you went to Russia last year, was it your first visit?
   B: No, I _____ there twice before.
9. *A:* Do you have any plans for the weekend?
   B: Yes, I _____ to a party on Saturday night.
10. *A:* Do you know what Steve's doing these days?
    B: No, I _____ him in ages.
11. *A:* Will you still be here by the time I get back?
    B: No, I _____ by then.

15 Robert is traveling around North America. He sends an e-mail to a friend in Winnipeg (Canada). Put the verb into the most appropriate form.

●○○   North American travels   ⊂⊃

To:	Chris
☰▾ Subject:	North American travels

Hi

(1) ___*I've just arrived*___ (I / just / arrive) in Minneapolis. (2) _____ (I / travel) for more than a month now, and (3) _____ (I / begin) to think about coming home. Everything (4) _____ (I / see) so far (5) _____ (be) really interesting, and (6) _____ (I / meet) some really kind people.

(7) _____ (I / leave) Kansas City a week ago. (8) _____ (I / stay) there with Emily, the aunt of a friend from college. She was really helpful and hospitable and although (9) _____ (I / plan) to stay only a couple of days, (10) _____ (I / end up) staying more than a week.

(11) _____ (I / enjoy) the trip from Kansas City to here. (12) _____ (I / take) the Greyhound bus and (13) _____ (meet) some really interesting people – everybody was really friendly.

So now I'm here, and (14) _____ (I / stay) here for a few days before (15) _____ _____ (I / continue) up to Canada. I'm not sure exactly when (16) _____ (I / get) to Winnipeg – it depends what happens while (17) _____ (I / be) here. But (18) _____ (I / let) you know as soon as (19) _____ (I / know) myself.

(20) _____ (I / stay) with a family here – they're friends of some people I know at home. Tomorrow (21) _____ (we / visit) some people they know who (22) _____ (build) a house on a lake. It isn't finished yet, but (23) _____ (it / be) interesting to see what it's like.

Anyway, that's all for now. (24) _____ (I / be) in touch again soon.

Robert

Modal Verbs (*can*/*must*/*would*, etc.)   Units 25–34, Appendix 4

16 Which alternatives are correct? Sometimes only one alternative is correct, and sometimes two of the alternatives are possible.

1. "What time will you be home tonight?" "I'm not sure. I ___*A or B*___ late."
   A may be   **B** might be   **C** can be   (both *A* and *B* are correct)
2. I can't find the theater tickets. They _____ out of my pocket.
   A must have fallen   **B** should have fallen   **C** had to fall
3. Somebody ran in front of the car as I was driving. Fortunately, I _____ just in time.
   A could stop   **B** could have stopped   **C** managed to stop
4. We've got plenty of time. We _____ yet.
   A must not leave   **B** couldn't leave   **C** don't have to leave
5. I _____ out but I didn't feel like it, so I stayed at home.
   A could go   **B** could have gone   **C** must have gone

6. I'm sorry I _____ to your party last week.
   A couldn't come   **B** couldn't have come   **C** wasn't able to come

7. "What do you think of my theory?" "I'm not sure. You _____ right."
   A could be   **B** must be   **C** might be

8. I couldn't wait for you any longer. I _____ , and so I went.
   A must go   **B** must have gone   **C** had to go

9. "Do you know where Liz is?" "No. I suppose she _____ shopping."
   A should have gone   **B** may have gone   **C** could have gone

10. At first they didn't believe me when I told them what had happened, but in the end
    I _____ them that I was telling the truth.
    A was able to convince   **B** managed to convince   **C** could convince

11. I promised I'd call Gary tonight. I _____ .
    A can't forget   **B** must not forget   **C** don't have to forget

12. Why did you leave without me? You _____ for me.
    A must have waited   **B** had to wait   **C** should have waited

13. Lisa called and suggested _____ lunch together.
    A we have   **B** having   **C** to have

14. You look nice in that jacket, but you hardly ever wear it. _____ it more often.
    A You'd better wear   **B** You should wear   **C** You ought to wear

15. Should I buy a car? What's your advice? What _____ ?
    A will you do   **B** would you do   **C** should you do

17   **Make sentences from the words in parentheses.**

1. Don't call them now. (they might / have / lunch)
   They might be having lunch.

2. I ate too much. Now I feel sick. (I shouldn't / eat / so much)
   I shouldn't have eaten so much.

3. I wonder why Tom didn't call me. (he must / forget)
   _____

4. Why did you go home so late? (you shouldn't / leave / so late)
   _____

5. You signed the contract. (it can't / change / now)
   _____

6. Why weren't you here earlier? (you could / get / here earlier)
   _____

7. "What's Linda doing?" "I'm not sure." (she may / watch / television)
   _____

8. Laura was standing outside the movie theater. (she must / wait / for somebody)
   _____

9. He was in prison at the time that the crime was committed. (he couldn't / do / it)
   _____

10. Why didn't you ask me to help you? (I would / help / you)
    _____

11. I'm surprised you weren't told that the road was dangerous. (you should / warn / about it)
    _____

12. Gary was in a strange mood yesterday. (he might not / feel / very well)
    _____

18 Complete B's sentences using *can/could/might/must/should/would* + the verb in parentheses. In some sentences you need to use *have*: *must have* . . . / *should have* . . . , etc. In some sentences you need the negative (*can't/couldn't*, etc.).

1. *A:* I'm hungry.
   B: But you just had lunch. You ___*can't be*___ hungry already. (be)
2. *A:* I haven't seen our neighbors in ages.
   B: Neither have I. They ___*must have gone*___ away. (go)
3. *A:* What's the weather like? Is it raining?
   B: Not right now, but it _____ later. (rain)
4. *A:* Where's Julia?
   B: I'm not sure. She _____ to the bank. (go)
5. *A:* I didn't see you at Michael's party last week.
   B: No, I had to work that night, so I _____ (go)
6. *A:* I saw you at Michael's party last week.
   B: No, you _____ me. I didn't go to Michael's party. (see)
7. *A:* What time will we get to Sue's house?
   B: Well, it's about a two-hour drive, so if we leave at 3:00, we _____ there by 5:00. (get)
8. *A:* When was the last time you saw Bill?
   B: Years ago. I _____ him if I saw him now. (recognize)
9. *A:* Did you hear the explosion?
   B: What explosion?
   A: There was a loud explosion about an hour ago. You _____ it. (hear)
10. *A:* We weren't sure which way to go. In the end we turned right.
    B: You went the wrong way. You _____ left. (turn)

If (conditional)   Units 24, 36–38

19 Put the verb into the correct form.

1. If you ___*found*___ a wallet in the street, what would you do with it? (find)
2. I have to hurry. My friend will be upset if I ___*'m not*___ on time. (not / be)
3. I didn't realize that Gary was in the hospital. If I ___*had known*___ he was in the hospital, I would have gone to visit him. (know)
4. If the phone _____ , can you answer it? (ring)
5. I can't decide what to do. What would you do if you _____ in my position? (be)
6. *A:* What should we do tomorrow?
   B: Well, if it _____ a nice day, we can go to the beach. (be)
7. *A:* Let's go to the beach.
   B: No, it's too cold. If it _____ warmer, I wouldn't mind going. (be)
8. *A:* Did you go to the beach yesterday?
   B: No, it was too cold. If it _____ warmer, we might have gone. (be)
9. If you _____ enough money to go anywhere in the world, where would you go? (have)
10. I'm glad we had a map. I'm sure we would have gotten lost if we _____ one. (not / have)
11. The accident was your fault. If you _____ more carefully, it wouldn't have happened. (drive)
12. *A:* Why do you read newspapers?
    B: Well, if I _____ newspapers, I wouldn't know what was happening in the world. (not / read)

20 Complete the sentences.

1. Liz is tired all the time. She shouldn't go to bed so late.
   If _Liz didn't go to bed so late, she wouldn't be tired all the time._

2. It's getting late. I don't think Sarah will come to see us now.
   I'd be surprised if Sarah _____

3. I'm sorry I disturbed you. I didn't know you were busy.
   If I'd known you were busy, I _____

4. I don't want them to be upset, so I've decided not to tell them what happened.
   They'd _____ if _____

5. The dog attacked you, but only because you frightened it.
   If _____

6. Unfortunately, I didn't have an umbrella, so I got very wet in the rain.
   I _____

7. Martin failed his driver's test last week. He was very nervous and that's why he failed.
   If he _____

21 Use your own ideas to complete the sentences.

1. I'd go out tonight if _____ .
2. I'd have gone out last night if _____ .
3. If you hadn't reminded me, _____ .
4. We wouldn't have been late if _____ .
5. If I'd been able to get tickets, _____ .
6. Who would you call if _____ ?
7. Cities would be nicer places if _____ .
8. If there were no television, _____ .

Passive   Units 40–43

22 Put the verb into the most appropriate passive form.

1. There's somebody behind us. I think we _are being followed_ (follow).
2. A mystery is something that _can't be explained_ (can't / explain).
3. We didn't play baseball yesterday. The game _____ (cancel).
4. The television _____ (repair). It's working again now.
5. In the middle of town there is a church, which _____ (restore)
   at this time. The work is almost finished.
6. The tower is the oldest part of the church. It _____ (believe) to
   be more than 100 years old.
7. If I didn't do my job right, I _____ (would / fire).
8. A: I left a newspaper on the desk last night and it isn't there now.
   B: It _____ (might / throw) away.
9. I learned to swim when I was very young. I _____ (teach) by
   my mother.
10. After _____ (arrest), I was taken to the police station.
11. "_____ (you / ever / arrest)?" "No, never."
12. *(TV news report)* Two people _____ (report) to _____
    (injure) in an explosion at a factory in Miami early this morning.

23 Put the verb into the correct form, active or passive.

1. This house is very old. It ___was built___ (build) over 100 years ago.
2. My grandfather was a builder. He ___built___ (build) this house many years ago.
3. "Is your car still for sale?" "No, I _____ (sell) it."
4. *A:* Is the house at the end of the street still for sale?
   B: No, it _____ (sell).
5. Sometimes mistakes _____ (make). It's inevitable.
6. I wouldn't leave your car unlocked. It _____ (might / steal).
7. My bag has disappeared. It _____ (must / steal).
8. I can't find my hat. Somebody _____ (must / take) it by mistake.
9. It's a serious problem. I don't know how it _____ (can / solve).
10. We didn't leave early enough. We _____ (should / leave) earlier.
11. Nearly every time I travel by plane, my flight _____ (delay).
12. A new bridge _____ (build) across the river. Work started last year
    and the bridge _____ (expect) to open next year.

24 Read these newspaper reports and put the verbs into the most suitable form.

1.
Fire at City Hall

City Hall (1) ___was damaged___ (damage) in a fire last night. The fire, which (2) _____ _____ (discover) at about 9:00 p.m., spread very quickly. Nobody (3) _____ (injure), but two people had to (4) _____ _____ (rescue) from an upstairs room. A large number of documents (5) _____ _____ (believe / destroy). It (6) _____ _____ (not / know) how the fire started.

3.
Road Delays

Repair work started yesterday on Route 22. The road (1) _____ (resurface), and there will be long delays. Drivers (2) _____ (ask) to use an alternate route if possible. The work (3) _____ (expect) to last two weeks. Next Sunday the road (4) _____ (close), and traffic (5) _____ (reroute).

2.
Convenience Store Robbery

A convenience store clerk (1) _____ _____ (force) to hand over $500 after (2) _____ (threaten) by a man with a gun. The man escaped in a car, which (3) _____ (steal) earlier in the day. The car (4) _____ _____ (later / find) in a parking lot, where it (5) _____ (abandon) by the thief. A man (6) _____ _____ (arrest) in connection with the robbery and (7) _____ _____ (still / question) by the police.

4.
Accident

A woman (1) _____ (take) to the hospital after her car collided with a truck on the freeway yesterday. She (2) _____ _____ (allow) to go home later that day after treatment. The road (3) _____ _____ (block) for an hour after the accident, and traffic had to (4) _____ _____ (reroute). A police investigator said afterward: "The woman was lucky. She could (5) _____ _____ (kill)."

Reported Speech

25 Complete the sentences using reported speech.

1.

> Can I speak to Paul, please?
>
> I'll try again later.
>
> Paul's gone out. I don't know when he'll be back. Do you want to leave a message?
>
> **You**

A woman called at lunchtime yesterday and asked _if she could speak to Paul_ . I told
_____ and _____
_____ . I asked _____
_____ , but she said _____ later. But she never did.

2.

> We have no record of a reservation in your name.
>
> We're sorry, but the hotel is full.
>
> Do you have any rooms available?
>
> RECEPTION

I went to New York recently, but my trip didn't begin well. I had reserved a hotel room, but when I
got to the hotel, they told _____ no _____ .
When I asked _____ ,
they said _____ , but _____ .
There was nothing I could do. I just had to look for somewhere else to stay.

3.

> Why are you visiting the country?
>
> How long do you intend to stay?
>
> Where will you be staying during your visit?
>
> We're on vacation.

After getting off the plane, we had to stand in line for an hour to get through immigration. Finally
it was our turn. The immigration official asked us _____
_____ , and we told _____ .
Then he wanted to know _____ and
_____ .
He seemed satisfied with our answers, checked our passports, and wished us a pleasant stay.

4.

> I'll call you from the airport when I arrive.
>
> **Sue**
>
> Don't come to the airport. I'll take the bus.

A: What time is Sue arriving this afternoon?

B: About three. She said _____
_____ .

A: Aren't you going to meet her?

B: No, she said _____ . She said
_____ .

310 ADDITIONAL EXERCISES

5.

A few days ago a man called from a marketing company and started asking me questions.

He wanted to know _____ and asked _____ .

I don't like people calling and asking questions like that, so I told _____

_____ and I put the phone down.

6. *now*

earlier

Louise   Sarah

Paul

Louise and Sarah are in a restaurant waiting for Paul.

Louise: I wonder where Paul is. He said _____ .

Sarah: Maybe he got lost.

Louise: I don't think so. He said _____ .

And I told _____ .

7.

Jane   Joe

Joe: Is there anything to eat?

Jane: You just said _____ .

Joe: Well, I am now. I'd love a banana.

Jane: A banana? But you said _____ .

You told _____ .

-ing and Infinitive

Units 51–64

26 **Put the verb into the correct form.**

1. How old were you when you learned ___to drive___ ? (drive)
2. I don't mind ___walking___ home, but I'd rather ___take___ a taxi. (walk / take)
3. I can't make a decision. I keep _____ my mind. (change)
4. He had made his decision and refused _____ his mind. (change)
5. Why did you change your decision? What made you _____ your mind? (change)
6. It was a really good vacation. I really enjoyed _____ by the ocean again. (be)
7. Did I really tell you I was unhappy? I don't remember _____ that. (say)
8. "Remember _____ Tom tomorrow." "OK. I won't forget." (call)
9. The water here is not very good. I'd avoid _____ it if I were you. (drink)
10. I pretended _____ interested in the conversation, but it was really very boring. (be)
11. I got up and looked out the window _____ what the weather was like. (see)
12. I have a friend who claims _____ able to speak five languages. (be)
13. I like _____ carefully about things before _____ a decision. (think / make)

14. I had an apartment downtown but I didn't like _____ there, so I decided _____ . (live / move)
15. Steve used _____ a hockey player. He had to stop _____ because of an injury. (be / play)
16. After _____ by the police, the man admitted _____ the car but denied _____ 100 miles an hour. (stop / steal / drive)
17. *A:* How do you make this machine _____ ? (work)
    B: I'm not sure. Try _____ that button and see what happens. (press)

27 **Make sentences from the words in parentheses.**

1. I can't find the tickets. (I / seem / lose / them)
   I seem to have lost them.
2. I don't have far to go. (it / not / worth / take / a taxi)
   It's not worth taking a taxi.
3. The game was getting boring. (we / stop / watch / after a while)
   _____
4. Tim isn't very reliable. (he / tend / forget / things)
   _____
5. I've got a lot of luggage. (you / mind / help / me?)
   _____
6. There's nobody at home. (everybody / seem / go out)
   _____
7. We don't like our apartment. (we / think / move)
   _____
8. The vase was very valuable. (I / afraid / touch / it)
   _____
9. Bill never carries money with him. (he / afraid / robbed)
   _____
10. I wouldn't go to see that movie. (it / not / worth / see)
    _____
11. I'm very tired after that long walk. (I / not / used / walk / so far)
    _____
12. Sue is on vacation. I received a postcard from her yesterday. (she / seem / enjoy / herself)
    _____
13. Dave had lots of vacation pictures. (he / insist / show / them to me)
    _____
14. I don't want to do the shopping. (I'd rather / somebody else / do / it)
    _____

28 **Complete the second sentence so that the meaning is similar to the first.**

1. I was surprised I passed the exam.
   I didn't expect _to pass the exam_ .
2. Did you manage to solve the problem?
   Did you succeed _in solving the problem_ ?
3. I don't read newspapers anymore.
   I've given up _____ .
4. I'd prefer not to go out tonight.
   I'd rather _____ .
5. He can't walk very well.
   He has trouble _____ .
6. Should I call you tonight?
   Do you want _____ ?
7. Nobody saw me come in.
   I came in without _____ .

8. They said I was a liar.
   I was accused _____ .
9. It will be good to see them again.
   I'm looking forward _____ .
10. What do you think I should do?
    What do you advise me _____ ?
11. It's too bad I couldn't go out with you.
    I'd like _____ .
12. I'm sorry that I didn't take your advice.
    I regret _____ .

---

a/an and *the*   Units 67–76

29 Put in *a/an* or *the* where necessary. Leave the space empty if the sentence is already complete.

1. I don't usually like staying at _____ hotels, but last summer we spent a few days at __*a*__ very nice hotel on __*the*__ ocean.
2. _____ tennis is my favorite sport. I play once or twice _____ week if I can, but I'm not _____ very good player.
3. I won't be home for _____ dinner this evening. I'm meeting some friends after _____ work, and we're going to _____ movies.
4. _____ unemployment is increasing, and it's very difficult for _____ people to find _____ work.
5. There was _____ accident as I was going _____ home last night. Two people were taken to _____ hospital. I think _____ most accidents are caused by _____ people driving too fast.
6. Carol is _____ economist. She used to work in _____ investment department of _____ Lloyds Bank. Now she works for _____ American bank in _____ United States.
7. *A:* What's _____ name of _____ hotel where you're staying?
   B: _____ Royal. It's on _____ West Street in _____ suburbs. It's near _____ airport.
8. I have two brothers. _____ older one is training to be _____ pilot with _____ Western Airlines. _____ younger one is still in _____ high school. When he finishes _____ school, he wants to go to _____ college to study _____ engineering.

Pronouns and Determiners   Units 80–89

30 Which alternatives are correct? Sometimes only one alternative is correct, and sometimes two alternatives are possible.

1. I don't remember __*A*__ about the accident. (*A* is correct)
   A anything   **B** something   **C** nothing
2. Chris and I have known _____ for quite a long time.
   A us   **B** each other   **C** ourselves
3. "How often do the buses run?"   "_____ 20 minutes."
   A All   **B** Each   **C** Every
4. I shouted for help, but _____ came.
   A nobody   **B** no one   **C** anybody
5. Last night we went out with some friends of _____ .
   A us   **B** our   **C** ours
6. It didn't take us a long time to get here. _____ traffic.
   A It wasn't much   **B** There wasn't much   **C** It wasn't a lot
7. Can I have _____ milk in my coffee, please?
   A a little   **B** any   **C** some
8. Sometimes I find it difficult to _____ .
   A concentrate   **B** concentrate me   **C** concentrate myself

9. There's _____ on at the movies that I want to see, so there's no point in going.

   A something   **B** anything   **C** nothing

10. I drink _____ water every day.

   A much   **B** a lot of   **C** lots of

11. _____ in the mall are open on Sunday.

   A Most of stores   **B** Most of the stores   **C** The most of the stores

12. There were about 20 people in the photo. I didn't recognize _____ of them.

   A any   **B** none   **C** either

13. I've been waiting _____ for Sarah to call.

   A all morning   **B** the whole morning   **C** all the morning

14. I can't afford to buy anything in this store. _____ so expensive.

   A All is   **B** Everything is   **C** All are

Adjectives and Adverbs

Units 96–105

31 There are mistakes in some of these sentences. Correct the sentences where necessary. Write *OK* if the sentence is already correct.

1. The building was (total destroyed) in the fire.   *totally destroyed*
2. I didn't like the book. It was such a stupid story.   *OK*
3. The city is very polluted. It's the more polluted place I've ever been to.   _____
4. I was disappointing that I didn't get the job. I was well qualified and the interview went well.   _____
5. Could you walk a little more slowly?   _____
6. Joe works hardly, but he doesn't get paid very much.   _____
7. The company's offices are in a modern large building.   _____
8. Dan is a very fast runner. I wish I could run as fast as him.   _____
9. I missed the three last days of the course because I was sick.   _____
10. You don't look happy. What's the matter?   _____
11. The weather has been unusual cold for this time of year.   _____
12. The water in the pool was too dirty to swim in it.   _____
13. I got impatient because we had to wait so long time.   _____
14. Is this box big enough, or do you need a bigger one?   _____
15. This morning I got up more early than usual.   _____

Conjunctions

Units 24, 36, 109–115

32 Which is correct?

1. I'll try to be on time, but don't worry if / ~~when~~ I'm late. (*if* is correct)
2. Don't throw that bag away. If / When you don't want it, I'll take it.
3. Please go to the reception desk if / when you arrive at the hotel.
4. We've arranged to play tennis tomorrow, but we won't play if / when it's raining.
5. Jennifer is in her final year at school. She still doesn't know what she's going to do if / when she graduates.
6. What would you do if / when you lost your keys?
7. I hope I'll be able to come to the party, but I'll let you know if / unless I can't.
8. I don't want to be disturbed, so don't call me if / unless it's something important.
9. Please sign the contract if / unless you're happy with the conditions.
10. I like traveling by ship as long as / unless the sea is not rough.
11. You might not remember the name of the hotel, so write it down if / in case you forget it.
12. It's not cold now, but take your coat with you if / in case it gets cold later.

13. Take your coat with you, and then you can put it on <u>if / in case</u> it gets cold later.
14. They always have the television on, <u>even if / if</u> nobody is watching it.
15. <u>Even / Although</u> we played very well, we lost the game.
16. <u>Despite / Although</u> we've known each other a long time, we're not especially close friends.
17. "When did you graduate from high school?" "<u>As / When</u> I was 18."
18. I think Ann will be very pleased <u>as / when</u> she hears the news.

Prepositions (time) Units 13, 116–119

33 Put in one of the following: **at on in during for since by until**

1. Jack is out of town. He'll be back <u> in </u> a week.
2. We're having a party _____ Saturday. Can you come?
3. I've got an interview next week. It's _____ 9:30 _____ Tuesday morning.
4. Sue isn't usually here _____ weekends. She goes away.
5. The train service is very good. The trains are nearly always _____ time.
6. It was a confusing situation. Many things were happening _____ the same time.
7. I couldn't decide whether or not to buy the sweater. _____ the end I decided not to.
8. The road is busy all the time, even _____ night.
9. I met a lot of nice people _____ my stay in New York.
10. I saw Helen _____ Friday, but I haven't seen her _____ then.
11. Brian has been doing the same job _____ five years.
12. Lisa's birthday is _____ the end of March. I'm not sure exactly which day it is.
13. We have some friends staying with us _____ the moment. They're staying _____ Friday.
14. If you're interested in applying for the job, your application must be received _____ Friday.
15. I'm just going out. I won't be long – I'll be back _____ 10 minutes.

Prepositions (position and other uses) Units 120–125

34 Put in the missing preposition.

1. I'd love to be able to visit every country _____ the world.
2. Jessica White is my favorite author. Have you read anything _____ her?
3. "Is there a bank near here?" "Yes, there's one _____ the end of this block."
4. Tim is out of town at the moment. He's _____ vacation.
5. We live _____ the country, a long way from the nearest town.
6. I've got a stain _____ my jacket. I'll have to have it cleaned.
7. We went _____ a party _____ Linda's house on Saturday.
8. Boston is _____ the East Coast of the United States.
9. Look at the leaves _____ that tree. They're a beautiful color.
10. "Have you ever been _____ Tokyo?" "No, I've never been _____ Japan."
11. Mozart died _____ Vienna in 1791 _____ the age of 35.
12. "Are you _____ this photograph?" "Yes, that's me, _____ the left."
13. We went _____ the theater last night. We had seats _____ the front row.
14. "Where's the light switch?" "It's _____ the wall _____ the door."
15. It was late when we arrived _____ the hotel.
16. I couldn't decide what to eat. There was nothing _____ the menu that I liked.
17. We live _____ a high rise. Our apartment is _____ the fifteenth floor.
18. *A:* What did you think of the movie?
    B: Some parts were a little stupid, but _____ the whole I enjoyed it.
19. "When you paid the hotel bill, did you pay cash?" "No, I paid _____ credit card."
20. "How did you get here? _____ the bus?" "No, _____ car."
21. *A:* I wonder what's _____ TV tonight. Do you have a newspaper?
    B: Yes, the TV listings are _____ the back page.

22. Helen works for a telecommunications company. She works _____ the customer service department.
23. Anna spent two years working _____ Chicago before returning _____ Italy.
24. "Did you enjoy your trip _____ the beach?" "Yes, it was great."
25. Next summer we're going _____ a trip to Canada.

Noun/Adjective + Preposition   Units 126–128

35 Put in the missing preposition.

1. The plan has been changed, but nobody seems to know the reason _____ this.
2. Don't ask me to decide. I'm not very good _____ making decisions.
3. Some people say that Sue is unfriendly, but she's always very nice _____ me.
4. What do you think is the best solution _____ the problem?
5. There has been a big increase _____ the price of land recently.
6. He lives a rather lonely life. He doesn't have much contact _____ other people.
7. Paul is a wonderful photographer. He likes taking pictures _____ people.
8. Michael got married _____ a woman he met when he was in college.
9. He's very brave. He's not afraid _____ anything.
10. I'm surprised _____ the amount of traffic today. I didn't think it would be so heavy.
11. Thank you for lending me the guidebook. It was full _____ useful information.
12. Please come in and sit down. I'm sorry _____ the mess.

Verb + Preposition   Units 129–133

36 Complete each sentence with a preposition where necessary. If no preposition is necessary, leave the space empty.

1. She works very hard. You can't accuse her _____ being lazy.
2. Who's going to look _____ your children while you're at work?
3. The problem is becoming serious. We have to discuss _____ it.
4. The problem is becoming serious. We have to do something _____ it.
5. I prefer this chair _____ the other one. It's more comfortable.
6. I have to call _____ the office to tell them I won't be at work today.
7. The river divides the city _____ two parts.
8. "What do you think _____ your new boss?" "She's all right, I guess."
9. Can somebody please explain _____ me what I have to do?
10. I said hello to her, but she didn't answer _____ me.
11. "Do you like staying at hotels?" "It depends _____ the hotel."
12. "Have you ever been to Borla?" "No, I've never heard _____ it. What is it?"
13. You remind me _____ somebody I knew a long time ago. You look just like her.
14. This is wonderful news! I can't believe _____ it.
15. George is not an idealist – he believes _____ being practical.
16. What's so funny? What are you laughing _____ ?
17. What have you done with all the money you had? What did you spend it _____ ?
18. If Kevin asks _____ you _____ money, don't give him any.
19. I apologized _____ Sarah _____ keeping her waiting so long.
20. Lisa was very helpful. I thanked _____ her _____ everything she'd done.

37 A says something and B replies. Which goes with which?

A

1. ~~I'd like to apply for a license.~~
2. I'm too warm with my coat on.
3. This jacket looks nice.
4. My phone number is 555-9320.
5. I don't think my car will fit in that space.
6. I'm glad we have a plan.
7. How did you find the mistake?
8. I'm not sure whether to accept their offer or not.
9. I don't know how to put this toy together.
10. It's a subject he doesn't like to talk about.
11. I don't know what this word means.

B

a. I can back up and give you more room.
b. Let me try. I'm sure I can figure it out.
c. Kate pointed it out.
d. ~~Sure, just fill out this form.~~
e. Yes, why don't you try it on?
f. OK, I won't bring it up.
g. Just a minute. I'll write it down.
h. Why don't you take it off then?
i. You can look it up.
j. I think you should turn it down.
k. Yes, now let's work out the details.

1. __d__   2. _____   3. _____   4. _____   5. _____   6. _____
7. _____   8. _____   9. _____   10. _____   11. _____

38 Only one alternative is correct. Which is it?

1. Nobody believed Paul at first but he __B__ to be right. (*B* is correct)
   A came out   **B** turned out   **C** worked out   **D** carried out
2. Here's some good news. It will _____ .
   A turn you up   **B** put you up   **C** blow you up   **D** cheer you up
3. I was annoyed with the way the children were behaving, so I _____ .
   A told them up   **B** told them off   **C** told them out   **D** told them over
4. The club committee is _____ of the president, the secretary, and seven other members.
   A set up   **B** made up   **C** set out   **D** made out
5. When you are finished with those board games, please _____ ?
   A put them away   **B** put them out   **C** turn them off   **D** turn them away
6. We moved the table to another room. It _____ too much space here.
   A took in   **B** took up   **C** took off   **D** took over
7. Barbara started taking classes in college, but she _____ after six months.
   A went out   **B** fell out   **C** turned out   **D** dropped out
8. You can't predict everything. Often things don't _____ the way you expect.
   A make out   **B** break out   **C** work out   **D** get out
9. Why are all these people here? What's _____ ?
   A going off   **B** getting off   **C** going on   **D** getting on
10. It's a very busy airport. There are planes _____ or landing every few minutes.
    A going up   **B** taking off   **C** getting up   **D** driving off
11. The traffic was moving slowly because a bus had _____ and was blocking the road.
    A broken down   **B** fallen down   **C** fallen over   **D** broken up
12. Pat feels different from other kids at her school. She doesn't think she _____ .
    A hands in   **B** turns in   **C** drops in   **D** fits in

39 Complete the sentences. Use two words each time.

1. Keep __away from__ the edge of the pool. You might fall in.
2. I didn't notice that the two pictures were different until Liz pointed it _____ me.
3. I asked Dan if he had any suggestions about what we should do, but he didn't come _____ anything.
4. I'm glad Sarah is coming to the party. I'm really looking _____ seeing her again.
5. Things are changing all the time. It's difficult to keep _____ all these changes.
6. I don't want to run _____ food for the party. Are you sure we have enough?
7. Don't let me interrupt you. Go _____ your work.

8. I'd love to go to your party, but I promised to go see my grandparents this weekend, and I can't get _____ it. They'd be disappointed if I didn't go.
9. I've had enough of being treated like this. I'm not going to put _____ it anymore.
10. I didn't enjoy the trip very much at the time, but when I look _____ it now, I realize it was a good experience and I'm glad I went on it.
11. The wedding was supposed to be a secret, so how did you find _____ it? Did Jenny tell you?
12. There is a very nice atmosphere in the office where I work. Everybody gets _____ everybody else.

40 Complete each sentence using a phrasal verb that means the same as the words in parentheses.

1. The football game had to be _called off_ because of the weather. (canceled)
2. The story Kate told wasn't true. She _made it up_ . (invented it)
3. A bomb _____ near the station, but no one was injured. (exploded)
4. George finally _____ nearly an hour late. (arrived)
5. Here's an application form. Can you _____ and sign it, please? (complete it)
6. A number of buildings are going to be _____ to make way for the new road. (demolished)
7. Since my father became ill, my older brother has _____ more responsibilities in the family. (accepted)
8. Be positive! You must never _____ ! (stop trying)
9. I was very tired and _____ in front of the television. (fell asleep)
10. After eight years together, they've decided to _____ . (separate)
11. The noise is terrible. I can't _____ any longer. (tolerate it)
12. We don't have a lot of money, but we have enough to _____ . (manage)
13. I'm sorry I'm late. The meeting _____ longer than I expected. (continued)
14. We need to make a decision today. We can't _____ any longer. (delay it)

41 Complete the sentences. Use one word each time.

1. You're driving too fast. Please _slow_ down.
2. It was only a small fire, and I managed to _____ it out with a bucket of water.
3. The house is empty at the present time, but the new tenants are _____ in next week.
4. I've _____ on weight. My clothes don't fit any more.
5. Their house is really nice now. They've _____ it up really well.
6. I was talking to the woman sitting next to me on the plane, and it _____ out that she works for the same company as my brother.
7. "Do you know what happened?" "Not yet, but I'm going to _____ out."
8. There's no need to get angry. _____ down!
9. Come and see us more often. You can _____ in any time you like.
10. Sarah has just called to say that she'll be late. She's been _____ up.
11. You've written my name wrong. It's Martin, not Marin — you _____ out the T.
12. My mom wants me to take her downtown and _____ her off at city hall this morning.
13. We had a really interesting discussion, but Jane didn't _____ in. She just listened.
14. Jonathan is in good shape. He _____ out at the gym every day.
15. Jenny said she would help me move, but she never came. I can't believe that she _____ me down.
16. We are still discussing the contract. There are a few things we need to _____ out.
17. My alarm clock _____ off in the middle of the night and _____ me up.

Study Guide

This guide will help you decide which units you need to study. The sentences in the guide are grouped together (Present and Past, Articles and Nouns, etc.) in the same way as the units in the *Contents* (pages iii–vi).

Each sentence can be completed using one or more of the alternatives (A, B, C, etc.). There are between two and five alternatives each time. IN SOME SENTENCES MORE THAN ONE ALTERNATIVE IS POSSIBLE.

If you don't know or if you are not sure which alternatives are correct, then you probably need to study the unit(s) in the list on the right. You will also find the correct sentence in this unit. (If two or three units are listed, you will find the correct sentence in the first one.)

There is an Answer Key to this Study Guide on page 362.

IF YOU ARE NOT SURE WHICH ANSWER IS RIGHT, STUDY UNIT(S)

Present and Past

1.1 At first I didn't like my job, but _____ to enjoy it now.
    A I'm beginning   **B** I begin   **1, 3**

1.2 I don't understand this sentence. What _____ ?
    A does mean this word   **B** does this word mean   **C** means this word   **2, 4, 7**

1.3 Robert _____ away two or three times a year.
    A is going usually   **B** is usually going   **C** usually goes   **D** goes usually   **2, 3, 107**

1.4 How _____ now? Better than before?
    A you are feeling   **B** do you feel   **C** are you feeling   **4**

1.5 It was a boring weekend. _____ anything.
    A I didn't   **B** I don't do   **C** I didn't do   **5**

1.6 Matt _____ while we were having dinner.
    A called   **B** was calling   **C** has called   **6, 9**

Present Perfect and Past

2.1 Everything is going well. We _____ any problems so far.
    A didn't have   **B** don't have   **C** haven't had   **7**

2.2 Sarah has lost her passport again. It's the second time this _____ .
    A has happened   **B** happens   **C** happened   **D** is happening   **7**

2.3 "Are you hungry?" "No, _____ lunch."
    A I just had   **B** I just have   **C** I've just had   **8**

2.4 It _____ raining for a while, but now it's raining again.
    A stopped   **B** has stopped   **C** was stopped   **8**

2.5 My mother _____ in Chile.
    A grew up   **B** has grown up   **C** had grown up   **8, 14**

2.6 _____ a lot of candy when you were a child?
    A Have you eaten   **B** Had you eaten   **C** Did you eat   **9**

2.7 John _____ in New York for 10 years. Now he lives in Los Angeles.
    A lived   **B** has lived   **C** has been living   **9, 12**

2.8 You're out of breath. _____ ?
    A Are you running?   **B** Have you run?   **C** Have you been running?   **10**

2.9 Where's the book I gave you? What _____ with it?
    A have you done   **B** have you been doing   **C** are you doing   **11**

2.10 *A:* _____ each other for a long time?
      B: Yes, since we were in high school.
      A Do you know   **B** Have you known   **C** Have you been knowing

      12, 11

2.11 Kelly has been working here _____ .
      A for six months   **B** since six months   **C** six months ago

      13

2.12 It's been two years _____ Joe.
      A that I don't see   **B** that I haven't seen   **C** since I didn't see
      D since I saw

      13

2.13 The man sitting next to me on the plane was very nervous. He
      _____ before.
      A hasn't flown   **B** didn't fly   **C** hadn't flown   **D** wasn't flying

      14

2.14 Stephanie was sitting in an armchair resting. She was tired because
      _____ very hard.
      A she was working   **B** she's been working   **C** she'd been working

      15

2.15 _____ a car when they were living in Miami?
      A Do they have   **B** Were they having   **C** Have they had
      D Did they have

      16, 9

2.16 I _____ tennis a lot, but I don't play very often now.
      A was playing   **B** was used to play   **C** used to play

      17

Future

3.1 I'm tired. _____ to bed now. Good night.
     A I go   **B** I'm going

     18

3.2 _____ tomorrow, so we can go out somewhere.
     A I'm not working   **B** I don't work   **C** I won't work

     18, 20

3.3 That bag looks heavy. _____ you with it.
     A I'm helping   **B** I help   **C** I'll help

     20

3.4 I think the weather _____ be nice this afternoon.
     A will   **B** shall   **C** is going to

     22, 21

3.5 "Ann is in the hospital." "Yes, I know. _____ her tonight."
     A I visit   **B** I'm going to visit   **C** I'll visit

     22, 19

3.6 We're late. The movie _____ by the time we get to the theater.
     A will already start   **B** will be already started   **C** will already have started

     23

3.7 Don't worry _____ late tonight.
     A if I'm   **B** when I'm   **C** when I'll be   **D** if I'll be

     24

Modals

4.1 The fire spread through the building very quickly, but fortunately everybody
     _____ .
     A was able to escape   **B** managed to escape   **C** could escape

     25

4.2 I'm so tired I _____ for a week.
     A can sleep   **B** could sleep   **C** could have slept

     26

4.3 The story _____ be true, but I don't think it is.
     A might   **B** can   **C** could   **D** may

     26, 28

4.4 Why did you stay at a hotel when you were in Paris? You _____
     with Julia.
     A can stay   **B** could stay   **C** could have stayed

     26

4.5 "I've lost one of my gloves." "You _____ it somewhere."

A must drop   **B** must have dropped   **C** must be dropping

D must have been dropping

27

4.6 *A:* I was surprised that Sarah wasn't at the meeting yesterday.

B: She _____ about it.

A might not know   **B** may not know

C might not have known   **D** may not have known

28

4.7 What was the problem? Why _____ leave early?

A had you to   **B** did you have to   **C** must you   **D** you had to

30

4.8 You missed a great party last night. You _____ . Why didn't you?

A must have come   **B** should have come   **C** ought to come

D had to come

31

4.9 Lisa _____ some new clothes.

A suggested that Mary buy   **B** suggested that Mary buys

C suggested Mary to buy

32

4.10 You're always at home. You _____ out more often.

A should go   **B** had better go   **C** had better to go

33

4.11 It's late. It's time _____ home.

A we go   **B** we must go   **C** we should go   **D** we went

33

4.12 _____ a little longer, but I really have to go now.

A I'd stay   **B** I'll stay   **C** I can stay   **D** I'd have stayed

34

If and *Wish*

5.1 I'm not tired enough to go to bed. If I _____ to bed now,
I wouldn't sleep.

A go   **B** went   **C** had gone   **D** would go

36

5.2 If I were rich, _____ a yacht.

A I'll have   **B** I can have   **C** I'd have   **D** I had

37

5.3 I wish I _____ have to work tomorrow, but unfortunately I do.

A don't   **B** didn't   **C** wouldn't   **D** won't

37, 39

5.4 The view was wonderful. If _____ a camera with me, I would
have taken some photos.

A I had   **B** I would have   **C** I would have had   **D** I'd had

38

5.5 The weather is horrible. I wish it _____ raining.

A would stop   **B** stopped   **C** stops   **D** will stop

39

Passive

6.1 We _____ by a loud noise during the night.

A woke up   **B** are woken up   **C** were woken up   **D** were waking up

40

6.2 A new supermarket is going to _____ next year.

A build   **B** be built   **C** be building   **D** building

41

6.3 There's somebody walking behind us. I think _____ .

A we are following   **B** we are being following

C we are followed   **D** we are being followed

41

6.4 "Where _____ ?" "In Los Angeles."

A were you born   **B** are you born   **C** have you been born

D did you born

42

6.5 There was a fight at the game, but nobody _____ .   **42**
A was hurt   **B** got hurt   **C** hurt

6.6 Jane _____ to call me last night, but she didn't.   **43**
A supposed   **B** is supposed   **C** was supposed

6.7 Where _____ ? Which hairdresser did you go to?   **44**
A did you cut your hair   **B** have you cut your hair
C did you have cut your hair   **D** did you have your hair cut

Reported Speech

7.1 Paul left the room suddenly. He said he _____ to go.   **46, 45**
A had   **B** has   **C** have

7.2 Hi, Joe. I didn't expect to see you today. Sonia said you _____ in   **46, 45**
the hospital.
A are   **B** were   **C** was   **D** should be

7.3 Ann _____ and left.   **46**
A said goodbye to me   **B** said me goodbye   **C** told me goodbye

Questions and Auxiliary Verbs

8.1 "What time _____ ?" "At 8:30."   **47**
A begins the film   **B** does begin the film   **C** does the film begin

8.2 "Do you know where _____ ?" "No, he didn't say."   **48**
A Tom has gone   **B** has Tom gone   **C** has gone Tom

8.3 The police officer stopped us and asked us where _____ .   **48**
A were we going   **B** are we going   **C** we are going   **D** we were going

8.4 "Do you think it will rain?" "_____"   **49**
A I hope not.   **B** I don't hope.   **C** I don't hope so.

8.5 "You don't know where Lauren is, _____ ?" "Sorry, I have no idea."   **50**
A don't you   **B** do you   **C** is she   **D** are you

-ing and the Infinitive

9.1 Suddenly everybody stopped _____ . There was silence.   **51**
A talking   **B** talk   **C** to talk   **D** that they talked

9.2 I have to go now. I promised _____ late.   **52, 34**
A not being   **B** not to be   **C** to not be   **D** I wouldn't be

9.3 Do you want _____ with you, or do you want to go alone?   **53**
A me coming   **B** me to come   **C** that I come   **D** that I will come

9.4 I know I locked the door. I clearly remember _____ it.   **54**
A locking   **B** to lock   **C** to have locked

9.5 She tried to be serious, but she couldn't help _____ .   **55**
A laughing   **B** to laugh   **C** that she laughed   **D** laugh

9.6 Paul lives in Vancouver now. He likes _____ there.   **56**
A living   **B** to live

9.7 It's not my favorite job, but I like _____ the kitchen as often   **56**
as possible.
A cleaning   **B** clean   **C** to clean   **D** that I clean

9.8 I'm tired. I'd rather _____ out tonight, if you don't mind.   **57**
A not going   **B** not to go   **C** don't go   **D** not go

9.9 "Should I stay here?" "I'd rather _____ with us."

A you come   **B** you to come   **C** you came   **D** you would come

57

9.10 Are you looking forward _____ on vacation?

A going   **B** to go   **C** to going   **D** that you go

58, 60

9.11 When Lisa went to Japan, she had to get used _____ on the left.

A driving   **B** to driving   **C** to drive

59

9.12 I'm thinking _____ a house. Do you think that's a good idea?

A to buy   **B** of to buy   **C** of buying

60, 64

9.13 I had no _____ a place to live. In fact it was surprisingly easy.

A difficulty to find   **B** difficulty finding

C trouble to find   **D** trouble finding

61

9.14 A friend of mine called _____ me to a party.

A for invite   **B** to invite   **C** for inviting   **D** for to invite

62

9.15 Jim doesn't speak very clearly. _____

A It is hard to understand him.   **B** He is hard to understand.

C He is hard to understand him.

63

9.16 The sidewalk was icy, so we walked very carefully. We were afraid

_____ .

A of falling   **B** from falling   **C** to fall   **D** to falling

64

9.17 I didn't hear you _____ in. You must have been very quiet.

A come   **B** to come   **C** came

65

9.18 _____ a hotel, we looked for somewhere to have dinner.

A Finding   **B** After finding   **C** Having found   **D** We found

66

Articles and Nouns

10.1 It wasn't your fault. It was _____ .

A accident   **B** an accident   **C** some accident

67

10.2 Where are you going to put all your _____ ?

A furniture   **B** furnitures

68

10.3 "Where are you going?" "I'm going to buy _____."

A a bread   **B** some bread   **C** a loaf of bread

68

10.4 Sandra is _____ . She works at a large hospital.

A nurse   **B** a nurse   **C** the nurse

69, 70

10.5 Helen works six days _____ week.

A in   **B** for   **C** a   **D** the

70

10.6 There are millions of stars in _____ .

A space   **B** a space   **C** the space

71

10.7 Every day _____ starts at 9:00 and ends at 3:00.

A school   **B** a school   **C** the school

72

10.8 _____ a problem in most big cities.

A Crime is   **B** The crime is   **C** The crimes are

73

10.9 When _____ invented?

A was telephone   **B** were telephones

C were the telephones   **D** was the telephone

74

10.10 Have you been to _____ ?
    A Canada or United States   **B** the Canada or the United States
    C Canada or the United States   **D** the Canada or United States
75

10.11 On our first day in Moscow, we visited _____ .
    A Kremlin   **B** a Kremlin   **C** the Kremlin
76

10.12 What time _____ on television?
    A is the news   **B** are the news   **C** is news   **D** is the new
77, 68

10.13 It took us quite a long time to get here. It was _____ trip.
    A three hour   **B** a three-hours   **C** a three-hour
78

10.14 This isn't my book. It's _____ .
    A my sister   **B** my sister's   **C** from my sister
    D of my sister   **E** of my sister's
79

Pronouns and Determiners

11.1 What time should we _____ tomorrow?
    A meet   **B** meet us   **C** meet ourselves
80

11.2 I'm going to a wedding on Saturday. _____ is getting married.
    A A friend of me   **B** A friend of mine   **C** One my friends
81

11.3 They live on a busy street. _____ a lot of noise from the traffic.
    A It must be   **B** It must have   **C** There must have   **D** There must be
82

11.4 He's lazy. He never does _____ work.
    A some   **B** any   **C** no
83

11.5 *A:* What would you like to eat?
    B: I don't care. _____ – whatever you have.
    A Something   **B** Anything   **C** Nothing
83

11.6 We couldn't buy anything because _____ of the stores were open.
    A all   **B** no one   **C** none   **D** nothing
84

11.7 We went shopping and spent _____ money.
    A a lot of   **B** much   **C** lots of   **D** many
85

11.8 _____ don't visit this part of the town.
    A The most tourists   **B** Most of tourists   **C** Most tourists
86

11.9 I asked two people the way to the station, but _____ of them could help me.
    A none   **B** either   **C** both   **D** neither
87

11.10 _____ enjoyed the party. It was great.
    A Everybody   **B** All   **C** All of us   **D** Everybody of us
88

11.11 The bus service is excellent. There's a bus _____ 10 minutes.
    A each   **B** every   **C** all
88, 89

Relative Clauses

12.1 I don't like stories _____ have unhappy endings.
    A that   **B** they   **C** which   **D** who
90

12.2 I didn't believe them at first, but in fact everything _____ was true.
    A they said   **B** that they said   **C** what they said
91

12.3 What's the name of the man _____ ?   **92**
   A you borrowed his car   **B** which car you borrowed
   C whose car you borrowed   **D** his car you borrowed

12.4 Brad told me about his new job, _____ very much.   **93**
   A that he's enjoying   **B** which he's enjoying   **C** he's enjoying
   D he's enjoying it

12.5 Sarah couldn't meet us, _____ was a shame.   **94**
   A that   **B** it   **C** what   **D** which

12.6 George showed me some pictures _____ by his father.   **95, 90**
   A painting   **B** painted   **C** that were painted   **D** they were painted

Adjectives and Adverbs

13.1 Jane doesn't enjoy her job anymore. She's _____ because every day   **96**
   she does exactly the same thing.
   A boring   **B** bored

13.2 Lisa was carrying a _____ bag.   **97**
   A black small plastic   **B** small and black plastic
   C small black plastic   **D** plastic small black

13.3 Maria's English is excellent. She speaks _____ .   **98**
   A perfectly English   **B** English perfectly
   C perfect English   **D** English perfect

13.4 He _____ to find a job, but he had no luck.   **99**
   A tried hard   **B** tried hardly   **C** hardly tried

13.5 I haven't seen her for _____ , I've forgotten what she looks like.   **100**
   A so long   **B** so long time   **C** a such long time   **D** such a long time

13.6 We haven't got _____ on vacation at the moment.   **101**
   A money enough to go   **B** enough money to go
   C money enough for going   **D** enough money for going

13.7 The test was fairly easy – _____ I expected.   **102**
   A more easy that   **B** more easy than   **C** easier than   **D** easier as

13.8 The more electricity you use, _____ .   **103**
   A your bill will be higher   **B** will be higher your bill
   C the higher your bill will be   **D** higher your bill will be

13.9 Patrick is a fast runner. I can't run as fast as _____ .   **104**
   A he   **B** him   **C** he can

13.10 The film was really boring. It was _____ I've ever seen.   **105**
   A most boring film   **B** the more boring film
   C the film more boring   **D** the most boring film

13.11 Ben likes walking. _____   **106**
   A Every morning he walks to work.   **B** He walks to work every morning.
   C He walks every morning to work.   **D** He every morning walks to work.

13.12 Joe never calls me. _____   **107**
   A Always I have to call him.   **B** I always have to call him.
   C I have always to call him.   **D** I have to call always him.

13.13 Lucy _____ . She left last month.   **108**
A still doesn't work here   B doesn't still work here
C no more works here   D doesn't work here anymore

13.14 _____ she can't drive, she has bought a car.   **109, 110**
A Even   B Even when   C Even if   D Even though

Conjunctions and Prepositions

14.1 I couldn't sleep _____ very tired.   **110**
A although I was   B despite I was   C despite of being
D in spite of being

14.2 You should register your bike _____ stolen.   **111**
A in case it will be   B if it will be   C in case it is   D if it is

14.3 The club is for members only. You _____ you're a member.   **112**
A can't go in if   B can go in only if   C can't go in unless
D can go in unless

14.4 _____ the day went on, the weather got worse.   **113**
A When   B As   C While   D Since

14.5 "What's that noise?" "It sounds _____ a baby crying."   **114, 115**
A as   B like   C as if   D as though

14.6 They are very kind to me. They treat me _____ their own son.   **115**
A like I'm   B as if I'm   C as if I was   D as if I were

14.7 I'll be in Toronto next week. I hope to see Tom _____ there.   **116**
A while I'll be   B while I'm   C during my visit   D during I'm

14.8 Fred is away at the moment. I don't know exactly when he's coming back, but I'm   **117**
sure he'll be back _____ Monday.
A by   B until

Prepositions

15.1 Goodbye! I'll see you _____ .   **118**
A at Friday morning   B on Friday morning
C in Friday morning   D Friday morning

15.2 I'm going away _____ the end of January.   **119**
A at   B on   C in

15.3 When we were in Chile, we spent a few days _____ Santiago.   **120, 122**
A at   B to   C in

15.4 Our apartment is _____ the second floor of the building.   **121**
A at   B on   C in   D to

15.5 I saw Steve _____ a concert on Saturday.   **122**
A at   B on   C in   D to

15.6 When did they _____ the hotel?   **123**
A arrive to   B arrive at   C arrive in   D get to   E get in

15.7 I'm going _____ vacation next week. I'll be away for two weeks.   **124**
A at   B on   C in   D for

15.8 We came _____ 6:45 train, which arrived at 8:30.   **125**
A in the   B on the   C by the   D by

15.9 *A:* Have you read anything _____ Ernest Hemingway?
B: No, what sort of books did he write?
A of   **B** from   **C** by

125

15.10 The accident was my fault, so I had to pay for the damage _____ the other car.
A of   **B** for   **C** to   **D** on   **E** at

126

15.11 I like them very much. They have always been very nice _____ me.
A of   **B** for   **C** to   **D** with

127

15.12 I'm not very good _____ fixing things.
A at   **B** for   **C** in   **D** about

128

15.13 I don't understand this sentence. Can you _____ ?
A explain to me this word   **B** explain me this word
C explain this word to me

129

15.14 If you're worried about the problem, you should do something _____ it.
A for   **B** about   **C** against   **D** with

130

15.15 "Who is Tom Hart?" "I have no idea. I've never heard _____ him."
A about   **B** from   **C** after   **D** of

131

15.16 *A:* What time will you be home?
B: I don't know. It depends _____ the traffic.
A of   **B** for   **C** from   **D** on

132

15.17 I prefer tea _____ coffee.
A to   **B** than   **C** against   **D** over

133, 57

Phrasal Verbs

16.1 These shoes are uncomfortable. I'm going to _____ .
A take off   **B** take them off   **C** take off them

134

16.2 We're playing a game. Why don't you _____ ?
A join in   **B** come in   **C** get in   **D** break in

135

16.3 Nobody believed Paul at first, but he _____ to be right.
A worked out   **B** came out   **C** found out   **D** turned out

136

16.4 We can't _____ making a decision. We have to decide now.
A put away   **B** put over   **C** put off   **D** put out

137

16.5 The party _____ until 4:00 in the morning.
A went by   **B** went to   **C** went on   **D** went off

138

16.6 You can always rely on Pete. He'll never _____ .
A put you up   **B** let you down   **C** take you over   **D** see you off

139

16.7 Children under 16 _____ half the population of the city.
A make up   **B** put up   **C** take up   **D** bring up

140

16.8 I'm surprised to hear that Sue and Paul have _____ . They seemed very happy together the last time I saw them.
A broken up   **B** ended up   **C** finished up   **D** split up

141

16.9 I parked in a no-parking zone, but I _____ it.
A came up with   **B** got away with   **C** made off with   **D** got along with

142

Answer Key to Exercises

In some of the exercises you have to use your own ideas to write sentences. Example answers are given in the Answer Key. If possible, check your answers with somebody who speaks English well.

UNIT 1

1.1
2. 'm looking (am looking)
3. 's getting (is getting)
4. 're staying (are staying)
5. is losing
6. 's starting (is starting)
7. 're making (are making)
   'm trying (am trying)
8. 's happening (is happening)

1.2
3. 'm not listening (am not listening)
4. 's having (is having)
5. 'm not eating (am not eating)
6. 's studying (is studying)
7. aren't speaking / 're not speaking
   (are not speaking)
8. 'm getting (am getting)
9. isn't working / 's not working
   (is not working)

1.3
1. What's he studying
   Is he enjoying
   he's learning
2. is your new job going
   it's getting
   he isn't enjoying / he's not enjoying
   he's beginning

1.4
2. is changing
3. 's getting (is getting)
4. is rising
5. is beginning

UNIT 2

2.1
2. drink
3. opens
4. causes
5. live
6. take
7. connects

2.2
2. do the banks close
3. don't watch (do not watch)
4. does Ricardo come
5. do you do
6. takes . . . does it take
7. does this word mean
8. doesn't exercise (does not exercise)

2.3
3. rises
4. make
5. don't eat

6. doesn't believe
7. translates
8. don't tell
9. flows

2.4
2. Does . . . play tennis?
3. Which newspaper do you read?
4. What does your brother do?
5. How often do you go to the
   movies?
6. Where do your grandparents live?

2.5
2. I promise
3. I insist
4. I apologize
5. I recommend

UNIT 3

3.1
3. is trying
4. are they talking
5. OK
6. It's getting (It is getting)
7. OK
8. I'm coming (I am coming)
9. is it going
10. He always gets
11. OK

3.2
3. 's waiting (is waiting)
4. Are you listening
5. Do you listen
6. flows
7. 's flowing (is flowing)
8. grow . . . aren't growing / 're
   not growing (are not growing)
9. 's improving (is improving)
10. 's staying (is staying) . . . stays
11. 'm starting (am starting)
12. 'm learning (am learning) . . .
    's teaching (is teaching)
13. finish . . . 'm working
    (am working)
14. live . . . do your parents live
15. 's looking (is looking) . . . 's
    staying (is staying)
16. does your brother do . . . isn't
    working / 's not working
    (is not working)
17. enjoy . . . 'm not enjoying
    (am not enjoying)

3.3
2. 's always breaking down.
3. 'm always making the same
   mistake. / . . . that mistake.

4. You're always forgetting your
   glasses.

UNIT 4

4.1
2. Do you believe
3. OK
4. It tastes
5. I think

4.2
2. What are you doing? I'm thinking.
3. Who does this umbrella belong to?
4. Dinner smells good.
5. Is anybody sitting there?
6. These gloves don't fit me.

4.3
2. 'm using
3. need
4. does he want
5. is he looking
6. believes
7. don't remember or can't
   remember
8. 'm thinking
9. think . . . don't use
10. consists

4.4
2. is being
3. 's
4. are you being
5. Is he

UNIT 5

5.1
2. had
3. walked to work
4. took her (about) half an hour
5. She started work
6. She didn't have / She didn't eat
   (She did not have/eat)
7. She finished work
8. She was . . . she got
9. She cooked
10. She didn't go
11. She went to bed
12. She slept

5.2
2. taught
3. sold
4. fell . . . hurt
5. threw . . . caught
6. spent . . . bought . . . cost

5.3

2. did you travel / did you go
3. did it take (you) / were you there
4. did you stay
5. How was the weather?
6. Did you go to / Did you see / Did you visit

5.4

3. didn't disturb
4. left
5. didn't sleep
6. flew
7. didn't cost
8. didn't have
9. were

UNIT 6

6.1

Example answers:

3. I was working.
4. I was in bed asleep. / I was sleeping.
5. I was getting ready to go out.
6. I was watching TV at home.

6.2

Example answers:

2. was taking a shower
3. were driving to work
4. was reading the paper
5. was watching it

6.3

1. didn't see . . . was looking
2. met . . . were going . . . was going . . . talked . . . were waiting *or* waited
3. was riding . . . stepped . . . was going . . . managed . . . didn't hit

6.4

2. were you doing
3. Did you go
4. were you driving . . . happened
5. took . . . wasn't looking
6. didn't know
7. saw . . . was trying
8. was walking . . . heard . . . was following . . . started
9. wanted
10. dropped . . . was doing . . . didn't break

UNIT 7

7.1

2. . . . you ever been to Mexico?
3. Have you ever run [in] a marathon?
4. Have you ever spoken to a famous person?
5. . . . the most beautiful place you've ever visited? (. . . you have ever visited?)

7.2

2. haven't seen (have not seen)
3. haven't eaten (have not eaten . . .)
4. I haven't played (I have not played)
5. I've had / I have had
6. I've never read (I have never)
7. I've never been / I haven't been
8. 's been (has been)
9. I've never tried / I have never tried
10. it's happened / it has happened
11. I've never seen / I have never seen

7.3

2. haven't read one / haven't read a newspaper
3. it hasn't made a profit
4. she hasn't worked hard this semester
5. it hasn't snowed [a lot] this winter
6. haven't won many/any games this season

7.4

2. you played tennis before? time I've played tennis.
3. Have you ridden a horse before? / Have you been on a horse before?
No, this is the first time I've ridden a horse. / . . . I've been on a horse.
4. Have you been in Los Angeles before?
No, this is the first time I've been in Los Angeles.

UNIT 8

8.1

2. has changed
3. forgot
4. went
5. had
6. 've lost / have lost

8.2

3. *both*
4. a.
5. b.
6. *both*
7. *both*
8. *both*
9. b.
10. a.

8.3

2. he just went out *or* he's just gone out
3. I didn't finish yet. *or* I haven't finished yet.
4. I already did it. *or* I've already done it.

5. Did you find a place to live yet? *or* Have you found a place to live yet?
6. I didn't decide yet. *or* I haven't decided yet.
7. she just came back *or* she's just come back
8. already invited me *or* has already invited me

UNIT 9

9.1

3. *OK*
4. I bought
5. were you
6. graduated
7. *OK*
8. *OK*
9. *OK*
10. was this book

9.2

2. has been cold recently.
3. was cold last week.
4. didn't read a newspaper yesterday.
5. I haven't read a newspaper today.
6. Kate has made a lot of money this year.
7. She didn't make so much last year.
8. Have you taken a vacation recently?

9.3

2. got . . . was . . . went
3. Did you eat . . . We've been
4. weren't (were not)
5. worked
6. 's lived (has lived)
7. Did you go . . . was . . . was
8. died . . . never met
9. 've never met (have never met)
10. haven't seen
11. have you lived / have you been living . . . did you live . . . did you live

9.4

Example answers:

2. I haven't bought anything today.
3. I didn't watch TV yesterday.
4. I went out with some friends last night.
5. I haven't been to the movies recently. / I haven't gone to . . .
6. I've read a lot of books recently.

UNIT 10

10.1

2. 's been watching television (has been watching)
3. 've been playing tennis (have been playing)
4. 's been running (has been running) / has been jogging

10.2

2. Have you been waiting long?
3. What have you been doing?
4. How long have you been working there?
5. How long have you been selling computers?

10.3

2. 've been waiting (have been waiting)
3. 've been studying Spanish (have been studying Spanish)
4. She's been working there (She has been working there)
5. They've been going there (They have been going there)

10.4

2. I've been looking (I have been looking)
3. are you looking
4. She's been teaching (She has been teaching)
5. I've been thinking (I have been thinking)
6. she's working (she is working)
7. She's been working (She has been working)

UNIT 11

11.1

2. 's been traveling for three months. / has been traveling . . .
   She's visited six countries so far. / She has visited . . .
3. He's won the national championships four times. / He has won . . .
   He's been playing tennis since he was 10. / He has been playing . . .
4. 've made five movies since they finished college. / have made . . .
   They've been making movies since they finished college. / They have been making . . .

11.2

2. you been waiting long?
3. Have you caught any fish?
4. How many people have you invited?
5. How long have you been teaching?
6. How many books have you written?
   How long have you been writing books?
7. How long have you been saving? How much money have you saved?

11.3

2. Somebody's broken / Somebody has broken
3. Have you been working
4. Have you ever worked
5. 's gone / has gone
6. He's appeared / He has appeared
7. I haven't been waiting
8. it's stopped / it has stopped
9. I've lost / I have lost . . . Have you seen
10. I've been reading / I have been reading . . . I haven't finished
11. I've read / I have read

UNIT 12

12.1

3. have been married
4. *OK*
5. It's been raining / It has been raining
6. have you been living
7. has been working
8. *OK*
9. I haven't drunk
10. have you had

12.2

2. How long have you been teaching English? / How long have you taught . . .
3. How long have you known Carol?
4. How long has your brother been in Costa Rica?
5. How long have you had that car?
6. How long has Scott been working at the airport? / How long has Scott worked . . .
7. How long have you been taking guitar lessons?
8. Have you always lived in Chicago?

12.3

3. 's been / has been
4. 've been waiting / have been waiting
5. 've known / have known
6. haven't played
7. 's been watching / has been watching
8. haven't watched
9. 've had / have had
10. hasn't been
11. 've been feeling / have been feeling *or* 've felt / have felt
12. 's lived / has lived *or* 's been living / has been living
13. haven't been
14. 've always wanted / have always wanted

UNIT 13

13.1

2. since
3. for
4. for
5. since
6. for / in
7. since
8. since
9. for

13.2

2. How long has Kate been studying Japanese?
   When did Kate start studying Japanese?
3. How long have you known Jeff?
   When did you first meet Jeff? / When did you and Jeff first meet?
4. How long have Rebecca and David been married?
   When did Rebecca and David get married?

13.3

3. been sick since
4. been sick for
5. married a year ago
6. had a headache since
7. to France three weeks ago.
8. been working in a hotel for six months. / I've worked in a hotel for six months.

13.4

2. No, I haven't seen Laura/her for/in about a month.
3. No, I haven't been to the movies for/in a long time.
4. No, I haven't eaten out in ages. / No, I haven't been to a restaurant in ages.
6. been about a month since I (last) saw Laura/her.
7. it's been a long time since I (last) went to the movies.
8. No, it's been ages since I (last) ate out. *or* . . . since I went to a restaurant.

UNIT 14

14.1

2. It had changed a lot.
3. She'd made plans to do something else. (She had made plans . . .)
4. The movie had already begun.
5. I hadn't seen him in five years.
6. She'd just had breakfast. (She had just had . . .)

14.2

2. 'd never seen her (had never seen . . .)
3. 'd never played (tennis) before. (had never played . . .)
4. 'd never been there before. (had never been . . .)

14.3

1. called the police
2. there was . . . had gone
3. He'd . . . come back from (He had . . . come back from)
   He looked
4. got a phone call . . . was
   'd sent her (had sent her)
   'd never answered them (had never answered them)

14.4

2. went
3. had gone
4. broke
5. saw . . . had broken . . . stopped

UNIT 15

15.1

2. They'd been playing soccer. (They had been playing . . .)
3. I'd been looking forward to it. (I had been looking forward . . .)
4. She'd been dreaming. (She had been dreaming.)
5. He'd been watching a DVD. (He had been watching . . .)

15.2

2. 'd been waiting . . . [suddenly] realized that I was in . . . *or* . . . that I had come to . . .
3. closed down, . . . had been working . . .
4. had been playing for about 10 minutes . . . a man in the audience started shouting.
5. *Example answer:*
   'd been driving along the road for about 10 minutes . . . the car behind me started honking its horn.

15.3

3. was walking
4. 'd been running (had been running)
5. were eating
6. 'd been eating (had been eating)
7. was looking
8. was waiting . . . 'd been waiting (had been waiting)
9. 'd had (had had)
10. 'd been traveling (had been traveling)

UNIT 16

16.1

3. I don't have a ladder. / I haven't got a ladder.
4. didn't have enough time.
5. He didn't have a map.
6. She doesn't have any money.
7. I don't have enough energy.
8. They didn't have a camera.

16.2

2. Do you have / Have you got
3. Did you have
4. Do you have / Have you got
5. Do you have / Have you got
6. did you have
7. Did you have

16.3

Example answers:

2. don't have a bike (now). had a bike (10 years ago).
3. I have a cell phone / I've got a cell phone (now). I didn't have a cell phone (10 years ago).
4. I don't have a dog (now). I didn't have a dog (10 years ago).
5. I have a guitar / I've got a guitar (now). I had a guitar (10 years ago).
6. I don't have long hair (now). I didn't have long hair (10 years ago).
7. I have a driver's license / I've got a driver's license (now). I didn't have a driver's license (10 years ago).

16.4

2. have a talk
3. had a party
4. have a look
5. 's having a nice time (is having . . .)
6. had a dream
7. Did you have trouble
8. had a baby
9. were having dinner
10. Did you have a good flight?

UNIT 17

17.1

2. used to have/ride
3. used to live
4. used to eat/like/love
5. used to be
6. used to take [me]
7. used to be
8. did you use to go

17.2

3.–6.
   He used to go to bed early.
   He didn't use to go out every night.

He used to run three miles every morning.
He didn't use to spend much money. /. . . a lot of money.

17.3

2.–10.
   used to have lots of friends, . . . she doesn't see many people these days.
   used to be very lazy, . . . she works very hard these days.
   didn't use to like cheese, . . . she eats lots of cheese now.
   used to be a hotel desk clerk, . . . she works in a bookstore now.
   used to play the piano, . . . she hasn't played the piano for years.
   never used to read newspapers, . . . she reads a newspaper every day now.
   didn't use to drink tea, . . . she likes it now.
   used to have a dog, . . . it died two years ago.
   used to go to a lot of parties, . . . she hasn't been to a party for ages.

UNIT 18

18.1

2. How long are you staying?
3. When are you leaving?
4. Are you going alone?
5. Are you traveling by car?
6. Where are you staying?

18.2

2. 'm working late. / 'm working till 9:00.
3. I'm going to the theater.
4. I'm meeting Julia.

18.3

Example answers:

2. 'm working tomorrow morning.
3. I'm not doing anything tomorrow night.
4. I'm playing football next Sunday.
5. I'm going to a party this evening.

18.4

3. 're having / are having
4. opens
5. 'm not going / am not going . . . 'm staying / am staying
6. Are you doing
7. 're going / are going . . . starts
8. 'm leaving / am leaving
9. 're meeting / are meeting
10. does this train get
11. 'm going / am going . . . Are you coming
12. does it end
13. 'm not using / am not using
14. 's coming / is coming . . . 's flying / is flying . . . arrives

UNIT 19

19.1
2. What are you going to wear?
3. Where are you going to put it?
4. Who are you going to invite?

19.2
2. I'm going to take it back.
3. I'm not going to take it.
4. I'm going to call her tonight.
5. I'm going to complain.

19.3
2. 's going to be late. (is going to be late.)
3. is going to sink.
4. 're going to run out of gas. (are going to . . .)

19.4
2. was going to buy
3. were going to play
4. was going to call
5. was going to quit
6. were going to have

UNIT 20

20.1
2. I'll turn / I'll put
3. I'll go
4. I'll do
5. I'll show / I'll teach
6. I'll have
7. I'll send
8. I'll give / I'll bring
9. I'll stay / I'll wait

20.2
2. I'll go to bed.
3. I'll walk.
4. I'll play tennis (today).
5. I don't think I'll go swimming.

20.3
3. I'll meet
4. I'll lend
5. I'm having
6. I won't forget
7. does your plane leave
8. won't tell
9. Are you doing
10. Will you come

20.4
2. shall I give/buy/get
3. I'll do / I will do
4. shall we go?
5. I won't tell
6. I'll try

UNIT 21

21.1
2. I'm going
3. will get
4. is coming

5. we are going
6. It won't hurt

21.2
2. 'll look / will look
3. 'll like / will like
4. 'll get / will get
5. will live
6. 'll see / will see
7. 'll come / will come
8. will take

21.3
2. won't
3. 'll / will
4. won't
5. 'll / will
6. 'll / will
7. won't
8. 'll / will

21.4
Example answers:
2. I'll be in bed.
3. I'll be at work.
4. I'll probably be at home.
5. I don't know where I'll be this time next year.

21.5
2. think it will rain?
3. think it will end?
4. do you think it will cost?
5. you think they'll get married? / . . . they will get married?
6. do you think you'll be back? / . . . you will be back?
7. do you think will happen?

UNIT 22

22.1
2. I'll lend
3. I'll get
4. I'm going to wash
5. are you going to paint
6. I'm going to buy
7. I'll show
8. I'll do
9. it's going to fall
10. He's going to take . . . he's going to start

22.2
2. I'm going to take . . . I'll join
3. you'll find
4. I'm not going to apply
5. You'll wake
6. I'll take . . . we'll leave . . . Ann is going to take

UNIT 23

23.1
2. b *is true*
3. a *and* c *are true*
4. b *and* d *are true*

5. c *and* d *are true*
6. c *is true*

23.2
2. We'll have finished
3. we'll be playing
4. I'll be working
5. the meeting will have ended
6. he'll have spent
7. you'll still be doing
8. she'll have traveled
9. I'll be staying
10. Will you be seeing

UNIT 24

24.1
2. goes
3. 'll tell / will tell . . . come
4. see . . . won't recognize / will not recognize
5. Will you miss . . . 'm/am
6. 's/is
7. 'll wait / will wait . . . 're/are
8. 'll be / will be . . . gets
9. is
10. calls . . . 'm/am

24.2
2. 'll give you my address . . . I find a place to live. *or* . . . I've found a place to live.
3. I'll come straight home . . . I do the shopping. *or* . . . I've done the shopping.
4. Let's go home . . . it gets dark.
5. I won't speak to her . . . she apologizes. *or* . . . she has apologized.

24.3
2. you go / you leave
3. you decide *or* you've decided / you have decided
4. you're in Hong Kong / you are in Hong Kong
5. build the new road / 've built the new road / have built the new road

24.4
2. If
3. When
4. if
5. If
6. when
7. if
8. if

UNIT 25

25.1
3. can
4. be able to
5. been able to
6. can
7. be able to

25.2

Example answers:
2. I used to be able to run fast.
3. I'd like to be able to play the piano.
4. I've never been able to get up early.

25.3
2. could run
3. can wait
4. couldn't eat
5. can't hear
6. couldn't sleep

25.4
2. was able to finish it
3. were able to find it
4. was able to get away

25.5
4. couldn't
5. managed to
6. could
7. managed to
8. could
9. managed to
10. couldn't

UNIT 26

26.1
2. could have fish.
3. could call (her) now.
4. You could give her a book.
5. We could go on Friday.

26.2
3. I could scream.
4. OK – could have *is also possible*
5. I could stay here all day
6. it could be in the car (may/ might *are also possible*)
7. OK
8. OK – could borrow *is also possible*
9. it could change later (may/ might *are also possible*)

26.3
2. could have come/gone
3. could apply
4. could have been
5. could have taken
6. could come

26.4
3. couldn't wear
4. couldn't have found
5. couldn't get
6. couldn't have been
7. couldn't have come/gone

UNIT 27

27.1
2. must
3. must not
4. must
5. must not
6. must

27.2
3. be
4. have been
5. go
6. be going
7. have taken / have stolen / have moved
8. have been
9. be following

27.3
3. It must have been very expensive.
4. I must have left it in the restaurant last night.
5. The exam must not have been very difficult.
6. She must have listened to our conversation.
7. She must not have understood what I said.
8. I must have forgotten to turn it off.
9. The neighbors must have been having a party.

27.4
3. can't
4. must not
5. can't
6. must not

UNIT 28

28.1
2. She might/may be busy.
3. She might/may be working.
4. She might/may want to be alone.
5. She might/may have been sick yesterday.
6. She might/may have gone home early.
7. She might/may have had to go home early.
8. She might/may have been working yesterday.
9. She might/may not want to see me.
10. She might/may not be working today.
11. She might/may not have been feeling well yesterday.

28.2
2. be
3. have been
4. be waiting
5. have

28.3
2. a) She might be watching TV in her room.
   b) She might have gone out.
3. a) It might be in the car.
   b) You might have left it in the restaurant last night.
4. a) He might not have heard the doorbell.

b) He might have been in the shower.
You can use **may** *instead of* **might** *in all these sentences.*

28.4
3. might not have received it
4. couldn't have been an accident
5. couldn't have tried
6. might not have been Chinese

UNIT 29

29.1
2. might/may buy a Toyota.
3. I might/may go to the movies.
4. He might/may come on Saturday.
5. I might/may hang it in the dining room.
6. She might/may go to college.

29.2
2. might wake up
3. might bite
4. might need
5. might slip
6. might break
You can use **may** *instead of* **might** *in all these sentences.*

29.3
2. might be able to meet/see
3. might have to work
4. might have to go/leave
You can use **may** *instead of* **might** *in all these sentences.*

29.4
2. might not go out tonight.
3. might not like the present you bought him. *or* ...bought for him.
4. Sue might not be able to get together with us tonight.
You can use **may** *instead of* **might** *in all these sentences.*

29.5
2. might as well go to the concert.
3. might as well paint the bathroom.
4. We might as well watch the movie.
You can use **may** *instead of* **might** *in all these sentences.*

UNIT 30

30.1
2. had to
3. have to
4. have to
5. has to
6. had to
7. had to
8. have to

30.2

2. do you have to go
3. Did you have to wait
4. do you have to be
5. Does he have to travel

30.3

3. have to make
4. had to ask
5. doesn't have to shave
6. didn't have to go
7. has to make
8. don't have to do

30.4

3. might have to
4. will have to
5. might have to
6. won't have to

30.5

3. don't have to
4. must not
5. don't have to
6. must not
7. doesn't have to
8. must not
9. don't have to

UNIT 31

31.1

2. should look for another job.
3. shouldn't go to bed so late.
4. should take a photo.
5. shouldn't use her car so much.
6. should put some pictures on the walls.

31.2

2. I don't think you should go out tonight.
3. you should apply for the job.
4. I don't think the government should raise taxes.

31.3

3. should come
4. should do
5. should have done
6. should have won
7. should be
8. should have arrived

31.4

3. should have reserved a table.
4. The store should be open by now.
   or The store should have opened by now.
5. shouldn't be driving so fast. / ... 50 miles an hour. *or* should be driving 30 miles an hour.
6. should have written it down
7. I shouldn't have been driving right behind another car.
8. I should have looked where I was going. *or* I should have been looking ...

UNIT 32

32.1

3. I stay a little longer.
4. she visit the museum after lunch.
5. I see a specialist.
6. I not lift anything heavy.
7. we pay the rent by Friday.
8. I go away for a few days.
9. I not give my children snacks before mealtime.
10. we have dinner early.

32.2

3. spend / take
4. apologize
5. be
6. wait
7. be
8. wear
9. have / be given
10. remember / not forget
11. drink / have

32.3

2. walk to work in the morning.
3. that he eat more fruit and vegetables.
4. suggested that he take vitamins.

UNIT 33

33.1

2. You'd better put a bandage on it. (You had better put ...)
3. 'd better make a reservation. (had better make a reservation ...)
4. You'd better not go to work (You had better not go ...)
5. I'd better pay the phone bill (soon). (I had better pay ...)
6. 'd better not go out (yet). (had better not go out ...)
7. We'd better take/get a taxi. (We had better take ...)

33.2

3. 'd better (had better)
4. should
5. should
6. 'd better (had better)
7. should
8. should

33.3

1. b) 'd (had)
   c) close/shut
2. a) did
   b) was done
   c) thought

33.4

2. took / had a vacation
3. It's time the train left.
4. It's time I/we had a party.
5. It's time some changes were made.
6. It's time he tried something else.

UNIT 34

34.1

Example answers:

2. I wouldn't like to be a teacher.
3. I'd love to learn to fly a plane. (I would love to learn ...)
4. It would be nice to have a big garden.
5. I'd like to go to Mexico. (I would like to go ...)

34.2

2. 'd enjoy (would enjoy)
3. would have enjoyed
4. would ... do
5. would have stopped
6. would have been
7. 'd be (would be)
8. would have passed
9. would have

34.3

2. e
3. b
4. f
5. a
6. d

34.4

2. he'd call. (he would call)
3. promised you wouldn't tell her.
4. promised they'd wait (for us).

34.5

2. wouldn't tell
3. wouldn't speak / talk
4. wouldn't let

34.6

2. would shake
3. would ... help
4. would share
5. would ... forget

UNIT 35

35.1

2. Can/Could I leave a message (for her)? *or* Can/Could you give her a message?
3. Can/Could you tell me how to get to the post office? *or* ... the way to the post office? *or* ... where the post office is?
4. Can/Could I try on these pants? *or* Can/Could I try these [pants] on?
5. Can/Could you give me a ride home? *or* Can/Could I [please] have a ride home?

35.2

3. Do you think you could check this letter (for me)? / ... check my letter?
4. Do you mind if I leave work early?

5. Do you think you could turn the music down? / . . . turn it down?
6. Is it OK if I come and see the apartment today?
7. Do you think I could have a look at your newspaper?

35.3
2. Can/Could/Would you show me? *or* Do you think you could show me? *or* . . . do it for me?
3. Would you like to sit down? *or* Would you like a seat? *or* Can I offer you a seat?
4. Can/Could/Would you slow down? *or* Do you think you could . . . ?
5. Can/Could/May I/we have the check, please? *or* Do you think I/we could have . . . ? *or* Can I get . . .
6. Would you like to borrow it?

UNIT 36

36.1
3. 'd take (would take)
4. closed down
5. wouldn't get
6. pressed
7. refused
8. 'd be (would be)
9. didn't come
10. borrowed
11. walked
12. would understand

36.2
2. would you do if you lost your passport?
3. What would you do if there was/were a fire in the building?
4. What would you do if you were in an elevator and it stopped between floors?

36.3
2. took the driver's test, he'd fail (it). / . . . he would fail (it).
3. we stayed at a hotel, it would cost too much.
4. she applied for the job, she wouldn't get it.
5. we told them the truth, they wouldn't believe us.
6. If we invited Bill, we'd have to invite his friends, too. (. . . we would have to . . .)

36.4
Example answers:
2. somebody broke into my house.
3. I'd have a much nicer day than usual.
4. you were invited?

5. you'd save a lot of time.
6. I didn't go out with you this evening?

UNIT 37

37.1
3. 'd help (would help)
4. lived
5. 'd live (would live)
6. would taste
7. were/was
8. wouldn't wait . . . 'd go (would go)
9. didn't go
10. weren't . . . wouldn't be

37.2
2. buy it . . . it weren't/wasn't so expensive. *or* . . . if it were/was cheaper.
3. 'd go out to eat more often if we could afford it. (We would go out . . .)
4. I didn't have to work late, I could meet you tomorrow. *or* . . . I'd meet (I would meet . . .) *or* . . . I'd be able to meet . . .
5. could have lunch on the patio if it weren't raining / wasn't raining.
6. I wanted his advice, I'd ask for it. (I would ask . . .)

37.3
2. I had a cell phone.
3. I wish Amanda was/were here.
4. I wish it weren't/wasn't so cold.
5. I wish I didn't live in a big city.
6. I wish I could go to the party.
7. I wish I didn't have to work tomorrow.
8. I wish I knew something about cars.
9. I wish I was feeling / were feeling better.

37.4
Example answers:
2. I wish I had a big garden.
3. I wish I could tell jokes. *or* I wish I was/were able to . . .
4. I wish I was/were taller.

UNIT 38

38.1
2. he'd missed (he had missed) . . . , he would have been.
3. I would have forgotten . . . you hadn't reminded
4. I'd had (I had had) . . . I would have sent
5. we would have enjoyed . . . the weather had been
6. It would have been . . . I had walked
7. I was / I were
8. I'd been (I had been)

38.2
2. hadn't been icy, the accident wouldn't have happened.
3. had known [that Matt had to get up early], I would have woken him up.
4. If Jim hadn't lent me the money, I wouldn't have been able to buy the car. *or* . . . I couldn't have bought the car.
5. If Michelle hadn't been wearing a seat belt, she would have been injured [in the crash].
6. If you had had (some) breakfast, you wouldn't be hungry now.
7. If I had had (some) money, I would have taken a taxi.

38.3
2. 'd applied (had applied) for the job.
3. I wish I'd learned to play a musical instrument [when I was younger]. (I wish I had learned . . .)
4. I wish I hadn't painted it red. *or* . . . the door red.
5. I wish I'd brought my camera. (I wish I had brought . . .)
6. I wish they'd called first [to say they were coming]. (I wish they had called) *or* I wish I'd known they were coming. (I wish I had known . . .)

UNIT 39

39.1
2. hope
3. wish
4. wished
5. hope
6. wish . . . hope

39.2
2. Jane/she would come. *or* . . . would hurry up.
3. would give me a job.
4. I wish the/that baby would stop crying.
5. wouldn't drive so fast.
6. I wish you wouldn't leave the door open [all the time].
7. wouldn't drop litter in the street.

39.3
2. *OK*
3. I wish I had more free time.
4. I wish our house was/were a little bigger.
5. *OK*
6. *OK*
7. I wish everything wasn't/weren't so expensive.

39.4
3. I knew
4. I'd taken (I had taken)
5. I could come
6. I wasn't / I weren't
7. they'd hurry (they would hurry)
8. we didn't have
9. we could have stayed
10. it wasn't/weren't
11. he'd decide (he would decide)
12. we hadn't gone

UNIT 40

40.1
2. is made
3. was damaged
4. were invited
5. are shown
6. are held
7. was written . . . was translated
8. were passed
9. is surrounded

40.2
2. When was television invented?
3. How are mountains formed?
4. When was Neptune discovered?
5. What is silver used for?

40.3
3. covers
4. is covered
5. are locked
6. was mailed . . . arrived
7. sank . . . was rescued
8. died . . . were brought up
9. grew up
10. was stolen
11. disappeared
12. did Sue quit
13. was Bill fired
14. is owned
15. called . . . was injured . . . wasn't needed
16. were these picture taken . . . Did you take

40.4
2. flights were canceled because of fog.
3. This road isn't used much.
4. was accused of stealing money.
5. are languages learned?
6. We were warned not to go out alone.

UNIT 41

41.1
2. can't be broken
3. it can be eaten
4. it can't be used
5. it can't be seen
6. it can be carried

41.2
3. be made
4. be spent
5. have been repaired
6. be carried
7. be woken up
8. have been arrested
9. have been caused

41.3
2. is being used right now.
3. our conversation was being recorded.
4. the game had been canceled.
5. A new highway is being built around the city.
6. A new hospital has been built near the airport.

41.4
3. was stolen! *or* It has been stolen! (It's been)
4. took it! *or* Somebody has taken it!
5. furniture had been moved.
6. hasn't been seen since then.
7. haven't seen her for ages.
8. the computers were being used.
9. 's being redecorated.
10. 's working again. (is working . . .) . . . It's been repaired. (It has been repaired)
11. Have you ever been mugged?

UNIT 42

42.1
2. was asked some difficult questions at the interview.
3. was given a present by her colleagues when she retired.
4. told about the meeting.
5. be paid for your work?
6. should have been offered the job.
7. been shown what to do?

42.2
2. being invited
3. being given
4. being hit
5. being treated
6. being paid

42.3
2.–6.
Beethoven was born in 1770.
John Lennon was born in 1940.
Galileo was born in 1564.
Mahatma Gandhi was born in 1869.
Martin Luther King Jr. was born in 1929.
Elvis Presley was born in 1935.
Leonardo da Vinci was born in 1452.
William Shakespeare was born in 1564.
7. was born in . . .

42.4
2. got stung
3. get used
4. got stolen
5. get paid
6. got stopped
7. get damaged
8. get asked

UNIT 43

43.1
3. are reported to be homeless after the floods.
4. is alleged to have robbed the store of $3,000.
5. is reported to have been badly damaged by the fire.
6. a) is said to be losing a lot of money.
   b) is believed to have lost a lot of money last year.
   c) is expected to lose money this year.

43.2
2. is supposed to know a lot of famous people. (He's supposed . . .)
3. He is supposed to be very rich.
4. He is supposed to have 12 children.
5. He is supposed to have been an actor when he was younger.

43.3
2. 're supposed to be my friend.
3. 'm supposed to be on a diet. (am supposed . . .)
4. was supposed to be a joke.
5. 's supposed to be a flower. (is supposed . . .)
6. 're supposed to be working. (are supposed . . .)

43.4
2. 're supposed to start (are supposed . . .)
3. was supposed to call
4. aren't / 're not supposed to block (are not supposed . . .)
5. was supposed to arrive

UNIT 44

44.1
1. b
2. a
3. a
4. b

44.2
2. have my jacket cleaned.
3. To have my watch repaired.
4. To have my eyes tested.

44.3
2. had it cut.
3. had it painted.
4. He had it built.
5. I had them delivered.

44.4

2. have another key made.
3. had your hair cut
4. Do you have a newspaper delivered
5. 're having a garage built
6. have your eyes checked
8. get it cleaned
9. get your ears pierced
10. got it repaired *or* 've gotten it repaired
12. had her purse stolen
13. had his nose broken

UNIT 45

45.1

2. his father wasn't very well.
3. said [that] Amanda and Paul were getting married next month.
4. He said [that] his sister had had a baby.
5. He said [that] he didn't know what Eric was doing.
6. He said [that] he'd seen Nicole at a party in June and she'd seemed fine / he had seen . . . she had seemed fine *or* He said [that] he saw Nicole . . . and she seemed . . .
7. He said [that] he hadn't seen Diane recently.
8. He said [that] he wasn't enjoying his job very much.
9. He said [that] I could come and stay at his place if I was ever in Chicago.
10. He said [that] his car had been stolen a few days ago. *or* . . . his car was stolen a few days ago.
11. He said [that] he wanted to take a trip, but [he] couldn't afford it.
12. He said [that] he'd tell Amy he'd seen me. / . . . he would tell . . . he had seen *or* . . . he saw me.

45.2

Example answers:

2. wasn't coming / . . . was going somewhere else / . . . was staying at home
3. she didn't like him
4. you didn't know anybody / you didn't know many people
5. she wouldn't be here / she would be away / she was going away
6. you were staying at home / you weren't going out
7. you couldn't speak (any) French / were fluent in French
8. you went to the movies last week / you had gone to the movies last week

UNIT 46

46.1

2. you said you didn't like fish.
3. But you said you couldn't drive.
4. But you said she had a very well-paid job.
5. But you said you didn't have any brothers or sisters.
6. But you said you'd never been to Peru. (you had never been)
7. But you said you were working tomorrow night.
8. But you said she was a friend of yours.

46.2

2. Tell
3. Say
4. said
5. told
6. said
7. tell . . . said
8. tell . . . say
9. told
10. said

46.3

2. her to slow down
3. her not to worry
4. asked Tom to give me a hand *or* . . . to help me
5. asked me to open my bag
6. told him to mind his own business
7. asked her to marry him
8. told her not to wait [for me] if I was late

UNIT 47

47.1

2. Were you born there?
3. Are you married?
4. How long have you been married?
5. Do you have (any) children? *or* Have you got (any) children?
6. How old are they?
7. What do you do?
8. What does your wife do?

47.2

3. paid the bill?
4. happened?
5. What did she/Diane say?
6. Who does it/this book belong to?
7. Who lives in that house? / Who lives there?
8. What did you fall over?
9. What fell on the floor?
10. What does it/this word mean?
11. Who did you borrow it/the money from?
12. What are you worried about?

47.3

2. How is cheese made?
3. When was the computer invented?
4. Why isn't Sue working today?
5. What time are your friends coming?
6. Why was the concert canceled?
7. Where was your mother born?
8. Why didn't you come to the party?
9. How did the accident happen?
10. Why doesn't this machine work?

47.4

2. Don't you like him?
3. Isn't it good?
4. Don't you have any?

UNIT 48

48.1

2. where the post office is?
3. what time it is.
4. what this word means.
5. if/whether the plane has left?
6. if/whether Sue is going out tonight.
7. where Carol lives?
8. where I parked the car.
9. if/whether there is a bank near here?
10. what you want.
11. why Kelly didn't come to the party.
12. how much it costs to park here?
13. who that woman is.
14. if/whether Ann got my letter?
15. how far it is to the airport?

48.2

1. Amy is?
2. when she'll be back. (. . . she will be back)
3. if/whether she went out alone?

48.3

2. where I'd been. (. . . where I had been)
3. asked me how long I'd been back. (. . . how long I had been back)
4. He asked me what I was doing now.
5. He asked me why I'd come back. (. . . why I had come back) *or* . . . why I came back.
6. He asked me where I was living.
7. He asked me if/whether I was glad to be back.
8. He asked me if/whether I had plans to stay for a while.
9. He asked me if/whether I could lend him some money.

UNIT 49

49.1
2. doesn't
3. was
4. will
5. am . . . isn't *or* 'm not . . . is
6. should
7. won't
8. do
9. could
10. would . . . could . . . can't

49.2
3. You do? I don't.
4. You didn't? I did.
5. You haven't? I have.
6. You did? I didn't.

49.3
Example answers:
3. So did I. *or* You did? What did you watch?
4. Neither will I. *or* You won't? Where will you be?
5. So do I. *or* You do? What kind of books do you like?
6. So would I. *or* You would? Where would you like to live?
7. Neither can I. *or* You can't? Why not?

49.4
2. I guess so.
3. I don't think so.
4. I hope so.
5. I'm afraid not.
6. I'm afraid so.
7. I hope not.
8. I think so.
9. I suppose so.

UNIT 50

50.1
3. haven't you
4. were you
5. does she
6. isn't he
7. has he
8. can't you
9. will he
10. aren't there
11. shall we
12. is it
13. aren't I
14. would you
15. will you
16. should I
17. had he

50.2
2. 's (very) expensive, isn't it?
3. was great, wasn't it?
4. 've had your hair cut, haven't you? *or* You had your hair cut, didn't you?
5. has a good voice, doesn't she? *or* She's got / has got . . . / . . . doesn't/hasn't she?
6. doesn't look very good, does it?
7. isn't very safe, is it?

50.3
2. don't have paper bags, do you?
3. don't know where Ann is, do you? *or* . . . haven't seen Ann, have you?
4. you haven't got a bicycle pump, have you? *or* . . . you don't have a bicycle pump, do you?
5. you haven't seen my keys, have you? *or* you didn't see my keys, did you?
6. you couldn't take me to the station, could you? *or* you couldn't give me a lift to the station, could you?

UNIT 51

51.1
2. making
3. listening
4. applying
5. reading
6. paying
7. using
8. forgetting
9. writing
10. being
11. trying
12. losing

51.2
2. driving too fast.
3. going swimming *or* going for a swim
4. breaking the DVD player
5. waiting a few minutes

51.3
2. traveling during rush hour
3. leaving . . . tomorrow
4. turning the radio down
5. not interrupting me all the time

51.4
Example answers:
2. standing
3. having a picnic
4. laughing
5. breaking down

UNIT 52

52.1
2. to help him
3. to carry her bags (for her)
4. to meet at 8:00
5. to tell him her name / to give him her name
6. not to tell anyone

52.2
2. to go
3. to get
4. waiting
5. to eat
6. to use
7. barking
8. to call
9. having
10. to say / say
11. missing
12. to find

52.3
2. to be worried about something.
3. seem to know a lot of people.
4. My English seems to be getting better.
5. That car appears to have broken down.
6. David tends to forget things.
7. They claim to have solved the problem.

52.4
2. how to use
3. what to do
4. how to ride
5. what to say
6. whether to go

UNIT 53

53.1
2. me to lend you some
3. like me to shut it
4. you like me to show you (how)
5. you want me to repeat it
6. you want me to wait

53.2
2. to stay with them
3. him use her phone
4. her to be careful
5. her to give him a hand

53.3
2. it to rain.
3. him do what he wants.
4. him look older.
5. you to know the truth.
6. me to call my sister.
7. me to apply for the job.
8. me not to say anything to the police.
9. not to believe everything he says.
10. you to get around more easily.

53.4
2. to go
3. to do
4. cry
5. to study
6. eating
7. read
8. to make
9. think

UNIT 54

54.1
2. driving
3. to go
4. to go
5. raining
6. to win
7. asking
8. asking
9. to answer
10. breaking
11. to pay
12. losing *or* to lose
13. to tell
14. crying *or* to cry
15. to get
16. meeting . . . to see

54.2
2. He can remember crying on his first day of school.
3. He can't remember wanting to be a doctor.
4. He can remember going to Miami when he was eight.
5. He can't remember falling into a river.
6. He can't remember being bitten by a dog.

54.3
1. b) lending
   c) to call
   d) to say
   e) leaving/putting
2. a) saying
   b) to say
3. a) to become
   b) working
   c) reading

UNIT 55

55.1
2. turning it the other way.
3. tried taking an aspirin?
4. try calling his office?

55.2
2. It needs painting. / needs to be painted.
3. needs cutting. / needs to be cut.
4. They need tightening. / need to be tightened.
5. It needs emptying. / to be emptied.

55.3
1. b) knocking
   c) to put
   d) asking
   e) to reach
   f) to concentrate
2. a) to go
   b) to be looked *or* looking
   c) to be washed *or* washing
   d) to be cut *or* cutting

e) to iron . . . to be ironed *or* to iron . . . ironing
3. a) overhearing
   b) get *or* to get
   c) smiling
   d) make *or* to make

UNIT 56

56.1
Example answers:
2. I don't mind playing cards.
3. I don't like being alone. *or* . . . to be alone.
4. I enjoy going to museums.
5. I love cooking. *or* I love to cook.

56.2
2. likes teaching biology.
3. He likes taking photographs. *or* He likes to take photographs.
4. I didn't like working there.
5. She likes studying medicine.
6. He doesn't like being famous.
7. She doesn't like taking risks. *or* She doesn't like to take risks.
8. I like to know things ahead of time.

56.3
2. to sit
3. waiting
4. going *or* to go
5. to get *or* getting
6. being
7. to come / to go
8. living
9. to talk
10. to hear / hearing / to be told

56.4
2. I would like / I'd like to have seen the program.
3. I would hate / I'd hate to have lost my watch.
4. I would love / I'd love to have met your parents.
5. I wouldn't like to have been alone.
6. I would prefer / I'd prefer to have traveled by train. *or* I would have preferred to travel . . .

UNIT 57

57.1
Example answers:
2. tennis to soccer.
3. prefer calling people . . . sending e-mails.
4. I prefer going to the movies to watching videos at home.
6. call people rather than send e-mails.
7. I prefer to go to the movies rather than watch videos at home.

57.2
3. I'd rather listen to some music.
4. I'd prefer to eat at home.
5. I'd rather wait a few minutes.
6. I'd rather go for a swim.
7. I'd prefer to think about it for a while.
8. I'd rather stand.
9. I'd prefer to go alone.
11. rather than play tennis.
12. than go to a restaurant.
13. rather than decide now.
14. than watch TV.

57.3
2. I told her
3. would you rather I went / did it
4. would you rather I called her

57.4
2. stayed/remained/waited
3. stay
4. didn't
5. were
6. didn't

UNIT 58

58.1
2. applying for the job
3. remembering names
4. passing the exam
5. being late
6. eating at home, we went to a restaurant
7. having to wait in line *or* waiting in line
8. playing well

58.2
2. by standing on a chair
3. by turning a key
4. by borrowing too much money
5. by driving too fast
6. by putting some pictures on the walls

58.3
2. paying
3. going
4. using
5. going
6. being/traveling/sitting
7. asking/telling/consulting
8. doing/having
9. turning/going
10. taking

58.4
2. looking forward to seeing her/ Diane.
3. looking forward to going to the dentist (tomorrow).
4. She's looking forward to graduating (next summer).
5. I'm looking forward to playing tennis (tomorrow).

UNIT 59

59.1

1. When Juan first went to Canada, he **wasn't used to having** dinner so early, but after a while he **got used to** it. Now he finds it normal. He is **used to eating / is used to having dinner** at 6:00.

2. She **wasn't used to working** nights and it took her a few months to **get used to** it. Now, after a year, she's pretty happy. She **is used to working** nights.

59.2

2. 'm used to sleeping on the floor.
3. 'm used to working long hours.
4. I'm not used to going to bed so late.

59.3

2. get used to living
3. got used to her. / ... to the/ their new teacher.
4. *Example answers:*
   get used to the weather. / ... to the food. / ... to speaking a foreign language.

59.4

3. drink
4. eating
5. having
6. have
7. go
8. be
9. being

UNIT 60

60.1

2. doing
3. coming/going
4. doing/trying
5. buying/getting
6. hearing
7. going
8. having/using
9. being
10. watching
11. inviting/asking

60.2

2. in solving
3. of living
4. of causing
5. (from) walking
6. for interrupting
7. of spending
8. from escaping
9. on carrying
10. to seeing

60.3

2. on driving Ann to the station / ... on taking Ann ...
3. on getting married
4. Sue for coming to see her
5. (to me) for not calling earlier
6. me of being selfish

UNIT 61

61.1

2. There's no point in working if you don't need money.
3. There's no point in trying to study if you feel tired.
4. There's no point in hurrying if you've got plenty of time.

61.2

2. asking Dave
3. in going out
4. calling her
5. complaining (about what happened)
6. taking
7. keeping

61.3

2. remembering people's names
3. getting a job
4. getting a ticket for the game
5. understanding him

61.4

2. reading
3. packing / getting ready
4. watching
5. going/climbing/walking
6. applying
7. getting / being

61.5

2. went swimming
3. go skiing
4. goes riding
5. 's gone shopping / went shopping

UNIT 62

62.1

2. to get some money.
3. 'm saving money to go to Canada.
4. I went into the hospital to have an operation.
5. I'm wearing two sweaters to keep warm.
6. I called the police to report that my car had been stolen.

62.2

2. to read
3. to walk
4. to drink
5. to put / to carry
6. to discuss / to talk about
7. to buy / to get
8. to talk / to speak
9. to wear / to put on
10. to celebrate
11. to help

62.3

2. for
3. to
4. to
5. for
6. to
7. for
8. for ... to

62.4

2. warm clothes so that I wouldn't be cold.
3. left Dave my phone number so that he could contact me. / ... would be able to contact me.
4. We whispered so that ... else would hear our conversation. / ... so that nobody could hear ... / would be able to hear ...
5. arrive early so that we can start the meeting on time. / ... so that we'll be able to start ...
6. Jennifer locked the door so that she wouldn't be disturbed.
7. I slowed down so that the car behind me could pass. / ... would be able to pass.

UNIT 63

63.1

2. easy to use.
3. was very difficult to open.
4. are impossible to translate.
5. car is expensive to maintain.
6. chair isn't safe to stand on.

63.2

2. easy mistake to make.
3. nice place to live. *or* ... a nice place to live in.
4. good game to watch.

63.3

2. 's careless of you to make the same mistake again and again.
3. It was nice of them to invite me (to stay with them). / It was nice of Dan and Jenny to ...
4. It's inconsiderate of them to make so much noise (at night). / It's inconsiderate of the neighbors to ...

63.4

2. am glad to hear *or* was glad to hear
3. were surprised to see
4. 'm/am sorry to hear *or* was sorry to hear

63.5

2. last (person) to arrive.
3. the only student to pass (the exam). / . . . the only one to pass (the exam).
4. the second customer/person to complain.
5. the first person/man to walk on the moon.

63.6

2. 're/are bound to be
3. 's/is sure to forget
4. 's/is not likely to rain   *or* isn't likely to rain
5. 's/is likely to be

UNIT 64

64.1

3. I'm afraid of losing it.
4. I was afraid to tell her.
5. We were afraid of missing our train.
6. We were afraid to look.
7. I was afraid of dropping it.
8. a) I was afraid to eat it.
   b) I was afraid of getting sick.

64.2

2. in starting
3. to read
4. in getting
5. to know
6. in looking

64.3

2. sorry to hear
3. sorry for saying / sorry about saying
4. sorry to bother
5. sorry for losing / sorry about losing

64.4

1. b) to leave
   c) from leaving
2. a) to solve
   b) in solving
3. a) of/about going
   b) to go
   c) to go
   d) to going
4. a) to buy
   b) to buy
   c) on buying
   d) of buying

UNIT 65

65.1

2. arrive
3. take it / do it
4. it ring
5. him play / him playing
6. you lock it / you do it
7. her fall

65.2

2. playing tennis.
3. Claire eating
4. Bill playing his guitar.
5. smell the dinner burning.
6. We saw Linda jogging/running.

65.3

3. tell
4. crying
5. riding
6. say
7. run . . . climb
8. explode
9. crawling
10. slam
11. sleeping

UNIT 66

66.1

2. in an armchair reading a book.
3. opened the door carefully trying not to make any noise.
4. Sarah went out saying she would be back in an hour.
5. Linda was in London for two years working as a teacher.
6. Mary walked around the town looking at the sights and taking pictures.

66.2

2. fell asleep watching television.
3. slipped and fell getting off a bus.
4. got very wet walking home in the rain.
5. Laura had an accident driving to work yesterday.
6. Two kids got lost hiking in the woods.

66.3

2. Having bought our tickets, we went into the theater.
3. Having had dinner, they continued their trip.
4. Having done the shopping, I stopped for a cup of coffee.

66.4

2. Thinking they might be hungry, I offered them something to eat.
3. Being a vegetarian, Sally doesn't eat meat of any kind.
4. Not knowing his e-mail address, I wasn't able to contact him.
5. Having traveled a lot, Sarah knows a lot about other countries.
6. Not being able to speak the local language, I had trouble communicating.
7. Having spent nearly all our money, we couldn't afford to stay in a hotel.

UNIT 67

67.1

3. We went to **a** very nice restaurant . . .
4. *OK*
5. I use **a** toothbrush . . .
6. . . . if there's **a** bank near here?
7. . . . for **an** insurance company
8. *OK*
9. *OK*
10. . . . we stayed in **a** big hotel.
11. . . . I hope we come to **a** gas station soon.
12. . . . I have **a** problem.
13. . . . It's **a** very interesting idea.
14. John has **an** interview for **a** job tomorrow.
15. . . . It's **a** good game.
16. *OK*
17. Jane was wearing **a** beautiful necklace.

67.2

3. a key
4. a coat
5. sugar
6. a cookie
7. electricity
8. an interview
9. blood
10. a question
11. a minute
12. a decision

67.3

2. days
3. meat
4. a line
5. letters
6. friends
7. people
8. air
9. patience
10. an umbrella
11. languages
12. space

UNIT 68

68.1

2. a) a paper
   b) paper
3. a) a light
   b) Light
4. a) time
   b) a wonderful time
5. a nice room
6. advice
7. nice weather
8. bad luck
9. job
10. trip
11. total chaos
12. some

13. doesn't
14. Your hair is . . . it
15. The damage

68.2
2. information
3. chairs
4. furniture
5. hair
6. progress
7. job
8. work
9. permission
10. advice
11. experience
12. experiences

68.3
2. some information about places to see in the city.
3. some advice about which courses to take? / . . . courses I can take?
4. is the news on (TV)?
5. 's a beautiful view, isn't it?
6. horrible/awful weather!

UNIT 69

69.1
3. It's a vegetable.
4. It's a game. / It's a board game.
5. They're musical instruments.
6. It's a (tall/high) building.
7. They're planets.
8. It's a flower.
9. They're rivers.
10. They're birds.
12. He was a writer / a poet / a playwright / a dramatist.
13. He was a scientist / a physicist.
14. They were U.S. presidents / American presidents / presidents of the U.S.
15. She was an actress / a movie actress / a movie star.
16. They were singers.
17. They were painters / artists.

69.2
2. 's a waiter.
3. 's a travel agent.
4. He's a surgeon.
5. He's a chef.
6. She's a journalist.
7. He's a plumber.
8. She's an interpreter.

69.3
4. a
5. an
6. – (Do you collect stamps?)
7. a
8. Some
9. – (Do you enjoy going to concerts?)
10. – (I've got sore feet.)

11. a
12. some
13. a . . . a
14. – (Those are nice shoes.)
15. some
16. a . . . some
17. a . . . – (Her parents were teachers, too.)
18. a . . . – (He's always telling lies.)

UNIT 70

70.1
1. . . . and **a** magazine. **The** newspaper is in my briefcase, but I can't remember where I put **the** magazine.
2. I saw **an** accident this morning. **A** car crashed into **a** tree. **The** driver of **the** car wasn't hurt, but **the** car was badly damaged.
3. . . . **a** blue one and **a** gray one. **The** blue one belongs to my neighbors; I don't know who **the** owner of **the** gray one is.
4. My friends live in **an** old house in **a** small town. There is **a** beautiful garden behind **the** house. I would like to have **a** garden like that.

70.2
1. b) the
   c) the
2. a) a
   b) a
   c) the
3. a) a
   b) the
   c) the
4. a) an . . . The
   b) the
   c) the
5. a) the
   b) a
   c) a

70.3
2. **the** dentist
3. **the** door
4. **a** mistake
5. **the** bus station
6. **a** problem
7. **the** post office
8. **the** floor
9. **the** book
10. **a** job at **a** bank
11. **a** small apartment near **the** hospital
12. **a** supermarket on **the** corner

70.4
Example answers:
3. About once a year.
4. Once or twice a year.
5. About 55 miles an hour.

6. About seven hours a night.
7. Two or three times a week.
8. About two hours a day.

UNIT 71

71.1
2. *A:* a; *B:* the
3. *A:* the; *B:* the
4. *A:* the; *B:* a
5. *A:* –; *B:* the
6. *A:* the; *B:* –
7. *A:* a; *B:* the
8. *A:* –; *B:* –
9. *A:* –; *B:* the
10. *A:* the; *B:* a

71.2
2. the . . . the
3. –
4. The
5. the
6. –
7. the . . . the . . . –
8. the

71.3
2. in a small town in the country
3. The moon goes around the earth every 27 days.
4. the same thing
5. a very hot day . . . the hottest day of the year
6. eat a good breakfast
7. live in a foreign country . . . learn the language
8. on the wrong platform
9. The next train

71.4
2. the ocean
3. question 8
4. the movies
5. breakfast
6. the gate
7. Gate 21

UNIT 72

72.1
2. to school
3. at home
4. to work
5. in high school
6. in bed
7. to prison

72.2
1. c) school
   d) school
   e) . . . school . . . The school
   f) school
   g) the school
2. a) college
   b) college
   c) the college

3. a) church
   b) church
   c) the church
4. a) class
   b) the class
   c) class
   d) the class
5. a) prison
   b) the prison
   c) prison
6. a) bed
   b) home
   c) work
   d) bed
   e) work
   f) work

UNIT 73

73.1
Example answers:
2.–5.
   I like cats.
   I don't like zoos.
   I don't mind fast-food
   restaurants.
   I'm not interested in football.

73.2
3. spiders
4. meat
5. the questions
6. the people
7. History
8. lies
9. the hotels
10. The water
11. the grass
12. patience

73.3
3. Apples
4. the apples
5. Women . . . men
6. tea
7. The vegetables
8. Life
9. skiing
10. the people
11. people . . . aggression
12. All the books
13. the beds
14. war
15. The First World War
16. the Pyramids
17. the history . . . modern art
18. the marriage
19. Most people . . . marriage . . .
    family life . . . society

UNIT 74

74.1
1. b) the cheetah
   c) the kangaroo (and the rabbit)
2. a) the swan
   b) the penguin
   c) the owl

3. a) the wheel
   b) the laser
   c) the telescope
4. a) the rupee
   b) the (Canadian) dollar
   c) the . . .

74.2
2. a
3. the
4. a
5. the
6. the
7. a
8. The

74.3
2. the injured
3. the unemployed
4. the sick
5. the rich . . . the poor

74.4
2. a German   Germans
3. a Frenchman/Frenchwoman
   the French
4. a Russian   Russians
5. a Chinese   the Chinese
6. a Brazilian   Brazilians
7. a Japanese man/woman
   the Japanese
8. . . .

UNIT 75

75.1
2. the
3. the . . . the
4. – (President Kennedy was
   assassinated in 1963.)
5. the
6. – (Do you know Professor
   Brown's phone number?)

75.2
3. OK
4. the United States
5. The south of India. . . the north
6. OK
7. the Channel
8. the Middle East
9. OK
10. the Swiss Alps
11. The UK
12. The Seychelles . . . the Indian
    Ocean
13. OK
14. The Hudson River . . . the
    Atlantic Ocean

75.3
2. (in) South America
3. the Nile
4. Sweden
5. the United States
6. the Rockies
7. the Mediterranean
8. Australia

9. the Pacific
10. the Indian Ocean
11. the Thames
12. the Mississippi
13. Thailand
14. the Panama Canal
15. the Amazon

UNIT 76

76.1
2. Turner's on Carter Road
3. the Crown (Hotel) on Park
   Road
4. St. Paul's on Market Street
5. the City Museum on George
   Street
6. Blackstone's on Forest Avenue
7. Lincoln Park at the end of
   Market Street
8. The China House on Park
   Road *or* Mario's Pizza on
   George Street

76.2
2. The Eiffel Tower
3. The Taj Mahal
4. The White House
5. The Kremlin
6. Broadway
7. The Acropolis
8. Buckingham Palace

76.3
2. Central Park
3. St. James's Park
4. The Ramada Inn . . . Main Street
5. O'Hare Airport
6. McGill University
7. Harrison's
8. the Ship Inn
9. The Statue of Liberty . . .
   New York Harbor
10. the Science Museum
11. IBM . . . General Electric
12. The Classic
13. the Great Wall
14. The Washington Post
15. Cambridge University Press

UNIT 77

77.1
3. shorts
4. a means
5. means
6. some scissors *or* a pair of
   scissors
7. a series
8. series
9. species

77.2
2. politics
3. economics
4. physics
5. gymnastics
6. electronics

77.3
2. don't
3. want
4. was
5. aren't
6. wasn't
7. isn't
8. they
9. are
10. Do
11. is

77.4
3. . . . wearing black jeans.
4. very nice people.
5. *OK*
6. . . . buy some new pajamas. *or*
. . . buy a new pair of pajamas.
7. There was a police officer / a
policeman / a policewoman . . .
8. *OK*
9. These scissors aren't . . .
10. . . . two days is enough . . .
11. Many people have . . .

UNIT 78

78.1
3. a computer magazine
4. vacation pictures
5. milk chocolate
6. a factory inspector
7. a race horse
8. a horse race
9. a Los Angeles lawyer
10. exam results
11. the dining room carpet
12. an oil company scandal
13. a five-story building
14. a traffic plan
15. a five-day course
16. a two-part question
17. a seven-year-old girl

78.2
2. room number
3. seat belt
4. credit card
5. weather forecast
6. newspaper editor
7. shop window

78.3
3. 20-dollar
4. 15-minute
5. 60 minutes
6. two-hour
7. five courses
8. two-year
9. 500-year-old
10. five days
11. six miles
12. six-mile

UNIT 79

79.1
3. your friend's umbrella
4. *OK*
5. Charles's daughter
6. Mary and Dan's son
7. *OK*
8. yesterday's newspaper
9. *OK*
10. *OK*
11. Your children's friends
12. Our neighbors' garden
13. *OK*
14. Bill's hair
15. Catherine's party
16. *OK*
17. Mike's parents' car
18. *OK*
19. *OK* (the government's
economic policy *is also correct*)

79.2
2. a boy's name
3. children's clothes
4. a girls' school
5. a bird's nest
6. a women's magazine

79.3
2. week's storm caused a lot of
damage.
3. town's only movie theater has
closed down.
4. Chicago's weather is very
changeable.
5. The region's main industry is
tourism.

79.4
2. a year's salary
3. four weeks' pay
4. five hours' sleep
5. a minute's rest

UNIT 80

80.1
2. hurt himself
3. blame herself
4. Put yourself
5. enjoyed themselves
6. burn yourself
7. express myself

80.2
2. me
3. myself
4. us
5. yourself
6. you
7. ourselves
8. themselves
9. them

80.3
2. dried herself
3. concentrate
4. defend yourself
5. meeting
6. relax

80.4
2. themselves
3. each other
4. each other
5. themselves
6. each other
7. ourselves
8. each other
9. ourselves . . . each other

80.5
2. it himself.
3. mail/do it myself.
4. told me herself. / herself told
me. / did herself.
5. call him yourself? / do it yourself?

UNIT 81

81.1
2. relative of yours.
3. borrowed a book of mine.
4. invited some friends of hers to
her place.
5. We had dinner with a neighbor
of ours.
6. I took a trip with two friends
of mine.
7. Is that man a friend of yours?
8. I met a friend of Amy's at the
party.

81.2
2. his own opinions
3. her own business
4. its own (private) beach
5. our own words

81.3
2. your own fault
3. her own ideas
4. your own problems
5. his own decisions

81.4
2. makes her own clothes
3. bake/make our own bread
4. writes his own songs

81.5
2. my own
3. myself
4. himself
5. his own
6. herself
7. her own
8. yourself
9. our own
10. herself

UNIT 82

82.1
3. Is there . . . there's / there is
4. there was . . . It was
5. It was
6. There was
7. is it
8. It was
9. It's / It is
10. there wasn't
11. Is it . . . it's / it is
12. there was . . . There was
13. It was
14. There wasn't
15. There was . . . it wasn't

82.2
2. is a lot of salt
3. There was nothing
4. There was a lot of violence in the movie. / There was a lot of fighting . . .
5. There were a lot of people in the stores / the shopping mall.
6. There is a lot to do in this town. / There is a lot happening in this town.

82.3
2. There might be
3. there will be / there'll be *or* there are going to be
4. There's going to be / There is going to be
5. There used to be
6. there should be
7. there wouldn't be

82.4
2. . . . and there was a lot of snow.
3. There used to be a church here.
4. There must have been a reason.
5. *OK*
6. There's sure to be a parking lot somewhere.
7. . . . there will be an opportunity . . .
8. *OK*
9. . . . there would be somebody . . . but there wasn't anybody.
10. There has been no change.
11. *OK*

UNIT 83

83.1
2. some
3. any
4. any . . . some
5. some
6. any
7. any
8. some
9. any
10. any

83.2
2. somebody/someone
3. anybody/anyone
4. anything
5. something
6. somebody/someone . . . anybody/anyone
7. something . . . anybody/anyone
8. Anybody/Anyone
9. anybody/anyone
10. anywhere
11. somewhere
12. anywhere
13. anybody/anyone
14. something
15. Anybody/Anyone
16. something
17. anybody/anyone . . . anything

83.3
2. Any day
3. Anything
4. anywhere
5. Any job *or* Anything
6. Any time
7. Anybody/Anyone
8. Any newspaper *or* Any one

UNIT 84

84.1
3. no
4. any
5. None
6. none
7. No
8. any
9. any
10. none
11. no

84.2
2. Nobody/No one.
3. None.
4. Nowhere.
5. None.
6. Nothing.
8. I wasn't talking to anybody/anyone.
9. I don't have any luggage.
10. I'm not going anywhere.
11. I didn't make any mistakes.
12. I didn't pay anything.

84.3
2. nobody/no one
3. Nowhere
4. anything
5. Nothing. I couldn't find anything . . .
6. Nothing
7. anywhere
8. Nobody/No one said anything.

84.4
2. nobody
3. anyone
4. Anybody
5. Nothing
6. Anything
7. anything

UNIT 85

85.1
3. a lot of salt
4. *OK*
5. It cost a lot
6. *OK*
7. many people *or* a lot of people
8. I use the phone a lot
9. *OK*
10. a lot of money

85.2
2. plenty of money.
3. plenty of room.
4. plenty to learn.
5. are plenty of things to see.
6. There are plenty of hotels.

85.3
2. little
3. many
4. much
5. few
6. little
7. many

85.4
3. a few dollars
4. *OK*
5. a little time
6. *OK*
7. only a few words
8. a few months

85.5
2. a little
3. a few
4. few
5. little
6. a little
7. little
8. a few

UNIT 86

86.1
3. –
4. of
5. –
6. –
7. of
8. of
9. –
10. –

86.2
3. of my spare time
4. accidents
5. of the buildings
6. of her friends
7. of the population
8. birds
9. of my teammates
10. of her opinions
11. large cities
12. (of) my dinner

86.3
Example answers:
2. the time / the day
3. my friends
4. (of) the questions
5. the photos / the photographs / the pictures
6. (of) the money

86.4
2. All of them
3. none of us
4. some of it
5. none of them
6. None of it
7. Some of them
8. all of it

UNIT 87

87.1
2. Neither
3. both
4. Either
5. Neither

87.2
2. either
3. both
4. Neither of
5. neither . . . both / both the / both of the
6. both / both of

87.3
2. either of them
3. both of them
4. neither of us
5. neither of them

87.4
3. Both Joe and Sam are on vacation.
4. Neither Joe nor Sam has a car.
5. Brian neither watches TV nor reads newspapers.
6. The movie was both boring and long.
7. That man's name is either Richard or Robert.
8. neither the time nor the money to go on vacation.
9. We can leave either today or tomorrow.

87.5
2. either
3. any
4. none
5. any
6. either
7. neither

UNIT 88

88.1
3. Everybody/Everyone
4. Everything
5. all/everything
6. everybody/everyone
7. everything
8. All
9. everybody/everyone
10. All
11. everything/all
12. Everybody/Everyone
13. All
14. everything

88.2
2. whole team played well.
3. the whole box (of chocolates).
4. searched the whole house.
5. whole family plays tennis.
6. Ann/She worked the whole day.
7. rained the whole week.
8. worked all day.
9. It rained all week.

88.3
2. every four hours
3. every four years
4. every five minutes
5. every six months

88.4
2. every day
3. all day
4. The whole building
5. every time
6. all the time
7. all my luggage

UNIT 89

89.1
3. Each
4. Every
5. Each
6. every
7. each
8. every

89.2
3. Every
4. Each
5. every
6. every
7. each
8. every
9. every

10. each
11. Every
12. each

89.3
2. had 10 dollars each / each had 10 dollars
3. postcards cost 40 cents each / postcards are 40 cents each
4. paid $195 each / each paid $195

89.4
2. everyone
3. every one
4. Everyone
5. every one

UNIT 90

90.1
2. who breaks into a house to steal things.
3. A customer is someone who buys something from a store.
4. A shoplifter is someone who steals from a store.
5. A coward is someone who is not brave.
6. An atheist is someone who doesn't believe in God.
7. A pessimist is someone who expects the worst to happen.
8. A tenant is someone who pays rent to live in a room or apartment.

90.2
2. waitress who/that served us was impolite and impatient.
3. building that/which was destroyed in the fire has now been rebuilt.
4. people who/that were arrested have now been released.
5. bus that/which goes to the airport runs every half hour.

90.3
2. who/that runs away from home
3. that/which were on the wall
4. that/which cannot be explained
5. who/that stole my car
6. that/which gives you the meanings of words
7. who/that invented the telephone
8. that/which can support life

90.4
3. that/which sells
4. who/that caused
5. *OK (who took is also correct)*
6. that/which is changing
7. *OK (which were is also correct)*
8. that/which won

UNIT 91

91.1
3. *OK (the people who/that we met is also correct)*
4. The people who/that work in the office
5. *OK (the people who/that I work with is also correct)*
6. *OK (the money that/which I gave you is also correct)*
7. the money that/which was on the table
8. *OK (the worst film that/which you've ever seen is also correct)*
9. the best thing that/which has ever happened to you

91.2
2. you're wearing *or* that/which you're wearing
3. you're going to see *or* that/which you're going to see
4. I/we wanted to visit *or* that/which I/we wanted to visit
5. I/we invited to the party *or* who/whom/that we invited . . .
6. you had to do *or* that/which you had to do
7. I/we rented *or* that/which I/we rented
8. Tom had recommended (to us) *or* that/which Tom had recommended . . .

91.3
2. we were invited to *or* that/which we were invited to
3. I work with *or* who/that I work with
4. you told me about *or* that/which you told me about
5. we went to last night *or* that/which we went to . . .
6. I applied for *or* that/which I applied for
7. you can rely on *or* who/that you can rely on
8. I saw you with *or* who/that I saw you with

91.4
3. – (that *is also correct*)
4. what
5. that
6. what
7. – (that *is also correct*)
8. what
9. – (that *is also correct*)

UNIT 92

92.1
2. whose wife is an English teacher
3. who owns a restaurant
4. whose ambition is to climb Everest
5. who have just gotten married / just got married
6. whose parents used to work in a circus

92.2
2. where I can buy some postcards
3. where I work
4. where Sue is staying
5. where I/we play baseball

92.3
2. where
3. who
4. whose
5. whom
6. where
7. whose
8. whom

92.4
Example answers:
2. I'll never forget the time we got stuck in an elevator.
3. The reason I didn't write to you was that I didn't know your address.
4. Unfortunately I wasn't at home the evening you called.
5. The reason they don't have a car is that they don't need one.
6. 1996 was the year Amanda got married.

UNIT 93

93.1
3. We often go to visit our friends in New York, which is not very far away.
4. I went to see the doctor, who told me to rest for a few days.
5. John, who/whom I've known for a very long time, is one of my closest friends.
6. Sheila, whose job involves a lot of travel, is away from home a lot.
7. The new stadium, which can hold 90,000 people, will be opened next month.
8. Alaska, where my brother lives, is the largest state in the United States.
9. A friend of mine, whose father is the manager of a company, helped me to get a job.

93.2
3. which began 10 days ago, is now over.
4. the book I was looking for this morning. *or* . . . the book that/which I was looking for.
5. which was once the largest city in the world, is now decreasing.
6. the people who/that applied for the job had the necessary qualifications.
7. a picture of her son, who is a police officer.

93.3
2. My office, which is on the second floor, is very small.
3. *OK (The office that/which I'm using . . . is also correct)*
4. Ben's father, who used to be a teacher, now works for a TV company.
5. *OK (The doctor who examined me . . . is also correct)*
6. The sun, which is one of millions of stars in the universe, provides us with heat and light.

UNIT 94

94.1
2. of which he's very proud
3. with whom we went on vacation
4. to which only members of the family were invited

94.2
2. most of which was useless
3. neither of which she has received
4. none of whom was suitable
5. one of which she hardly ever uses
6. half of which he gave to his parents
7. both of whom are teachers
8. only a few of whom I knew
9. (the) sides of which were lined with trees
10. the aim of which is to save money

94.3
2. doesn't have a phone, which makes it difficult to contact her.
3. Neil has passed his exams, which is good news.
4. Our flight was delayed, which meant we had to wait three hours at the airport.
5. Kate offered to let me stay at her house, which was very nice of her.
6. The street I live on is very noisy at night, which makes it difficult to sleep sometimes.
7. Our car has broken down, which means we can't take our trip tomorrow.

UNIT 95

95.1
2. man sitting next to me on the plane
3. taxi taking us to the airport
4. path leading to the river
5. factory employing 500 people
6. a brochure containing the information I needed

95.2
2. damaged in the storm
3. suggestions made at the meeting
4. paintings stolen from the museum
5. the man arrested by the police

95.3
3. living
4. offering
5. named
6. blown
7. sitting . . . reading
8. driving . . . selling

95.4
3. is somebody coming.
4. There were a lot of people traveling.
5. There was nobody else staying there.
6. There was nothing written on it.
7. There's a new course beginning next Monday.

UNIT 96

96.1
2. a) exhausting
   b) exhausted
3. a) depressing
   b) depressed
   c) depressed
4. a) exciting
   b) exciting
   c) excited

96.2
2. interested
3. exciting
4. embarrassing
5. embarrassed
6. amazed
7. astonishing
8. amused
9. terrifying . . . shocked
10. bored . . . boring
11. boring . . . interesting

96.3
2. bored
3. confusing
4. disgusting
5. interested
6. annoyed
7. boring
8. exhausted
9. excited
10. amusing
11. interesting

UNIT 97

97.1
2. an unusual gold ring
3. a beautiful old house
4. black leather gloves
5. an old Italian film

6. a long thin face
7. big black clouds
8. a lovely sunny day
9. an ugly yellow dress
10. a long wide avenue
11. a little old red car
12. a nice new green sweater
13. a small black metal box
14. a big fat black cat
15. a charming little old country inn
16. beautiful long black hair
17. an interesting old French painting
18. an enormous red and yellow umbrella

97.2
2. tastes/tasted awful
3. feel fine
4. smell nice
5. look wet
6. sounds/sounded interesting

97.3
2. happy
3. happily
4. violent
5. terrible
6. properly
7. good
8. slow

97.4
3. the last two days
4. the first two weeks of May
5. the next few days
6. the first three questions (on the exam)
7. the next two years
8. the last three days of our vacation

UNIT 98

98.1
2. badly
3. easily
4. patiently
5. unexpectedly
6. regularly
7. perfectly . . . slowly . . . clearly

98.2
3. selfishly
4. terribly
5. sudden
6. colorfully
7. colorful
8. badly
9. badly
10. safe

98.3
2. careful
3. continuously
4. happily
5. fluent
6. specially
7. complete

8. perfectly
9. nervous
10. financially *or* completely

98.4
2. seriously ill
3. absolutely enormous
4. slightly damaged
5. unusually quiet
6. completely changed
7. unnecessarily long
8. badly planned

UNIT 99

99.1
2. good
3. well
4. good
5. well
6. well
7. good
8. well
9. good
10. well

99.2
2. well known
3. well maintained
4. well written
5. well informed
6. well dressed
7. well paid

99.3
2. *OK*
3. *OK*
4. hard
5. *OK*
6. slowly

99.4
2. hardly hear
3. hardly slept
4. hardly speak
5. hardly said
6. hardly changed
7. hardly recognized

99.5
2. hardly any
3. hardly anything
4. hardly anybody/anyone
5. hardly ever
6. Hardly anybody/anyone
7. hardly anywhere
8. hardly *or* hardly ever
9. hardly any
10. hardly anything . . . hardly anywhere

UNIT 100

100.1
4. so
5. so
6. such a
7. so

8. such
9. such a
10. such a
11. so
12. so . . . such
13. so
14. such a
15. such a

100.2
3. I was so tired (that) I couldn't keep my eyes open.
4. We had such a good time on vacation (that) we didn't want to come home.
5. She speaks English so well (that) you would think it was her native language. *or* She speaks such good English (that) . . .
6. I've got such a lot to do (that) I don't know where to begin. *or* I've got so much to do (that) . . .
7. The music was so loud (that) you could hear it from miles away.
8. I had such a big breakfast (that) I didn't eat anything else for the rest of the day.
9. It was such terrible weather (that) we spent the whole day indoors.
10. I was so surprised (that) I didn't know what to say.

100.3
Example answers:
2. a) friendly
   b) a nice person
3. a) lively
   b) an exciting place
4. a) exhausting
   b) a difficult job
5. a) long
   b) a long time

UNIT 101

101.1
3. enough money
4. enough milk
5. warm enough
6. enough room
7. well enough
8. enough time
9. qualified enough
10. big enough
11. enough cups

101.2
2. too busy to talk
3. too late to go
4. warm enough to sit
5. too shy to be
6. enough patience to be
7. too far away to hear
8. enough English to read

101.3
2. too hot to drink.
3. was too heavy to move.
4. aren't / are not ripe enough to eat.
5. is too complicated (for me) to explain.
6. was too high (for us) to climb over.
7. isn't / is not big enough for three people (to sit on).
8. things are too small to see without a microscope.

UNIT 102

102.1
2. stronger
3. smaller
4. more expensive
5. warmer/hotter
6. more interesting / more exciting
7. nearer/closer
8. more difficult / more complicated
9. better
10. worse
11. longer
12. more quietly
13. more often
14. farther/further
15. happier

102.2
3. more serious than
4. thinner
5. bigger
6. more interested
7. more important than
8. simpler / more simple
9. more crowded than
10. more peaceful than
11. more easily
12. higher than

102.3
2. longer by train than by car.
3. further/farther than Dave.
4. worse than Chris (on the test).
5. arrived earlier than I expected.
6. run more often than the trains. *or* The buses run more frequently than . . .
7. were busier than usual (at work today). *or* We were busier at work today than usual.

UNIT 103

103.1
2. much bigger
3. much more complicated than
4. a little cooler
5. far more interesting than
6. a little more slowly
7. a lot easier
8. slightly older

103.2
2. any sooner / any earlier
3. no higher than / no more expensive than
4. any farther/further
5. no worse than

103.3
2. bigger and bigger
3. heavier and heavier
4. more and more nervous
5. worse and worse
6. more and more expensive
7. better and better
8. more and more talkative

103.4
2. the more I liked him *or* the more I got to like him
3. the more profit you (will) make *or* the higher your profit (will be) *or* the more your profit (will be)
4. the harder it is to concentrate
5. the more impatient she became

103.5
2. older
3. older *or* elder
4. older

UNIT 104

104.1
2. as high as yours.
3. know as much about cars as me. *or* . . . as I do.
4. as cold as it was yesterday.
5. feel as tired as I did yesterday. *or* . . . as I felt yesterday.
6. lived here as long as us. *or* . . . as we have.
7. as nervous (before the interview) as I usually am. *or* . . . as usual.

104.2
3. as far as I thought.
4. less than I expected.
5. go out as much as I used to. *or* . . . as often as I used to.
6. have longer hair.
7. know them as well as me. *or* . . . as I do.
8. as many people at this meeting as at the last one.

104.3
2. as well as
3. as long as
4. as soon as
5. as often as
6. as quietly as
7. just as comfortable as
8. just as well qualified as
9. just as bad as

104.4

2. is the same color as mine
3. arrived at the same time as you did
4. birthday is the same day as Tom's *or* birthday is the same as Tom's

104.5

2. than him / than he does
3. as me / as I do
4. than us / than we were
5. than her / than she is
6. as them / as they have been

UNIT 105

105.1

2. the cheapest restaurant in the town.
3. the happiest day of my life.
4. 's the most intelligent student in the class.
5. 's the most valuable painting in the gallery.
6. 's the busiest time of the year.
8. of the richest men in the world.
9. 's one of the oldest houses in the city.
10. 's one of the best colleges in the state.
11. was one of the worst experiences of my life.
12. 's one of the most dangerous criminals in the country.

105.2

3. larger
4. the smallest
5. better
6. the worst
7. the most popular
8. ... the highest mountain in the world ... It is higher than ...
9. the most enjoyable
10. more comfortable
11. the quickest
12. The oldest *or* The eldest

105.3

2. the funniest joke I've ever heard.
3. is the best coffee I've ever tasted.
4. 's the most generous person I've ever met.
5. 's the furthest/farthest I've ever run.
6. 's the worst mistake I've ever made. *or* was the worst ...
7. 's the most famous person you've ever met?

UNIT 106

106.1

3. Jim doesn't like basketball very much.
4. *OK*
5. I ate my breakfast quickly and ...
6. ... a lot of people to the party?

7. *OK*
8. Did you go to bed late last night?
9. *OK*
10. I met a friend of mine on my way home.

106.2

2. We won the game easily.
3. I closed the door quietly.
4. Diane speaks Chinese quite well.
5. Tim watches TV all the time.
6. Please don't ask that question again.
7. Does Ken play golf every weekend?
8. I borrowed some money from a friend of mine.

106.3

2. go to the supermarket every Friday.
3. did you come home so late?
4. takes her children to school every day.
5. been to the movies recently.
6. write your name at the top of the page.
7. remembered her name after a few minutes.
8. walked around the town all morning.
9. didn't see you at the party on Saturday night.
10. found some interesting books in the library.
11. left her umbrella in a restaurant last night.
12. are building a new hotel across from the park.

UNIT 107

107.1

3. I usually take ...
4. *OK*
5. Steve hardly ever gets angry.
6. ... and I also went to the bank.
7. Jane always has to hurry ...
8. We were all ... / *OK*
9. *OK*

107.2

2. a) We were all on vacation in Spain.
   b) We were all staying at the same hotel.
   c) We all enjoyed ourselves.
3. Catherine is always very generous.
4. I don't usually have to work on Saturdays.
5. Do you always watch TV in the evenings?
6. ... is also studying Japanese.
7. a) The new hotel is probably very expensive.
   b) It probably costs a lot to stay there.

8. a) I can probably help you.
   b) I probably can't help you.

107.3

2. usually take
3. am usually
4. has probably gone
5. were both born
6. can also sing
7. often sleeps
8. have never spoken
9. always have to wait
10. can only read
11. will probably be leaving
12. probably won't be
13. is hardly ever
14. are still living
15. would never have met
16. always am

UNIT 108

108.1

3. He doesn't write poems anymore.
4. He still wants to be a teacher.
5. He isn't / He's not interested in politics anymore.
6. He's still single.
7. He doesn't go fishing anymore.
8. He doesn't have a beard anymore.
10.–12.
   He no longer writes poems.
   He is / He's no longer interested in politics.
   He no longer goes fishing.
   He no longer has a beard.

108.2

2. hasn't left yet.
3. haven't finished (repairing the road) yet.
4. They haven't woken up yet.
5. Has she found a place to live yet?
6. I haven't decided (what to do) yet.
7. It hasn't taken off yet.

108.3

5. I don't want to go out yet.
6. she doesn't work there anymore
7. I still have a lot of friends there. *or* I've still got ...
8. We've already met.
9. Do you still live in the same place
10. have you already eaten
11. He's not here yet.
12. he still isn't here (he isn't here yet *is also possible*)
13. are you already a member
14. I can still remember it very clearly
15. These pants don't fit me anymore.
16. "Have you finished with the paper yet?" "No, I'm still reading it." *or* Are you finished with ... ?

UNIT 109

109.1
2. even Amanda
3. not even Julie
4. even Amanda
5. even Sarah
6. not even Amanda

109.2
2. even painted the floor.
3. 's even met the president.
   or even met . . .
4. could even hear it from two
   blocks away. *or* You could
   even hear the noise from . . .
6. I can't even remember her name.
7. There isn't even a movie theater.
8. He didn't even tell his wife
   (where he was going).
9. I don't even know the people
   next door.

109.3
2. even older
3. even better
4. even more difficult
5. even worse
6. even less

109.4
2. if
3. even if
4. even
5. even though
6. Even
7. even though
8. even if
9. Even though

UNIT 110

110.1
2. Although I had never seen her
   before
3. although it was quite cold
4. although we don't like them
   very much
5. Although I didn't speak the
   language
6. Although the heat was on
7. although I'd met her twice before
8. although we've known each
   other a long time

110.2
2. a) In spite of (*or* Despite)
   b) Although
3. a) because
   b) although
4. a) because of
   b) in spite of (*or* despite)
5. a) although
   b) because of
Example answers:
6. a) he hadn't studied very hard
   b) he had studied very hard

7. a) I was hungry
   b) being hungry / my hunger /
   the fact (that) I was hungry

110.3
2. In spite of having very little
   money, they are happy. *or* In
   spite of the fact (that) they
   have very little money . . .
3. Although my foot was injured,
   I managed to walk to the
   nearest town. *or* I managed
   to walk to the nearest town
   although my . . .
4. I enjoyed the movie in spite
   of the silly story. / . . . in spite
   of the story being silly. / . . . in
   spite of the fact (that) the story
   was silly. *or* In spite of . . . , I
   enjoyed the movie.
5. Despite living on the same
   street, we hardly ever see each
   other. *or* Despite the fact (that)
   we live on . . . *or* We hardly
   ever see each other despite . . .
6. Even though I was only out for
   five minutes, I got very wet in
   the rain. *or* I got very wet in
   the rain even though I was . . .

110.4
2. It's very windy, though.
3. We ate it, though.
4. I don't like her husband, though.

UNIT 111

111.1
2.–5.
   a map with you in case you get lost.
   Take a raincoat with you in
   case it rains.
   Take a camera with you in
   case you want to take some
   pictures/photos.
   Take some water with you in
   case you're thirsty. *or*
   . . . you get thirsty.

111.2
2. in case I don't see you again
   (before you go)
3. check the list in case we forgot
   something *or* . . . forgot
   anything
4. your files in case the computer
   crashes

111.3
2. the name (of the book) in case
   he forgot it
3. my parents in case they were
   worried (about me)
4. (Liz) another e-mail in case she
   hadn't received the first one
5. them my address in case they
   came to New York (one day)

111.4
3. If
4. if
5. in case
6. if
7. if
8. in case
9. in case

UNIT 112

112.1
2. unless you listen carefully.
3. I'll never speak to her again unless
   she apologizes to me. *or* Unless
   she apologises to me, I'll . . .
4. He won't be able to understand
   you unless you speak very
   slowly. *or* Unless you speak
   very slowly, he . . .
5. The company will have to
   close unless business improves
   soon. *or* Unless business
   improves soon, the company . . .

112.2
2. (to the party) unless you go, too.
3. won't attack you unless you
   move suddenly.
4. won't speak to you unless you
   ask him something.
5. won't see you unless it's an
   emergency.

112.3
2. unless
3. providing
4. as long as
5. unless
6. unless
7. provided
8. Unless
9. unless
10. as long as

112.4
Example answers:
2. it's not too hot
3. there isn't too much traffic
4. it isn't raining
5. I'm in a hurry
6. you have something else to do
7. you pay it back next week
8. you take risks

UNIT 113

113.1
2. We all smiled as we posed for
   the photograph.
3. I burned myself as I was taking
   a hot dish out of the oven.
4. The crowd cheered as the two
   teams ran onto the field.
5. A dog ran out in front of the car
   as we were driving along the road.

113.2

3. because
4. at the same time as
5. at the same time as
6. because
7. because

Example answers:

9. Since I was tired, I went to bed early.
10. We decided to go out to eat since we had no food at home.
11. Since we don't use the car very often, we've decided to sell it.

113.3

3. *OK*
4. when I was asleep
5. When I finished high school
6. *OK*
7. when I was a child

113.4

Example answers:

1. you were getting into your car.
2. we started playing tennis.
3. I had to walk home.
4. somebody walked in front of the camera.

UNIT 114

114.1

3. like her mother
4. people like him
5. *OK*
6. like most of his friends
7. like talking to the wall
8. *OK*
9. *OK*
10. *OK*
11. like a bomb exploding
12. like a fish

114.2

2. like blocks of ice
3. like a beginner
4. as a tour guide
5. like a church
6. as a birthday present
7. like winter
8. like a child

114.3

2. like
3. as
4. like
5. like
6. as (like *is also possible*)
7. like
8. as
9. as
10. like
11. like
12. as
13. as
14. Like

15. as
16. As
17. like
18. as (like *is also possible*)

UNIT 115

115.1

2. look like you've seen a ghost.
3. sound like you're enjoying yourself.
4. feel like I've (just) run a marathon.

115.2

2. looks like it's going to rain.
3. It sounds like they're having an argument.
4. It looks like there's been an accident.
5. It looks like we'll have to walk.
6. It sounds like you should see a doctor.

115.3

2. as if he meant what he said
3. as if she hurt her leg
4. as if he hadn't eaten for a week
5. as if she was enjoying it
6. as if I'm going to be sick
7. as if she didn't want to come
8. as if I didn't exist

115.4

2. as if [I] was/were
3. as if she was/were
4. as if it was/were

UNIT 116

116.1

3. during
4. for
5. during
6. for
7. for
8. for
9. during
10. for
11. for
12. for
13. during
14. for

116.2

3. while
4. While
5. During
6. while
7. during
8. During
9. while
10. during
11. while
12. during
13. while
14. while

116.3

Example answers:

3. I was doing the housework.
4. I make a quick phone call?
5. the lesson.
6. the interview.
7. the car is moving.
8. we were having dinner.
9. the game.
10. we were walking home.

UNIT 117

117.1

2. by 8:30.
3. by Saturday whether you can come to the party.
4. you're here by 2:00.
5. we should arrive by lunchtime.

117.2

2. by
3. by
4. until
5. until . . . by
6. by
7. until
8. by
9. by
10. until
11. By
12. by

117.3

Example answers:

3. until I come back
4. by 5:00
5. by next Friday
6. until midnight

117.4

2. By the time I got to the station / By the time I'd gotten to the station
3. By the time I finished (my work) / By the time I'd finished (my work)
4. By the time the police arrived
5. By the time we got to the top / By the time we'd gotten to the top

UNIT 118

118.1

2. at night
3. in the evening
4. on July 21, 1969
5. at the same time
6. in the 1920s
7. in about 20 minutes
8. at the moment
9. in the Middle Ages
10. in 11 seconds
11. (on) Saturdays

118.2

2. on
3. in
4. On

5. on
6. in
7. in
8. at
9. on
10. at
11. in
12. at
13. on
14. in
15. On . . . at
16. at . . . in
17. on . . . in
18. on . . . in

118.3
3. a
4. *both*
5. b
6. b
7. *both*
8. a
9. b
10. a

UNIT 119

119.1
2. on time
3. in time
4. on time
5. in time
6. on time
7. in time
8. in time
9. on time

119.2
2. got home just in time.
3. stopped him just in time.
4. got to the theater just in time for the beginning of the film.

119.3
2. at the end of the month
3. at the end of the course
4. at the end of the race
5. at the end of the interview

119.4
2. In the end she resigned (from her job).
3. In the end I gave up (trying to learn German).
4. In the end we decided not to go (to the party). *or* In the end we didn't go (to the party).

119.5
2. In
3. at . . . at
4. in
5. in
6. at
7. in
8. at
9. in

UNIT 120

120.1
2. On his arm. *or* On the man's arm.
3. At the traffic light.
4. a) On the door.
   b) In the door.
5. On the wall.
6. In Paris.
7. a) At the front desk.
   b) On the desk.
8. On/At the beach.

120.2
2. on my guitar
3. at the next gas station
4. in your coffee
5. on that tree
6. in the mountains
7. on the island
8. at the window

120.3
2. on
3. at
4. on
5. in
6. on
7. at
8. in . . . in
9. on
10. in
11. on . . . in
12. at

UNIT 121

121.1
2. On the second floor.
3. At/On the corner.
4. In the corner.
5. At the top of the stairs.
6. In the back of the car.
7. In the front.
8. On the left.
9. In the back row.
10. On a farm.

121.2
2. on the right
3. in the world
4. on the way to work
5. on the West Coast
6. in the front row
7. in/at the back of the class
8. on the back of this card

121.3
2. in
3. in
4. in/at
5. in
6. on
7. At . . . on
8. in
9. in

10. on
11. in
12. on
13. in
14. on . . . on

UNIT 122

122.1
2. on a train
3. at a conference
4. in the hospital
5. at the hairdresser's
6. on his bike
7. in New York
8. at the Ford Theater

122.2
2. in a taxi
3. at the party
4. on the plane
5. at school
6. at the gym
7. in the hospital
8. in/at the airport
9. in prison

122.3
2. at
3. in
4. at
5. at/in . . . in
6. in
7. on
8. at
9. in
10. at
11. in
12. at . . . at
13. in
14. in . . . at

UNIT 123

123.1
3. at
4. to
5. to
6. into
7. at *or* –
8. to
9. into
10. to
11. at
12. to
13. into
14. to
15. – . . . to
16. to . . . in
17. in . . . to . . . in

123.2
Example answers:
2.–4.
   I've been to Hong Kong once.
   I've never been to Tokyo.
   I've been to Paris a few times.

123.3
2. in
3. –
4. at
5. to
6. –

123.4
2. got on the bus.
3. I got out of the car.
4. I got off the train.
5. I got into the taxi. *or* I got in the taxi.
6. I got off the plane.

UNIT 124

124.1
2. in cold weather
3. in pencil
4. in love
5. in capital letters
6. in the shade
7. in my opinion

124.2
2. on strike
3. on a tour
4. on television
5. on purpose
6. on a diet
7. on business
8. on vacation
9. on the phone
10. on the whole

124.3
2. on
3. on
4. at
5. in
6. on
7. for
8. on
9. at
10. at
11. on
12. In . . . on
13. on
14. on
15. on
16. at
17. on
18. in

UNIT 125

125.1
2. by mistake
3. by hand
4. by credit card
5. by satellite

125.2
2. on
3. by
4. by . . . on

5. in
6. on
7. by

125.3
Example answers:
3.–5.
    Ulysses is a novel by James Joyce.
    "Yesterday" is a song by Paul McCartney.
    Guernica is a painting by Pablo Picasso.

125.4
2. by
3. with
4. by
5. by
6. by . . . in
7. by . . . with . . . on

125.5
2. traveling by bus *or* traveling on the bus *or* traveling on buses
3. taken with a very good camera
4. this music is by Beethoven
5. pay cash *or* pay in cash
6. a mistake by one of our players

125.6
2. by 25 cents.
3. by two votes.
4. her/Kate by five minutes.

UNIT 126

126.1
2. to the problem
3. with her brother
4. in the cost of living
5. to your question
6. for a new road
7. in/to working at home
8. in the number of people without jobs
9. for shoes like these any more
10. between your job and mine

126.2
2. invitation to
3. contact with
4. key to
5. cause of
6. reply to
7. connection between
8. pictures of
9. reason for
10. damage to

126.3
2. to
3. in
4. for
5. of
6. in *or* to
7. for
8. to *or* toward
9. with

10. in
11. to
12. of
13. for . . . in
14. to
15. with

UNIT 127

127.1
2. nice of
3. was generous of him.
4. wasn't very nice of them.
5. That's very kind of
6. That wasn't very polite of him.
7. That's a little childish of them.

127.2
2. kind to
3. sorry for
4. nervous about
5. upset about
6. impressed by/with
7. bored with *or* bored by
8. astonished at/by

127.3
2. of
3. to . . . to
4. of
5. of
6. with
7. to
8. with
9. at/by
10. with
11. about
12. about
13. for/about . . . at
14. at/with . . . for
15. about
16. about
17. at/by
18. by/with
19. about
20. about
21. for

UNIT 128

128.1
2. of furniture
3. for this mess
4. of time
5. at tennis
6. to a Russian (man)
7. of him / of Robert
8. from yours / than yours

128.2
2. similar to
3. afraid of
4. interested in
5. responsible for
6. proud of
7. different from/than

128.3

2. for
3. of
4. of
5. in
6. to
7. of . . . of
8. on
9. of
10. with
11. of
12. of
13. in
14. of
15. of
16. at
17. of
18. to
19. of

128.4

Example answers:

2. I'm hopeless at telling jokes.
3. I'm not very good at mathematics.
4. I'm pretty good at remembering names.

UNIT 129

129.1

3. this question to me? / Can you explain it to me?
4. you explain the problem to me? / Can you explain it to me?
5. Can you explain to me how this machine works?
6. Can you explain to me what I have to do?

129.2

3. to
4. –
5. to
6. to
7. –
8. –
9. to
10. –

129.3

3. speaking to
4. point . . . at
5. glanced at
6. listen to
7. throw . . . at
8. throw . . . to

129.4

2. at
3. at
4. to
5. to
6. at
7. at
8. to
9. at

10. at
11. to

UNIT 130

130.1

2. for
3. for
4. to
5. for
6. about
7. –
8. about
9. –
10. for
11. for
12. about
13. for
14. for

130.2

2. waiting for
3. talk about
4. asked . . . for
5. applied for
6. do . . . about
7. looks after *or* has looked after
8. left . . . for

130.3

2. for
3. about
4. of
5. for
6. of
7. about
8. –

130.4

2. looking for
3. looked after
4. looking for
5. look for
6. looks after

UNIT 131

131.1

2. about
3. to . . . about
4. of
5. of
6. about . . . about . . . about . . . about
7. of
8. about
9. about/of

131.2

2. complaining about
3. think about
4. warn . . . about
5. heard of
6. dream of
7. reminded . . . about
8. remind . . . of

131.3

2. hear about
3. heard from
4. heard of
5. hear from
6. hear about
7. heard of

131.4

2. think about
3. think of
4. think of
5. thinking of/about
6. think of
7. thought about
8. think . . . of
9. thinking about/of

UNIT 132

132.1

2. for the misunderstanding
3. on winning the tournament
4. from/against his enemies
5. of nine players
6. on bread and eggs

132.2

2. for everything
3. for the economic crisis
4. on television
5. is to blame for the economic crisis
6. television is to blame for the increase in violent crime

132.3

2. paid for
3. accused of
4. depends on
5. live on
6. congratulated . . . on
7. apologize to

132.4

2. from
3. on
4. of/from
5. for
6. for
7. –
8. on
9. on
10. – *or* on
11. from/against
12. of

UNIT 133

133.1

2. small towns to big cities
3. with all the information I needed
4. $70 on a pair of shoes

133.2

2. happened to
3. invited to
4. divided into
5. believe in

6. fill . . . with
7. drove into
8. Concentrate on
9. succeeded in

133.3
2. to
3. on
4. in
5. to
6. in
7. with
8. into
9. in
10. on
11. into
12. to
13. –
14. into
15. on
16. from . . . into
17. to . . . on
18. into
19. with

133.4
Example answers:
2. on CDs
3. into a wall
4. to volleyball
5. into many languages

UNIT 134

134.1
2. sit down
3. flew away
4. get out
5. run out
6. get by
7. gone up
8. looked around

134.2
2. back at
3. up to
4. forward to
5. away with
6. up at
7. in through
8. along with

134.3
2. wake me up
3. get it out
4. give them back
5. turn it on
6. take them off

134.4
3. them back
4. the television off *or* off the television
5. it over
6. her up
7. *Example answers:*
   your coat on *or* on your coat

8. it out
9. my shoes off *or* off my shoes
10. the light(s) on *or* on the light(s)

UNIT 135

135.1
2. eats
3. moved
4. drop
5. checked
6. cut
7. plug
8. fit
9. fill
10. hand / turn
11. leave
12. dropped

135.2
2. into
3. in
4. out
5. into
6. out of

135.3
2. dropped out
3. moved in
4. left out
5. joined in
6. eating out *or* to eat out
7. fits in
8. dropped in
9. get out of

135.4
2. Fill them out
3. handed it in
4. left them out
5. let us in

UNIT 136

136.1
2. a mistake
3. a candle
4. an order
5. a campfire
6. a new product
7. a problem

136.2
2. works out
3. carried out
4. ran out
5. work out
6. find out
7. tried out
8. pointed out
9. work out
10. went out
11. turned out
12. figure out
13. find out
14. put out

136.3
2. giving/handing out
3. turned out nice/fine/sunny
4. working out
5. run out
6. figure out . . . use the camera / her new camera

136.4
2. try it out
3. figure him out
4. pointing it out

UNIT 137

137.1
2. put the heat on
3. put the radio on
4. put the light on
5. put a DVD on

137.2
2. going on
3. take off
4. turned off
5. drove off / went off
6. put on
7. had on
8. put off
9. called off
10. put on
11. see . . . off

137.3
2. took off
3. tried on a/the hat *or* tried a/the hat on
4. was called off
5. see him off
6. put them on

UNIT 138

138.1
2. went on
3. went on walking
4. dozed off / dropped off / nodded off
5. go on working
6. went off
7. keeps on calling me

138.2
2. went off
3. dropped off
4. taken on
5. ripped off
6. goes on
7. dozed off / dropped off / nodded off
8. told off
9. lay off
10. going off
11. keep on
12. go on
13. showing off
14. hold on / hang on

138.3
2. dragging on
3. were ripped off
4. go off
5. move on / go on
6. go on with
7. tell them off
8. laid off

UNIT 139

139.1
2. turn it down
3. calm him down
4. put them up
5. let her down
6. turned it down

139.2
2. took them down
3. stand up
4. turned it up
5. put their bags down
6. were blown/knocked down
7. wrote it down
8. bent down . . . picked them up

139.3
2. calm down
3. slowed down
4. was turned down
5. broken down
6. cut down
7. let down
8. (has) closed down
9. be torn down
10. turned down
11. burned down
12. broken down

UNIT 140

140.1
2. went up to / walked up to
3. catch up with
4. keep up with

140.2
2. used up
3. backed up
4. grow up
5. turn up
6. gave up
7. taking up
8. give up
9. ended up
10. takes up
11. make up

140.3
3. set it up
4. keep up with
5. was brought up / grew up
6. keep it up
7. backed up
8. went up to
9. was made up of
10. backing me up

UNIT 141

141.1
2. D
3. E
4. C
5. G
6. A
7. B

141.2
2. held up
3. fixed it up
4. cheer him up

141.3
2. blew up
3. beaten up
4. broken up / split up
5. came up
6. clears up
7. mixed up

141.4
2. look it up
3. put up with
4. made it up
5. come up with
6. tear it up
7. saving up for
8. clean it up

UNIT 142

142.1
2. Pay
3. throw
4. gets
5. be
6. look
7. gave
8. get

142.2
2. be away / have gone away
3. be back
4. ran away
5. smile back
6. get away
7. Keep away

142.3
2. blew away
3. put it back
4. walked away
5. threw it back (to her)
6. threw them away

142.4
2. throw it away
3. take them back
4. pay you back / pay it back
5. gave them away
6. call back / call me back

Answer Key to Additional Exercises

(see page 296)

1

3. 'm getting / am getting
4. do you do
5. arrived . . . was raining
6. calls . . . didn't call
7. were thinking . . . decided
8. are you looking
9. doesn't rain
10. rang . . . were having
11. went . . . was studying . . . didn't want . . . didn't stay
12. told . . . didn't believe . . . thought . . . was joking

2

2. didn't go
3. is wearing
4. went
5. haven't heard
6. is being
7. wasn't reading
8. didn't have
9. It's beginning
10. got
11. wasn't
12. you've been
13. I've been doing
14. did she go
15. I've been playing
16. do you come
17. since I saw her
18. for 20 years

3

3. are you going
4. Do you watch
5. have you lived / have you been living / have you been
6. Did you have
7. Have you seen
8. was she wearing
9. Have you been waiting / Have you been here
10. does it take
11. Have you ridden
12. Have you (ever) been

4

2. 've known each other / have known each other or 've been friends / have been friends
3. I've ever had / I've ever been on / I've had in ages (etc.)
4. He left / He went home / He went out
5. I've worn it
6. I was playing
7. been swimming for or gone swimming for

8. since I've been / since I (last) went
9. did you buy / did you get

5

1. got . . . was already waiting . . . had arrived
2. was lying . . . wasn't watching . . . 'd fallen / had fallen . . . was snoring . . . turned . . . woke
3. 'd just gone / had just gone . . . was reading . . . heard . . . got . . . didn't see . . . went
4. missed . . . was standing . . . realized . . . 'd left / had left . . . had . . . got
5. met . . . was walking . . . 'd been / had been . . . 'd been playing / had been playing . . . were going . . . invited . . . 'd arranged / had arranged . . . didn't have

6

2. Somebody's taken it. / Somebody has taken it.
3. They'd only known / They had only known each other (for) a few weeks.
4. It's been raining / It has been raining all day. or It's rained / It has rained all day.
5. I'd been dreaming. / I had been dreaming.
6. I'd had / I had had a big breakfast.
7. They've been going / They have been going there for years.
8. I've had it / I have had it since I got up.
9. He's been training / He has been training very hard for it.

7

1. I haven't seen
2. You look   or   You're looking
3. are you going
4. are you meeting
5. I'm going
6. Do you travel a lot
7. are you going
8. I'm meeting
9. has been   or   was
10. I've been waiting
11. has just started   or   just started
12. is she doing
13. Does she like
14. she thinks
15. Are you working   or   Do you work
16. spoke
17. you were working
18. went

19. I started / I had started
20. I lost
21. you haven't had
22. I've had
23. have you seen
24. has he been
25. I saw
26. he left
27. He'd been
28. he decided / he'd decided
29. He was really looking forward
30. is he doing
31. I haven't heard
32. he left

8

1. invented
2. it's ended / it has ended / it ended
3. had gone . . . left
4. did you do . . . Did you go
5. have you had
6. was looking
7. She's been teaching / She has been teaching
8. I bought . . . I haven't worn
9. I saw . . . was . . . I'd seen / I had seen . . . I remembered . . . he was
10. Have you heard . . . She was . . . died . . . She wrote . . . Have you read
11. does this word mean . . . I've never seen
12. Did you get . . . it had already begun
13. knocked . . . was . . . she'd gone / she had gone . . . she didn't want
14. He'd never used / He had never used . . . he didn't know
15. went . . . She needed . . . she'd been sitting / she had been sitting

9

3. used to drive
4. was driving
5. were working
6. used to have
7. was living
8. was playing
9. used to play
10. was wearing

10

2. I'm going to the dentist.
3. No, we're going to rent a car.
4. I'll take care of the children.
5. I'm having lunch with Sue.
6. What are you going to have?
7. I'll turn on the light.
8. I'm going to turn on the light.

11

2. I'll go
3. should/shall we meet
4. starts
5. I'll meet
6. I'm seeing
7. Should/Shall I ask
8. I'll see
9. are going
10. does the movie start
11. Are you meeting
12. I'll be

12

1. (2) Are you going to take
   (3) it starts
   (4) you'll enjoy
   (5) it will / it's going to be
2. (1) you're going
   (2) We're going
   (3) you have
   (4) I'll send
   (5) I'll get
   (6) I get
3. (1) I'm having / I'm going to have
   (2) are coming
   (3) they'll have left
   (4) they're
   (5) I won't be / I will not be
   (6) you know
   (7) I'll call
4. (1) should/shall we meet
   (2) I'll be waiting
   (3) you arrive
   (4) I'll be sitting
   (5) I'll be wearing
   (6) Is Agent 307 coming / Is Agent 307 going to come / Will Agent 307 be coming
   (7) Should/Shall I bring
   (8) I'll explain
   (9) I see
   (10) I'll try

13

1. I'll have
2. Are you going
3. should/shall I call
4. It's going to land
5. it's / it is
6. I'll miss / I'm going to miss . . . you go (or you've gone)
7. Should/Shall I give . . . I give . . . will you send
8. does it end
9. I'm going . . . is getting
10. I'll tell . . . I'm . . . I won't be
11. I'm going to have / I'm having
12. she apologizes
13. we'll be living
14. you finish

14

2. 've had
3. I bought *or* I got
4. 'll come
5. 've been *or* 've eaten
6. used to play
7. haven't been waiting *or* haven't been here
8. 'd been
9. 'm going
10. haven't seen *or* haven't heard from
11. 'll have gone *or* 'll have left

15

2. I've been traveling
3. I'm beginning
4. I've seen
5. has been
6. I've met
7. I left
8. I stayed *or* I was staying
9. I'd planned *or* I was planning
10. I ended up
11. I enjoyed
12. I took
13. met
14. I'm staying *or* I'm going to stay *or* I'll be staying *or* I'll stay
15. I continue
16. I'll get
17. I'm
18. I'll let
19. I know
20. I'm staying
21. we're going to visit *or* we're visiting
22. are building *or* have been building
23. it will be
24. I'll be

16

2. A
3. C
4. C
5. B
6. A *or* C
7. A *or* C
8. C
9. B *or* C
10. A *or* B
11. A *or* B
12. C
13. A *or* B
14. B *or* C
15. B

17

3. He must have forgotten.
4. You shouldn't have left so late.
5. It can't be changed now.

6. You could have gotten here earlier.
7. She may be watching television.
8. She must have been waiting for somebody.
9. He couldn't have done it.
10. I would have helped you.
11. You should have been warned about it.
12. He might not have been feeling very well. *or* He might not have felt . . .

18

3. could rain / might rain
4. might have gone / could have gone
5. couldn't go
6. couldn't have seen / can't have seen
7. should get
8. wouldn't recognize / might not recognize
9. must have heard
10. should have turned

19

4. rings
5. were
6. 's / is
7. was/were
8. had been
9. had
10. hadn't had
11. 'd driven / had driven *or* 'd been driving / had been driving
12. didn't read

20

2. came (to see us now).
3. wouldn't have disturbed you.
4. be upset . . . I told them what happened.
5. you hadn't frightened the dog, it wouldn't have attacked you.
6. wouldn't have gotten (so) wet if I'd had an umbrella. *or* . . . if I had had an umbrella.
7. hadn't been (so) nervous, he wouldn't have failed (his driver's test).

21

Example answers:
1. I wasn't feeling so tired
2. I hadn't had so much to do
3. I would have forgotten Jane's birthday
4. you hadn't taken so long to get ready
5. I would have gone to the concert
6. you were in trouble
7. there was less traffic
8. people would go out more

22

3. was canceled
4. has been repaired
5. is being restored
6. 's believed / is believed
7. 'd be fired / would be fired
8. might have been thrown
9. was taught
10. being arrested / having been arrested
11. Have you ever been arrested
12. are reported . . . have been injured *or* be injured

23

3. sold *or* 've sold / have sold
4. 's been sold / has been sold
5. are made
6. might be stolen
7. must have been stolen
8. must have taken
9. can be solved
10. should have left
11. is delayed
12. is being built . . . is expected

24

Fire at City Hall
2. was discovered
3. was injured
4. be rescued
5. are believed to have been destroyed
6. is not known

Convenience Store Robbery
1. was forced
2. being threatened
3. had been stolen
4. was later found
5. had been abandoned
6. has been arrested / was arrested
7. is still being questioned

Road Delays
1. is being resurfaced
2. are asked / are being asked / have been asked
3. is expected
4. will be closed
5. will be rerouted

Accident
1. was taken
2. was allowed
3. was blocked
4. be rerouted
5. have been killed

25

1. I told **her** (**that**) **Paul had gone out** and **I didn't know when he'd be back**. I asked (**her**) **if/ whether she wanted to leave a message**, but she said (**that**) **she'd try again** later.

2. I had reserved a hotel room, but when I got to the hotel, they told **me** (**that**) **they had** no **record of a reservation in my name**. When I asked (**them**) **if/whether they had any rooms available**, they said (**that**) **they were sorry**, but **the hotel was full**.

3. The immigration official asked us **why we were visiting the country**, and we told **him** (**that**) **we were on vacation**. Then he wanted to know **how long we intended to stay** and **where we would be staying during our visit**.

4. She said (**that**) **she'd call us from the airport when she arrived**. *or* She said (**that**) **she'll call us from the airport when she arrives**. No, she said **not to come to the airport**. She said (**that**) **she'd take the bus**. *or* She said (**that**) **she'll take the bus**.

5. He wanted to know **what my job was** and asked (**me**) **how much I made**. *or* He wanted to know **what my job is** and asked (**me**) **how much I made**. . . . so I told **him to mind his own business** and I put the phone down.

6. He said (**that**) **he'd be at the restaurant at 7:30**. He said (**that**) **he knew where the restaurant was**. And I told **him to call me if there was any problem**.

7. You just said (**that**) **you weren't hungry**. But you said (**that**) **you didn't like bananas**. You told **me not to buy any**.

26

3. changing
4. to change
5. change
6. being
7. saying
8. to call
9. drinking
10. to be
11. to see
12. to be
13. to think . . . making
14. living . . . to move
15. to be . . . playing
16. being stopped . . . to stealing . . . driving
17. work . . . pressing

27

3. We stopped watching after a while.
4. He tends to forget things.
5. Would you mind helping me? / Do you mind helping me?
6. Everybody seems to have gone out.
7. We're thinking of moving.
8. I was afraid to touch it.
9. He's / He is afraid of being robbed.
10. It's not worth seeing.
11. I'm not used to walking so far.
12. She seems to be enjoying herself.
13. He insisted on showing them to me.
14. I'd rather somebody else did it.

28

3. reading newspapers
4. not go out tonight / . . . stay at home tonight
5. walking
6. me to call you tonight
7. anybody seeing me / . . . without being seen
8. of being a liar/ . . . of lying
9. to seeing them again
10. to do
11. to have gone out with you
12. not taking your advice / . . . that I didn't take your advice

29

2. Tennis . . . twice a week . . . a very good player
3. for dinner . . . after work . . . to the movies
4. Unemployment . . . for people . . . find work
5. an accident . . . going home . . . taken to the hospital. I think most accidents . . . by people driving
6. an economist . . . in the investment department of Lloyds Bank . . . for an American bank . . . in the United States
7. the name of the hotel . . . The Royal . . . on West Street in the suburbs . . . near the airport.
8. The older one . . . a pilot with Western Airlines . . . The younger one . . . in high school. . . . he finishes school . . . go to college . . . study engineering.

30

2. B
3. C
4. A *or* B
5. C
6. B
7. A *or* C
8. A
9. C
10. B *or* C

11. B
12. A
13. A *or* B
14. B

31

3. It's the most polluted place . . .
4. I was disappointed that . . .
5. *OK*
6. Joe works hard, but . . .
7. . . . in a large modern building.
8. *OK* (as fast as he can *is also correct*)
9. I missed the last three days . . .
10. *OK*
11. The weather has been
    unusually cold . . .
12. The water in the pool was too
    dirty to swim in.
13. . . . to wait such a long time. (so
    long *is also correct*)
14. *OK*
15. . . . I got up earlier than usual.

32

2. If
3. when
4. if
5. when
6. if
7. if
8. unless
9. if
10. as long as
11. in case
12. in case
13. if
14. even if
15. Although
16. Although
17. When
18. when

33

2. on
3. at . . . on
4. on
5. on
6. at
7. In
8. at
9. during
10. on . . . since
11. for
12. at
13. at . . . until
14. by
15. in

34

1. in
2. by
3. at
4. on
5. in

6. on
7. to . . . at
8. on
9. on
10. to . . . to
11. in . . . at
12. in . . . on
13. to . . . in
14. on . . . by
15. at
16. on
17. in . . . on
18. on
19. by
20. On . . . by
21. on . . . on
22. in
23. in . . . to
24. to
25. on

35

1. for
2. at
3. to
4. to
5. in
6. with
7. of
8. to
9. of
10. at/by
11. of
12. about

36

1. of
2. after
3. – *(no preposition)*
4. about
5. to
6. – *(no preposition)*
7. into
8. of
9. to
10. – *(no preposition)*
11. on
12. of
13. of
14. – *(no preposition)*
15. in
16. at (about *is also possible*)
17. on
18. – *(no preposition)* . . . for
19. to . . . for
20. – *(no preposition)* . . . for

37

2. h
3. e
4. g
5. a
6. k
7. c

8. j
9. b
10. f
11. i

38

2. D
3. B
4. B
5. A
6. B
7. D
8. C
9. C
10. B
11. A
12. D

39

2. out to
3. up with
4. forward to
5. up with
6. out of
7. on with
8. out of
9. up with
10. back on
11. out about
12. along with

40

3. went off
4. turned up / showed up
5. fill it out / fill it in
6. torn down / knocked down
7. taken on
8. give up
9. dozed off / dropped off / nodded
   off
10. split up / break up
11. put up with it
12. get by
13. went on
14. put it off

41

2. put
3. moving
4. put
5. fixed
6. turned / turns
7. find
8. Calm
9. drop
10. held
11. left *or* 've left / have left
12. drop
13. join
14. works
15. let
16. work
17. went . . . woke

Answer Key to Study Guide

(see page 319)

Present and Past

1.1 A
1.2 B
1.3 C
1.4 B, C
1.5 C
1.6 A

Present Perfect and Past

2.1 C
2.2 A
2.3 A, C
2.4 A
2.5 A
2.6 C
2.7 A
2.8 C
2.9 A
2.10 B
2.11 A
2.12 D
2.13 C
2.14 C
2.15 D
2.16 C

Future

3.1 B
3.2 A
3.3 C
3.4 A, C
3.5 B
3.6 C
3.7 A

Modals

4.1 A, B
4.2 B
4.3 A, C, D
4.4 C
4.5 B
4.6 C, D
4.7 B
4.8 B
4.9 A
4.10 A
4.11 D
4.12 A

If and Wish

5.1 B
5.2 C
5.3 B
5.4 D
5.5 A

Passive

6.1 C
6.2 B
6.3 D
6.4 A
6.5 A, B
6.6 C
6.7 D

Reported Speech

7.1 A
7.2 B
7.3 A

Questions and Auxiliary Verbs

8.1 C
8.2 A
8.3 D
8.4 A
8.5 B

-ing and the Infinitive

9.1 A
9.2 B, D
9.3 B
9.4 A
9.5 A
9.6 A
9.7 C
9.8 D
9.9 C
9.10 C
9.11 B
9.12 C
9.13 B, D
9.14 B
9.15 A, B
9.16 A
9.17 A
9.18 B, C

Articles and Nouns

10.1 B
10.2 A
10.3 B, C
10.4 B
10.5 C
10.6 A
10.7 A
10.8 A
10.9 D
10.10 C
10.11 C
10.12 A
10.13 C
10.14 B

Pronouns and Determiners

11.1 A
11.2 B
11.3 D
11.4 B
11.5 B
11.6 C
11.7 A, C
11.8 C
11.9 D
11.10 A, C
11.11 B

Relative Clauses

12.1 A, C
12.2 A, B
12.3 C
12.4 B
12.5 D
12.6 B, C

Adjectives and Adverbs

13.1 B
13.2 C
13.3 B, C
13.4 A
13.5 A, D
13.6 B
13.7 C
13.8 C
13.9 B, C
13.10 D
13.11 A, B
13.12 B
13.13 D
13.14 D

Conjunctions and Prepositions

14.1 A, D
14.2 C
14.3 B, C
14.4 B
14.5 B
14.6 C, D
14.7 B, C
14.8 A

Prepositions

15.1 B, D
15.2 A
15.3 C
15.4 B
15.5 A
15.6 B, D
15.7 B
15.8 B
15.9 C
15.10 C
15.11 C
15.12 A
15.13 C
15.14 B
15.15 D
15.16 D
15.17 A

Phrasal Verbs

16.1 B
16.2 A
16.3 D
16.4 C
16.5 C
16.6 B
16.7 A
16.8 A, D
16.9 B

Index

The numbers in the index are unit numbers, not page numbers.